Applications of Computational Science in Artificial Intelligence

Anand Nayyar
Duy Tan University, Da Nang, Vietnam

Sandeep Kumar
CHRIST University (Deemed), Bangalore, India

Akshat Agrawal
Amity University, Guragon, India

A volume in the Advances in
Computational Intelligence and
Robotics (ACIR) Book Series

Published in the United States of America by
    IGI Global
    Engineering Science Reference (an imprint of IGI Global)
    701 E. Chocolate Avenue
    Hershey PA, USA 17033
    Tel: 717-533-8845
    Fax: 717-533-8661
    E-mail: cust@igi-global.com
    Web site: http://www.igi-global.com

Library of Congress Cataloging-in-Publication Data

Names: Nayyar, Anand, editor. | Kumar, Sandeep, 1983- editor. | Agrawal,
    Akshat, 1986- editor.
Title: Applications of computational science in artificial intelligence /
    Anand Nayyar, Sandeep Kumar, and Akshat Agrawal, editors.
Description: Hershey, PA : Engineering Science Reference, an imprint of IGI
    Global, [2022] | Includes bibliographical references and index. |
    Summary: "This book delivers technological solutions to improvise smart
    technologies architecture, healthcare, and environment sustainability
    covering diverse aspects regarding: Computational solutions, computation
    framework, smart prediction, healthcare solutions using computational
    informatics and many more"-- Provided by publisher.
Identifiers: LCCN 2021038001 (print) | LCCN 2021038002 (ebook) | ISBN
    9781799890126 (h/c) | ISBN 9781799890133 (s/c) | ISBN 9781799890140
    (ebook)
Subjects: LCSH: Machine learning. | Artificial intelligence.
Classification: LCC Q325.5 .A6595 2022 (print) | LCC Q325.5 (ebook) | DDC
    006.3/1--dc23
LC record available at https://lccn.loc.gov/2021038001
LC ebook record available at https://lccn.loc.gov/2021038002

This book is published in the IGI Global book series Advances in Computational Intelligence and Robotics (ACIR) (ISSN: 2327-0411; eISSN: 2327-042X)

British Cataloguing in Publication Data
A Cataloguing in Publication record for this book is available from the British Library.

All work contributed to this book is new, previously-unpublished material.
The views expressed in this book are those of the authors, but not necessarily of the publisher.

For electronic access to this publication, please contact: eresources@igi-global.com.

Advances in Computational Intelligence and Robotics (ACIR) Book Series

ISSN:2327-0411
EISSN:2327-042X

Editor-in-Chief: Ivan Giannoccaro University of Salento, Italy

MISSION

While intelligence is traditionally a term applied to humans and human cognition, technology has progressed in such a way to allow for the development of intelligent systems able to simulate many human traits. With this new era of simulated and artificial intelligence, much research is needed in order to continue to advance the field and also to evaluate the ethical and societal concerns of the existence of artificial life and machine learning.

The **Advances in Computational Intelligence and Robotics (ACIR) Book Series** encourages scholarly discourse on all topics pertaining to evolutionary computing, artificial life, computational intelligence, machine learning, and robotics. ACIR presents the latest research being conducted on diverse topics in intelligence technologies with the goal of advancing knowledge and applications in this rapidly evolving field.

COVERAGE

- Agent technologies
- Computer Vision
- Computational Intelligence
- Pattern Recognition
- Intelligent Control
- Natural Language Processing
- Artificial Life
- Adaptive and Complex Systems
- Neural Networks
- Robotics

IGI Global is currently accepting manuscripts for publication within this series. To submit a proposal for a volume in this series, please contact our Acquisition Editors at Acquisitions@igi-global.com or visit: http://www.igi-global.com/publish/.

Titles in this Series

For a list of additional titles in this series, please visit:
www.igi-global.com/book-series/advances-computational-intelligence-robotics/73674

Challenges and Applications for Hand Gesture Recognition
Lalit Kane (School of Computer Science, University of Petroleum and Energy Studies, India) Bhupesh Kumar Dewangan (School of Engineering, University of Petroleum and Energy Studies, India) and Tanupriya Choudhury (School of Computer Science, University of Petroleum and Energy Studies, India)
Engineering Science Reference • © 2022 • 249pp • H/C (ISBN: 9781799894346) • US $195.00

Real-Time Applications of Machine Learning in Cyber-Physical Systems
Balamurugan Easwaran (University of Africa, Toru-Orua, Nigeria) Kamal Kant Hiran (Sir Padampat Singhania University, India) Sangeetha Krishnan (University of Africa, Toru-Orua, Nigeria) and Ruchi Doshi (Azteca University, Mexico)
Engineering Science Reference • © 2022 • 307pp • H/C (ISBN: 9781799893080) • US $245.00

Handbook of Research on New Investigations in Artificial Life, AI, and Machine Learning
Maki K. Habib (The American University in Cairo, Egypt)
Engineering Science Reference • © 2022 • 565pp • H/C (ISBN: 9781799886860) • US $345.00

Biomedical and Business Applications Using Artificial Neural Networks and Machine Learning
Richard S. Segall (Arkansas State University, USA) and Gao Niu (Bryant University, USA)
Engineering Science Reference • © 2022 • 394pp • H/C (ISBN: 9781799884552) • US $245.00

Integrating AI in IoT Analytics on the Cloud for Healthcare Applications
D. Jeya Mala (School of CS&IT, Jain University, Bangalore, India)
Engineering Science Reference • © 2022 • 312pp • H/C (ISBN: 9781799891321) • US $245.00

For an entire list of titles in this series, please visit:
www.igi-global.com/book-series/advances-computational-intelligence-robotics/73674

701 East Chocolate Avenue, Hershey, PA 17033, USA
Tel: 717-533-8845 x100 • Fax: 717-533-8661
E-Mail: cust@igi-global.com • www.igi-global.com

Table of Contents

Detailed Table of Contents

Chapter 1
    Emine Ela Küçük, Giresun University, Turkey
    Dilek Küçük, Tübitak Marmara Research Center, Turkey

COVID-19 pandemic has a significant impact in the world. It has led to different measures taken by governments to prevent its spread, such as school closures, employment of e-learning, and complete lockdowns. Together with the pandemic, these measures also affected many people, economically and psychologically. This chapter assesses the attitudes of undergraduate nursing students in Turkey during the COVID-19 pandemic, using automatic natural language processing (NLP) techniques. NLP is a branch of artificial intelligence, and it facilitates automatic analysis of natural language texts. Machine translation and sentiment analysis are among significant NLP techniques. Data collection is performed using an online questionnaire, filled by 101 students from three different universities in Turkey. Machine translation is used to translate responses of the students to English, and then sentiment analysis is performed on these translations. The sentiment analysis results can be used by related nursing educators and health professionals.

Chapter 2
    Çağla Çelemoğlu, Ondokuz Mayis University, Turkey
    Selime Beyza Özçevik, Ondokuz Mayıs University, Turkey
    Şenol Eren, Ondokuz Mayıs University, Turkey

Here, first of all, the authors investigated power Fibonacci sequence modulo k and formulas for the periods of these sequences, based on the period of the Fibonacci sequence modulo k. And then, the authors described a new power sequence for positive integer modulus. They named these sequences power Pell sequences modulo k. After that the authors determined those positive integer moduli for which this sequence exists and the number of such sequences for a given modulo k. In addition, the authors provide formulas for the periods of these sequences, based on the period of the Pell sequence modulo k, and they studied sequence/subsequence relationships between power Pell sequences. Finally, the authors examined ElGamal cryptosystem which is one of the asymmetric cryptographic systems and ElGamal cryptosystem which is obtained by using some power sequences. And they obtained asymmetric cryptographic applications by using power Pell sequences which the authors described.

Chapter 3

Sasikaladevi N., School of Computing, SASTRA University (Deemed),
India
Revathi A., School of EEE, SASTRA University (Deemed), India

The proposed system is based on a diagnosis of COVID from x-ray images. In the respiratory system, 17 different viral infections are possible. Accurately discriminating COVID from other viral infections is necessary today as it spreads rapidly. The proposed system differentiates COVID infection accurately from other viral infections. The convolutional neural network (CNN) provides superior performance for disease diagnosis based on images in the deep learning era. In this chapter, to solve this issue, the authors propose a hypergraph-based convolutional neural network-based fast and accurate diagnosis system for COVID. In this work, the hypergraph represents the sophisticated features of a lung x-ray image to diagnose COVID. In-depth features are extracted from the x-ray images using residual neural networks. In order to discriminate COVID viral infection from other viral infections, the hypergraph fusion approach is used.

Chapter 4

Sasikaladevi N., School of Computing, SASTRA University (Deemed),
India
Revathi A., School of EEE, SASTRA University (Deemed), India

The outbreak of human-to-human transmissible COVID-19 has caused approximately 64,000 deaths around the world and keeps continuously increasing in an exponential order that has provoked global alarm. To control the spread of the disease, screening large numbers of suspected cases for appropriate quarantine and treatment measures is of higher priority. Since clinical laboratory testing with precise accuracy for huge samples in the infected region remains a great challenge that demands complementary diagnostic methods to combat the disease. In this work, the authors have identified a new AI-based deep learning framework named CORONATE based on neural architecture space search network (NASNET) as a competent choice that can extract graphical features from radiography images referred from the public dataset of x-ray images. This observation endorses that CORONATE model can administer a faster clinical diagnosis well ahead of pathogenic tests with higher accuracy and can empower the medical team to ensure a good control on the outbreak by saving critical diagnosis time.

Chapter 5

Trieu Minh Vu, Institute for Nanomaterials, Advanced Technologies, and
Innovation, Technical University of Liberec, Czech Republic
Reza Moezzi, Institute for Nanomaterials, Advanced Technologies, and
Innovation, Technical University of Liberec, Czech Republic
Jindrich Cyrus, Institute for Nanomaterials, Advanced Technologies,
and Innovation, Technical University of Liberec, Czech Republic
Jaroslav Hlava, Faculty of Mechatronics, Informatics, and
Interdisciplinary Studies, Technical University of Liberec, Czech
Republic
Michal Petru, Institute for Nanomaterials, Advanced Technologies, and
Innovation, Technical University of Liberec, Czech Republic

Autonomous driving vehicles are developing rapidly; however, the control systems for autonomous driving vehicles tracking smoothly in high speed are still challenging. This chapter develops non-linear model predictive control (NMPC) schemes for controlling autonomous driving vehicles tracking on feasible trajectories. The optimal control action for vehicle speed and steering velocity is generated online using NMPC optimizer subject to vehicle dynamic and physical constraints as well as the surrounding obstacles and the environmental side-slipping conditions. NMPC subject to softened state constraints provides a better possibility for the optimizer to generate a feasible solution as real-time subject to online dynamic constraints and to maintain the vehicle stability. Different parameters of NMPC are simulated and analysed to see the relationships between the NMPC horizon prediction length and the weighting values. Results show that the NMPC can control the vehicle tracking exactly on different trajectories with minimum tracking errors and with high comfortability.

Chapter 6

Satheeshkumar B., Annamalai University, India
Sathiyaprasad B., Annamalai University, India

A metaheuristic-based data optimization algorithm with machine learning-based feature extraction and classification architectures is proposed. The medical data collected from hospital database and public health dataset are input to analyze abnormalities through IoT. The data optimization is carried out using metaheuristic-based gravitational search algorithm. When the data is optimized, the loss function during the feature extraction, classification will be minimized for ML architecture. The feature extraction has been carried out for the medical data using Bi-LSTM-based RNN architecture, and the extracted data has been classified using a deep belief network with CNN (DBN-CNN). Collected data have been classified for prediction of abnormal and normal data range. Experimental results show the efficiency of the proposed method when compared to existing techniques, namely accuracy, precision, recall, and F1-score. Confusion matrix shows actual class and predicted class of normal and abnormal data predicted from input data.

Chapter 7

Detection of similar images taken in different perspectives is a big concern in digital image processing. Fast and robust methods have been proposed in this area. In this chapter, a novel image matching approach is proposed by using speeded-up robust features (SURF). SURF is a local feature detector and descriptor that can be used for tasks such as object recognition or registration or classification or 3D reconstruction. Successful detection of the images is achieved by finding and matching corresponding interest points using SURF features. The task of finding correspondences between two images is performed through using a novel brute-force method which uniformly generates random pairs for matching similarity. Experimental results show that the proposed method yields better results than conventional brute force methods in which at least 5% accuracy increment is obtained.

Movies have become a significant part of today's generation. In this chapter, the authors worked on data mining and ML techniques like random forest regression, decision tree regression, support vector regression, and predict the success of the movies on the basis of ratings from IMDb and data retrieved from comments on social media platforms. Based on ML techniques, the chapter develops a model that will predict movie success before the release of the movie and thereby decrease the risk. Twitter sentimental analysis is used to retrieve data from Twitter, and polarity and subjectivity of the movie is calculated based on the user reviews, and those retrieved data machine learning algorithms are used to predict the IMDb rating. A predictive model is developed by using three algorithms, decision tree regression, SVR, and random forest regression. The chapter compared the results using three different techniques to get the movie success prediction at a reasonable accuracy.

Chapter 9

Parita Jain, KIET Group of Institutions, India
Puneet Kumar Aggarwal, ABES Engineering College, India
Kshirja Makar, HMR Institute of Technology and Management, India
Riya Garg, HMR Institute of Technology and Management, India
Jaya Mehta, HMR Institute of Technology and Management, India
Poorvi Chaudhary, HMR Institute of Technology and Management,
India

Evolution of technology summons risks. With the use of complex prototypes and methods, not only the decision-making propensity of the machines increases but also the risk assessment reduces and frauds increased. Machine learning (ML) is considered an appropriate solution for the management of risks as it can produce the desired solution with less human effort. So, to minimize the possibility of risks, certain methods are adopted that benefited through ML. The chapter provides an insight into various applications of ML techniques in the field of risk analysis. The application of ML in this sector has led to a fact that these methods can be used to analyze huge amounts of data with efficient predictive analysis. Moreover, the future of machine learning in risk analysis and management is presented bringing out the positive picture. As a conclusion, one can just say that humans will be seeing an era which will make even complex problems easy to solve with efficiency. The chapter concludes with some limitations which need to be fixed for better risk management.

Chapter 10

Tanvi Arora, CGC College of Engineering, India

The world has been put to a standstill by the COVID-19 pandemic, which has been caused by the SARS-CoV-2 (initially called 2019-nCoV) infecting agent. Moreover, this pandemic is spreading like a wildfire. Even the developed nations are running short of hospital beds and ventilators to treat the critically ill. Considering the total population of the world and the pace at which this pandemic is spreading, it not possible to hospitalize all the positive patients with intensive care facilities. In the chapter, the authors present a machine learning-based approach that will categorize the COVID-19 positive patients into five different categories, namely asymptomatic, mild, moderate, severe, and critical. The proposed system is capable of classifying the COVID-19-affected patients into five distinct categories using selected features of age, gender, ALT, hemoglobin, WBC, heart disease, hypertension, fever, muscle ache, shortness of breath with 97.5% accuracy.

Chapter 11

Web recommendation is the process of providing personalization recommendations to the requirements of specific users. A lot of research is conducted on recommender systems by a broad range of communities including computer scientists and interdisciplinary researchers. In response, a lot of recommender systems have been developed so far. However, the complexity of these systems can lead to information overload and decreased utility for the users. For these reasons, researchers have sought to apply the techniques of recommender systems to deliver personalized views of social annotation systems. In this chapter, the authors cover recent improvements in recommender systems and explore the major challenges. This chapter finally presents a prototype for adaptation to end-users. The model emphasizes an annotation-based recommendation system for generating recommendations.

Preface

Computational science deals with using computers to solve complex problems in science and engineering. Usually, computational science refers to computer science and applied mathematics. Various statistical techniques are used to sculpt and simulate complicated systems in this field.

In collaboration with engineering, Computational Science acts as a bridge between hypothesis and experimentation. Nowadays, most current research areas need to use computational methods to automate the processes. Some significant industries viz: biological, semiconductor, and automobile rely on advanced modelling and simulation. It also contributes to policy and decisions related to human health, resources, transportation, and defence. Computational science is inherently interdisciplinary. Its objectives relate to identifying and evaluating complicated systems, foreseeing their performance, and enhancing procedures and strategies.

This book has a collection of twelve chapters. A brief description of each of the chapters follows:

Chapter 1 uses natural language processing (NLP) to assess nursing students' attitudes. Here authors processed an approach to analysing the responses of nursing students to questions about the COVID-19 pandemic and the nursing profession, using automatic NLP techniques. Data has been collected online using a questionnaire in Turkish. During data analysis, a machine translation system was first used to translate the students' responses into English and then utilized a sentiment analyser for English on the translated responses to obtain the students' opinions automatically. Chapter 2 discussed a new power sequence in the positive integer modulo, and they named this sequence power Pell sequence modulo k. In addition, the authors determined those positive integer moduli for which this sequence exists and the number of such sequences for a given modulo.

Chapter 3 proposed a system based on hypergraph, fused hypergraph, learning from hypergraph representation, and the hypergraph convolution neural network for diagnosing COVID from X-ray images. The proposed system differentiates COVID infection accurately from other viral infections. A hypergraph-based convolutional neural network proposed for fast and accurate diagnosis system of COVID. Chapter 4 identified a new AI-based deep learning framework named CORONATE (COROna using Neural ArchiTecture sEarch) based on neural architecture space search network (NASNET) as a competitive choice to extract graphical features from radiography images referred from the public dataset of X-ray images. The proposed CORONATE model has ascertained with 98.3% accuracy, 96.7% sensitivity, and 100% specificity.

Chapter 5 introduced a model predictive control (MPC) schemes for controlling vehicle tracking on different trajectories. Simulations show that MPC algorithms can control the tracking vehicle very well since they can solve the optimal control actions subject to constraints. It shows that performance, stabilization, and robustness of the MPC controller can be regulated by varying its parameters and modifying its objective functions to softened constraints or constraint regions. Chapter 6 proposed a metaheuristic-based data optimization algorithm with machine learning-based feature extraction and classification architectures. Here the data optimization is carried out using gravitational search algorithm. The feature extraction has been carried out for the medical data using Bi-LSTM based RNN architecture in extracting the feature of input medical data, and this extracted data has been classified using a deep belief network with convolutional neural networks (DBN-CNN). The experimental results obtained by proposed technique as accuracy of 97.5%, precision of 94.5%, recall of 89.9% and F-1 score of 87.6%.

Chapter 7 proposed a new approach to image matching using Speeded-Up Robust Features (SURF). In the empirical studies, a broad set of experimental results indicates that the proposed method yields better and more reliable results than the traditional brute force method, which achieves an accuracy improvement of at least 5%. Chapter-8 highlights data mining and machine learning techniques like random forest regression, decision tree, and support vector machine and predicted the success of the movies based on ratings from IMDb and data retrieved from comments on social media platforms. Based on machine learning techniques, the proposed work develops a model that will help predict movie success before the release of the movie and thereby decreasing the risk somehow. The polarity and subjectivity of the movie are calculated based on the user reviews, and on those retrieved data, machine learning algorithms are used to predict the IMDb rating.

Chapter 9 discussed various aspects and techniques of machine learning that are engaged in the fields of risk assessment to ameliorate this process. Chapter 10 presented an ML-based approach to categorize the COVID 19 patients into five categories: asymptomatic, mild, moderate, severe, and critical. Then based upon the severity of the patient and availability of the space in intensive care units, the asymptomatic, mild, and moderate patients can be kept in isolation without intensive care equipment, and the severe and critical patients can be kept in the ICUs. Chapter 11 covered recent improvements in recommender systems and explored the significant challenges. This chapter finally presents a prototype for adaptation to end-users.

The model emphasizes an annotation-based recommendation system for generating recommendations.

Anand Nayyar
Duy Tan University, Da Nang, Vietnam

Sandeep Kumar
CHRIST University (Deemed), Bangalore, India

Akshat Agrawal
Amity University, Guragon, India

Chapter 1
Using Natural Language Processing Techniques to Assess the Attitudes of Nursing Students During the COVID–19 Pandemic

Emine Ela Küçük
Giresun University, Turkey

Dilek Küçük
Tübitak Marmara Research Center, Turkey

ABSTRACT

COVID-19 pandemic has a significant impact in the world. It has led to different measures taken by governments to prevent its spread, such as school closures, employment of e-learning, and complete lockdowns. Together with the pandemic, these measures also affected many people, economically and psychologically. This chapter assesses the attitudes of undergraduate nursing students in Turkey during the COVID-19 pandemic, using automatic natural language processing (NLP) techniques. NLP is a branch of artificial intelligence, and it facilitates automatic analysis of natural language texts. Machine translation and sentiment analysis are among significant NLP techniques. Data collection is performed using an online questionnaire, filled by 101 students from three different universities in Turkey. Machine translation is used to translate responses of the students to English, and then sentiment analysis is performed on these translations. The sentiment analysis results can be used by related nursing educators and health professionals.

DOI: 10.4018/978-1-7998-9012-6.ch001

INTRODUCTION

At the time of writing this chapter, the novel Coronavirus Disease 2019 (COVID-19) pandemic is still effective all over the world. This global pandemic has started in 2019 and since then it has affected all individuals and countries in the world. Lockdowns, school closures, using masks and complying with the social distancing rules are among the measures proposed and applied to decrease the negative effects of the pandemic. Remote education and remote working have become widespread. Many health professionals and scientists have worked hard to treat the infected and develop vaccines and drugs against the disease. Vaccines against COVID-19 have emerged at the end of this endeavor. The aforementioned change in the education and working style have been considered positively by some of the people concerned while some people have considered these changes negatively.

The aim of this study is to use automatic natural language processing (NLP) techniques to assess the attitudes of nursing students towards the COVID-19 pandemic and nursing profession at the initial stages of this global pandemic. NLP is a significant branch of artificial intelligence (AI) with application opportunities in diverse domains (Chowdhury, 2003, Jurafsky and Martin, 2020). NLP, and hence AI, is increasingly being used by recommender systems, in healthcare applications, in information retrieval systems, and in finance applications, among others. It is known that automatic NLP methods can be used to improve public health surveillance on the Web and other textual health-related sources (Natsiavas et al., 2016; Küçük et al., 2017; Baclic et al., 2020).

In this book chapter, the data is obtained online from 101 undergraduate nursing students between May 21, 2020 and July 5, 2020, with a questionnaire of open-ended questions published on Google Forms[1]. The questions (in Turkish) are about the opinions of the students regarding the recent COVID-19 pandemic, their coping strategies with stress during the pandemic and their personal development strategies, as well as their ideas regarding the nursing profession.

Within the course of this study, various NLP techniques are applied to the collected data (in natural language) in order to automatically extract the sentiments of the students towards the pandemic and towards the nursing profession alike.

Hence, an important NLP task considered in the current study is sentiment analysis (opinion mining) which estimates the opinion of a text owner (using the text) as a classification output in the form of these polarity classes: Positive, Negative, and Neutral (Feldman, 2013; Hemmatian and Sohrabi, 2019). We have used a high-performance sentiment analyzer for English texts (Hutto and Gilbert, 2014) for this purpose. However, before sentiment analysis, we have used another NLP technique, machine translation, to translate our original texts in Turkish into English. For this purpose, Google Translate (Wu et al., 2016) is employed.

Our study is significant as it is important to automatically infer plausible pieces of information from natural language texts, using NLP techniques, particularly at a time of a global pandemic affecting each and every person in the world.

Additionally, the opinions of undergraduate nursing students towards their future profession are valuable to improve nursing education and health education in general. Hence, we believe that sentiment analysis experiments in these settings constitute an important practical application of NLP (and AI). That is, using information processing and AI techniques such as those of NLP can contribute significantly to the related decision making processes.

Additionally, most previous work on the opinions of nursing students has performed manual analysis of the collected data. Our study differs from previous work in the sense that it applies NLP (and hence, AI) techniques in an automated manner on the answers of open-ended questions where the answers are given in natural language.

Currently, we have used machine translation and sentiment analysis techniques as our NLP techniques, yet, based on the current study, other recent and popular NLP techniques such as stance detection (Küçük et al., 2017) and controversy detection (Küçük et al., 2021) can also be employed on our dataset to enrich the sentiment results.

Main objectives of the current book chapter include the following items:

- This chapter aims to automatically determine the opinions of nursing students regarding the recent COVID-19 pandemic and regarding the nursing profession.
- For this purpose, NLP techniques, particularly, sentiment analysis and machine translation are employed to determine the opinions of the students.
- Another aim is to discuss the plausibility of the automatically obtained sentiment analysis results.

The rest of our book chapter is organized as follows: we first present a review of the related literature in the Background section. Next, we describe our data collection procedure and the results of our NLP techniques on the collected data in the Main Focus of the Chapter section. We provide discussions of the sentiment analysis results in the Solutions and Recommendations section. Future work based on the current study is presented in Future Research Directions section. Finally, our book chapter is concluded with a summary of the main points in the last (Conclusion) section.

BACKGROUND

The novel Coronavirus disease (COVID-19) pandemic, which has started in 2019, has drastically changed the common practices of people and governments. The emergence of this pandemic has boosted related research to better cope with it and to lessen its effects. These research papers tackle with different aspects of the disease and the pandemic. To name a few, data visualization strategies for COVID-19 data are presented in (Devi and Nayyar, 2021). Different technologies to combat with the COVID-19 pandemic are reviewed in (Al-Turjman et al., 2021) where these technologies include deep learning, big data, and robotics. Sharma et al. (2021) present optimization models for scheduling the movements of drones to be used to transfer COVID-19 medications. Similarly, drone-based case studies are described for measurement and monitoring of the pandemic and pandemic related prevention measures in (Kumar et al., 2021). Current pandemic trends are analyzed and automatic forecasting technologies based on time-series analysis are used in (Sobti et al., 2020) to predict future trends of the pandemic in India. Taneja et al. (2021) present a method to detect face mask wearing among individuals where the proposed method is based on a convolutional neural network (CNN) which is a deep learning method. Zivkovic et al. (2021) propose a hybrid method to predict COVID-19 cases. The proposed and evaluated method is based on machine learning and a nature inspired algorithm (Zivkovic et al., 2021). Laguarta et al. (2020) develop an artificial intellinge based voice analysis approach to detect COVID-19 cases based on their cough recordings. They report that their approach can achieve an accuracy of about 98.5% including asymptomatic COVID-19 cases (Laguarta et al., 2020). Tripathy et al. (2022) present a tool model called Smart COVID-19 shield which employs Internet of Things (IoT) technology in order to automatically detect common symptoms of COVID-19. The model is equipped with related sensors and is also capable of checking whether social distance measurements are followed (Tripathy et al., 2022).

The application opportunities of different artificial intelligence technologies, such as traditional machine learning and deep learning methods, within the context of the COVID-19 pandemic are studied and reviewed extensively in the related literature (Alakus and Turkoglu, 2020; Alimadadi et al., 2020; Jamshidi et al., 2020; Jin et al., 2020; Oh et al., 2020; Vaishya et al., 2020).

As the COVID-19 pandemic has a very deep impact on societies, there are several studies that are conducted to uncover the effects of the pandemic on different groups of people in societies. Students and particularly students from health-related faculties constitute a significant group where they are affected both as individuals and also due to the fact that the pandemic is directly related to their profession.

Cao et al. (2020) has explored the effects of the COVID-19 pandemic on the anxiety levels of medical college students in China. They have used Generalized Anxiety Disorder (GAD-7) scale (Spitzer et al., 2006) during data collection. It has been found that 0.9% of the participating students have suffered from severe anxiety, 2.7% of them have moderate anxiety, and 21.3% of them have mild anxiety (Cao et al., 2020). In (Cervera-Gasch et al., 2020), the intentions and the knowledge of the medicine and nursing students regarding the COVID-19 pandemic are analyzed. It is found that the students are willing to care for COVID-19 patients, however, it is also observed that a low percentage of students report that they have the required training (Cervera-Gasch et al., 2020). Cleland et al. (2020) have summarized the opinions and experiences of related experts on the topic of teaching at medical schools during the COVID-19 pandemic. They have determined the main areas of concern as: campus-based learning/teaching, clinical learning/teaching, selection/ assessment, and finally, the needs of the educators (Cleland et al., 2020). In (Dos Santos, 2020), the effects of the COVID-19 pandemic on the sense of belonging, opinions, and decision-making of nursing students in South Korea are considered. Data collection is carried out with interview questions asked online through a social media platform. At the end of the study, it is concluded that financial considerations constitute the main reason for choosing the nursing profession by the students. Another finding of the study is that almost all of the participating students have expressed their intention to quit the nursing profession due to the COVID-19 pandemic (Dos Santos, 2020). Ellis et al. (2020) have studied the impact of the COVID-19 pandemic on the stress levels of adolescents in Canada. After data collection through online surveys, it is found that the participating adolescents show a high level of concern for the pandemic, and that they are worried about schooling and peer relationships during the pandemic. It is also reported that COVID-19 related stress is associated with more loneliness and depression, particularly for those adolescents who are inclined to spend more time on social media platforms (Ellis et al., 2020). Lovrić et al. (2020) has similarly collected data from 33 nursing students through an online survey, about their perceptions about the COVID-19 pandemic. It is reported in this study that the students are aware of the spread of misinformation regarding the pandemic on social media. It is also observed that while the students have a mild fear of infection in classrooms, they are more concerned about being infected with the disease during their visits to the related clinics (Lovrić et al., 2020). In (Nearchou et al., 2020), a review of the studies carried out about the impact of the COVID-19 pandemic on the mental health of children and adolescents. It is summarized in this review paper that the COVID-19 pandemic has led to important mental health issues among children and adolescents, the most common of them being anxiety and depression (Nearchou et al., 2020). Puljak et al. (2020) have explored the opinions and ideas of the students of health sciences in Croatia about the e-learning process employed during the COVID-19 pandemic. Data is collected from 2.520 students by sending them a questionnaire form through e-mail. It is observed that while most of the students are satisfied with the e-learning settings during the pandemic, there are also students who have expressed their concerns about the lack of practical lessons during this period (Puljak et al., 2020).

In (Alici and Copur, 2021), the authors aim to determine the anxiety and fear of nursing students during the COVID-19 pandemic. 234 nursing students participated in the study and during data collection, Beck Anxiety Inventory and Fear of COVID-19 scale are used. It is addressed in the study that the fear and anxiety levels of nursing students are high (Alici and Copur, 2021). In (Aslan and Pekince, 2021), the stress levels of nursing students during pandemic are explored. 662 students have participated in the study and data is collected with an information form and with Perceived Stress Scale. It is concluded that the participating students have a moderate level of stress and that their stress levels vary with respect to their age, gender, and pandemic-related variables (Aslan and Pekince, 2021). Bączek et al. (2021) has explored the perception of online (electronic) learning during the COVID-19 pandemic by Polish medical students. After the analysis of the questionnaire filled by medical students; it is found that 69% of the students express that staying at home and continuous access to online course materials are the main advantages of e-learning. 70% of the students claim that the lack of interaction with the patients is the main disadvantage while 54% of the students claim that technical problems is the main disadvantage of e-learning (Bączek et al., 2021). In another related study (Belingheri et al., 2021); the intention of nursing students towards being vaccinated against the COVID-19 is examined. A related questionnaire is filled by 422 nursing students, and about 81% of the students have expressed their intention to get vaccinated. The main reason for the expressions in favor of being vaccinated is to protect family and friends. The main reason for being against vaccination is the fear of the adverse effects of vaccines (Belingheri et al., 2021). De Gagne et al. (2021) analyzed tweets posted by nursing students during the COVID-19 pandemic in three countries: the US, the UK, and South Korea. At the end of the analysis of over 8,000 tweets by nursing students, it is reported that the students have shared their concerns about the effects of the COVID-19 pandemic on their education in addition to sharing information about their lives and they have engaged in social interactions on Twitter for support and information sharing as well (De Gagne et al., 2021). Lim et al. (2021) has examined the opinions of university students in Singapore towards the COVID-19 vaccines. After data collection from the students through an online survey, it is found that 32% of the students have expressed vaccine hesitancy. Possible side effects and safety issues are found to be the main reasons of vaccine hesitancy in the study (Lim et al., 2021). In (Majrashi et al., 2021), a scoping review of the studies conducted on stress sources for the nursing students and their coping strategies with these stress sources during the time of the COVID-19 pandemic. After an analysis of 13 related studies, it is pointed out that the nursing students suffer from anxiety and depression, due to reasons such as e-learning, clinical training, and course workloads. In order to cope with stress, the students are reported to search for information and consultation, and to stay optimistic (Majrashi et al., 2021). Anxiety levels of nursing students in Israel during the COVID-19 pandemic and their strategies to cope with this anxiety are studied in (Savitsky et al., 2021). GAD-7 scale (Spitzer et al., 2006) is used to collect data from 244 nursing students. At the end of the study, it is observed that the prevalence of severe anxiety among the students is 13.1% and the prevalence of moderate anxiety is 42.8% (Savitsky et al., 2021). In another related work by Mulyadi et al. (2021), a systematic review of the studies conducted on the mental health problems and sleeping disturbances of nursing students that are observed during the COVID-19 pandemic is presented. After the analysis of 17 related papers, it is reported that the prevalence of depression among nursing students is 52%, the prevalence of fear is 41%, the prevalence of anxiety is 32%, that of stress is 30%, and finally, the prevalence of sleeping disturbances is 27% (Mulyadi et al., 2021).

Natural language processing (NLP) is a subtopic of artificial intelligence. NLP is defined in the related literature as the computational treatment of natural language texts and speech to automatically manipulate and understand the natural language and speech (Chowdhury, 2003). There are several different NLP problems ranging from parsing, text classification and text clustering, information extraction, and information retrieval to automatic machine translation and question answering (Jurafsky and Martin, 2020). Rule-based, lexicon-based, traditional machine learning based and more recently deep learning techniques are commonly utilized for different NLP tasks (Küçük and Arıcı, 2018; Jurafsky and Martin, 2020).

Machine translation is an NLP technique where natural language texts produced in one language are automatically translated into other languages (Lopez, 2008; Papineni et al., 2002). Google Translate is one of the best performing machine translation systems presented so far (Wu et al., 2016). Deep learning based neural network systems are known to achieve high performance rates recently (Wu et al., 2016; Vaswani et al., 2018).

Sentiment analysis and stance detection are also among the popular and recent research topics of NLP (Küçük, 2021). Sentiment analysis is particularly a well-studied topic where the polarity of the underlying text is usually sought (Feldman, 2013; Hemmatian and Sohrabi, 2019). These polarity classes are "positive" and "negative" while the third "neutral" class is also commonly considered. Sentiment analysis is also considered as a problem in affective computing (Picard, 2003; Tao and Tan, 2005). Affective computing can be defined as the class of automatic computing technologies that deal with the analysis and generation of features related to affect or emotion (Tao and Tan, 2005).

NLP techniques have also been used to extract useful information from natural language texts about the COVID-19 pandemic. In (Low et al., 2020); different language-based features are used to train models for trend analysis, classification, and clustering of Reddit posts in order to uncover the vulnerable mental health support groups and anxiety levels during the COVID-19 pandemic. It is reported in this study that these NLP and machine learning techniques employed help reveal patterns of mental health problems expressed in natural language as well as the related concerns of the Reddit users (Low et al., 2020). Mostafa (2020) has used word2vec (Mikolov et al., 2013) and a number of machine learning algorithms to determine the sentiments of Egyptian students towards the e-learning scheme employed during the time of COVID-19 pandemic. The author concludes that this study helps better understand the opinions of the students about the related processes (Mostafa, 2020). In (Oyebode et al., 2020), COVID-19 related comments from six different social media platforms are collected and analyzed using NLP techniques such as keyphrase extraction and sentiment analysis. Later, the extracted information is used to categorize the comments into themes (Oyebode et al., 2020). Finally, Klein et al. (2021) analyzed English tweets including keywords related to COVID-19 in order to determine COVID-19 cases that are self-reported by Twitter users. Bidirectional Encoder Representations from Transformers (BERT) (Devlin et al., 2018) is used in this system to classify the tweets. BERT is a pre-trained deep learning model commonly used for many NLP problems. It is reported in the study that an F-score of 76% is achieved using their approach based on BERT, which is proposed to identify those tweets that self-report COVID-19 cases (Klein et al., 2021).

As reviewed above, considerable research effort has been devoted to using artificial intelligence and related technologies to decrease the negative effects of the COVID-19 pandemic and to improve the quality of life of populations in the world during the period of the pandemic. Yet, we believe that further and extensive studies should be conducted to automatically determine opinions and ideas of people during the pandemic. Results of such studies will be of critical importance in order to achieve improved public health surveillance. Hence, in the current book chapter, we present one such study targeting at the automatic determination of the opinions of nursing students about the pandemic. Our study will help public health professionals, education authorities, and health-related policy makers.

MAIN FOCUS OF THE CHAPTER

In this section, we describe our dataset and data analysis methods. The first subsection below elaborates the data collection method to arrive at the final dataset and the second subsection describes the application of automatic data analysis methods on the collected dataset.

Data Collection

Data is collected with an online questionnaire form which is made available to the nursing students through Google Forms. The open-ended questions from the questionnaire (which are considered within this book chapter) are provided below:

1. How does the COVID-19 pandemic affect you?
2. What do you do to cope with stress during the COVID-19 pandemic?
3. What do you do for your professional development during the COVID-19 pandemic?
4. How do you assess the nursing profession during the COVID-19 pandemic?
5. How do you think the COVID-19 pandemic affect nursing profession?

The link to the online questionnaire form is shared with nursing students from three different universities in Turkey. Those students who volunteer and agree to fill in the online form are included in the study. A total of 101 students from three different universities have agreed to participate and voluntarily filled in the form between May 21st, 2020 and July 5th, 2020.

83% of the students are female and 17% of are male nursing students. 18% of the students are 1st grade students, 31% of them are 2nd grade, 21% of them are 3rd grade, and 30% of them are 4th grade students. Due to the e-learning strategy employed during the time of data collection due to the COVID-19 pandemic, the places of residence of the participating students constitute 15 different cities in Turkey. The average age of the participating students is 21.55.

The answers to these five questions (given in natural language) are considered within the course of the current study.

Data Analysis Using Natural Language Processing

As mentioned previously in the Background section, sentiment analysis (also known as opinion mining) is an important NLP task and aims to determine the sentiment or opinion of the text producer using rule-based, lexicon-based, machine learning based, and deep learning based methods. The output of the sentiment analysis procedure is a polarity class (usually) from this set: {positive, negative, neutral} (Hutto and Gilbert, 2014).

Sentiment analysis is a significant process to automatically determine the opinions of people, particularly at the time of a global pandemic. Automatic sentiment

Figure 1. NLP pipeline for the sentiment analysis on the responses of nursing students

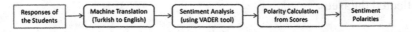

analysis schemes are employed to infer the opinions and ideas of people about the COVID-19 pandemic in several studies including (Barkur and Vibha, 2020; Chakraborty et al., 2020; de Las Heras-Pedrosa et al., 2020; Naseem et al., 2021; Rahman and Islam, 2022).

Valence Aware Dictionary for sEntiment Reasoning (VADER) is a rule based sentiment analyzer that is commonly employed as a practical tool in the related literature (Hutto and Gilbert, 2014). VADER outputs a compound sentiment score and the score can be used to perform sentiment classification, using the following rules[2]:

If (score >= 0.05) then positive sentiment,

If (score > -0.05) and (score < 0.05) then neutral sentiment,

If (score <= -0.05) then negative sentiment

VADER is made publicly available on the Web as a Python library. However, its versions written in other programming languages are also available. In this study, we have used the Java implementation of VADER[3].

The responses of the students are in Turkish language. Hence, in order to apply VADER to Turkish content, we first use the machine translation tool, Google Translate, to translate the responses of the students from Turkish to English, then apply the VADER sentiment analysis, and finally turn the compound sentiment scores obtained into actual sentiment classes. Hence, our pipeline to determine the sentiments from the student responses is given in Figure 1.

We start with the answers to the first question and feed these answers to the NLP pipeline given in Figure 1. That is, we first translate these sentences into English. Then, the resulting English translations are given as input to the VADER sentiment analysis tool. And finally, the compound scores determined by the sentiment analyzer are turned into actual sentiment class labels of positive, negative, and neutral.

At the end of this processing stage, we observe that 11% of the answers (to the first question) have a positive sentiment, 78% of the answers have negative sentiment, and 11% of them have neutral sentiment.

Table 1. Questions and sentiment analysis results on the responses of students to these questions

No.	Question	Positive Sentiment	Negative Sentiment	Neutral Sentiment
1	How does the COVID-19 pandemic affect you?	11%	78%	11%
2	What do you do to cope with stress during the COVID-19 pandemic?	22%	9%	69%
3	What do you do for your professional development during the COVID-19 pandemic?	15%	4%	81%
4	How do you assess the nursing profession during the COVID-19 pandemic?	47%	16%	37%
5	How do you think the COVID-19 pandemic affect nursing profession?	57%	25%	18%

The same NLP pipeline has been applied to the answers to the second, third, fourth, and fifth questions. The results obtained on responses to the remaining four questions are presented below:

1. The sentiment polarities of the responses to the second question are as follows: the polarities of 22% of the responses are found to be positive, 9% of the responses are negative, and 69% of the responses are neutral.
2. The resulting polarities calculated for the third question are as follows: 15% of the responses have positive sentiment, 4% of the responses are negative, and remaining 81% of them have neutral sentiment.
3. The polarities of the responses to the fourth question are as follows: 47% of the responses are classified as positive, 16% of the responses are classified as negative, and 37% of the responses are classified with neutral sentiment.
4. Finally, the polarities of the responses to the fifth question are found to as follows: 57% of the responses to this question have positive sentiment, 25% of them have negative sentiment, and 18% of them have neutral sentiment.

SOLUTIONS AND RECOMMENDATIONS

The considered five questions asked to nursing students and their final sentiment analysis results are summarized in Table 1.

The first question explores the opinions of nursing students about the COVID-19 pandemic. It can be observed that the responses of the students are mostly negative (78%). It is an expected result and comparable with the related results in the literature.

Only about 11% of the responses of the students have positive sentiment, while the remaining 11% of the responses have neutral sentiment.

The second and third questions are about the coping strategies of the students with the COVID-19 pandemic and about their professional development strategies during the pandemic. For the responses of both of these two questions, the most common sentiment class is neutral (69% and 81%, respectively). Additionally, the prevalence of positive sentiment is also higher that the prevalence of negative sentiment for both of these questions. That is, the prevalence of negative sentiment for these two questions is quite low (9% and 4%, respectively). It can be concluded that the participating students tend to use a neutral and positive language when responding to questions about their coping strategies with stress and personal development strategies during the time of the COVID-19 pandemic.

The last two questions are about the perceptions of the nursing students about the nursing profession itself, during the COVID-19 pandemic. The most prevalent sentiment of the students' responses for both of these two questions is positive. The prevalence of the positive sentiment is 47% for the fourth question, and the corresponding prevalence is 57% for the last question. Neutral sentiment is the second most common sentiment for the fourth question (37%) while negative sentiment is the second most common sentiment for the last question (15%). It can be concluded that the nursing students have a positive attitude towards the nursing profession and health care professionals during this global pandemic.

Overall, we can argue that the sentiments of the students about the COVID-19 pandemic itself are mostly negative. Their sentiments about their coping strategies with stress and personal development strategies are mostly neutral. Finally, the sentiments observed in responses to questions about the nursing profession are mostly positive.

It will be fruitful to extend the size of the dataset by collecting data from a larger set of students and also from students of other health-related professions and then conduct similar experiments on the extended forms of the dataset.

FUTURE RESEARCH DIRECTIONS

Future work based on the current study includes the employment of other NLP techniques such as stance detection and controversy detection on the responses of the nursing students. Stance detection is a research topic in NLP that is related to sentiment analysis and it aims to determine the position (stance) of a text owner towards a particular target. The resulting stance classes include Favor, Against, and None (Küçük, 2017; Küçük, 2021). Controversy detection aims to automatically determine controversial topics in texts (Küçük et al., 2021). There are several controversial issues in health-related tasks including complementary and alternative medicine, and different types of vaccines. The existing sentiment information automatically obtained within the course of the current book chapter can be enriched with the results of automatic stance detection and controversy detection.

CONCLUSION

COVID-19 pandemic has affected many aspects of the lives of the humans, ranging from education to working styles. It can be argued that it has affected both the personal and professional lives of health professionals and students at health-related universities. People are commonly expressing their opinions about the COVID-19 pandemic on the Internet and on other platforms using their natural language. Automatic NLP techniques offer important opportunities when processing these texts to extract valuable information. In this book chapter, we have processed the responses of nursing students to questions about the COVID-19 pandemic and about the nursing profession, using automatic NLP techniques. Data has been collected online using a questionnaire in Turkish. During data analysis, we have first used a machine translation system to translate the responses of the students into English and then utilized a sentiment analyzer for English on the translated responses, to automatically obtain the opinions of the students. The results show that, although the sentiments of the students towards the COVID-19 pandemic are mostly negative, their sentiments towards the nursing profession are mostly positive. The results can be used by nursing educators to improve the related education strategies and also by other health professionals. Future work includes using other NLP techniques to automatically elicit richer information from the feedbacks of the nursing students.

REFERENCES

Al-Turjman, F., Devi, A., & Nayyar, A. Emerging Technologies for Battling COVID-19. *Studies in Systems, Decision and Control*, 324.

Alakus, T. B., & Turkoglu, I. (2020). Comparison of deep learning approaches to predict COVID-19 infection. *Chaos, Solitons, and Fractals*, *140*, 110120. doi:10.1016/j.chaos.2020.110120 PMID:33519109

Alici, N. K., & Copur, E. O. (n.d.). Anxiety and fear of COVID-19 among nursing students during the COVID-19 pandemic: A descriptive correlation study. *Perspectives in Psychiatric Care*.

Alimadadi, A., Aryal, S., Manandhar, I., Munroe, P. B., Joe, B., & Cheng, X. (2020). Artificial intelligence and machine learning to fight COVID-19. *Physiological Genomics*, *52*(4), 200–202. doi:10.1152/physiolgenomics.00029.2020 PMID:32216577

Aslan, H., & Pekince, H. (2021). Nursing students' views on the COVID-19 pandemic and their percieved stress levels. *Perspectives in Psychiatric Care*, *57*(2), 695–701. doi:10.1111/ppc.12597 PMID:32808314

Baclic, O., Tunis, M., Young, K., Doan, C., Swerdfeger, H., & Schonfeld, J. (2020). Artificial intelligence in public health: Challenges and opportunities for public health made possible by advances in natural language processing. *Canada Communicable Disease Report*, *46*(6), 161–168. doi:10.14745/ccdr.v46i06a02 PMID:32673380

Bączek, M., Zagańczyk-Bączek, M., Szpringer, M., Jaroszyński, A., & Wożakowska-Kapłon, B. (2021). Students' perception of online learning during the COVID-19 pandemic: A survey study of Polish medical students. *Medicine*, *100*(7), e24821. doi:10.1097/MD.0000000000024821 PMID:33607848

Barkur, G., Vibha, G. B. K., & Kamath, G. B. (2020). Sentiment analysis of nationwide lockdown due to COVID 19 outbreak: Evidence from India. *Asian Journal of Psychiatry*, *51*, 102089. doi:10.1016/j.ajp.2020.102089 PMID:32305035

Belingheri, M., Ausili, D., Paladino, M. E., Luciani, M., Di Mauro, S., & Riva, M. A. (2021). Attitudes towards COVID-19 vaccine and reasons for adherence or not among nursing students. *Journal of Professional Nursing*, *37*(5), 923–927. doi:10.1016/j.profnurs.2021.07.015 PMID:34742523

Cao, W., Fang, Z., Hou, G., Han, M., Xu, X., Dong, J., & Zheng, J. (2020). The psychological impact of the COVID-19 epidemic on college students in China. *Psychiatry Research*, *287*, 112934. doi:10.1016/j.psychres.2020.112934 PMID:32229390

Cervera-Gasch, Á., González-Chordá, V. M., & Mena-Tudela, D. (2020). COVID-19: Are Spanish medicine and nursing students prepared? *Nurse Education Today*, *92*, 104473. doi:10.1016/j.nedt.2020.104473 PMID:32497867

Chakraborty, K., Bhatia, S., Bhattacharyya, S., Platos, J., Bag, R., & Hassanien, A. E. (2020). Sentiment Analysis of COVID-19 tweets by Deep Learning Classifiers—A study to show how popularity is affecting accuracy in social media. *Applied Soft Computing*, *97*, 106754. doi:10.1016/j.asoc.2020.106754 PMID:33013254

Chowdhury, G. G. (2003). Natural language processing. *Annual Review of Information Science & Technology*, *37*(1), 51–89. doi:10.1002/aris.1440370103

Cleland, J., McKimm, J., Fuller, R., Taylor, D., Janczukowicz, J., & Gibbs, T. (2020). Adapting to the impact of COVID-19: Sharing stories, sharing practice. *Medical Teacher*, *42*(7), 772–775. doi:10.1080/0142159X.2020.1757635 PMID:32401079

De Gagne, J. C., Cho, E., Park, H. K., Nam, J. D., & Jung, D. (2021). A qualitative analysis of nursing students' tweets during the COVID-19 pandemic. *Nursing & Health Sciences*, *23*(1), 273–278. doi:10.1111/nhs.12809 PMID:33404157

de Las Heras-Pedrosa, C., Sánchez-Núñez, P., & Peláez, J. I. (2020). Sentiment analysis and emotion understanding during the COVID-19 pandemic in Spain and its impact on digital ecosystems. *International Journal of Environmental Research and Public Health*, *17*(15), 5542. doi:10.3390/ijerph17155542 PMID:32751866

Devi, A., & Nayyar, A. (2021). Perspectives on the Definition of Data Visualization: A Mapping Study and Discussion on Coronavirus (COVID-19) Dataset. In *Emerging Technologies for Battling Covid-19* (pp. 223–240). Springer. doi:10.1007/978-3-030-60039-6_11

Devlin, J., Chang, M. W., Lee, K., & Toutanova, K. (2018). *BERT: Pre-training of deep bidirectional transformers for language understanding*. arXiv preprint arXiv:1810.04805.

Dos Santos, L. M. (2020). How does COVID-19 pandemic influence the sense of belonging and decision-making process of nursing students: The study of nursing students' experiences. *International Journal of Environmental Research and Public Health*, *17*(15), 5603. doi:10.3390/ijerph17155603 PMID:32756506

Ellis, W. E., Dumas, T. M., & Forbes, L. M. (2020). Physically isolated but socially connected: Psychological adjustment and stress among adolescents during the initial COVID-19 crisis. *Canadian Journal of Behavioural Science/Revue Canadienne des Sciences du Comportement*, *52*(3), 177.

Feldman, R. (2013). Techniques and applications for sentiment analysis. *Communications of the ACM*, *56*(4), 82–89. doi:10.1145/2436256.2436274

Hemmatian, F., & Sohrabi, M. K. (2019). A survey on classification techniques for opinion mining and sentiment analysis. *Artificial Intelligence Review*, *52*(3), 1495–1545. doi:10.100710462-017-9599-6

Hutto, C., & Gilbert, E. (2014). VADER: A parsimonious rule-based model for sentiment analysis of social media text. In *Proceedings of the International AAAI Conference on Web and Social Media* (*Vol. 8*, No. 1). AAAI.

Jamshidi, M., Lalbakhsh, A., Talla, J., Peroutka, Z., Hadjilooei, F., Lalbakhsh, P., Jamshidi, M., La Spada, L., Mirmozafari, M., Dehghani, M., & Sabet, A. (2020). Artificial intelligence and COVID-19: Deep learning approaches for diagnosis and treatment. *IEEE Access: Practical Innovations, Open Solutions*, 8, 109581–109595. doi:10.1109/ACCESS.2020.3001973 PMID:34192103

Jin, C., Chen, W., Cao, Y., Xu, Z., Tan, Z., Zhang, X., Deng, L., Zheng, C., Zhou, J., Shi, H., & Feng, J. (2020). Development and evaluation of an artificial intelligence system for COVID-19 diagnosis. *Nature Communications*, *11*(1), 1–14. doi:10.103841467-020-18685-1 PMID:33037212

Jurafsky, D., & Martin, J. H. (2020). *Speech and language processing: An introduction to natural language processing, computational linguistics, and speech recognition.* Prentice Hall.

Klein, A. Z., Magge, A., O'Connor, K., Amaro, J. I. F., Weissenbacher, D., & Hernandez, G. G. (2021). Toward using Twitter for tracking COVID-19: A natural language processing pipeline and exploratory data set. *Journal of Medical Internet Research*, *23*(1), e25314. doi:10.2196/25314 PMID:33449904

Küçük, D. (2017). Stance detection in Turkish tweets. *Proceedings of the International Workshop on Social Media World Sensors (SIDEWAYS) of ACM Hypertext Conference*.

Küçük, D. (2021). Sentiment, stance, and intent detection in Turkish tweets. In *New Opportunities for Sentiment Analysis and Information Processing* (pp. 206–217). IGI Global. doi:10.4018/978-1-7998-8061-5.ch011

Küçük, D., & Arıcı, N. (2018). Doğal dil işlemede derin öğrenme uygulamaları üzerine bir literatür çalışması [A literature study on deep learning applications in natural language processing]. *Uluslararası Yönetim Bilişim Sistemleri ve Bilgisayar Bilimleri Dergisi*, *2*(2), 76–86.

Küçük, E. E., Takır, S., & Küçük, D. (2021). Controversy detection on health-related tweets. In *Proceedings of the 14th International Symposium on Health Informatics and Bioinformatics* (p. 60). Academic Press.

Küçük, E. E., Yapar, K., Küçük, D., & Küçük, D. (2017). Ontology-based automatic identification of public health-related Turkish tweets. *Computers in Biology and Medicine*, *83*, 1–9. doi:10.1016/j.compbiomed.2017.02.001 PMID:28187367

Kumar, A., Sharma, K., Singh, H., Srikanth, P., Krishnamurthi, R., & Nayyar, A. (2021). Drone-Based Social Distancing, Sanitization, Inspection, Monitoring, and Control Room for COVID-19. In *Artificial Intelligence and Machine Learning for COVID-19* (pp. 153–173). Springer. doi:10.1007/978-3-030-60188-1_8

Laguarta, J., Hueto, F., & Subirana, B. (2020). COVID-19 artificial intelligence diagnosis using only cough recordings. *IEEE Open Journal of Engineering in Medicine and Biology, 1*, 275–281. doi:10.1109/OJEMB.2020.3026928 PMID:34812418

Lim, L. J., Lim, A. J., Fong, K. K., & Lee, C. G. (2021). Sentiments regarding COVID-19 vaccination among graduate students in Singapore. *Vaccines, 9*(10), 1141. doi:10.3390/vaccines9101141 PMID:34696249

Lopez, A. (2008). Statistical machine translation. *ACM Computing Surveys, 40*(3), 1–49. doi:10.1145/1380584.1380586

Lovrić, R., Farčić, N., Mikšić, Š., & Včev, A. (2020). Studying during the COVID-19 pandemic: A qualitative inductive content analysis of nursing students' perceptions and experiences. *Education Sciences, 10*(7), 188. doi:10.3390/educsci10070188

Low, D. M., Rumker, L., Talkar, T., Torous, J., Cecchi, G., & Ghosh, S. S. (2020). Natural language processing reveals vulnerable mental health support groups and heightened health anxiety on Reddit during COVID-19: Observational study. *Journal of Medical Internet Research, 22*(10), e22635. doi:10.2196/22635 PMID:32936777

Majrashi, A., Khalil, A., Nagshabandi, E. A., & Majrashi, A. (2021). Stressors and coping strategies among nursing students during the COVID-19 pandemic: Scoping review. *Nursing Reports, 11*(2), 444–459. doi:10.3390/nursrep11020042 PMID:34968220

Mikolov, T., Chen, K., Corrado, G., & Dean, J. (2013). *Efficient estimation of word representations in vector space*. arXiv preprint arXiv:1301.3781.

Mostafa, L. (2020). Egyptian student sentiment analysis using word2vec during the coronavirus (Covid-19) pandemic. In *International Conference on Advanced Intelligent Systems and Informatics* (pp. 195-203). Springer.

Mulyadi, M., Tonapa, S. I., Luneto, S., Wei-Ting, L. I. N., & Lee, B. O. (2021). Prevalence of mental health problems and sleep disturbances in nursing students during the COVID-19 pandemic: A systematic review and meta-analysis. *Nurse Education in Practice, 57*, 103228. doi:10.1016/j.nepr.2021.103228 PMID:34653783

Naseem, U., Razzak, I., Khushi, M., Eklund, P. W., & Kim, J. (2021). Covidsenti: A large-scale benchmark Twitter data set for COVID-19 sentiment analysis. *IEEE Transactions on Computational Social Systems, 8*(4), 1003–1015. doi:10.1109/TCSS.2021.3051189

Natsiavas, P., Maglaveras, N., & Koutkias, V. (2016). A public health surveillance platform exploiting free-text sources via natural language processing and linked data: application in adverse drug reaction signal detection using PubMed and Twitter. In *Knowledge Representation for Health Care* (pp. 51–67). Springer.

Nearchou, F., Flinn, C., Niland, R., Subramaniam, S. S., & Hennessy, E. (2020). Exploring the impact of COVID-19 on mental health outcomes in children and adolescents: A systematic review. *International Journal of Environmental Research and Public Health, 17*(22), 8479. doi:10.3390/ijerph17228479 PMID:33207689

Oh, Y., Park, S., & Ye, J. C. (2020). Deep learning COVID-19 features on CXR using limited training data sets. *IEEE Transactions on Medical Imaging, 39*(8), 2688–2700. doi:10.1109/TMI.2020.2993291 PMID:32396075

Oyebode, O., Ndulue, C., Mulchandani, D., Suruliraj, B., Adib, A., Orji, F. A., . . . Orji, R. (2020). *COVID-19 pandemic: identifying key issues using social media and natural language processing*. arXiv preprint arXiv:2008.10022.

Papineni, K., Roukos, S., Ward, T., & Zhu, W. J. (2002). Bleu: a method for automatic evaluation of machine translation. In *Proceedings of the 40th Annual Meeting of the Association for Computational Linguistics* (pp. 311-318). Academic Press.

Picard, R. W. (2003). Affective computing: Challenges. *International Journal of Human-Computer Studies, 59*(1-2), 55–64. doi:10.1016/S1071-5819(03)00052-1

Puljak, L., Čivljak, M., Haramina, A., Mališa, S., Čavić, D., Klinec, D., Aranza, D., Mesarić, J., Skitarelić, N., Zoranić, S., Majstorović, D., Neuberg, M., Mikšić, Š., & Ivanišević, K. (2020). Attitudes and concerns of undergraduate university health sciences students in Croatia regarding complete switch to e-learning during COVID-19 pandemic: A survey. *BMC Medical Education, 20*(1), 1–11. doi:10.118612909-020-02343-7 PMID:33167960

Rahman, M., & Islam, M. N. (2022). Exploring the performance of ensemble machine learning classifiers for sentiment analysis of covid-19 tweets. In *Sentimental Analysis and Deep Learning* (pp. 383–396). Springer. doi:10.1007/978-981-16-5157-1_30

Savitsky, B., Findling, Y., Ereli, A., & Hendel, T. (2020). Anxiety and coping strategies among nursing students during the Covid-19 pandemic. *Nurse Education in Practice, 46*, 102809. doi:10.1016/j.nepr.2020.102809 PMID:32679465

Sharma, K., Singh, H., Sharma, D. K., Kumar, A., Nayyar, A., & Krishnamurthi, R. (2021). Dynamic models and control techniques for drone delivery of medications and other healthcare items in COVID-19 hotspots. In *Emerging Technologies for Battling Covid-19* (pp. 1–34). Springer. doi:10.1007/978-3-030-60039-6_1

Sobti, P., Nayyar, A., & Nagrath, P. (2020). Time Series Forecasting for Coronavirus (COVID-19). In *Proceedings of International Conference on Futuristic Trends in Networks and Computing Technologies* (pp. 309-320). Springer.

Spitzer, R. L., Kroenke, K., Williams, J. B., & Löwe, B. (2006). A brief measure for assessing generalized anxiety disorder: The GAD-7. *Archives of Internal Medicine*, *166*(10), 1092–1097. doi:10.1001/archinte.166.10.1092 PMID:16717171

Taneja, S., Nayyar, A., & Nagrath, P. (2021). Face Mask Detection Using Deep Learning during COVID-19. In *Proceedings of Second International Conference on Computing, Communications, and Cyber-Security* (pp. 39-51). Springer. 10.1007/978-981-16-0733-2_3

Tao, J., & Tan, T. (2005). Affective computing: A review. In *Proceedings of International Conference on Affective Computing and Intelligent Interaction* (pp. 981-995). Springer. 10.1007/11573548_125

Tripathy, H. K., Mishra, S., Suman, S., Nayyar, A., & Sahoo, K. S. (2022). Smart COVID-shield: An IoT driven reliable and automated prototype model for COVID-19 symptoms tracking. *Computing*, 1–22. doi:10.100700607-021-01039-0

Vaishya, R., Javaid, M., Khan, I. H., & Haleem, A. (2020). Artificial Intelligence (AI) applications for COVID-19 pandemic. *Diabetes & Metabolic Syndrome*, *14*(4), 337–339. doi:10.1016/j.dsx.2020.04.012 PMID:32305024

Vaswani, A., Bengio, S., Brevdo, E., Chollet, F., Gomez, A. N., Gouws, S., . . . Uszkoreit, J. (2018). *Tensor2tensor for neural machine translation*. arXiv preprint arXiv:1803.07416.

Wu, Y., Schuster, M., Chen, Z., Le, Q. V., Norouzi, M., Macherey, W., . . . Dean, J. (2016). *Google's neural machine translation system: Bridging the gap between human and machine translation*. arXiv preprint arXiv:1609.08144.

Zivkovic, M., Bacanin, N., Venkatachalam, K., Nayyar, A., Djordjevic, A., Strumberger, I., & Al-Turjman, F. (2021). COVID-19 cases prediction by using hybrid machine learning and beetle antennae search approach. *Sustainable Cities and Society*, *66*, 102669. doi:10.1016/j.scs.2020.102669 PMID:33520607

ENDNOTES

[1]   http://forms.google.com/

[2]   https://github.com/cjhutto/vaderSentiment

[3] https://github.com/apanimesh061/VaderSentimentJava

Chapter 2
Power Pell Sequences, Some Periodic Relations of These Sequences, and a Cryptographic Application With Power Pell Sequences

Çağla Çelemoğlu
Ondokuz Mayis University, Turkey

Selime Beyza Özçevik
Ondokuz Mayis University, Turkey

Şenol Eren
Ondokuz Mayis University, Turkey

ABSTRACT

Here, first of all, the authors investigated power Fibonacci sequence modulo k and formulas for the periods of these sequences, based on the period of the Fibonacci sequence modulo k. And then, the authors described a new power sequence for positive integer modulus. They named these sequences power Pell sequences modulo k. After that the authors determined those positive integer moduli for which this sequence exists and the number of such sequences for a given modulo k. In addition, the authors provide formulas for the periods of these sequences, based on the period of the Pell sequence modulo k, and they studied sequence/subsequence relationships between power Pell sequences. Finally, the authors examined ElGamal cryptosystem which is one of the asymmetric cryptographic systems and ElGamal cryptosystem which is obtained by using some power sequences. And they obtained asymmetric cryptographic applications by using power Pell sequences which the authors described.

DOI: 10.4018/978-1-7998-9012-6.ch002

INTRODUCTION

The Fibonacci sequence, $\{F_n\}_0^\infty$, is a sequence of numbers, beginning with the integer couple 0 and 1, in which the value of any element is computed by taking the summation of the two antecedent numbers. If so, for $n \geq 2$, $F_n = F_{n-1} + F_{n-2}$ (Koshy, 2001). The first eight terms of this sequence are $1, 1, 2, 3, 5, 8, 13, 21$.

There have been many studies in the literature dealing with the Fibonacci sequences. Some authors obtained generalization of the Fibonacci sequence by changing only the first two terms of the sequence or with minor changes only the recurrence relation, while others obtained generalizations of the Fibonacci sequence by changing both of them. In addition, the Fibonacci sequence $F = 0, 1, 1, 2, 3, 5, 8, \ldots$ has come to the fore for centuries, as it seems there is no end to its many surprising properties. It is seen that the popular number sequence has been found to have important properties when the sequence reduced under a modulus. It is well known, the Fibonacci sequence and the other sequences which is obtained by changing the recurrence relation or the first two terms of Fibonacci sequence under a modulus is periodic. $\pi(k)$ denote the period of the Fibonacci sequence modulo k, formulas are known for computing $\pi(k)$ based on the prime factorization of k. But if k is prime number, there is no formula for $\pi(k)$. On the other hand, some equations are provided. For example, if k is prime number and if $k \equiv \pm 1 \pmod{10}$, $\pi(k) \mid k - 1$ and if $k \equiv \pm 3 \pmod{10}$, $\pi(k) \mid 2(k+1)$ (Renault, 2013).

In this study, the authors used Pell sequence which is obtained by changing only the recurrence relation of Fibonacci sequence, power Fibonacci sequence modulo k, the relationship of periods of these sequences as material. These structures the authors used in this article are introduced as follows:

Definition 1. The Pell sequence (P_n) is defined recursively by the equation $P_n = 2P_{n-1} + P_{n-2}$ for $n \geq 1$, where $P_0 = 0$ and $P_1 = 1$ (Koshy, 2001).

Definition 2. Let G be a bi-infinite integer sequence providing the recurrence relation $G_n = G_{n-1} + G_{n-2}$. Providing $G \equiv 1, \alpha, \alpha^2, \alpha^3, \ldots \pmod{k}$ for some modulus k, then G is named a power Fibonacci sequence modulo k (Ide and Renault, 2012).

Example 1. For modulo $k = 29$, the two power Fibonacci sequences are following:

1, 6, 7, 13, 20, 4, 24, 28, 23, 22, 16, 9, 25, 5, 1, 6, 7, ... and 1, 24, 25, 20, 16, 7, 23, 1, 24, ...

Theorem 1. There is precisely one power Fibonacci sequence modulo 5. For $k \neq 5$, there exist power Fibonacci sequences modulo k certainly when k has prime factorization $k = q_1^{t_1} . q_2^{t_2} \ldots q_s^{t_s}$ or $k = 5q_1^{t_1} . q_2^{t_2} \ldots q_s^{t_s}$, where each $q_i \equiv \mp 1 \pmod{10}$; in either case there are definitely 2^s power Fibonacci sequences modulo k (Ide and Renault, 2012).

The Periods of Power Fibonacci Sequences

It is known that $\pi(k)$ denote the period of the Fibonacci sequence modulo k and there is no known explicit formula for $\pi(k)$. But, providing $(k, l) = 1$ then $\pi(kl) = \left[\pi(k), \pi(l)\right]$ (Wall, 1960). It is easily seen that if S is any periodic sequence mod kl and $(k, l) = 1$, then its period is the least common multiple of the period of S taken mod k and the period of S taken mod l. For $k > 2$, $\pi(k)$ is even (Wall, 1960; Renault, 1996).

In addition, it is known that $\pi(k)$ denote the period of the Fibonacci sequence know that Ide and Renault establishes a relationship between $\pi(k)$ and the period of power Fibonacci sequences modulo k. And, they obtained following theorems:

Theorem 2. Let q be a prime of the form $q \equiv \mp 1 \pmod{10}$ and let γ and σ be two roots of $f(x) = x^2 - x - 1 \pmod{q^t}$. Suppose $|\gamma| \geq |\sigma|$.

1. If $\pi(q^t) \equiv 0 \pmod 4$, then $|\gamma| = |\sigma| = \pi(q^t)$.
2. If $\pi(q^t) \equiv 2 \pmod 4$, then $|\gamma| = 2|\sigma| = \pi(q^t)$ (Ide and Renault, 2012).

Theorem 3. Let $k = q_1^{t_1} . q_2^{t_2} \ldots q_s^{t_s}$ be the product of the primes of the form $q_i \equiv \mp 1 \pmod{10}$.

1. If $\pi(k) \equiv 0 \pmod 4$, then modulo k, each power Fibonacci sequence has period $\pi(k)$.
2. If $\pi(k) \equiv 2 \pmod 4$, then modulo k, one power Fibonacci sequence has (odd) period $\dfrac{\pi(k)}{2}$ and the others have period $\pi(k)$.

3. If $\pi(k) \equiv 0 \pmod 4$, then modulo $5k$, each power Fibonacci sequence has period $\pi(k)$.

4. $\pi(k) \equiv 2 \pmod 4$, then modulo $5k$, each power Fibonacci sequence has period $2\pi(k)$ (Ide and Renault, 2012).

Also, in this study, the authors aim to use power Pell sequences in cryptography.

Cryptography and the Types of Cryptography

All of the methods used to make an understandable message incomprehensible to undesirable parties are called cryptography (Çimen vd. 2007). That is, cryptography is all of the mathematical methods that try to ensure information security notions like confidentiality, integrity, authentication and non-denial. The most focused issue of cryptography among these methods is privacy.

The main purpose of cryptography is to ensure the two which are usually referred to as Alice and Bob in order to get into touch over an insecure canal such that a rival, Oscar, can't understand. The information which is sent is called as plaintext, and the information is selected arbitrary (Stinson 2002). This communication takes place as follows:

Alice encrypts the plaintext, using a predetermined key, and sends ciphertext over the insecure channel. Oscar, by seeing the ciphertext in the channel, can't determine what the the message was; but Bob who knows the encryption key, can decrypt the ciphertext and revive the plaintext or the message. These situations are identified by using the following mathematical notation.

Definition 3. A cryptosystem is a five–tuple (P, C, K, E, D) where the following conditions are satisfied:

1. P is a finite set of possible plaintexts (or the messages);
2. C is a finite set of possible ciphertexts (or encrypted messages);
3. K is a finite set of possible keys;
4. For each $K \in K$, there is an encryption function $e_K : P \to C$ ($e_K \in E$) and a decryption function $d_K : C \to P$ ($d_K \in D$) such that $d_K(e_K(x)) = x$ for every plaintext element $x \in P$ (Stinson, 2002).

Every algorithms use a key to audit encryption and decryption, and a message may only be decrypted when the key meets the encryption key used. So the most important issue in encryption is the key. Cryptography is divided into two according to key structure.

In secret key cryptosystems which is the first of these, like Vernam cipher, is based on the fact that the key used when encrypting a message is known only between the sender and the receiver and this key is secret. In other words, this secret key, which both parties should know, was used in both encryption and decryption process. Therefore, in order for confidential messaging to occur, this key must be securely shared with the message between the sender and the receiver. In these systems, someone who doesn't know the key should try all possible keys to get the correct plaintext from the ciphertext. But in public key cryptosystems which is last of these, like ElGamal cryptosystem, both public and private keys are used. That is, distinct keys are used encryption scheme and decryption scheme. In this systems, no problems like key exchange (ElGamal 1985, Stinson 2002).

At the very heart of cryptography is the notion of one way function, which was shown to be necessary and sufficient for many cryptographic primitives.

A one-way function (OWF) is a function f such that for each x in the domain of f, it is easy to compute $f(x)$; but for essentially all y in the range of f, it is computationally infeasible to find any x such that $y = f(x)$. But, only a one-way function is not used in public-key cryptography. Because, in this situation, the receiver can't also make sense of the message. So a trapdoor one-way function is needed. A trapdoor one-way function is a one-way function where the inverse direction is easy, given a certain piece of information (the trapdoor), but difficult otherwise. Public-key cryptosystems are based on trapdoor one-way functions. The public key that everyone knows gives information about the particular instance of the function; the private key which known only to the receiver gives information about the trapdoor (Zhu, 2001).

In this paper, discrete logarithm problem, generalized discrete logarithm problem ElGamal and the generalized ElGamal encryption method has been used as the method. Definitions of these notions which were used in the study are given below:

Definition 4. Given a generator α of $\mathbb{Z}_q^*$ for most appropriately large prime q, $f(v) = \alpha^v (\mathrm{mod}\, q)$ is a one-way function. $f(v)$ is easily computed given α, v, and q; but for most choices q it is difficult, given $(y; q; \alpha)$, to find an v in the range $1 \leq v \leq q - 1$ such that $\alpha^v (\mathrm{mod}\, q) = y$. The difficult direction is known as the discrete logarithm problem.

Definition 5. Let q be a prime number such that the discrete logarithm problem in $(\mathbb{Z}_q^*, .)$ is infeasible, and let $\alpha \in \mathbb{Z}_q^*$ be a primitive element. Let $P = \mathbb{Z}_q^*$, $C = \mathbb{Z}_q^* \times \mathbb{Z}_q^*$ and define

$$K = \left\{ (q, \alpha, v, \beta) : \beta \equiv \alpha^v (\mathrm{mod}\, q) \right\}.$$

The values q, α, β are the public key, and v is the private key. For $K = \left(q, \alpha, v, \beta\right)$, and for a (secret) random number $u \in \mathbb{Z}_{q-1}$, define $e_K(x, u) = \left(y_1, y_2\right)$, where

$$y_1 = \alpha^u (\operatorname{mod} q)$$
$$y_2 = x\beta^u (\operatorname{mod} q)$$

For $y_1, y_2 \in \mathbb{Z}_q^*$, define $d_K(y_1, y_2) = y_2(y_1^{v})^{-1} \operatorname{mod} q$ (Stinson, 2002)

Definition 6. Established a finite cyclic group G of order n, a generator α of G, and an element $\beta \in G$ find the integer a, $0 \leq a \leq n-1$, such that $\alpha^a = \beta$. The hard problem is accepted as the generalized discrete logarithm problem (Menezes et al. 1996).

Definition 7. Let G be a finite cyclic group such that the generalized discrete logarithm problem is infeasible, and let α be a generator of G. Let define $K = \left\{\left(\alpha, a, \beta\right) : \beta = \alpha^a\right\}$. The values α, β are the public key, and $a(1 \leq a \leq n-1)$ is the private key. For $K = \left(\alpha, a, \beta\right)$, and for a (secret) random number $k(1 \leq k \leq n-1)$, introduce $e_K(x, k) = \left(y_1, y_2\right)$, where $y_1 = \alpha^k$ and $y_2 = x\beta^k$. For (y_1, y_2), introduce $d_K(y_1, y_2) = y_2(y_1^{a})^{-1}$. The system which is basically depended on generalized discrete logarithm problem is accepted as generalized ElGamal cryptosystem (Menezes et al. 1996).

The organization of this chapter is as follows. In this chapter, the authors aimed to describe a new power sequence for positive integer modulus and to find the period of new power sequence. According to this purpose, firstly, the authors researched the studies on power sequences and their use in cryptography in literature review. In line with research, the authors described a new power sequence for positive integer modulus and determined those positive integer modulus for which this sequence exists and the number of such sequences for a given modulo k in the proposed work. The authors named these sequences power Pell sequences modulo k. In addition, in the proposed work, the authors provide formulas for the periods of these sequences, based on the period of the Pell sequence modulo k and they studied sequence/subsequence relationships between power Pell sequences. Also, in the same section, the authors used power Pell sequences in asymmetric cryptographic applications. And they made some samples. Then, in analysis, what has been done in this study examined by comparing it with previous studies in the literature from different perspectives. As a result of this comparison, the authors obtained that the systems obtained with the power sequences in this study are more advantageous. Finally, suggestions for future research on this subject have been made.

LITERATURE REVIEW

The Fibonacci number sequence which was previously found by Indian mathematicians in the sixth century. But the sequence was introduced by Fibonacci as a result of calculating the problem related to the reproduction of rabbits in the book named Liber Abaci in 1202. Fibonacci has not done any work using these sequences. In fact, the first researches on these sequences were made about 600 years later. However, the subsequent research has increased substantially. There have been many studies in the literature dealing with the Fibonacci sequences. Some authors obtained generalization of the Fibonacci sequence by changing only the first two terms of the sequence or with minor changes only the recurrence relation, while others obtained generalizations of the Fibonacci sequence by changing both of them. Some of these sequences are chronologically as follows:

Lucas, Pell, Pell Lucas, Jacobsthal and Jacobsthal–Lucas sequences, k – Fibonacci and k – Lucas, generalized Fibonacci sequence with two real parameters used non-linear recurrence relation, generalized k – Fibonacci and generalized k – Lucas, generalized Fibonacci sequence with four real parameters used nonlinear recurrence relation, generalized k – Horadam (Edson and Yayenie, 2009; Falcon and Plaza, 2007; Horadam, 1965; Ide and Renault, 2012; Klein and Ben-Nissan, 2010; Lee, 2000; Lucas, 1878; Öcal et al, 2005; Sloane, 1973; Taşçı and Kılıç, 2008; Taşkara et al, 2010; Uslu et al, 2011; Vajda, 1989; Yazlık and Taşkara, 2012; Yayenie, 2011; Yılmaz and Bozkurt, 2009)

In addition, it is studied on the period of Fibonacci sequence and the sequences obtained Fibonacci sequence. Firstly, in 1960, Wall discussed the period of Fibonacci sequence modulo k (Wall, 1960). Then, in 1968, Shah and in 1989, Ehrlich discussed a somewhat related question of the existence of a complete residue system mod k in the Fibonacci sequence (Shah, 1968; Ehrlich, 1989). In 2013, Renault studied the period of (a, b) - Fibonacci sequence mod k (Renault, 2013). Studies on the periods of recurrence sequences still continue today.

Also, all of these sequences are based on the Fibonacci sequence and Fibonacci sequence has many impressive features. Different sequences are also defined using Fibonacci sequence. For example, in 2010, it is described the second order Gopala Hemachandra sequences and codes (Basu and Prasad, 2010). And in 2012, it is obtained that the power Fibonacci sequence modulo k (Ide and Renault, 2012) which is based on Fibonacci sequence and is one of the reccurent sequences. There are quite a lot implementations of these number sequences different areas like engineering, nature and cryptography and coding theory.

The first examples of cryptography are encountered in some unusual hieroglyphic samples belonging to the period of the Old Kingdom, Egypt around 1900 BC.

Again, around 60-50 BC, an encryption method was designed by Julius Caesar by changing the places of the letters in the normal alphabet and this method was used in state communication. In 1917, the Vernam cipher was found by Gilbert Vernam, and afterwards, it was determined by Joseph Mauborgne, the major in charge of communications in the US military, that using the Vernam cipher at once, that is, changing the key after each encryption, would make the system much more secure. This cipher, which is the perfect encryption method, is called 'one-time pad'. In all of the ciphers mentioned so far, the encryption scheme is based on the fact that the key used when encrypting a message is known only between the sender and the receiver and that this key is secret. In other words, this secret key, which both sender and the receiver should know, is used in both encryption and decryption. Therefore, this key must also be securely shared between the sender and the receiver in order for confidential messaging to take place. These systems are known *secret key cryptosystems or symmetric cryptography* (Çimen et al, 2007; Stinson, 2002; Zhu, 2001). In 1976, with an algorithm designed by Whitfield Diffie and Martin Hellman, the public key cryptosystem, namely asymmetric cryptography, emerged and cryptography took a different direction. With this algorithm, a solution to the key sharing problem of secret key cryptosystems is also provided. In 1978, a public key encryption algorithm called RSA was discovered by Rivest, Shamir and Adleman. This system is currently used in the security systems of some banks. In 1984, Another asymmetric encryption algorithm called ElGamal cryptosystem and based on Diffie-Hellman key exchange was proposed by Taher Elgamal. In public key cryptosystems, like ElGamal cryptosystem or RSA, both public and private key are used. That is, different keys are used encryption and decryption. In this systems, no problems like key exchange (Diffie and Hellman, 1976; El-Gamal, 1985; Menezes, 1996; Stinson, 2002; Zhu, 2001).

In addition, in 2015, it is described the third order Gopala Hemachandra sequences and codes and it is made symmetric cryptographic applications by using the third order Gopala Hemachandra codes (Nalli and Ozyilmaz, 2015).

Also, various applications have been made on the RSA or ElGamal cryptosystem which are asymmetric cryptographic systems. It is obtained extensions of RSA cryptosystem using polynomials over finite fields (El-Kassar et al, 2017). Also, it is obtained different extensions of ElGamal cryptosystem using some polynomials or ElGamal-like cryptosystem for enciphering large messages (El-Kassar and Haraty, 2005; Hwang et al, 2002).

PROPOSED WORK

The Power Pell Sequences in Positive Integer Modulo and the Number of These Sequences

In this section, the authors examined Pell sequences and power Fibonacci sequence modulo k and the authors defined power Pell sequence modulo k as follows:

Definition 8. Let P^* be a bi-infinite integer sequence satisfying the recurrence relation $P_n^* = 2P_{n-1}^* + P_{n-2}^*$. If $P^* \equiv 1, \alpha, \alpha^2, \alpha^3, \dots \pmod{k}$ for some positive integer modulus, then P^* is called a power Pell sequence modulo k.

Example 2. Modulo $k = 7$, there are two power Pell sequences:

$$1, 4, 2, 1, 4, \quad \text{and} \quad 1, 5, 4, 6, 2, 3, 1, 5,$$

Theorem 4. There is exactly one power Pell sequence modulo 2. For $k \neq 2$, there exist power Pell sequences modulo k precisely when k has prime factorization $k = q_1^{t_1}.q_2^{t_2} \dots q_s^{t_s}$ or $= 2q_1^{t_1}.q_2^{t_2} \dots q_s^{t_s}$, where each $q_i \equiv \mp 1 \pmod 8$; in either case there are definitely 2^s power Fibonacci sequences modulo k.

Proof. If $p(x) = x^2 - 2x - 1$ where α is a root of $p(x)$, $1, \alpha, \alpha^2$ is a power Pell sequence modulo k. The roots of $p(x)$ are those residues of the form $(1 + r)$ where $r^2 \equiv 2 \pmod k$. Let $p(x) = x^2 - 2$. Counting the number of solutions to $p(x) \equiv 0 \pmod k$.

For $k = 2$, the only solution to $x^2 \equiv 2 \pmod 2$ is 0 and there are no solutions to $x^2 \equiv 2 \pmod 4$. Thus, $x^2 \equiv 2 \pmod{2^t}$ has a solution only when $t = 1$ and that solution $x = 0 \pmod 2$. The corresponding power Pell sequence is $1,1,1,1,1\dots$. For $k \neq 2$, by use of the law of quadratic reciprocity, is found that 2 is a quadratic residue modulo primes of the form $q \equiv \pm 1 \pmod 8$. Thus, if $q \equiv \pm 1 \pmod 8$, then $p(x) \pmod k$ has two distinct roots. Moreover, with $p(x) = x^2 - 2$ and q is a prime of the form $q \equiv \pm 1 \pmod 8$, if x_1 is a root of $p(x) \pmod q$, then $p'(x_1) = 2x_1 \not\equiv 0 \pmod q$. By Hensel's Lemma (Niven et al, 1991), the authors obtained that $p(x) \pmod{q^t}$ has two distinct roots for every positive integer t.

Lastly, if k and k' are relatively prime, if $p(x) \equiv 0 \pmod{k}$ has m solutions and $p(x) \equiv 0 \pmod{k'}$ has m' solutions, by Chinese Remainder Theorem, then $p(x) \equiv 0 \pmod{kk'}$ has $m.m'$ solutions.

The Periods of Power Pell Sequences

In this section, the authors studied on the period of power Pell sequences the authors described and obtained some results. Here, the period of Pell sequences modulo k is denoted by $\tau(k)$.

Firstly, the authors investigated the period of power Pell sequences. And the authors obtained following results:

Theorem 5. The prime number q is in the form of $q \equiv \pm 1 \pmod{8}$, and and let θ and μ be the two roots of

$$p(x) = x^2 - 2x - 1 \pmod{q^t}.$$

Suppose $|\theta| \geq |\mu|$.

1.   For $\tau(q^t) \equiv 0 \pmod{4}$, $|\theta| = |\mu| = \tau(q^t)$
2.   For $\tau(q^t) \equiv 2 \pmod{4}$, $|\theta| = 2|\mu| = \tau(q^t)$.

Proof. Due to θ and μ are roots of

$$p(x) = x^2 - 2x - 1 \pmod{q^t}, \; \theta.\mu \equiv -1$$

and

$$(\theta.\mu)^n \equiv \theta^n \mu^n \equiv (-1)^n \pmod{p^e}$$

for any n. So, the proof of theorem 5 can be easily obtained similarly to the proof of lemma in (Ide and Renault, 2012).

Theorem 6. Let $k = q_1^{t_1}.q_2^{t_2}\ldots q_s^{t_s}$ in the form of $q_i \equiv \pm 1 \pmod{8}$.

1.   For $\tau(k) \equiv 0 \pmod 4$, the period of each power Pell sequence modulo k and modulo $2k$ is $\tau(k)$.

2.   For $\tau(k) \equiv 2 \pmod 4$, the period of one of power Pell sequences modulo k and modulo $2k$ is $\dfrac{1}{2}\tau(k)$, and the periods of others are $\tau(k)$.

Proof. Firstly, if $k = q^t$, then it can be easily seen that the conditions i and ii has been provided according to Theorem 5. Let u and v be relatively prime, and for induction, suppose that theorem is provided for modulo u and v. Now, if the authors show that it holds for modulo $u.v$, then the conditions i and ii will be proved.

Denote the roots of

$$p(x) = x^2 - 2x - 1 \pmod u$$

by $a_1, a_2, \quad a_s$ and denote the roots of

$$p(x) = x^2 - 2x - 1 \pmod v$$

by $b_1, b_2, \ldots b_{s'}$. Then the $s.s'$ roots of $p(x) \pmod{u.v}$ are represented d_{ij} for $1 \le i \le s, 1 \le j \le s'$ with root d_{ij} satisfying the following congruences

$$d_{ij} \equiv a_i \pmod u$$

$$d_{ij} \equiv b_j \pmod v.$$

One easily sees that $\left| d_{ij} \right|_{u.v} = \left[\left| a_i \right|_u, \left| b_j \right|_v \right]$.

To build i in theorem, assume that either $\tau(u) \equiv 0 \pmod 4$ or $\tau(v) \equiv 0 \pmod 4$. Then

$$\left| d_{ij} \right|_{u.v} = \left[\left| a_i \right|_u, \left| b_j \right|_v \right] \text{ or } \left[\tau(u), \frac{1}{2}\tau(v) \right] \text{ or } \left[\frac{1}{2}\tau(u), \tau(v) \right],$$

but from all these results it is seen that

$$\left|d_{ij}\right|_{u.v} = \tau\left(uv\right) \equiv 0\left(\mathrm{mod}\,4\right).$$

Moreover, the only root of $p\left(x\right)$ (mod 2) is the residue 1 and the roots of $p\left(x\right)$ mod $2k$ can be denoted as d_j, $\left|d_j\right|_{2k} = \left[\left|1\right|_2, \left|b_j\right|_k\right]$. If $\pi\left(u\right) \equiv 0\,(\mathrm{mod}4)$, then $\left|d_j\right|_k = \tau\left(k\right) \equiv 0\,(\mathrm{mod}4)$. Thus $\left|d_j\right|_{2k} = \left[1, \tau\left(k\right)\right] = \tau\left(k\right)$.

To prove ii in theorem, suppose that either $\tau\left(u\right) \equiv 2\left(\mathrm{mod}\,4\right)$ or $\tau\left(v\right) \equiv 2\left(\mathrm{mod}\,4\right)$. If

$$\left|d_{ij}\right|_{u.v} = \left[\left|a_i\right|_u, \left|b_j\right|_v\right] \text{ or } \left[\tau\left(u\right), \frac{1}{2}\tau\left(v\right)\right] \text{ or } \left[\frac{1}{2}\tau\left(u\right), \tau\left(v\right)\right]$$

then the authors have

$$\left|d_{ij}\right|_{u.v} = \tau\left(uv\right) \equiv 2\left(\mathrm{mod}\,4\right)$$

for all these cases. The one remaining case is

$$\left|d_{ij}\right|_{u.v} = \left[\frac{1}{2}\tau\left(u\right), \frac{1}{2}\tau\left(v\right)\right] = \frac{1}{2}\tau\left(uv\right).$$

In addition to, because of

$$\left|d_j\right|_{2k} = \left[\left|1\right|_2, \left|b_j\right|_k\right] = \left[1, \left|b_j\right|_k\right] = \tau\left(u\right),$$

one of the periods of power Pell sequences are equals to $\dfrac{1}{2}\tau\left(u\right)$ for modulo $2k$, the others have period $\tau\left(u\right)$.

Subsequence Relationships Among Power Pell Sequences

Theorem 7. θ and μ be the conjugate two roots of

$$p\left(x\right) = x^2 - 2x - 1\left(\mathrm{mod}\,k\right).$$

Suppose $|\theta| \geq |\mu|$. Let

$$T \equiv 1, \theta, \theta^2, \theta^3, \ldots (\mod k)$$

and let

$$M \equiv 1, \mu, \mu^2, \mu^3, \ldots (\mod k).$$

1. For $|\theta| > |\mu|$, M is a subsequence of T.
2. For $|\theta| = |\mu|$, and $k = q^t$ such that q be a prime number in $q \equiv \pm 1 (\mod 8)$, M and T are subsequences of each other.

Proof. Let assume that $|\theta| = 2n$. If $\theta^n \equiv -1 (\mod k)$ then T is a subsequence of M. Firstly, by multiplying the congruence with θ^{-1}, the authors get $\theta^{n-1} \equiv -\theta^{-1}$. Because of $\theta.\mu \equiv -1 (\mod k)$, it is obtained $-\theta^{-1} \equiv \mu$ and thus the authors obtain that $\theta^{n-1} \equiv \mu$. As a result, M is a subsequence of T.

To build i in theorem, assume $|\theta| > |\mu|$. According to Theorem 5, $|\theta| = 2|\mu| = 2n$ and n is odd here. Due to of $\theta.\mu \equiv -1 (\mod k)$, it can be written $(\theta.\mu)^n \equiv (-1)^n$ and since $\mu^n \equiv 1$, it is got $\theta^n \equiv -1$. According to claim in the first part of the proof, M is a subsequence of T.

To build ii in theorem, Firstly it can be observed that $(\theta^n)^2 = \theta^{2n} \equiv 1 (\mod q^e)$ and then it can be obtained $\theta^n \equiv -1 (\mod q^e)$ According to the claim at the beginning of the proof, the authors conclude M is a subsequence of T. Because of $|\theta| = |\mu|$ if switch the roles of θ and μ with the same proof, the authors can obtain that T is a subsequence of M.

Example 3. Modulo $k = 17$, there are two power Pell sequences:

$1, 7, 15, 3, 4, 11, 9, 12, 16, 10, 2, 14, 13, 6, 8, 5, 1, 7,$

and

$1, 12, 8, 11, 13, 3, 2, 7, 16, 5, 9, 6, 4, 14, 15, 10, 1, 12,$

$|\theta| = |\mu|$, then these sequences are subsequences of each other.

On the other hand, Modulo $k = 23$, there are two power Pell sequences:

$$1, 19, 16, 5, 3, 11, 2, 15, 9, 10, 6, 22, 4, 7, 18, 20, 12, 21, 8, 14, 13, 17, 1, 19,$$

and

$$1, 6, 13, 9, 8, 2, 12, 3, 18, 16, 4, 1, 6,$$

$|\theta| > |\mu|$, then second sequence is a subsequence of the other.

An Application of Power Pell Sequences to Cryptography

In this section, the authors used power Pell sequences in asymmetric cryptography. And the authors redefined the discrete logarithm problem and ElGamal cryptosystem which based on the discrete logarithm problem by using the power Pell sequences modulo k.

ElGamal Cryptosystem Obtained With Power Pell Sequence

Definition 9. Got a generator α of a chosen subgroup of $\mathbb{Z}_k^*$ for most appropriately large k, $f(\lambda) = \alpha^\lambda \pmod{k}$ is a one-way function. $f(\lambda)$ is easily computed given λ, α, and k; but for most choices k it is difficult, given (y; k; α), to find an λ such that $\alpha^\lambda \pmod{k} = y$. This difficult problem is called as the discrete logarithm problem with power Pell sequence modulo k.

Now, the authors will obtain public-key cryptosystem based on the discrete logarithm problem with power Pell sequence modulo k. The authors particularly called the cryptosystem as the ElGamal cryptosystem with power Pell sequence modulo k.

Definition 10. Let k be a positive integer such that the discrete logarithm problem with power Fibonacci sequence modulo k in a chosen subgroup of ($\mathbb{Z}_k^*$, .) is infeasible, and let

$$\alpha \in (the\ chosen\ subgroup\ of\ \mathbb{Z}_k^*)$$

be a primitive element (generator). Let $P = \mathbb{Z}_k \setminus \{0\}$,

$C = (the\ chosen\ subgroup\ of\ \mathbb{Z}^*_k) \times (\mathbb{Z}_k \setminus \{0\})$

and define

$$K = \left\{ (k, \alpha, \lambda, \beta) : \beta \equiv \alpha^\lambda \left(\bmod\, k \right) \right\}.$$

The values k, α, β are the public key, and λ is the private key. For $K = (k, \alpha, \lambda, \beta)$, and for a (secret) random number $u \in \mathbb{Z}_{the\ order\ of\ the\ chosen\ subgroup}$, define $e_K(x, k) = (y_1, y_2)$, where $\begin{array}{l} y_1 = \alpha^u (\bmod\, k) \\ y_2 = x\beta^u (\bmod\, k) \end{array}$. For $(y_1, y_2) \in C$, define

$d_K(y_1, y_2) = y_2 (y_1^\lambda)^{-1} \bmod k$.

Example 4. Suppose that $k = 914$ which provides Theorem 4 and so, modulo $k = 914$, there are two power Pell sequences:

- 1, 81, 163, 407, 63, 533, 215, 49, 313, 675, 749, 345, 525, 481, 573, 713, 171, 141, 453, 133, 719, 657, 205, 153, 511, 261, 119, 499, 203, 905, 185, 361, 907, 347, 687, 807, 473, 839, 323, 571, 551, 759, 241, 327, 895, 289, 559, 493, 631, 841, 485, 897, 451, 885, 393, 757, 79, 1, 81, 163, … and
- 1, 835, 757, 521, 885, 463, 897, 429, 841, 283, 493, 355, 289, 19, 327, 673, 759, 363, 571, 591, 839, 441, 807, 227, 347, 7, 361, 729, 905, 711, 499, 795, 261, 403, 153, 709, 657, 195, 133, 461, 141, 743, 713, 341, 481, 389, 345, 165, 675, 601, 49, 699, 533, 851, 407, 751, 81, 913, 79, 157, 393, 29, 451, 17, 485, 73, 631, 421, 559, 625, 895, 587, 241, 759, 155, 343, 323, 75, 473, 107, 687, 567, 907, 553, 185, 9, 203, 415, 119, 653, 511, 761, 205, 257, 719, 781, 453, 773, 171, 201, 573, 433, 525, 569, 749, 239, 313, 865, 215, 381, 63, 507, 163, 833, 1, 835, 757, …

It can be choosed one of these sequences with higher order.

Thus, {1, 835, 757, 521, 885, 463, 897, 429, 841, 283, 493, 355, 289, 19, 327, 673, 759, 363, 571, 591, 839, 441, 807, 227, 347, 7, 361, 729, 905, 711, 499, 795, 261, 403, 153, 709, 657, 195, 133, 461, 141, 743, 713, 341, 481, 389, 345, 165, 675, 601, 49, 699, 533, 851, 407, 751, 81, 913, 79, 157, 393, 29, 451, 17, 485, 73, 631, 421, 559, 625, 895, 587, 241, 759, 155, 343, 323, 75, 473, 107, 687, 567, 907, 553, 185, 9, 203, 415, 119, 653, 511, 761, 205, 257, 719, 781, 453, 773, 171, 201, 573, 433, 525, 569, 749, 239, 313, 865, 215, 381, 63, 507, 163, 833} is a power Pell sequence for modulo 914. α is a primitive element of the chosen subgroup of $\mathbb{Z}_k^*$. So, the primitive element $\alpha = 835$. Let's assume that the private key chosen by the receiver is $\lambda = 92$, so

$$\beta = 835^{92} \, (\bmod\, 914) = 205.$$

Then, suppose that the sender wishes to send the message $x = 759$ to receiver and the random integer which the sender chooses is $u = 86$. Hence, the sender computes

$$y_1 = \alpha^u (\bmod\, k) = 835^{86} (\bmod\, 914) = 203,$$
$$y_2 = x\beta^u (\bmod\, k) = 759.205^{86} (\bmod\, 914) = 759.345 = 451.$$

and sends $y = \left(y_1, y_2\right) = (203, 451)$ to the receiver.

The receiver calculates the sent message as follows:

$$x = y_2 (y_1^\lambda)^{-1} \bmod k = 451.(203^{92})^{-1} \bmod 914$$
$$= 451.(345)^{-1} \bmod 914$$
$$= 451.559 \bmod 914$$
$$= 759$$

Also, the authors compared that ElGamal cryptosystem and ElGamal cryptosystem with power Pell sequence in terms of cryptography. And the authors found that ElGamal cryptosystem with power Pell sequence modulo k is more advantageous than ElGamal cryptosystem in terms of cryptography. Because in the ElGamal cryptosystem, while the plaintext must be less than $q - 1$, in ElGamal cryptosystem with power Pell sequence modulo k, the plaintext must be less than $k - 1$. In addition it is known that if in ElGamal cryptosystem in $\mathbb{Z}_q^*$, q is a large prime number, in ElGamal cryptosystem with power Pell sequence modulo k, k is more large number ($k = q_1^{t_1}.q_2^{t_2} \ldots q_s^{t_s}$ or $k = 2q_1^{t_1}.q_2^{t_2} \ldots q_s^{t_s}$ in the form of $q_i \equiv \pm 1 \left(\bmod\, 8\right)$).

ANALYSIS

In this section, what has been done in this study will be analyzed by comparing it with previous studies in the literature from different perspectives. In this study, firstly, it is described a new power sequence modulo k (power Pell sequence modulo k) and it is determined as follows those positive integer modulus for which this sequence exists and the number of such sequences for a given modulo k. There is exactly one power Pell sequence modulo 2. For $k \neq 2$, there exist power Pell sequences modulo k precisely when k has prime factorization $k = q_1^{t_1} . q_2^{t_2} \ldots q_s^{t_s}$ or $= 2q_1^{t_1} . q_2^{t_2} \ldots q_s^{t_s}$, where each $q_i \equiv \mp 1 \pmod 8$; in either case there are definitely 2^s power Fibonacci sequences modulo k. In 2012, it is determined as follows those positive integer modulus for which power Fibonacci sequence exists and the number of such sequences for a given modulo k. There is precisely one power Fibonacci sequence modulo 5. For $k \neq 5$, there exist power Fibonacci sequences modulo k certainly when k has prime factorization $k = q_1^{t_1} . q_2^{t_2} \ldots q_s^{t_s}$ or $k = 5q_1^{t_1} . q_2^{t_2} \ldots q_s^{t_s}$, where each $q_i \equiv \mp 1 \pmod{10}$; in either case there are definitely 2^s power Fibonacci sequences modulo k (Ide and Renault, 2012). In 2020, it is determined as follows those positive integer modulus for which power Jacobsthal sequence exists and the number of such sequences for a given modulo k. For $k \geq 3$, there precisely exist power Jacobsthal sequences modulo k.

In addition, for the number of the power Jacobsthal sequences modulo k, there is exactly one power Jacobsthal sequence modulo 3 and for $k3$, when k has prime factorization $k = 3^t q_1^{t_1} . q_2^{t_2} \ldots q_s^{t_s}$, there are exactly 2^s power Jacobsthal sequences for $t = 0, 1$, 3.2^s power Jacobsthal sequences for $t = 2$, 6.2^s power Jacobsthal sequences modulo k for $t > 2$ (Ozyilmaz and Nalli, 2020). When the authors compare power Fibonacci, power Pell and power Jacobsthal sequences in terms of the modulo k which these sequences exist, they get that power Jacobsthal sequence exist for every modulo $k \geq 3$. So, it is obtained the most advantageous power sequence is power Jacobsthal sequence in terms of its presence in modulos.

Then, in this study, it is investigated as follows the periods of power Pell sequences and formulated the periods of power Pell sequences, based on the period of Pell sequence modulo k. The period of power Pell sequences is equal to $\tau(k)$ or $\frac{1}{2}\tau(k)$ ($\tau(k)$ is denoted the period of Pell sequences modulo k). Also, in 2012, it is obtained the period of power Fibonacci sequences is equal to $\pi(k)$ or $\frac{1}{2}\pi(k)$ ($\pi(k)$ is denoted the period of Fibonacci sequences modulo k) (Ide and Renault, 2012). Similarly, it is easily seen that the same periodic relationship will be found for power Jacobsthal sequences. Hence, when the authors compare the periodic relationship between power Fibonacci, power Pell and power Jacobsthal sequences and Fibonacci, Pell, Jacobsthal sequence, they get that similar equations are obtained for these three sequences.

After that, in this study, the authors examined sequence/subsequence relationships between power Pell sequences and obtained according to the roots of the characteristic equation of the Pell sequence, either only one of the sequences is a subsequence of the other or both of the sequences are subsequences of the other. In 2012, Ide and Renault examined sequence/subsequence relationships between power Fibonacci sequences and they got same relationship (Ide and Renault, 2012). Similarly, it is easily seen that the same sequence/subsequence relationships will be found for power Jacobsthal sequences. Thus, it is obtained that the same sequence/subsequence relations for all three sequences.

Finally, in this study, the authors used power Pell sequences in ElGamal cryptosystem which is one of the asymmetric cryptographic systems. And the authors obtained ElGamal cryptosystem with power Pell sequences and made some cryptographic applications by using this cryptosystem. In 2019, the authors obtained ElGamal cryptosystem with power Fibonacci sequences and they made some cryptographic applications by using this cryptosystem (Ozyilmaz and Nalli, 2019). In 2020, the authors obtained ElGamal cryptosystem with power Jacobsthal sequences and they made some cryptographic applications by using this cryptosystem (Ozyilmaz and Nalli, 2020). When each of the cryptosystems obtained with these three power sequences is compared cryptographically with the ElGamal system, it is seen that the systems obtained with the power sequences are more advantageous. Since, while only prime modules are used in the ElGamal system, the powers of the primes and the modules of the products of these powers are used in ElGamal systems obtained with these three sequences.

CONCLUSION AND FUTURE SCOPE

In here, firstly, the authors described a new power sequence in the positive integer modulo and they named this sequence as power Pell sequence modulo k. In addition, the authors determined those positive integer modulus for which this sequence exists and the number of such sequences for a given modulo.

Then, they examined the periods of power Pell sequences and built formulas for the periods of these sequences, based on the period of the Pell sequence modulo k. And, the authors studied sequence/subsequence relationships between power Pell sequences. After that, the authors what has been done in this study analyzed by comparing it with previous studies in the literature from different perspectives. As a result of this analyzed, the authors obtained following:

- The most advantageous power sequence is power Jacobsthal sequence in terms of its presence in modulos.
- The period of power Pell sequences is equal to the period of Pell sequences or half the period of Pell sequences as in power Fibonacci and power Jacobsthal sequences.
- Sequence/subsequence relationships between power Pell sequences are the same as power Fibonacci and power Jacobsthal sequences.

Finally, the authors used power Pell sequences in asymmetric cryptographic applications. And, they compared that ElGamal cryptosystem and ElGamal cryptosystem with power Pell sequence in terms of cryptography. And they found that ElGamal cryptosystem with power Pell sequence modulo k is more advantageous than ElGamal cryptosystem in terms of cryptography.

In addition, the following can be done as future research directions. New power sequences are described. And it can be investigated in which modulus these new power sequences exist. Then, the periods of these new power sequences can be examined. And the equations which found can be compared with periods of other power sequences. In addition new cryptographic systems can be built with these new power sequences and applications can be made. And also these cryptographic applications are comparable with each other.

ACKNOWLEDGMENT

This research received no specific grant from any funding agency in the public, commercial, or not-for-profit sectors.

REFERENCES

Basu, M., & Prasad, B. (2010). Long range variant of Fibonacci universal code. *Journal of Number Theory*, *130*(9), 1925–1931. doi:10.1016/j.jnt.2010.01.013

Çimen, C., Akleylek, S., & Akyıldız, E. (2007). Şifrelerin Matematiği: Kriptografi. Ankara: ODTÜ Yayıncılık.

Diffie, W., & Hellman, M. E. (1976). New Directions In Cryptography. *IEEE Transactions on Information Theory*, *22*(6), 644–654. doi:10.1109/TIT.1976.1055638

Edson, M., & Yayenie, O. (2009). A New Generalization of Fibonacci Sequence Extended Binet's Formula. *Integers: Electronic Journal of Combinatorial Number Theory*, *9*(6), 639–654. doi:10.1515/INTEG.2009.051

Ehrlich, A. (1989). On the Periods of the Fibonacci Sequence Modulo M. *Fibonacci Quarterly*, *27*, 11–13.

El-Kassar, A. N., & Haraty, R. A. (2005). ElGamal Public-Key cryptosystem in multiplicative groups of quotient rings of polynomials over finite fields. *Computer Science and Information Systems*, *2*(1), 63–77. doi:10.2298/CSIS0501063E

El-Kassar, A. N., Haraty, R. A., Awad, Y. A., & Debnath, N. C. (2005, November). Modified RSA in the Domains of Gaussian Integers and Polynomials Over Finite Fields. In CAINE (pp. 298-303). Academic Press.

ElGamal, T. (1985). A public key cryptosystem and a signature scheme based on discrete logarithms. *IEEE Transactions on Information Theory*, *31*(4), 469–472. doi:10.1109/TIT.1985.1057074

Falcon, S., & Plaza, A. (2007). On the Fibonacci $k-$. *Chaos, Solitons, and Fractals*, *32*(5), 1615–1624. doi:10.1016/j.chaos.2006.09.022

Horadam, A. F. (1965). Basic Properties of A Certain Generalized Sequence of Numbers. *The Fibonacci Quaterly*, *3*(3), 161–176.

Hwang, M. S., Chang, C. C., & Hwang, K. F. (2002). An ElGamal-like cryptosystem for enciphering large messages. *IEEE Transactions on Knowledge and Data Engineering*, *14*(2), 445–446. doi:10.1109/69.991728

Ide, J., & Renault, M. S. (2012). Power Fibonacci Sequences. *The Fibonacci Quarterly*, *50*(2), 175–180.

Klein, S. T., & Ben-Nissan, M. K. (2010). On the usefulness of Fibonacci Compression Codes. *The Computer Journal*, *53*(6), 701–716. doi:10.1093/comjnl/bxp046

Koshy, T. (2001). *Fibonacci and Lucas Numbers with Applications*. Wiley. doi:10.1002/9781118033067

Lee, G.Y. (2000). Fibonacci $k-$Lucas Numbers and Associated Bipartite Graphs. *Lineer Algebra and its Applications, 320*, 51–61.

Lucas, E. (1878). Théorie des fonctions numériques simplement périodiques. *American Journal of Mathematics*, *1*(4), 289–321. doi:10.2307/2369373

Menezes, A. J., Oorschot, P. C., & Vanstone, S. A. (1996). *Handbook of Applied Cryptography*. CRC Press.

Nalli, A., & Ozyilmaz, C. (2015). The third order variations on the Fibonacci universal code. *Journal of Number Theory*, *149*, 15–32. doi:10.1016/j.jnt.2014.07.010

Niven, I., Zuckerman, H. S., & Montgomery, H. L. (1991). *An introduction to the theory of numbers*. John Wiley & Sons.

Öcal, A. A., Tuglu, N., & Altinişik, E. (2005). On the Representation of $k-$Generalized Fibonacci and Lucas Numbers. *Applied Mathematics and Computation*, *170*, 584–596.

Ozyilmaz, C., & Nalli, A. (2019). Restructuring Of Discrete Logarithm Problem And Elgamal Cryptosystem By Using The Power Fibonacci Sequence Module M. *Journal of Science and Arts*, (1), 61–70.

Özyılmaz, Ç., & Nallı, A. (2020). Composite Discrete Logarithm Problem and a Reconstituted ElGamal Cryptosystem Based on the Problem: New ElGamal Cryptosystems With Some Special Sequences and Composite ElGamal Cryptosystem. In Implementing Computational Intelligence Techniques for Security Systems Design. IGI Global.

Renault, M. (1996). *The Fibonacci sequence under various moduli* (Master Thesis). Wake Forest University, Institute of Science.

Renault, M. (2013). The period, rank, and order of the (a, b)-Fibonacci sequence mod m. *Mathematics Magazine*, *86*(5), 372–380. doi:10.4169/math.mag.86.5.372

Rivest, R. L., Shamir, A., & Adleman, L. (1978). A method for obtaining digital signatures and public-key cryptosystems. *Communications of the ACM*, *21*(2), 120–126. doi:10.1145/359340.359342

Shah, A. P. (1968). Fibonacci sequence modulo m. *Fibonacci Quarterly*, *6*, 139–141.

Sloane, N. J. A. (1973). *A Handbook of Integer Sequences*. Academic Press.

Stinson, D. R. (2002). *Cryptography Theory and Practice*. Chapman & Hall / CRC.

Taşçi, D., & Kilic, E. (2004). On the Order $k-$. *Applied Mathematics and Computation*, *155*(3), 637–641. doi:10.1016/S0096-3003(03)00804-X

Taşkara, N., Uslu, K., & Güleç, H. H. (2010). On the Properties of Lucas Numbers with Binomial Coefficients. *Applied Mathematics Letters*, *23*(1), 68–72. doi:10.1016/j.aml.2009.08.007

Uslu, K., Taskara, N., & Kose, H. (2011). The Generalized $k-$Fibonacci and Lucas Number. *Ars Combinatoria*, *99*, 25–32.

Vajda, S. (1989). *Fibonacci and Lucas Numbers and the Golden Section*. Ellis Horwood.

Wall, D. D. (1960). Fibonacci Series Modulo m. *The American Mathematical Monthly*, *67*(6), 525–532. doi:10.1080/00029890.1960.11989541

Yayenie, O. (2011). A Note on Generalized Fibonacci Sequences. *Applied Mathematics and Computation*, *217*(12), 5603–5611. doi:10.1016/j.amc.2010.12.038

Yazlik, Y., & Taşkara, N. (2012). A Note on Generalized $k-$. *Computers & Mathematics with Applications (Oxford, England)*, *63*(1), 36–41. doi:10.1016/j.camwa.2011.10.055

Yilmaz, F., & Bozkurt, D. (2009). The Generalized Order $k-$ Jacobsthal Numbers. Int. *J. Contemp. Math. Sciences*, *4*(34), 1685–1694.

Zhu, H. (2001). *Survey of Computational Assumptions Used in Cryptography Broken or Not by Shor's Algoritm* (Master Thesis). McGill University School of Computer Science, Montreal.

ADDITIONAL READING

Hoffstein, J., Pipher, J., Silverman, J. H., & Silverman, J. H. (2008). *An introduction to mathematical cryptography* (Vol. 1). Springer.

Hungerfold, T. W. (1987). *Algebra*. Springer-Verlag.

Jones, G. A., & Jones, J. M. (1998). *Elementary number theory*. Springer Science & Business Media. doi:10.1007/978-1-4471-0613-5

Katz, J., Menezes, A. J., Van Oorschot, P. C., & Vanstone, S. A. (1996). *Handbook of Applied cryptography*. CRC press.

Klein, S. T., & Ben-Nissan, M. K. (2009). On the usefulness of Fibonacci compression codes. *The Computer Journal*, *53*(6), 701–716. doi:10.1093/comjnl/bxp046

KEY TERMS AND DEFINITIONS

Cryptography: It is a process of protecting information and communications such that the only one for whom the information is intended can understand.

Cyclic Group: It is a group which is generated the only one element.

Fibonacci Sequence: It is a recurrence sequence that beginning with the integer couple 0 and 1, in which the value of any element is computed by taking the summation of the two antecedent numbers.

Generator: It is an element in the group in which all the different powers of that element give all the different elements of the group.

One Way Function: It is a function that is easy to compute on every input, but it is hard to invert given the image of a random input.

Pell Sequence: It is a recurrence sequence that beginning with the integer couple 0 and 1, in which the value of any element is computed by taking the summation of twice the previous term and two previous terms.

Period: The period of a sequence is the number of terms within the repeated part of a sequence.

Power Fibonacci Sequence Modulo k **:** If a sequence that satisfying the Fibonacci recurrence relation also provides $\equiv 1, \alpha, \alpha^2, \alpha^3, \ldots (\mod k)$ for some modulus k, then this sequence is named a power Fibonacci sequence modulo k.

Quadratic Residue: An integer a is called a quadratic residue modulo n if there exists an integer x such that $x^2 \equiv a (\mod n)$.

Recurrence Sequences: Recurrence sequence is a sequence of numbers indexed by an integer and generated by solving a recurrence equation.

Trapdoor: It is special information which is used to find inverse.

Chapter 3
Robust Diagnostic System for COVID–19 Based on Chest Radiology Images

Sasikaladevi N.
School of Computing, SASTRA University (Deemed), India

Revathi A.
School of EEE, SASTRA University (Deemed), India

ABSTRACT

The proposed system is based on a diagnosis of COVID from x-ray images. In the respiratory system, 17 different viral infections are possible. Accurately discriminating COVID from other viral infections is necessary today as it spreads rapidly. The proposed system differentiates COVID infection accurately from other viral infections. The convolutional neural network (CNN) provides superior performance for disease diagnosis based on images in the deep learning era. In this chapter, to solve this issue, the authors propose a hypergraph-based convolutional neural network-based fast and accurate diagnosis system for COVID. In this work, the hypergraph represents the sophisticated features of a lung x-ray image to diagnose COVID. In-depth features are extracted from the x-ray images using residual neural networks. In order to discriminate COVID viral infection from other viral infections, the hypergraph fusion approach is used.

DOI: 10.4018/978-1-7998-9012-6.ch003

INTRODUCTION

According to the World Health Organization (WHO) report, millions of people are affected by the coronavirus. There is a need to repeat the test for confirmation (Chu, 2019). As it is a fast-spreading pandemic, there is a demand for rapid and accurate diagnostic systems. Based on Fang's (Fang, 2020) study, lung radiology image-based diagnostics outperformed all other screening methods. With a strong suggestion, a diagnostic with radiological images could be a first step in monitoring the COVID (Li, 2020). Early diagnosis of 2019-nCoV is crucial for disease treatment and control. Compared to a Reverse transcription-polymerase chain reaction (RT-PCR), chest X-ray imaging may be a more reliable, practical, and rapid method to diagnose and assess COVID, especially in the pandemic region. Even though radiology images-based COVID diagnosis is faster than PCR, it requires the Artificial Intelligence (AI) based diagnosis to gain a rapid and accurate explication over the X-ray images (Kermany, 2018).

Respiratory illness includes H1NI viral infection, H5N1, Enterovirus, and viral pneumonia. Among these infections, coronavirus infection is severe as it mutates easily and rapidly. There are three basic types of coronavirus infection such as SARS, MERS, and COVID-19. There is a demand to discriminate these three viral infections from other viral pneumonia. This paper proposes the hyper graph-based approach to discriminate coronavirus infection from other virus infections in the lungs based on X-ray images.

The proposed system is based on a diagnosis of COVID from X-ray images. In the respiratory system, 17 different viral infections are possible. Accurately discriminating COVID from other viral infections is necessary today as it spreads rapidly. The proposed system differentiates COVID infection accurately from other viral infections. The Convolutional Neural Network (CNN) provides superior performance for disease diagnosis based on images in the deep learning era. Diagnosis of COVID from X-ray images needs a much more complex representational model as there is a demand to classify the images based on highly sophisticated features. In this paper, to solve this issue, we propose a Hypergraph-based convolutional Neural network-based Fast and Accurate Diagnosis system for COVID. In this work, the Hypergraph represents the sophisticated features of a lung x-ray image to diagnose COVID. In-depth features are extracted from the X-ray images using Residual neural networks. In order to discriminate COVID viral infection from other viral infections, the Hypergraph fusion is approach is used. The proposed model is evaluated based on the COVID dataset

RELATED WORK

This section analyzes various state-of-the-art methods to detect COVID from X-ray images. These methods can be classified into four different categories. Some researchers used the pre-trained neural network in X-ray images for classification. The second category is transfer learning, in which the pre-trained neural network is customized and then used for classification. Few researchers proposed deep learning and machine learning methods to predict COVID from the x-ray image dataset by designing the network from scratch. Finally, very few research works are based on extracting the in-depth features from the X-ray images, and then these extracted features are used for classification by using machine learning or deep learning models.

COVID-Net, a deep convolutional neural network design tailored to detect COVID-19, is proposed by Wang et al. (Wang, 2020). Apostolopoulos (Apostolopoulos, 2020) evaluated the performance of state-of-the-art convolutional neural network architectures proposed over the recent years for medical image classification. A pneumonia chest x-ray detection based on generative adversarial networks (GAN) with a fine-tuned deep transfer learning for a limited dataset will be presented in (Khalifa 2021). Pre-trained Resnet50 and VGG16 were tuned or trained on a balanced set of COVID-19 and pneumonia chest X-rays (Ahmed, 2021). CoroNet - a Deep Neural Network for Detection and Diagnosis of Covid-19 from Chest X-ray Images is proposed in (Khan, 2020). Apostolopoulos (Apostolopoulos, 2020) used a Convolutional Neural Network called Mobile Net and trained from scratch to investigate the importance of the extracted features for the classification task. In (Chowdhury 2020), different pre-trained networks are analyzed with the COVID X-ray image dataset. Zhang (Zhang, 2020) developed a new deep anomaly detection model for the fast, reliable screen. Horry investigated different pertained neural networks with COVID X-ray image datasets (Horry, 2020). Kausani (Kassania, 2021) extracted in-depth features from the pre-trained networks and classified them using machine learning algorithms. Deep Learning Classifiers to Diagnose COVID-19 in X-Ray Images is proposed in (Karar 2021). A 3-step technique is proposed to fine-tune a pre-trained ResNet-50 architecture (Keles 2021).

Basu proposed a method to detect abnormalities and extract key features of the altered lung parenchyma, which may be related to specific signatures of the COVID (Basu, 2020). In (Ucar, 2020) proposed deep- Bayes squeeze net for COVID diagnosis. Deep Learning Model for COVID-19 Patterns Detection in X-ray Images proposed in (Luz, 2021). Nasser et al. (Nasser, 2020) proposed using pre-trained knowledge to improve the diagnostic performance using transfer learning techniques and compared the performance of different CNN architectures. Deep neural networks (DNN)-based method for automatically detecting COVID-19 symptoms from CXR images is proposed in (Karim 2020). Minaee (Minaee, 2020) proposed deep learning models to detect COVID-19 patients from their chest radiography images. Madrid (Maghdid, 2021) proposed a deep and transfer learning algorithm to detect COVID in X-ray images. Nour et al. (Nour, 2020) extracted in-depth features from pre-trained networks and classified them using different machine learning algorithms. Rahimzadeh (Rahimzadeh, 2021) extracted in-depth features from X-ray images, and then pre-trained neural networks were used for classification. Arora et al. (2021) extracted in-depth features from the X-ray images and then classified them using a machine learning approach. Ozkaya (Özkaya, 2020) extracted in-depth features from X-ray images using a pre-trained network and classified them using a support vector machine.

PROPOSED SYSTEM FOR COVID DIAGNOSIS

This section introduces the framework for a Hypergraph fusion-based system to accurately discriminate COVID infection from other virus infections in the lungs by using lung x-ray images. In the first phase, in-depth features are extracted from the pre-trained deep neural networks, and the extracted deep features are used to construct the Hypergraphs. Hyper graph fusion approach is used to correlate high order correlation in the deep features. In the next phase, the high order complex correlation in the deep features is optimized by learning the Hypergraph. Finally, Hypergraph based convolutional neural network method is used to perform fast and accurate COVID diagnosis.

Phase 1: Hypergraph Construction Based on the Deep Features Extracted from X-ray Images

In this phase, the Hypergraph is constructed to represent the complex deep features extracted from COVID x-ray images based on pre-trained deep neural networks. A hypergraph is defined as $G = \left(V, \mathcal{E}, W\right)$ where V is a set of vertices, $\mathcal{E}$ is a set of hyperedges, W is the weight for each hyperedge.

The hypergraph G is denoted by a $\left|V\right| * \left|\mathcal{E}\right|$ incidence matrix H, with entries defined as,

$$h\left(v, e\right) = \begin{cases} 0 \, v \, not \in e \\ 1 \, v \in e \end{cases}$$

where $v \in V, e \in \mathcal{E}$. D_e, D_v represents the diagonal matrices of the edge degrees and the vertex degrees, respectively. The degree of the vertex v is defined as,

$$d(v) = \sum_{e \in \mathcal{E}} \omega(e) h(v, e) \tag{2}$$

where $\omega(e)$ is the weight of the hyperedge e. The degree of the hyperedge is denoted as,

$$\delta(e) = \sum_{v \in V} h(v, e) \mathrm{x} \tag{3}$$

For the COVID diagnosis task, the in-depth features of N data are represented as $X = \left[x_1, x_2 \dots x_N \right]^T$. The Hypergraph is formulated based on the distance between the deep features. The distance of any two feature data i and j is represented as $d(x_i, x_j)$, and it is estimated based on the Euclidean distance between the deep features.

Phase 2: Hypergraph Fusion Method to Enhance the Emphasis on Deep Features

After constructing individual hypergraphs, the hypergraph fusion approach emphasizes high order correlations. n_f number of hypergraphs

$$G_1 = (V_1, \mathcal{E}_1), G_2 = (V_2, \mathcal{E}_2), \dots G_{n_f} = (V_{n_f}, \mathcal{E}_{n_f}),$$

are generated for each x-ray image based on extracted deep features as given in phase 1. Each Hypergraph is assigned with the weight α_i s.t $\sum_{i=1}^{n_f} \alpha_i = 1$.

Representational Learning Using Hypergraph Spectral Clustering

The task of learning is to predict the labels of the remaining unlabeled vertices. There are N samples, three categories of features such as normal, affected by a non-COVID virus infection, and COVID viral infection. The classification process is represented as a regularization problem defined in (Zhou, 2006), and it is represented as,

$$\arg\min_{F} \left\{ R_{emp}(F) + \lambda \Omega(F) \right\} \tag{4}$$

Where $F = \{f_1, f_2\}$ is the target vector with conference score of samples. $R_{emp}(F)$ is used to minimize the difference between the labels of the training features and the target estimation, and it is represented as,

$$R_{emp}(F) = \sum_{k=1}^{3} f_k - y_k^{2} \tag{5}$$

Where $\square_\square$ is the label vector for the two categories, COVID-affected and COVID-not-affected? Y is the label matrix of size N*2.

$$Y_{i,j} = \begin{cases} 0, normal \\ 1, Non\,Covid\,Infection \\ 2, Covid\,Infection \end{cases}$$

In the second component of the equation, λ is the trade-off parameter, and Ω is the regularization parameter (Shi, 2018).

$$\Omega(F) = \frac{1}{2} \sum_{i=1}^{n_f} \alpha_i \sum_{e \in \mathcal{E}_i} \sum_{u,v \in V_i} \frac{W_i(e) h_i(u,e) h_i(v,e)}{\delta_i(e)} * \left(\frac{f(u)}{\sqrt{d_i(u)}} - \frac{f(v)}{\sqrt{d_i(v)}} \right)^2 \tag{6}$$

$$\Omega(f) = \sum_{i=1}^{n_f} \alpha_i f^T (I - \theta_i) f \tag{7}$$

$$\Omega(f) = f^T \Delta f$$

Where,

$$\Delta = \sum_{i=1}^{n_f} \alpha_i \left(I - \theta_i \right), \theta = D_v^{-\frac{1}{2}} HWD_e^{-1} H^T D_v^{-\frac{1}{2}}$$

where Δ is a Laplacian, the positive semi define matrix. Now, the objective function re-defined as,

$$\arg\min_F \sum_{k=1}^{2} f_k - y_k^2 + \lambda[tr\left(F^T \Delta F\right)\} \tag{7}$$

The following equation is derived by differentiating the objective function of F

$$F - Y + \lambda\left(F - \Delta F\right) = 0 \tag{8}$$

Then,

$$F = \left(I^N + \lambda\Delta\right)^{-1} Y \tag{9}$$

Assign, $Y = I^N$, and obtain $A^H = \left(I^N + \lambda\Delta\right)^{-1} I^N$ denotes the high order complex correlation in the deep features of the Covid images.

EXPERIMENTAL ANALYSIS

This section explains the experimental setting, dataset, evaluation criteria, and comparison methods. This experiment is conducted in the Intel Core i7-2.2 GHz processor with 12GB RAM, Graphical Processing Unit (GPU) NVIDIA GTX 1050. The proposed FAT system is implemented in Python with Tensor flow 2.0 and Keras package. The datasets consist of 5949 chest radiography images for 2839 patient cases. The dataset includes 2000 normal, 2000 lung pneumonia, and 1000 COVID-infected cases. Fig. 1 shows the sample of normal, viral pneumonia and COVID affected person's x-ray images.

In the first phase of the proposed system, deep features are extracted from the X-ray images based on the pre-trained deep neural networks such as Resnet50 and Inception-v3. The feature vector is of size 1000. Evaluation criteria such as Accuracy, specificity, sensitivity, precision, recall, F1 score, true positive rate, and false-negative rate are computed for the proposed system.

Figure 1. Sample X-Ray image data set

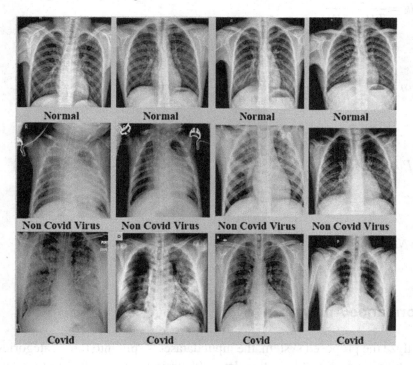

$$Accuracy = \frac{TP + TN}{TP + FP + FN + TN} \qquad (11)$$

$$Specificity = \frac{TN}{TN + FP} \qquad (12)$$

$$Sensitivity = \frac{TP}{TP + FN} \qquad (13)$$

$$Precision = \frac{TP}{TP + FP} \qquad (14)$$

$$Recall = \frac{TP}{TP + FN} \tag{15}$$

$$F1\,Score = 2 * \frac{Recall * Precision}{Recall + Precision} \tag{16}$$

$$True\,Positive\,Rate = \frac{TP}{TP + FN} \tag{17}$$

$$False\,Negative\,Rate = \frac{FN}{FN + TP} \tag{18}$$

Performance Analysis

To analyze the proposed system, the input dataset is split into three categories such as 80% training data + 20% testing data, 70% training data + 30% testing data, and 60% training data + 40% testing data. Accuracy is estimated for each category and projected in Fig. 2. It shows that the proposed system yields 100% accuracy for the split of 80%-20%. Furthermore, it also shows that even with category three 60%-40% split, the proposed system exhibits higher and consistently accurate results.

Figure 2. Accuracy of the FAT system

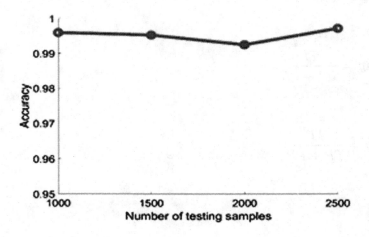

Stability of Precision, Recall, Sensitivity, and Specificity

Covid screening demands ideal recall as it is a rapidly spreading disease. The proposed system provides the recall value in the range of .98 to 1.0. If the recall is 1.0, it will find all the patients with the COVID infection. The precision value is also significantly high with the proposed FAT system. However, in cases where we want to find an optimal blend of precision and recall, we can combine the two metrics using the metric F1 score. Sensitivity and specificity are stable regardless of the likelihood of COVID in the population tested. Sensitivity is used to test the system's performance in the COVID-present subgroup Specificity is used to test the system's performance in the normal (no-COVID) subgroup. However, an unusual population may alter sensitivity and specificity by increasing FNs or FPs, respectively. The table 1 shows the proposed system's sensitivity, specificity, and precision stability.

Table 1. Precision, sensitivity and specificity analysis

			Covid	Virus Pneumonia	Normal
Category-1	Training samples: 4000 Testing samples: 1000	Specificity	0.995	1.000	1.000
		Sensitivity	1.000	0.999	1.000
		Precision	0.983	1.000	1.000
Category-2	Training samples: 3500 Testing samples: 1500	Specificity	0.994	1.000	1.000
		Sensitivity	1.000	0.988	1.000
		Precision	0.977	1.000	1.000
Category-3	Training samples: 3000 Testing samples: 2000	Specificity	0.996	0.991	1.000
		Sensitivity	0.975	0.994	1.000
		Precision	0.987	0.987	1.000
Category-4	Training samples: 2500 Testing samples: 2500	Specificity	0.996	1.000	1.000
		Sensitivity	1.000	0.993	1.000
		Precision	0.986	1.000	1.000

Confusion Matrix

The confusion matrix is computed based on TP, TN, FP, and FN. The more accurate system should exhibit a higher value for TP and TN and a lesser value for FP and FN. As it is a prediction system for a rapidly growing pandemic, there is a demand to have the ideal value for FN. Fig. 3 shows the confusion matrix with the varying sample rate. It provides the FN as 0 for all the cases.

Figure 3. Confusion matrix

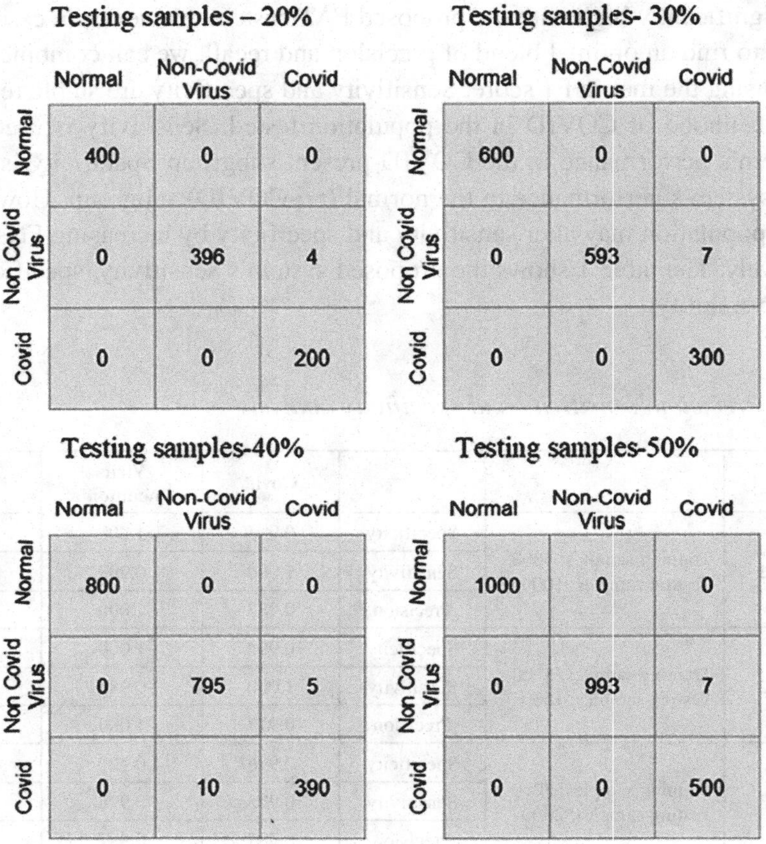

Testing samples – 20%

	Normal	Non-Covid Virus	Covid
Normal	400	0	0
Non Covid Virus	0	396	4
Covid	0	0	200

Testing samples- 30%

	Normal	Non-Covid Virus	Covid
Normal	600	0	0
Non Covid Virus	0	593	7
Covid	0	0	300

Testing samples-40%

	Normal	Non-Covid Virus	Covid
Normal	800	0	0
Non Covid Virus	0	795	5
Covid	0	10	390

Testing samples-50%

	Normal	Non-Covid Virus	Covid
Normal	1000	0	0
Non Covid Virus	0	993	7
Covid	0	0	500

ROC Curve

A Receiver Operating Characteristic (ROC) curve is a graphical plot that illustrates the diagnostic ability of a multi classifier system as its discrimination threshold is varied. Fig. 4 shows the ROC curve with the various number of testing samples. Even with varying testing samples, the ROC plot for each category shows the ideal measure. The average Area Under Curve (AUC) is 99.5%.

Figure 4. ROC plot for varying testing sample size

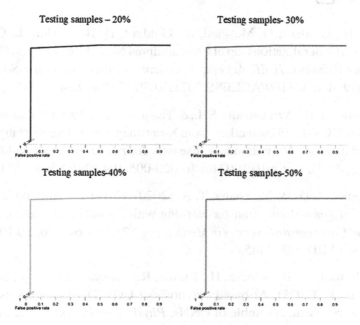

CONCLUSION

This proposed model is based on Hypergraph, fused Hypergraph, learning from hypergraph representation, and the hypergraph convolution neural network. Pre-trained deep neural networks extracted in-depth features from the X-ray images. These in-depth features are complex and highly correlated. Hence, these features are represented in the form of a Hypergraph. In order to increase the complex high order correlation of in-depth features, Hypergraph from different deep features are weighted to construct a fused Hypergraph. The transductive inference is used to learn the high order correlation in the features from the fused hypergraph representation. Finally, the hypergraph convolution neural network is constructed to train the system. Experimental results clearly show that the proposed system diagnose COVID rapidly and accurately. It provides 99.9% accuracy, 99% sensitivity, and specificity.

REFERENCES

Ahmed, K. B., Goldgof, G. M., Paul, R., Goldgof, D. B., & Hall, L. O. (2021). Discovery of a Generalization Gap of Convolutional Neural Networks on COVID-19 X-Rays Classification. *IEEE Access: Practical Innovations, Open Solutions*, *9*, 72970–72979. doi:10.1109/ACCESS.2021.3079716 PMID:34178559

Apostolopoulos, I. D., Aznaouridis, S. I., & Tzani, M. A. (2020). Extracting possibly representative COVID-19 biomarkers from X-ray images with deep learning approach and image data related to pulmonary diseases. *Journal of Medical and Biological Engineering*, *40*(3), 1. doi:10.100740846-020-00529-4 PMID:32412551

Apostolopoulos, I. D., & Mpesiana, T. A. (2020). Covid-19: Automatic detection from x-ray images utilizing transfer learning with convolutional neural networks. *Physical and Engineering Sciences in Medicine*, *43*(2), 635–640. doi:10.100713246-020-00865-4 PMID:32524445

Arora, R., Bansal, V., Buckchash, H., Kumar, R., Sahayasheela, V. J., Narayanan, N., ... Raman, B. (2021). AI-based diagnosis of COVID-19 patients using X-ray scans with a stochastic ensemble of CNNs. *Physical and Engineering Sciences in Medicine*, 1-15.

Basu, S., Mitra, S., & Saha, N. (2020, December). Deep learning for screening covid-19 using chest x-ray images. In *2020 IEEE Symposium Series on Computational Intelligence (SSCI)* (pp. 2521-2527). IEEE. 10.1109/SSCI47803.2020.9308571

Chowdhury, M. E., Rahman, T., Khandakar, A., Mazhar, R., Kadir, M. A., Mahbub, Z. B., Islam, K. R., Khan, M. S., Iqbal, A., Emadi, N. A., Reaz, M. B. I., & Islam, M. T. (2020). Can AI help in screening viral and COVID-19 pneumonia? *IEEE Access: Practical Innovations, Open Solutions*, *8*, 132665–132676. doi:10.1109/ACCESS.2020.3010287

Chu, D. K., Pan, Y., Cheng, S. M., Hui, K. P., Krishnan, P., Liu, Y., Ng, D. Y. M., Wan, C. K. C., Yang, P., Wang, Q., Peiris, M., & Poon, L. L. (2020). Molecular diagnosis of a novel coronavirus (2019-nCoV) causing an outbreak of pneumonia. *Clinical Chemistry*, *66*(4), 549–555. doi:10.1093/clinchem/hvaa029 PMID:32031583

Fang, Y., Zhang, H., Xie, J., Lin, M., Ying, L., Pang, P., & Ji, W. (2020). Sensitivity of chest CT for COVID-19: Comparison to RT-PCR. *Radiology*, *296*(2), E115–E117. doi:10.1148/radiol.2020200432 PMID:32073353

Germany, D. S., Goldbaum, M., Cai, W., Valentim, C. C., Liang, H., Baxter, S. L., ... Zhang, K. (2018). Identifying medical diagnoses and treatable diseases by image-based deep learning. *Cell, 172*(5), 1122–1131. doi:10.1016/j.cell.2018.02.010 PMID:29474911

Horry, M. J., Chakraborty, S., Paul, M., Ulhaq, A., Pradhan, B., Saha, M., & Shukla, N. (2020). COVID-19 detection through transfer learning using multimodal imaging data. *IEEE Access: Practical Innovations, Open Solutions, 8,* 149808–149824. doi:10.1109/ACCESS.2020.3016780 PMID:34931154

Karar, M. E., Hemdan, E. E. D., & Shouman, M. A. (2021). Cascaded deep learning classifiers for computer-aided diagnosis of COVID-19 and pneumonia diseases in X-ray scans. *Complex & Intelligent Systems, 7*(1), 235–247. doi:10.100740747-020-00199-4 PMID:34777953

Karim, M. R., Döhmen, T., Cochez, M., Beyan, O., Rebholz-Schuhmann, D., & Decker, S. (2020, December). DeepCOVIDExplainer: Explainable COVID-19 diagnosis from chest X-ray images. In *2020 IEEE International Conference on Bioinformatics and Biomedicine (BIBM)* (pp. 1034-1037). IEEE. 10.1109/BIBM49941.2020.9313304

Kassania, S. H., Kassanib, P. H., Wesolowskic, M. J., Schneidera, K. A., & Detersa, R. (2021). Automatic detection of coronavirus disease (COVID-19) in X-ray and CT images: A machine learning-based approach. *Biocybernetics and Biomedical Engineering, 41*(3), 867–879. doi:10.1016/j.bbe.2021.05.013 PMID:34108787

Keles, A., Keles, M. B., & Keles, A. (2021). COV19-CNNet and COV19-ResNet: Diagnostic inference Engines for early detection of COVID-19. *Cognitive Computation,* 1–11. doi:10.100712559-020-09795-5 PMID:33425046

Khalifa, N. E. M., Manogaran, G., Taha, M. H. N., & Loey, M. (2021). A deep learning semantic segmentation architecture for COVID-19 lesions discovery in limited chest CT datasets. *Expert Systems: International Journal of Knowledge Engineering and Neural Networks,* 12742. doi:10.1111/exsy.12742 PMID:34177038

Khan, A. I., Shah, J. L., & Bhat, M. M. (2020). CoroNet: A deep neural network for detecting and diagnosing COVID-19 from chest x-ray images. *Computer Methods and Programs in Biomedicine, 196,* 105581. doi:10.1016/j.cmpb.2020.105581 PMID:32534344

Li, Y., & Xia, L. (2020). Coronavirus disease 2019 (COVID-19): Role of chest CT in diagnosis and management. *AJR. American Journal of Roentgenology, 214*(6), 1280–1286. doi:10.2214/AJR.20.22954 PMID:32130038

Luz, E., Silva, P., Silva, R., Silva, L., Guimarães, J., Miozzo, G., Moreira, G., & Menotti, D. (2021). Towards an effective and efficient deep learning model for COVID-19 patterns detection in X-ray images. *Research on Biomedical Engineering*, 1–14. doi:10.100742600-021-00151-6

Maghdid, H. S., Asaad, A. T., Ghafoor, K. Z., Sadiq, A. S., Mirjalili, S., & Khan, M. K. (2021, April). Diagnosing COVID-19 pneumonia from X-ray and CT images. In Multimodal Image Exploitation and Learning 2021 (Vol. 11734). International Society for Optics and Photonics.

Minaee, S., Kafieh, R., Sonka, M., Yazdani, S., & Soufi, G. J. (2020). Deep-covid: Predicting covid-19 from chest x-ray images using deep transfer learning. *Medical Image Analysis*, *65*, 101794. doi:10.1016/j.media.2020.101794 PMID:32781377

Nasser, N., Emad-ul-Haq, Q., Imran, M., Ali, A., Razzak, I., & Al-Helali, A. (2021). A smart healthcare framework for detecting and monitoring COVID-19 using IoT and cloud computing. *Neural Computing & Applications*, 1–15. PMID:34522068

Nour, M., Cömert, Z., & Polat, K. (2020). A novel medical diagnosis model for COVID-19 infection detection based on in-depth features and Bayesian optimization. *Applied Soft Computing*, *97*, 106580. doi:10.1016/j.asoc.2020.106580 PMID:32837453

Özkaya, U., Öztürk, Ş., & Barstugan, M. (2020). Coronavirus (COVID-19) classification using deep features fusion and ranking technique. In *Big Data Analytics and Artificial Intelligence Against COVID-19: Innovation Vision and Approach* (pp. 281–295). Springer.

Rahimzadeh, M., Attar, A., & Sakhaei, S. M. (2021). A fully automated deep learning-based network detecting covid-19 from a new and large lung ct scan dataset. *Biomedical Signal Processing and Control*, *68*, 102588. doi:10.1016/j.bspc.2021.102588 PMID:33821166

Ucar, F., & Korkmaz, D. (2020). COVIDiagnosis-Net: Deep Bayes-SqueezeNet based diagnosis of the coronavirus disease 2019 (COVID-19) from X-ray images. *Medical Hypotheses*, *140*, 109761. doi:10.1016/j.mehy.2020.109761 PMID:32344309

Wang, L., Lin, Z. Q., & Wong, A. (2020). Covid-net: A tailored deep convolutional neural network design for detecting covid-19 cases from chest x-ray images. *Scientific Reports*, *10*(1), 1–12. doi:10.103841598-020-76550-z PMID:31913322

Zhang, J., Xie, Y., Pang, G., Liao, Z., Verjans, J., Li, W., Sun, Z., He, J., Li, Y., Shen, C., & Xia, Y. (2020). Viral pneumonia screening on chest x-rays using Confidence-Aware anomaly detection. *IEEE Transactions on Medical Imaging*, *40*(3), 879–890. doi:10.1109/TMI.2020.3040950 PMID:33245693

Zhou, D., Huang, J., & Schölkopf, B. (2006). Learning with hypergraphs: Clustering, classification, and embedding. *Advances in Neural Information Processing Systems*, *19*, 1601–1608.

Chapter 4
Neural Architecture Search Network for the Diagnosis of COVID From the Radiographic Images

Sasikaladevi N.
School of Computing, SASTRA University (Deemed), India

Revathi A.
School of EEE, SASTRA University (Deemed), India

ABSTRACT

The outbreak of human-to-human transmissible COVID-19 has caused approximately 64,000 deaths around the world and keeps continuously increasing in an exponential order that has provoked global alarm. To control the spread of the disease, screening large numbers of suspected cases for appropriate quarantine and treatment measures is of higher priority. Since clinical laboratory testing with precise accuracy for huge samples in the infected region remains a great challenge that demands complementary diagnostic methods to combat the disease. In this work, the authors have identified a new AI-based deep learning framework named CORONATE based on neural architecture space search network (NASNET) as a competent choice that can extract graphical features from radiography images referred from the public dataset of x-ray images. This observation endorses that CORONATE model can administer a faster clinical diagnosis well ahead of pathogenic tests with higher accuracy and can empower the medical team to ensure a good control on the outbreak by saving critical diagnosis time.

DOI: 10.4018/978-1-7998-9012-6.ch004

INTRODUCTION

Fast and precise screening of massive numbers of cases infected with viral pneumonia symptoms is highly demanded to initiate the treatment procedure and quarantine to control the spread of Corona Virus Disease (COVID-19). Pathogenic laboratory testing is the diagnostic gold standard, but it is time-consuming with significant false-positive results. Computed tomography (CT) and radiography have emerged as practical diagnostic tools for the preliminary identification of COVID-19. However, the intense and widespread outbreak of this disease and relatively inadequate radiologists instigate the need for a computer-aided diagnosis system. Although typical images may help early screening of suspected cases, the images of various viral pneumonia are similar and overlap with other infectious and inflammatory lung diseases. Advance Artificial intelligence technologies involving deep learning models might extract COVID-19's graphical features and provide a clinical diagnosis to accurately confirm suspected cases by screening the samples faster to identify the infected persons and start the quarantine and treatment procedures.

According to the World Health Organization (WHO) report, millions of people are affected by the coronavirus. There is a need to repeat the test for confirmation (Chu, 2019). As it is a fast-spreading pandemic, there is a demand for rapid and accurate diagnostic systems. Based on Fang's (Fang, 2020) study, lung radiology image-based diagnostics outperformed all other screening methods. With a strong suggestion, a diagnostic with radiological images could be a first step in monitoring the COVID (Li, 2020). Early diagnosis of 2019-nCoV is crucial for disease treatment and control. Compared to a Reverse transcription-polymerase chain reaction (RT-PCR), chest X-ray imaging may be a more reliable, practical, and rapid method to diagnose and assess COVID, especially in the pandemic region. Even though radiology images-based COVID diagnosis is faster than PCR, it requires the Artificial Intelligence (AI) based diagnosis to gain a rapid and accurate explication over the X-ray images (Kermany, 2018).

Respiratory illness includes H1NI viral infection, H5N1, Enterovirus, and viral pneumonia. Among these infections, coronavirus infection is severe as it mutates easily and rapidly. There are three basic types of coronavirus infection such as SARS, MERS, and COVID-19. There is a demand to discriminate these three viral infections from other viral pneumonia. This paper proposes the hyper graph-based approach to discriminate coronavirus infection from other virus infections in the lungs based on X-ray images.

Deep leaning and machine learning models are playing an important role in computer vision and pattern recognition. As the low radiation x-ray images are poor quality images, it is very difficult to infer the decision by radiologists. Hence, there is a demand for the deep learning technique to perfectly extract the in-depth features from low quality chest x-ray images for better prediction of COVID. Several researchers proposed different types of deep learning models for COVID diagnosis. COVID-ResNet has been employed to classify COVID-19 and three other infection types (Al-Waisy, 2020). They trained the COVID-X-ray dataset using ResNet and have claimed good accuracy but cannot be directly employed for clinical diagnosis as it needs to be validated for the more extensive data set. Automated methods (El Asnaoui 2021) were used to classify the chest X-ray using various Deep Learning architectures, namely a baseline CNN, VGG16, VGG19, DenseNet201 Inception_ResNet_V2, Inception_V3, Xception, Resnet50, and MobileNet_V2. They conducted experiments using chest X-Ray & CT datasets and evaluated their result using various performance metrics. They claimed accuracy of around 84% by the Resnet50, MobileNet_V2, and Inception_Resnet_V2 models compared to architectures cited in their paper. A deep learning framework named COVIDX-Net was introduced by (Karar 2021) to assist radiologists in auto-diagnosing the presence of COVID-19 in X-ray images and have claimed f1-scores that combine precision and recall values yielding 0.89 and 0.91 for normal and COVID-19, respectively. A deep convolutional neural network (COVID-Net has been designed by (Wang 2020) to detect COVID-19. They pre-trained on the ImageNet dataset and then trained on the COVIDx dataset using the Adam optimizer using a learning rate policy and applying some hyperparameters. A deep anomaly detection model for reliability speeding up the screening process has been introduced (Zhang, 2020). They have evaluated their model with 100 chest X-ray images of 70 patients confirmed with COVID-19 from the Github repository. They need to focus on reducing the false-negative rate and false-positive rate. DeTraC model (Abbas 2021) can deal with any irregularities in the image dataset by investigating class boundaries using a class decomposition mechanism. They have applied data augmentation techniques to increase the sample size by flipping in all directions, rotating at different angles. To change the contrast of each image, they have applied the histogram modification technique.

Drop weights based Bayesian Convolutional Neural Networks (BCNN) have been investigated in (Kassania 2021) to estimate uncertainty in Deep Learning solutions. They have used a publicly available COVID-19 chest X-ray dataset and claimed that the uncertainty in prediction is strongly correlated with the accuracy of the prediction. They used a pre-trained ResNet50V2 model, and the limitation of their model is the availability of limited labeled data for the experimentation. An automatic prediction of COVID-19 using deep convolution neural network-based pre-trained transfer models has been mentioned (Narin, 2021). They used Chest X-ray images for their experimentation. An end-to-end structure without manual feature extraction and selection methods have been employed. Prevention and control management along with diagnosis and treatment process is elaborately compiled in (Liang, 2020) that gives an excellent insight to handle unprecedented global war.

The design of a new search space called NASNet search space (Zoph, 2018) authorizes transferability. It searches for the best convolution cell and applies it to the ImageNet dataset by stacking multiple copies of this cell, each with its parameters to configure convolutional architecture. This approach can automate eliciting optimization methods with the intent of deep learning architectures. The basic knowledge to calculate sensitivity, specificity, positive predictive value, and negative predictive value can be referred from (Parikh, 2008). They have analyzed the merits and limitations of these critical measures to assess the prediction process.

The outbreak of human-to-human transmissible COVID 19 has caused approximately 64,000 deaths worldwide and keeps continuously increasing in an exponential order that has provoked a global alarm. Coronaviruses are hazardous viruses that may induce Severe Acute Respiratory Syndrome (SARS). To control the spread of the disease, screening large numbers of suspected cases for appropriate quarantine and treatment measures is of higher priority. Clinical laboratory testing with precise accuracy for huge samples in the infected region remains a significant challenge that demands complementary diagnostic methods to combat the disease. In this work, we have identified a new AI-based deep learning framework named CORONATE (COROna using Neural ArchiTecture sEarch) based on Neural Architecture Space Search Network NASNET as a competent choice that can extract graphical features from radiography images referred from the public dataset of X-ray images. The proposed CORONATE model has ascertained with 98.3% accuracy, 96.7% sensitivity, and 100% specificity, which ratifies the claim of our proposal. This observation endorses that the CORONATE model can administer a faster clinical diagnosis well ahead of pathogenic test with higher accuracy and empower the medical team to ensure a reasonable control on the outbreak by saving critical diagnosis time. In this study, we have developed a NASNET based CORONATE diagnosis of lung images to detect the patients with COVID-19, which can automatically extract radiographic features of novel pneumonia, especially the ground-glass opacity (GGO), from radiographs and can report the result with 98.3% accuracy.

DATASET AND EXPERIMENTAL SETUP

The proposed CORONATE uses the public dataset of X-ray images provided by Dr. Joseph Cohen1 and Dr. Adrian Rosebrock2 to classify negative and positive COVID-19 cases. The dataset includes 200 X-ray images, divided into 100 normal and 100 positive COVID-19 images. Fig. 2 shows a sample of normal and COVID-19 images extracted from the dataset. The X-ray images for confirmed COVID-19 disease reveal a pattern of ground-glass opacification with occasional consolidation in the patchy, peripheral, and bilateral areas. The original size of tested images

Figure 1. Normal images

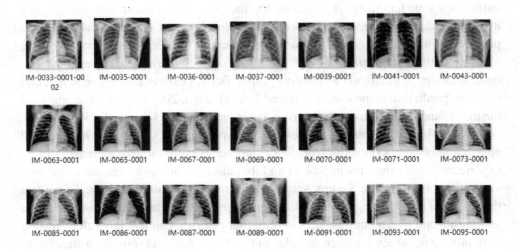

ranges from 1112 x 624 to 2170 x 1953 pixels. All images were scaled to 331 × 331 pixels for the experimental setup. The CORONATE framework, including deep learning classifiers, has been implemented using Python and the Keras package with TensorFlow2 on Intel(R) Core(TM) i7-2.2 GHz processor. In addition, the experiments were conducted with the graphical processing unit (GPU) NVIDIA GTX 1050 Ti and RAM with 4 GB and 16 GB, respectively.

NEURAL ARCHITECTURE SEARCH NETWORK

In the early days of neural network research, human engineers developed network architectures to achieve their goals. Nowadays, some pioneering work on neural architecture search where computers can be automated to search for appropriate networks to achieve better performance. This technique can automate the design of ANN (Artificial Neural Network), which is a prevalently employed model for automated machine learning. NASNET is prominent for hyper-parameter optimization that enables networks to attain their goals. It is categorized into three components: the search space to define the type of ANN that can be designed and optimized, the search strategy that explains the methodology to explore the search space, and the performance estimation strategy to estimate the performance of possible performance ANN from the design.

The search strategy of this model selects architecture A from a predefined search space. This architecture is then passed to a performance estimation strategy

Figure 2. COVID infected images

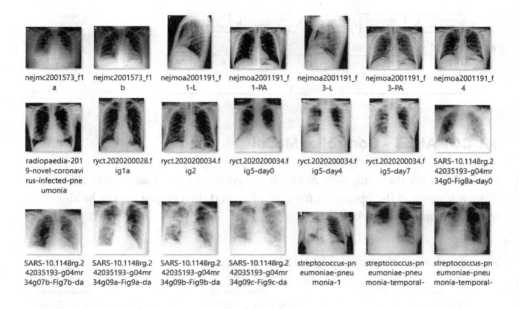

that can assess the performance of this architecture and can be returned as per the requirement; hence, this model is claimed to be adaptive.

Neural Architecture Search (NAS) is the process of automating architecture engineering that helps to develop the design of the machine learning model. If the dataset and the task are submitted, it can build the best architecture for the given task that can be trained and verified the input dataset. This attempt to use the NASNET model is unique as it has been identified as a subfield of AutoML and has a significant overlap with hyperparameter optimization. It learns and chooses the best architecture by adopting a search strategy to maximize performance. The highlight of this work is the deployment of the search method Neural Architecture Search (NAS) framework proposed by (Bello 2017). In NAS, the controller will sample child networks with various architectures. The child networks are then finely trained to converge at the best architecture over time.

Figure 3. NASNET architecture

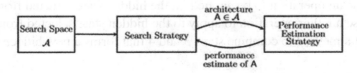

Figure 4. CORANATE controller

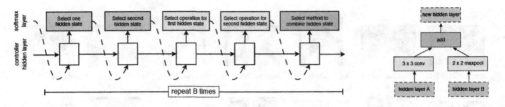

3.1 CORANET - Controller Model

Fig. 4 Portrays the controller model in a layered format that selects the various hidden states and the operation for each state and then combines the hidden states to derive a new hidden layer.

Figure 5. Schematic diagram of NASNET search space

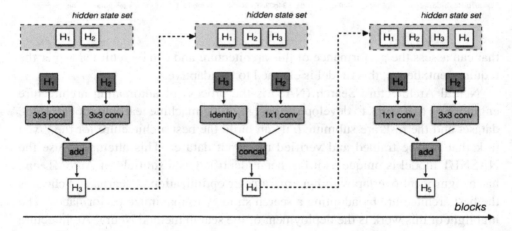

The controller recursively predicts the structure of the cell from the initially hidden states as per the following procedure:

- Select the hidden state Hj from Hj-1 created in previous blocks.
- Select a second hidden state as mentioned in the previous step.
- Choose an operation to be applied on the hidden state selected from step 1.
- Choose another operation to apply to the hidden state selected from step 2.
- Select a method to combine steps 3 and 4 that forms a new hidden state.

Box 1.

Identity 1*7 then 7*1 convolution 3 * 3 average pooling 5 * 5 max pooling 1 * 1 convolution 3 * 3 depth-wise separable conv 7 * 7 depth-wise separable conv	1*3 then 3*1 convolution 3*3 dilated convolution 3 * 3 max pooling 7 * 7 max pooling 3 * 3 convolution 5 * 5 depth-wise separable conv

The operations shown in Box 1 can be selected.

Network motifs are recursively constructed in each stage termed as blocks. Each block consists of the controller selecting a pair of hidden states (dark gray), operations to perform on those hidden states (yellow), and a combination operation (green). The resulting hidden state is retained in the set of potential hidden states to be selected on subsequent blocks. NASNets has been selected as the best model for this work as it can achieve state-of-the-art performances with fewer floating-point operations and parameters than the alternate model.

PROPOSED CORANATE FRAMEWORK

Figure 6. CORONATE framework

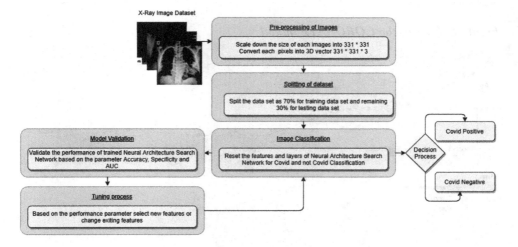

The proposed CORANTE framework shown in Fig. 6 uses X-ray images and is preprocessed by scaling down the size of each image and then represented as a

Figure 7. Accuracy of the CORONATE model

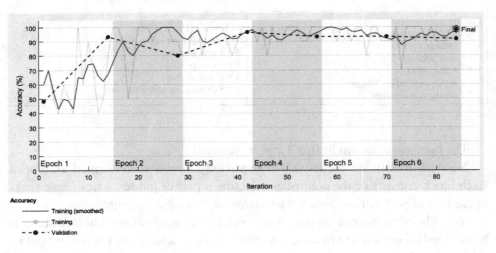

3D vector. The preprocessed data set was then split to 7-% and 30% for training and testing, respectively. The features and layers of the Neural architecture space network (NASNET) are made adaptive to detect the presence of COVID. The proposed framework is validated and evaluated for accuracy, specificity, and AUC. This outcome is then used to tune the performance of the NASNET in the respective layers by reselecting the dominating features from the images.

Training process is shown in Figure 7 and 8.

Figure 8. Loss of the CORONATE model

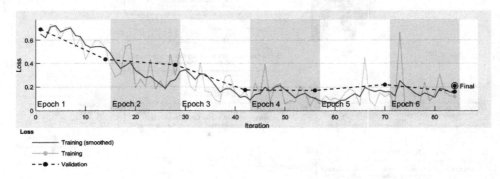

Fig. 7 and Fig. 8 portray the accuracy and the loss measured over six epochs, and for both the measures, the model gives abstract measures between the fourth

Figure 9. Confusion matrix template

	True class		Measures
	Positive	**Negative**	**Measures**
Predicted class — Positive	True positive TP	False positive FP	Positive predictive value (PPV) $\frac{TP}{TP+FP}$
Predicted class — Negative	False negative FN	True negative TN	Negative predictive value (NPV) $\frac{TN}{FN+TN}$
Measures	Sensitivity $\frac{TP}{TP+FN}$	Specificity $\frac{TN}{FP+TN}$	Accuracy $\frac{TP+TN}{TP+FP+FN+TN}$

and sixth epoch. Higher accuracy values and lower loss make the proposed model efficient for the auto-detection process.

Fig. 9 exhibits the confusion matrix template that displays the essential measures used to evaluate the proposed model, and the observed values for each of the respective measures are tabulated in Fig. 10. It is desirable to obtain a 100% positive predictive value (PPV) and specificity with an overall claim of 98.3% accuracy. The sensitivity and Negative Predictive value also fall above 96.5%, which can validate the proposed model. The PPV measure and NPV are good indicators to project the prevalence of COVID.

A receiver operating characteristic curve (ROC) curve, which is a graphical plot that illustrates the diagnostic ability of the proposed binary classifier, is presented in Fig. 11. It summarizes the trade-off between the detection and false-positive rates for the proposed CORONATE predictive model. From the curve, it is evident that smaller values on the x-axis of the plot (0) signal lower false positives and higher true negatives, and similarly more significant values on the y-axis of the plot (0.98) indicate higher true positives and lower false negatives which substantiates the desirable value for the proposed CORANTE model for the screening process.

Figure 10. Confusion Matrix values for the CORONATE model

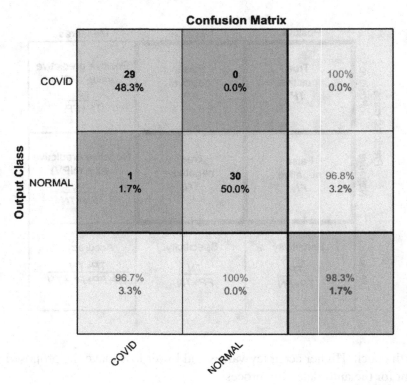

CONCLUSION

The promising results achieved by the proposed CORONATE on the public dataset of chest radiography images ascertain that the proposed model can accelerate the design of precise detection of the presence of COVID as a deep learning solution. We can achieve an accuracy of 98.3% and 100% for both PPV and specificity that validates the resulting learned architecture to accomplish the binary classification of the input images with idealistic values for most performance assessment measures, namely accuracy, sensitivity, and sensitivity specificity. The fundamental advantage of the underlying SPACE net architecture implanted in the proposed model is disclosed to outperform the divergent streamlined, targeted architectures. The proposed model can be used to precisely detect the virus as the best automated and complementary tool for the medical experts to aid the triaging and quarantining process for early treatment safe and speedy recovery.

Figure 11. ROC plot for the CORONATE predictive model

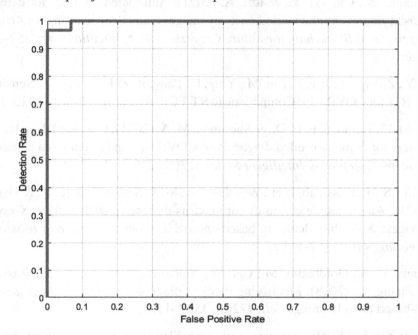

REFERENCES

Abbas, A., Abdelsamea, M. M., & Gaber, M. M. (2021). Classification of COVID-19 in chest X-ray images using DeTraC deep convolutional neural network. *Applied Intelligence*, *51*(2), 854–864. doi:10.100710489-020-01829-7 PMID:34764548

Al-Waisy, A. S., Al-Fahdawi, S., Mohammed, M. A., Abdulkareem, K. H., Mostafa, S. A., Maashi, M. S., ... Garcia-Zapirain, B. (2020). COVID-CheXNet: Hybrid deep learning framework for identifying COVID-19 virus in chest X-rays images. *Soft Computing*, 1–16.

Bello, I., Zoph, B., Vasudevan, V., & Le, Q. V. (2017, July). Neural optimizer search with reinforcement learning. In *International Conference on Machine Learning* (pp. 459-468). PMLR.

Chu, D. K., Pan, Y., Cheng, S. M., Hui, K. P., Krishnan, P., Liu, Y., ... Poon, L. L. (2020). Molecular diagnosis of a novel coronavirus (2019-nCoV) causing an outbreak of pneumonia. *Clinical Chemistry*, *66*(4), 549–555.

El Asnaoui, K., Chawki, Y., & Idri, A. (2021). Automated methods for detecting and classifying pneumonia based on x-ray images using deep learning. In *Artificial Intelligence and Blockchain for Future Cybersecurity Applications* (pp. 257–284). Springer.

Fang, Y., Zhang, H., Xie, J., Lin, M., Ying, L., Pang, P., & Ji, W. (2020). Sensitivity of chest CT for COVID-19: Comparison to RT-PCR. *Radiology*, *296*(2), E115–E117.

Karar, M. E., Hemdan, E. E. D., & Shouman, M. A. (2021). Cascaded deep learning classifiers for computer-aided diagnosis of COVID-19 and pneumonia diseases in X-ray scans. *Complex & Intelligent Systems*, *7*(1), 235–247.

Kassania, S. H., Kassanib, P. H., Wesolowskic, M. J., Schneidera, K. A., & Detersa, R. (2021). Automatic detection of coronavirus disease (COVID-19) in X-ray and CT images: A machine learning-based approach. *Biocybernetics and Biomedical Engineering*, *41*(3), 867–879.

Kermany, D. S., Goldbaum, M., Cai, W., Valentim, C. C., Liang, H., Baxter, S. L., ... Zhang, K. (2018). Identifying medical diagnoses and treatable diseases by image-based deep learning. *Cell*, *172*(5), 1122–1131.

Li, Y., & Xia, L. (2020). Coronavirus disease 2019 (COVID-19): Role of chest CT in diagnosis and management. *AJR. American Journal of Roentgenology*, *214*(6), 1280–1286.

Liang, T. (2020). Handbook of COVID-19 prevention and treatment. The First Affiliated Hospital, Zhejiang University School of Medicine.

Narin, A., Kaya, C., & Pamuk, Z. (2021). Automatic detection of coronavirus disease (covid-19) using x-ray images and deep convolutional neural networks. *Pattern Analysis & Applications*, 1–14.

Parikh, R., Mathai, A., Parikh, S., Sekhar, G. C., & Thomas, R. (2008). Understanding and using sensitivity, specificity, and predictive values. *Indian Journal of Ophthalmology*, *56*(1), 45.

Wang, L., Lin, Z. Q., & Wong, A. (2020). Covid-net: A tailored deep convolutional neural network design for detecting covid-19 cases from chest x-ray images. *Scientific Reports*, *10*(1), 1–12.

Zhang, J., Xie, Y., Pang, G., Liao, Z., Verjans, J., Li, W., ... Xia, Y. (2020). Viral pneumonia screening on chest x-rays using Confidence-Aware anomaly detection. *IEEE Transactions on Medical Imaging*, *40*(3), 879–890.

Zoph, B., Vasudevan, V., Shlens, J., & Le, Q. V. (2018). Learning transferable architectures for scalable image recognition. In *Proceedings of the IEEE conference on computer vision and pattern recognition* (pp. 8697-8710). IEEE.

Chapter 5

Autonomous Vehicle Tracking Based on Non-Linear Model Predictive Control Approach

Trieu Minh Vu
Institute for Nanomaterials, Advanced Technologies, and Innovation, Technical University of Liberec, Czech Republic

Jaroslav Hlava
Faculty of Mechatronics, Informatics, and Interdisciplinary Studies, Technical University of Liberec, Czech Republic

Reza Moezzi
Institute for Nanomaterials, Advanced Technologies, and Innovation, Technical University of Liberec, Czech Republic

Michal Petru
Institute for Nanomaterials, Advanced Technologies, and Innovation, Technical University of Liberec, Czech Republic

Jindrich Cyrus
Institute for Nanomaterials, Advanced Technologies, and Innovation, Technical University of Liberec, Czech Republic

ABSTRACT

Autonomous driving vehicles are developing rapidly; however, the control systems for autonomous driving vehicles tracking smoothly in high speed are still challenging. This chapter develops non-linear model predictive control (NMPC) schemes for controlling autonomous driving vehicles tracking on feasible trajectories. The optimal control action for vehicle speed and steering velocity is generated online using NMPC optimizer subject to vehicle dynamic and physical constraints as well as the surrounding obstacles and the environmental side-slipping conditions. NMPC subject to softened state constraints provides a better possibility for the optimizer

DOI: 10.4018/978-1-7998-9012-6.ch005

to generate a feasible solution as real-time subject to online dynamic constraints and to maintain the vehicle stability. Different parameters of NMPC are simulated and analysed to see the relationships between the NMPC horizon prediction length and the weighting values. Results show that the NMPC can control the vehicle tracking exactly on different trajectories with minimum tracking errors and with high comfortability.

INTRODUCTION

The rapid and widespread development of advanced technologies on robotics, automation, IT and high-speed communication networks has made the application of autonomous driving vehicles growing constantly and changing the society. Autonomous vehicles have been received considerable attention in recent years and the needs are arising for the mechatronic systems to control the vehicle tracking from any given start points to any given destination points online generated from the global positioning system (GPS) and subject to the vehicle physical constraints.

This book chapter develops a real-time control system for an autonomous ground vehicle directed online from the GPS maps or/and from unmanned aerial vehicles (UAVs) images. This system can be applied for auto traveling on road or off road for unmanned ground vehicles. The system can also be used for auto parking and auto driving vehicles.

Motivation for the use of MPC is its ability to handle the constraints online within its open-loop optimal control problems while many other control techniques are conservative in handling online constraints or even try to avoid activating them, thus, losing the best performance that may be achievable. MPC can make the close loop system operating near its limits and hence, produce much better performance.

However, MPC regulator is designed for online implementation, any infeasible solution of the optimization problems cannot be allowed. To improve the system's stability once some constraints are violated, some kinds of softened constraints or tolerant regions can be developed whereas the output constraints are not strictly imposed and can be violated somewhat during the evolution of the performance.

To deal with the system uncertainties and the model-plant mismatches, robust MPC algorithms can be built accounting for the modelling errors at the controller design. Robust MPC can forecast all possible models in the plant uncertainty set and the optimal actions then can be determined through the min-max optimization.

The reference feasible trajectories can be generated online using solver for ordinary differential equations (ODEs) with the flatness or polynomial equations presented in (Minh V.T, 2013). Algorithms for robust MPC tracking set points are referred in Minh V.T and Hashim F.B (2011), where the system's uncertainties are demonstrated by a set of multiple models via a tree trajectory and its branches and the robust MPC problem is to find the optimal control actions that, once implemented, cause all branches to converge to a robust control invariant set.

Application of MPC in controlling vehicle speed and engine torque is referred to in Minh V.T and Hashim F.B (2012), where a real time transition strategy with MPC is achieved for quick and smooth clutch engagements. Essential knowledge on vehicle handling and steering calculations is referred to in Minh V.T (2012), in chapter 8 and chapter 9, where the vehicle dynamic behaviours are analysed and applied for designing a fee-error feedback controller for its autonomous tracking.

Robust MPC schemes for input saturated and softened state constraints are referred from Minh V.T and Afzulpurkar N (2005), where uncertain systems are used with linear matrix inequalities (LMIs) subject to input and output saturated constraints. Nonlinear MPC (NMPC) algorithms are referred to in Minh V.T and Afzulpurkar N (2006), where three NMPC regulators of zero terminal region, quasi-infinite horizon, and softened state constraints are presented and compared. In NMPC, all solution for the regulator is implemented for close-lope control by solving on-line the ODEs repeatedly.

Control of vehicle tracking with MPC can be referred to in some several latest research papers. However, the idea of an MPC for online tracking optimal trajectories generated from flatness or polynomial equations is still not available. Some of MPC schemes for autonomous ground vehicle can be seen in Falcon P. *et al* (2008), where an initial frame work based on MPC for a simplified vehicle is presented. However, the research has ignored the real-time solving of the vehicle ODEs equations and failed to generate the optimal controlled inputs for the vehicle linear velocity and its steering velocity. Similarly, another recent paper on optimal MPC for path tracking of autonomous vehicles by Lei L. *et al* (2011) is presented where the vehicle's equations of motion are approximately linearized by the vehicle coordinates and the heading angle. The paper failed to include the steering angle in its equations.

Scheme for a robust MPC applied to mobile vehicle trajectory control can be seen also from Baharonian M. *el al* (2011) with an assumption that there is a virtual reference moving according to the desired reference trajectory and then, the control problem becomes too simple and too trivial. An adaptive trajectory tracking control of wheeled mobile is considered by Wang J. *et al* (2011), however the paper does not mention on how a feasible trajectory can be generated and how some optimal control actions can be achieved for the best trajectory tracking performance. Another reference by Shim T. *et al* (2912) derives algorithms for MPC to control the front steering velocity and the wheel torque for autonomous ground vehicle. However, the paper failed to implement the on-line solving ODEs equations of NMPC. Another scheme of robust MPC to control fast vehicle dynamics with approximately linearized model is developed by Peni T and Bokor J (2006) from some unrealistic assumptions that the vehicle velocity is a constant, and so that the system is always linear. The latest development of MPC and autonomous vehicle tracking are referred to in Vu Trieu Minh et al. (2020), Minh, V.T. et al (2019), VT Minh (2011), Vu Trieu Minh and Wan Mansor Wan Muhamad (2010), andVu Trieu Minh, John Pumwa (2012).

So, the idea of this chapter is to generate comprehensive schemes for MPC to track reference trajectories generated online by ODEs from the vehicle kinematics. Vehicle location data can be collected and processed online from GPS or UAV. Then, the vehicle can automatically generate optimal feasible trajectory subject to feasible constraints on speed, steering, sideslip, obstacles, etc., and track exactly on these paths. The chapter is constructed as follows: Section 2 describes the system kinematic equations; Section 3 develops MPC schemes; Section 4 presents MPC using linearized model; Section 5 develops MPC using nonlinear model; Section 6 presents the MPC performances comparison; Finally, some study remarks are concluded in section 7.

SYSTEM MODELING

This part briefly presents concept of nonholonomic system and definition of Lie bracket of two vector fields $X_1(q)$ and $X_2(q)$ in the matrix form corresponding to the Cartesian (x, y) coordinate system:

$$\left[X_1, X_2\right](p) = \frac{\partial X_2}{\partial q} X_1\bigg|_p - \frac{\partial X_1}{\partial q} X_2\bigg|_p = \left[X_2(f)X_1 - X_1(f)X_2\right] \tag{1}$$

where $\dfrac{\partial X_1}{\partial q}$, $\dfrac{\partial X_2}{\partial q}$ are Jacobian matrices, X_1 and X_2 are vector fields on a smooth m - dimensional manifold M of $(q^1, q^2, ..., q^m)$ around some point $p \in M$ and $\left[X_1, X_2\right]$ is the Lie bracket. The nonlinear motions of the vehicle can be presented via the following Lie bracket vector field.

Once a vehicle is rolling without slipping; the vehicle dynamic can be represented in a set of first-order differential constraints on its configuration variables. If the vehicle has the rear-wheel driving, the kinematic model can be derived in equation (2) and shown in figure 1.

In figure 1, r is the vehicle wheel radius and l is the distance between the wheels; x and y are the Cartesian coordinates of the rear wheel, θ measures the orientation of the vehicle body with respect to the x axis, and φ is the steering angle.

Figure 1. A simplified vehicle model

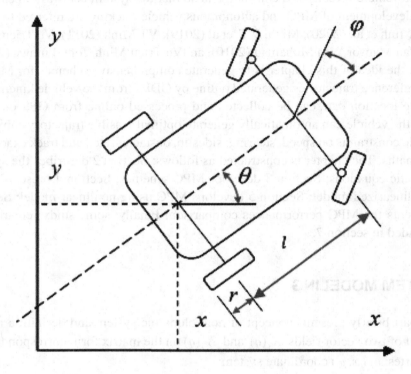

$$\begin{bmatrix} \dot{x} \\ \dot{y} \\ \dot{\theta} \\ \dot{\varphi} \end{bmatrix} = \underbrace{\begin{bmatrix} \cos\theta \\ \sin\theta \\ \dfrac{\tan\varphi}{l} \\ 0 \end{bmatrix}}_{X_1} u_1 + \underbrace{\begin{bmatrix} 0 \\ 0 \\ 0 \\ 1 \end{bmatrix}}_{X_2} u_2 \qquad (2)$$

In equation (2), the vehicle motion is controlled by two inputs, u_1 is the linear driving velocity, and, u_2 is the angular steering velocity. There are four (4) coordinates or state variables, namely the position of the vehicle $x_1 = x$ and $x_2 = y$; the angle, $x_3 = \theta$, of the vehicle body orientation with respect to the x axis; and the steering angle, $x_4 = \varphi$.

A useful tool to test the controllability of this nonlinear system is the Lie brackets rank condition as referred to in De Luca *et al.* (1998).

$$rank\left[X_1, X_2, X_3, X_4\right] = \left[X_1, X_2, [X_1, X_2], [X_1, [X_1, X_2]]\right] = 4 \tag{3}$$

The four components of function X_1 from equation (2) are: $X_1^1 = \cos\theta$, $X_1^2 = \sin\theta$, $X_1^3 = \dfrac{\tan\varphi}{l}$, and $X_1^4 = 0$.

For the feasible control of this dynamical system, the Lie brackets in (1) must be transferred and satisfied equations in (3). It can be seen that Jacobian matrix of the function X_1 is:

$$J_F(x, y, \theta, \varphi) = X_1(f) = \begin{bmatrix} \dfrac{\partial X_1^1}{\partial x} & \dfrac{\partial X_1^1}{\partial y} & \dfrac{\partial X_1^1}{\partial \theta} & \dfrac{\partial X_1^1}{\partial \varphi} \\ \dfrac{\partial X_1^2}{\partial x} & \dfrac{\partial X_1^2}{\partial y} & \dfrac{\partial X_1^2}{\partial \theta} & \dfrac{\partial X_1^2}{\partial \varphi} \\ \dfrac{\partial X_1^3}{\partial x} & \dfrac{\partial X_1^3}{\partial y} & \dfrac{\partial X_1^3}{\partial \theta} & \dfrac{\partial X_1^3}{\partial \varphi} \\ \dfrac{\partial X_1^4}{\partial x} & \dfrac{\partial X_1^4}{\partial y} & \dfrac{\partial X_1^4}{\partial \theta} & \dfrac{\partial X_1^4}{\partial \varphi} \end{bmatrix} = \begin{bmatrix} 0 & 0 & -\sin\theta & 0 \\ 0 & 0 & \cos\theta & 0 \\ 0 & 0 & 0 & \dfrac{1}{l\cos^2\varphi} \\ 0 & 0 & 0 & 0 \end{bmatrix}$$

The four components of function X_2 from equation (2) are: $X_2^1 = 0$, $X_2^2 = 0$, $X_2^3 = 0$, and $X_2^4 = 1$.

And Jacobian matrix of the function X_2 is:

$$J_F(x, y, \theta, \varphi) = X_2(f) = \begin{bmatrix} \dfrac{\partial X_1^1}{\partial x} & \dfrac{\partial X_1^1}{\partial y} & \dfrac{\partial X_1^1}{\partial \theta} & \dfrac{\partial X_1^1}{\partial \varphi} \\ \dfrac{\partial X_2^2}{\partial x} & \dfrac{\partial X_2^2}{\partial y} & \dfrac{\partial X_2^2}{\partial \theta} & \dfrac{\partial X_2^2}{\partial \varphi} \\ \dfrac{\partial X_2^3}{\partial x} & \dfrac{\partial X_2^3}{\partial y} & \dfrac{\partial X_2^3}{\partial \theta} & \dfrac{\partial X_2^3}{\partial \varphi} \\ \dfrac{\partial X_2^4}{\partial x} & \dfrac{\partial X_2^4}{\partial y} & \dfrac{\partial X_2^4}{\partial \theta} & \dfrac{\partial X_2^4}{\partial \varphi} \end{bmatrix} = \begin{bmatrix} 0 & 0 & 0 & 0 \\ 0 & 0 & 0 & 0 \\ 0 & 0 & 0 & 0 \\ 0 & 0 & 0 & 0 \end{bmatrix}$$

From equation (1), the Lie bracket of vector field $X_3 = \left[X_1, X_2\right]$ is:

$$X_3 = \left[X_1, X_2\right] = \left[X_2(f)X_1 - X_1(f)X_2\right]$$

$$= \begin{bmatrix} 0 & 0 & 0 & 0 \\ 0 & 0 & 0 & 0 \\ 0 & 0 & 0 & 0 \\ 0 & 0 & 0 & 0 \end{bmatrix} \begin{bmatrix} \cos\theta \\ \sin\theta \\ \dfrac{\tan\varphi}{l} \\ 0 \end{bmatrix} - \begin{bmatrix} 0 & 0 & -\sin\theta & 0 \\ 0 & 0 & \cos\theta & 0 \\ 0 & 0 & 0 & \dfrac{1}{l\cos^2\varphi} \\ 0 & 0 & 0 & 0 \end{bmatrix} \begin{bmatrix} 0 \\ 0 \\ 0 \\ 1 \end{bmatrix} = \begin{bmatrix} 0 \\ 0 \\ -\dfrac{1}{l\cos^2\varphi} \\ 0 \end{bmatrix} \tag{4}$$

And the Lie bracket of vector field $X_4 = \left[X_1\left[X_1, X_2\right]\right]$ is:

$$X_4 = \left[X_1\left[X_1, X_2\right]\right] =$$

$$= \begin{bmatrix} 0 & 0 & 0 & 0 \\ 0 & 0 & 0 & 0 \\ 0 & 0 & 0 & -\dfrac{2\tan\varphi}{l\cos^2\varphi} \\ 0 & 0 & 0 & 0 \end{bmatrix} \begin{bmatrix} \cos\theta \\ \sin\theta \\ \dfrac{\tan\varphi}{l} \\ 0 \end{bmatrix} - \begin{bmatrix} 0 & 0 & -\sin\theta & 0 \\ 0 & 0 & \cos\theta & 0 \\ 0 & 0 & 0 & \dfrac{1}{l\cos^2\varphi} \\ 0 & 0 & 0 & 0 \end{bmatrix} \begin{bmatrix} 0 \\ 0 \\ -\dfrac{1}{l\cos^2\varphi} \\ 0 \end{bmatrix} = \begin{bmatrix} -\dfrac{\sin\theta}{l\cos^2\varphi} \\ \dfrac{\cos\theta}{l\cos^2\varphi} \\ 0 \\ 0 \end{bmatrix} \tag{5}$$

Check the determinant of this 4x4 Jacobi-Lie bracket matrix from (3):

$$\det\left(X_1 X_2 X_3 X_4\right) = \begin{vmatrix} \cos\theta & 0 & 0 & -\dfrac{\sin\theta}{l\cos^2\varphi} \\ \sin\theta & 0 & 0 & \dfrac{\cos\theta}{l\cos^2\varphi} \\ \dfrac{\tan\varphi}{l} & 0 & -\dfrac{1}{l\cos^2\varphi} & 0 \\ 0 & 1 & 0 & 0 \end{vmatrix} = \dfrac{1}{l^2\cos^4\varphi} \tag{6}$$

So, if $\varphi \neq \dfrac{\pi}{2}$, then $\det\left[X_1 X_2 X_3 X_4\right]$ is well defined and the system in (2) is non-holonomic. This means that the dynamical system in (2) can be transformed from any given state to any other state or all of its position parameters are under controlled by the input vectors. Or it is possible to express all state variables as a function of the inputs.

In the next part, an approximate linearized system and its discretized form from continuous derivative equations in (2) will be developed. The discretized form of this system will be used for the MPC open loop optimization calculation.

The vehicle model in (2) is nonlinear and has the first order derivative form:

$$\dot{X} = f(x, u) \tag{7}$$

where the state variables are $x \triangleq \left[x, y, \theta, \varphi\right]'$, and the inputs are $u = \left[u_1, u_2\right]'$. The nonlinear equation in (7) can be expanded in Taylor series around the referenced point (x_r, u_r) at $\dot{X}_r = f(x_r, u_r)$, that:

$$\dot{X} \approx f(x_r, u_r) + f_{x,r}(x - x_r) + f_{u,r}(u - u_r) \tag{8}$$

where $f_{x,r}$ and $f_{r,x}$ are the Jacobean of f corresponding to x and u, evaluated around the referenced points (x_r, u_r).

Subtraction of (8) and $\dot{X}_r = f(x_r, u_r)$ results a linear approximation to the system at the reference points for a continuous time (t) model:

$$\dot{\tilde{X}}(t) = A(t)\tilde{X}(t) + B(t)\tilde{u}(t) \tag{9}$$

where

$$\tilde{X}(t) = X(t) - X_r(t) = \begin{bmatrix} x(t) - x_r(t) \\ y(t) - y_r(t) \\ \theta(t) - \theta_r(t) \\ \varphi(t) - \varphi_r(t) \end{bmatrix},$$

and

$$\tilde{u}(t) = u(t) - u_r(t) = \begin{bmatrix} u_1(t) - u_{r1}(t) \\ u_2(t) - u_{r2}(t) \end{bmatrix},$$

$$A(t) = \begin{bmatrix} 0 & 0 & -u_{r1}(t)\sin\theta_r(t) & 0 \\ 0 & 0 & u_{r1}(t)\cos\theta_r(t) & 0 \\ 0 & 0 & 0 & \dfrac{u_{r1}(t)}{l\cos^2\varphi_r(t)} \\ 0 & 0 & 0 & 0 \end{bmatrix}, \; B(t) = \begin{bmatrix} \cos\theta_r(t) & 0 \\ \sin\theta_r(t) & 0 \\ \dfrac{\tan\varphi_r(t)}{l} & 0 \\ 0 & 1 \end{bmatrix}$$

The continuous approximation of $\dot{\tilde{X}}(t)$ in (9) can be represented in the discrete-time (k) with time $k+1 = k + \Delta t$ and Δt is the length of sampling interval. The inputs $u(k)$ are held constant during the time interval $(k+1)$ and (k). The symbols of $x_k = x(k)$ and $u_k = u(k)$ are also used:

$$\tilde{X}(k+1) = A(k)\tilde{X}(k) + B(k)\tilde{u}(k)$$

$$\tilde{Y}(k) = C(k)\tilde{X}(k) \tag{10}$$

where

$$A(k) = \begin{bmatrix} 1 & 0 & -u_{r1}(k)\sin\theta_r(k)(\Delta t) & 0 \\ 0 & 1 & u_{r1}(k)\cos\theta_r(k)(\Delta t) & 0 \\ 0 & 0 & 1 & \dfrac{u_{r1}(k)}{l\cos^2\varphi_r(k)}(\Delta t) \\ 0 & 0 & 0 & 1 \end{bmatrix},$$

$$B(k) = \begin{bmatrix} \cos\theta_r(k)(\Delta t) & 0 \\ \sin\theta_r(k)(\Delta t) & 0 \\ \dfrac{\tan\varphi_r(k)}{l}(\Delta t) & 0 \\ 1 & (\Delta t) \end{bmatrix},$$

$$C(k) = \begin{bmatrix} 1 & 0 & 0 & 0 \\ 0 & 1 & 0 & 0 \\ 0 & 0 & 1 & 0 \\ 0 & 0 & 0 & 1 \end{bmatrix},$$

and,

$$\tilde{X}(k) = X(k) - X_r(k) = \begin{bmatrix} x(k) - x_r(k) \\ y(k) - y_r(k) \\ \theta(k) - \theta_r(k) \\ \varphi(k) - \varphi_r(k) \end{bmatrix}, \; \tilde{u}(k) = u(k) - u_r(k) = \begin{bmatrix} u_1(k) - u_{r1}(k) \\ u_2(k) - u_{r2}(k) \end{bmatrix}$$

In the above discretized model, the two control inputs are the difference in the actual and the desired vehicle linear velocity, $u_1(k) - u_{r1}(k)$, and the difference of the actual and desired steering angular velocity, $u_2(k) - u_{r2}(k)$. The four outputs, $y(k) = \tilde{Y}(k) = C(k)\tilde{X}(k)$, are totally measured and updated in each real-time scanning interval. It is important to note that the vehicle linearized model in (10) is a time variant system with its transfer function is depending on its positions and the scanning speeds.

The approximate linearized equations (10) are used to develop MPC algorithms in the next part.

MODEL PREDICTIVE CONTROL

This part presents the design of MPC algorithms for the discretized linearized model. MPC works out the optimal open-loop optimization problem that minimizes the difference between the predicted plant behaviour and the desired plant behaviour. MPC differs from other control techniques in that the optimal control problem is solved on-line for the current state of the plant, rather than off-line determined as the feedback policy. MPC has been widely applied in the robotic technologies because of its ability to handle input and output constrains in the optimal control problem.

MPC algorithms are now designed to control the two inputs of the vehicle driving velocity, $u_1(k)$, and, its steering velocity, $u_2(k)$, in order to achieve the desired outputs of the vehicle coordinate position, $x_1(k) = x(k)$, and $x_2(k) = y(k)$; the vehicle orientation body angle with respect to the x axis, $x_3(k) = \theta(k)$; and the steering angle, $x_4(k) = \varphi(k)$. All of these outputs are set to tract exactly on the given trajectory reference set points of $x_r(k)$, $y_r(k)$, $\theta_r(k)$, and $\varphi_r(k)$ at each discrete-time (k).

From (10), the prediction horizon for the outputs, $y_{k+i|k}$, and the input increments, $\Delta u_{k+i|k}$, can be rewritten as,

$$
\begin{bmatrix} y_{k+1|k} \\ y_{k+2|k} \\ \vdots \\ y_{k+N_y|k} \end{bmatrix} = \begin{bmatrix} CA \\ CA^2 \\ \vdots \\ CA^{N_y} \end{bmatrix} x_{k|k} + \begin{bmatrix} CB \\ CAB + CB \\ \vdots \\ \sum_{i=1}^{N_y} CA^{i-1}B \end{bmatrix} u_{k-1}
$$

$$
+ \begin{bmatrix} CB & 0 & \cdots & 0 \\ CAB + CB & CB & 0 & 0 \\ \vdots & \vdots & \ddots & \vdots \\ \sum_{i=1}^{N_y} CA^{i-1}B & \sum_{i=1}^{N_y-1} CA^{i-1}B & \cdots & \sum_{i=1}^{N_y-N_u+1} CA^{i-1}B \end{bmatrix} \begin{bmatrix} \Delta u_k \\ \Delta u_{k+1} \\ \vdots \\ \Delta u_{k+N_u-1} \end{bmatrix}
$$

Then, the tracking set points MPC objective function with hard constraints is:

$$
\min_{U \triangleq \left\{ \Delta u_k, \ldots, \Delta u_{k+N_u-1} \right\}} \left\{ J(U, x(k)) = \sum_{i=0}^{N_y-1} \left[(y_{k+i|k} - r_{k+i|k})' Q(y_{k+i|k} - r_{k+i|k}) + \Delta u'_{k+i|k} R \Delta u_{k+i|k} \right] \right\},
$$

subject to:

$$
u_k \in \mathcal{U}, \text{ and } u_{k+i} \in \left[u_{\min}, u_{\max} \right], \Delta u_{k+i} \in \left[\Delta u_{\min}, \Delta u_{\max} \right], \text{ for } i = 0, 1, \ldots, N_u - 1,
$$

$$
y_k \in \mathcal{Y}, \text{ and } y_{k+i|k} \in \left[y_{\min}, y_{\max} \right], \text{ for } i = 0, 1, \ldots, N_y - 1,
$$

$$
\Delta u_k = u_k - u_{k-1} \in \Delta \mathcal{U}, \text{ and } \Delta u_{k+i} = 0, \text{ for } i \geq N_u,
$$

$$
x_{k|k} = x(k) \quad , \qquad\qquad x_{k+i+1|k} = A(k)x_{k+i|k} + B(k)u_{k+i} \quad ,
$$

$$
u_{k+i|k} = u_{k+i-1|k} + \Delta u_{k+i|k}, y_{k+i|k} = C(k)x_{k+i|k} \tag{11}
$$

where $x(k)$ denotes the state variables at the current discrete time (k):

$$
U \triangleq \left\{ \Delta u_k, \ldots, \Delta u_{k+N_u-1} \right\}
$$

is the solution of input increments, N_u is the inputs predictive horizon; N_y is the outputs predictive horizon; $y_{k+i|k}$ are the predictive outputs at the current discrete time (k), $r_{k+i|k}$ are the corresponding reference output setpoints; $\Delta u_{k+i|k}$ are the input increments prediction with

$$\Delta u_{k+i|k} = u_{k+i|k} - u_{k+i-1|k}\,;\ Q = Q' \geq 0,\ R = R' > 0$$

are the weighting penalty matrices for predicted outputs and input increments, respectively.

The MPC regulator computes the optimal solution,

$$U^* \triangleq \left\{\Delta u_k^*,...,\Delta u_{k+N_{u-1}}^*\right\}$$

and the new inputs

$$u_{k+i|k} = u_{k+i-1|k} + \Delta u_{k+i|k}\,,$$

from the objective function (11), then applies only the first element of the current inputs increment, Δu_k^*, and calculate the current optimal inputs,

$$u^*(k) = u_{k-1} + \Delta u_k^*\,,$$

and inserts this $u^*(k)$ into the system. After having inserted the current optimal inputs at time k, the MPC regulator repeats the optimization, $u^*(k+1)$, for the next interval time, $k+1$, based on the new calculation of the update state variables $x(k+1)$. This way, the closed loop control strategy is obtained by solving on-line the open loop optimization problem.

By substituting

$$x_{k+N_y|k} = A^{N_y}(k)x(k) + \sum_{i=0}^{N_y-1} A^i(k)B(k)u_{k+N_y-1-i}\,,$$

equation (11) can be rewritten as a function of only the current state $x(k)$ and the current set points $r(k)$:

$$\Psi\big(x(k),r(k)\big) = \frac{1}{2}x'(k)Yx(k) + \min_U\left\{\frac{1}{2}U'HU + x'(k)r(k)FU\right\},\qquad (12)$$

subject to the hard combined constraints of $GU \leq W + Ex(k)$, where the column vector

$$U \triangleq \left[\Delta u_k, \ldots, \Delta u_{k+N_p-1}\right]' \in \Delta \mathcal{U}$$

is the prediction optimization vector; $H = H' > 0$, and H, F, Y, G, W and E are matrices obtained from Q, R and given constraints in (11). As only the optimizer U is needed, the term involving Y is usually removed from (12). Then, the optimization problem in (12) is a quadratic program and depends only on the current state $x(k)$ and the current set points $r(k)$ subject to the hard combined constraints. The implementation of MPC requires the on-line solution of this quadratic program at each time interval (k).

In reality, the system would have both input and output constraints and the difficulty will arise due to the inability to satisfy the output constraints due to the input constraints. Since MPC is designed for on-line implementation, any infeasible solution of the online optimization problem in (12) cannot be allowed. Normally the input constraints are based on the physical limits of the vehicle and can be considered as hard constraints. If the outputs constraints are the tracking positions which are not strictly imposed and can be violated somewhat during the evolution of the performance. To guarantee the system stability once the outputs violate the constraints, the hard constrained optimization in (11) can be modified to a new MPC objective function with softened constraints as:

$$\min_{U \triangleq \left\{\Delta u_k, \ldots, \Delta u_{k+N_u-1}\right\}} \left\{ J(U, x(k)) = \sum_{i=0}^{N_y-1} \left[\begin{array}{l} (y_{k+i|k} - r_{k+i|k})' Q(y_{k+i|k} - r_{k+i|k}) \\ + \Delta u'_{k+i|k} R \Delta u_{k+i|k} + \varepsilon'_i(k) \Lambda \varepsilon_i(k) \end{array} \right] \right\} \tag{13}$$

where $\varepsilon_i(k) \geq 0$ are the new penalty terms added to the MPC objective function,

$$\varepsilon_i(k) = \left[\varepsilon_y; \varepsilon_u\right], \ y_{\min} - \varepsilon_y \leq y_{k+i|k} \leq y_{\max} + \varepsilon_y$$

and

$$u_{\min} - \varepsilon_u \leq u_{k+i|k} \leq u_{\max} + \varepsilon_u.$$

And $\Lambda = \Lambda^{'} \geq 0$ is the new penalty matrix (usually $\Lambda > 0$ and set with small values). These terms, $\varepsilon_{i}(k)$, will keep the constrained violations at low values until the solution is returned. A new MPC algorithm for softened constraints to select the optimal inputs $u^{*}(k+i \mid k)$ can be conducted similarly to (12) with the new added penalty terms $\varepsilon_{i}^{'}(k)\Lambda\varepsilon_{i}(k)$.

Furthermore, in order to increase the possibility of the MPC to find out online solution in critical time, some output set points can be temporally deleted because the deletion of some output set points can make the system looser and the probability that the MPC optimizer can find a solution will increase. Deletion of some output set points can be conducted via temporally assigning zeros in the penalty matrices Q and R. For example, the above MPC controller has four outputs $y = \left[y_{1}, y_{2}, y_{3}, y_{4}\right]^{'}$, if we select the 4 by 4 penalty matrix $Q = diag\{1,1,1,1\}$, implying that all four outputs are required to reach set points. However, if we want to delete the output set points for y_{3}, y_{4} or it is required that only the two outputs, y_{1}, y_{2}, to reach the set points, we can choose a new penalty matrix $Q = diag\{1,1,0,0\}$. In other words, the new controlled variables now become $y = \left[y_{1}, y_{2}\right]^{'}$.

Robustness of MPC can be also increased if some set points can be relaxed into regions rather than in some specific values. Then, a new MPC algorithm can be developed if the set points $r(k)$ now can be changed into some regions. An output region is defined by the minimum and maximum values of a desired range. The minimum value is the lower limit, and the maximum value is the upper limit and satisfied $y_{lower} \leq y_{k+i|k} \leq y_{upper}$. The modified objective function for the MPC with output regions is:

$$\min_{U \triangleq \{\Delta u_{k}, \ldots, \Delta u_{k+N_{u}-1}\}} \left\{ J(U, x(k)) = \sum_{i=0}^{N_{y}-1} \left[z_{k+i|k}^{'} Q z_{k+i|k} + \Delta u_{k+i|k}^{'} R \Delta u_{k+i|k} \right] \right\}, \quad (14)$$

where $z_{k+i|k} \geq 0$; $z_{k+i|k} = y_{k+i|k} - y_{upper}$ for $y_{k+i|k} > y_{upper}$;

$z_{k+i|k} = y_{lower} - y_{k+i|k}$ for $y_{k+i|k} < y_{lower}$; $z_{k+i|k} = 0$ for $y_{lower} \leq y_{k+i|k} \leq y_{upper}$

As long as the outputs still lie inside the desired regions, no control actions are taken because none of the control objectives have been violated, all $z_{k+i|k} = 0$. But when an output violates the desired region, the control objective in the MPC regulator will activate and push them back to the desired regions. This modified MPC objective

Figure 2. MPC control system

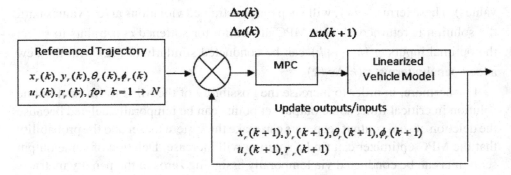

function can be applied for the autonomous tracking vehicle when the desired set points are changed to some desired regions. The tracking trajectory will become smoother and the controller tasks will be reduced to maintain the outputs in the desired regions.

Numerical experiments of the MPC schemes are presented in the following parts of this research.

MPC USING LINEARIZATION MODEL

This part presents the MPC performance for linearized vehicle model in (10). The diagram of the MPC control system is shown in figure 2.

For the trajectory tracking, a reference trajectory is generated by solving the trajectory differential equations in (2). The difference of the reference trajectory parameters (set points) and the actual current vehicle parameters is provided to the MPC regulator. The MPC regulator will calculate the optimized control input horizon. Only the first element of this optimal solution is fed to the linearized vehicle model to generate the next outputs of the vehicle. The update system outputs are now compared with the update set points in the reference trajectory for the next MPC regulator calculation repetition.

MPC for Tracking a Full Circle

For generating a full circle reference trajectory, the reference desired inputs are set at $u_1 = r\omega$ and $u_2 = 0$. The initial positions are selected as

Figure 3. Circular reference set points

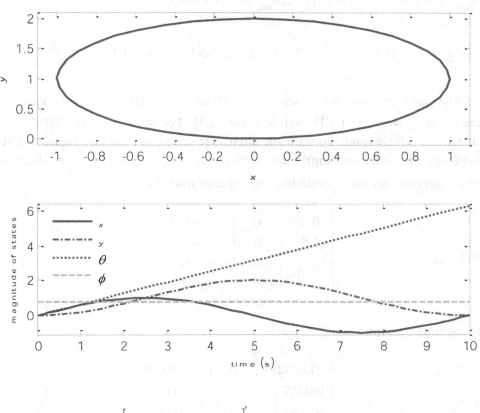

$$\begin{bmatrix} x_0 & y_0 & \theta_0 & \varphi_0 \end{bmatrix}' = \begin{bmatrix} 0 & 0 & 0 & \arctan\dfrac{r}{l} \end{bmatrix}'$$

(referred to figure 1). For this simulation, we use $r = 0.5m$, $l = 1.5m$, and $\omega = 1 rad\,/\,\sec$. The reference set points are generated using online ODE45 function in Matlab and shown in figure 3.

We now use the MPC control system in figure 2 to track the vehicle along the circular path in figure 3.

For this simulation, the initial positions of the vehicle are set at

$$X_0 = \begin{bmatrix} -0.5 & -0.5 & 0 & 0 \end{bmatrix}';$$

The constraints are set at

$$u_{\min} = \begin{bmatrix} -1, -1 \end{bmatrix}', \; u_{\max} = \begin{bmatrix} 1, 1 \end{bmatrix}', \; \Delta u_{\min} = \begin{bmatrix} -0.5, -0.5 \end{bmatrix}',$$

$$\Delta u_{\max} = \begin{bmatrix} 0.5, 0.5 \end{bmatrix}', \; y_{\min} = \begin{bmatrix} -1, -1, -1, -1 \end{bmatrix}', \text{ and } y_{\max} = \begin{bmatrix} 1, 1, 1, 1 \end{bmatrix}';$$

The predictive horizons are set at $N_u = 10$ and $N_y = 10$; The penalty matrices are set at $Q = diag\{1, 1, 1, 1\}$ and $R = diag\{1, 1\}$. Performance of the MPC with linearized vehicle model to track the circular reference is shown in figure 4. The MPC optimizer is minimizing the tracking errors $y_{k+i|k} - r_{k+i|k}$ at each points (discrete time intervals) during its evolution performance from the initial position,

$$error_{initial} = y_{k|0} - r_{k|0} = \begin{bmatrix} -0.5 \\ -0.5 \\ 0 \\ 0 \end{bmatrix} - \begin{bmatrix} 0 \\ 0 \\ 0 \\ 0.7854 \end{bmatrix} = \begin{bmatrix} -0.5 \\ -0.5 \\ 0 \\ -0.7854 \end{bmatrix}$$

to the final position,

$$error_{final} = y_{k|N} - r_{k|N} = \begin{bmatrix} -0.0202 \\ 0.0257 \\ 0.0094 \\ 0.7648 \end{bmatrix} - \begin{bmatrix} 0 \\ 0 \\ 0 \\ 0.7854 \end{bmatrix} = \begin{bmatrix} -0.0202 \\ 0.0257 \\ 0.0094 \\ -0.0206 \end{bmatrix},$$

or very small errors are left at the end of the tracking trajectory.

In MPC, if the prediction horizon is shortened, the calculation burden will be considerably reduced but will lead to incremental changes in the inputs and then, bad performance of the outputs. With shortened outputs and inputs predictions, the system may become instable. Figure 5 shows the MPC performance with shortened predictive horizons to $N_u = 4$ and $N_y = 4$.

Sufficient long prediction horizon will increase the MPC performance and its stability. However, the calculation burden will also be dramatically increased. The next simulation shown in figure 6 runs with $N_u = 20$ and $N_y = 20$. Performance of the tracking outputs is much improved as well as the inputs become smoother (easier to regulate the inputs to achieve the outputs).

Figure 4. Tracking MPC linearized model

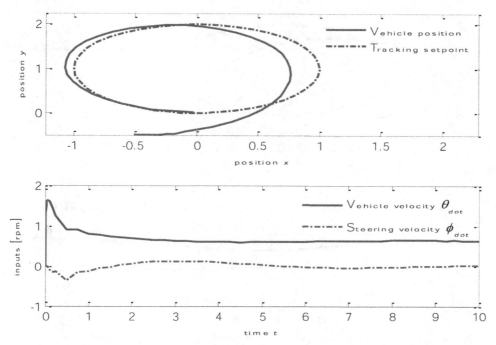

However, with too long horizon length, MPC will result too slow control increments and therefore deteriorate the controlled performance. The system becomes instable as shown in figure 7 with too long prediction horizon of $N_u = 23$ and $N_y = 23$.

Regulation of the penalty matrices can also affect the MPC performance. If we set $Q \gg R$ (Q is set much larger than R), then any small changes in the outputs will affect dramatically to the MPC objective function. It means that the inputs are set to be changed faster than the outputs. However, the vehicle inputs (speeds) are harder to be regulated or changed, so we can scarify some tracking output errors to gain some smoother inputs by setting $Q \ll R$. The next simulation runs with $N_u = 6$, $N_y = 6$, $Q = diag\{1,1,1,1\}$, and $R = diag\{10,10\}$. Figure 8 shows that the inputs become smoother (easier to control) but the output tracking errors become considerably larger.

For the case of $Q \gg R$, we set now $N_u = 6$, $N_y = 6$, $Q = diag\{10,10,10,10\}$, and $R = diag\{1,1\}$. Figure 9 shows the system becomes very sensitive to the input changes. Those faster input changes can be seen and resulted triangular in shape. These inputs shape is unrealistic since we cannot control the vehicle velocity on that shape. The conclusion is that that the system will be instability.

Figure 5. MPC linearized model with short horizon

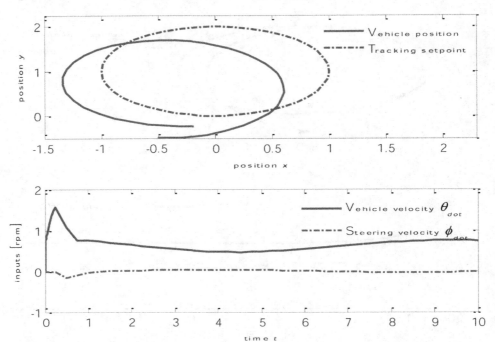

Another way to regulate the system is to change the reference set points $(y_{k+i|k} - r_{k+i|k})$. In the previous simulations, we set the set point errors at zeros, $r_k = y_k - y_r = [0, 0, 0, 0]'$, for all difference of the reference trajectory and the vehicle positions. To offset the vehicle sideslips or to compensate the model-plant mismatches, we can dynamically change these set point errors. For example, if we set $r_k = [0.1, 0.1, 0, 0]'$, the MPC performance is shown in figure 10, the final position of the vehicle becomes $[x_F, y_F] = [0.1, 0.1]$, but the vehicle tracks faster to the reference trajectory.

We can also assign the offsets to the vehicle orientation angle, θ, and steering angle, φ. For example, if we set the tracing errors at $r_k = [0, 0, 0.1, 0.1]'$, the MPC performance will be in figure 11. Due to the positive error offsets on the orientation and steering angles, the vehicle rotates in a smaller radius and also has the destination parameters of $[\theta_F, \varphi_F] = [0.1, 0.1]$.

All of the above MPC performances are set with the initial position of the vehicle,

Figure 6. MPC linearized model with long horizon

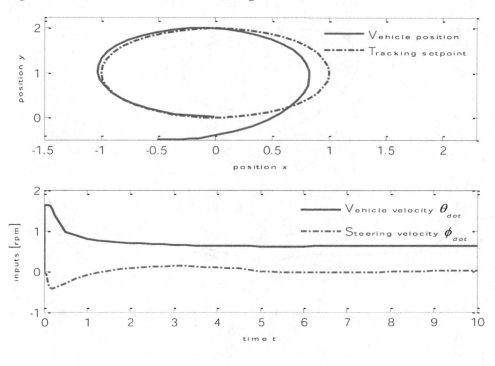

$$X_0^{\text{Vehicle}} = \begin{bmatrix} -0.5 & -0.5 & 0 & 0 \end{bmatrix}'.$$

It is quite different to the initial position of the reference trajectory,

$$X_0^{\text{Reference}} = \begin{bmatrix} 0 & 0 & 0 & \arctan\dfrac{r}{l} \end{bmatrix}'.$$

This difference can be considered as the measured output errors or the model-plant mismatches. MPC regulator can gradually minimize these tracking errors during its evolution and drive the vehicle closer to its reference set points. In the next parts, we will investigate the ability of the MPC to track the vehicle on any feasible paths from any given start points to any given destination points generated directly from the kinematic differential equations in (2).

Figure 7. MPC linearized model with too long horizon and instability

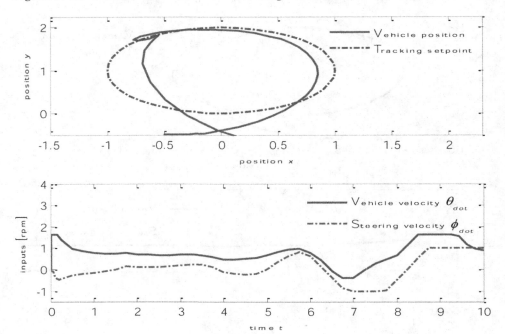

4.2. MPC for Tracking Flatness Trajectory

Flatness trajectory generation is presented in Minh V.T. (2013). Figure 12 shows a flatness trajectory for the vehicle from the initial position, $\left[x_0, y_0\right] = \left[0,0\right]$, to the final position, $\left[x_F, y_F\right] = \left[10,10\right]$, and the development of the orientation angle, θ, and steering angle, φ, during this travel. The time for completing this travel is set at $T = 100 \, \text{sec}$;

For this MPC tracking, the initial positions of the vehicle are set at

$$X_0 = \begin{bmatrix} 0 & -0.5 & 0 & 0 \end{bmatrix}';$$

The predictive horizons are set at short $N_u = 4$ and $N_y = 4$; Penalty matrices are set equally at $Q = diag\{1,1,1,1\}$ and $R = diag\{1,1\}$; The reference velocity inputs are $u_1 = 1$ (u_1 is set at 0 at the initial point, during the first 1/5 travelling time length, u_1 will gradually increase and maintain at 1 for 60 sec, during the final 1/5 traveling time length, u_1 will decrease back to 0), and $u_2 = 0$. Performance of

Figure 8. MPC linearized model with $Q \ll R$

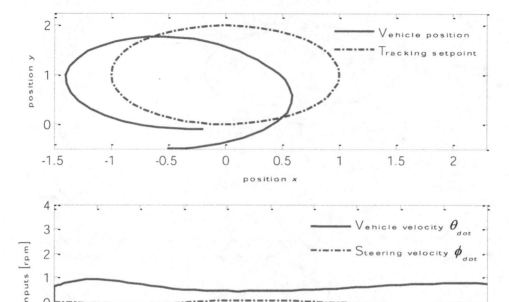

this MPC is shown in figure 13. The vehicle starts from an initial velocity of $u_1 = 0$ and from its initial positions of

$$X_0 = \begin{bmatrix} 0 & -0.5 & 0 & 0 \end{bmatrix}',$$

gradually tracks to the reference trajectory in 10 sec.

Next, we lengthen the horizon prediction to $N_u = 8$ and $N_y = 8$, we now can see that the too long prediction horizon can degrade the MPC performance. In this example, the system becomes instable as shown in figure 14.

The system's instability shown in figure 14 is due to the too incentive changes of the vehicle input velocities. If we increase penalty matrix values, R, or set $Q < R$, the input increments will be slower and the inputs will become smoother. Next simulation runs with $Q = diag\{1,1,1,1\}$ and $R = diag\{3,3\}$. The system returns stable due to the slower increment of inputs as shown in figure 15.

Figure 9. MPC linearized model with $Q \gg R$

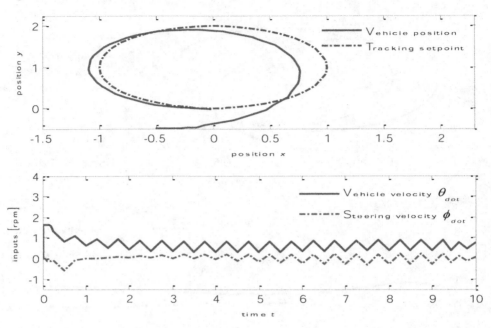

Figure 10. MPC linearized model with set point offsets variation

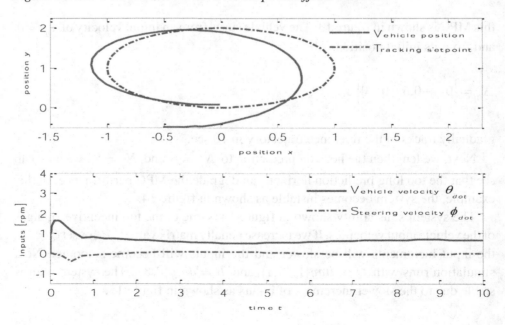

Figure 11. MPC linearized model with set point offsets in angles

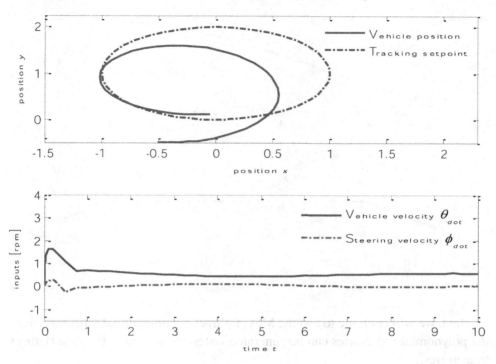

Figure 12. Flatness trajectory reference set points

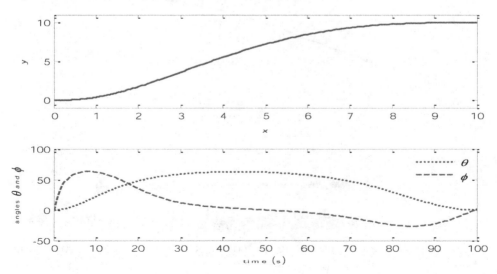

Figure 13. MPC for tracking flatness trajectory

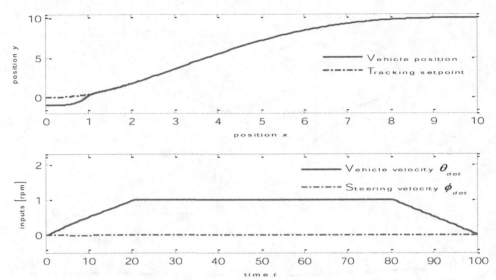

Next, we will continue to test the MPC for tracking polynomial trajectory since the polynomial trajectories can be generated faster and smoother than the flatness trajectories.

Figure 14. MPC with too long horizon

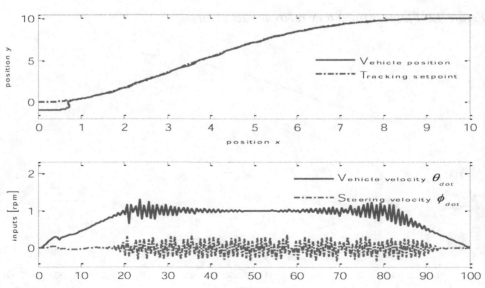

Figure 15. MPC with $Q < R$

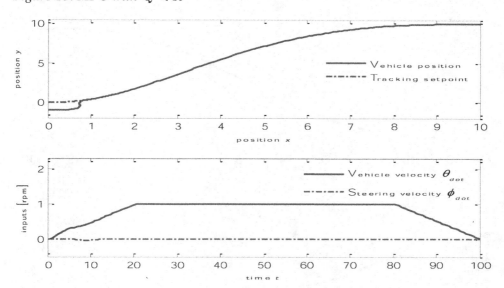

MPC for Tracking Polynomial Trajectory

Polynomial trajectory generation is presented in Minh V.T. (2013). Figure 16 shows the polynomial trajectory for the vehicle from the initial position, $[x_0, y_0] = [0, 0]$, to the final position, $[x_F, y_F] = [10, 10]$, and the changes of the orientation angle, θ, and steering angle, φ, during the travel. Similarly, the time for completing this path is set at $T = 100 \sec$;

The initial positions of the vehicle are set at

$$X_0 = \begin{bmatrix} 0 & -0.5 & 0 & 0 \end{bmatrix}';$$

The predictive horizons are set at short $N_u = 4$ and $N_y = 4$; Penalty matrices are set equally at $Q = diag\{1, 1, 1, 1\}$ and $R = diag\{1, 1\}$; The reference velocity inputs are $u_1 = 1$ (u_1 is set at 0 at the initial point, during the first 1/5 traveling time length, u_1 will gradually increase and maintain at 1, during the final 1/5 traveling time length, u_1 will decrease back to 0), and $u_2 = 0$. Performance of this MPC is shown in figure 17. The vehicle gradually tracks the reference trajectory set points in 20 sec.

Figure 16. Polynomial trajectory reference set points

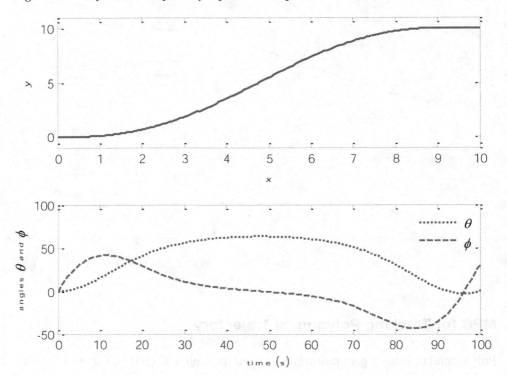

Next, we lengthen the horizon prediction to $N_u = 8$ and $N_y = 8$, we can see that the too long prediction horizon can degrade the MPC performance. The system becomes instable as shown in figure 18.

If we increase penalty matrix values, R, or set $Q < R$, the input increments will be slower and the inputs will become smoother. In the next simulation, we set the same horizon prediction lengths of $N_u = 8$ and $N_y = 8$, but increase the input penalty matrix values to $R = diag\{10,10\}$, and maintain the output penalty matrix at $Q = diag\{1,1,1,1\}$. The system returns back stable as shown in figure 19.

Vehicle can track the given trajectory by reversed speed. In this case, we set the reference velocity inputs u_1 as minus values. Then, the vehicle now is moving backward tracking on the path. Figure 20 shows the MPC performance for this vehicle reversing on the trajectory with the velocity of $u_1 = -1$.

We have known that this system is very sensitive to the vehicle velocity changes. If we double the vehicle reference speed, $u_1 = 2$, the system will become instable

Figure 17. MPC for tracking polynomial trajectory

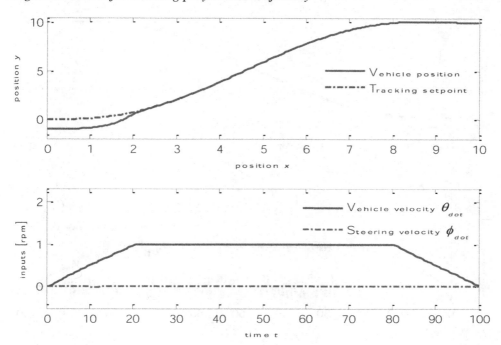

as shown in figure 21. The too fast velocity input can lead to bad performance or the system becomes instable.

In the next part, we will investigate the MPC performance using directly the nonlinear vehicle model.

MPC USING NONLINEAR MODEL

This part presents the MPC performance for the original nonlinear vehicle model in (2) since the linearized model can only approximate the dynamics of the true system. MPC schemes can guarantee the stability for nonlinear system by imposing the stabilized conditions on the open loop optimal regulator. These conditions take a terminal constrained region to the origin or with the terminal penalty of the softened constraints.

The diagram of the MPC control using nonlinear kinematic model is shown in figure 22.

The on-line optimization problem for this NMPC is taken place in real time. The MPC regulator determines an optimal future input trajectory that brings the

Figure 18. MPC with too long horizon

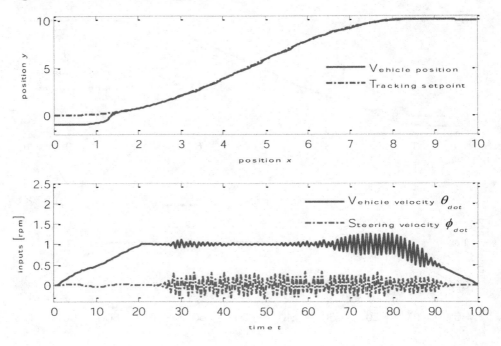

Figure 19. MPC with $R = 10Q$

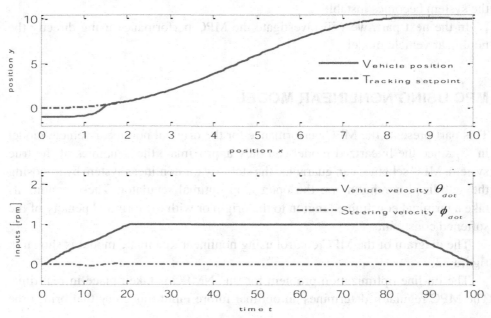

Figure 20. MPC for tracking in reverse direction

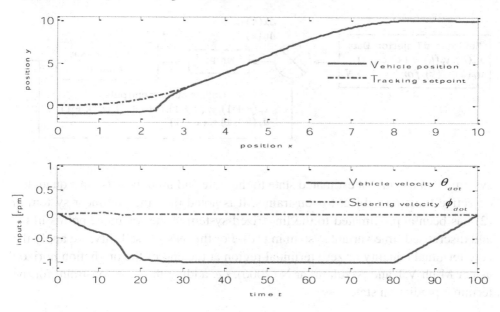

Figure 21. MPC with velocity $u_1 = 2$

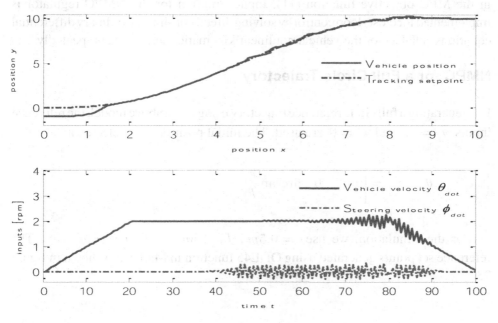

Figure 22. NMPC control system

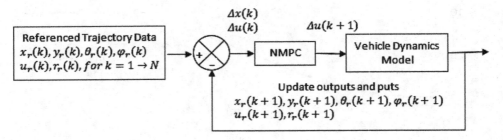

system from its current estimated state to the state and input targets via a quadratic objective function subject to constraints. It is noted that, the nonlinear system in (2) has been approximated to the linearized system at the reference points in (9) and discretised time variant system in (10). For this NMPC stability, we apply the zero terminal equality or zero terminal region at the end of the prediction horizon as per Minh V.T and Afzulpurkar N (2006), *i.e.* adding the zero constraint for the terminal prediction state

$$x_{k+i|k} = A^i(k)x_{k|k} + \sum_{\substack{i \geq N_u}}^{N_y-1} A^i(k)B(k)u_{k+N_y-1-i|k} = 0$$

in the MPC objective function (11). Inputs solution for the NMPC regulator is implemented for close-loop control by solving directly on-line the ordinary differential equations (ODEs) for the vehicle nonlinear kinematic model in (2) repeatedly.

NMPC for a Full Circle Trajectory

For generating a full circle reference trajectory using in the above model, the reference inputs $u_1 = r\omega$ and $u_2 = 0$ are used. The initial positions are selected as

$$\begin{bmatrix} x_0 & y_0 & \theta_0 & \varphi_0 \end{bmatrix}' = \begin{bmatrix} 0 & 0 & 0 & \arctan\dfrac{r}{l} \end{bmatrix}'.$$

For the simulation, we use $r = 0.5m$, $l = 1.5m$, and $\omega = 1rad / \sec$. The reference set points generated using ODE45 function in Matlab are shown in figure 23.

Figure 23. Circular reference set points

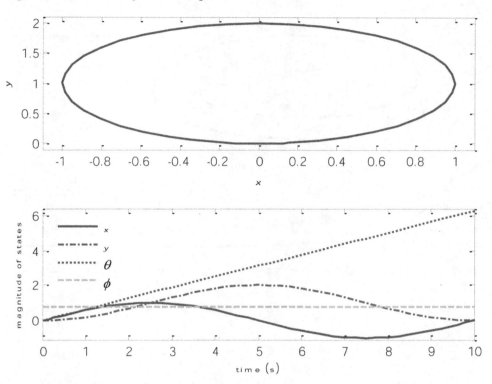

We now use the on-line MPC regulator in (11) to run the nonlinear vehicle kinematic model in (2) to track these circular reference set points. For this simulation, the initial positions of the vehicle are set at

$$X_0 = \begin{bmatrix} -0.5 & -0.5 & 0 & 0 \end{bmatrix}';$$

The constraints are set at

$$u_{\min} = \begin{bmatrix} -1, -1 \end{bmatrix}', \ u_{\max} = \begin{bmatrix} 1, 1 \end{bmatrix}', \ \Delta u_{\min} = \begin{bmatrix} -0.5, -0.5 \end{bmatrix}',$$

$$\Delta u_{\max} = \begin{bmatrix} 0.5, 0.5 \end{bmatrix}', \ y_{\min} = \begin{bmatrix} -1, -1, -1, -1 \end{bmatrix}', \text{ and } y_{\max} = \begin{bmatrix} 1, 1, 1, 1 \end{bmatrix}';$$

Figure 24. NMPC tracking

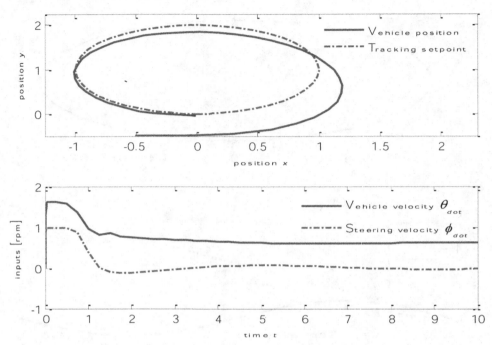

The predictive horizons are set at $N_u = 10$ and $N_y = 10$; Penalty matrices are set at $Q = diag\{1,1,1,1\}$ and $R = diag\{1,1\}$. Performance of the NMPC vehicle model to track the circular reference set points is shown in figure 24. The NMPC optimizer minimizes the tracking errors at each points and tracks the vehicle with very small errors left at the end of the trajectory. The inputs look good since they are physically smooth enough for controlling this vehicle.

In NMPC, if the prediction horizon is shortened, the calculation burden will be considerably reduced but will lead to sharp and faster changes in the inputs, then, causing bad performance of the outputs. With short prediction horizons, the system may become instable. Figure 25 shows the NMPC performance with shortened horizons to $N_u = 4$ and $N_y = 4$. We can see the worse performance from the final tracking errors and the sharp inputs movement at the starting time.

In NMPC, we can regulate the control performance by changing the predictive horizon length, penalty matrices, softened constraints or time scanning intervals. We can also regulate the system by changing reference set point errors $(y_{k+i|k} - r_{k+i|k})$ to offset the vehicle sideslip or to compensate the model-plant mismatches. In the previous simulations, we have set the set point errors at

Figure 25. NMPC with shortened horizon

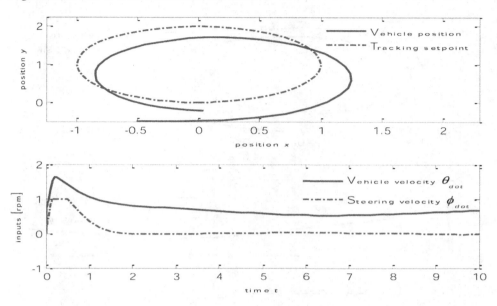

$$r_k = y_k - y_r = \begin{bmatrix} 0,0,0,0 \end{bmatrix}'.$$

To offset the vehicle sideslips or the model-plant mismatches, we can dynamically change these set point errors. For example, if we now set the set point errors at $r_k = \begin{bmatrix} -0.1, 0.3, 0, 0 \end{bmatrix}'$, the NMPC performance is shown in figure 26 and we can see some better tracking performances:

The above NMPC performances show that the vehicle can track a full circle with the initial positions of

$$X_0^{\text{Vehicle}} = \begin{bmatrix} -0.5 & -0.5 & 0 & 0 \end{bmatrix}'$$

other than the reference initial positions of

$$X_0^{\text{Reference}} = \begin{bmatrix} 0 & 0 & 0 & \arctan\dfrac{r}{l} \end{bmatrix}'.$$

This difference can be considered as the possible errors of the measured outputs or the initial model-plant mismatches. NMPC regulator can overcome those errors

Figure 26. NMPC with new set point offsets

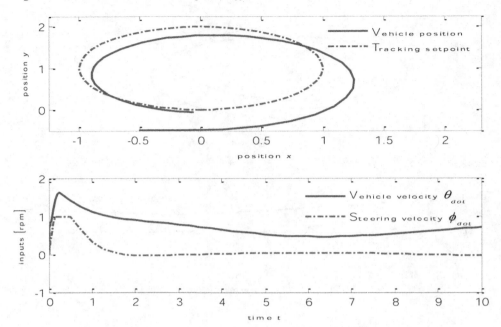

and track the vehicle exactly along the given reference set points. In the next part, we will investigate the ability of the NMPC to track the vehicle on any feasible generated directly from the original vehicle kinematic differential equations in (2).

NMPC for Tracking Flatness Trajectory

Flatness trajectory equations are presented in Minh V.T. (2013). Figure 27 shows a flatness trajectory for the vehicle from the initial position, $[x_0, y_0] = [0,0]$, to the final position, $[x_F, y_F] = [10,10]$, and the development of the orientation angle, θ, and steering angle, φ, during the travel. The time for completing this travel is set for $T = 100\sec$;

For this NMPC tracking, the initial positions of the vehicle are set at

$$X_0 = \begin{bmatrix} 0 & -0.5 & 0 & 0 \end{bmatrix}';$$

The predictive horizons are set at $N_u = 10$ and $N_y = 10$; Penalty matrices are set at $Q = diag\{1,1,1,1\}$ and $R = diag\{60,60\}$; The reference velocity inputs are

Figure 27. Flatness trajectory reference setpoints

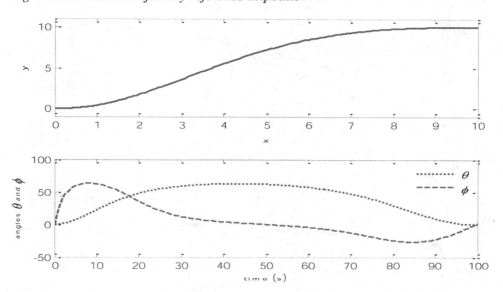

set at, $u_1 = \dfrac{1}{3}$ (u_1 is set at 0 at starting point, during the first 1/5 time length, u_1 will gradually increase and maintain at 1/3 for 60 sec, during the final 1/5 time length, u_1 will decrease back to 0), and, $u_2 = 0$. Performance of this NMPC tracking is shown in figure 28. The vehicle starts with an initial velocity of $u_1 = 0$ and from the initial position of

$$X_0 = \begin{bmatrix} 0 & -0.5 & 0 & 0 \end{bmatrix}'$$

gradually tracks to the reference tracking trajectory in 15 sec.

Next, we shorten the horizon prediction length to $N_u = 6$ and $N_y = 6$ while maintain other parameters unchanged. We can see that this shortened prediction horizon can degrade the performance because it causes the deterioration of the inputs. In this example, the system becomes infeasible for the inputs as shown in figure 29.

The above instable system is due to the too heavy penalty values imposed on the input matrix ($R = diag\{60, 60\}$). This heavy penalty causes too slow and too small changes in the inputs. If we release this penalty on the inputs to $R = diag\{1, 1\}$, the system returns stable as shown in figure 30.

Figure 28. NMPC for tracking flatness trajectory

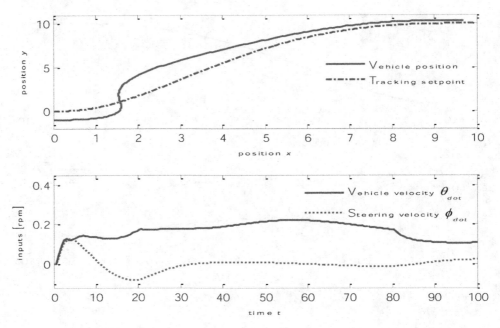

Figure 29. NMPC with too short horizon

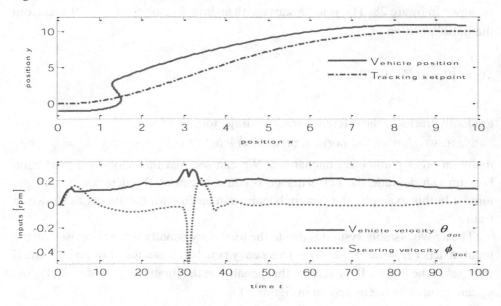

Figure 30. NMPC with $R = diag\{1,1\}$

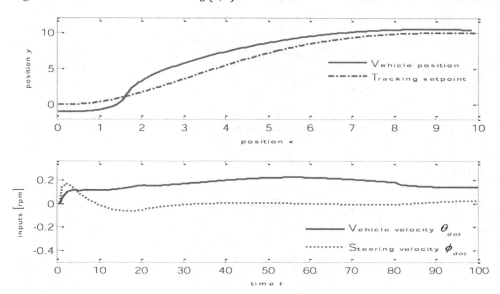

The above NMPC can run with longer predictive horizon and achieve better performance. Figure 31 shows this NMPC performance with $N_u = 16$ and $N_y = 16$. We can see the very small tracking errors at the end of the travel.

Next, we continue to test the NMPC for tracking the polynomial trajectory since the polynomial trajectories can be generated faster and smoother than the flatness trajectories.

NMPC for Tracking Polynomial Trajectory

Polynomial trajectory equations are presented in Minh V.T. (2013). Figure 32 shows a polynomial trajectory for the vehicle from the initial position, $[x_0, y_0] = [0, 0]$, to the final position, $[x_F, y_F] = [10, 10]$, and the development of its orientation angle, θ, and steering angle, φ, during the travel. Similarly, the time for completing this travel is set for $T = 100\,\text{sec}$;

The initial positions of the vehicle are set at

$$X_0 = \begin{bmatrix} 0 & -0.5 & 0 & 0 \end{bmatrix}';$$

Figure 31. NMPC with $N_u = 16$ *and* $N_y = 16$

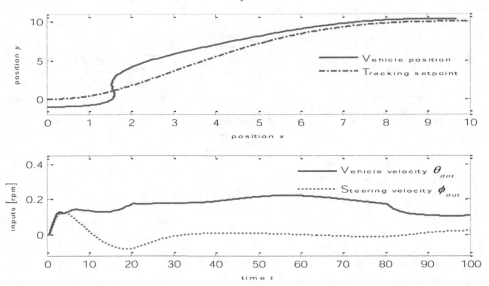

The predictive horizons are set at $N_u = 10$ and $N_y = 10$; Penalty matrices are set at $Q = diag\{1,1,1,1\}$ and $R = diag\{60,60\}$; The reference velocity inputs are set at $u_1 = 1$ (u_1 is set at 0 at the starting point, during the first 1/5 time length, u_1 will gradually increase and maintain at 1, during the final 1/5 time length, u_1 will

Figure 32. Polynomial trajectory reference set points

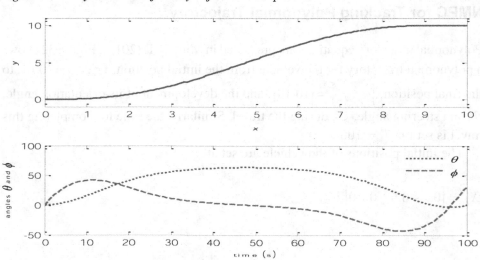

Figure 33. NMPC for tracking polynomial trajectory

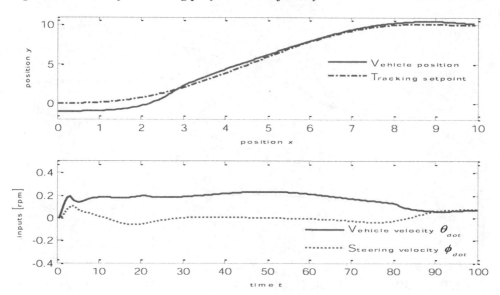

decrease back to 0), and, $u_2 = 0$. Performance of this NMPC tracking is shown in figure 33. The vehicle gradually tracks exactly the reference set points in 28 sec.

Next, we shorten the horizon prediction length to $N_u = 5$ and $N_y = 5$, we can see that the too short prediction horizon can degrade the performance. The system becomes instable as shown in figure 34. The performance is worse due to the sensitiveness of the inputs and the vehicle cannot reach the output set points.

The above shortened horizon NMPC becomes instable at the end of the trajectory since the input increments are too slow and too small due to the too heavy penalty imposed on the inputs matrix, $R = diag\{60, 60\}$. If we release this penalty and the inputs can variate more freely, the system will return stable with $R = diag\{1, 1\}$ as shown in figure 35.

Now we can lengthen the predictive horizon for the above NMPC to $N_u = 16$ and $N_y = 16$. The system performance becomes much better as shown in figure 36. The vehicle tracks rapidly and exactly on the reference set points in 28 sec.

In the next part, we compare the performances of linearized MPC and NMPC performances applying for the above different reference trajectories.

Figure 34. NMPC with shorten horizon

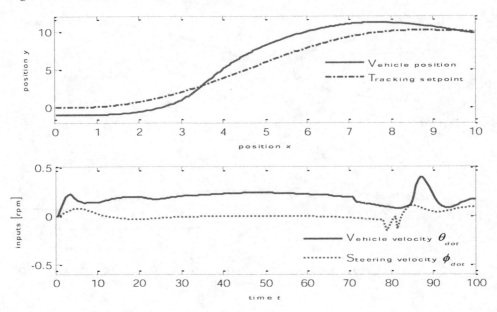

Figure 35. NMPC with $R = diag\{1,1\}$

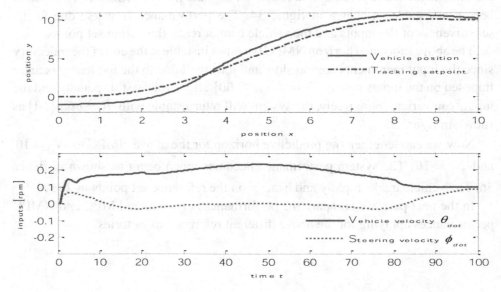

Figure 36. NMPC with lengthen horizon

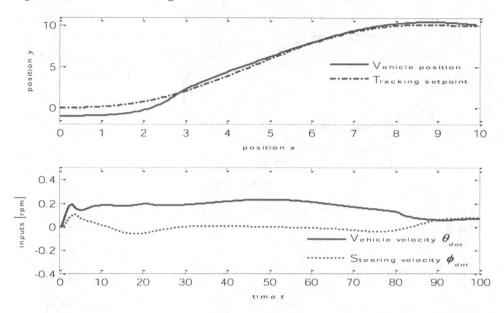

MPC PERFORMANCES COMPARISON

Compared for Tracking a Full Circle Trajectory

The two MPC schemes are compared for tracking a full circle trajectory. For this simulation, the initial positions of the vehicle are set at

$$X_0 = \begin{bmatrix} -0.5 & -0.5 & 0 & 0 \end{bmatrix}';$$

The constraints are set at

$$u_{min} = \begin{bmatrix} -1, -1 \end{bmatrix}', \ u_{max} = \begin{bmatrix} 1, 1 \end{bmatrix}', \ \Delta u_{min} = \begin{bmatrix} -0.5, -0.5 \end{bmatrix}',$$

$$\Delta u_{max} = \begin{bmatrix} 0.5, 0.5 \end{bmatrix}', \ y_{min} = \begin{bmatrix} -1, -1, -1, -1 \end{bmatrix}', \ \text{and} \ y_{max} = \begin{bmatrix} 1, 1, 1, 1 \end{bmatrix}';$$

115

Figure 37. MPCs tracking a full circle

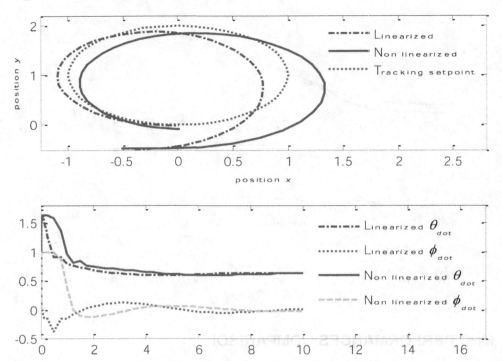

The predictive horizons are set at $N_u = 10$ and $N_y = 10$; Penalty matrices are set at $Q = diag\{1,1,1,1\}$ and $R = diag\{1,1\}$. Performances of the two MPC schemes are shown in figure 37.

The linearized MPC scheme drives the vehicle with a smaller rotating radius and goes faster and closer to the reference set points. However, the inputs the NMPC are smoother and really better in term of stability for the system performance. The CPU elapsed time for the two MPC schemes is almost the same. Elapsed CPU time for the linearized MPC is **0.74** sec and elapsed CPU time for the NMPC is **0.89** sec.

Compared for Tracking a Flatness Trajectory

The two MPC schemes are compared for tracking a flatness trajectory. The initial positions of the vehicle are set at

$$X_0 = \begin{bmatrix} 0 & -0.5 & 0 & 0 \end{bmatrix}';$$

Figure 38. MPCs tracking a flatness trajectory

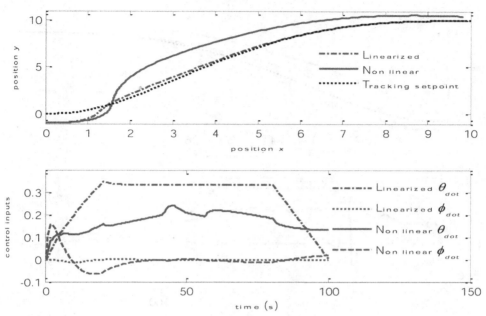

The predictive horizons are set at short of $N_u = 6$ and $N_y = 6$; Penalty matrices are set at $Q = diag\{1,1,1,1\}$ and $R = diag\{2,2\}$; The reference velocity inputs are set at $u_1 = \dfrac{1}{3}$ (u_1 is set at 0 at the starting point, during the first 1/5 time length, u_1 will gradually increase and maintain at 1/3, during the final 1/5 time length, u_1 will drop back to 0), and $u_2 = 0$. Performance of these MPCs is shown in 38.

The linearized MPC scheme drives the vehicle faster to track the reference trajectory as well as its inputs come closer to the input trajectory (easier to control) since the vehicle model is not real. It is only an approximation via its linearized model. In reality, the movement of the vehicle must be online calculated through its real nonlinear derivative equations. And then, the NMPC is slower and more difficult to track the trajectory because that its plant-model mismatches are more significant. The NMPC scheme becomes more difficult to control in term of its lower stable inputs. The CPU elapsed time for these two schemes is now becoming a big challenge since the elapsed CPU time for the NMPC is **4.27** sec, almost doubles the elapsed CPU time for the linearized MPC of only **2.45** sec for the whole travel calculation.

The NMPC scheme will become more difficult to control if we impose high values on the input penalty matrix since with too slow and small input increments, the system will become instable as shown in figure 39 if we set the input penalty

Figure 39. MPCs tracking a flatness trajectory with $R = diag\{60, 60\}$

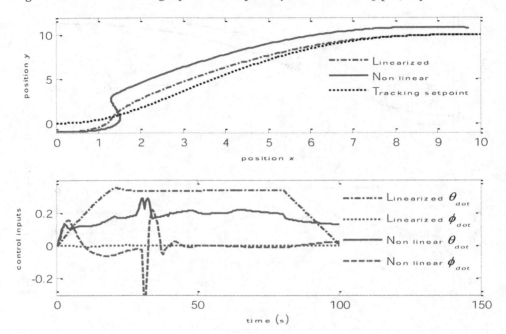

matrix of $R = diag\{60, 60\}$. The CPU elapsed time for the NMPC in this simulation is **3.61** sec, the elapsed CPU time for the linearized MPC is **1.61** sec for the whole travel calculation

Compared for Tracking a Polynomial Trajectory

The two MPC schemes are compared for tracking a polynomial trajectory. The initial positions of the vehicle are set at

$$X_0 = \begin{bmatrix} 0 & -0.5 & 0 & 0 \end{bmatrix}';$$

The predictive horizons are set at short of $N_u = 6$ and $N_y = 6$; Penalty matrices are set at $Q = diag\{1, 1, 1, 1\}$ and $R = diag\{2, 2\}$; The reference velocity inputs are set at, $u_1 = \dfrac{1}{3}$ (u_1 is set at 0 at the initial point, during the first 1/5 time length, u_1 will gradually increase and maintain at 1/3, during the final 1/5 time length, u_1 will

Figure 40. MPCs tracking a polynomial trajectory

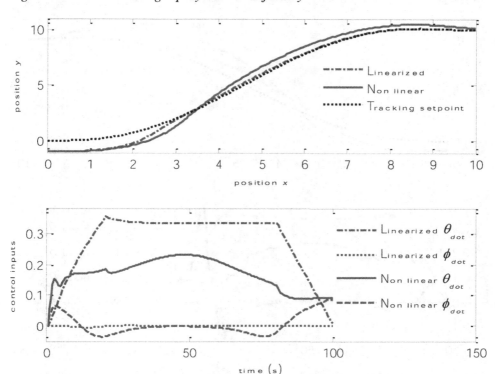

drop back to 0), and $u_2 = 0$. Performance of these MPCs tracking is shown in figure 40.

Similarly, the NMPC performance is slower and more difficult to track the trajectory due to the larger plant-model mismatches. The elapsed CPU time for the linearized MPC is **2.67** sec and the elapsed CPU time for the NMPC is **4.69** sec.

The inputs of the NMPC also are more sensitive to its stability. If we shorten the control horizon to $N_u = 5$ and $N_y = 5$, the NMPC scheme becomes instable dues to the sensitiveness of its inputs as shown in figure 41. In this simulation, the elapsed CPU time for the linearized MPC is **1.84** sec and the elapsed CPU time for the NMPC is **3.23** sec.

NMPC With Varying the Scanning Time Intervals

The amount of time between each measurement, called the sampling time interval, is one of critical factors for this type of discretized control system. If the scanning time is too short (too fast), the computer may not complete the calculation yet. Or

Figure 41. MPCs tracking a polynomial trajectory with shorten horizon

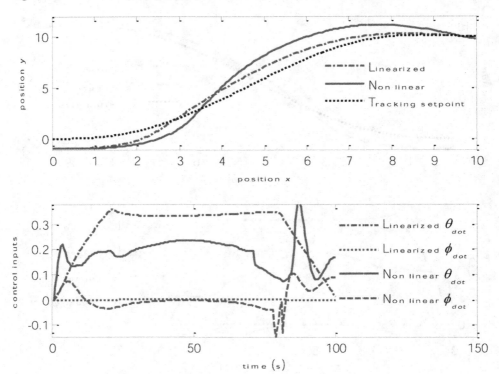

due to significant plant model mismatches, the too small and slow input increments can also deteriorate the system instability. On contrary, if the scanning time is too long, then the vehicle dynamics can also lead to undesirable performance. Therefore, appropriate scanning time length much be chosen via real experiments and depending on each real systems. In this part, we investigate some different sampling time intervals they may affect the performances of NMPC.

For Flatness Trajectory

The initial positions of the vehicle are set at

$$X_0 = \begin{bmatrix} 0 & -0.5 & 0 & 0 \end{bmatrix}';$$

The predictive horizons are set at short of $N_u = 10$ and $N_y = 10$; Penalty matrices are set at $Q = diag\{1,1,1,1\}$ and $R = diag\{60,60\}$; The reference velocity

Figure 42. NMPC tracking flatness trajectory with a short scanning time (0.1 sec)

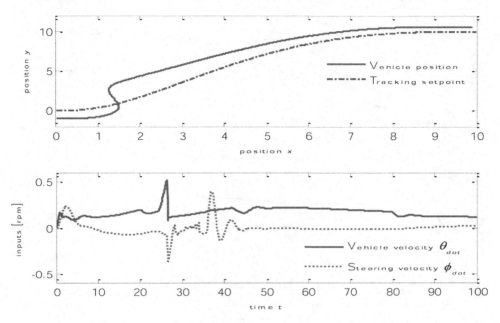

inputs $u_1 = \dfrac{1}{3}$ and $u_2 = 0$. The scanning time interval now is shortened to 0.1 sec. The system becomes instable due to the sensitiveness of the inputs as shown in figure 42. The elapsed CPU time of this simulation is 25.0482 sec (considerably increasing).

The above system returns stable if we lengthen the scanning interval to 0.5 sec as shown in figure 43. The elapsed CPC time now for this simulation is reduced to 4.1465 sec.

For this short time scanning interval (0.1 sec) but if we lengthen the prediction horizon to $N_u = 30$ and $N_y = 30$, the system becomes instable due to the too slow and too small input increments amid the significant model-plant mismatches as shown in figure 44. The elapsed CPU time for this simulation is 7.6514 sec.

Comparison of the two NMPC performances with short scanning time (0.1 sec) and long scanning time (0.5 sec) is shown in figure 45. The longer scanning time NMPC scheme tracks faster with smaller output errors but the shorter scanning time NMPC scheme requires smoother inputs and better stability.

For Polynomial Trajectory

The initial positions of the vehicle are set at

Figure 43. NMPC tracking flatness trajectory with a long scanning time (0.5 sec)

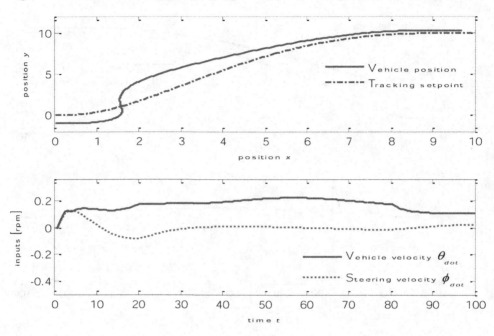

Figure 44. NMPC tracking flatness trajectory with lengthened prediction horizon

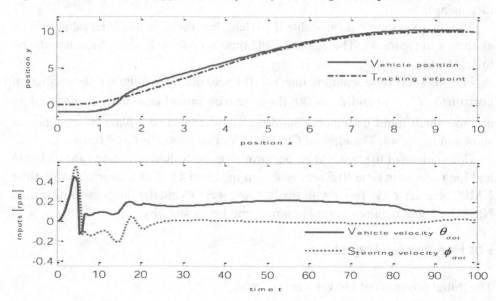

Figure 45. NMPC tracking flatness trajectory with long and short prediction horizon

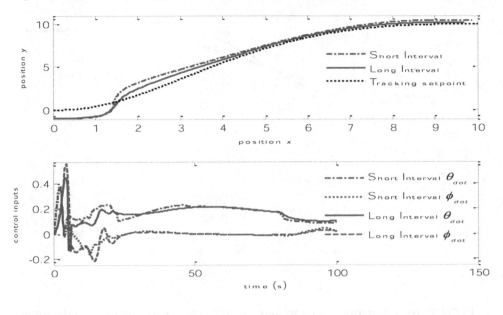

$$X_0 = \begin{bmatrix} 0 & -0.5 & 0 & 0 \end{bmatrix}';$$

The predictive horizons are set at short of $N_u = 6$ and $N_y = 6$; Penalty matrices are set at $Q = diag\{1,1,1,1\}$ and $R = diag\{60,60\}$; The reference velocity inputs are set at $u_1 = \dfrac{1}{3}$ and $u_2 = 0$. The scanning time interval now is set at short of 0.1 sec. The system becomes instable due to the high sensitiveness of the inputs as shown in figure 46. The elapsed CPU time of this simulation is 21.7409 sec.

The above system returns stable if we lengthen the scanning interval to 0.5 sec as seen in figure 47. The elapsed CPC time for this simulation is reducing to 4.1465 sec.

For this short scanning interval (0.1 sec) but if we lengthen the prediction horizon to $N_u = 15$ and $N_y = 15$, the system is still maintaining stable with the elapsed CPU time of 24.5552 sec as shown in figure 48. However, the system will become no longer stable if we lengthen the prediction horizon for $N_u > 15$ and $N_y > 15$.

Comparison of the two NMPC performances for short scanning time (0.1 sec) and long scanning time (0.5 sec) with the same other parameters is shown in figure 49. The longer scanning time NMPC scheme tracks the reference trajectory faster but the shorter scanning time NMPC scheme is required much smoother inputs and thus, more stable.

Figure 46. NMPC for polynomial trajectory with short scanning time (0.1 sec)

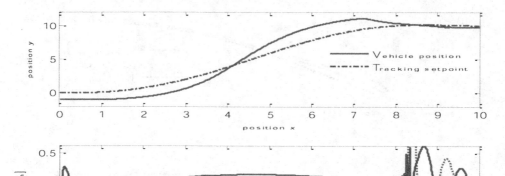

In the above simulation, since we have set the equal heavy penalty on the inputs with $R = diag\{60, 60\}$ on both input u_1 and input u_2. As we know that the vehicle velocity, u_1, is harder to control (regulate) than the steering velocity, u_2. Now we can test the system performances with a new input matrix of $R = diag\{60, 1\}$. It means that we set the penalty for any changes of u_1 is 60 times greater than the any

Figure 47. NMPC for polynomial trajectory with long scanning time (0.5 sec)

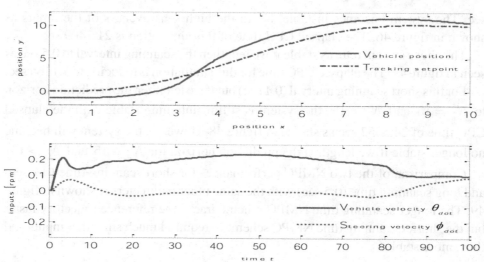

Figure 48. NMPC for polynomial trajectory with $N_u = 15$ and $N_y = 15$

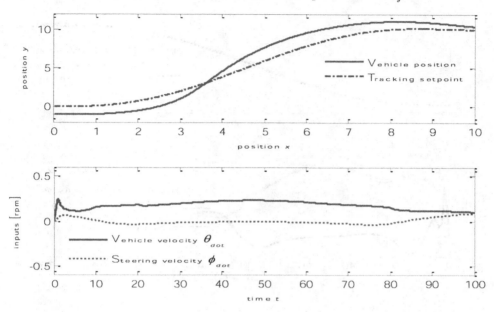

changes of u_2. In other words, the steering velocity, u_2, is set to move much more

Figure 49. NMPC for polynomial trajectory with long and short scanning interval

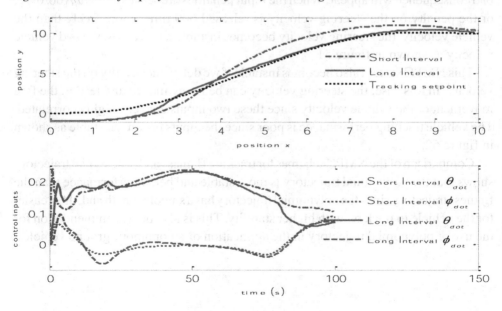

Figure 50. NMPC tracking polynomial trajectory with $R = diag\{60,1\}$

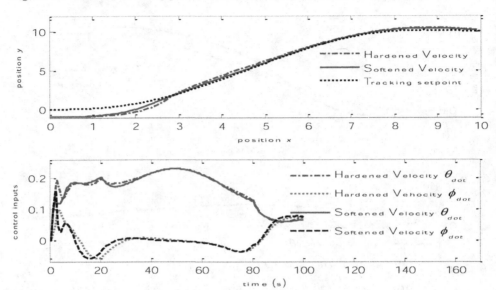

freely than the vehicle velocity, u_1. Simulation for this example is shown in figure 50. Both MPC performances have been significantly improved and both systems are stable and required much smoother inputs.

However if we set the penalty on the steering velocity with too small values, the bad consequence will appear. When the input penalties are set at $R = diag\{60, 0.1\}$, or the penalty on the steering velocity is released 600 times more freely than the vehicle velocity, the steering velocity becomes instable and leads to the bad vehicle velocity as shown in figure 51.

This NMPC system also becomes instable if we delete the penalty on the steering velocity. In this case, the steering velocity can be freely moved and lead to the free movement of the vehicle velocity since these two inputs are very highly correlated. The vehicle tracking performance is poor since the inputs become instable as shown in figure 52.

Comparison of the NMPC schemes for tracking flatness and polynomial trajectory shows that the polynomial trajectory is more stable and better performance than the flatness trajectory since the polynomial trajectory has a smoother path and, thus, easier for the vehicle to track on with higher stability. This is also out recommendation for the use of polynomial trajectory in the application of autonomous ground vehicles.

Figure 51. NMPC tracking polynomial trajectory with $R = diag\{60, 0.1\}$

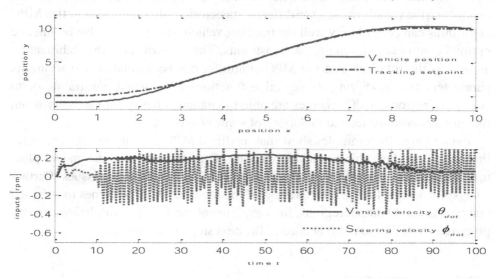

CONCLUSION

Figure 52. NMPC tracking polynomial trajectory with $R = diag\{1, 0\}$

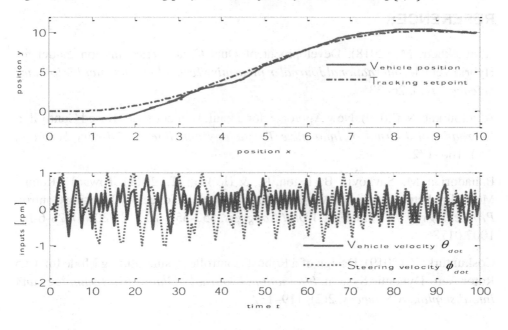

MPC schemes for linearized and nonlinear have been developed and tested for controlling the vehicle tracking on different trajectories. Simulations show that MPC algorithms can control very well the tracking vehicle since it can solve on line the optimal control actions subject to constraints. The performance, the stabilization as well as the robustness of the MPC controller can be regulated by varying its parameters and modifying its objective functions to softened constraints or to constraint regions. MPC schemes are able to guarantee the system stability when the initial conditions lead to violations of some constraints.

Even though the examples show that modified MPC algorithms are successful in controlling the vehicle tracking, model of uncertainty and the model-plant mismatches that may affect the closed loop stability are still open issues. Further analysis is needed for the effectiveness of the modified MPC schemes to softened constraints and to output regions. Real experiments and further validations for this proposed controller are also needed in the next step of the project.

ACKNOWLEDGMENT

The authors would like to confirm that there is no conflict of interests associated with this publication and there is no financial fund for this work that can affect the research outcomes.

REFERENCES

Abouelkheir, M. (2018). Development of Dual Clutch Transmission model for Hybrid Vehicle. *International Journal of Innovative Technology and Interdisciplinary Sciences*, *1*(1), 26–33.

Afzulpurkar, N. (2019). New Approach for a Fault Detect Model-Based Controller. *International Journal of Innovative Technology and Interdisciplinary Sciences*, *2*(2), 160–172.

Bahadorian, M., Savkovic, B., Eston, R., & Hesketh, T. (2011). Toward a Robust Model Predictive Controller Applied to Mobile Vehicle Trajectory Tracking Control. *Proceedings of the 18th IFAC World Congress*, 552-557. 10.3182/20110828-6-IT-1002.01786

Coskunturk, Y. (2019). Design of a Robust Controller Using Sliding Mode for Two Rotor Aero-Dynamic System. *International Journal of Innovative Technology and Interdisciplinary Sciences*, *2*(2), 119–132.

Falcone, P., Borrelli, F., Tseng, H., Asgari, J., & Hrovat, D. (2008). A Hierarchical Model Predictive Control Framework for Autonomous Ground Vehicles. *American Control Conference*, 3719-3724. 10.1109/ACC.2008.4587072

Israel, O. (2019). Study on Modeling and Simulation of HEV for Optimal Fuel Economy. *International Journal of Innovative Technology and Interdisciplinary Sciences*, 2(2), 133–146.

Katusin, N. (2019). Glove for Augmented and Virtual Reality. *International Journal of Innovative Technology and Interdisciplinary Sciences*, 2(2), 147–159.

Laumond, J. (1998). Robot Motion Planning and Control. In Feedback Control of a Nonholonomic Car-like Robot. Springer-Verlag.

Lei, L., Zhurong, J., Tingting, C., & Xinchung, J. (2011). Optimal Model Predictive Control for Path Tracking of Autonomous Vehicle. *3ʳᵈ International Conference on Measuring Technology and Mechatronics Automation*, 791-794. 10.1109/ICMTMA.2011.481

Minh, V. T. (2011). Conditions for stabilizability of linear switched systems. *AIP Conference Proceedings*, 1337(1), 108–112.

Minh, V. T. (2012). Advanced Vehicle Dynamics. Malaya Press.

Minh, V. T. (2013). Trajectory Generation for Autonomous Vehicles. In T. Březina & R. Jabloński (Eds.), *Mechatronics*. Springer.

Minh, V. T., & Afzulpurkar, N. (2005). Robust Model Predictive Control for Input Saturated and Softened State Constraints. *Asian Journal of Control*, 7(3), 323–329. doi:10.1111/j.1934-6093.2005.tb00241.x

Minh, V. T., & Afzulpurkar, N. (2006). A Comparative Study on Computational Schemes for Nonlinear Model Predictive Control. *Asian Journal of Control*, 8(4), 324–331. doi:10.1111/j.1934-6093.2006.tb00284.x

Minh, V. T., & Hashim, F. B. (2011). Tracking setpoint robust model predictive control for input saturated and softened state constraints. *International Journal of Control, Automation, and Systems*, 9(5), 958–965. doi:10.100712555-011-0517-4

Minh, V. T., Hashim, F. B., & Awang, M. (2012). Development of a Real-time Clutch Transition Strategy for a Parallel Hybridelectric Vehicle. *Proceedings of the Institution of Mechanical Engineers. Part I, Journal of Systems and Control Engineering*, 226(2), 188–203. doi:10.1177/0959651811414760

Minh, V. T., Katushin, N., & Pumwa, J. (2019). Motion tracking glove for augmented reality and virtual reality. *Paladyn: Journal of Behavioral Robotics*, *10*(1), 160–166.

Minh, V. T., & Pumwa, J. (2012). Simulation and control of hybrid electric vehicles. *International Journal of Control, Automation, and Systems*, *10*(2), 308–316.

Minh, V. T., Tamre, M., Musalimov, V., Kovalenko, P., Rubinshtein, I., Ovchinnikov, I., & Moezzi, R. (2020). Simulation of Human Gait Movements. *International Journal of Innovative Technology and Interdisciplinary Sciences*, *3*(1), 326–345.

Minh, V. T., Tamre, M., Safonov, A., & Monakhov, I. (2020). Design and implementation of a mechatronic elbow orthosis. *Mechatronic Systems and Control*, *48*(4), 231–238.

Minh, V. T., & Wan, M. W. M. (2010). Model Predictive Control of a Condensate Distillation Column. *International Journal of Systems Control*, *1*(1), 4–12.

Moezzi, R., Minh, V. T., & Tamre, M. (2018). Fuzzy Logic Control for a Ball and Beam System. *International Journal of Innovative Technology and Interdisciplinary Sciences*, *1*(1), 39–48.

Ovchinnikov, I., & Kovalenko, P. (2018). Predictive Control Model to Simulate Humanoid Gait. *International Journal of Innovative Technology and Interdisciplinary Sciences*, *1*(1), 9–17.

Parman, S. (2019). Fuzzy Logic Control of Clutch for Hybrid Vehicle. *International Journal of Innovative Technology and Interdisciplinary Sciences*, *2*(1), 78–86.

Peni, T., & Bokor, J. (2006). Robust Model Predictive Control for Controlling Fast Vehicle Dynamics. *14th Mediterranean Conference on Control and Automation*, 1-5. 10.1109/MED.2006.328864

Poulaiin, T. (2019). Path Generation and Control of Autonomous Robot. *International Journal of Innovative Technology and Interdisciplinary Sciences*, *2*(3), 200–211.

Pumwa, J. (2019). Time Variant Predictive Control of Autonomous Vehicles. *International Journal of Innovative Technology and Interdisciplinary Sciences*, *2*(1), 62–77.

Shim, T., Adireddy, G., & Yuan, H. (2012). Autonomous Vehicle Collision Avoidance System using Path Planning and Model Predictive Control Base Active Front Steering and Wheel Torque Control. *Journal of Automobile Engineering*, *226*(6), 767–778. doi:10.1177/0954407011430275

Suebsomran, A. (2019). Stabilizability Analysis of Multiple Model Control with Probabilistic. *International Journal of Innovative Technology and Interdisciplinary Sciences*, *2*(2), 173–180.

Tamre, M., Hudjakov, R., Shvarts, D., Polder, A., Hiiemaa, M., & Juurma, M. (2018). Implementation of Integrated Wireless Network and MATLAB System to Control Autonomous Mobile Robot. *International Journal of Innovative Technology and Interdisciplinary Sciences*, *1*(1), 18–25.

Trieu Minh, Vu., Tamre, M., Musalimov, V., Kovalenko, P., Rubinshtein, I., Ovchinnikov, I., Krcmarik, D., Moezzi, R., & Hlava, J. (2020). Model Predictive Control for Modeling Human Gait Motions Assisted by Vicon Technology. *Journal Européen des Systèmes Automatisés*, *53*(5), 589–600.

Wan Muhamad, W. M. (2019). Vehicle Steering Dynamic Calculation and Simulation. *International Journal of Innovative Technology and Interdisciplinary Sciences*, *2*(1), 87–97.

Wang, J., Lu, Z., Chen, W., & Wu, X. (2011). *An Adaptive Trajectory Tracking Control of Wheeled Mobile Robots. In Industrial Electronics and Applications*. ICIEA.

Yasin, H. (2019). Modelling and Control of Hybrid Vehicle. *International Journal of Innovative Technology and Interdisciplinary Sciences*, *2*(3), 212–222.

Chapter 6
Medical Data Analysis Using Feature Extraction and Classification Based on Machine Learning and Metaheuristic Optimization Algorithm

Satheeshkumar B.
Annamalai University, India

Sathiyaprasad B.
iD https://orcid.org/0000-0003-3531-6999
Annamalai University, India

ABSTRACT

A metaheuristic-based data optimization algorithm with machine learning-based feature extraction and classification architectures is proposed. The medical data collected from hospital database and public health dataset are input to analyze abnormalities through IoT. The data optimization is carried out using metaheuristic-based gravitational search algorithm. When the data is optimized, the loss function during the feature extraction, classification will be minimized for ML architecture. The feature extraction has been carried out for the medical data using Bi-LSTM-based RNN architecture, and the extracted data has been classified using a deep belief network with CNN (DBN-CNN). Collected data have been classified for prediction of abnormal and normal data range. Experimental results show the efficiency of the proposed method when compared to existing techniques, namely accuracy, precision, recall, and F1-score. Confusion matrix shows actual class and predicted class of normal and abnormal data predicted from input data.

DOI: 10.4018/978-1-7998-9012-6.ch006

INTRODUCTION

A better healthcare system is the main problem for a growing global population in the modern world. IoMT is a goal for a more comprehensive and accessible healthcare system. IoMT is the wireless integration of medical devices that allows for D2D communication. The most difficult issue in recent days has been the time required for web services by Nayyar et al., (2018). By keeping up with the current technology advances, three-dimensional (3D) video can be downloaded at random intervals. For reliable data measurement, the acquired voluminous data is obtained with minimum time. It will improve device resource allocation and provide faster speeds for diverse networks. Wi-Fi, Bluetooth, ZigBee, and other cellular platforms are among the heterogeneous networks that make up the IoMT. D2D communication is a critical component of the IoMT platform, as it is both efficient and reliable by Nayyar et al., (2018). The essential characteristics of an intelligent healthcare system are low delay, high throughput, and reliability, all of which are critical for accurate and successful diagnosis and consultation. For emergency healthcare applications, the critical time analysis is the most important parameter to consider. IoT-driven wearable devices can provide extremely dependable and delay-tolerant communication and data transmission by Nayyar et al., (2018).

In portioning clustering method, metaheuristic optimization methods are used. Based on particular measures, it partitions dataset into group of subsets. Nature of group formation is influenced by fitness function. To transfer partitioning process into optimization issue, fitness function is selected by Nayyar et al., (2019). Web text mining and image pattern recognition in computer science, portfolio management studies, medical anthropology to classify diseases based on a combination of patient records and genomic investigations, WSN for distributing sensors to improve lifetime and coverage area, and library mathematics for grouping publications by content by Rathee et al., (2019).

This research contribution is as follows:

- To develop Metaheuristic based data optimization algorithm with machine learning based feature extraction and classification architectures.
- To optimize the data using Metaheuristic based gravitational search algorithm
- To extract the features of medical data using Bi-LSTM based RNN architecture
- To classify the extracted data using deep belief network with convolutional neural networks (DBN-CNN). This classification results will show normal as well as abnormal range of data.
- Experimental results shows accuracy, precision, recall and F-1 score. The confusion matrix shows normal and abnormal data.

Paper organization is as follows, In Section 2 related works are presented. Section 3 shows proposed model for data optimization and medical data classification. Evaluation criteria discussed in Section 4. Finally, conclusion is presented in Section 5.

BACKGROUND

Machine learning is used in healthcare business for diagnosis, prognosis, and surveillance. Machine learning (ML), according to Health Catalyst, it is the life-saving technology that will alter healthcare. This technology challenges the traditional reactive approach to healthcare. In Alweshah et al study's by Mahapatra et al., (2019) a wrapper FS methodology using K-nearest neighbour (KNN) classifiers was used to run a new optimization technique, MBO (monarch butterfly optimization) method. Eighteen standard datasets were used in the study. El-Hasnony et al., (2020) proposed a new binary wrapper FS–GWO (grey wolf optimization) and PSO (particle swarm optimization). KNN classifiers with Euclidean separation matrices were used to find the best answer. A chaotic tent map aided in avoiding locked-to-optimal local problem method. To be suited for the challenges of the FS model, sigmoid function was utilised to change search space from continuous vectors to a binary one, and cross-validation K-fold was used to overcome over-fitting issue. BenSaid and Alimi (2021) presented a web-based FS method that addresses these issues. MOANOFS OFS (optimal feature selection) technique examines recent developments in online machine learning techniques and a dispute resolution mechanism (automated negotiation) to enhance classification performance of ultrahigh-dimension databases. The ensemble technique, CatBoost, RF, and XGBoost were used in Al-Sarem et al., (2021) study's to determine the primary feature for Parkinson's Disease (PD) prediction. Effects of this feature were investigated utilizing several thresholds to achieve best performance for PD prediction. Results showed that CatBoost approaches produced best results. To shed light on CT variation, Wang et al., (2020) developed a Big Data analytics (BDA) method for FS model for collecting each explanatory factor of computation time (CT). For the purpose of developing an observed network, relative analysis was performed between 2 candidate components utilising mutual data metrics. After that, by removing the effect of transitive connections from network. Shehab et al., (2021) proposed a new KNN-based hybrid FS cloud-based technique for unbalanced data. Approach provided here combines Euclidean as well as firefly distance metrics used by KNN. In compared to weighted nearest neighbour, the testing findings revealed a superior understanding of feature weights and time utilisation. Li et al., (2020) combined multimodal FS as well as grouped feature extraction into a novel quicker hybrid reduction dimension method, combining their advantages of reducing redundant as well as irrelevant data. Dataset's intrinsic dimension was first assessed utilizing maximum probability method. As a multimodal strategy for reducing incorrect features, the information Gain and Fisher score-based FS were used. They were classified into a given number of clusters using redundancy among the elected features as clustering requirements. Spencer et al., (2020) used a comparable FS model to examine the efficacy of the model obtained using the ML approach. To create unique feature sets, a Chi-squared test, PCA model, symmetrical uncertainty, and Relief were used to estimate the four commonly used heart disease datasets. Following that, numerous classification approaches were used to develop methods that were then linked to the search for the best feature combination to improve the accuracy of heart condition forecasts. To tackle the FS difficulties for classification purposes with the wrapper approach, Abdel-Basset et al., (2021) presented hybrid versions of the HHOBSA (hybrid Harris Hawks optimization technique-based simulated annealing) technique. Simulated annealing (SA) improves HHOBSA model's performance and aids in escape from the local ideal. As an evaluator for the novel solution, a typical wrapper model KNN utilising the Euclidean distance metric is used. Mohammed et al., (2020) provided a collection of hybrid and effective GA methods for tackling FS issues with large feature sizes in the processed data. In the evolution technique, the provided algorithm uses a novel gene-weighted method that can adoptively categorise features into weak or redundant features, unstable features, and strong relative features. Ability to detect which regions of country are experiencing an increase in disease was investigated by Alweshah et al., (2020). Ontologies were employed to conduct the experiment, which found that 62 percentage of the patient population had the condition. This study should be repeated on different patients for a new population proportion. The LR and RF algorithms were used by other researchers to forecast fresh data. The first study combined LR with PCA. In this scenario, Maleki et al., (2021) used UCI machine learning repository datasets to build a method to predict whether a person had cardiac disease. LR was initially taught all of the traits by the authors. Then, after deleting the least important features, they trained LR and proposed model called LR with PCA. Finally, the best accuracy was reached by LR with PCA, which was 86 percentages. The findings reveal whether or not cardiac disease exists at various levels of severity. Medical services that are suitable for everyone were proposed by Bichri et al., (2020). The scientists used the feature selection method to predict liver disease using a classification algorithm technique. The research was based on ILPD (Indian liver patient dataset) from University of California, Irvine database. Aurelia et al., (2021) combined LR and RF to predict cardiac disease in another study. The researchers utilized UCI heart illness dataset to forecast heart disease in its early stages in order to better manage the disease. Different categorization algorithms were used to conduct a comparative analysis. For RF with LM, the best accuracy rating is 88.4 percentages. In this case, we recommend using appropriate data pre-processing methods to improve the accuracy value. For the classification of fresh data, many researchers used the RF, KNN, SVM, NB, and R techniques alone or in combination with other algorithms. Ehatisham-ul-Haq et al., (2020) used a variety of supervised ML techniques and examined their accuracy in predicting cardiac disease. Except for MLP and KNN, all of the applied techniques had their importance scores calculated for each feature. A model based on the M-health dataset was proposed by Ye et al., (2021). The proposed method using RF and SVM classification techniques had maximum accuracy and effectiveness, according to results. With a large amount of data, the RF method is most efficient, resulting in a high accuracy value. Nandhini et al., (2020) used two standard datasets from UCI library, namely Cleveland and Hungarian, to create a data mining approach. The authors tested 5 various classification techniques, including RF, NN, NB, R, and SVM, among others. Regression classification was found to be the worst-performing method, while RF had a high accuracy of 98.136 percent. With a large amount of data, regression technique had lowest accuracy value. The Nave Bayes (NB) method was used in a study published by Nasiri et al., (2021). The writers came to the conclusion that as the amount of data grew, so did the accuracy. The model's accuracy declined as the amount of data rose. The accuracy of the NB technique was 98.7% in this trial. Furthermore, it is appropriate for tiny datasets. As a result, alternative algorithms should be tested in order to achieve a high level of accuracy. Ali et al., (2021) suggested an approach that used classification algorithms to divide the dataset into diabetes-affected and non-affected patients. The authors tested their method using real-world data collected from Pima Indian community. They used six different algorithms to train the model, including J48, MLP, HoeffdingTree, JRip, Bayes Net, and RF, and got a precision of 0.757 and a recall of 0.762.

The researchers suggested a medical text feature learning approach based on CNNs and intelligent recognition. Unstructured medical text features were extracted using a text analysis technique paired with a word vector and a CNN for illness risk assessment. Experiments on a number of diseases were conducted utilising data from a hospital patient. The experiment's findings confirmed the practicality of suggested method for disease risk assessment, as well as its adaptability. A multimodal medical data feature learning model was presented based on medical text feature learning model. Experiments have shown that in terms of training time as well as stability, the multi-modal data fusion disease risk assessment approach outperforms text disease risk assessment technique. While addressing variety of disease risk assessment models as well as intelligent identification based on text data and multimodal data fusion need more integration expertise in disease risk assessment application.

MAIN FOCUS OF THE CHAPTER

This section discusses about the proposed metaheuristic algorithms based on data optimization for medical data which leads to the predictive analysis of risk based on abnormal data range. The dataset has been obtained from public healthcare and this dataset includes over 100,000 records with 55 attributes. Gender, age, race, number of diagnoses, drugs, procedures, readmission, and other attributes are included in some of these attributes.

The data has been initially collected using IoMT module and the data has been optimized. Here we use Metaheuristic algorithms for data optimization in which gravitational search optimization algorithm has been used. Then using this optimized data, the features have been extracted using BiLSTM_RNN architecture. Here we establish deep belief architecture (DBA) where the classification is carried out using CNN. By this classification the normal range and abnormal range of data has been classified. The normal data range has been updated to the hospital database and for the abnormal data range, risk has been analysed by the parametric ranges. The proposed medical data analysis has been given in Figure 1.

Metaheuristic Based Gravitational Search Optimization Algorithm (MGSA)

Newtonian laws of gravity and motion inspired GSOA (Gravitational Search Optimization Algorithm), which is one of newest stochastic population based metaheuristics. A group of agents known as objects, are inserted in n-dimensional search space of issue to discover optimum solution through modelling of Newtonian laws of gravity as well as motion in basic model of GSOA, which was initially created to handle continuous optimization problems. In MGSA, each agent's position represents a potential solution to issue, and is thus denoted by vector Xi in problem's search space. Because a heavy item has a big effective attraction radius and thus a high intensity of attraction, agents with higher performance gain more gravitational mass. Using gravitational law and rules of motion, every agent adjusts its position Xi toward positions of MGSA's finest population agents over the course of its existence. Consider a model with s agents in which position of i-th agent is starting point for MGSA is defined by eq. (1):

$$X_i = \left(x_i^1, \ldots, x_i^d, \ldots, x_i^n \right); i = 1, 2, \ldots, s \tag{1}$$

Where x_i^d shows position of i-th agent in d-th dimension where n is search space dimension.

Figure 1. Overall architecture for proposed medical analysis

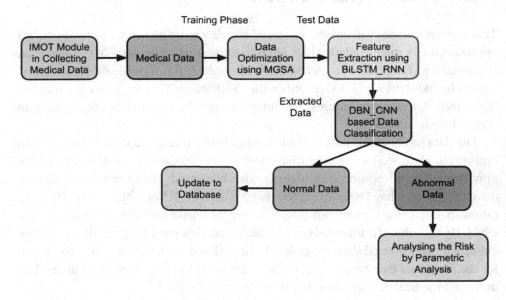

Gravitational mass of every agent is evaluated after estimating current data fitness given by eq. (2) and eq. (3):

$$q_i\left(t\right) = \frac{fit_i\left(t\right) - worst\left(t\right)}{best\left(t\right) - worst\left(t\right)} \qquad (2)$$

$$M_i\left(t\right) = \frac{q_i\left(t\right)}{\sum_{j=1}^{s} q_j\left(t\right)} \qquad (3)$$

where $M_i\left(t\right)$ and $fit_j\left(t\right)$ denotes gravitational mass as well as agent fitness value i at time t and worst(t) and best(t) are denoted by eq. (4) and eq.(5):

$$best\left(t\right) = \min_{j \in \{1,...,s\}} fit_j\left(t\right) \qquad (4)$$

$$worst\left(t\right) = \max_{j \in \{1,...,s\}} fit_j\left(t\right) \qquad (5)$$

Total forces from a collection of KGSA heavier agents (Kbest set) that apply to an agent is examined based on law of gravity using eq. (6) gives agent acceleration utilising equation of motion using eq. (7)

$$F_i^d\left(t\right) = \sum_{j \in K \text{ best}, j \neq i} \text{rand}_j G\left(t\right) \frac{M_j\left(t\right) M_i\left(t\right)}{R_{ij}\left(t\right) + \varepsilon}\left(x_j^d\left(t\right) - x_i^d\left(t\right)\right) \tag{6}$$

$$a_i^d\left(t\right) = \frac{F_i^d\left(t\right)}{M_i\left(t\right)} = \sum_{j \in Kbest, j \neq i} \text{rand}_j G\left(t\right) \frac{M_j\left(t\right)}{R_{ij}\left(t\right) + \varepsilon}\left(x_j^d\left(t\right) - x_i^d\left(t\right)\right) \tag{7}$$

Where,

In interval [0,1] rand_j is a uniformly distributed random number.

- R_{ij} (t) is Euclidean distance between i and j represented as kX$_i$(t), X$_j$(t)k2,
- Kbest is set of 1st KGSOA agents with best fitness value and largest gravitational mass. KGSOA is a function of time, with a K initial value at start and a reducing value through time, and
- G(t) is gravitational constant, which has a starting value, G$_{initial}$, and is lowered with time to an end value, G$_{end}$ given by eq. (8)

$$G\left(t\right) = G\left(G_{initial}, G_{end}, t\right) \tag{8}$$

After that, an agent's next velocity is determined as a percentage of its present velocity multiplied by its acceleration. Then, its next position is estimated using eq. (9) and eq. (10),

$$v_i^d\left(t+1\right) = \text{rand}_i * v_i^d\left(t\right) + a_i^d\left(t\right) \tag{9}$$

$$x_i^d\left(t+1\right) = x_i^d\left(t\right) + v_i^d\left(t+1\right) \tag{10}$$

BiLSTM_RNN Based Feature Extraction

The prototype uses the grid molded by the whole medical text group as the data. To pick the maximum proper dimension of convolution community, comparative assessments are finished. By then, RNN network is utilized for division to get multi-dimensional pieces of phrase route, which will be sent off BiLSTM system for learning. Super-limit regard is changed a couple of times to find a steadily expanding number of exact results differentiated and various prototypes. The potential gains of RNN in division and the advantages of BiLSTM in adjusting to gathering are united at once in enhancement of precision yield.

Two hidden states $h_t^{forward}$ and $h_t^{backward}$ are concatenated into a final hidden state h_t^{bilstm} given by eq. (11)

$$h_t^{bilstm} = h_t^{forward} \oplus h_t^{backward} \tag{11}$$

Where, $\oplus$ is concatenation operator.

1. BiLSTM Level

The BiLSTM level is the third level, and the new component vector obtained at previous level is used as data. The phrase vector is obviously employed as data, as opposed to the typical BiLSTM association. The multi-dimensional portion of the phrase vector is used as data for the prototype count. Learning subject to ascribes of the phrase trajectory of the multi-dimensional component, BiLSTM system progresses the accuracy of the yield and the viability of training. This level generally uses the potential gains of BiLSTM association to oversee timing issues as well as practices the removed novel part trajectories, handling the weakness of RNN association as well as growing the training limit of the association. The BiLSTM prototype is a modified LSTM prototype built by combining an ordinary RNN prototype with a collaborative period estimation. It can handle the issue that the standard RNN prototype is slanted to slant dissipating otherwise point impact when the gathering is extended, and can in like manner review and association the previous as well as upcoming information concluded the advancing also in conflicting elements. The architecture of Bi-LSTM in shown in Figure 2.

2. Establishing DBN Architecture

DNN seems like a simple neural network on the surface. It has a 'neurons' input layer and output layer, separated by a number of layers of hidden units. The DNN

Figure 2. Bi-LSTM architecture

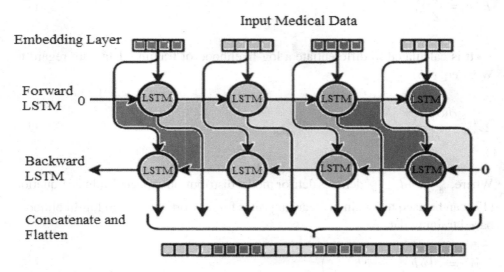

adjusts the weights across hidden layers using unsupervised learning approaches, allowing network to determine optimal internal representation (features) of inputs. As demonstrated in eq. (1), an RBM has general form of an energy function for a pair of visible and hidden vectors, v, h > and a matrix of weights W related to connection between v and h in eq. (12).

$$E\left(v,h\right) = -a^T v - b^T h - v^T W h \tag{12}$$

The bias weights for visible and concealed units are a and b, respectively. V and h probability distributions are formed, which is provided by eq. (13):

$$P\left(v,h\right) = \frac{1}{Z} e^{-E\left(v,h\right)} \tag{13}$$

Where Z is a normalizing constant represented in eq. (14):

$$Z = \sum_{v',h'} e^{-E\left(v',h\right)} \tag{14}$$

Probability of a vector v equals sum of above equation over hidden units given by eq. (15):

$$P\left(v\right) = \frac{1}{Z}\sum_{h} e^{-E\left(v,h\right)} \tag{15}$$

It is calculated to differentiate a log-likelihood of training data with regard to W by eq. (16):

$$\sum_{n=1}^{n=N} \frac{\partial \log P\left(v^n\right)}{\partial W_{ij}} = v_i h_{j\text{data}} - v_i h_{j\text{model}} \tag{16}$$

Where, $\cdot_{\text{data}}$ *and* $\cdot_{\text{model}}$ denotes data or model distribution expected values. Equation (17) can be used to obtain the learning rules for network weights in log-likelihood-based training data.

$$" W_{ij} = \varepsilon\left(v_i h_{j\text{data}} - v_i h_{j\text{model}}\right) \tag{17}$$

Where learning rate is denoted as ε. Unbiased samples are attained from $v_i h_{j\text{data}}$, hence there is no connection between neurons at either visible or hidden layer. Furthermore, the activations of hidden or visible units are conditionally independent. Then the conditional property is represented in eq. (18):

$$P\left(h\,v\right) = \prod_j P\left(h_j\,v\right) \tag{18}$$

Where, $h_j \in \left\{0,1\right\}$ and the probability of $h_j = 1$ is given by eq. (19):

$$P\left(h_j = 1\,v\right) = \sigma\left(b_j + \sum_i v_i W_{ij}\right) \tag{19}$$

Where, logistic function is denoted as σ which is represented by eq. (20):

$$\sigma\left(x\right) = \left(1 + e^{-x}\right)^{-1} \tag{20}$$

Conditional probability of $v_i = 1$ is evaluated by eq. (21):

$$P\left(v_i = 1\,v\right) = \sigma\left(a_i + \sum_j W_{ij} h_j\right) \tag{21}$$

Figure 3. Architecture of CNN in training faces

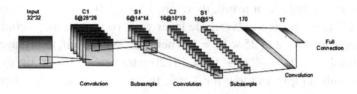

Using Gibbs sampling, all hidden units are updated in parallel using eq. (8), while visible units are updated using eq. (10). Finally, by determining expected value of multiplying updated values for hidden as well as visible units, proper sampling from ($v_i h_j$) could be attained. It should be noted that the DL technique employs a variety of supervised and unsupervised algorithms, although this work focuses solely on DBN because it is the most often used algorithm for diabetes data categorization.

CNN a deep learning model is a knowledge based NN, it extensively well shows methods to use image classification, it incorporates with linear layers convolutional (Conv) layer, FC layer, model with a non-linear function an activation function above linear and non-linear function impinges on every component of input, pooling minimize the final outcomes size, multiple perceptron to analyse the image inputs, it is trained with learnable weights and bias value to several parts of images to segregate pixel values. One main advantage of using CNN it uses a local spatial domain for the input images; it shares a few sharable parameters and less number of weights. This technique is predominately more efficient than other models due to less Computation complexity and less usage of memory.

Algorithm involves skill in architecture design as well as continual debugging in practical application to acquire best suited CNN architecture for a given application. Based on a 96 × 96 grey image as input, the pre-process stage converts the image to 32 × 32 pixels in size. Layer 7 convolution model's design depth is made up of the input layer, convolution layer C1, sub sampling layer S1, convolution layer C2, sampling layer S2, hidden layer H, and output layer F.

After pre-processing, there are 17 different images in 32 × 32 input. At this point, there are a total of $6 \times (5 \times 5 + 1) = 156$ parameters to train. The C1 layer for convolution employs six convolution kernels, each with a size of 5 × 5, and may generate six feature maps, each with $(32-5 + 1) \times (32-5 + 1) = 28 \times 28 = 784$ neurons. Each of the six feature maps in the S1 layer, which is used for subsampling, has $14 * 14 = 196$ neurons. C2 is a convolution layer with 16 feature graphs, each containing $(14-5 + 1)(14-5 + 1) = 100$ neurons and employing full connection. i.e., each characteristic figure used to be associated with its own set of six convolution kernels, which corresponded to the six characteristics of the sample layer S1 convolution and figure. As a result, there are $16 \times (150 + 1) = 150$ parameters to train in the C2 layer. S2 is a sub sample layer with 16 feature maps containing 5 5 neurons apiece, for a total of $25 \times 16 = 400$ neurons. As a result, the H layer's feature map has a total of $170 \times (400 + 1) = 48120$ parameters. Based on the standard figure of the sub sample window for 2×2, there are 32 trainable S2 parameters. Layer F outputs all connections, including 17 neurons. There will be $17 \times (170 + 1) = 2907$ parameters to train in total.

3. Forward Propagation

In i^{th} convolution layer, output of neuron of row k, column y, and k^{th} feature pattern given by eq. (22)

$$O_{x,y}^{(l,k)} = \tanh\left(\sum_{t=0}^{f-1}\sum_{r=0}^{k_+}\sum_{c=0}^{k_n} W_{(r,c)}^{(k,t)} O_{(x+r,x+c)}^{(l-1,)} + \text{Bias}^{(l,k)}\right) \tag{22}$$

The number of convolution cores in a feature pattern produced by a neuron in row x, column y in the lth sub sample layer is f, and the number of convolution cores in the kth feature pattern is eq. (23) among them.

$$O_{x,y}^{(l,k)} = \tanh\left(W^{(k)}\sum_{r=0}^{S_h}\sum_{c=0}^{S_n} O_{(xx_h+ry\times S_w+c)}^{(l-1,k)} + \text{Bias}^{(l,k)}\right) \tag{23}$$

j^{th} neuron output in l^{th} hiden layer H given by eq. (24)

$$O_{(l,j)} = \tanh\left(\sum_{k=0}^{s-1}\sum_{x=0}^{S_i}\sum_{y=0}^{S_z} W_{(x,y)}^{(jk)} O_{(x,y)}^{(l-1,k)} + \text{Bias}^{(l,j)}\right) \tag{24}$$

One of them is the sample layer's number of feature patterns. Layer F output of ith neuron given by eq. (25)

$$O_{(t,i)} = \tanh\left(\sum_{j=0}^{H} O_{(l-1,j)} W_{(i,j)}^{t} + \text{Bias}^{(l,i)}\right) \tag{25}$$

4. Back Propagation

In output layer O, k^{th} neuron output deviation is represented in eq.(26):

$$d\left(O_k^o\right) = y_k - t_k \tag{26}$$

In output layer, kth neuron input deviation is represented in eq. (27)

$$d\left(I_k^o\right) = \left(\overline{y_k} - t_k\right)\varphi\left(v_k\right) = \varphi\left(v_k\right)d\left(O_k^o\right) \tag{27}$$

In output layer, kth neuron bias and weight variation is given by eq. (28) and eq. (29):

$$\Delta W_{k,x}^o = d\left(I_k^o\right)y_{k,x} \tag{28}$$

$$\Delta \text{Bias}_k^o = d\left(I_k^o\right) \tag{29}$$

In H hidden layer, kth neuron output bias is given by eq. (30)

$$\Delta W_{m,x,y}^{H,k} = d\left(I_k^H\right)y_{x,y}^m \tag{30}$$

In H hidden layer, kth neuron input bias is given by eq. (31)

$$d\left(I_k^H\right) = \varphi\left(v_k\right)d\left(O_k^H\right) \tag{31}$$

In the mth feature pattern, weight and bias variation in row x, column y, and a former layer in front of k neurons in hide layer H given by eq. (32) and eq. (33)

$$\Delta W_{k,m,x}^o = d\left(I_k^o\right)y_{x,y} \tag{32}$$

$$\Delta \text{Bias}_k^h = d\left(I_k^n\right) \tag{33}$$

In the mth feature pattern, sub sample layer S, output bias of row x, column y given by eq. (34)

$$d\left(O_{x,y}^{s,m}\right) = \sum_{k}^{170} d\left(I_{m,x,y}^{H}\right) W_{m,x,y}^{H,k} \tag{34}$$

In the mth feature pattern, sub sample layer S, input bias of row x, column y given by eq. (35)

$$d\left(I_{x,y}^{s,m}\right) = \varphi\left(v_{k}\right) d\left(O_{x,y}^{s,m}\right) \tag{35}$$

In the mth feature pattern, sub sample layer S, weight and bias variation of row x, column y given by eq. (36)

$$\Delta W^{s,m} = \sum_{x=0}^{sm} \sum_{y=0}^{fi} d\left(I_{\lfloor x/2\rfloor, y/2}^{s,m}\right) O_{x,y}^{c,m} \tag{36}$$

C denotes convolution layer as shown in eq. (37).

$$\Delta \mathrm{Bias}^{s,m} = \sum_{x=0}^{fh} \sum_{y=0}^{fw} d\left(O_{x,y}^{s,m}\right) \tag{37}$$

In the kth feature pattern, output bias of row x, column y, convolution layer C from eq. (38)

$$d\left(O_{x,y}^{c,k}\right) = d\left(I_{\lfloor x/2\downarrow\downarrow/2}^{s,k}\right) W^{k} \tag{38}$$

In the kth feature pattern, input bias of row x, column y, convolution layer Cgiven by eq. (39)

$$d\left(I_{x,y}^{c,k}\right) = \varphi\left(v_{k}\right) d\left(O_{x,y}^{c,k}\right) \tag{39}$$

Row r, column c weight variation in the mth convolution core, corresponding to the kth feature pattern in the lth layer, convolution C given by eq. (40)

$$\Delta W_{r,c}^{k,m} = \sum_{x=0}^{m} \sum_{y=0}^{m} d\left(I_{x,y}^{c,k}\right) O_{x+r,y+c}^{l-1,m} \tag{40}$$

Convolution core total bias variation given by eq. (41)

$$\Delta \text{ Bias } \square^{c,k} = \sum_{x=0}^{m} \sum_{y=0}^{fix} d\left(I_{x,y}^{c,k}\right) \tag{41}$$

The output from the softmax layer will be classified to be normal and abnormal range of medical data and the abnormal range of data will be carried out for predictive analysis for risk has been analysed using parametric analysis in simulation.

Algorithm for Proposed Model

Input Training set $\left\{\left(x_1, y_1, \ldots, \left(x_n, y_n\right)\right)\right\}$

Step 1: Initialize, a single unlabeled node as T.

Step 2: While *T* is the unlabeled leaves **do**

Step 3: Navigation of data samples to its respective leaves.

Step 4: for all unlabeled leaves *v* in *T* **do**

Step 5: if the stopping criterion is satisfied by *v* **or** no samples are there to reach *v* **then**

Step 6: With the most frequent label *v is* labelled amongst the samples that reaches *v*

Step 7: else

Step 8: Select candidate splits for *v* and D is estimated for each of them.

Step 9: Split *v* with the highest estimated D amongst all possible candidate splits.

Step 10: end if

Step 11: end for

Step 12: end while

Input Primary training data set values as {(x1, y1). . . (x*n*, y*n*)}

Step 1: Initialize, a single unlabeled node as T.

Step 2: While *T* is the unlabeled leaves **do**

Step 3: for all unlabeled leaves *v* in *T* **do**

Step 4: if the stopping criterion is satisfied by *v* **or** no samples are there to reach *v* **then**

Step 5: With the most frequent label *v is* labelled amongst the samples that reaches *v*

Step 6: else

Step 7: Select candidate splits for *v* and estimate D for each of them.

Step 8: end if

Step 9: end for

Step 10: *v* unlabeled leaf *is* Split so, *nv*D is maximum amongst all unlabeled leaves and all possible candidate splits, where *nv*is the number of samples to reach *v*.

Step 11: end while

Flowchart for Proposed Model

See Figure 4.

Figure 4. Flowchart for proposed model

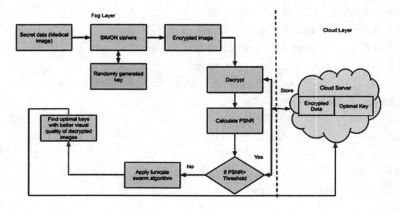

SOLUTIONS AND RECOMMENDATIONS

1. Performance Analysis

Performance analysis for various datasets for accuracy, precision, f1 score, recallis discussed. The comparative analysis has been made between existing and proposed technique. Using confusion matrix actual class and predicted class of data has been analysed and predict the risk.

The entire implementation of the proposed techniques done in Python tool and configurations for experimentation are: PC with Ubuntu, 4GB RAM, and Intel i3 processor.

a. Performance Metrics

The accuracy, precision, recall, and F1 – Score are parameters of evaluation considered by confusion matrix. The True Positive (TP), False Negative (FN), True Negative (TN), and False Positive (FP) are estimated values for evaluation of parameters stated.

Accuracy: Accuracy is defined number of values predicted correctly to total number of predictions and presented in equation (42)

$$Accuracy = \frac{TP + TN}{TP + TN + FP + FN} \tag{42}$$

Recall or Sensitivity: It is defined as the values predicted correctly to the value of total prediction and described in equation (43)

$$Recall = \frac{TP}{TP + FN} \tag{43}$$

Precision: It is described as the ratio of values of true positive to the total values predicted and given in equation (44)

$$Precision = \frac{TP}{TP + FP} \tag{44}$$

F1 - Score: It is stated as ratio between average mean of precision and recall and expressed in equation (45)

$$F1\text{-}Score = 2 * \frac{Precision * Recall}{Precision + Recall} \tag{45}$$

Confusion Matrix: The proposed model performance is provided by the comparative analysis of actual and predicted values. The analysis is dependent on TP, FN, FP, and TN estimation. It is represented in equation (46)

$$Confusion\ Matrix = \begin{bmatrix} TP & FP \\ FN & TN \end{bmatrix} \tag{46}$$

Figure 5. Confusion matrix for proposed medical data analysis

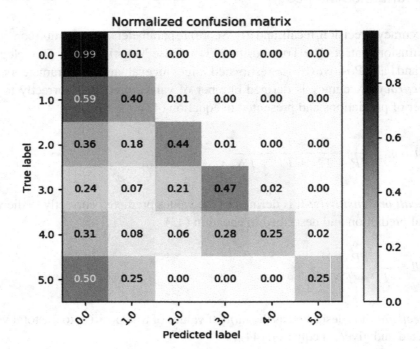

b. Confusion Matrix Diagram

Confusion matrix for medical data analysis using proposed method is shown in Figure 5. The confusion matrix has been calculated for actual class and predicted class based on the matrix normalization using proposed technique.

Table 1 shows the some of the observation evaluated from medical datasets instances, and then classifying the instances with same observation, then performance measures of various techniques of KNN, CNN, ANN are compared with proposed MGSA_BiLSTM RNN_DBNCNN method. Table1 shows Comparison of performance in Accuracy, Precision, Recall and F1-score.

The Figure 6 is graphical representation for Table 1. It shows comparison for various methods in terms of Accuracy. As shown in above figure the proposed MGSA_BiLSTMRNN_DBNCNN achieves Accuracy of 97.5% which is maximum percentage than existing techniques.

Figure 7 represents comparative analysis for precision. It shows the comparison for various methods in terms of precision. As shown in the above figure the proposed MGSA_BiLSTM RNN_DBNCNN achieves maximum results when compared to existing techniques. Whereas, the existing approaches has resulted to

Table 1. Comparison of performance of proposed MGSA_BiLSTM RNN_DBNCNN

Parameters	KNN	CNN	ANN	MGSA_BiLSTM RNN_DBNCNN
Accuracy	90.5	93.8	96.5	97.5
Precision	89.6	92.5	93.8	94.5
Recall	84.5	86.7	87.7	89.9
F1Score	80.5	81	83.7	87.6

worst performance with less precision rate. Finally, the proposed MGSA_BiLSTM RNN_DBNCNN method has high precision rate with 94.5% when compared to existing methods.

The above Figure-8 shows comparative analysis of recall for proposed medical data analysis and existing techniques. Based on the comparison, the proposed technique obtained recall of 89.9% which is optimized when compared with existing technique.

The above Figure 9 is comparative analysis for F-1 score between proposed and existing techniques. F-1 score obtained by proposed technique is 87.6% which is optimal and enhanced range in classifying medical data. These ranges of parameters will improve the risk prediction for abnormal range of proposed technique.

Figure 6. Comparative analysis of Accuracy

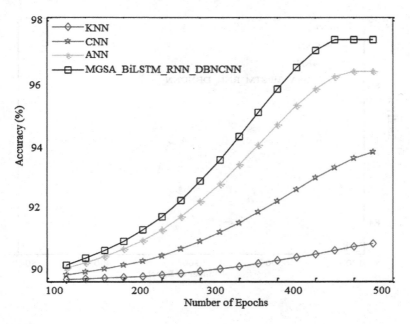

Figure 7. Comparative analysis of Precision

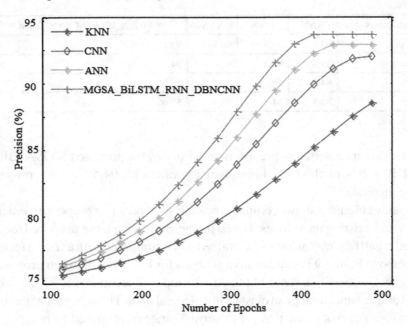

Figure 8. Comparative analysis of Recall

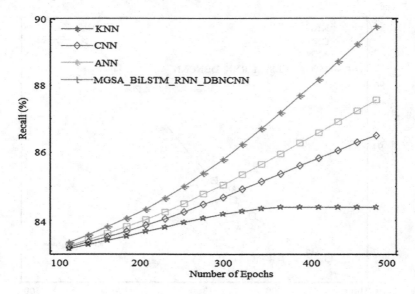

Figure 9. Comparative analysis for F1-Score

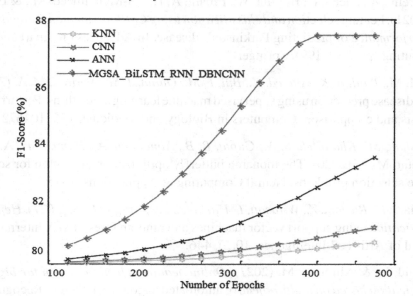

CONCLUSION

In this paper, metaheuristic algorithms based on data optimization with machine learning based feature extraction and classification architectures were proposed. Here the aim is to develop Metaheuristic based data optimization algorithm with machine learning based feature extraction and classification architectures. Then optimization of the data has been carried out using metaheuristic based gravitational search algorithm after this the data features has been extracted using Bi-LSTM based RNN architecture. Then it classifies the extracted data using deep belief network with convolutional neural networks (DBN-CNN). This classification results will show normal and abnormal range of data. Experimental results show the accuracy of 97.5%, precision of 94.5%, recall of 89.9% and F-1 score of 87.6%. Confusion matrix shows normal and abnormal data. In the future, mist layer of IoHT architecture will be executed with optimal resource allocation using advanced optimization techniques.

REFERENCES

Abdel-Basset, M., Ding, W., & El-Shahat, D. (2021). A hybrid Harris Hawks optimization algorithm with simu*lated annealing for feature selection. Artificial Intelligence Review, 54(1)*, 593–637.

Al-Sarem, M., Saeed, F., Boulila, W., Emara, A. H., Al-Mohaimeed, M., & Errais, M. (2021). Feature selec*tion and classification using CatBoost method for improving the performance* of predicting Parkinson's disease. In Advances on Smart and Soft Computing (pp. 189–199). Springer.

Ali, M. M.*, Paul, B. K., Ahmed, K., Bui, F. M., Quinn, J. M., & Moni, M. A. (2021).* Heart disease prediction using supervised machine learning algorithms: Performance analysis and comparison. Computers in Biology and Medicine, 136, 104672.

Alw*eshah, M., Khalaileh, S. A., Gupta, B. B., Almomani, A., Hammouri,* A. I., & Al-Betar, M. A. (2020). The monarch butterfly optimization algorithm for solving feature selection problems. Neural Computing & Applications, 1–15.

Aurelia, J. *E., Rustam, Z., Wirasati, I., Hartini, S., & Saragih, G. S. (2021). Hepatitis classification* using support vector machines and random forest. IAES International Journal of Artificial Intelligence, 10(2), 446.

BenSaid, F., & Alimi, A. M. (202*1). Online feature selection system for big data classification based on multi-objectiv*e automated negotiation. Pattern Recognition, 110, 107629.

Bichri, A., Kamzon, M. A., & Abderafi, S. (2020). Artificial neural network to predict the performance of the phosphoric acid production. *Procedia Computer Science, 177*, 444–449.

Ehatisham-ul-Haq, M., Malik, M. N., Azam, M. A., Naeem, U., Khalid, A., & Ghazanfar, M. A. (2020). Identifying Users with Wear*able Sensors based on Activity Patterns. Procedia C*omputer Science, 177, 8–15.

El-Hasnony, I. M., Barakat, S. I., Elhoseny, M., & Mostafa, R. R. (2020). Improved feature selection model for big data analytics. IEE*E Access: Practical I*nnovations, Open Solutions, 8, 66989–67004.

Li, M., Wang, H., Yang, L., Liang, Y., Shang, Z., & Wan, H. (2020). Fast hybrid dimensionality reduction method for classification based on feature selection and grouped feature extractio*n. Expert Systems with Applications,* 150, 113277.

Mahapatra, B., Krishnamurthi, R., & Nayyar, A. (2019). Healthcare models and algorithms for privacy and security in healthcare records. Security and Privacy of *Electronic Healthcare Records: Conc*epts, Paradigms and Solutions, 183.

Maleki, N., Zeinali, Y., & Niaki, S. T. A. (2021). A k-NN method for lung cancer prognosis with the use of a *genetic algorithm for feature* selection. Expert Systems with Applications, 164, 113981.

Mohammed, T. A., Bayat, O., Uçan, O. N., & Alhayali, S. (2020). Hybrid efficient genetic algorithm for big data feature selection problems. *Foundations of Science, 25(4), 1009*–1025.

Nandhini, S., & KS, J. M. (2020, February). Performance evaluation of machine learning algorithms for email spam detection. In 2020 International Confere*nce on Emerging T*rends in Information Technology and Engineering (ic-ETITE) (pp. 1-4). IEEE.

Nasiri, S., & Khosravani, M. R. (2021). Machine learning in predicting *mechanical behavior of additi*vely manufactured parts. Journal of Materials Research and Technology, 14, 1137-1153.

Nayyar, A., & Nguyen, N. G. (2018). Introduction to swarm intelligence. *Advances in Swarm Int*elligence for Optimizing Problems in Computer Science, 53-78.

Nayyar, A., Garg, S., Gupta, D., & Khanna, A. (2018). Evolutionary computation: theory and algorithms. In A*dvances in swarm intelligence fo*r opt*i*mizing problems in computer science (pp. 1–26). Chapman and Hall/CRC. doi:10.1201/9780429445927-1

Nayyar, A., Le, D. N., & Nguyen, N. G. (Eds.). (20*18). Advances in swarm int*elligence for optimizing problems in computer science. CRC Press. doi:10.1201/9780429445927

Nayyar, A., Puri, V., & Nguyen, N. G. (2019). BioSenHealth 1.0: a novel inter*net of medical things (IoMT)-based patient health moni*toring system. In International conference on innovative computing and communications (pp. 155-164). Springer. 10.1007/978-981-13-2324-9_16

Rathee, D., Ahuja, K., & Nayyar, A. (201*9). Sustainable future Io*T ser*v*ices with touch-enabled handheld devices. Security and Privacy of Electronic Healthcare Records: Concepts, Paradigms and Solutions, 131, 131-152.

Shehab, N., Badawy, M., & Ali, H. A. (2021). Toward featu*re selection in big data preprocessing based* on h*y*brid cloud-based model. The Journal of Supercomputing, 1–40.

Spencer, R., Thabtah, F., Abdelhamid, N., & Thompson, M. (2020). Exploring*feature selection and classification methods for predicting heart disease. Digital Health, 6.*

Wang, J., Zheng, P., & Zhang, J. (2020). Big data analytics for cycle time related feature selection in the semiconductor wafer fabrication system. Com*puters & Industrial Engineering, 143, 106362.*

Ye, Y., Shi, J., Zhu, D., Su, L., Huang, J., & Huang, Y. (2021). Management of medical and health big data based on integrated learning-based health care system: A review and comparative analysis. Computer Me*thods and Programs in Biomedicine, 209,* 106293.

Chapter 7
Robust Image Matching for Information Systems Using Randomly Uniform Distributed SURF Features

Ibrahim Furkan Ince

https://orcid.org/0000-0003-1570-875X

Nisantasi University, Turkey

ABSTRACT

Detection of similar images taken in different perspectives is a big concern in digital image processing. Fast and robust methods have been proposed in this area. In this chapter, a novel image matching approach is proposed by using speeded-up robust features (SURF). SURF is a local feature detector and descriptor that can be used for tasks such as object recognition or registration or classification or 3D reconstruction. Successful detection of the images is achieved by finding and matching corresponding interest points using SURF features. The task of finding correspondences between two images is performed through using a novel brute-force method which uniformly generates random pairs for matching similarity. Experimental results show that the proposed method yields better results than conventional brute force methods in which at least 5% accuracy increment is obtained.

INTRODUCTION

Detection of similar images taken in different perspectives is a big concern in digital image processing. Fast and robust methods have been proposed in this area. In

DOI: 10.4018/978-1-7998-9012-6.ch007

computer vision and image processing areas, the machine learning subject occupies an important position in rapidly evolving technology with cognitive applications being studied (Kashif et al., 2016). Object recognition applications, which are one of the basic functions of evolving robots, have become a system that has been intensively researched in recent years (Wang et al., 2022). However, for these systems to succeed in real-world applications, they must not be able to change quickly for certain changes (Satone et al., 2013) after enhancing the image quality (Küpeli et al., 2020), (Ince et al., 2019).

Visual characteristics are very important in computer vision and image processing (Dagher et al., 2006), (Bulut, 2021). The feature search process is used to highlight prominent visual cues in digital images (Ghazali et al., 2007). It is called the definition of the associated image primitive (point, line / curve, area, etc.) (Mazloum et al., 2012). Feature extraction is the process of recognizing a shape, extracting important properties of a shape, and getting a property vector (Li et al., 2010). Feature detectors and descriptions are often used in object recognition, object tracking, 3D reconstruction, image compositing, and visual mapping (Vinay et al., 2015).

The attribute detector selects points of interest with unique content in the image. The key to feature detection is to find features that do not change locally. Therefore, it is important to achieve invariant properties for all deformation conditions, such as rotation, scale, and lighting changes. The ideal functional detector should provide reproducibility, distinctiveness, locality, quantity, accuracy, and efficiency.

Speeded-Up Robust Features (SURF) is a local feature detector and descriptor that can be used for tasks such as object recognition or registration or classification or 3D reconstruction. SURF descriptors can be used to locate and recognize objects, people, or faces, to make 3D scenes, to track objects, and to extract points of interest (Loiseau–Witon et al., 2022). SURF has a comparable performance with the other existing detectors. It has a high repeatable mechanism that can recursively find the required points under different viewing conditions. Its methodological concept has been derived from David Lowe's SIFT (Gupta et al., 2021).

In this area, many studies have been released. Only a few of them which have been recently published are examined here. Verma et al. has proposed a method to match the objects using SURF features (Verma et al., 2016). To detect the proximities between two objects simultaneously and robustly, the proposed method starts by intelligently picking the SURF points based on proximity and stability in the prototype image. SURF points of the image are discovered and matched on the prototype image. The notion of FGV (Feature Grid Vector) and FGC (Feature Grid Cluster) is presented to the group the SURF.

Nawaz et al. has proposed a hybrid medical watermarking method through the SURF features and DCT (discrete cosine transform). In the experiments, the watermarking algorithm, named URF-DCT perceptual hashing, has maintained a robust mechanism against geometric and conventional attacks to protect the security of images (Nawaz et al., 2020).

Banwaskar et al. has used SURF features in summarizing videos using adaptive local thresholding. Successful experimental results are obtained in terms of precision, recall, and F1 measures on the I2V dataset videos. However, the performance controls are conducted by human observers (Banwaskar et al., 2020). Skin lesions and features are segmented automatically in a study proposed by Mardanisamani et al. by using a combination of Active Contour Model (ACM) and Speeded-Up Robust Features (SURF). They compared the proposed method with the Otsu thresholding algorithm by extracting HSV parameters. They claim that the presented method outperformed at a lower computational time (Mardanisamani et al., 2021).

Agrawal et al. present an approach of object counting using textural information. SURF is used for extracting textual information through FGV (Feature grid vectors) and FGC (feature grid clusters). Also, SVM (Support Vector Machine) as a classifier is used to detect true instances of a given object with fewer computations and high accuracy. In the experimental studies, this method gave better results in terms of illumination, rotation, and scale (Agrawal et al., 2020). Vardhan et al. presented an unsupervised learning approach for object matching using SURF for counting, identifying, and locating all instances of an object in a digital image. Homography transform is performed SURF features using a clustering method (Vardhan et al., 2015), (Bulut, 2021b)

Detection of similar images taken from different perspectives is a major concern in digital image processing, especially in medical areas (Ince et al., 2021). This article proposes a new approach to image matching using Speeded-Up Robust Features (SURF). SURF is a built-in function detector and descriptor that can be used for the tasks such as object recognition, registration, classification, and 3D reconstruction. Image recognition can be successful by using the SURF feature to find the points of interest.

In this paper, a novel image matching approach is proposed by using Speeded-Up Robust Features (SURF). SURF is a local feature detector and descriptor that can be used for tasks such as object recognition or registration or classification or 3D reconstruction. Successful detection of the images is achieved by finding and matching corresponding interest points using SURF features. The task of finding correspondences between two images is performed in which a conventional brute force matching algorithm is modified with randomly uniform feature pairs to calculate the similarity between two SURF features. To make the algorithm stable, the time-independent pseudo-random generator is used which generates all the time the same results depending on the predefined seed number. Since the pseudo-random generator creates uniformly distributed occurrences of the generations of random seeds, the brute force matching algorithm yields better results in terms of accuracy since the nature of the distributions is always uniform. According to experimental results, by using this method, there exists at least a 5% increment in the matching accuracy.

This paper has four more sections. In the second section, there is a technical background. In the third section, there is a definition of the proposed approach and its architecture. Experimental results are presented in the fourth section. In the last section, future study is presented and our contributions are summarized.

TECHNICAL BACKGROUND

In this section, some required information and description have been given as technical background. These are as follows: SURF, Google street view system, image alignment, taking a series of still photos, locating correspondence points in each pair of images, estimating a transformation matrix between related photographs to calculate a new location of images in the panorama, and lastly stitching photos together.

SURF: Feature Detection and Description

Feature detection is the process where the framework automatically examines an image to extract features that are unique to the objects in the image, in such a manner that the framework can detect an object based on its features in different images. This detection should ideally be possible when the image shows the object with different transformations, mainly scale, and rotation, or when parts of the object are occluded. In Figure 1, there is an overview of the SURF algorithm's process. The SURF processes can be divided into 3 overall steps.

1. Detection: Automatically identify interesting features, interest points this must be done robustly. The same feature should always be detected regardless of viewpoint.
2. Description: Each interest point should have a unique description that does not depend on the scale and rotation of the features.
3. Matching: Given an input image, determine which objects it contains, and possibly a transformation of the object, based on predetermined interest points.

In figure 2, there is an output of detecting common features between two images with different scales and cropping by using SURF.

Figure 1. Overview of SURF algorithm's process

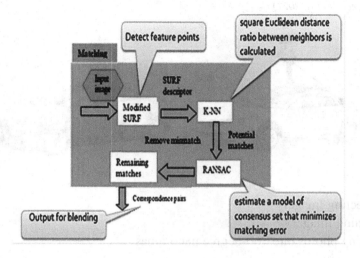

Current Systems and Architectures

Google Street View

Google Street View is a technology that provides panoramic views from positions along many streets in the world. In the proposed framework, it is planned to look more closely into how this technology operates. Shown in the figure below is a Street View Car (Google's Street Photos, 2021).

The steps of Google's publishing steps are summarized below:

Figure 2. Detecting common features between two images with different scales and cropping

Figure 3. Google street view cars
(Google's Street Photos, 2021)

- Collecting imagery
- Aligning imagery
- Turning photos into 360-degree panoramas

These geographic locations are stored periodically in the Google Services and delivered to the receivers by Google Maps API services (Erol et al., 2017), (Bulut, 2018).

Image Alignment

Algorithms for aligning images and stitching them into seamless photo-mosaics are among the oldest and most widely used in computer vision. There are two main methods used for image alignment and stitching, direct, and feature-based. Direct is a brute force method (Jakubović et al., 2018) that uses all the data in an image. It is more accurate since it takes in all the available information but requires inputs from a human operator to define the matching image pairs. It is also significantly slower from a computational standpoint (Szeliski et al., 1997).

The process of building a panoramic image consists of four principal stages including (Szeliski et al., 1997), (Ostiak et al., 2016), (Suen et al., 2007):

Figure 4. Process of creating panoramas

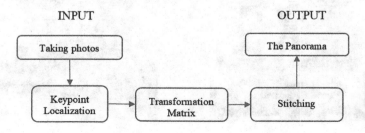

1ˢᵗ stage: Taking a series of still photos are in Figure 5.

Figure 5. Series of still photos that cover a 360-degree view

2ⁿᵈ stage: Locating correspondence points in each pair of images can be seen in Figure 6.

Some algorithms in computer vision detect and describe local features in images i.e. Scale-invariant feature transform (or SIFT) which was published by David Lowe in 1999 (Chau et al., 2014).

3ʳᵈ stage: Estimating a transformation matrix between related photographs to calculate a new location of images in the panorama is created. To compute a new position of pixels from an image B onto a final panorama A, the transformation matrix H is to be estimated as follows:

$$x' \sim Hx \tag{1}$$

where x is the position of a pixel in the image B, x' is the position of a pixel in the final panorama. The sign $\sim$ denotes similarity up to scale. H is a 3×3 matrix that can be estimated by using the Direct Linear Transform algorithm (Maghsoudi et al., 2017). Direct linear transform algorithm is

$$H = \begin{pmatrix} h_1 & h_2 & h_3 \\ h_4 & h_5 & h_6 \\ h_7 & h_8 & h_9 \end{pmatrix} \tag{2}$$

4ᵗʰ stage: Lastly, stitching photos together can be seen in Figure 7.

Figure 6. Detection of similar features in all still images

PROPOSED SYSTEM ARCHITECTURE

An image matching algorithm combined with Robust SURF features is proposed to overcome the unstable performance of the SURF algorithm. Based on the feature point detection of the SURF algorithm, corresponding interest points between images are found. Given below are the steps to find a correspondence between interest points from different images:

Figure 7. 3 images being combined to form a panorama

- SURF algorithm uses a global threshold value to the number of unique interest points that will be generated.
- After the generation of interest points, the proposed framework compares them to find the similarities between the points in both images. This is done by generating a descriptor for each interest point randomly uniform and getting the Euclidean distance between them. The smaller the Euclidean distance between the interest points' descriptors, the higher the similarity between them.
- Finally, the proposed framework creates one to one relationship between interest points in both images. If more than one interest point has the same corresponding interest point in the other image, the proposed framework selects the one that has the smallest Euclidean distance between their descriptors.

Figure 8 presents the flow chart and procedures about this proposed study in detail. The SURF processes have 3 main phases. The interest point detection, the description, and the matching phases are Figure 9, 10, and 11 respectively.

The initial stage of our project doesn't include an image database. However, after completing our implementation, it is aimed to take the framework further by turning it into an application. This application will include an image database that users can use to match various objects, places, etc.

The database is an organized collection of images. The data is typically organized to model aspects of reality in a way that supports processes requiring information,

Figure 8. Flow chart

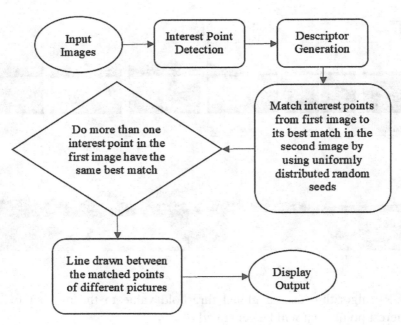

such as modeling the availability of finding the interest points in an image. The database handles the interaction of the user and the actual system. The image matching can be done by comparing an image the user has uploaded with the images from the database.

Content-based image retrieval (CBIR) is a framework to classify and analyze images (Li et al., 2021). In Figure 12, there is an integration model of CBIR and database.

Figure 9. 1. Interest point detection: Automatically identify interesting features, interest points must be done robustly. The same feature should always be detected regardless of viewpoint.

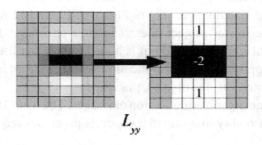

$$L_{yy}$$

Figure 10. 2. Descriptors: Each interest point should have a unique description that does not depend on the scale and rotation of the features.

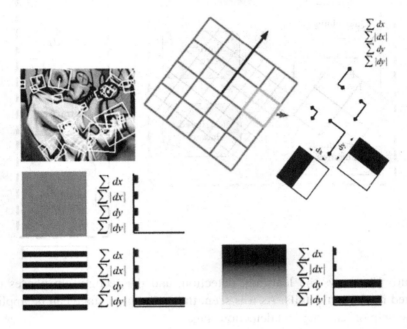

IMPLEMENTATION AND EXPERIMENTAL RESULTS

The Procedure of the Method

As an open-source environment that is available in the Java platform Processing Development Environment (PDE) has been used in the implementation. PDE has a compatible SURF library and in the proposed framework, a system that can be used be used to locate and recognize objects, people, or faces, to make 3D scenes, panorama generation, to track objects, and to extract points of interest is achieved.

Figure 11. 3. Matching: By comparing the descriptors obtained from different images, matching pairs can be found. A one-to-many correspondence is found between points.

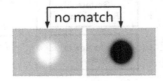

Figure 12. A CBIR System that is based on a feature database

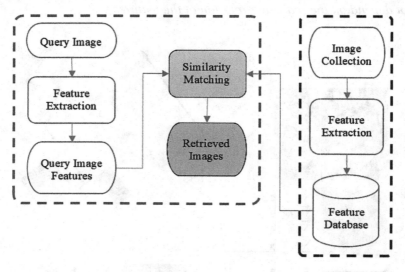

Figure 13. shows the learning, detection, and the recognition phases of the presented method in details. As it is seen, the recognition stage can be applicable with the help of learning and detection stages.

Figure 13. Possible future implementations

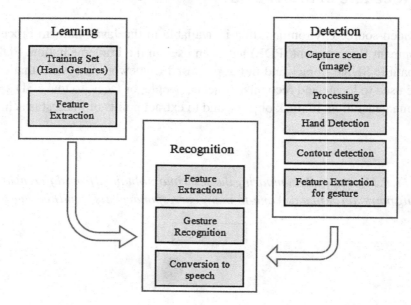

Assessments and Comparisons

According to the experimental results taken with the image comparison with a different rotation, scale, and translation of 20 numbers of images, a 5% increment in the matching accuracy is obtained. Apart from the performance increment, the proposed architecture includes several advantages concerning the existing conventional method as follows:

- Availability: The proposed system is intended to be an application that is based on image matching. It is planned to have a mobile application for the system. The application should be accessible anytime the customer wants to have access to it. Services are delivered whenever requested.
- Usability: The system is designed in a way to be user-friendly. The system is very easy to understand and to use. The end-user will be able to interact with the system via an application running on a mobile phone. The user is required to take two or more pictures of different places before he or she can use the system to either decide which place it is or which picture corresponds to another picture. The functions of the system are not complex. New users should be able to adapt to the application without needing help.
- High Performance: The proposed framework is going to consist of operations such as detection of points, generation of descriptors, and matching which means it will be very performance intensive. Optimizing the algorithm to make it faster is one of our priorities while developing it. Also, to avoid system failure whenever the application fails, it should be up in a minimum time.
- Maintainability: The entire project team must have an understanding of the codes and how it works. Codes must be readable and understandable for ease in changing/deleting some functionality of the system and improvements in the program. Modifications should be done in less time.

Additionally, in order to enrich the study, a classification framework especially based on supervised learning methods can be added to this proposed study to gain a better performance as presented in these studies (Alzubi et al., 2018), (Jain et al., 2020). Especially hybrid approaches of optimization methods in this area might give better performances (Uslu et al., 2020).

The mixture of supervised and unsupervised methods in expert systems using new transition functions might also produce satisfactory results (Bulut et al., 2016).

CONCLUSION AND FUTURE WORK

In the digital image and video processing areas, detection and recognition of the similar images taken from different perspectives are a major concern both in the literature and industry. Up to now fast and robust methods by researchers and developers have been proposed in this area.

In this regard, this article proposes a new approach to image matching using Speeded-Up Robust Features (SURF). SURF is a built-in feature detector and an identifier that you can use for tasks such as object recognition, registration, classification, and 3D reconstruction. Successful image recognition is achieved by using the SURF function to find and collate relevant points of interest. The task of finding similarities between two images is performed using a new brute force method that produces uniform random pairs that match the similarities. In the empirical studies, a broad set of experimental results indicates that the proposed method yields better and more reliable results than the traditional brute force method, which achieves an accuracy improvement of at least 5%.

For future work, it is planned to have the proposed framework apply to various areas such as allocating and recognizing the objects, people, or faces, to make 3D scenes, panorama generation, to track objects, and to extract points of interest.

REFERENCES

Agrawal, P., Sharma, T., & Verma, N. K. (2020). Supervised approach for object identification using speeded-up robust features. *International Journal of Advanced Intelligence Paradigms*, *15*(2), 165–182. doi:10.1504/IJAIP.2020.105142

Banwaskar, M. R., & Rajurkar, A. M. (2020). Creating Video Summary Using Speeded Up Robust Features. In *Applied Computer Vision and Image Processing* (pp. 308–317). Springer. doi:10.1007/978-981-15-4029-5_31

Bulut, F., & Amasyali, M. F. (2016). Katı kümeleme ve yeni bir geçiş fonksiyonuyla uzman karışımlarında sınıflandırma. *Gazi Üniversitesi Mühendislik Mimarlık Fakültesi Dergisi, 31*(4).

Bulut, F. (2021). Low dynamic range histogram equalization (LDR-HE) via quantized Haar wavelet transform. *The Visual Computer*, 1–17. doi:10.100700371-021-02281-5

Bulut, F. (2021b). Locally-Adaptive Naïve Bayes Framework Design via Density-Based Clustering for Large Scale Datasets. In *Handbook of Research on Machine Learning Techniques for Pattern Recognition and Information Security* (pp. 278–292). IGI Global. doi:10.4018/978-1-7998-3299-7.ch016

Bulut, F., & Erol, M. H. (2018). A real-time dynamic route control approach on google maps using integer programming methods. *International Journal of Next-Generation Computing*, *9*(3), 189–202.

Chau, H., & Karol, R. (2014). *Robust panoramic image stitching*. Department of Aeronautics and Astronautics Stanford University Stanford.

Dagher, I., & Nachar, R. (2006). Face recognition using IPCA-ICA algorithm. *IEEE Transactions on Pattern Analysis and Machine Intelligence*, *28*(6), 996–1000. doi:10.1109/TPAMI.2006.118 PMID:16724592

Erol, M. H., & Bulut, F. (2017, April). Real-time application of travelling salesman problem using Google Maps API. In 2017 Electric Electronics, Computer Science, Biomedical Engineerings' Meeting (EBBT) (pp. 1-5). IEEE. doi:10.1109/EBBT.2017.7956764

Ghazali, K. H., Mansor, M. F., Mustafa, M. M., & Hussain, A. (2007, December). Feature extraction technique using discrete wavelet transform for image classification. In *2007 5th Student Conference on Research and Development* (pp. 1-4). IEEE. 10.1109/SCORED.2007.4451366

Google's Street Photos. (2021). https://www.google.com/streetview/explore/

Gupta, S., Thakur, K., & Kumar, M. (2020). 2D-human face recognition using SIFT and SURF descriptors of face's feature regions. *The Visual Computer*, 1–10.

Ince, I. F., & Bulut, F. (2021). A Novel Image Segmentation Technique for Medical Decision Support Systems: Osteoarthritis (Oa) Knee Abnormality Detection from Hazy X-Ray Images Through Polygon Construction. *Advances in Machinery And Digitization*, *1*, 79–104.

Ince, I. F., Ince, O. F., & Bulut, F. (2019). MID Filter: An Orientation-Based Nonlinear Filter For Reducing Multiplicative Noise. *Electronics (Basel)*, *8*(9), 936. doi:10.3390/electronics8090936

Jakubović, A., & Velagić, J. (2018, September). Image feature matching and object detection using brute-force matches. In *2018 International Symposium ELMAR* (pp. 83-86). IEEE. 10.23919/ELMAR.2018.8534641

Kashif, M., Deserno, T. M., Haak, D., & Jonas, S. (2016). Feature description with SIFT, SURF, BRIEF, BRISK, or FREAK? A general question answered for bone age assessment. *Computers in Biology and Medicine*, *68*, 67–75. doi:10.1016/j.compbiomed.2015.11.006 PMID:26623943

Küpeli, C., & Bulut, F. (2020). Görüntüdeki Tuz Biber ve Gauss Gürültülerine Karşı Filtrelerin Performans Analizleri. *Haliç Üniversitesi Fen Bilimleri Dergisi, 3*(2), 211–239.

Li, X., Yang, J., & Ma, J. (2021). Recent developments of content-based image retrieval (CBIR). *Neurocomputing, 452,* 675–689. doi:10.1016/j.neucom.2020.07.139

Li, Y. A., Shen, Y. J., Zhang, G. D., Yuan, T., Xiao, X. J., & Xu, H. L. (2010, May). An efficient 3D face recognition method using geometric features. In *2010 2nd International Workshop on Intelligent Systems and Applications* (pp. 1-4). IEEE.

Loiseau–Witon, N., Kéchichian, R., Valette, S., & Bartoli, A. (2022). Learning 3D medical image keypoint descriptors with the triplet loss. *International Journal of Computer Assisted Radiology and Surgery, 17*(1), 141–146. doi:10.100711548-021-02481-3 PMID:34453284

Maghsoudi, O. H., Tabrizi, A. V., Robertson, B., & Spence, A. (2017, December). 3d modeling of running rodents based on direct linear transform. In 2017 IEEE signal processing in medicine and biology symposium (SPMB) (pp. 1-4). IEEE.

Mardanisamani, S., Karimi, Z., Jamshidzadeh, A., Yazdi, M., Farshad, M., & Farshad, A. (2021). *A New Approach for Automatic Segmentation and Evaluation of Pigmentation Lesion by using Active Contour Model and Speeded Up Robust Features.* arXiv preprint arXiv:2101.07195.

Mazloum, J., Jalali, A., & Amiryan, J. (2012, October). A novel bidirectional neural network for face recognition. In 2012 2nd International eConference on Computer and Knowledge Engineering (ICCKE) (pp. 18-23). IEEE. doi:10.1109/ICCKE.2012.6395345

Nawaz, S. A., Li, J., Bhatti, U. A., Mehmood, A., Shoukat, M. U., & Bhatti, M. A. (2020). Advance hybrid medical watermarking algorithm using speeded-up robust features and discrete cosine transform. *Plus One, 15*(6), e0232902.

Ostiak, P. (2006, April). Implementation of HDR panorama stitching algorithm. In *Proceedings of the 10th CESCG Conference* (pp. 24-26). Academic Press.

Satone, M., & Kharate, G. K. (2013). Selection of eigenvectors for face recognition. *International Journal of Advanced Computer Science and Applications, 4*(3). Advance online publication. doi:10.14569/IJACSA.2013.040316

Suen, S. T., Lam, E. Y., & Wong, K. K. (2007). Photographic stitching with optimized object and color matching based on image derivatives. *Optics Express, 15*(12), 7689–7696. doi:10.1364/OE.15.007689 PMID:19547097

Szeliski, R., & Shum, H. Y. (1997, August). Creating full view panoramic image mosaics and environment maps. In *Proceedings of the 24th annual conference on Computer graphics and interactive techniques* (pp. 251-258). 10.1145/258734.258861

Uslu, M. F., Uslu, S., & Bulut, F. (2020). *An adaptive hybrid approach: Combining genetic algorithm and ant colony optimization for integrated process planning and scheduling*. Applied Computing and Informatics.

Vardhan, A. H., Verma, N. K., Sevakula, R. K., & Salour, A. (2015, October). Unsupervised approach for object matching using speeded-up robust features. In 2015 IEEE Applied Imagery Pattern Recognition Workshop (AIPR) (pp. 1-8). IEEE. doi:10.1109/AIPR.2015.7444541

Verma, N. K., Goyal, A., Vardhan, A. H., Sevakula, R. K., & Salour, A. (2016). Object matching using speeded up robust features. In Intelligent and evolutionary systems (pp. 415-427). Springer. doi:10.1007/978-3-319-27000-5_34

Vinay, A., Hebbar, D., Shekhar, V. S., Murthy, K. B., & Natarajan, S. (2015). Two novel detector-descriptor based approaches for face recognition using sift and surf. *Procedia Computer Science*, *70*, 185–197. doi:10.1016/j.procs.2015.10.070

Wang, N., Wang, Y., & Er, M. J. (2022). Review on deep learning techniques for marine object recognition: Architectures and algorithms. *Control Engineering Practice*, *118*, 104458. doi:10.1016/j.conengprac.2020.104458

Chapter 8
Prediction of Movie Success Using Sentimental Analysis and Data Mining

Meenu Vijarania
Center of Excellence, K. R. Mangalam University, Gurugram, India

Ashima Gambhir
Amity University, Gurgaon, India

Deepthi Sehrawat
Amity University, Gurgaon, India

Swati Gupta
Center of Excellence, K. R. Mangalam University, Gurugram, India

ABSTRACT

Movies have become a significant part of today's generation. In this chapter, the authors worked on data mining and ML techniques like random forest regression, decision tree regression, support vector regression, and predict the success of the movies on the basis of ratings from IMDb and data retrieved from comments on social media platforms. Based on ML techniques, the chapter develops a model that will predict movie success before the release of the movie and thereby decrease the risk. Twitter sentimental analysis is used to retrieve data from Twitter, and polarity and subjectivity of the movie is calculated based on the user reviews, and those retrieved data machine learning algorithms are used to predict the IMDb rating. A predictive model is developed by using three algorithms, decision tree regression, SVR, and random forest regression. The chapter compared the results using three different techniques to get the movie success prediction at a reasonable accuracy.

DOI: 10.4018/978-1-7998-9012-6.ch008

INTRODUCTION

Movies are one of the convenient ways of one's entertainment. Irrespective of age love for movies remains the same, whether he is an older man or a schoolboy. Movie industry produces a lot of movies every year, but a few become a success, few gain medium exposure while rest come under the category of a flop. A lot of investment takes place in completing and finalizing a movie having many star casts and many workers working day and night for the success of it. The revenue that will be generated by the movie after it's release depends on many factors like casts of the movie, budget of the movie, review given by the critics, rating of the movie, the year movie released, time of the release etc. The parameters involved in predicting the movie success made it difficult to find a direct formula for the prediction of the success. However, a model can be built by choosing those parameters which can directly affect the forecast, which will be beneficial for the businessmen also and the viewers even. Based on the past experiences and reviews of similar movies and casts, it can be predicted whether a movie will be a success or a flop. It will help the stakeholders to invest correctly and will be beneficial for the audiences also in selecting a movie. They may be able to make the decision before the release of the movie.

Based on machine learning techniques, the proposed work develops a model which will help in the prediction of movie success before the release of the movie and thereby decreasing the risk somehow. The best way to know about movies and its revenue generation is IMDb ratings. In this model, Sentimental Analysis is done on the Twitter data, and the relation between polarity and subjectivity is calculated. On that calculated information, three Machine learning Algorithms are applied and compared to get the best accuracy in prediction of the IMDb ratings. The dataset has been taken from Kaggle.com Vast amount of data is present there about the movies, there gross collection, critics reviews, working cast members and factors influencing their work. Machine learning techniques enabled us to discover many aspects which is helpful in the prediction of success or failure of upcoming movies based on some information provided beforehand. Here we tried to develop a model which will predict movie success rate with more accuracy and precision. This model will predict the IMDb rating of Hollywood as well as Bollywood movies. Python programming language is used for making this model. We divide the dataset into a training set and testing set for the same. From the result we get, we can easily conclude that the movie will be successful or not. There is a twofold outcome of this research, firstly providing tools and techniques which can transform data into a suitable format for machine learning, secondly, provides selected information taken from this refined data.

The main objective of this chapter to design the model to predict whether the given movie will be a success or will be a failure before the date of the release. A predictive model is being developed by using three algorithms, Decision Tree Regression, SVR, and Random Forest regression. Compare the Results using three different techniques to get the movie success prediction at a reasonable accuracy rate and can invest their time and money accordingly.

This chapter is organised in following structure: Section 2 presents the Literature Review. Section 3 explains the material and methods used for proposed model. Section 4 describes the methodology and design of model which will predict movie success rate with more accuracy and precision. Section 5 discusses the result and implications based on proposed model. Section 6 describes the conclusion and future scope of the proposed model.

LITERATURE REVIEW

The fact of how the movie has been justified primarily decides the success of a movie. Initially, many people considered gross collection as the major point for movie success. But now many factors affect the same like a review of the movie, background story, box office collection, likes and comments about the movies. Many used regression models and considered revenues and applied binary classification for the forecast. At the same time, few adopted applications of Natural Language Processing for sentimental analysis and gathered movie reviews for their testing. There are many works done, predicting the success or failure of the movie. Some were predicting result after the movie is released, while some were predicting before release. We have studied multiple papers which we are discussing below:

The author predicting movie success or movie failure by developing a mathematical model, which was based on multiple factors (Ahmad et. al, 2017). Their model was based on an interesting relation between attributes. They used various attributes such as budget, actors, directors, producers, cast, release date etc. Simulated data were used; they cleaned, integrated, and transformed hundreds of records for their analysis. Their model was based on chi-square (X^2 analysis), which find a correlation between various factors. With a degree of freedom as 8, they calculated 64.39 as expected frequency for the relationship between genre and ratings. With a degree of freedom as one, their expected frequency was 20.6 for the relationship between actors and genre. With a degree of freedom as one, the frequency was 11.57 for the relation between actors and ratings.

The main concern of this chapter to review a system where a website was used in which registered users write their reviews (Upadhyay et. al, 2018). For the prediction of movie whether it will be a success or will be a failure, they used this review system.

They developed a custom dictionary which was comprised of those words which was commonly used in the movie review and which was later to be matched for the corresponding weightage. By classifying the movies into Hit, Average, Flop, their goal was to provide an algorithm which can give accurate result and movie success or failure can be predicted. They used Sentimental Analysis to analyse opinions about a particular topic. For the overall rating, the mean of the average of reviews and ratings was calculated. These ratings can be affected by the season like major festivals, weekends, and holidays. Based on the overall rating movies were labelled as Hit, Average, Flop.

The author proposed a system predicting the success or failure which was based upon data mining techniques(Meenakshi et. al, 2018). They tried to reduce the risk of decision making by making a system which can predict the past and future of the movie. Data Collection, Data Cleaning, Data Transfer, Data Analysis and Prediction were used as the components of their methodology. In their proposed system, they used two techniques to study the dataset, first was K-Means and second was the Decision Tree algorithm. For the output, they analyse the trends and patterns by these two techniques.

The researcher proposed a model where they can predict movie success (Darekar, 2018). They divide their dataset into classical factors and social factors so that they can predict the success of the movie. They use multiple data mining techniques for predicting social and critics ratings. They use multiple machine learning algorithms like Linear Regression, Polynomial Regression, KNN, ID3, to do the same. They took only social factors randomly for the prediction and got a good result.

Model is designed for predicting movie success or movie failure by used different data mining and ML techniques(Dhir, 2018). Methods used are Support Vector Machine Classification, AdABoost, Gradient Boost, Random Forest, KNN classification. They proposed to give a better accuracy model than the previous existing model. After comparing all the methods adopted for predicting the success of a movie, they found out that Random Forest gave the best result out of all. The dataset is prepared and structured such that it represents all the movies and their approaches accurately and should be feasible to all machine learning algorithms and methods for analysis also. They compared their result with the previous prediction based on Korean movies (58% accuracy) and accuracy on IMDb date between 2000-2012, which gave only 50.7% of accuracy. Their accuracy was close to 60%, which was better than these. They proposed to work in the field of MLP and Bagging on the existing dataset summation with a dataset from YouTube and Twitter.

The researchers designed a model which can predict movie success to those movies which were released in the USA only (Cizmeci, 2018). Their model works only for Hollywood movies. Factorization machine approach (MSE and R2) were used by them to predict the success of the movie. They achieved the best performance metric. MSE gave them a score of 1.24, and R2 gave them a score of 0.88.

The author analysed different attributes from different sources to predict movie success using various mining algorithms and also study the similarities between movies (Kudagamage, 2018). Four algorithms were used (SVM, ANN, Naïve Bayes, Decision Tree), and also they use an Ensemble approach to predict the success of the movie. On the basis of the results obtained from the classifiers, SVM with 89.61% predicts the highest accuracy. An accuracy of 71.42%, 76.62%, 86.66% were produced by Decision Tree, Naïve Bayes, and Neural Networks, respectively. Later the accuracy produced was increased to 92.85% using an Ensemble approach. They also had a mathematical approach which produced an accuracy of 85-90%.

A model is proposed which is used for the prediction of a Bollywood movie (Verma, 2019). They use ML algorithms like Random Forest, Decision Tree, SVM, Adaptive Tree Boosting, Logistic Regression, and Artificial Neural Network and compare the results of those algorithms to get the best result of the used algorithms. Their model consists of multiple parameters to predict the outcome. Most of their models get an accuracy range of 80-90%, but two of their techniques, Logistic regression and Random Forest achieved an accuracy of 92%. The result they get indicated that the important predictors were music's song, screen used for release and IMDb ratings.

A comparative model is designed which can predict the movie success and compare their results to choose the best accuracy result (Khandelwala, 2019). They do a comparative analysis of different algorithms to get a better result. For the data, they perform data mining technique on current data only. They used multiple algorithms for their prediction model and perform a comparative analysis on AdaBoost, Decision Tree, Logistic Regression, Naive Bayes, and KNN to get the best out of them.

In their work, author relate the music rating of a movie with the sense of being to predict a movie success or a flop long before the release of a movie(Verma, 2019). They used many machine learning methods like Logistic Regression, Multiple Regression, Discriminant Analysis, ANN etc. With an accuracy of about 80%, their model can predict the success of the movie. They used IBM SPSS21.0 so that they can process and analyse those data and able to develop an LR model. Three different predictors were used for getting the prediction which made it possible to get the forecast close to 80%. Predictors used were Screens, IMDb ratings, Music rating. The base for taking LR Model as a working model was generated from the Hosmer and Lemeshow Test, which compared different methods.

After having reviewed over multiple papers, there are certain loopholes ascertained with the author works. There has not been any model that can predict both Hollywood and Bollywood movie from the same model. Every author either has used a model for Bollywood movie or Hollywood movie or their language's movie. Some has used small dataset, and some has used social factors only, every author has taken different parameters for their model to predict the success. Because of these reasons, we were encouraged to choose this topic and work on this.

MATERIAL AND METHODS

- **Materials:** The required dataset for our project is collected from Kaggle database from where we downloaded the dataset and used as input. This dataset consists of both Hollywood and Bollywood movies which are more than ten years old. Hollywood dataset is from another source, and Bollywood dataset is from another source, so these datasets need to be integrated and transformed to make the combined dataset much simpler to use and easily read by ML algorithms for the prediction of the success of the movie. Large amount of data is present there about the movies, there gross collection, critics reviews, and working cast members and factors influencing their work. We divide the dataset into a training set and testing set for the same. From the result we get, we can easily conclude that the movie will be successful or not.
- **Methods:** In this chapter, We have used three different techniques Decision Tree Regression, SVR, and Random Forest regression for proposed model to predict the movie success.

Random Forest Regression is a supervised learning algorithm. It is basically used for both classification as well as regression. This algorithm selects the sample from dataset and prepare multiple decision trees for each and every sample and predict the result.

Decision Tree algorithm is a classifier which can also be used for both classification and regression analysis. Decision Tree algorithm uses tree representation for solving a problem. It follows the split approach and divides the dataset on the given condition.

Support Vector Machine is also used as a regression model. SVR has few minor differences in the principle used by SVM. Support Vector Regression is used to predict continuous variables. SVR plots variables in a predefined value.

In this model, data is collected from kaggel.com. Data which is collected from different sources contains much irrelevant details which was of no use. Firstly, data is to be cleaned and get relevant data. The data was extracted and the converted into .csv file format. Then three different techniques Decision Tree Regression, SVR, and Random Forest regression used to predict the movie success or failure. The user can enter the information mentioned like movie name, name of 1st and 2nd actor, year of release movie and another structure in Fig. 4 shows the predicted result after the user has entered the data. This model will help the audience to choose the movie before investing their time and money wisely.

METHODOLOGY AND DESIGN

Figure 1. Overview of the model

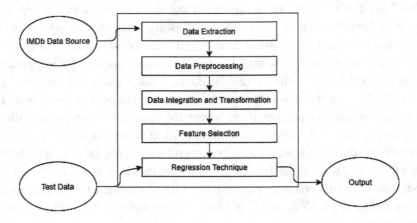

A. Data Extraction

The data was collected from sources like Kaggle.com and various social media platforms. There was no such data available which include all the attributes which can be used for the prediction of the movie success. To properly get our result of prediction, we have to consider several relevant datasets. Therefore, we opt for a different dataset provider.

B. Data Pre-processing

The data we got contains much irrelevant information which was of no use. The data contained missing values and was very noisy. So, these data need to be cleaned to get relevant and noise-free data. The data was then converted to a .csv file format.

C. Data Integration and Transformation

The data came from various sources. Hollywood dataset is from another source, and Bollywood dataset is from another source, so these datasets need to be integrated

Figure 2. Flowchart of the working of the model

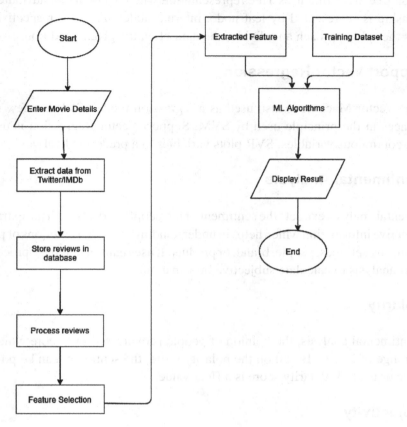

and transformed to make the combined dataset much simpler to use and easily read by ML algorithms for the prediction of the success of the movie.

D. Random Forest

A Random Forest is a supervised learning algorithm. It is used for both classifications as well as regression. This algorithm selects random samples from the given dataset and construct multiple decision trees for every sample and predict the result. Voting is performed, and most voted result is selected as the final predicted result.

E. Decision Tree

Decision Tree algorithm is a classifier which can be used for both classification and regression analysis and is a supervised ML algorithm. For solving a problem,

Decision tree algorithm uses Tree representation where Class label, attributes and relationship is represented by leaf node, internal node and edges respectively. It follows the split approach and divides the dataset on the given condition.

F. Support Vector Regression

Support Vector Machine is also used as a regression model. SVR has few minor differences in the principle used by SVM. Support Vector Regression is used to predict continuous variables. SVR plots variables in a predefined value.

G. Sentimental Analysis

Sentimental analysis extracts the sentiment of the people. It deals with the extraction of subjective information which helps in understanding the social emotions of people related to any services, people, brand, or product. It uses natural language processing and text analysis to calculate subjective information.

H. Polarity

In a sentimental analysis, the opinion of people is expressed in a score which lies in the range of [-1, 1]. Based on the polarity score, the sentiment can be positive, negative or neutral. Polarity score is a float value.

I. Subjectivity

Subjectivity refers to how any person's emotion, personal opinion shape any judgement. Subjectivity score lies in a range of (0, 1).

As shown in Fig. 3, a frame where the user can enter the information mentioned, and another structure in Fig. 4 shows the predicted result after the user has entered the data. This model will help the audience to choose the movie before investing their time and money wisely.

RESULTS

A predictive model is being developed by using three algorithms, Decision Tree Regression, SVR, and Random Forest regression. A frame has been developed where user can enter the details of the movie which they want to get information about the movie. The results of the model and frame are shown below.

Figure 3. A frame of the model

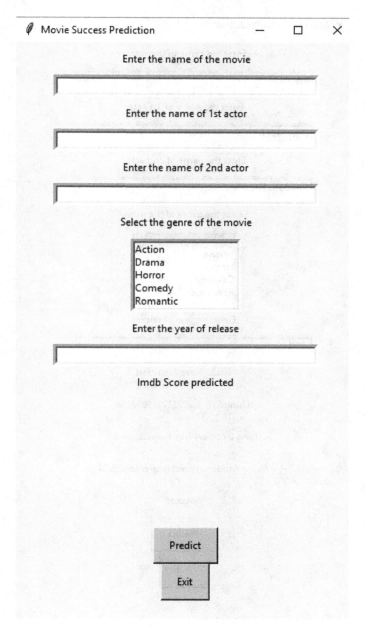

As shown in Fig. 5, the first model is developed by using Decision Tree Regression technique which is producing an overall accuracy of 73-78%.

Figure 4. Frame showing predicted result

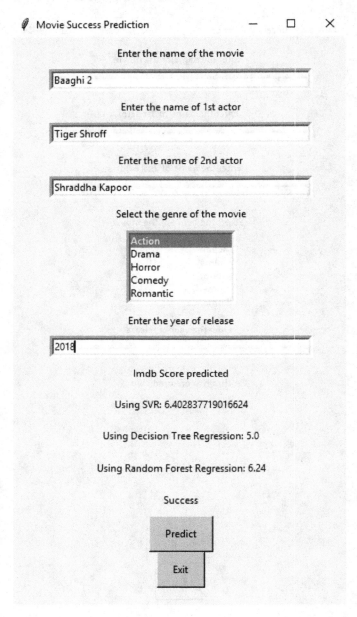

By using Random Forest Regression technique, the next model has achieved an overall accuracy of 78-83%. The result of this model is shown in Fig. 6.

Figure 5. Relation between original and predicted rating of decision tree

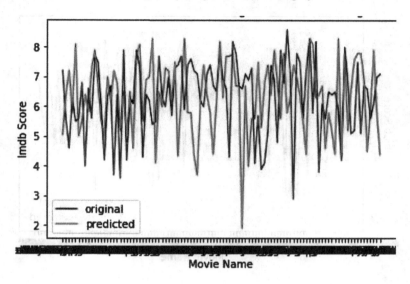

Fig. 7 depicts the result of the third model, based on SVR. This model has an accuracy of 80-85%.

From the above results, comparing the three models shown, we can conclude that the SVR has produced the maximum accuracy out of the three outcomes. User can use this model to get the movie success prediction at a reasonable accuracy rate and can invest their time and money accordingly.

Figure 6. Relation between original and predicted rating of random forest

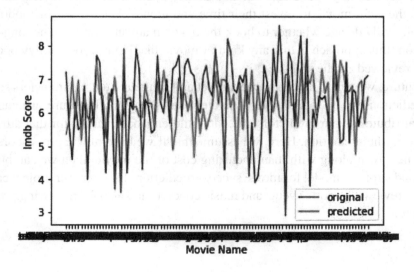

Figure 7. The relation between original and predicted rating of SVR

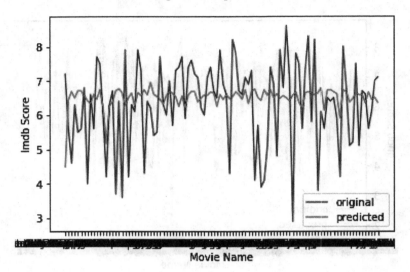

CONCLUSION AND FUTURE SCOPE

In this business world, where everything starts with risk and involvement of money and time, there is an opportunity to reduce the uncertainty in the future. This chapter contains the model to predict whether the given movie will be a success or will be a failure before the date of the release. This chapter establishes the relation between various factors which can be helpful in making this predictive model. This model will help all the stakeholders connected with the movie to make a wise decision. This model not only saves time but also money of the audience and help them to choose the right movie to invest their time and money. Due to this methodology, user can easily decide whether to book the ticket in advance or not. The long-term gain from this approach is that any kind of movie like Hollywood, Bollywood, etc can be reviewed on the website.

In future, we will work on a large dataset and can relate more parameters so that the prediction can be made more accurately and precisely. In future, we can add many attributes as our predictors and can build enhanced model for that attribute to perform the prediction. Here, we assume that if we have movie gross score and movie net profit along with manufacturing cost of the movie, then we can build a better and stronger model for movie success prediction. In future our project can be used for reviewing sports events and music concerts and also for reviewing product sales, etc.

REFERENCES

Ahmad, J., Duraisamy, P., Yousef, A., & Buckles, B. (2017, July). Movie success prediction using data mining. In *2017 8th International Conference on Computing, Communication and Networking Technologies (ICCCNT)* (pp. 1-4). IEEE. 10.1109/ICCCNT.2017.8204173

Ahuja, R., Solanki, A., & Nayyar, A. (2019, January). Movie recommender system using K-Means clustering and K-Nearest Neighbor. In *2019 9th International Conference on Cloud Computing, Data Science & Engineering (Confluence)* (pp. 263-268). IEEE.

Alzubi, J., Nayyar, A., & Kumar, A. (2018, November). Machine learning from theory to algorithms: An overview. *Journal of Physics: Conference Series, 1142*(1), 012012.

Bane, K. (n.d.). *Success of Bollywood Movie Using Machine Techniques: A Literature Review*. Academic Press.

Bhave, A., Kulkarni, H., Biramane, V., & Kosamkar, P. (2015, January). Role of different factors in predicting movie success. In *2015 International Conference on Pervasive Computing (ICPC)* (pp. 1-4). IEEE.

Cizmeci, B., & Ögüdücü, Ş. G. (2018, September). Predicting IMDb ratings of pre-release movies with factorization machines using social media. In *2018 3rd International Conference on Computer Science and Engineering (UBMK)* (pp. 173-178). IEEE.

Darekar, S., Kadam, P., Patil, P., Tawde, C., & Student, B. E. (2018). Movie Success Prediction based on Classical and Social Factors. *International Journal of Engineering Science and Computing, 50-62.*

Dhir, R., & Raj, A. (2018, December). Movie success prediction using machine learning algorithms and their comparison. In *2018 First International Conference on Secure Cyber Computing and Communication (ICSCCC)* (pp. 385-390). IEEE.

Gaikar, D., Solanki, R., Shinde, H., Phapale, P., & Pandey, I. (2019). Movie Success Prediction Using Popularity Factor from Social Media. *International Research Journal of Engineering and Technology, 6*(4), 5184–5190.

Gaikar, D. D., Marakarkandy, B., & Dasgupta, C. (2015). Using Twitter data to predict the performance of Bollywood movies. *Industrial Management & Data Systems*.

Jain, A., & Nayyar, A. (2020). Machine learning and its applicability in networking. In *New age analytics* (pp. 57–79). Apple Academic Press.

Kaur, A., & Kaur, A. G. (2013). Predicting Movie Success: Review of Existing Literature. *International Journal of Advanced Research in Computer Science and Software Engineering, 3*(6), 1694–1697.

Khandelwal, R., & Virwani, H. (2019, February). Comparative analysis for prediction of success of bollywood movie. In *Proceedings of International Conference on Sustainable Computing in Science, Technology and Management (SUSCOM)*. Amity University Rajasthan.

Kudagamage, U. P., Kumara, B. T. G. S., & Baduraliya, C. H. (2018). Data mining approach to analysis and prediction of movie success. *International Conference on Business Innovation (ICOBI)*.

Latif, M. H., & Afzal, H. (2016). Prediction of movies popularity using machine learning techniques. *International Journal of Computer Science and Network Security, 16*(8), 127.

Lee, K., Park, J., Kim, I., & Choi, Y. (2018). Predicting movie success with machine learning techniques: Ways to improve accuracy. *Information Systems Frontiers, 20*(3), 577–588.

Meenakshi, K., Maragatham, G., Agarwal, N., & Ghosh, I. (2018, April). A Data mining Technique for Analyzing and Predicting the success of Movie. []. IOP Publishing.]. *Journal of Physics: Conference Series, 1000*(1), 012100.

Peerzada, S. A., Padhy, N., Sheetlani, J., & Hassan, G. (2020, March). Predict the Performance of Students and School on Educational kegga (U-DISE). In *2020 International Conference on Computer Science, Engineering and Applications (ICCSEA)* (pp. 1-6). IEEE.

Priya, B. G. (2019). *Sentiment Analysis for Online Movie Reviews using SVM*. Academic Press.

Quader, N., Gani, M. O., Chaki, D., & Ali, M. H. (2017, December). A machine learning approach to predict movie box-office success. In *2017 20th International Conference of Computer and Information Technology (ICCIT)* (pp. 1-7). IEEE.

Saraee, M., White, S., & Eccleston, J. (2004). A data mining approach to analysis and prediction of movie ratings. *WIT Transactions on Information and Communication Technologies, 33*.

Sharda, R., & Delen, D. (2006). Predicting box-office success of motion pictures with neural networks. *Expert Systems with Applications, 30*(2), 243–254.

Singh, T., Nayyar, A., & Solanki, A. (2020). Multilingual opinion mining movie recommendation system using RNN. In *Proceedings of First International Conference on Computing, Communications, and Cyber-Security (IC4S 2019)* (pp. 589-605). Springer.

Sutton, R. S., & Barto, A. G. (2018). *Reinforcement learning: An introduction.* MIT Press.

Upadhyay, A., Kamath, N., Shanghavi, S., Mandvikar, T., & Wagh, P. (2018). Movie Success Prediction Using Data Mining. Department of Information Technology, Shah & Anchor Kutchhi Engineering College, 6(4).

Verma, G., & Verma, H. (2019, February). Predicting Bollywood movies success using machine learning technique. In *2019 Amity International Conference on Artificial Intelligence (AICAI)* (pp. 102-105). IEEE.

Verma, H., & Verma, G. (2020). Prediction model for Bollywood movie success: A comparative analysis of performance of supervised machine learning algorithms. *The Review of Socionetwork Strategies, 14*(1), 1–17. doi:10.100712626-019-00040-6

Chapter 9
Machine Learning for Risk Analysis

Parita Jain
KIET Group of Institutions, India

Puneet Kumar Aggarwal
ABES Engineering College, India

Kshirja Makar
*HMR Institute of Technology and
Management, India*

Riya Garg
*HMR Institute of Technology and
Management, India*

Jaya Mehta
*HMR Institute of Technology and
Management, India*

Poorvi Chaudhary
*HMR Institute of Technology and
Management, India*

ABSTRACT

Evolution of technology summons risks. With the use of complex prototypes and methods, not only the decision-making propensity of the machines increases but also the risk assessment reduces and frauds increased. Machine learning (ML) is considered an appropriate solution for the management of risks as it can produce the desired solution with less human effort. So, to minimize the possibility of risks, certain methods are adopted that benefited through ML. The chapter provides an insight into various applications of ML techniques in the field of risk analysis. The application of ML in this sector has led to a fact that these methods can be used to analyze huge amounts of data with efficient predictive analysis. Moreover, the future of machine learning in risk analysis and management is presented bringing out the positive picture. As a conclusion, one can just say that humans will be seeing an era which will make even complex problems easy to solve with efficiency. The chapter concludes with some limitations which need to be fixed for better risk management.

DOI: 10.4018/978-1-7998-9012-6.ch009

INTRODUCTION

Machine Learning (ML) is the new utterance of technology. It has the proficiency of replacing emphatic programming of the devices. It is generally hinged on the conception that a substantial amount of data is provided and on the basis of that data and some algorithms the machine is trained, and different machine modules are fabricated. The decisions made by the machines based on data provided are immensely efficient and accurate. With the commencement of the contemporary aeon of technology, ingenious crimes and risks are also escalating. In the modern world the most important constituent to take off is the risk management and its intensifying production. This chapter comprises all the information regarding how machine learning has palliated in risk assessment (Aggarwal et al., 2021; Apostolakis,2004; Aven,2012).

Large scale organizations, companies, and institutions are prone to risks like frauds consequently they are sticking to various machine learning techniques that can prevent or abate these frauds or risks. The chapter is an amalgamation of various strategies for changing the perspective of risk assessment. On the basis of risk assessment with machine learning various case studies sheathing different aspects has been covered in the chapter. These case studies have effectively engulfed the seriousness of risk assessment. Case studies are basically an inspiration of the future consequently elucidating constructing techniques to diminish risks. Several applications are also incorporated in this chapter as well that lead us to the significance of risk assessment in several industries and organizations for protection from copious frauds and deceptions altogether with the integration of machine learning in this peculiar field (Chen et al., 2008; Cheng et al., 2016).

The resonance of this chapter is related to the arguments that can be a sense of salvation from risks that can emerge abundant provenances followed by a conclusion which covers the mantle of machine learning in the field of risk management as a whole.

Machine Learning

Machine learning can be described as a subcategory of the Artificial Intelligence (AI) field which has its main focus on examining and recognizing patterns and arrangements in data to facilitate features such as training, thinking, decision making, learning, and researching without interference. Machine learning allows the user to pack an enormous sum of data with a computer algorithm, allows the computer to examine and analyze the data to make recommendations based on the input received. If some features require redesigning, they are classified and improved for a better

Figure 1. Machine learning algorithm process

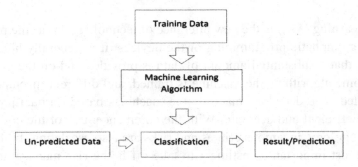

design for the future (Creedy, 2011; Alzubi et al., 2018; Comfort, 2019; Jain et al., 2020; Aggarwal et al., 2021; Singh et al., 2021).

The main aim of the technology is to produce an easy to use a mechanism which works on making decisions by the computational algorithm. Variables, algorithms, and innovations are accountable for making decisions. Awareness towards the solution is needed for the better learning of the systems working and thus helps in understanding the path to reach the result.

In the initial stages of implementation of the algorithm, input or data is provided to the machine provided that the result is already known for that set of feed data. The changes are then made to produce the result (Diekmann, 1992; Durga et al., 2009; Goodfellow et al., 2016). The efficiency of the result depends on the amount and the quantity of the data that is fed to the machine as shown in Figure 1.

Risk Analysis

Risk is referred to as the occurrence of undesired events while running a project which creates a negative impact on the achievement of the goals of that project. Risk is the possibility of an unwanted or harmful event. Risk analysis is the analysis done by adopting different methods in order to check the probability of the happening of the risk and it is performed in order to remove the chances or minimize the probability of the occurrence of the harmful events. Risk analysis is desirable as the occurrence of risk is directly proportional to the amount of losses faced in a project. Every technology or project has an equal chance of being successful as well as becoming a failure and hence the analysis is done to reduce this chance, what is called the risk of failure (Kaplan Kaplan and Garrick, 1981; Hastie et al., 2009; Hauge et al., 2015; Haugen and Vinnem, 2015; Khakzad, 2015).

Risk analysis includes identifying the type of hazard that can be associated with the project which may be chemical hazard, mechanical hazard, or even technical hazard. It is a process which is analytical in nature and is aimed to know all the desired information related to undesirable events. It involves analysis of the hazards that have occurred in the past and also which have the probability of occurring in future (Khakzad et al., 2013a; 2013b). It not only analyses the hazards but also their consequences on the system so that appropriate measures can be taken. The main objective is to increase the chances of success and at the same time minimize the cost or investment on the project. As important risk analysis is, it is even more difficult to be performed. The traditional method of using employees requires a lot of time to complete the process (King and Zeng, 2001; Kongsvik et al., 2015; Landucci and Paltrinieri, 2016a, 2016b). But now with the growth of industries the amount of data generated is more, operations performed on a project are more but the time to complete that project is less. So, in order to fulfil the demand vs. time ratio industries use technical and more reliable methods such as ML. There are different methods in which risk analysis can be done. These methods are:

1. *Qualitative methods:* It is a method which is generally used in the process of decision making or before decision making. It involves various predictions based on previous experiences; different judgments are passed by different members of the project. This is not a very accurate method and is generally done at the initial state of the project (Jain et al., 2018; Jain and Sharma, 2019). The major aim is to improve the quality of the project based on past experiences. This method is suggested when there is no time constraint, and the risk level is quite low. This method does not make use of any algorithms or numerical data. It is performed through brainstorming or by questionnaire or interviews.

2. *Quantitative methods:* This method is way more numerical and reliable than the qualitative methods. In these different numerical values can be assigned to different risks identified based on the probability of their occurrences and the algorithms are performed to calculate the level of the risk of the project (Aggarwal et al., 2018; Aggarwal et al., 2019; Jain et al., 2020, Chaudhary et al., 2021; Makar et al., 2021). In this method they do not pre- assume the things. It involves analyzing the probability of number of occurrences, analysis of the consequences as well as the aftereffects of the solution. This method is a little expensive as it requires machines and computer systems, but it is very accurate in results.

3. *Semi- Quantitative methods:* These methods are neither fully qualitative nor completely numerical or algorithm based. This is a mid-way method adapted according to the needs of the project and clients. The method used depends on the level of risk of the project. In this various project are classified into low, middle, or high-risk level projects. This method is used in small scale projects

or where the client is not sure about the requirements and hence is not able to predict the exact level of risk associated.

Figure 2. Components of risk analysis

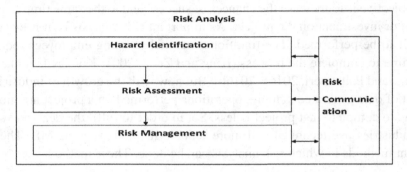

The major components of risk analysis include hazard identification, risk assessment, risk management, risk communication (Nivolianitou et al., 2004; Nobre, 2009; Musgrave, 2013; Lasi et al., 2014). The step-by-step process is shown in Figure 2.

1. *Hazard Identification:* The primary step to proceed towards risk analysis is the identification of the problems or risks or hazards that can be faced in the future. The no. of hazards determines the level of risk for the project. More are the no. of hazards higher is the level of risk. Once the identification is done this stage is followed by risk perception which means the acceptance of the risk identified. How the risk is perceived depends on person to person and also upon the characteristics of the risk. If the client wants the project to be successful and earn profit, then he/she is bound to accept the risk and also take appropriate measures in order to minimize it. In order to cure the problem first one needs to know the problem similarly in order to remove the risks first the hazard needs to be identified as well as accepted and not ignored.

2. *Risk Assessment:* When the level of risk increases it becomes necessary to assess these risks in order to find solutions at the right time. This is done to ensure the safety of the project as well as the workers, users etc. (Paltrinieri et al., 2015).

3. *Risk Management:* this refers to manage the risks that are being assessed and analyzed. There are different strategies which are used to manage the risks.

These strategies aim to remove the negative effects of the risk and increase the productivity (Pasman and Reniers, 2014).

4. *Risk Communication:* It refers to making this process interactive between the clients, developers, and users by exchanging and transferring the information of risk with each other. This stage involves active participation of all those who are associated with a project directly or indirectly that is from the lower to higher level in order to make the process efficient and fulfill the demands of all stages. It is important because it makes the decision-making process easier as the decision involving lowest risk probability is chosen. It is done by discussion and analyzing different hazards and its impact. It reduces the gap between the expectations and results provided. And also, it gives a voice to the users to address their disappointments which are also kind of a risk (Aven and Krohn, 2014; Bucelli et al., 2017).

The main objective is to understand the aspects and techniques of machine learning that are engaged in the fields of risk assessment. The succeeding time of machine learning in risk assessment is skillfully acknowledged in the chapter. Various use cases have also been discussed such as supervision of conduct and market abuse in trading, fraud detection and credit risk to understand the use of ML in risk assessment.

The rest of the chapter is organized into different sections. The next section discusses about the concept of risk assessment and risk management and how it works. Then, in next section it is discussed how the business world manage the risks. After that, various ML techniques and algorithms are discussed that may be applied for assessing risk. Then, different case studies are discussed to understand the concept in depth. And at last, conclusions are drawn from the chapter. Finally references at last.

RISK ASSESSMENT AND RISK MANAGEMENT

When the level of risk increases it becomes necessary to assess these risks in order to find solutions at the right time. This is done to ensure the safety of the project as well as the workers, users etc. For example, mechanical project risks can be dangerous for workers, which are technology related project risks that can prove to be dangerous for users' data. To assess the hazards, one must figure out the origin, consequences, and the results. To identify the origin all, the sources must be assessed to understand where the things could go wrong. Then, figure out how much are these risks exposed to the outside environment. This stage is known as risk estimation in which individual systems are assessed to know the contributions of each source and functionality towards the risk (Oien et al., 2011; Noh et al., 2014; Nyvlt et al., 2015)

Understanding the individual systems helps in forming connections and links of the sources with the risk being produced while development. If the risk is assessed during the development process only it can be easily cured and removed (Nyvlt and Rausand, 2012). It also helps to predict which features can produce failures in future and they can be continuously monitored and managed. Hence the qualitative analysis of risk assessment includes detailed study of logical flow of the data and the system functionalities.

Generally, the risks that are assessed are represented in the form of diagrams, flow charts, decision trees etc. for better understanding. For risk assessment some factors such as the equipment used, the software developed, the functionalities produced, and target audience must be kept in mind. This step is very important in order to build the gap between the risk that is being predicted and that is being perceived (Paltrinieri and Reniers, 2017). This is because the risk predicted is generally statistical in nature and is based on the theory of probability and number of assumptions. So, in order to bridge this gap quantitative and numerical approach must be adapted rather than estimating the factors on the basis of their frequency. This stage of analyzing the prediction with the result is called risk evaluation and is a part of risk assessment. Different tests are performed, and various test drives are run to assess and predict the risk, so the final product is safe and successful. Also, various data sets are created in order to keep the tracks of failures produced in the past and to ensure that same hazards are not produced in future.

Risk Management

Now the next step that comes is to manage the risks that are being assessed and analyzed. There are different strategies which are used to manage the risks. These strategies aim to remove the negative effects of the risk and increase the productivity. Some people tend to manage the risk by avoiding it but it is not the correct way to deal with the hazards as if they are not dealt with at the earlier stage they will grow into something serious. So, the correct way of managing risks is first of all accepting them (Paltrinieri et al., 2019). The risk management is done on the basis of priority that means the risk with highest probability of occurrence or the risk that can cause maximum amount of damage needs to be dealt first and the risks which are expected to cause lower loss are prioritized in descending order. Hence, first it needs classification of the risks based on loss and probability.

Generally, the amount of loss faced is given more priority than the frequency of its occurrence. It is the most important step because if the risks are not managed properly then there is no point in identifying and assessing them. The unmanaged risks reduce the rate of profit, durability, quality, and reliability of the project. It can also affect the brand value of a company and decrease the trust of users. The problem or limitation faced by this phase is the limited amount of technique and resources available to manage the hazards and the increase in cost due to risk management. Steps required in risk management are:

1. Identification of the risk and its resource and domain
2. Considering the impact of this on the system
3. Probability of occurrence
4. Impact on effective cost
5. Consequences on the project
6. Classification on the basis of priority
7. Assessing the constraints that can be faced
8. Describing the need of users and agenda for doing this activity
9. Doing discussions and communications to decide the managing technique.
10. Finally developing an analytical approach in order to manage the risk.
11. Organizing the resources and cost required for managing process.

Thus, Risk Management is done on the basis of results obtained from Risk Assessment and then the appropriate techniques are chosen by managers.

RISK IN THE BUSINESS WORLD

As one all know that any business be it small or big is prone to risk. Some of them even cause loss of profits to extend bankruptcy. The large firms have expanded their sections of risk management. The smaller firms or businesses are still not able to find systematic ways to handle the issue. Comprehensive business plans are required to have a successful business, but the plans need to be updated with time (Svozil et al., 1997). With changes in the market and its standards, the old methods of risk management and analysis require modification. The major risks that the firms face are:

1. *Strategic Risk:* As the name suggests Strategically Risk is a strategy related in which the planning is not appropriate for the successful development of the business. This is due to the technological changes in the society, new competitors with modern technologies entering the market, rapid changes in the customer demand section, an increase in the cost of raw material. Studies show the example of firms that suffered strategic risk. Some trained their models to gain success, and some did not. An example of the same is Kodak, which had a decent position in the photography firm that when the engineers developed the digital camera, it marked the shift as a threat to its center marketing model and failed to modify it. If Kodak had considered the strategic risk more thoroughly,

it could have led to a better future for the company. Handling a strategic risk is not always destructive as there are examples of brands which were able to see it as a chance of change like Xerox. It became a success with a single and satisfactory product i.e., a photocopy machine. The company tried to add a laser printer to enhance the business model and was ready to face the statistical risk. The company saw the positive side of the change due to good planning.

2. *Compliance Risk:* The company tries to increase their profits and business empires, but they have to obey a certain amount of laws while doing the same. The laws are constantly changed with time and regulation is required. For example, a person makes cosmetic products in his factory and sells it to a country. The person is doing so well in the industry and thus wants to expand the business to another country. Now the business is under the compliance risk. The countries have some rules regarding the import of products and the rules and regulation which may cost money and may not give a bigger margin in profits in comparison to the expected margins. The same condition may arise if the product line is changed.

3. *Operational Risk:* This type of risk is due to the unexpected failure in the way the company operates. The risks include mechanical failure, technical failure or failure due to people. If a person has a salary of ₹10,000 and is given a check of ₹1000 then it is a failure of process and people. This may look like a small problem in the example but in the big industry, it can cause issues with bigger amounts. Other problems like natural disasters and power cuts which can cause operational damage. From these examples, a definition of Operational Risk can be defined as any issue or risk that damages the function or operation of a business (Villa et al., 2016a, 2016b).

4. *Financial Risk:* Most of the times the risk that the firm faces is categorized as Financial Risk i.e. a risk having a financial issue leading to low revenue and decreased profits. Let us assume that a client has the credit extension of 30 days and is a large source of the company's revenue (Marchi and Ravetz,1999). The company, in this case, is under financial risk as a great deal of trouble can be caused if the payment is not done on time. Similar is the case when a particular company is in great debt. International businesses undergo huge financial risks. One can go back to the example of cosmetics where the person wanted to sell the products in the international market and if the person tries to sell the goods in USA, UK, France, and India the company may have to bear the conversion charges of these different currencies. This type of example comes under financial risk.

5. *Reputational Risk:* One thing which is common to all the businesses is their Reputation, be it a small size business or a multinational firm if the reputation is positive then the selling of commodity and recruitment of employees become

easier. If the reputation is damaged then there is an immediate loss in revenue and the employees might leave the company too, the advertising agencies may not show interest in the work related to the company and so on (Yang and Haugen, 2015).

MODELS IN THE FIELD OF RISK MANAGEMENT

Various models have been proposed for managing risks in different scenarios (Mahajan et al., 2021). Some of the models are explained as:

1. *Interpretability:* Machine learning designs have a character of signifying results that is hard to understand or evaluate. To increase the interpretability some models which are used are as follow:
    a. Linear monotonic models: linear coefficients act as a huge support for the exhibition of the output. Linear regression models come under this category.
    b. Nonlinear monotonic models: restraining data so that one can see either a falling or a rising global relationship where the variables are simplified for producing the result. Gradient boosting model is an example of the same.
    c. Nonlinear no monotonic model: methodologies such as local interpretable model-agnostic explanations or Shapley values help ensure local interpretability. The examples include models like unconstrained deep learning models.
2. *Bias:* This feature takes care of the trueness of the system. The validation takes care of the proper implementation of rules for fairness in the mechanism. Four approaches are generally used depending on the requirements:
    a. Demographic blindness: settlements are composed utilizing a restricted assortment of characteristics that are related to the preserved classes.
    b. Demographic parity: for each protected class results are proportionally the same.
    c. Equal opportunity: for each protected class true positive standards are similar.
    d. Equal odds: for each protected class true positive and false positive rate are equal.
3. *Feature Engineering:* It is the method of managing data to create innovations that execute with the help of machine learning algorithms. It is the process of selecting significant characteristics from a fresh pool of data and converting them into forms that are fit for machine learning. Feature engineering

model development in ML is complicated in comparison to the models used traditionally. The first reason for this is that machine learning models can combine a higher amount of information. Second is that there is a need for feature engineering that is required for disorganized data references at the pre-processing level before that training method can start.

4. *Hyper Parameters:* The variables which define the system composition and decide the network training method are the hyper parameters. It is very important to understand the variables and determine the appropriate selection of hyper parameters. The approaches for the selection of hyper parameters include the latest practices used in the industry and expert judgment.

5. *Production Readiness:* Machine-learning models, despite being algorithmic, require a lot of computation. This element is generally viewed in the process of model development. The validation is done previously to evaluate a variety of model risks connected with its usage and for machine learning they expand their scope. There is a requirement of setting a limitation on the data flow through the model, keeping in mind the run time and the architecture of the model.

6. *Dynamic Model Calibration:* Sometimes there is a dynamic change in the parameters of some types of models depicting the data patterns. The validators can easily decide which dynamic calibration is best suited for the firm. The factors that are evaluated include the development of a monitoring plan, ensuring proper control to reduce risk in accordance with the usage of the model.

MACHINE LEARNING TECHNIQUES FOR RISK MANAMGEMENT AND ASSESSMENT

There are two types of ML techniques which are used in risk analysis namely Supervised ML technique in which the input is pre-decided under supervised conditions and generates an expected output (Wolpert, 2002; Jain et al., 2020, Kumar et al., 2020). The other technique is Unsupervised ML technique in which various kinds of inputs are given in undefined sets and an unexpected output is generated.

1. *Supervised Technique:* It is further divided into regression and classification. Regression technique is used to define the relationship between the variable assigned to the risks predicted during the assessment. For example, a regression equation for a credit-based assessment can be defined as the variable assigned to non- payment of the loan taken which is further analyzed and sorted using a long range of variables which are independent which are assigned to functions like employment condition sort the person, past payment history, property etc.

This method is very useful as the independent variables facilitate in the management process and it is much better than the traditional method as it is self-explanatory and less theoretical and more practical. This method is suitable for big data sets as the variables which are not in use are deleted automatically. The other main technique is classification technique. It is the most commonly used technique in which risks are prioritized and represented in the form of decision trees and data flow diagrams. This method is easy and more comprehensive due to the visual representation and hence requires less time in management.

This model is understood by both technical and non-technical members. The risks are branched into various categories according to the percentages which indicate the probability of the occurrence of the various risks and hazards. This categorization and subdivision technique helps to determine the later consequences as well. This makes the sorting possible in less time as it contains only decision based yes / no type's questions. The only limitation of this module is that predictive power is low, which means it helps in analyzing but not in predicting when compared to the traditional methods.

2.   *Unsupervised Technique:* This method is further categorized into clustering. This is also based in subdivision, but it forms similar subgroups and does not predict any output. This is kind of a grouping technique with no prediction function. The example of this technique is Spam detection in emails. This means all the similar looking mails form a cluster that is if a mail is considered spam, then all the similar looking mails will be clustered as spam. This assignment of variables is lacking which does not allow it to detect or predict anything. This just helps the analysts to figure out the patterns and similarities between the functions.

The ML techniques form various models which are quite complex in nature as it has use of too many variables and other parameters in comparison of the output generated which make it heavy as well as complex as shown in Figure 3. Due to the complexity in design the interpretation time also increases which is undesirable. A good predictive model is generally hard to analyze. For efficient risk assessment and management interpretation is as important as prediction. So, some methods can be applied on these models to overweight the observations in comparison to parameters or inputs so that more and more outputs can be generated. Such a method is called "Boosting". Another way is running a model on different datasets many times so that it produces different predictions for the same dataset. This is called Bagging. The final desirable model is the average of boosting and bagging so that it can both predict as well as interpret at the same time.

Figure 3. Machine learning assessment model techniques

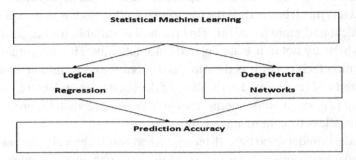

In order to remove all the complexities machine learning is combining with some techniques of deep learning which lead to advancement in the technology. These are generally referred to practical approach or theory free approach as it does not involve much of explanation as they are mostly self-explanatory. In deep learning all the algorithms are equipped in such a way that they represent a particular aspect of data and enhance the prediction of that part of data. This is how the data can be easily predicted by using ML techniques and interpreted with a little help of deep learning techniques without any increase in the complexity. This allows easy interpretation of even low quality and unstructured data which is present in huge datasets and makes the understanding easy for both analysts and non-technical users (Aggarwal et al., 2021). This integrated approach allows all the features to run together as system and perform a relevant analysis. Various ML algorithms applied by distinguish researchers to solve various risk is explained in Table 1.

Challenges of Machine Learning in Risk Management

Apart from all the use cases and advantages of using ML in risk analysis and management, there exist some of the major issues that need to be taken into consideration. Some of the challenges of machine learning in risk management that the industry faces are as follows:

1. *Availability of Data:* One of the most significant challenges is to obtain relevant as well as suitable data for processing. There is a lot of potential for machine learning packages for performing multiple tasks such as processing images and natural language by reading all types of data, but it is becoming difficult to maintain the discipline in the data internally (Jain et al., 2020). Moreover, the sharing of data is tough as the information is stored in different systems

Table 1. ML algorithms for risk management

Risk Type	ML Algorithms
Credit Risk	Neural Networks, SVM, KNN, Random Forest, Lasso regression, Cluster analysis.
Liquidity Risk	SVM, ANN, Bayesian Networks
Market Risk	GELM, Cluster analysis, SOM, Gaussian Mixtures, Cluster Analysis.
Operational Risk	Non-linear clustering method, Neural Networks, k-Nearest Neighbor, Naïve Bayesian, Decision Tree.
RegTech Risk	SVM

with different restrictions that makes the information retrieval even more challenging. Also, perhaps the information may not be stored formally.

2. *Availability of Skilled Staff:* With the evolution of new techniques, the requirement of skilled labor is quite demanding. The implementation, understanding and working of advanced features and solutions is of utter importance. Since, providing training to the unskilled staff is time consuming, therefore, there are some attempts made to solve this problem providing the course to aspirants by building a campus with around 7000 people in India where there is frequent presence of these skills.

3. *Accuracy of Machine Learning Techniques:* It is not as simple as just applying various machine learning techniques to manage the potential risk rather it requires continuous evaluation of the process in order to obtain optimal current solution. In order to ensure the feasibility, multiple testing of the technique is required.

4. *Transparency and Ethics:* This is one of the popular issues that usually occur. It is evident from the fact that the models work between the layers and remain hidden in the initial input and final output. This can lead to compliance problems while validating the model. It may even turn into the loss of a firm or convergence of the uniform ideal for trading resulting in a lot of risk. There are many ethical issues as well such as unequal lending decision due to gender, race, and sexual discrimination.

Machine Learning use Cases Under Financial Sector

This section analyzes and gives a detailed description of various use cases of machine learning in the field of risk management under the financial sector such as fraud detection, credit risk and supervision of conduct and market abuse in trading (Tanwar et al., 2020).

1.   *Fraud Detection:* Machine learning is now being used for a lot of time in the field of fraud detection mainly credit card fraud in the banking system. It has resulted in higher significant success rate till now. Banks have set up various monitoring and surveillance systems in order to ensure security. These systems keep a track on the payment fraud activities that take place more often. The fraud model engine works on the traditional historical payment algorithm that blocks the fraudulent trade as soon as it detects it (Aggarwal et al., 2014; Aggarwal et al., 2018; Jain et al.,2021).

Machine learning algorithms training, testing and authorization becomes possible because of large data sets provided by the credit card payments. Moreover, various classification algorithms are trained with the help of historical data with identified fraud and non-fraud tags. This training is done with the help of large historical non fraudulent data. The above historical payment datasets generate a clear view of features of the card by distinguishing them on the basis of transactions, owner and history of the payment.

2.   *Credit Risk:* The term credit risk signifies the prospects of loss because of unsuccessful payments made by the lender. Therefore, the Credit Risk Management System (CRMS) is implemented in order to meet the losses by analyzing the fairness of the bank and its capital along with the loan loss section at any instant of time. This system has enhanced the transparency as demanded by the financial crises. Transparency is carried by paying more emphasis on the regular examination of the knowledge of banks for its customers and credit risks.

Suitable credit risk management improves the entire performance of the system and provides a competitive benefit. Various prediction models are made in order to make predictions regarding the kind of lender. This is where the machine learning techniques are implemented. These machine learning algorithms are providing positive results and greater success rates in solving the problems including credit risks as well.

3.   *Supervision of conduct and market abuse in trading:* Another use case of Machine Learning in the risk management system is the surveillance of the performance loopholes generated mainly by the traders working in the financial institutions. The various trading illegalities often lead to economic as well as status failure. In order to overcome such crimes and shortcomings, numerous self-operating systems have been developed in order to provide a check on

the trading behaviors of dealers with increased accuracy and distinct ways to identify them.

Earlier, in the initial stages, the system's performance was limited to check the behavior of a single trade. But with time, various new machine learning approaches are applied and the machines can now identify huge and complicated data and analyze the entire portfolios. Apart from analyzing, the systems are also able to link distinct trading facts via email flux, calendar items, developing check in and checkout-times, and calls as well. The automatic analysis is performed using deep learning and text mining techniques which makes the system machine readable.

CASE STUDIES TO UNDERSTAND THE ROLE OF MACHINE LEARNING IN RISK MANAGEMENT

There are number of case studies available in literature from which some are really important to understand the impact of machine learning on risk analysis.

Case Study 1: Banks

On average banks are prone to various risks such as credit risk, market risk, foreign exchange risk, foreign risk, frauds, etc. These risks are treacherous for the reputation of the banks and their worthwhile procedures. These risks are dormant privation to the banks, and they can be questioned for the obligations on them. Risks are unpredictable and can develop irrespective of time. How well would it be if the risk can be specified or predicted? To specify the upcoming risks in advance, machine learning can be implemented. All the possible risks are first analyzed and reviewed. During the process of analysis of these risks a large amount of data is collected which is basically unstructured in nature. This data is collected from market information, customer reviews, metadata etc.

Machine learning is all about working with data. It processes this data for working machines. The machines will produce a desired output on the basis of the input processed. When machine learning along with some algorithms will be implemented on the large amount of unstructured data. The machine will interact on the basis of the data and the output will be generated. This generated output that can be a sort of prediction for the upcoming risk that might rise up in the near future.

For the accurate results from the system, it is important the training of the large amount of unstructured data that is collected is done in a perfect way. After the training is finished the data is converted into structured data or the labeled data. On this final set of data various algorithms are processed. These algorithms basically

Figure 4. Role of machine learning in the risk management for Disaster Management

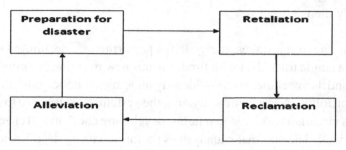

mold the data into a framework of a process to take place on the basis of which the final output is generated. The type of data collected in the final output will also be of the same category.

Machine learning is compatible, dynamic and can prevent a bank from such cunning risks. Several problems can be easily fathom with the help of machine learning in the fields of risk assessment.

Case Study 2: Disaster Management

Disaster can be defined as the natural affliction that can lead to various human, environmental and property losses. These disasters are unpredictable but there are several technologies which are operated today to predict an approximate time for such calamities. The labeled data which is collected for machine learning is used to predict the disaster in the form of a sequence of their occurrence. There are various processes which can forecast the occurrence of the disasters on the basis of their probability of occurrence as shown in Figure 4. During these processes there is a chance that several fallacies occur. This measure indicates misfiring of appliance or apparatus, preservation excess, quantity of supplementary worked, etc.

These machines that predict the upcoming disasters and the human generation cannot afford risks in these indicators as everyone relies on their final output. Consequently, the role of risk assessment in fields like disaster management becomes necessary for protection of a specific area from sudden tragedy and irreplaceable losses. Machine learning includes several techniques that look after the prevention of such risks in this area.

Apart from all the issues and problems, looking at the positives in a situation is a much more crucial segment. Considering the future of machine learning in risk management is worthy. This is evident from the fact that the cost of development is reduced. Moreover, the time-consuming nature of this process has also decreased at a higher scale. One such instance is that of Banco Bilbao Viscera Argentaria

(BBVA), is a financial service company in Spain. This multinational corporation is investing heavily in compliance-based workers. Therefore, various machine learning techniques are used in order to reduce this outlay. This technology makes the repetitive tasks automatic. Along with the organization, data clustering as well as recovering of advanced data are some of the abilities of machine learning that will provide a huge benefit to the companies.

CONCLUSION

Throughout the chapter various aspects and techniques of machine learning that are engaged in the fields of risk assessment to ameliorate this process has been discussed. The succeeding time of machine learning in risk assessment is skillfully acknowledged. The pasture of machine learning has the potential to create wonders in risk assessment by incorporating methodical procedures and models that can fabricate accurate results for risk analysis by effectively monitoring large and complex datasets. The application of machine learning in this sector has led to a fact that these methods or techniques can be used to analyze huge amounts of data with efficient predictive analysis. Various use cases have also been discussed such as supervision of conduct and market abuse in trading, fraud detection and credit risk.

The description of various models and the case studies that are covered in the chapter is a blueprint of the utilization of machine learning in different industries and organizations in the fields like risk management in banks, and risk management in disaster management. The major issue that can be addressed in technology is encounter of risks for this machine learning provides various models and techniques that can minimize or prevent these risks. These techniques and models change with different sets of labeled data as per the convenience of the procedure. It provides the stability in the field and the protection of human and national information that can be considered as highly confidential information. Still research is going on in the area of risk assessment and several measures are already implemented. There are still many areas left to work and provide measures to. It can ease the exertion of several industries and organizations to identify the potential risk and to involve methods if the probability of risk encounter is strong.

In the end, one can just say that humans will be seeing an era which will make even complex problems easy to solve with efficiency and they will solve it for sure, which will be time saving and will be economically beneficial. In today's era, technologies such as AI and ML are treated as a solution to almost every problem.

REFERENCES

Aggarwal, P. K., Grover, P. S., & Ahuja, L. (2018). Exploring Quality Aspects of Smart Mobile Phones Applications. *Journal of Advanced Research in Dynamical and Control Systems*, *11*, 292–297.

Aggarwal, P. K., Grover, P. S., & Ahuja, L. (2018). Security Aspect in Instant Mobile Messaging Applications. *Proceedings of IEEE International Conference on Recent Advances on Engineering, Technology and Computational Sciences (RAETCS)*, 1-5. 10.1109/RAETCS.2018.8443844

Aggarwal, P. K., Grover, P. S., & Ahuja, L. (2019). Assessing Quality of Mobile Applications Based On a Hybrid MCDM Approach. *International Journal of Open Source Software and Processes*, *10*(3), 51–65. doi:10.4018/IJOSSP.2019070104

Aggarwal, P. K., & Jain, P. (2014). Adaptive approach for Information Hiding in WWW Pages. *Proceedings of International Conference on Issues and Challenges in Intelligent Computing Techniques (ICICT)*. 10.1109/ICICICT.2014.6781262

Aggarwal, P. K., Jain, P., Chaudhary, P., Garg, R., Makar, K., & Mehta, J. (2021). AIIoT for Development of Test Standards for Agricultural Technology. In Intelligence of Things: AI-IoT Based Critical-Applications and Innovations (pp. 77-99). doi:10.1007/978-3-030-82800-4_4

Aggarwal, P. K., Jain, P., Mehta, J., Garg, R., Makar, K., & Chaudhary, P. (2021). Machine Learning, Data Mining and Big Data Analytics for 5G-Enabled IoT. In Blockchain for 5G enabled IoT: The new wave for Industrial Automation. Springer. doi:10.1007/978-3-030-67490-8_14

Aggarwal, P. K., & Sharma, S. (2021). Gaps Identification for User Experience for Model Driven Engineering. *Proceedings of the International Conference on Cloud Computing, Data Science & Engineering- Confluence*, 196-199.

Alzubi, J., Nayyar, A., & Kumar, A. (2018). Machine learning from theory to algorithms: an overview. In *Journal of physics: conference series*. IOP Publishing. doi:10.1088/1742-6596/1142/1/012012

Apostolakis, G. E. (2004). How useful is quantitative risk assessment? In Risk Analysis: An official publication of the Society for Risk Analysis. Wiley. doi:10.1111/j.0272-4332.2004.00455.x

Aven, T. (2012). The risk concept—Historical and recent development trends. *Reliability Engineering & System Safety*, *99*, 33–44. doi:10.1016/j.ress.2011.11.006

Aven, T., & Krohn, B. S. (2014). A new perspective on how to understand, assess and manage risk and the unforeseen. *Reliability Engineering & System Safety*, *121*, 1–10. doi:10.1016/j.ress.2013.07.005

Bucelli, M., Paltrinieri, N., & Landucci, G. (2017). Integrated risk assessment for oil and gas installations in sensitive areas. *Ocean Engineering*, *150*, 377–390. doi:10.1016/j.oceaneng.2017.12.035

Chaudhary, P., Goel, S., Jain, P., Singh, M., & Aggarwal, P. K. (2021). The Astounding Relationship: Middleware, Frameworks, and API. *Proceedings of the International Conference on Reliability, Infocom Technologies and Optimization (Trends and Future Directions) (ICRITO)*, 1-4.

Chen, H., Moan, T., & Verhoeven, H. (2008). Safety of dynamic positioning operations on mobile offshore drilling units. *Reliability Engineering & System Safety*, *93*(7), 1072–1090. doi:10.1016/j.ress.2007.04.003

Cheng, H.-T., Koc, L., Harmsen, J., Shaked, T., Chandra, T., Aradhye, H., Anderson, G., Corrado, G., Chai, W., & Ispir, M. (2016). Wide & deep learning for recommender systems. In *Proceedings of the 1st Workshop on Deep Learning for Recommender Systems*. ACM. 10.1145/2988450.2988454

Comfort, L. K. (2019). *The Dynamics of Risk: Changing Technologies, Complex Systems, and Collective Action in Seismic Policy*. Princeton University Press.

Creedy, G. D. (2011). Quantitative risk assessment: How realistic are those frequency assumptions? *Journal of Loss Prevention in the Process Industries*, *24*(3), 203–207. doi:10.1016/j.jlp.2010.08.013

De Marchi, B., & Ravetz, J. R. (1999). Risk management and governance: A post-normal science approach. *Futures*, *31*(7), 743–757. doi:10.1016/S0016-3287(99)00030-0

Diekmann, E. J. (1992). Risk analysis: Lessons from artificial intelligence. *International Journal of Project Management*, *10*(2), 75–80. doi:10.1016/0263-7863(92)90059-I

Durga Rao, K., Gopika, V., Sanyasi Rao, V. V. S., Kushwaha, H. S., Verma, A. K., & Srividya, A. (2009). Dynamic fault tree analysis using Monte Carlo simulation in probabilistic safety assessment. *Reliability Engineering & System Safety*, *94*(4), 872–883. doi:10.1016/j.ress.2008.09.007

Goodfellow, I. J., Bengio, Y., & Courville, A. (2016). *Deep Learning*. The MIT Press.

Hastie, T., Tibshirani, R., & Friedman, J. (2009). Unsupervised learning. In *The Elements of Statistical Learning* (pp. 485–585). Springer. doi:10.1007/978-0-387-84858-7_14

Hauge, S., Okstad, E., Paltrinieri, N., Edwin, N., Vatn, J., & Bodsberg, L. (2015). *Handbook for monitoring of barrier status and associated risk in the operational phase*. Center for Integrated Operations in the Petroleum Industry.

Haugen, S., & Vinnem, J. E. (2015). Perspectives on risk and the unforeseen. *Reliability Engineering & System Safety*, *137*, 1–5. doi:10.1016/j.ress.2014.12.009

Jain, A., & Nayyar, A. (2020). Machine learning and its applicability in networking. In *New age analytics* (pp. 57–79). Apple Academic Press. doi:10.1201/9781003007210-3

Jain, P., Aggarwal, P. K., Chaudhary, P., Makar, K., Mehta, J., & Garg, R. (2021). Convergence of IoT and CPS in Robotics. In Emergence of Cyber Physical Systems and IoT in Smart Automation and Robotics. Springer. doi:10.1007/978-3-030-66222-6_2

Jain, P., Sharma, A., & Aggarwal, P. K. (2020). Key Attributes for a Quality Mobile Application. *Proceedings of the International Conference on Cloud Computing, Data Science & Engineering Confluence*, 50-54. 10.1109/Confluence47617.2020.9058278

Jain, P., Sharma, A., Aggarwal, P. K., Makar, K., Shrivastava, V., & Maitrey, S. (2020). Machine Learning for Web Development: A Fusion. *Proceedings of 2nd International Conference on AI and Speech Technology*.

Jain, P., Sharma, A., & Ahuja, L. (2018). The Impact of Agile Software Development Process on the quality of Software Product. *Proceedings of the International Conference on Reliability, Infocom Technologies and Optimization (Trends and Future Directions) (ICRITO)*, 812-815. 10.1109/ICRITO.2018.8748529

Jain, P., & Sharma, S. (2019). Prioritizing Factors Used in Designing of Test Cases: An ISM-MICMAC Based Analysis. *Proceedings of International Conference on Issues and Challenges in Intelligent Computing Techniques (ICICT)*. 10.1109/ICICT46931.2019.8977643

Jain, P., Singhal, A., Chawla, D., & Shrivastava, V. (2020). Image Recognition and Segregation using Image Processing Techniques. *TEST Engineering and Management*, *83*, 2404–2410.

Kaplan, S., & Garrick, B. J. (1981). On the quantitative definition of risk. *Risk Analysis*, *1*(1), 11–27. doi:10.1111/j.1539-6924.1981.tb01350.x PMID:11798118

Khakzad, N. (2015). Application of dynamic Bayesian network to risk analysis of domino effects in chemical infrastructures. *Reliability Engineering & System Safety*, *138*, 263–272. doi:10.1016/j.ress.2015.02.007

Khakzad, N., Khan, F., & Amyotte, P. (2013a). Risk-based design of process systems using discrete-time Bayesian networks. *Reliability Engineering & System Safety*, *109*, 5–17. doi:10.1016/j.ress.2012.07.009

Khakzad, N., Khan, F., & Amyotte, P. (2013b). Quantitative risk analysis of offshore drilling operations: A Bayesian approach. *Safety Science*, *57*, 108–117. doi:10.1016/j.ssci.2013.01.022

King, G., & Zeng, L. (2001). Logistic regression in rare events data. *Political Analysis*, *9*(2), 137–163. doi:10.1093/oxfordjournals.pan.a004868

Kongsvik, T., Almklov, P., Haavik, T., Haugen, S., Vinnem, J. E., & Schiefloe, P. M. (2015). Decisions and decision support for major accident prevention in the process industries. *Journal of Loss Prevention in the Process Industries*, *35*, 85–94. doi:10.1016/j.jlp.2015.03.018

Kumar, A., Sangwan, S. R., & Nayyar, A. (2020). Multimedia social big data: Mining. In *Multimedia big data computing for IoT applications* (pp. 289–321). Springer. doi:10.1007/978-981-13-8759-3_11

Landucci, G., & Paltrinieri, N. (2016a). A methodology for frequency tailorization dedicated to the Oil & Gas sector. *Process Safety and Environmental Protection*, *104*, 123–141. doi:10.1016/j.psep.2016.08.012

Landucci, G., & Paltrinieri, N. (2016b). Dynamic evaluation of risk: From safety indicators to proactive techniques. *Chemical Engineering Transactions*, *53*, 169–174.

Lasi, H., Fettke, P., Kemper, H.-G., Feld, T., & Hoffmann, M. (2014). Industry 4.0. *Business & Information Systems Engineering*, *6*(4), 239–242. doi:10.100712599-014-0334-4

Mahajan, S., Nayyar, A., Raina, A., Singh, S. J., Vashishtha, A., & Pandit, A. K. (2021). A Gaussian process-based approach toward credit risk modeling using stationary activations. *Concurrency and Computation*, 6692.

Makar, K., Goel, S., Kaur, P., Singh, M., Jain, P., & Aggarwal, P. K. (2021). Reliability of Mobile Applications: A Review and Some Perspectives. *Proceedings of the International Conference on Reliability, Infocom Technologies and Optimization (Trends and Future Directions) (ICRITO)*, 11-14.

Musgrave, G. L. (2013). James Owen Weatherall, The Physics of Wall Street: A Brief History of Predicting the Unpredictable. *Business Economics (Cleveland, Ohio)*, *48*(3), 203–204. doi:10.1057/be.2013.17

Nivolianitou, Z. S., Leopoulos, V. N., & Konstantinidou, M. (2004). Comparison of techniques for accident scenario analysis in hazardous systems. *Journal of Loss Prevention in the Process Industries*, *17*(6), 467–475. doi:10.1016/j.jlp.2004.08.001

Nobre, F. S. (2009). *Designing Future Information Management Systems*. IGI Global.

Noh, Y., Chang, K., Seo, Y., & Chang, D. (2014). Risk-based determination of design pressure of LNG fuel storage tanks based on dynamic process simulation combined with Monte Carlo method. *Reliability Engineering & System Safety*, *129*, 76–82. doi:10.1016/j.ress.2014.04.018

Nývlt, O., Haugen, S., & Ferkl, L. (2015). Complex accident scenarios modelled and analysed by Stochastic Petri Nets. *Reliability Engineering & System Safety*, *142*, 539–555. doi:10.1016/j.ress.2015.06.015

Nývlt, O., & Rausand, M. (2012). Dependencies in event trees analyzed by Petri nets. *Reliability Engineering & System Safety*, *104*, 45–57. doi:10.1016/j.ress.2012.03.013

Oien, K., Utne, I. B., & Herrera, I. A. (2011). Building safety indicators: Part 1 – theoretical foundation. *Safety Science*, *49*(2), 148–161. doi:10.1016/j.ssci.2010.05.012

Paltrinieri, N., Khan, F., & Cozzani, V. (2015). Coupling of advanced techniques for dynamic risk management. *Journal of Risk Research*, *18*(7), 910–930. doi:10.1080/13669877.2014.919515

Paltrinieri, N., & Reniers, G. (2017). Dynamic risk analysis for Seveso sites. *Journal of Loss Prevention in the Process Industries*, *49*, 111–119. doi:10.1016/j.jlp.2017.03.023

Paltrinieria, N., Comfortb, L., & Reniers, G. (2019). Learning about risk: Machine learning for risk assessment. *Safety Science*, *118*, 475–486. doi:10.1016/j.ssci.2019.06.001

Pasman, H., & Reniers, G. (2014). Past, present and future of Quantitative Risk Assessment (QRA) and the incentive it obtained from Land-Use Planning (LUP). *Journal of Loss Prevention in the Process Industries*, *28*, 2–9. doi:10.1016/j.jlp.2013.03.004

Singh, M., Sukhija, N., Sharma, A., Gupta, M., & Aggarwal, P. K. (2021). *Security and Privacy Requirements for IoMT-Based Smart Healthcare System*. Big Data Analysis for Green Computing. doi:10.1201/9781003032328-2

Svozil, D., Kvasnicka, V., & Pospichal, J. (1997). Introduction to multi-layer feed-forward neural networks. *Chemometrics and Intelligent Laboratory Systems*, *39*(1), 43–62. doi:10.1016/S0169-7439(97)00061-0

Tanwar, S., Bhatia, Q., Patel, P., Kumari, A., Singh, P. K., & Hong, W. C. (2020). Machine Learning Adoption in Blockchain-Based Smart Applications: The Challenges, and a Way Forward. *IEEE Access: Practical Innovations, Open Solutions*, *8*, 474–488. doi:10.1109/ACCESS.2019.2961372

Villa, V., Paltrinieri, N., Khan, F., & Cozzani, V. (2016a). Towards dynamic risk analysis: A review of the risk assessment approach and its limitations in the chemical process industry. *Safety Science*, *89*, 77–93. doi:10.1016/j.ssci.2016.06.002

Villa, V., Paltrinieri, N., Khan, F., & Cozzani, V. (2016b). A Short Overview of Risk Analysis Background and Recent Developments. In *Dynamic Risk Analysis in the Chemical and Petroleum Industry*. Evolution and Interaction with Parallel Disciplines in the Perspective of Industrial Application. doi:10.1016/B978-0-12-803765-2.00001-9

Wolpert, D.H. (2002). The supervised learning no-free-lunch theorems. *Soft Computing and Industry*, 25–42.

Yang, X., & Haugen, S. (2015). Classification of risk to support decision-making in hazardous processes. *Safety Science*, *80*, 115–126. doi:10.1016/j.ssci.2015.07.011

Chapter 10
Machine Learning– Based Categorization of COVID–19 Patients

Tanvi Arora

ⓘD https://orcid.org/0000-0002-8454-6005
CGC College of Engineering, India

ABSTRACT

The world has been put to a standstill by the COVID-19 pandemic, which has been caused by the SARS-CoV-2 (initially called 2019-nCoV) infecting agent. Moreover, this pandemic is spreading like a wildfire. Even the developed nations are running short of hospital beds and ventilators to treat the critically ill. Considering the total population of the world and the pace at which this pandemic is spreading, it not possible to hospitalize all the positive patients with intensive care facilities. In the chapter, the authors present a machine learning-based approach that will categorize the COVID-19 positive patients into five different categories, namely asymptomatic, mild, moderate, severe, and critical. The proposed system is capable of classifying the COVID-19-affected patients into five distinct categories using selected features of age, gender, ALT, hemoglobin, WBC, heart disease, hypertension, fever, muscle ache, shortness of breath with 97.5% accuracy.

INTRODUCTION

The *SARS-CoV-2* (initially called 2019-nCoV) infecting agent is zoonotic and is spreading from one infectious person to another. Moreover, the symptoms of the infection becomes evident over a while, till that time the carrier of the virus

DOI: 10.4018/978-1-7998-9012-6.ch010

unknowingly comes in contact with several other persons. To date no firm vaccine has been developed to curtail the effect of this disease, prevention is the only viable escape. Since this disease emerged at such a large scale over a short duration of time, and has spread the world over. The world is not prepared to handle this pandemic.

Coronaviruses are a family of viruses that are known since the 1960s and they can infect humans as well as animals. They have been seen to cause respiratory infections. Towards the end of the year 2019, all of a sudden there was a surge of pneumonia patients in the Wuhan city of Hubei province of China and most of the patients that reported that diseases had a connection with the seafood market of Wuhan. The disease has been named as "2019 novel Coronavirus"(Suganthan, 2019).

This novel virus has been recognized as similar to SARS-CoV(Severe Acute Respiratory Syndrome Coronavirus) based upon the phylogeny and taxonomy of the past studies therefore it has been renamed as SARS-CoV-2(Gorbalenya, 2020).

The COVID 19 infection can spread like a wildfire from one human to human. Therefore whoever is found positive with COVID 19, he is isolated from others to stop the spread of the disease. The persons who have come in contact with the COVID 19 patient are also put in quarantine, as a precautionary measure, as the symptoms of the infection does not appear instantaneously, the virus is believed to have an average incubation period of 5 days and the maximum period of 14 days. The patients thus put in quarantine are said to be the suspected cases. On the contrary the patients who exhibit pneumonia-like symptoms like fever, short breathlessness, dry cough are also termed as suspected cases and are also monitored by putting in isolation(Zhang et al., 2020).

The COVID 19 infection is confirmed by carrying out a laboratory test of the suspected case, by taking a swap of the patient's nose or the back of the throat as the nose and back of the throat are the hot sites where the virus is replicating. The swabs are then put into a solution that helps to release the cells from the swab, then the genetic code of the COVID 19 is matched with the cells captured from the swab. (Tian et al., 2020)(Xiong et al., 2020).

Considering the total population of the world and the pace at which this pandemic is spreading, it not just possible to hospitalize all the positive patients with intensive care facilities In the proposed work we are presenting a machine learning-based approach, that will categorize the COVID 19 tested positive patients into five different categories namely Asymptomatic, Mild, Moderate, Severe, and Critical. Then based upon the severity of the patient and availability of the space in the Intensive Care Units, the Asymptomatic, Mild and Moderate patients can be kept in isolation without intensive care equipment and the severe and critical patients can be kept in the ICU's. In this study a dataset of 3567 COVID 19 patients has been taken from the hospitals located in Wuhan, China. The Random Forest-based machine learning model has been trained using the medical records of 2567 patients and the rest of the records have been used for testing the model using the medical history, laboratory test results and current symptoms. The proposed system is capable of classifying the COVID 19 affected patients into five distinct categories with 97.5% accuracy using features of ALT, hypertension, shortness of breath and gender.

The paper has been organized as: section 1 presents an introduction, Literature review is deliberated in section 2, section 3 presents materials and methods, experiments and results are described in section 4, discussion of the results is done in section 5 and finally conclusion is presented in section 6.

LITERATURE REVIEW

The COVID 19 pandemic has emerged just a couple of months ago, and the researchers have put in much effort to study the characteristics of the widespread disease. Although much work in the domain of machine learning has not yet been carried out in this work. But the researchers have tried to detect the presence of the COVID 19 pandemic by evaluating the Chest X-ray images(WANG, 2020) or the CT images of the chest(Ai et al., 2020)(Bai et al., 2020)(Pan et al., 2020)(Shen et al., 2020) using the features of the images of the lungs captured.

It has been reported in (Singhal, 2020) that the COVID 19 infection is transmitted from individual to individual either by inhalation of the water droplets in the air or by direct physical contact with the carrier of the infection human being or the surfaces where the carrier have touched. The incubation period of the virus varies between 2 to 14 days. The typical symptoms of the infected are high temperature, dry cough, throat that is soar, lethargy and difficulty breathing.

To avoid the waiting time of the pathogen testing a CT scan of the lungs is performed and the CT images are being used to create the hypothesis about the presence of COVID 19 using the deep learning modalities. As the graphical features learned from the CT images can firm the presence of COIVD 19. The early detection and action prevents the spread of the viral infection. (Wang et al., 2020)

A machine learning algorithm has been used to improve possible case identifications of COVID-19 quickly by using a mobile phone-based web survey. This will also reduce the spread in the susceptible populations. (Rao & Vazquez, 2020). The volumetric chest CT images have been used to extract the visual traits and deep learning models along with COVNet have been used to detect the presence of COVID 19 (Li et al., 2020).

The artificial intelligence-powered methods have been used to analyze the data associated with the COVID 19, which can be further used for decision making and treatment plans and can also be used to forecast the spread of the disease. (Santosh, 2020)

The machine learning-based supervised methods have been proposed for the classification of the genomes of the COVID 19. The methods are very fast, scalable and accurate. In this approach the signal processing of the genome is carried out using the machine learning modalities that are supervised. (Randhawa et al., 2020)

A machine learning technique for predicting the survival rate of critically ill patients has been proposed that uses three main clinical traits namely lactic dehydrogenase (LDH), lymphocyte and High-sensitivity C-reactive protein (hsCRP) to predict the survival(Yan et al., 2020).

A review of the different machine learning modalities for predicting the disease using the health care data. (Uddin, Khan, Hossain, & Moni, 2019) The studies have shown that Random Forest and SVM based classifiers give the most promising results.

Recently an artificial intelligence-based framework based upon the data of Chinese patients have been proposed, that predicts the severity of the COVID 19 by using a set of features for the severely ill patients with an accuracy of 70% using the Alanine aminotransferase(ALT) feature using the decision trees and an accuracy of 80% using features of ALT, gender, temperature, sodium, potassium, myalgias, hemoglobin, lymphocyte count, creatinine level, age and white blood cell counts(Jiang, Coffee, Bari, Wang, & Jiang, 2020).

Based upon the literature survey it can be concluded that although over a short span of few months, researchers have proposed many techniques to predict the presence of COVID 19, using imaging modalities or by studying the genome and some have tried to use artificial intelligence to predict the severity of the COVID 19. Most of the work is focused on using image-based modalities to confirm the presence of the COVID 19. But still, not much work has been proposed so far to predict the severity of COVID 19, so that the intensive care treatment which is a limited resource these days, owing to the emergence of a large number of cases should only be recommended for the person who have critical and severe condition, while the other patients who have although tested positive, they may be kept in isolated wards or quarantine at their homes so that the ones who need more medical supervision are not devoid of the care and medical attention, that is required for them.

MATERIALS AND METHODS

Dataset

In this study the dataset has been generated using the case reports of the 3567 COVID 19 patients admitted in different hospitals located in Wuhan, China. The records of 2567 patients have been used to train the model and 1000 records have been used for testing the model. The testing set had records of 335 asymptomatic patients (33.5%),

324 patients (32.4%) who had mild symptoms, 298 patients (29.8%) with moderate symptoms, 34 patients(3.4%) had severe symptoms and remaining 9 patients(0.9%) had critical condition. The dataset contains personal parameters, current symptoms, previous medical history and laboratory test results of all the patients.

The features that have been considered for our study are as follows:

Personal Parameters

1. Age: The patients have been categorized into different slabs of age, 0-10, 11-20, 21-30,31-40,41-50,51-60,61-70,71-80,81-90,91-100.
2. Gender: Male, Female
3. International Travel: the value of 1 if the patient has either a foreign travel history or has come in contact with someone returned from foreign lands and a value of 0 if the patient has no foreign travel history or has not contacted any person who returned from foreign lands.

Current Symptoms: All the patients were recorded for their current symptoms on the parameters of fever, cough (wet, dry or no cough), Nasal congestion, Sore Throat, blood in the mucous, Wheezing, Muscle Ache, shortness of breath, Diarrhea. If any of the above symptoms is true then it is represented by value 1, otherwise, that value for that symptom is marked as 0.

Previous Medical History: All the patients we recorded for their prior medical conditions namely Hypertension, Hepatitis B, Diabetes, heart disease, organ transplant. If any of the above conditions is true then it is represented by value 1, otherwise, that value for that condition is marked as 0.

Laboratory Test Results: For each patient a set of tests were performed to judge the functioning of the various vital organs. The values that are recorded are the count of white blood cells, Lymphocyte count, Neutrophils count, Hemoglobin level, platelet count, ESR, CRP, ALT, AST, Sodium, Potassium, Creatinine, Creatinine kinase, Lactate dehydrogenase, glucose, Fio2, Tropponon-I, Cycle threshold values, BNP, procalcitonin. Any parameter that is not in the normal range as specified is marked with 1 and the normal parameter is marked with 0.

In short for each patient three personal parameters, nine current symptoms, five previous medical history parameters and twenty laboratory test results are recorded. That is a total of thirty-seven features have been recorded.

Methods

Feature Selection

Features are the distinguishable properties of the entities. They are used by the machine learning methods for classification. An object can have a large number of distinguishing features, but all of them are not relevant for the task of classification. In the domain of computer-assisted learning or statistics, the task of optimal feature selection is very important. It aims at selecting the subset of relevant and class determining features to make the task of classification simpler, faster and generalized thereby minimizing the overfitting.

The feature selection approach aims to choose a subset of distinguishing features, that can very efficiently predict the class labels of the input data. The most discriminating features are to be selected; therefore the dependent variables are removed that reduce the feature set. If the domain knowledge is limited then in some cases the variables that are not correlated with the class serve as noise and may deteriorate the classification results.

It is not possible to evaluate all the subsets of the features of the objects. It may become an NP-hard problem, for a large number of features. So, therefore, there is a need to use an alternative approach which can help to select the most relevant and class determining features and remove the redundant and non-contributing features. The feature selection methods have been broadly classified as filter-based methods, wrapper based methods and embedded methods.

The feature selection helps to reduce overfitting, improves the accuracy and reduces the training time. The feature selection process is a two-step process. In the first step all the subsets of the attributes are evaluated for building a model and accuracy evaluation of the proposed model. The second step searches the space of all the subsets in a structured manner based upon subset evaluation.

In the proposed work the feature selection has been carried out using the Correlation-based feature selection approach(Hall, 1999) that uses a filter-based approach. It selects the features based upon heuristic rules, that find the appropriate features based upon correlation. This algorithm is quite proficient at finding the duplicate, non-contributing features. The CFS approach selects those features that have more class determining capabilities and the least correlation amongst the feature set.

In this work the feature selection has been done using the machine learning tool: WEKA. In the experiments the best first approach with forward selection heuristic method has been used for the correlation-based feature selection. It has assumed that if after five iterations there is no change in the subset of the features selected then the algorithm should stop. Then the merit of each of the subset of features is carried out and the subset that has the highest merit is selected. For our work, we have used the feature set that has a merit of 0.523 and the subset of the features that has been created for predicting the severity of COVID 19 are Age, Gender, ALT, Hemoglobin, WBC, Heart Disease, Hypertension, Fever, Muscle Ache, Shortness of Breath.

Classification

Classification is the process of assigning the class labels to the new observations based upon the previously known observations, for which the class labels are known. The classification task is very easy for a human to perform, but it is a challenging task from the perspective of the computer. In this work we have tried to create a data driver classifier, that is trained based upon the previous data available for which the class labels are known. Then the trained model can be tested upon the test set and predict the class labels. Then by comparing the output of the trained model and the pre-existing results, the accuracy of the classifier can be determined.

In the proposed work the random forest classifier(Breiman, 2001) has been used to classify the COVID, 19 patients, into five different categories namely asymptomatic, mild, moderate, severe and critical patients, based upon the set of features selected by the Correlation-based feature section approach, as illustrated in the previous section. In random forest classifiers there are a group of trees that are derived to do the predictions that are done based upon the randomly generated vectors that are sampled independently and they also have a similar distribution for the trees taken in the forest. To see if the random forest is the ideal choice, the experimental results have been compared with other machine learning classifiers namely

The Naïve Bayes classifiers learn from the training database upon the conditional probability of the of all the features that are contributing to the determination of the class category. Finally, the classifier does the classification using the Bayes Rule to determine the posterior probability(Friedman, Geiger, & Goldszmit, 1997). The Radial Basis Function(RBF) network(Oyang, Hwang, Ou, Chen, & Chen, 2005), that approximate the probability density function on the training data for the class objects of the dataset. The k nearest neighbor classification algorithm works by finding the k nearest neighbors, then it tries to find the distance between the k nearest neighbors and then it sorts the distances between the neighbors, find the category of the nearest neighbor and then use the majority as the class label for the classification process(Serbanescu, 2010), The SVM (J, 1998) classifier works by applying a mapping function to categorize data even if it is not linearly separable. It finds a separator in between the different categories and finally the data under consideration is transformed in such a manner so that the separator thus found can draw a hyperplane to categorize the data. the Multilayer Perceptron(Lek & Park, 2008)is a learning process that is based upon the non-linear mapping structure. It has been proven to be one of the most flexible approximation functions that can be used with any type of data. It is quite useful when the underlying relationships among the underlying data is not known.

EXPERIMENTS AND RESULTS

Performance Evaluation Metrics

The performance of the classifiers has been measured based upon the parameters of Accuracy, Recall & Precision as illustrated in(Arora & Dhir, 2020)(Arora & Dhir, 2016)(Soni, Kumar, & Chand, 2019). The performance evaluation parameters have been calculated using the following equations and values:

True Positive: Positive Patients marked as Positive
False Positive: Negative Patients marked as Positive
True Negative: Negative Patients marked as Negative
False Negative: Positive Patients marked as Negative
Precision: It is the percentage of the patients retrieved that are positive.

$$Precision = \frac{True\,Positive}{True\,Positive + Fasle\,Negative} \tag{1}$$

Recall: It is the percentage of successful retrieval of the positive patients. It is used to measure the completeness of the results.

$$Recall = \frac{True\,Positive}{True\,Positive + False\,Positive} \tag{2}$$

F-Measure: It is the measure of the harmonic means of precision and recall.

$$F\,Measure = \frac{2 * Precission * Recall}{Precission + Recall} \tag{3}$$

Accuracy: It is the percentage of the current results retrieved

$$Accuracy = \frac{True\ Positive + True\ Negative}{True\ Positive + True\ Negative + False\ Positive + False\ Negative}$$

(4)

The performance is estimated by doing k fold cross-validation(Bengio & Grandvalet, 2004). The experimental work has been carried out by testing and trying different parameters so that the best results are obtained.

Comparative Performance Evaluation

In this work the results of the random forest classifier have been shown considering the personal parameters, current symptoms, previous medical history and laboratory test results of the patients, then the results are compared by considering the selected features using the correlation-based feature selection approach. The results thus obtained have been compared with the other state of art classifiers firstly by considering all the features and then considering the selected features.

Classification Performance With Different Type of Features Using Random Forest Classifier

The random forest classifier has been used to categorize the records of 1000 COVID 19 positive tested patients into five different categories using the features of personal parameters, considering age, gender, international travel history within the last few days. The random forest classifier was able to classify them with 48% accuracy. When the current symptoms of the patient viz fever, cough, nasal congestion, sore throat, blood in mucous, wheezing, muscle ache, shortness of breath, diarrhea were considered, the random forest classifier classified the patients with 56.3% accuracy. The previous medical history of the patients was used to categorize the patients and the random forest classifier was able to classify patients with 54.9% accuracy considering the features of hypertension, Hepatitis B, Diabetes, heart disease and organ transplant. But when the patients were classified with the features of the laboratory test's such as count of white blood cells, Lymphocyte count, Neutrophils count, Hemoglobin level, platelet count, ESR, CRP, ALT, AST, Sodium, Potassium, Creatinine, Creatinine kinase, Lactate dehydrogenase, glucose, Fio2, Tropponon-I, Cycle threshold values, BNP, procalcitonin, the random forest classified the patients with 88.6% accuracy. But when the patients were categorized with all the thirty-seven features together then the accuracy of the classification results jumped to 96.6%. The results are presented in Table1.

Table 1. Classification Performance with different type of features using Random Forest Classifier

Model		Confusion Matrix					True Positive	False Positive	Precision	Recall	F-Measure	Accuracy (%)
		Asymptomatic	Mild	Moderate	Severe	Critical						
Personal Parameters,	Asymptomatic	103	89	74	57	12	0.307	0.073	0.682	0.307	0.423	48%
	Mild	18	191	54	54	7	0.589	0.182	0.612	0.589	0.600	
	Moderate	18	28	170	17	52	0.596	0.189	0.561	0.596	0.578	
	Severe	12	2	5	10	5	0.294	0.135	0.071	0.294	0.115	
	Critical	0	2	0	1	6	0.666	0.077	0.073	0.666	0.131	
Current Symptoms,	Asymptomatic	179	46	63	42	5	0.534	0.102	0.724	0.534	0.615	56.3%
	Mild	24	192	53	48	7	0.592	0.133	0.680	0.592	0.633	
	Moderate	26	36	190	14	32	0.637	0.178	0.603	0.637	0.619	
	Severe	17	4	8	1	4	0.029	0.109	0.009	0.029	0.014	
	Critical	1	4	1	2	1	0.111	0.048	0.020	0.111	0.034	
Previous Medical History	Asymptomatic	165	53	67	43	7	0.492	0.105	0.693	0.492	0.575	54.9%
	Mild	27	191	54	46	6	0.589	0.141	0.658	0.589	0.622	
	Moderate	28	38	191	16	49	0.593	0.185	0.595	0.593	0.594	
	Severe	18	3	7	1	5	0.029	0.107	0.009	0.029	0.014	
	Critical	0	5	2	1	1	0.111	0.066	0.014	0.111	0.025	
Laboratory Test Results	Asymptomatic	314	6	3	11	1	0.937	0.018	0.963	0.937	0.950	88.6%
	Mild	0	288	23	10	3	0.888	0.050	0.894	0.888	0.891	
	Moderate	6	23	256	7	6	0.859	0.041	0.898	0.859	0.878	
	Severe	6	4	2	21	1	0.617	0.028	0.428	0.617	0.506	
	Critical	0	1	1	0	7	0.777	0.011	0.388	0.777	0.518	
All the features	Asymptomatic	321	4	6	2	2	0.958	0.012	0.975	0.958	0.966	96.6%
	Mild	2	318	1	2	1	0.981	0.008	0.981	0.981	0.981	
	Moderate	4	1	289	3	1	0.969	0.011	0.973	0.969	0.971	
	Severe	2	1	1	29	1	0.852	0.007	0.805	0.852	0.828	
	Critical	0	0	0	0	9	1	0.005	0.642	1	0.782	

Classification Performance With Individual and Combined Selected Features Using Random Forest Classifier

The features were selected using the correlation-based feature selection and then the random forest classifier has been used to categorize the records of 1000 COVID 19 positive tested patients into five different categories using the selected features of personal parameters, considering gender and age, random forest classifier was able to classify the records with 56.3% accuracy. When the selected feature of current symptoms i.e shortness of breath, fever, muscle ace has been considered, the random forest classifier classified the patients into five distinct categories with 68.1% accuracy. The selected feature of the previous medical history of the patients has been used to categorize the patients, the random forest classifier was able to classify patients with 55.7% accuracy considering the features of hypertension and heart disease. But when the patients were classified with the selected features of the laboratory tests such as count of white blood cells, Hemoglobin level, ALT, the random forest classified the patients with 92.8% accuracy. But when the patients were categorized with selected features amongst all the features considered together, the classification accuracy of 97.5% was achieved considering the features of Age, Gender, ALT, Hemoglobin, WBC, Heart Disease, Hypertension, Fever, Muscle Ache, Shortness of Breath. The results are presented in Table 2.

Classification Performance With Other Classifiers

To validate the superiority of the random forest classifier, its performance has been compared with five other classifiers namely Naïve Bayes, Multilayer perceptron, Radial Basis Function network, k Nearest Neighbor and Support Vector Machine based classifiers using all the 37 features. The namely Naïve Bayes classifier classified with an accuracy of 82.3%, the Multilayer perceptron classifier classified with 67.9%, the Radial Basis Function network classified with 54.9%, the k Nearest Neighbor classified with 61.8% accuracy and Support Vector Machines can achieve an accuracy of 92.4%. But the overall best accuracy of 96.6% has been shown by Random forest-based classifier. The results are depicted in Table 3.

Classification Performance of Selected Features With Different Classifiers

To validate the superiority of the random forest classifier with the selected set of features, its performance has been compared with five other classifiers as well. The Naïve Bayes classifier classified with an accuracy of 83%, the Multilayer perceptron classifier classified with 69%, the Radial Basis Function network classified with

Table 2. Classification performance with individual and combined selected features using Random Forest Classifier

Model	Features Selected		Confusion Matrix					True Positive	False Positive	Precision	Recall	F-Measure	Accuracy (%)
			Asymptomatic	Mild	Moderate	Severe	Critical						
Personal Parameters,	Age Gender	Asymptomatic	119	89	76	45	6	0.355	0.040	0.815	0.355	0.494	56.3%
		Mild	8	214	44	52	6	0.660	0.168	0.652	0.660	0.656	
		Moderate	12	23	203	14	46	0.681	0.175	0.622	0.681	0.650	
		Severe	7	1	3	20	3	0.588	0.115	0.151	0.588	0.240	
		Critical	0	1	0	1	7	0.777	0.061	0.102	0.777	0.181	
Current Symptoms,	Fever Muscle Ache Shortness of Breath	Asymptomatic	245	24	42	22	2	0.731	0.100	0.785	0.731	0.757	68.1%
		Mild	22	218	41	40	3	0.672	0.0709	0.819	0.672	0.738	
		Moderate	26	16	216	17	23	0.724	0.130	0.701	0.724	0.712	
		Severe	17	5	8	1	4	0.028	0.083	0.012	0.028	0.017	
		Critical	2	3	1	2	1	0.111	0.032	0.0303	0.1111	0.047	
Previous Medical History	Heart Disease Hypertension	Asymptomatic	178	43	75	33	6	0.531	0.096	0.735	0.531	0.616	55.7%
		Mild	23	199	58	41	3	0.614	0.127	0.698	0.614	0.653	
		Moderate	27	36	171	14	50	0.573	0.202	0.546	0.573	0.559	
		Severe	14	4	8	4	4	0.117	0.091	0.043	0.117	0.063	
		Critical	0	3	1	0	5	0.555	0.063	0.073	0.555	0.129	
Laboratory Test Results	ALT Hemoglobin WBC	Asymptomatic	323	2	3	6	1	0.964	0.033	0.930	0.964	0.947	92.8%
		Mild	8	286	15	13	2	0.882	0.035	0.916	0.882	0.899	
		Moderate	14	20	286	12	14	0.826	0.029	0.931	0.826	0.875	
		Severe	2	3	1	27	1	0.794	0.030	0.465	0.794	0.586	
		Critical	0	1	2	0	6	0.666	0.017	0.25	0.666	0.363	
Combined Selected Features	Age, Gender, ALT, Hemoglobin, WBC, Heart Disease, Hypertension Fever, Muscle Ache, Shortness of Breath,	Asymptomatic	326	2	5	1	1	0.973	0.007	0.984	0.973	0.978	97.5%
		Mild	2	318	1	2	1	0.981	0.007	0.984	0.981	0.982	
		Moderate	2	3	290	2	0	0.976	0.008	0.979	0.976	0.978	
		Severe	1	0	0	33	0	0.970	0.006	0.846	0.970	0.904	
		Critical	0	0	0	1	8	0.888	0.002	0.8	0.888	0.842	

Table 3. Classification performance of all features using different classifiers

Classifier		Confusion Matrix					True Positive	False Positive	Precision	Recall	F-Measure	Accuracy (%)
		Asymptomatic	Mild	Moderate	Severe	Critical						
Naive Bayes	Asymptomatic	293	12	7	10	13	0.874	0.023	0.930	0.874	0.901	
	Mild	15	252	32	14	11	0.777	0.040	0.868	0.777	0.820	82.5%
	Moderate	2	18	262	261	12	0.472	0.065	0.850	0.472	0.607	
	Severe	3	4	6	17	4	0.5	0.233	0.056	0.5	0.100	
	Critical	2	4	1	1	1	0.111	0.032	0.024	0.111	0.04	
MLP	Asymptomatic	135	87	67	34	12	0.402	0.051	0.798	0.402	0.535	
	Mild	14	264	18	9	19	0.814	0.161	0.707	0.814	0.757	67.9%
	Moderate	16	12	260	4	6	0.872	0.123	0.749	0.872	0.806	
	Severe	1	7	1	18	7	0.529	0.048	0.276	0.529	0.363	
	Critical	3	3	1	0	2	0.222	0.044	0.043	0.222	0.072	
RBF Network	Asymptomatic	165	53	67	43	7	0.492	0.105	0.693	0.492	0.575	
	Mild	27	191	54	46	6	0.589	0.141	0.658	0.589	0.622	54.9%
	Moderate	28	38	191	16	49	0.593	0.185	0.595	0.593	0.594	
	Severe	18	3	7	1	5	0.029	0.107	0.009	0.029	0.014	
	Critical	0	5	2	1	1	0.111	0.066	0.014	0.111	0.025	
kNN	Asymptomatic	179	64	56	22	14	0.534	0.037	0.877	0.534	0.664	
	Mild	14	189	47	56	18	0.583	0.126	0.689	0.583	0.632	61.8%
	Moderate	8	19	218	34	17	0.736	0.152	0.670	0.736	0.702	
	Severe	2	1	2	28	1	0.823	0.117	0.198	0.823	0.32	
	Critical	1	1	2	1	4	0.444	0.050	0.074	0.444	0.126	
SVM	Asymptomatic	304	3	14	13	1	0.907	0.038	0.921	0.907	0.914	
	Mild	17	296	4	2	5	0.913	0.008	0.980	0.913	0.945	92.4%
	Moderate	3	1	296	5	1	0.967	0.031	0.930	0.967	0.948	
	Severe	4	2	3	23	2	0.676	0.021	0.522	0.676	0.589	
	Critical	2	0	1	1	5	0.555	0.009	0.357	0.555	0.434	
Random Forest	Asymptomatic	321	4	6	2	2	0.958	0.012	0.975	0.958	0.966	
	Mild	2	318	1	2	1	0.981	0.008	0.981	0.981	0.981	96.6%
	Moderate	4	1	289	3	1	0.969	0.011	0.973	0.969	0.971	
	Severe	2	1	1	29	1	0.852	0.007	0.805	0.852	0.828	
	Critical	0	0	0	0	9	1	0.005	0.642	1	0.782	

Table 4. Classification performance of selected features with different classifiers

Classifier		Confusion Matrix					True Positive	False Positive	Precision	Recall	F-Measure	Accuracy (%)
		Asymptomatic	Mild	Moderate	Severe	Critical						
Naïve Bayes	Asymptomatic	326	2	5	1	1	0.973	0.015	0.973	0.973	0.973	83%
	Mild	2	201	18	2	1	0.897	0.031	0.905	0.897	0.901	
	Moderate	2	13	281	2	0	0.942	0.046	0.909	0.942	0.925	
	Severe	2	5	4	19	4	0.558	0.006	0.76	0.558	0.644	
	Critical	3	1	1	1	3	0.333	0.006	0.333	0.333	0.333	
MLP	Asymptomatic	135	87	67	34	12	0.402	0.049	0.803	0.402	0.536	69%
	Mild	12	272	14	16	10	0.839	0.159	0.715	0.839	0.772	
	Moderate	18	13	260	5	2	0.872	0.118	0.758	0.872	0.811	
	Severe	2	5	1	19	7	0.558	0.056	0.256	0.558	0.351	
	Critical	1	3	1	0	4	0.444	0.031	0.114	0.444	0.181	
RBF Network	Asymptomatic	217	25	54	37	2	0.647	0.111	0.745	0.647	0.693	58.5%
	Mild	37	174	45	56	12	0.537	0.071	0.783	0.537	0.637	
	Moderate	26	18	186	12	56	0.624	0.163	0.617	0.624	0.621	
	Severe	10	2	15	5	2	0.147	0.109	0.045	0.147	0.068	
	Critical	1	3	1	1	3	0.333	0.072	0.04	0.333	0.071	
kNN	Asymptomatic	193	58	49	23	12	0.576	0.037	0.885	0.576	0.698	62.1%
	Mild	12	178	57	63	14	0.549	0.116	0.692	0.549	0.612	
	Moderate	10	19	218	34	17	0.731	0.156	0.664	0.731	0.696	
	Severe	2	1	2	28	1	0.823	0.125	0.187	0.823	0.306	
	Critical	1	1	2	1	4	0.444	0.044	0.083	0.444	0.140	
SVM	Asymptomatic	304	3	14	13	1	0.907	0.010	0.977	0.907	0.941	94.7%
	Mild	4	316	1	1	2	0.975	0.008	0.981	0.975	0.978	
	Moderate	1	2	292	2	1	0.979	0.025	0.941	0.979	0.960	
	Severe	1	1	2	29	1	0.852	0.017	0.630	0.852	0.725	
	Critical	1	0	1	1	6	0.666	0.005	0.545	0.666	0.6	
Random Forest	Asymptomatic	326	2	5	1	1	0.973	0.007	0.984	0.973	0.978	97.5%
	Mild	2	318	1	2	1	0.981	0.007	0.984	0.981	0.982	
	Moderate	2	3	290	2	0	0.976	0.008	0.979	0.976	0.978	
	Severe	1	0	0	33	0	0.970	0.006	0.846	0.970	0.904	
	Critical	0	0	0	1	8	0.888	0.002	0.8	0.888	0.842	

58%, the k Nearest Neighbor classified with 62.1% accuracy and Support Vector Machines can achieve an accuracy of 94.7%. But the overall best accuracy of 97.5% has been shown by Random forest-based classifier. The results are depicted in Table 4.

DISCUSSION

The COVID 19 pandemic has spread to the whole of the world, and by each passing day the number of persons that are infected by it is increasing at an exponential rate. The medical and research fraternity is working day and night to develop the ways to subside the ill effects of the pandemics. The rate at which this pandemic is spreading, even the developed nations like the United States of America, Italy, Spain, etc does not have enough medical infrastructure to cater to the medical needs of the patients that need to be hospitalized, as this pandemic has infected millions worldwide. If proper categorization of the COVID 19 patients is carried out, then it can be ascertained that who needs to be hospitalized and who just needs to be placed in isolation wards. As per the data available so far, only 20% of the patients get under the critically ill and sever complication category, those need intensive care treatment, nearly 80% of the people are having a mild effect. This will result in the efficient utilization of the available limited resources of hospitals.

In this work WEKA machine learning tool has been used to classify the patients into five distinct categories, depending upon the severity of the COVID 19 infection. Thirty-seven features of personal attributes, current symptoms, previous medical history, laboratory tests have been used to classify using the Random Forest classifier. It has been observed that an individual category of features is not capable enough to ascertain the severity of cases into five different categories. As personal features can classify with 48% accuracy and when the features are selected the classification accuracy increase to 56.3%. The current symptoms can classify with 56.3% and when the class determining features are considered then the accuracy increases to 68.1%. The previous medical history features can classify with 54.9% but when the selected features are used, then the classification accuracy increases to 55.7%. It can be seen that the feature selection increases the classification accuracy. The features of gender, shortness of breath, hypertension and ALT are the best predictors to categorize the patients into five different categories based upon the severity of the infection.

Further the random forest classifier has been able to assign correct class labels for the feature set of thirty-seven features and four features. The classification results of the random forest classifier have been compared with Naïve Bayes, Multilayer Perceptron, Radial Basis Function, k Nearest Neighbor and Support Vector Machine classifier. The Naïve Bayes can classify with an accuracy of 82.3% with all the features and with an accuracy of 83% with a selected set of features. The Multilayer Perceptron classifier can classify with 67.9% using all features and 69% with selected features. The Radial Basis Function network can classify with 54.9% with all features and 58.5% with selected features. The k nearest neighbor is capable of classifying with 61.8% with all the features and 62.1% with selected set f features. The Support Vector Machine classifier classifies with 92.4% considering all the features and with 94.7% accuracy with a selected set of features. But the overall best performance has been given by the Random Forest classifier with 96.6% accuracy with thirty-seven features and 97.5% accuracy with the selected ten features. It can be observed that the Random Forest classifier is the best classifier to classify the COVID 19 infected patients with the best overall accuracy.

CONCLUSION

The proposed system is capable of classifying the COVID 19 into five different categories depending upon the severity of the symptoms present in them. The method is based upon the personal features, current symptoms, prior medical history, laboratory tests performed. The machine learning-based random forest has been efficient enough to classify the patients into five different categories considering ten distinct features of Age, Gender, ALT, Hemoglobin, WBC, Heart Disease, Hypertension, Fever, Muscle Ache, Shortness of Breath, the classification accuracy of 97.5% has been achieved. The major shortfall of the proposed study is that the features have been taken from one city only, where the infection first originated. But considering the spread of the infection world over, if the features of the patients from different countries are considered, then better and more efficient results can be achieved with a reduced number of features.

FUTURE SCOPE

The proposed work can be further extended to include the covid 19 symptoms of the different variants of the virus that has emerged and do the comparative study of different variants and the complications.

COMPLIANCE WITH ETHICAL STANDARDS

Conflict of Interest: None.

Ethical approval: All procedures performed in studies involving human participants were in accordance with the ethical standards of the institutional and/or national research committee and with the 1964 Helsinki declaration and its later amendments or comparable ethical standards.

Informed consent: Informed consent was obtained from all individual participants included in the study.

REFERENCES

Ai, T., Yang, Z., Hou, H., Zhan, C., Chen, C., Lv, W., Tao, Q., Sun, Z., & Xia, L. (2020). Correlation of Chest CT and RT-PCR Testing in Coronavirus Disease 2019 (COVID-19) in China: A Report of 1014 Cases. *Radiology*, *296*(2), E32–E40. Advance online publication. doi:10.1148/radiol.2020200642 PMID:32101510

Arora, T., & Dhir, R. (2016). Correlation Based Feature Selection & Classification Via Regression of Segmented Chromosomes using Geometric Features. *Medical & Biological Engineering & Computing*, *55*(5), 733–745. doi:10.100711517-016-1553-2 PMID:27474041

Arora, T., & Dhir, R. (2020). Geometric feature-based classification of segmented human chromosomes. *International Journal of Image and Graphics*, *20*(01), 2050006. Advance online publication. doi:10.1142/S0219467820500060

Bai, H. X., Hsieh, B., Xiong, Z., Halsey, K., Choi, J. W., Tran, T. M. L., Pan, I., Shi, L.-B., Wang, D.-C., Mei, J., Jiang, X.-L., Zeng, Q.-H., Egglin, T. K., Hu, P.-F., Agarwal, S., Xie, F.-F., Li, S., Healey, T., Atalay, M. K., & Liao, W.-H. (2020). Performance of radiologists in differentiating COVID-19 from viral pneumonia on chest CT. *Radiology*, *296*(2), E46–E54. Advance online publication. doi:10.1148/radiol.2020200823 PMID:32155105

Bengio, Y., & Grandvalet, Y. (2004). No Unbiased Estimator of the Variance of K-Fold Cross-Validation. *Journal of Machine Learning Research*, *5*, 1089–1105.

Breiman, L. (2001). Random Forests. *Machine Learning*, *45*(1), 5–32. doi:10.1023/A:1010933404324

Devi, A., & Nayyar, A. (2021). Perspectives on the Definition of Data Visualization: A Mapping Study and Discussion on Coronavirus (COVID-19) Dataset. *Emerging Technologies for Battling Covid-19: Applications and Innovations*, 223-240.

Friedman, N., Geiger, D., & Goldszmit, M. (1997). Bayesian Network Classifiers. *Machine Learning*, 29(2/3), 131–163. doi:10.1023/A:1007465528199

Gorbalenya, A. E. (2020). Severe acute respiratory syndrome-related coronavirus – The species and its viruses, a statement of the Coronavirus Study Group. *bioRxiv*. doi:10.1101/2020.02.07.937862

Hall, M. (1999). *Correlation-based feature selection for machine learning* [Ph.D. Thesis]. Department of Computer Science, Waikato University, New Zealand.

J, P. (1998). *Sequential minimal optimization: a fast algorithm for training support vector machines*. Academic Press.

Jiang, X., Coffee, M., Bari, A., Wang, J., Jiang, X., Huang, J., Shi, J., Dai, J., Cai, J., Zhang, T., Wu, Z., He, G., & Huang, Y. (2020). Towards an Artificial Intelligence Framework for Data-Driven Prediction of Coronavirus Clinical Severity. doi:10.32604/cmc.2020.010691

Lek, S., & Park, Y. S. (2008). Multilayer Perceptron. In Encyclopedia of Ecology (pp. 2455–2462). doi:10.1016/B978-008045405-4.00162-2

Li, L., Qin, L., Xu, Z., Yin, Y., Wang, X., Kong, B., ... Xia, J. (2020). Artificial Intelligence Distinguishes COVID-19 from Community-Acquired Pneumonia on Chest CT. *Radiology*. Advance online publication. doi:10.1148/radiol.2020200905 PMID:32191588

Oyang, Y.-J., Hwang, S.-C., Ou, Y.-Y., Chen, C.-Y., & Chen, Z.-W. (2005). Data classification with radial basis function networks based on a novel kernel density estimation algorithm. *IEEE Transactions on Neural Networks*, 16(1), 225–236. doi:10.1109/TNN.2004.836229 PMID:15732402

Pan, F., Ye, T., Sun, P., Gui, S., Liang, B., Li, L., ... Zheng, C. (2020). Time Course of Lung Changes On Chest CT During Recovery From 2019 Novel Coronavirus (COVID-19) Pneumonia. *Radiology*. Advance online publication. doi:10.1148/radiol.2020200370 PMID:32053470

Randhawa, G. S., Soltysiak, M. P. M., El Roz, H., de Souza, C. P. E., Hill, K. A., & Kari, L. (2020). Machine learning using intrinsic genomic signatures for rapid classification of novel pathogens: COVID-19 case study. *bioRxiv*. doi:10.1101/2020.02.03.932350

Rao, A. S. R. S., & Vazquez, J. A. (2020). Identification of COVID-19 Can be Quicker through Artificial Intelligence framework using a Mobile Phone-Based Survey in the Populations when Cities/Towns Are under Quarantine. *Infection Control and Hospital Epidemiology*, *41*(7), 826–830. Advance online publication. doi:10.1017/ice.2020.61

Santosh, K. C. (2020). AI-Driven Tools for Coronavirus Outbreak: Need of Active Learning and Cross-Population Train/Test Models on Multitudinal/Multimodal Data. *Journal of Medical Systems*, *44*(5), 93. Advance online publication. doi:10.100710916-020-01562-1 PMID:32189081

Serbanescu, M. S. (2010). *A k-nearest neighbor approach for chromosome shape classification.* Academic Press.

Shen, C., Yu, N., Cai, S., Zhou, J., Sheng, J., Liu, K., Zhou, H., Guo, Y., & Niu, G. (2020). Quantitative computed tomography analysis for stratifying the severity of Coronavirus Disease 2019. *Journal of Pharmaceutical Analysis*, *10*(2), 123–129. Advance online publication. doi:10.1016/j.jpha.2020.03.004 PMID:32292624

Singhal, T. (2020). A Review of Coronavirus Disease-2019 (COVID-19). *Indian Journal of Pediatrics*, *87*(4), 281–286. Advance online publication. doi:10.100712098-020-03263-6 PMID:32166607

Sobti, P., Nayyar, A., & Nagrath, P. (2020, October). Time Series Forecasting for Coronavirus (COVID-19). In *International Conference on Futuristic Trends in Networks and Computing Technologies* (pp. 309-320). Springer.

Soni, R., Kumar, B., & Chand, S. (2019). Text detection and localization in natural scene images based on text awareness score. *Applied Intelligence*, *49*(4), 1376–1405. Advance online publication. doi:10.100710489-018-1338-4

Suganthan, N. (2019). COVID-19. *Jaffna Medical Journal.* doi:10.4038/jmj.v31i2.72

Tian, S., Hu, N., Lou, J., Chen, K., Kang, X., Xiang, Z., Chen, H., Wang, D., Liu, N., Liu, D., Chen, G., Zhang, Y., Li, D., Li, J., Lian, H., Niu, S., Zhang, L., & Zhang, J. (2020). Characteristics of COVID-19 infection in Beijing. *The Journal of Infection*, *80*(4), 401–406. Advance online publication. doi:10.1016/j.jinf.2020.02.018 PMID:32112886

Uddin, S., Khan, A., Hossain, M. E., & Moni, M. A. (2019). Comparing different supervised machine learning algorithms for disease prediction. *BMC Medical Informatics and Decision Making*, *19*(1), 281. Advance online publication. doi:10.118612911-019-1004-8 PMID:31864346

Wang, J. (2020). Procedures for health protection and control for COVID-19 during X-ray imaging examinations in Jiangsu province. *Chinese Journal of Radiological Medicine and Protection*.

Wang, S., Kang, B., Ma, J., Zeng, X., Xiao, M., Guo, J., & Xu, B. (2020). *A deep learning algorithm using CT images to screen for coronavirus disease (COVID-19)*. MedRxiv; doi:10.1101/2020.02.14.20023028

Xiong, Z., Fu, L., Zhou, H., Liu, J. K., Wang, A. M., Huang, Y., ... Liao, W. H. (2020). Construction and evaluation of a novel diagnosis process for 2019-Corona Virus Disease. *Zhonghua Yi Xue Za Zhi*. Advance online publication. doi:10.3760/cma.j.cn112137-20200228-00499 PMID:32157849

Yan, L., Zhang, H.-T., Xiao, Y., Wang, M., Sun, C., Liang, J., & Yuan, Y. (2020). *Prediction of survival for severe COVID-19 patients with three clinical features: development of a machine learning-based prognostic model with clinical data in Wuhan*. MedRxiv; doi:10.1101/2020.02.27.20028027

Zhang, Dong, Cao, Yuan, Dong, Yang, Bin, Qin, ... Gao. (2020). Clinical characteristics of 140 patients infected with SARS-CoV-2 in Wuhan, China. *Allergy: European Journal of Allergy and Clinical Immunology*. doi:10.1111/all.14238

Zivkovic, M., Bacanin, N., Venkatachalam, K., Nayyar, A., Djordjevic, A., Strumberger, I., & Al-Turjman, F. (2021). COVID-19 cases prediction by using hybrid machine learning and beetle antennae search approach. *Sustainable Cities and Society*, 66, 102669.

Chapter 11
Designing a Hybrid Approach for Web Recommendation Using Annotation

Sunny Sharma
University of Jammu, Kathua, India

Vijay Rana
Dr. Yashwant Singh Parmar University of Horticulture and Forestry, India

Vivek Kumar
Arni University, India

ABSTRACT

Web recommendation is the process of providing personalization recommendations to the requirements of specific users. A lot of research is conducted on recommender systems by a broad range of communities including computer scientists and interdisciplinary researchers. In response, a lot of recommender systems have been developed so far. However, the complexity of these systems can lead to information overload and decreased utility for the users. For these reasons, researchers have sought to apply the techniques of recommender systems to deliver personalized views of social annotation systems. In this chapter, the authors cover recent improvements in recommender systems and explore the major challenges. This chapter finally presents a prototype for adaptation to end-users. The model emphasizes an annotation-based recommendation system for generating recommendations.

DOI: 10.4018/978-1-7998-9012-6.ch011

Figure 1. Web mining

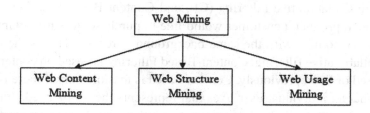

INTRODUCTION

With the abundant amount of data present on the web, it becomes very hectic for users to retrieve the intended information. At that time, prominent and sophisticated frameworks like Semantic Web and Web Recommender systems played a significant role to mine valuable information. The Semantic Web i.e. a web of information is an expansion of the current web which aims to make this huge information machine-understandable (Sharma et al., 2021). On the other side, Web recommender systems are advanced tools that are exploited to analyze the user behavior for generating recommendations. These information retrieval tools fall under Web Mining.

Web Mining is the process of providing useful and desired information from the web (Stumme et al., 2006; Aquin et al., 2011). It is enriched with the three mining standards which are depicted in figure 2. Web Content Mining (WCM), Usage Mining (WUM), and Web Structure Mining (WSM). Content Mining is the process of analyzing the contents of web pages. WSM is the process of mining the knowledge about the web pages like the ranking of web pages, how these web pages are interlinked with one another (Sharma et al., 2021). In WUM, information about a user is analyzed while the user surfs the web (Hug, 2020). This usage information is further used to predict the future needs of the user and for the neighboring users. Nevertheless, the abundant amount of information available on the web creates a challenge to both the customers and the companies. The customer is presented with multiple choices of products for a specific need which leads to product overload. Consequently, the need for computing-based advertising strategies like one-to-one marketing and Client Relationship Management (CRM) has been stressed by both researchers and companies. An effective strategy to overcome this product overload is by providing personalized web recommendations in which the user is interested.

Web Recommender Systems (Srivastava et al. 2009; Jannach et al., 2021; Webster et al., 2006) inherit a filtering process to predict the need of users which the users might tend to express. For instance, think of the Netflix model where the users are recommended the contents based on their past behaviors, or how products are shown on Amazon. A general view of such recommendation techniques is depicted in figure 1. The two most popular and recommended methods to make a recommender method are Collaborative Filtering (CF) and Content Based Filtering (CBF). To predict which product a customer would like to purchase, it is important to know what other customers with the same background purchase. This is the main idea behind collaborative filtering. Content-Based Filtering is based on content the user has browsed or liked previously. Content-based is feasible only if there is data that defines what an individual user likes that represents the user's needs (Gao, 2021; Beheshti et al., 2020). A hybrid recommender system can achieve better performance.

The necessity to integrate recommendation techniques is to achieve peak performance. Every known recommendation technique has advantages and disadvantages, and several researchers have decided to combine techniques in various ways. This article proposes a design of a novel hybrid recommendation technique and explores the spectrum of hybridization strategies that have been proposed, as well as the many recommendation techniques that are being explored. This paper is organized as follows: In Section 2, we present the state of art. The different techniques of web mining along with the concept of web personalization are presented. The existing work performed so far in the personalization field is described in Section 3. The motivation to work is presented in Section 4. In the Section 5, we demonstrate the working of our model for generating the recommendation. Finally, we draw conclusions in Section 6.

The significant commitment of this paper is:

1. To design an algorithm for content extraction.
2. To design a hybrid approach for personalized content recommendation.
3. Performance evaluation of proposed algorithm.

THE STATE OF ART: WEB MINING AND WEB PERSONALIZATION

Through the integration of various existing web technologies (like data mining, text mining, web mining, ontology expansion, and semantic personalization), the exponential improvement in web technologies has enabled web users to experience enhanced personalized services & information. The mixture of web mining techniques and techniques for web recommendations plays an essential role in these circumstances (Heidari, 2009).

Figure 2. Taxonomy of recommender system

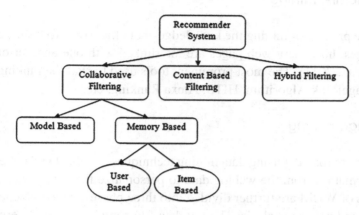

Web Mining

Web mining (WM) is the process of exploiting data mining as well as text mining techniques to retrieve information from the web. Due to the remarkable growth of information sources, this area of research is very popular today. With the amount of data increasing on the Internet every year, the techniques of data mining are employed to change this data into information. For this work, prominent data mining techniques like clustering, classification, association, statistical analysis, etc are used significantly for effective web analysis.

The three categories of Web Mining are also presented in this section. WCM is the method of analyzing the contents of the web pages whereas WSM is the process of mining the knowledge about the web pages like the ranking of a web page, how those web pages are interlinked with one another (Sharma et al., 2011). In WUM, information about a user is analyzed while the user surfs the web. This usage information is further used to predict the future needs of the user and for the neighboring users.

Web Content Mining

WCM is a process of analyzing the contents of web pages, images, videos, etc. The techniques of web content mining are comparable to text mining and data mining. The major difference is that in Web content mining, the data over the web is available in a semi- structured form.

Web Structure Mining

WSM is the process of mining the knowledge about the web pages such as ranking of web pages, how these web pages are interlinked with one another on the web (Sharma et al., 2011). The most prominent tools used to find the ranking of a web page are PageRank Algorithm, HITS, Alexa Ranking, etc.

Web Usage Mining

WUM is an approach of using data mining techniques to collect and understand the usage information from the weblog data to personalize the contents of a website. The phases of WUM are further divided into three phases: data collection, pattern discovery, and pattern analysis. The log data file contains usage patterns of users which can be stored either on the server-side or client-side. A log file contains information about a user like clicked documents, referrer pages, access time for a website, etc. By analyzing such data, a webmaster can conclude the lifetime value of customers. In WUM, all information about a user is analyzed while the user surfs the web. This usage information is further used to predict the future needs of the user and for the neighboring users. Nevertheless, the abundant amount of information available on the web creates a challenge to both the customers and the companies. The customer is presented with multiple choices of products for a specific need which leads to product overload. An effective strategy to overcome this product overload is by recommending personalized web recommendations in which the user is most interested.

Web Personalization

Web Personalization was presented over two decades back and many eminent researchers have presented various techniques to make the process of personalization as convenient as possible. Web Personalization research exploits many other research areas like Artificial Intelligence, Machine Learning, Natural Language Processing (NLP), and Web Mining. The whole process of web personalization can be described in three phases: Learning, Matching, and Recommendation. The Learning phase is further subdivided into two types: Implicit Learning and Explicit Learning. The second phase is matching. The matching phase includes filtration processes which are Collaborative Filtering (CF), Content-Based Filtering (CBF), Rule-Based and Hybrid Filtering. The last phase, the recommendation phase is responsible for providing the set of personalized results to the users. Web Recommender Systems (Burke, 2007; Sharma & Rana, 2017) inherit a filtering process to predict the need of users which the users might tend to express. For instance, think of Netflix models where the users are recommended the contents based on their past behaviors, or how products are shown on Amazon (Karimi et al., 2018) A general view of such recommendation techniques is depicted in figure 2. The two most popular and recommended approaches to building a recommender system are: Collaborative Filtering (CF) and Content-Based Filtering (CBF). To predict which product a customer would like to purchase, it is important to know what other customers with the same background purchase. This is the main idea behind collaborative filtering. Content-Based Filtering is based on content the user has browsed or liked previously.

BACKGROUND

A literature review is an important part of the research. It describes the work of researchers and highlights the research challenges which need to be addressed.

Malik et al. (Malik & Fyfe, 2012) describe web personalization in three different phases: Learning, Matching, and Recommendation. The Learning phase is further subdivided into two types: Implicit Learning and Explicit Learning. The second phase is matching. The matching phase includes filtration processes which are Collaborative Filtering (CF), Content-Based Filtering (CBF), and Hybrid Filtering. The last phase, the recommendation phase is responsible for providing the set of personalized results to the users.

Samaret et al. (2017) proposed an approach for emotion detection from text with keywords semantic similarity. In this supervised learning-based approach, the keywords are labeled with one of the six Ekman emotion categories with Ontology. The presented methodology depends on the syntax, semantic analysis, and meaning of each sentence.

Heidari et al. (2003) insist on the importance of semantic web technologies and emphasize that modern web technology has the ability to extremely encourage the prospect of improvement on the internet.

Santra A et al. (2012) proposed a personalization recommendation model. To improve the accuracy of the proposed model, optimization function and proposed evaluation are applied. Data mining techniques like the Naïve Bayes method and Neural Networks method are exploited to prove that the accuracy of prediction is better.

Wu F et al. (2015) aims to predict the user's behavior in some particular situation and subsequently offers personalized recommendations for example target ads, events, and movement prediction. More generally he focuses on mobile devices and modern positioning technology. The shared data on social media such as location-based tweets can generate data about some events and locations. The social media platforms such as Twitter, fb, foursquare generate abundant amounts of information.

Twitter alone generates 1 million geo-based tweets every day. These tweets can be used to predict the nature of an event, users visited location and the set of tweets can reveal the true purpose of a user to visit the particular place.

Ali et al. (2016) presented that available book recommender systems face several issues because most of these systems merely consider descriptions of the books along with Metadata. In response, the author developed a hybrid book recommender system that provides recommendations by using a table of contents along with association rule mining. The paper also urges that problems like cold start and Sparsity can be mitigated by using the proposed approach.

Hassan et al. (2015) proposed a semantic enhanced hybrid recommendation approach by incorporating the semantic of the items to the item-based collaborative filtering approach for improving the recommendation in E-government domains. Further, a new ontology-based semantic similarity approach is proposed to find the similarity between the ontology instances The authors finally show the efficiency of the framework by using a case study of Australian e-government tourism services. The evaluation of the results shows that the proposed study outperforms the competent approaches like recommendation results.

Sepliarskaia et al. (2017) described an approach for integrating the click behavior into the web ranking using click models as well page ranking approaches. The author presented that by training a click model, the proposed approach performs better than the existing approaches that rely on feature engineering.

Joseph et al. (2019) proposed the shortest entity distance algorithm based on content-based filtering for the recommending news. The author urged that the proposed algorithm performs better even in cold start examined conditions. Moreover, this entity distance algorithm also infers the highest correlation of graph traversal algorithms.

PROBLEM DEFINITION

Identifying the nature of the user is tedious due to the dynamic nature of the user. Web users often exhibit different intentions at different intervals of time. The Information Retrieval system needs to identify the nature of the user to filter out the irrelevant results.

Web 2.0 contains information in such a way that only humans can interpret the information precisely. But despite the abundant amount of information available on the web, humans can't touch all this information. So the solution is that information on the web must be stored in such a way that machines can understand the information. The Recommendation based web mining is operating on this idea. Despite the huge success of recommendation techniques, these techniques suffer from several limitations. Some challenges which are associated with Collaborative Filtering are

Table 1. Research gap

Year	Author	Objective	Technique	Characteristics/ Future Scope
2019	Joseph et al. (2020)	Recommends news using a content-based news recommendation system	Graph traversal algorithm, a human-annotated data set	The proposed algorithm is Limited to up to 2 context words.
2017	Sepliarskaia et al. (2017)	Improves content-based Web result ranking by considering personal behavioral signals	Global click frequency	The algorithm is applicable only for previously advanced pages.
2016	Ali & Ullah (2016)	Provides relevant book recommendations.	Opinions of similar users, Association Rule Mining, Collaborative Filtering.	The precision can be enhanced by incorporating ontology for user profiling.
2017	Fathy et al. (2017)	Finds the emotion Detection from Text using sentiment analysis.	Semantic Similarity, Text Mining	Find the emotion of text with help of the proposed algorithm
2016	Jiao (2016)	To improve the precision and recall measures by providing the accurate recommendations	Semantic quantitative analysis	Neural Network-based filtering is supposed to exploit in the future work
2015	Fei et al. (2015)	It presents a study on semantics behind people's movement, i.e., understanding what is the reason for a person to move to a location at a particular time.	Geo-tagged tweets, Kernel Density Estimation.	Location-aware Deep Collaborative Filtering can be used to provide better recommendations.
2015	Dou (2015)	To Improve data mining	Domain Knowledge, Semantic Similarity	It improves data mining by incorporating ontology
2012	Santra et al. (2012)	Studies the behavior of the interested users.	Naïve Bayes method and Neural Networks	With data on uncertain attributes, it is very complicated to construct decision tree classifiers.
2006	Warren et al. (2006)	Automatically Extract Meaningful Information	Web Personalization	Able to maintain knowledge in a dynamic environment
2001	Lee et al. (2001)	Provide Personalized Product Service	Collaborative Filtering, Naïve Bayes	It adopted collaborative filtering, data mining techniques

Cold Start Problem, Sparsity, and Scalability (Himeur et al., 2021). The quality of recommendations provided by these techniques is reduced due to these problems.

RESEARCH METHODOLOGY

The main purpose to implement a hybrid model (Behavior Evaluation and Web Personalization (BEWP)) is to tackle the challenges arising in CF and CBF techniques and thus produce accurate results. The ontology is used to save the user's interactions to the user profile. The user profile is utilized by content-based filtering techniques to provide recommendations. Ontology is acting as knowledge-based which maintains the data in a hierarchy and provides information about how the different type of data is interlinked with another. Recommending the web users with the relevant information based on user requirements is one of the important tasks of this approach. If these requirements are quickly familiar, the best recommendations can be offered to the user instantly.

Behavior Evaluation and Web Personalization (BEWP)

BEWP system comprises of four modules namely User Profiling Module (UIM), Content Processing Module (CPM), Context Similarity and Domain Analysis Module (CSDAM), and Pattern Discovery and Analysis Module (PDAM).

User Profiling (UP)

Web personalization is an intuitive way to personalize a website or provide personalizing results to the users according to their needs. The first step in web personalization is to identify a user on the web and to construct a user profile for an individual. User profiling is the process of collecting, extracting, and identifying structured information. There are two ways to perform user profiling: Implicit user profile and Explicit user profile. In implicit user profiles, the system automatically collects user information without user intervention. In contrast, while performing explicit user profiling, the users provide feedback to the system like ratings, name, place, gender, etc. User profiling assists recommendation systems to operate according to the user. Therefore user profiling is one of the most important steps to solve the problems of recommender systems.

Figure 3. High-level view of proposed approach

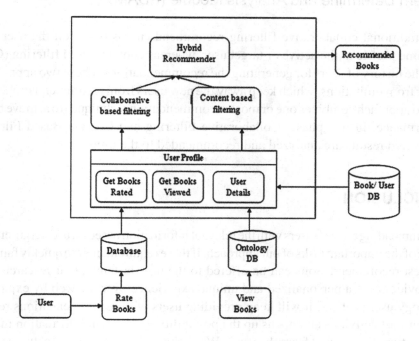

Content Processing Module (CPM)

After user profiling and identification of a user, the next step is content processing. The content-based technique requires proper methods for document representation, user profiling, and technique for comparing user-profiles and represented items. Content-based recommender systems require a technique for document representation for keyword matching. Our approach intends to exploit the Vector Space Model (VSM) with basic TF-IDF weighting. VSM is a basic method for representing text documents in space. In VSM, every document is represented by a vector in an n-dimensional space, where each term from the given document is assigned a dimension. More generally each document is viewed as a vector of term weights, where each weight in the document represents the correlation among the terms and the documents.

Context Similarity and Domain Analysis Module (CSDAM)

The third phase is CSDAM, where similarity measures are exploited for Collaborative Filtering as well as Content-Based filtering to find matching patterns.

Pattern Determine and Analysis Module (PDAM)

The traditional collaborative filtering recommends items based on the user with the same profile to the active or target user, whereas content-based filtering (CBF) uses the history of users for generating the recommendations. These two approaches suffer from limitations, which keep away the new users from recommendations. The hybrid approach combines one or more recommendation techniques to achieve better performance. In this phase, Collaborative Filtering and Content-Based Filtering discovered results are analyzed and recommended to the users.

CONCLUSION

Recommending the web users with the relevant information based on user requirements is one of the important tasks of our approach. If these requirements are quickly familiar, the best recommendations can be offered to the user instantly. Our research aims to provide users a personalized and unique experience over the web by exploiting ontology user profiles. It will keep providing users with recommendations related to their past activities and opens up the possibility that certain information may be unintentionally escaped from the users. We exclusively confine user feature vectors in this paper, neglecting the item side. If we can discover some connections between the items, we can add item regularization terms to our framework to increase prediction accuracy even further. In the future, this would be an interesting social search problem to explore.

REFERENCES

Al-Hassan, M., Lu, H., & Lu, J. (2015). A semantic enhanced hybrid recommendation approach: A case study of e-Government tourism service recommendation system. *Decision Support Systems*, *72*, 97–109. doi:10.1016/j.dss.2015.02.001

Ali, Z., Khusro, S., & Ullah, I. (2016, May). A hybrid book recommender system based on table of contents (toc) and association rule mining. In *Proceedings of the 10th International Conference on Informatics and Systems* (pp. 68-74). ACM. 10.1145/2908446.2908481

Aquin, D. (2011). Watson, more than a semantic web search engine. *Semantic Web*, *2*(1), 55–63. doi:10.3233/SW-2011-0031

Beheshti, A., Yakhchi, S., Mousaeirad, S., Ghafari, S. M., Goluguri, S. R., & Edrisi, M. A. (2020). Towards cognitive recommender systems. *Algorithms*, *13*(8), 176. doi:10.3390/a13080176

Burke, R. (2007). Hybrid web recommender systems. In *The adaptive web* (pp. 377–408). Springer. doi:10.1007/978-3-540-72079-9_12

Dou, D., Wang, H., & Liu, H. (2015, February). Semantic data mining: A survey of ontology-based approaches. In *Proceedings of the 2015 IEEE 9th international conference on semantic computing (IEEE ICSC 2015)* (pp. 244-251). IEEE. 10.1109/ICOSC.2015.7050814

Eirinaki, M., & Vazirgiannis, M. (2003). Web mining for web personalization. *ACM Transactions on Internet Technology*, *3*(1), 1–27. doi:10.1145/643477.643478

Fathy, S., El-Haggar, N., & Haggag, M. H. (2017). A Hybrid Model for Emotion Detection from Text. *International Journal of Information Retrieval Research*, *7*(1), 32–48. doi:10.4018/IJIRR.2017010103

Gao, C., Lei, W., He, X., de Rijke, M., & Chua, T. S. (2021). Advances and challenges in conversational recommender systems: A survey. *AI Open*, *2*, 100–126. doi:10.1016/j.aiopen.2021.06.002

Heidari, K. (2009). The impact of semantic web on e-commerce. *World Academy of Science, Engineering and Technology*, *51*.

Himeur, Y., Alsalemi, A., Al-Kababji, A., Bensaali, F., Amira, A., Sardianos, C., Dimitrakopoulos, G., & Varlamis, I. (2021). A survey of recommender systems for energy efficiency in buildings: Principles, challenges and prospects. *Information Fusion*, *72*, 1–21. doi:10.1016/j.inffus.2021.02.002

Hug, N. (2020). Surprise: A Python library for recommender systems. *Journal of Open Source Software*, *5*(52), 2174. doi:10.21105/joss.02174

Jannach, D., Manzoor, A., Cai, W., & Chen, L. (2021). A survey on conversational recommender systems. *ACM Computing Surveys*, *54*(5), 1–36. doi:10.1145/3453154

Jiao, M. H., Chen, X. F., Su, Z. H., & Chen, X. (2016, May). Research on personalized recommendation optimization of E-commerce system based on customer trade behaviour data. In *2016 Chinese Control and Decision Conference (CCDC)* (pp. 6506-6511). IEEE. 10.1109/CCDC.2016.7532169

Joseph, K., & Jiang, H. (2019, May). Content based news recommendation via shortest entity distance over knowledge graphs. In *Companion Proceedings of The 2019 World Wide Web Conference* (pp. 690-699). 10.1145/3308560.3317703

Karimi, M., Jannach, D., & Jugovac, M. (2018). News recommender systems–Survey and roads ahead. *Information Processing & Management, 54*(6), 1203–1227. doi:10.1016/j.ipm.2018.04.008

Lei, Y., Uren, V., & Motta, E. (2006, October). Semsearch: A search engine for the semantic web. In EKAW (Vol. 4248, pp. 238-245). doi:10.1007/11891451_22

Leung, K. W. T., Lee, D. L., & Lee, W. C. (2010, March). Personalized web search with location preferences. In *Data Engineering (ICDE), 2010 IEEE 26th International Conference on* (pp. 701-712). IEEE. 10.1109/ICDE.2010.5447911

Malik, Z. K., & Fyfe, C. (2012). Review of web personalization. *Journal of Emerging Technologies in Web Intelligence, 4*(3), 285–296. doi:10.4304/jetwi.4.3.285-296

Milano, S., Taddeo, M., & Floridi, L. (2020). Recommender systems and their ethical challenges. *AI & Society, 35*(4), 957–967. doi:10.100700146-020-00950-y

Santra, A. K., & Jayasudha, S. (2012). Classification of web log data to identify interested users using Naïve Bayesian classification. *International Journal of Computer Science Issues, 9*(1), 381.

Sepliarskaia, A., Radlinski, F., & de Rijke, M. (2017, April). Simple personalized search based on long-term behavioral signals. In *European Conference on Information Retrieval* (pp. 95-107). Springer. 10.1007/978-3-319-56608-5_8

Sharma, K., Shrivastava, G., & Kumar, V. (2011, April). Web mining: Today and tomorrow. In *Electronics Computer Technology (ICECT), 2011 3rd International Conference on* (Vol. 1, pp. 399-403). IEEE.

Sharma, S., & Rana, V. (2017). Web personalization through semantic annotation system. *Advances in Computational Sciences and Technology, 10*(6), 1683–1690.

Sharma, S., Rana, V., & Malhotra, M. (2021). Automatic recommendation system based on hybrid filtering algorithm. *Education and Information Technologies*, 1–16.

Srivastava, J., Cooley, R., Deshpande, M., & Tan, P. N. (2000). Web usage mining: Discovery and applications of usage patterns from web data. *SIGKDD Explorations, 1*(2), 12–23. doi:10.1145/846183.846188

Stumme, G., Hotho, A., & Berendit, B. (2006). Semantic Web Mining. *Semantic Web Mining, Elsevier, 4*(2), 124–143. doi:10.1016/j.websem.2006.02.001

Wang, S., Hu, L., Wang, Y., Cao, L., Sheng, Q. Z., & Orgun, M. (2019). *Sequential recommender systems: challenges, progress and prospects*. arXiv preprint arXiv:2001.04830. doi:10.24963/ijcai.2019/883

Webster, D., Huang, W., Mundy, D., & Warren, P. (2006, May). Context-orientated news filtering for web 2.0 and beyond. In *Proceedings of the 15th international conference on World Wide Web* (pp. 1001-1002). 10.1145/1135777.1135985

Wu, F., Li, Z., Lee, W. C., Wang, H., & Huang, Z. (2015, May). Semantic annotation of mobility data using social media. In *Proceedings of the 24th International Conference on World Wide Web* (pp. 1253-1263). 10.1145/2736277.2741675

Wu, F., Wang, H., Li, Z., Lee, W. C., & Huang, Z. (2015, May). SemMobi: A semantic annotation system for mobility data. In *Proceedings of the 24th International Conference on World Wide Web* (pp. 255-258). ACM. 10.1145/2740908.2742837

Compilation of References

Abbas, A., Abdelsamea, M. M., & Gaber, M. M. (2021). Classification of COVID-19 in chest X-ray images using DeTraC deep convolutional neural network. *Applied Intelligence*, *51*(2), 854–864. doi:10.100710489-020-01829-7 PMID:34764548

Abdel-Basset, M., Ding, W., & El-Shahat, D. (2021). A hybrid Harris Hawks optimization algorithm with simulated annealing for feature selection. *Artificial Intelligence Review*, *54*(1), 593–637.

Abouelkheir, M. (2018). Development of Dual Clutch Transmission model for Hybrid Vehicle. *International Journal of Innovative Technology and Interdisciplinary Sciences*, *1*(1), 26–33.

Afzulpurkar, N. (2019). New Approach for a Fault Detect Model-Based Controller. *International Journal of Innovative Technology and Interdisciplinary Sciences*, *2*(2), 160–172.

Aggarwal, P. K., & Sharma, S. (2021). Gaps Identification for User Experience for Model Driven Engineering. *Proceedings of the International Conference on Cloud Computing, Data Science & Engineering- Confluence*, 196-199.

Aggarwal, P. K., Jain, P., Chaudhary, P., Garg, R., Makar, K., & Mehta, J. (2021). AIIoT for Development of Test Standards for Agricultural Technology. In Intelligence of Things: AI-IoT Based Critical-Applications and Innovations (pp. 77-99). doi:10.1007/978-3-030-82800-4_4

Aggarwal, P. K., Jain, P., Mehta, J., Garg, R., Makar, K., & Chaudhary, P. (2021). Machine Learning, Data Mining and Big Data Analytics for 5G-Enabled IoT. In Blockchain for 5G enabled IoT: The new wave for Industrial Automation. Springer. doi:10.1007/978-3-030-67490-8_14

Aggarwal, P. K., Grover, P. S., & Ahuja, L. (2018). Exploring Quality Aspects of Smart Mobile Phones Applications. *Journal of Advanced Research in Dynamical and Control Systems*, *11*, 292–297.

Aggarwal, P. K., Grover, P. S., & Ahuja, L. (2018). Security Aspect in Instant Mobile Messaging Applications. *Proceedings of IEEE International Conference on Recent Advances on Engineering, Technology and Computational Sciences (RAETCS)*, 1-5. 10.1109/RAETCS.2018.8443844

Aggarwal, P. K., Grover, P. S., & Ahuja, L. (2019). Assessing Quality of Mobile Applications Based On a Hybrid MCDM Approach. *International Journal of Open Source Software and Processes*, *10*(3), 51–65. doi:10.4018/IJOSSP.2019070104

Aggarwal, P. K., & Jain, P. (2014). Adaptive approach for Information Hiding in WWW Pages. *Proceedings of International Conference on Issues and Challenges in Intelligent Computing Techniques (ICICT)*. 10.1109/ICICICT.2014.6781262

Agrawal, P., Sharma, T., & Verma, N. K. (2020). Supervised approach for object identification using speeded-up robust features. *International Journal of Advanced Intelligence Paradigms*, *15*(2), 165–182. doi:10.1504/IJAIP.2020.105142

Ahmad, J., Duraisamy, P., Yousef, A., & Buckles, B. (2017, July). Movie success prediction using data mining. In *2017 8th International Conference on Computing, Communication and Networking Technologies (ICCCNT)* (pp. 1-4). IEEE. 10.1109/ICCCNT.2017.8204173

Ahmed, K. B., Goldgof, G. M., Paul, R., Goldgof, D. B., & Hall, L. O. (2021). Discovery of a Generalization Gap of Convolutional Neural Networks on COVID-19 X-Rays Classification. *IEEE Access: Practical Innovations, Open Solutions*, *9*, 72970–72979. doi:10.1109/ACCESS.2021.3079716 PMID:34178559

Ahuja, R., Solanki, A., & Nayyar, A. (2019, January). Movie recommender system using K-Means clustering and K-Nearest Neighbor. In *2019 9th International Conference on Cloud Computing, Data Science & Engineering (Confluence)* (pp. 263-268). IEEE.

Ai, T., Yang, Z., Hou, H., Zhan, C., Chen, C., Lv, W., Tao, Q., Sun, Z., & Xia, L. (2020). Correlation of Chest CT and RT-PCR Testing in Coronavirus Disease 2019 (COVID-19) in China: A Report of 1014 Cases. *Radiology*, *296*(2), E32–E40. Advance online publication. doi:10.1148/radiol.2020200642 PMID:32101510

Alakus, T. B., & Turkoglu, I. (2020). Comparison of deep learning approaches to predict COVID-19 infection. *Chaos, Solitons, and Fractals*, *140*, 110120. doi:10.1016/j.chaos.2020.110120 PMID:33519109

Al-Hassan, M., Lu, H., & Lu, J. (2015). A semantic enhanced hybrid recommendation approach: A case study of e-Government tourism service recommendation system. *Decision Support Systems*, *72*, 97–109. doi:10.1016/j.dss.2015.02.001

Alici, N. K., & Copur, E. O. (n.d.). Anxiety and fear of COVID-19 among nursing students during the COVID-19 pandemic: A descriptive correlation study. *Perspectives in Psychiatric Care*.

Ali, M. M., Paul, B. K., Ahmed, K., Bui, F. M., Quinn, J. M., & Moni, M. A. (2021). Heart disease prediction using supervised machine learning algorithms: Performance analysis and comparison. *Computers in Biology and Medicine*, *136*, 104672.

Alimadadi, A., Aryal, S., Manandhar, I., Munroe, P. B., Joe, B., & Cheng, X. (2020). Artificial intelligence and machine learning to fight COVID-19. *Physiological Genomics*, *52*(4), 200–202. doi:10.1152/physiolgenomics.00029.2020 PMID:32216577

Ali, Z., Khusro, S., & Ullah, I. (2016, May). A hybrid book recommender system based on table of contents (toc) and association rule mining. In *Proceedings of the 10th International Conference on Informatics and Systems* (pp. 68-74). ACM. 10.1145/2908446.2908481

Al-Sarem, M., Saeed, F., Boulila, W., Emara, A. H., Al-Mohaimeed, M., & Errais, M. (2021). Feature selection and classification using CatBoost method for improving the performance of predicting Parkinson's disease. In *Advances on Smart and Soft Computing* (pp. 189–199). Springer.

Al-Turjman, F., Devi, A., & Nayyar, A. Emerging Technologies for Battling COVID-19. *Studies in Systems, Decision and Control*, 324.

Al-Waisy, A. S., Al-Fahdawi, S., Mohammed, M. A., Abdulkareem, K. H., Mostafa, S. A., Maashi, M. S., ... Garcia-Zapirain, B. (2020). COVID-CheXNet: Hybrid deep learning framework for identifying COVID-19 virus in chest X-rays images. *Soft Computing*, 1–16.

Alweshah, M., Khalaileh, S. A., Gupta, B. B., Almomani, A., Hammouri, A. I., & Al-Betar, M. A. (2020). The monarch butterfly optimization algorithm for solving feature selection problems. *Neural Computing & Applications*, 1–15.

Alzubi, J., Nayyar, A., & Kumar, A. (2018). Machine learning from theory to algorithms: an overview. In *Journal of physics: conference series*. IOP Publishing. doi:10.1088/1742-6596/1142/1/012012

Alzubi, J., Nayyar, A., & Kumar, A. (2018, November). Machine learning from theory to algorithms: An overview. *Journal of Physics: Conference Series*, *1142*(1), 012012.

Apostolakis, G. E. (2004). How useful is quantitative risk assessment? In Risk Analysis: An official publication of the Society for Risk Analysis. Wiley. doi:10.1111/j.0272-4332.2004.00455.x

Apostolopoulos, I. D., Aznaouridis, S. I., & Tzani, M. A. (2020). Extracting possibly representative COVID-19 biomarkers from X-ray images with deep learning approach and image data related to pulmonary diseases. *Journal of Medical and Biological Engineering*, *40*(3), 1. doi:10.100740846-020-00529-4 PMID:32412551

Apostolopoulos, I. D., & Mpesiana, T. A. (2020). Covid-19: Automatic detection from x-ray images utilizing transfer learning with convolutional neural networks. *Physical and Engineering Sciences in Medicine*, *43*(2), 635–640. doi:10.100713246-020-00865-4 PMID:32524445

Aquin, D. (2011). Watson, more than a semantic web search engine. *Semantic Web*, *2*(1), 55–63. doi:10.3233/SW-2011-0031

Arora, R., Bansal, V., Buckchash, H., Kumar, R., Sahayasheela, V. J., Narayanan, N., ... Raman, B. (2021). AI-based diagnosis of COVID-19 patients using X-ray scans with a stochastic ensemble of CNNs. *Physical and Engineering Sciences in Medicine*, 1-15.

Arora, T., & Dhir, R. (2016). Correlation Based Feature Selection & Classification Via Regression of Segmented Chromosomes using Geometric Features. *Medical & Biological Engineering & Computing*, *55*(5), 733–745. doi:10.100711517-016-1553-2 PMID:27474041

Arora, T., & Dhir, R. (2020). Geometric feature-based classification of segmented human chromosomes. *International Journal of Image and Graphics*, *20*(01), 2050006. Advance online publication. doi:10.1142/S0219467820500060

Aslan, H., & Pekince, H. (2021). Nursing students' views on the COVID-19 pandemic and their percieved stress levels. *Perspectives in Psychiatric Care, 57*(2), 695–701. doi:10.1111/ppc.12597 PMID:32808314

Aurelia, J. E., Rustam, Z., Wirasati, I., Hartini, S., & Saragih, G. S. (2021). Hepatitis classification using support vector machines and random forest. *IAES International Journal of Artificial Intelligence, 10*(2), 446.

Aven, T. (2012). The risk concept—Historical and recent development trends. *Reliability Engineering & System Safety, 99*, 33–44. doi:10.1016/j.ress.2011.11.006

Aven, T., & Krohn, B. S. (2014). A new perspective on how to understand, assess and manage risk and the unforeseen. *Reliability Engineering & System Safety, 121*, 1–10. doi:10.1016/j.ress.2013.07.005

Baclic, O., Tunis, M., Young, K., Doan, C., Swerdfeger, H., & Schonfeld, J. (2020). Artificial intelligence in public health: Challenges and opportunities for public health made possible by advances in natural language processing. *Canada Communicable Disease Report, 46*(6), 161–168. doi:10.14745/ccdr.v46i06a02 PMID:32673380

Bączek, M., Zagańczyk-Bączek, M., Szpringer, M., Jaroszyński, A., & Wożakowska-Kapłon, B. (2021). Students' perception of online learning during the COVID-19 pandemic: A survey study of Polish medical students. *Medicine, 100*(7), e24821. doi:10.1097/MD.0000000000024821 PMID:33607848

Bahadorian, M., Savkovic, B., Eston, R., & Hesketh, T. (2011). Toward a Robust Model Predictive Controller Applied to Mobile Vehicle Trajectory Tracking Control. *Proceedings of the 18th IFAC World Congress*, 552-557. 10.3182/20110828-6-IT-1002.01786

Bai, H. X., Hsieh, B., Xiong, Z., Halsey, K., Choi, J. W., Tran, T. M. L., Pan, I., Shi, L.-B., Wang, D.-C., Mei, J., Jiang, X.-L., Zeng, Q.-H., Egglin, T. K., Hu, P.-F., Agarwal, S., Xie, F.-F., Li, S., Healey, T., Atalay, M. K., & Liao, W.-H. (2020). Performance of radiologists in differentiating COVID-19 from viral pneumonia on chest CT. *Radiology, 296*(2), E46–E54. Advance online publication. doi:10.1148/radiol.2020200823 PMID:32155105

Bane, K. (n.d.). *Success of Bollywood Movie Using Machine Techniques: A Literature Review*. Academic Press.

Banwaskar, M. R., & Rajurkar, A. M. (2020). Creating Video Summary Using Speeded Up Robust Features. In *Applied Computer Vision and Image Processing* (pp. 308–317). Springer. doi:10.1007/978-981-15-4029-5_31

Barkur, G., Vibha, G. B. K., & Kamath, G. B. (2020). Sentiment analysis of nationwide lockdown due to COVID 19 outbreak: Evidence from India. *Asian Journal of Psychiatry, 51*, 102089. doi:10.1016/j.ajp.2020.102089 PMID:32305035

Basu, M., & Prasad, B. (2010). Long range variant of Fibonacci universal code. *Journal of Number Theory, 130*(9), 1925–1931. doi:10.1016/j.jnt.2010.01.013

Basu, S., Mitra, S., & Saha, N. (2020, December). Deep learning for screening covid-19 using chest x-ray images. In *2020 IEEE Symposium Series on Computational Intelligence (SSCI)* (pp. 2521-2527). IEEE. 10.1109/SSCI47803.2020.9308571

Beheshti, A., Yakhchi, S., Mousaeirad, S., Ghafari, S. M., Goluguri, S. R., & Edrisi, M. A. (2020). Towards cognitive recommender systems. *Algorithms*, *13*(8), 176. doi:10.3390/a13080176

Belingheri, M., Ausili, D., Paladino, M. E., Luciani, M., Di Mauro, S., & Riva, M. A. (2021). Attitudes towards COVID-19 vaccine and reasons for adherence or not among nursing students. *Journal of Professional Nursing*, *37*(5), 923–927. doi:10.1016/j.profnurs.2021.07.015 PMID:34742523

Bello, I., Zoph, B., Vasudevan, V., & Le, Q. V. (2017, July). Neural optimizer search with reinforcement learning. In *International Conference on Machine Learning* (pp. 459-468). PMLR.

Bengio, Y., & Grandvalet, Y. (2004). No Unbiased Estimator of the Variance of K-Fold Cross-Validation. *Journal of Machine Learning Research*, *5*, 1089–1105.

BenSaid, F., & Alimi, A. M. (2021). Online feature selection system for big data classification based on multi-objective automated negotiation. *Pattern Recognition*, *110*, 107629.

Bhave, A., Kulkarni, H., Biramane, V., & Kosamkar, P. (2015, January). Role of different factors in predicting movie success. In *2015 International Conference on Pervasive Computing (ICPC)* (pp. 1-4). IEEE.

Bichri, A., Kamzon, M. A., & Abderafi, S. (2020). Artificial neural network to predict the performance of the phosphoric acid production. *Procedia Computer Science*, *177*, 444–449.

Breiman, L. (2001). Random Forests. *Machine Learning*, *45*(1), 5–32. doi:10.1023/A:1010933404324

Bucelli, M., Paltrinieri, N., & Landucci, G. (2017). Integrated risk assessment for oil and gas installations in sensitive areas. *Ocean Engineering*, *150*, 377–390. doi:10.1016/j.oceaneng.2017.12.035

Bulut, F., & Amasyali, M. F. (2016). Katı kümeleme ve yeni bir geçiş fonksiyonuyla uzman karışımlarında sınıflandırma. *Gazi Üniversitesi Mühendislik Mimarlık Fakültesi Dergisi, 31*(4).

Bulut, F. (2021). Low dynamic range histogram equalization (LDR-HE) via quantized Haar wavelet transform. *The Visual Computer*, 1–17. doi:10.100700371-021-02281-5

Bulut, F. (2021b). Locally-Adaptive Naïve Bayes Framework Design via Density-Based Clustering for Large Scale Datasets. In *Handbook of Research on Machine Learning Techniques for Pattern Recognition and Information Security* (pp. 278–292). IGI Global. doi:10.4018/978-1-7998-3299-7.ch016

Bulut, F., & Erol, M. H. (2018). A real-time dynamic route control approach on google maps using integer programming methods. *International Journal of Next-Generation Computing*, *9*(3), 189–202.

Burke, R. (2007). Hybrid web recommender systems. In *The adaptive web* (pp. 377–408). Springer. doi:10.1007/978-3-540-72079-9_12

Cao, W., Fang, Z., Hou, G., Han, M., Xu, X., Dong, J., & Zheng, J. (2020). The psychological impact of the COVID-19 epidemic on college students in China. *Psychiatry Research*, *287*, 112934. doi:10.1016/j.psychres.2020.112934 PMID:32229390

Cervera-Gasch, Á., González-Chordá, V. M., & Mena-Tudela, D. (2020). COVID-19: Are Spanish medicine and nursing students prepared? *Nurse Education Today*, *92*, 104473. doi:10.1016/j.nedt.2020.104473 PMID:32497867

Chakraborty, K., Bhatia, S., Bhattacharyya, S., Platos, J., Bag, R., & Hassanien, A. E. (2020). Sentiment Analysis of COVID-19 tweets by Deep Learning Classifiers—A study to show how popularity is affecting accuracy in social media. *Applied Soft Computing*, *97*, 106754. doi:10.1016/j.asoc.2020.106754 PMID:33013254

Chaudhary, P., Goel, S., Jain, P., Singh, M., & Aggarwal, P. K. (2021). The Astounding Relationship: Middleware, Frameworks, and API. *Proceedings of the International Conference on Reliability, Infocom Technologies and Optimization (Trends and Future Directions) (ICRITO)*, 1-4.

Chau, H., & Karol, R. (2014). *Robust panoramic image stitching*. Department of Aeronautics and Astronautics Stanford University Stanford.

Cheng, H.-T., Koc, L., Harmsen, J., Shaked, T., Chandra, T., Aradhye, H., Anderson, G., Corrado, G., Chai, W., & Ispir, M. (2016). Wide & deep learning for recommender systems. In *Proceedings of the 1st Workshop on Deep Learning for Recommender Systems*. ACM. 10.1145/2988450.2988454

Chen, H., Moan, T., & Verhoeven, H. (2008). Safety of dynamic positioning operations on mobile offshore drilling units. *Reliability Engineering & System Safety*, *93*(7), 1072–1090. doi:10.1016/j.ress.2007.04.003

Chowdhury, G. G. (2003). Natural language processing. *Annual Review of Information Science & Technology*, *37*(1), 51–89. doi:10.1002/aris.1440370103

Chowdhury, M. E., Rahman, T., Khandakar, A., Mazhar, R., Kadir, M. A., Mahbub, Z. B., Islam, K. R., Khan, M. S., Iqbal, A., Emadi, N. A., Reaz, M. B. I., & Islam, M. T. (2020). Can AI help in screening viral and COVID-19 pneumonia? *IEEE Access: Practical Innovations, Open Solutions*, *8*, 132665–132676. doi:10.1109/ACCESS.2020.3010287

Chu, D. K., Pan, Y., Cheng, S. M., Hui, K. P., Krishnan, P., Liu, Y., Ng, D. Y. M., Wan, C. K. C., Yang, P., Wang, Q., Peiris, M., & Poon, L. L. (2020). Molecular diagnosis of a novel coronavirus (2019-nCoV) causing an outbreak of pneumonia. *Clinical Chemistry*, *66*(4), 549–555. doi:10.1093/clinchem/hvaa029 PMID:32031583

Çimen, C., Akleylek, S., & Akyıldız, E. (2007). Şifrelerin Matematiği: Kriptografi. Ankara: ODTÜ Yayıncılık.

Cizmeci, B., & Ögüdücü, Ş. G. (2018, September). Predicting IMDb ratings of pre-release movies with factorization machines using social media. In *2018 3rd International Conference on Computer Science and Engineering (UBMK)* (pp. 173-178). IEEE.

Cleland, J., McKimm, J., Fuller, R., Taylor, D., Janczukowicz, J., & Gibbs, T. (2020). Adapting to the impact of COVID-19: Sharing stories, sharing practice. *Medical Teacher, 42*(7), 772–775. doi:10.1080/0142159X.2020.1757635 PMID:32401079

Comfort, L. K. (2019). *The Dynamics of Risk: Changing Technologies, Complex Systems, and Collective Action in Seismic Policy.* Princeton University Press.

Coskunturk, Y. (2019). Design of a Robust Controller Using Sliding Mode for Two Rotor Aero-Dynamic System. *International Journal of Innovative Technology and Interdisciplinary Sciences, 2*(2), 119–132.

Creedy, G. D. (2011). Quantitative risk assessment: How realistic are those frequency assumptions? *Journal of Loss Prevention in the Process Industries, 24*(3), 203–207. doi:10.1016/j.jlp.2010.08.013

Dagher, I., & Nachar, R. (2006). Face recognition using IPCA-ICA algorithm. *IEEE Transactions on Pattern Analysis and Machine Intelligence, 28*(6), 996–1000. doi:10.1109/TPAMI.2006.118 PMID:16724592

Darekar, S., Kadam, P., Patil, P., Tawde, C., & Student, B. E. (2018). Movie Success Prediction based on Classical and Social Factors. *International Journal of Engineering Science and Computing,* 50-62.

De Gagne, J. C., Cho, E., Park, H. K., Nam, J. D., & Jung, D. (2021). A qualitative analysis of nursing students' tweets during the COVID-19 pandemic. *Nursing & Health Sciences, 23*(1), 273–278. doi:10.1111/nhs.12809 PMID:33404157

de Las Heras-Pedrosa, C., Sánchez-Núñez, P., & Peláez, J. I. (2020). Sentiment analysis and emotion understanding during the COVID-19 pandemic in Spain and its impact on digital ecosystems. *International Journal of Environmental Research and Public Health, 17*(15), 5542. doi:10.3390/ijerph17155542 PMID:32751866

De Marchi, B., & Ravetz, J. R. (1999). Risk management and governance: A post-normal science approach. *Futures, 31*(7), 743–757. doi:10.1016/S0016-3287(99)00030-0

Devi, A., & Nayyar, A. (2021). Perspectives on the Definition of Data Visualization: A Mapping Study and Discussion on Coronavirus (COVID-19) Dataset. *Emerging Technologies for Battling Covid-19: Applications and Innovations,* 223-240.

Devi, A., & Nayyar, A. (2021). Perspectives on the Definition of Data Visualization: A Mapping Study and Discussion on Coronavirus (COVID-19) Dataset. In *Emerging Technologies for Battling Covid-19* (pp. 223–240). Springer. doi:10.1007/978-3-030-60039-6_11

Devlin, J., Chang, M. W., Lee, K., & Toutanova, K. (2018). *BERT: Pre-training of deep bidirectional transformers for language understanding.* arXiv preprint arXiv:1810.04805.

Dhir, R., & Raj, A. (2018, December). Movie success prediction using machine learning algorithms and their comparison. In *2018 First International Conference on Secure Cyber Computing and Communication (ICSCCC)* (pp. 385-390). IEEE.

Diekmann, E. J. (1992). Risk analysis: Lessons from artificial intelligence. *International Journal of Project Management, 10*(2), 75–80. doi:10.1016/0263-7863(92)90059-I

Diffie, W., & Hellman, M. E. (1976). New Directions In Cryptography. *IEEE Transactions on Information Theory, 22*(6), 644–654. doi:10.1109/TIT.1976.1055638

Dos Santos, L. M. (2020). How does COVID-19 pandemic influence the sense of belonging and decision-making process of nursing students: The study of nursing students' experiences. *International Journal of Environmental Research and Public Health, 17*(15), 5603. doi:10.3390/ijerph17155603 PMID:32756506

Dou, D., Wang, H., & Liu, H. (2015, February). Semantic data mining: A survey of ontology-based approaches. In *Proceedings of the 2015 IEEE 9th international conference on semantic computing (IEEE ICSC 2015)* (pp. 244-251). IEEE. 10.1109/ICOSC.2015.7050814

Durga Rao, K., Gopika, V., Sanyasi Rao, V. V. S., Kushwaha, H. S., Verma, A. K., & Srividya, A. (2009). Dynamic fault tree analysis using Monte Carlo simulation in probabilistic safety assessment. *Reliability Engineering & System Safety, 94*(4), 872–883. doi:10.1016/j.ress.2008.09.007

Edson, M., & Yayenie, O. (2009). A New Generalization of Fibonacci Sequence Extended Binet's Formula. *Integers: Electronic Journal of Combinatorial Number Theory, 9*(6), 639–654. doi:10.1515/INTEG.2009.051

Ehatisham-ul-Haq, M., Malik, M. N., Azam, M. A., Naeem, U., Khalid, A., & Ghazanfar, M. A. (2020). Identifying Users with Wearable Sensors based on Activity Patterns. *Procedia Computer Science, 177*, 8–15.

Ehrlich, A. (1989). On the Periods of the Fibonacci Sequence Modulo M. *Fibonacci Quarterly, 27*, 11–13.

Eirinaki, M., & Vazirgiannis, M. (2003). Web mining for web personalization. *ACM Transactions on Internet Technology, 3*(1), 1–27. doi:10.1145/643477.643478

El Asnaoui, K., Chawki, Y., & Idri, A. (2021). Automated methods for detecting and classifying pneumonia based on x-ray images using deep learning. In *Artificial Intelligence and Blockchain for Future Cybersecurity Applications* (pp. 257–284). Springer.

ElGamal, T. (1985). A public key cryptosystem and a signature scheme based on discrete logarithms. *IEEE Transactions on Information Theory, 31*(4), 469–472. doi:10.1109/TIT.1985.1057074

El-Hasnony, I. M., Barakat, S. I., Elhoseny, M., & Mostafa, R. R. (2020). Improved feature selection model for big data analytics. *IEEE Access: Practical Innovations, Open Solutions, 8*, 66989–67004.

El-Kassar, A. N., Haraty, R. A., Awad, Y. A., & Debnath, N. C. (2005, November). Modified RSA in the Domains of Gaussian Integers and Polynomials Over Finite Fields. In CAINE (pp. 298-303). Academic Press.

El-Kassar, A. N., & Haraty, R. A. (2005). ElGamal Public-Key cryptosystem in multiplicative groups of quotient rings of polynomials over finite fields. *Computer Science and Information Systems*, 2(1), 63–77. doi:10.2298/CSIS0501063E

Ellis, W. E., Dumas, T. M., & Forbes, L. M. (2020). Physically isolated but socially connected: Psychological adjustment and stress among adolescents during the initial COVID-19 crisis. *Canadian Journal of Behavioural Science/Revue Canadienne des Sciences du Comportement*, 52(3), 177.

Erol, M. H., & Bulut, F. (2017, April). Real-time application of travelling salesman problem using Google Maps API. In 2017 Electric Electronics, Computer Science, Biomedical Engineerings' Meeting (EBBT) (pp. 1-5). IEEE. doi:10.1109/EBBT.2017.7956764

Falcone, P., Borrelli, F., Tseng, H., Asgari, J., & Hrovat, D. (2008). A Hierarchical Model Predictive Control Framework for Autonomous Ground Vehicles. *American Control Conference*, 3719-3724. 10.1109/ACC.2008.4587072

Falcon, S., & Plaza, A. (2007). On the Fibonacci $k-$. *Chaos, Solitons, and Fractals*, 32(5), 1615–1624. doi:10.1016/j.chaos.2006.09.022

Fang, Y., Zhang, H., Xie, J., Lin, M., Ying, L., Pang, P., & Ji, W. (2020). Sensitivity of chest CT for COVID-19: Comparison to RT-PCR. *Radiology*, 296(2), E115–E117. doi:10.1148/radiol.2020200432 PMID:32073353

Fathy, S., El-Haggar, N., & Haggag, M. H. (2017). A Hybrid Model for Emotion Detection from Text. *International Journal of Information Retrieval Research*, 7(1), 32–48. doi:10.4018/IJIRR.2017010103

Feldman, R. (2013). Techniques and applications for sentiment analysis. *Communications of the ACM*, 56(4), 82–89. doi:10.1145/2436256.2436274

Friedman, N., Geiger, D., & Goldszmit, M. (1997). Bayesian Network Classifiers. *Machine Learning*, 29(2/3), 131–163. doi:10.1023/A:1007465528199

Gaikar, D. D., Marakarkandy, B., & Dasgupta, C. (2015). Using Twitter data to predict the performance of Bollywood movies. *Industrial Management & Data Systems*.

Gaikar, D., Solanki, R., Shinde, H., Phapale, P., & Pandey, I. (2019). Movie Success Prediction Using Popularity Factor from Social Media. *International Research Journal of Engineering and Technology*, 6(4), 5184–5190.

Gao, C., Lei, W., He, X., de Rijke, M., & Chua, T. S. (2021). Advances and challenges in conversational recommender systems: A survey. *AI Open*, 2, 100–126. doi:10.1016/j.aiopen.2021.06.002

Germany, D. S., Goldbaum, M., Cai, W., Valentim, C. C., Liang, H., Baxter, S. L., ... Zhang, K. (2018). Identifying medical diagnoses and treatable diseases by image-based deep learning. *Cell*, *172*(5), 1122–1131. doi:10.1016/j.cell.2018.02.010 PMID:29474911

Ghazali, K. H., Mansor, M. F., Mustafa, M. M., & Hussain, A. (2007, December). Feature extraction technique using discrete wavelet transform for image classification. In *2007 5th Student Conference on Research and Development* (pp. 1-4). IEEE. 10.1109/SCORED.2007.4451366

Goodfellow, I. J., Bengio, Y., & Courville, A. (2016). *Deep Learning*. The MIT Press.

Google's Street Photos. (2021). https://www.google.com/streetview/explore/

Gorbalenya, A. E. (2020). Severe acute respiratory syndrome-related coronavirus – The species and its viruses, a statement of the Coronavirus Study Group. *bioRxiv*. doi:10.1101/2020.02.07.937862

Gupta, S., Thakur, K., & Kumar, M. (2020). 2D-human face recognition using SIFT and SURF descriptors of face's feature regions. *The Visual Computer*, 1–10.

Hall, M. (1999). *Correlation-based feature selection for machine learning* [Ph.D. Thesis]. Department of Computer Science, Waikato University, New Zealand.

Hastie, T., Tibshirani, R., & Friedman, J. (2009). Unsupervised learning. In *The Elements of Statistical Learning* (pp. 485–585). Springer. doi:10.1007/978-0-387-84858-7_14

Haugen, S., & Vinnem, J. E. (2015). Perspectives on risk and the unforeseen. *Reliability Engineering & System Safety*, *137*, 1–5. doi:10.1016/j.ress.2014.12.009

Hauge, S., Okstad, E., Paltrinieri, N., Edwin, N., Vatn, J., & Bodsberg, L. (2015). *Handbook for monitoring of barrier status and associated risk in the operational phase*. Center for Integrated Operations in the Petroleum Industry.

Heidari, K. (2009). The impact of semantic web on e-commerce. *World Academy of Science, Engineering and Technology*, 51.

Hemmatian, F., & Sohrabi, M. K. (2019). A survey on classification techniques for opinion mining and sentiment analysis. *Artificial Intelligence Review*, *52*(3), 1495–1545. doi:10.100710462-017-9599-6

Himeur, Y., Alsalemi, A., Al-Kababji, A., Bensaali, F., Amira, A., Sardianos, C., Dimitrakopoulos, G., & Varlamis, I. (2021). A survey of recommender systems for energy efficiency in buildings: Principles, challenges and prospects. *Information Fusion*, *72*, 1–21. doi:10.1016/j.inffus.2021.02.002

Horadam, A. F. (1965). Basic Properties of A Certain Generalized Sequence of Numbers. *The Fibonacci Quaterly*, *3*(3), 161–176.

Horry, M. J., Chakraborty, S., Paul, M., Ulhaq, A., Pradhan, B., Saha, M., & Shukla, N. (2020). COVID-19 detection through transfer learning using multimodal imaging data. *IEEE Access: Practical Innovations, Open Solutions, 8*, 149808–149824. doi:10.1109/ACCESS.2020.3016780 PMID:34931154

Hug, N. (2020). Surprise: A Python library for recommender systems. *Journal of Open Source Software, 5*(52), 2174. doi:10.21105/joss.02174

Hutto, C., & Gilbert, E. (2014). VADER: A parsimonious rule-based model for sentiment analysis of social media text. In *Proceedings of the International AAAI Conference on Web and Social Media* (*Vol. 8*, No. 1). AAAI.

Hwang, M. S., Chang, C. C., & Hwang, K. F. (2002). An ElGamal-like cryptosystem for enciphering large messages. *IEEE Transactions on Knowledge and Data Engineering, 14*(2), 445–446. doi:10.1109/69.991728

Ide, J., & Renault, M. S. (2012). Power Fibonacci Sequences. *The Fibonacci Quarterly, 50*(2), 175–180.

Ince, I. F., & Bulut, F. (2021). A Novel Image Segmentation Technique for Medical Decision Support Systems: Osteoarthritis (Oa) Knee Abnormality Detection from Hazy X-Ray Images Through Polygon Construction. *Advances in Machinery And Digitization, 1*, 79–104.

Ince, I. F., Ince, O. F., & Bulut, F. (2019). MID Filter: An Orientation-Based Nonlinear Filter For Reducing Multiplicative Noise. *Electronics (Basel), 8*(9), 936. doi:10.3390/electronics8090936

Israel, O. (2019). Study on Modeling and Simulation of HEV for Optimal Fuel Economy. *International Journal of Innovative Technology and Interdisciplinary Sciences, 2*(2), 133–146.

J, P. (1998). *Sequential minimal optimization: a fast algorithm for training support vector machines.* Academic Press.

Jain, P., Aggarwal, P. K., Chaudhary, P., Makar, K., Mehta, J., & Garg, R. (2021). Convergence of IoT and CPS in Robotics. In Emergence of Cyber Physical Systems and IoT in Smart Automation and Robotics. Springer. doi:10.1007/978-3-030-66222-6_2

Jain, P., Sharma, A., & Ahuja, L. (2018). The Impact of Agile Software Development Process on the quality of Software Product. *Proceedings of the International Conference on Reliability, Infocom Technologies and Optimization (Trends and Future Directions) (ICRITO)*, 812-815. 10.1109/ICRITO.2018.8748529

Jain, A., & Nayyar, A. (2020). Machine learning and its applicability in networking. In *New age analytics* (pp. 57–79). Apple Academic Press.

Jain, P., Sharma, A., & Aggarwal, P. K. (2020). Key Attributes for a Quality Mobile Application. *Proceedings of the International Conference on Cloud Computing, Data Science & Engineering Confluence*, 50-54. 10.1109/Confluence47617.2020.9058278

Jain, P., Sharma, A., Aggarwal, P. K., Makar, K., Shrivastava, V., & Maitrey, S. (2020). Machine Learning for Web Development: A Fusion. *Proceedings of 2nd International Conference on AI and Speech Technology.*

Jain, P., & Sharma, S. (2019). Prioritizing Factors Used in Designing of Test Cases: An ISM-MICMAC Based Analysis. *Proceedings of International Conference on Issues and Challenges in Intelligent Computing Techniques (ICICT).* 10.1109/ICICT46931.2019.8977643

Jain, P., Singhal, A., Chawla, D., & Shrivastava, V. (2020). Image Recognition and Segregation using Image Processing Techniques. *TEST Engineering and Management, 83,* 2404–2410.

Jakubović, A., & Velagić, J. (2018, September). Image feature matching and object detection using brute-force matches. In *2018 International Symposium ELMAR* (pp. 83-86). IEEE. 10.23919/ELMAR.2018.8534641

Jamshidi, M., Lalbakhsh, A., Talla, J., Peroutka, Z., Hadjilooei, F., Lalbakhsh, P., Jamshidi, M., La Spada, L., Mirmozafari, M., Dehghani, M., & Sabet, A. (2020). Artificial intelligence and COVID-19: Deep learning approaches for diagnosis and treatment. *IEEE Access: Practical Innovations, Open Solutions, 8,* 109581–109595. doi:10.1109/ACCESS.2020.3001973 PMID:34192103

Jannach, D., Manzoor, A., Cai, W., & Chen, L. (2021). A survey on conversational recommender systems. *ACM Computing Surveys, 54*(5), 1–36. doi:10.1145/3453154

Jiang, X., Coffee, M., Bari, A., Wang, J., Jiang, X., Huang, J., Shi, J., Dai, J., Cai, J., Zhang, T., Wu, Z., He, G., & Huang, Y. (2020). Towards an Artificial Intelligence Framework for Data-Driven Prediction of Coronavirus Clinical Severity. doi:10.32604/cmc.2020.010691

Jiao, M. H., Chen, X. F., Su, Z. H., & Chen, X. (2016, May). Research on personalized recommendation optimization of E-commerce system based on customer trade behaviour data. In *2016 Chinese Control and Decision Conference (CCDC)* (pp. 6506-6511). IEEE. 10.1109/CCDC.2016.7532169

Jin, C., Chen, W., Cao, Y., Xu, Z., Tan, Z., Zhang, X., Deng, L., Zheng, C., Zhou, J., Shi, H., & Feng, J. (2020). Development and evaluation of an artificial intelligence system for COVID-19 diagnosis. *Nature Communications, 11*(1), 1–14. doi:10.103841467-020-18685-1 PMID:33037212

Joseph, K., & Jiang, H. (2019, May). Content based news recommendation via shortest entity distance over knowledge graphs. In *Companion Proceedings of The 2019 World Wide Web Conference* (pp. 690-699). 10.1145/3308560.3317703

Jurafsky, D., & Martin, J. H. (2020). *Speech and language processing: An introduction to natural language processing, computational linguistics, and speech recognition.* Prentice Hall.

Kaplan, S., & Garrick, B. J. (1981). On the quantitative definition of risk. *Risk Analysis, 1*(1), 11–27. doi:10.1111/j.1539-6924.1981.tb01350.x PMID:11798118

Karar, M. E., Hemdan, E. E. D., & Shouman, M. A. (2021). Cascaded deep learning classifiers for computer-aided diagnosis of COVID-19 and pneumonia diseases in X-ray scans. *Complex & Intelligent Systems*, *7*(1), 235–247. doi:10.100740747-020-00199-4 PMID:34777953

Karimi, M., Jannach, D., & Jugovac, M. (2018). News recommender systems–Survey and roads ahead. *Information Processing & Management*, *54*(6), 1203–1227. doi:10.1016/j.ipm.2018.04.008

Karim, M. R., Döhmen, T., Cochez, M., Beyan, O., Rebholz-Schuhmann, D., & Decker, S. (2020, December). DeepCOVIDExplainer: Explainable COVID-19 diagnosis from chest X-ray images. In *2020 IEEE International Conference on Bioinformatics and Biomedicine (BIBM)* (pp. 1034-1037). IEEE. 10.1109/BIBM49941.2020.9313304

Kashif, M., Deserno, T. M., Haak, D., & Jonas, S. (2016). Feature description with SIFT, SURF, BRIEF, BRISK, or FREAK? A general question answered for bone age assessment. *Computers in Biology and Medicine*, *68*, 67–75. doi:10.1016/j.compbiomed.2015.11.006 PMID:26623943

Kassania, S. H., Kassanib, P. H., Wesolowskic, M. J., Schneidera, K. A., & Detersa, R. (2021). Automatic detection of coronavirus disease (COVID-19) in X-ray and CT images: A machine learning-based approach. *Biocybernetics and Biomedical Engineering*, *41*(3), 867–879. doi:10.1016/j.bbe.2021.05.013 PMID:34108787

Katusin, N. (2019). Glove for Augmented and Virtual Reality. *International Journal of Innovative Technology and Interdisciplinary Sciences*, *2*(2), 147–159.

Kaur, A., & Kaur, A. G. (2013). Predicting Movie Success: Review of Existing Literature. *International Journal of Advanced Research in Computer Science and Software Engineering*, *3*(6), 1694–1697.

Keles, A., Keles, M. B., & Keles, A. (2021). COV19-CNNet and COV19-ResNet: Diagnostic inference Engines for early detection of COVID-19. *Cognitive Computation*, 1–11. doi:10.100712559-020-09795-5 PMID:33425046

Khakzad, N. (2015). Application of dynamic Bayesian network to risk analysis of domino effects in chemical infrastructures. *Reliability Engineering & System Safety*, *138*, 263–272. doi:10.1016/j.ress.2015.02.007

Khakzad, N., Khan, F., & Amyotte, P. (2013a). Risk-based design of process systems using discrete-time Bayesian networks. *Reliability Engineering & System Safety*, *109*, 5–17. doi:10.1016/j.ress.2012.07.009

Khakzad, N., Khan, F., & Amyotte, P. (2013b). Quantitative risk analysis of offshore drilling operations: A Bayesian approach. *Safety Science*, *57*, 108–117. doi:10.1016/j.ssci.2013.01.022

Khalifa, N. E. M., Manogaran, G., Taha, M. H. N., & Loey, M. (2021). A deep learning semantic segmentation architecture for COVID-19 lesions discovery in limited chest CT datasets. *Expert Systems: International Journal of Knowledge Engineering and Neural Networks*, 12742. doi:10.1111/exsy.12742 PMID:34177038

Khan, A. I., Shah, J. L., & Bhat, M. M. (2020). CoroNet: A deep neural network for detecting and diagnosing COVID-19 from chest x-ray images. *Computer Methods and Programs in Biomedicine*, *196*, 105581. doi:10.1016/j.cmpb.2020.105581 PMID:32534344

Khandelwal, R., & Virwani, H. (2019, February). Comparative analysis for prediction of success of bollywood movie. In *Proceedings of International Conference on Sustainable Computing in Science, Technology and Management (SUSCOM)*. Amity University Rajasthan.

King, G., & Zeng, L. (2001). Logistic regression in rare events data. *Political Analysis*, *9*(2), 137–163. doi:10.1093/oxfordjournals.pan.a004868

Klein, A. Z., Magge, A., O'Connor, K., Amaro, J. I. F., Weissenbacher, D., & Hernandez, G. G. (2021). Toward using Twitter for tracking COVID-19: A natural language processing pipeline and exploratory data set. *Journal of Medical Internet Research*, *23*(1), e25314. doi:10.2196/25314 PMID:33449904

Klein, S. T., & Ben-Nissan, M. K. (2010). On the usefulness of Fibonacci Compression Codes. *The Computer Journal*, *53*(6), 701–716. doi:10.1093/comjnl/bxp046

Kongsvik, T., Almklov, P., Haavik, T., Haugen, S., Vinnem, J. E., & Schiefloe, P. M. (2015). Decisions and decision support for major accident prevention in the process industries. *Journal of Loss Prevention in the Process Industries*, *35*, 85–94. doi:10.1016/j.jlp.2015.03.018

Koshy, T. (2001). *Fibonacci and Lucas Numbers with Applications*. Wiley. doi:10.1002/9781118033067

Küçük, E. E., Takır, S., & Küçük, D. (2021). Controversy detection on health-related tweets. In *Proceedings of the 14th International Symposium on Health Informatics and Bioinformatics* (p. 60). Academic Press.

Küçük, D. (2017). Stance detection in Turkish tweets. *Proceedings of the International Workshop on Social Media World Sensors (SIDEWAYS) of ACM Hypertext Conference*.

Küçük, D. (2021). Sentiment, stance, and intent detection in Turkish tweets. In *New Opportunities for Sentiment Analysis and Information Processing* (pp. 206–217). IGI Global. doi:10.4018/978-1-7998-8061-5.ch011

Küçük, D., & Arıcı, N. (2018). Doğal dil işlemede derin öğrenme uygulamaları üzerine bir literatür çalışması [A literature study on deep learning applications in natural language processing]. *Uluslararası Yönetim Bilişim Sistemleri ve Bilgisayar Bilimleri Dergisi*, *2*(2), 76–86.

Küçük, E. E., Yapar, K., Küçük, D., & Küçük, D. (2017). Ontology-based automatic identification of public health-related Turkish tweets. *Computers in Biology and Medicine*, *83*, 1–9. doi:10.1016/j.compbiomed.2017.02.001 PMID:28187367

Kudagamage, U. P., Kumara, B. T. G. S., & Baduraliya, C. H. (2018). Data mining approach to analysis and prediction of movie success. *International Conference on Business Innovation (ICOBI)*.

Kumar, A., Sangwan, S. R., & Nayyar, A. (2020). Multimedia social big data: Mining. In *Multimedia big data computing for IoT applications* (pp. 289–321). Springer. doi:10.1007/978-981-13-8759-3_11

Kumar, A., Sharma, K., Singh, H., Srikanth, P., Krishnamurthi, R., & Nayyar, A. (2021). Drone-Based Social Distancing, Sanitization, Inspection, Monitoring, and Control Room for COVID-19. In *Artificial Intelligence and Machine Learning for COVID-19* (pp. 153–173). Springer. doi:10.1007/978-3-030-60188-1_8

Küpeli, C., & Bulut, F. (2020). Görüntüdeki Tuz Biber ve Gauss Gürültülerine Karşı Filtrelerin Performans Analizleri. *Haliç Üniversitesi Fen Bilimleri Dergisi, 3*(2), 211–239.

Laguarta, J., Hueto, F., & Subirana, B. (2020). COVID-19 artificial intelligence diagnosis using only cough recordings. *IEEE Open Journal of Engineering in Medicine and Biology, 1*, 275–281. doi:10.1109/OJEMB.2020.3026928 PMID:34812418

Landucci, G., & Paltrinieri, N. (2016a). A methodology for frequency tailorization dedicated to the Oil & Gas sector. *Process Safety and Environmental Protection, 104*, 123–141. doi:10.1016/j.psep.2016.08.012

Landucci, G., & Paltrinieri, N. (2016b). Dynamic evaluation of risk: From safety indicators to proactive techniques. *Chemical Engineering Transactions, 53*, 169–174.

Lasi, H., Fettke, P., Kemper, H.-G., Feld, T., & Hoffmann, M. (2014). Industry 4.0. *Business & Information Systems Engineering, 6*(4), 239–242. doi:10.100712599-014-0334-4

Latif, M. H., & Afzal, H. (2016). Prediction of movies popularity using machine learning techniques. *International Journal of Computer Science and Network Security, 16*(8), 127.

Laumond, J. (1998). Robot Motion Planning and Control. In Feedback Control of a Nonholonomic Car-like Robot. Springer-Verlag.

Lee, G.Y. (2000). Fibonacci k − Lucas Numbers and Associated Bipartite Graphs. *Lineer Algebra and its Applications, 320*, 51–61.

Lee, K., Park, J., Kim, I., & Choi, Y. (2018). Predicting movie success with machine learning techniques: Ways to improve accuracy. *Information Systems Frontiers, 20*(3), 577–588.

Lei, L., Zhurong, J., Tingting, C., & Xinchung, J. (2011). Optimal Model Predictive Control for Path Tracking of Autonomous Vehicle. *3rd International Conference on Measuring Technology and Mechatronics Automation*, 791-794. 10.1109/ICMTMA.2011.481

Lei, Y., Uren, V., & Motta, E. (2006, October). Semsearch: A search engine for the semantic web. In EKAW (Vol. 4248, pp. 238-245). doi:10.1007/11891451_22

Lek, S., & Park, Y. S. (2008). Multilayer Perceptron. In Encyclopedia of Ecology (pp. 2455–2462). doi:10.1016/B978-008045405-4.00162-2

Leung, K. W. T., Lee, D. L., & Lee, W. C. (2010, March). Personalized web search with location preferences. In *Data Engineering (ICDE), 2010 IEEE 26th International Conference on* (pp. 701-712). IEEE. 10.1109/ICDE.2010.5447911

Li, Y. A., Shen, Y. J., Zhang, G. D., Yuan, T., Xiao, X. J., & Xu, H. L. (2010, May). An efficient 3D face recognition method using geometric features. In *2010 2nd International Workshop on Intelligent Systems and Applications* (pp. 1-4). IEEE.

Liang, T. (2020). Handbook of COVID-19 prevention and treatment. The First Affiliated Hospital, Zhejiang University School of Medicine.

Li, L., Qin, L., Xu, Z., Yin, Y., Wang, X., Kong, B., ... Xia, J. (2020). Artificial Intelligence Distinguishes COVID-19 from Community-Acquired Pneumonia on Chest CT. *Radiology*. Advance online publication. doi:10.1148/radiol.2020200905 PMID:32191588

Li, M., Wang, H., Yang, L., Liang, Y., Shang, Z., & Wan, H. (2020). Fast hybrid dimensionality reduction method for classification based on feature selection and grouped feature extraction. *Expert Systems with Applications*, *150*, 113277.

Lim, L. J., Lim, A. J., Fong, K. K., & Lee, C. G. (2021). Sentiments regarding COVID-19 vaccination among graduate students in Singapore. *Vaccines*, *9*(10), 1141. doi:10.3390/vaccines9101141 PMID:34696249

Li, X., Yang, J., & Ma, J. (2021). Recent developments of content-based image retrieval (CBIR). *Neurocomputing*, *452*, 675–689. doi:10.1016/j.neucom.2020.07.139

Li, Y., & Xia, L. (2020). Coronavirus disease 2019 (COVID-19): Role of chest CT in diagnosis and management. *AJR. American Journal of Roentgenology*, *214*(6), 1280–1286. doi:10.2214/AJR.20.22954 PMID:32130038

Loiseau–Witon, N., Kéchichian, R., Valette, S., & Bartoli, A. (2022). Learning 3D medical image keypoint descriptors with the triplet loss. *International Journal of Computer Assisted Radiology and Surgery*, *17*(1), 141–146. doi:10.100711548-021-02481-3 PMID:34453284

Lopez, A. (2008). Statistical machine translation. *ACM Computing Surveys*, *40*(3), 1–49. doi:10.1145/1380584.1380586

Lovrić, R., Farčić, N., Mikšić, Š., & Včev, A. (2020). Studying during the COVID-19 pandemic: A qualitative inductive content analysis of nursing students' perceptions and experiences. *Education Sciences*, *10*(7), 188. doi:10.3390/educsci10070188

Low, D. M., Rumker, L., Talkar, T., Torous, J., Cecchi, G., & Ghosh, S. S. (2020). Natural language processing reveals vulnerable mental health support groups and heightened health anxiety on Reddit during COVID-19: Observational study. *Journal of Medical Internet Research*, *22*(10), e22635. doi:10.2196/22635 PMID:32936777

Lucas, E. (1878). Théorie des fonctions numériques simplement périodiques. *American Journal of Mathematics*, *1*(4), 289–321. doi:10.2307/2369373

Luz, E., Silva, P., Silva, R., Silva, L., Guimarães, J., Miozzo, G., Moreira, G., & Menotti, D. (2021). Towards an effective and efficient deep learning model for COVID-19 patterns detection in X-ray images. *Research on Biomedical Engineering*, 1–14. doi:10.100742600-021-00151-6

Maghdid, H. S., Asaad, A. T., Ghafoor, K. Z., Sadiq, A. S., Mirjalili, S., & Khan, M. K. (2021, April). Diagnosing COVID-19 pneumonia from X-ray and CT images. In Multimodal Image Exploitation and Learning 2021 (Vol. 11734). International Society for Optics and Photonics.

Maghsoudi, O. H., Tabrizi, A. V., Robertson, B., & Spence, A. (2017, December). 3d modeling of running rodents based on direct linear transform. In 2017 IEEE signal processing in medicine and biology symposium (SPMB) (pp. 1-4). IEEE.

Mahajan, S., Nayyar, A., Raina, A., Singh, S. J., Vashishtha, A., & Pandit, A. K. (2021). A Gaussian process-based approach toward credit risk modeling using stationary activations. *Concurrency and Computation*, 6692.

Mahapatra, B., Krishnamurthi, R., & Nayyar, A. (2019). Healthcare models and algorithms for privacy and security in healthcare records. *Security and Privacy of Electronic Healthcare Records: Concepts, Paradigms and Solutions*, 183.

Majrashi, A., Khalil, A., Nagshabandi, E. A., & Majrashi, A. (2021). Stressors and coping strategies among nursing students during the COVID-19 pandemic: Scoping review. *Nursing Reports*, *11*(2), 444–459. doi:10.3390/nursrep11020042 PMID:34968220

Makar, K., Goel, S., Kaur, P., Singh, M., Jain, P., & Aggarwal, P. K. (2021). Reliability of Mobile Applications: A Review and Some Perspectives. *Proceedings of the International Conference on Reliability, Infocom Technologies and Optimization (Trends and Future Directions) (ICRITO)*, 11-14.

Maleki, N., Zeinali, Y., & Niaki, S. T. A. (2021). A k-NN method for lung cancer prognosis with the use of a genetic algorithm for feature selection. *Expert Systems with Applications*, *164*, 113981.

Malik, Z. K., & Fyfe, C. (2012). Review of web personalization. *Journal of Emerging Technologies in Web Intelligence*, *4*(3), 285–296. doi:10.4304/jetwi.4.3.285-296

Mardanisamani, S., Karimi, Z., Jamshidzadeh, A., Yazdi, M., Farshad, M., & Farshad, A. (2021). *A New Approach for Automatic Segmentation and Evaluation of Pigmentation Lesion by using Active Contour Model and Speeded Up Robust Features*. arXiv preprint arXiv:2101.07195.

Mazloum, J., Jalali, A., & Amiryan, J. (2012, October). A novel bidirectional neural network for face recognition. In 2012 2nd International eConference on Computer and Knowledge Engineering (ICCKE) (pp. 18-23). IEEE. doi:10.1109/ICCKE.2012.6395345

Meenakshi, K., Maragatham, G., Agarwal, N., & Ghosh, I. (2018, April). A Data mining Technique for Analyzing and Predicting the success of Movie. []. IOP Publishing.]. *Journal of Physics: Conference Series*, *1000*(1), 012100.

Menezes, A. J., Oorschot, P. C., & Vanstone, S. A. (1996). *Handbook of Applied Cryptography*. CRC Press.

Mikolov, T., Chen, K., Corrado, G., & Dean, J. (2013). *Efficient estimation of word representations in vector space.* arXiv preprint arXiv:1301.3781.

Milano, S., Taddeo, M., & Floridi, L. (2020). Recommender systems and their ethical challenges. *AI & Society, 35*(4), 957–967. doi:10.100700146-020-00950-y

Minaee, S., Kafieh, R., Sonka, M., Yazdani, S., & Soufi, G. J. (2020). Deep-covid: Predicting covid-19 from chest x-ray images using deep transfer learning. *Medical Image Analysis, 65,* 101794. doi:10.1016/j.media.2020.101794 PMID:32781377

Minh, V. T. (2012). Advanced Vehicle Dynamics. Malaya Press.

Minh, V. T. (2011). Conditions for stabilizability of linear switched systems. *AIP Conference Proceedings, 1337*(1), 108–112.

Minh, V. T. (2013). Trajectory Generation for Autonomous Vehicles. In T. Březina & R. Jabloński (Eds.), *Mechatronics.* Springer.

Minh, V. T., & Afzulpurkar, N. (2005). Robust Model Predictive Control for Input Saturated and Softened State Constraints. *Asian Journal of Control, 7*(3), 323–329. doi:10.1111/j.1934-6093.2005. tb00241.x

Minh, V. T., & Afzulpurkar, N. (2006). A Comparative Study on Computational Schemes for Nonlinear Model Predictive Control. *Asian Journal of Control, 8*(4), 324–331. doi:10.1111/j.1934-6093.2006.tb00284.x

Minh, V. T., & Hashim, F. B. (2011). Tracking setpoint robust model predictive control for input saturated and softened state constraints. *International Journal of Control, Automation, and Systems, 9*(5), 958–965. doi:10.100712555-011-0517-4

Minh, V. T., Hashim, F. B., & Awang, M. (2012). Development of a Real-time Clutch Transition Strategy for a Parallel Hybridelectric Vehicle. *Proceedings of the Institution of Mechanical Engineers. Part I, Journal of Systems and Control Engineering, 226*(2), 188–203. doi:10.1177/0959651811414760

Minh, V. T., Katushin, N., & Pumwa, J. (2019). Motion tracking glove for augmented reality and virtual reality. *Paladyn: Journal of Behavioral Robotics, 10*(1), 160–166.

Minh, V. T., & Pumwa, J. (2012). Simulation and control of hybrid electric vehicles. *International Journal of Control, Automation, and Systems, 10*(2), 308–316.

Minh, V. T., Tamre, M., Musalimov, V., Kovalenko, P., Rubinshtein, I., Ovchinnikov, I., & Moezzi, R. (2020). Simulation of Human Gait Movements. *International Journal of Innovative Technology and Interdisciplinary Sciences, 3*(1), 326–345.

Minh, V. T., Tamre, M., Safonov, A., & Monakhov, I. (2020). Design and implementation of a mechatronic elbow orthosis. *Mechatronic Systems and Control, 48*(4), 231–238.

Minh, V. T., & Wan, M. W. M. (2010). Model Predictive Control of a Condensate Distillation Column. *International Journal of Systems Control, 1*(1), 4–12.

Moezzi, R., Minh, V. T., & Tamre, M. (2018). Fuzzy Logic Control for a Ball and Beam System. *International Journal of Innovative Technology and Interdisciplinary Sciences, 1*(1), 39–48.

Mohammed, T. A., Bayat, O., Uçan, O. N., & Alhayali, S. (2020). Hybrid efficient genetic algorithm for big data feature selection problems. *Foundations of Science, 25*(4), 1009–1025.

Mostafa, L. (2020). Egyptian student sentiment analysis using word2vec during the coronavirus (Covid-19) pandemic. In *International Conference on Advanced Intelligent Systems and Informatics* (pp. 195-203). Springer.

Mulyadi, M., Tonapa, S. I., Luneto, S., Wei-Ting, L. I. N., & Lee, B. O. (2021). Prevalence of mental health problems and sleep disturbances in nursing students during the COVID-19 pandemic: A systematic review and meta-analysis. *Nurse Education in Practice, 57*, 103228. doi:10.1016/j.nepr.2021.103228 PMID:34653783

Musgrave, G. L. (2013). James Owen Weatherall, The Physics of Wall Street: A Brief History of Predicting the Unpredictable. *Business Economics (Cleveland, Ohio), 48*(3), 203–204. doi:10.1057/be.2013.17

Nalli, A., & Ozyilmaz, C. (2015). The third order variations on the Fibonacci universal code. *Journal of Number Theory, 149*, 15–32. doi:10.1016/j.jnt.2014.07.010

Nandhini, S., & KS, J. M. (2020, February). Performance evaluation of machine learning algorithms for email spam detection. In *2020 International Conference on Emerging Trends in Information Technology and Engineering (ic-ETITE)* (pp. 1-4). IEEE.

Narin, A., Kaya, C., & Pamuk, Z. (2021). Automatic detection of coronavirus disease (covid-19) using x-ray images and deep convolutional neural networks. *Pattern Analysis & Applications*, 1–14.

Naseem, U., Razzak, I., Khushi, M., Eklund, P. W., & Kim, J. (2021). Covidsenti: A large-scale benchmark Twitter data set for COVID-19 sentiment analysis. *IEEE Transactions on Computational Social Systems, 8*(4), 1003–1015. doi:10.1109/TCSS.2021.3051189

Nasiri, S., & Khosravani, M. R. (2021). Machine learning in predicting mechanical behavior of additively manufactured parts. *Journal of Materials Research and Technology, 14*, 1137-1153.

Nasser, N., Emad-ul-Haq, Q., Imran, M., Ali, A., Razzak, I., & Al-Helali, A. (2021). A smart healthcare framework for detecting and monitoring COVID-19 using IoT and cloud computing. *Neural Computing & Applications*, 1–15. PMID:34522068

Natsiavas, P., Maglaveras, N., & Koutkias, V. (2016). A public health surveillance platform exploiting free-text sources via natural language processing and linked data: application in adverse drug reaction signal detection using PubMed and Twitter. In *Knowledge Representation for Health Care* (pp. 51–67). Springer.

Nawaz, S. A., Li, J., Bhatti, U. A., Mehmood, A., Shoukat, M. U., & Bhatti, M. A. (2020). Advance hybrid medical watermarking algorithm using speeded-up robust features and discrete cosine transform. *Plus One, 15*(6), e0232902.

Nayyar, A., & Nguyen, N. G. (2018). Introduction to swarm intelligence. *Advances in Swarm Intelligence for Optimizing Problems in Computer Science*, 53-78.

Nayyar, A., Garg, S., Gupta, D., & Khanna, A. (2018). Evolutionary computation: theory and algorithms. In *Advances in swarm intelligence for optimizing problems in computer science* (pp. 1–26). Chapman and Hall/CRC. doi:10.1201/9780429445927-1

Nayyar, A., Le, D. N., & Nguyen, N. G. (Eds.). (2018). *Advances in swarm intelligence for optimizing problems in computer science*. CRC Press. doi:10.1201/9780429445927

Nayyar, A., Puri, V., & Nguyen, N. G. (2019). BioSenHealth 1.0: a novel internet of medical things (IoMT)-based patient health monitoring system. In *International conference on innovative computing and communications* (pp. 155-164). Springer. 10.1007/978-981-13-2324-9_16

Nearchou, F., Flinn, C., Niland, R., Subramaniam, S. S., & Hennessy, E. (2020). Exploring the impact of COVID-19 on mental health outcomes in children and adolescents: A systematic review. *International Journal of Environmental Research and Public Health, 17*(22), 8479. doi:10.3390/ijerph17228479 PMID:33207689

Niven, I., Zuckerman, H. S., & Montgomery, H. L. (1991). *An introduction to the theory of numbers*. John Wiley & Sons.

Nivolianitou, Z. S., Leopoulos, V. N., & Konstantinidou, M. (2004). Comparison of techniques for accident scenario analysis in hazardous systems. *Journal of Loss Prevention in the Process Industries, 17*(6), 467–475. doi:10.1016/j.jlp.2004.08.001

Nobre, F. S. (2009). *Designing Future Information Management Systems*. IGI Global.

Noh, Y., Chang, K., Seo, Y., & Chang, D. (2014). Risk-based determination of design pressure of LNG fuel storage tanks based on dynamic process simulation combined with Monte Carlo method. *Reliability Engineering & System Safety, 129*, 76–82. doi:10.1016/j.ress.2014.04.018

Nour, M., Cömert, Z., & Polat, K. (2020). A novel medical diagnosis model for COVID-19 infection detection based on in-depth features and Bayesian optimization. *Applied Soft Computing, 97*, 106580. doi:10.1016/j.asoc.2020.106580 PMID:32837453

Nývlt, O., Haugen, S., & Ferkl, L. (2015). Complex accident scenarios modelled and analysed by Stochastic Petri Nets. *Reliability Engineering & System Safety, 142*, 539–555. doi:10.1016/j.ress.2015.06.015

Nývlt, O., & Rausand, M. (2012). Dependencies in event trees analyzed by Petri nets. *Reliability Engineering & System Safety, 104*, 45–57. doi:10.1016/j.ress.2012.03.013

Öcal, A. A., Tuglu, N., & Altinişik, E. (2005). On the Representation of k − Generalized Fibonacci and Lucas Numbers. *Applied Mathematics and Computation, 170*, 584–596.

Oh, Y., Park, S., & Ye, J. C. (2020). Deep learning COVID-19 features on CXR using limited training data sets. *IEEE Transactions on Medical Imaging*, *39*(8), 2688–2700. doi:10.1109/TMI.2020.2993291 PMID:32396075

Oien, K., Utne, I. B., & Herrera, I. A. (2011). Building safety indicators: Part 1 – theoretical foundation. *Safety Science*, *49*(2), 148–161. doi:10.1016/j.ssci.2010.05.012

Ostiak, P. (2006, April). Implementation of HDR panorama stitching algorithm. In *Proceedings of the 10th CESCG Conference* (pp. 24-26). Academic Press.

Ovchinnikov, I., & Kovalenko, P. (2018). Predictive Control Model to Simulate Humanoid Gait. *International Journal of Innovative Technology and Interdisciplinary Sciences*, *1*(1), 9–17.

Oyang, Y.-J., Hwang, S.-C., Ou, Y.-Y., Chen, C.-Y., & Chen, Z.-W. (2005). Data classification with radial basis function networks based on a novel kernel density estimation algorithm. *IEEE Transactions on Neural Networks*, *16*(1), 225–236. doi:10.1109/TNN.2004.836229 PMID:15732402

Oyebode, O., Ndulue, C., Mulchandani, D., Suruliraj, B., Adib, A., Orji, F. A., . . . Orji, R. (2020). *COVID-19 pandemic: identifying key issues using social media and natural language processing*. arXiv preprint arXiv:2008.10022.

Özkaya, U., Öztürk, Ş., & Barstugan, M. (2020). Coronavirus (COVID-19) classification using deep features fusion and ranking technique. In *Big Data Analytics and Artificial Intelligence Against COVID-19: Innovation Vision and Approach* (pp. 281–295). Springer.

Özyılmaz, Ç., & Nallı, A. (2020). Composite Discrete Logarithm Problem and a Reconstituted ElGamal Cryptosystem Based on the Problem: New ElGamal Cryptosystems With Some Special Sequences and Composite ElGamal Cryptosystem. In Implementing Computational Intelligence Techniques for Security Systems Design. IGI Global.

Ozyilmaz, C., & Nalli, A. (2019). Restructuring Of Discrete Logarithm Problem And Elgamal Cryptosystem By Using The Power Fibonacci Sequence Module M. *Journal of Science and Arts*, (1), 61–70.

Paltrinieria, N., Comfortb, L., & Reniers, G. (2019). Learning about risk: Machine learning for risk assessment. *Safety Science*, *118*, 475–486. doi:10.1016/j.ssci.2019.06.001

Paltrinieri, N., Khan, F., & Cozzani, V. (2015). Coupling of advanced techniques for dynamic risk management. *Journal of Risk Research*, *18*(7), 910–930. doi:10.1080/13669877.2014.919515

Paltrinieri, N., & Reniers, G. (2017). Dynamic risk analysis for Seveso sites. *Journal of Loss Prevention in the Process Industries*, *49*, 111–119. doi:10.1016/j.jlp.2017.03.023

Pan, F., Ye, T., Sun, P., Gui, S., Liang, B., Li, L., ... Zheng, C. (2020). Time Course of Lung Changes On Chest CT During Recovery From 2019 Novel Coronavirus (COVID-19) Pneumonia. *Radiology*. Advance online publication. doi:10.1148/radiol.2020200370 PMID:32053470

Papineni, K., Roukos, S., Ward, T., & Zhu, W. J. (2002). Bleu: a method for automatic evaluation of machine translation. In *Proceedings of the 40th Annual Meeting of the Association for Computational Linguistics* (pp. 311-318). Academic Press.

Parikh, R., Mathai, A., Parikh, S., Sekhar, G. C., & Thomas, R. (2008). Understanding and using sensitivity, specificity, and predictive values. *Indian Journal of Ophthalmology*, *56*(1), 45.

Parman, S. (2019). Fuzzy Logic Control of Clutch for Hybrid Vehicle. *International Journal of Innovative Technology and Interdisciplinary Sciences*, *2*(1), 78–86.

Pasman, H., & Reniers, G. (2014). Past, present and future of Quantitative Risk Assessment (QRA) and the incentive it obtained from Land-Use Planning (LUP). *Journal of Loss Prevention in the Process Industries*, *28*, 2–9. doi:10.1016/j.jlp.2013.03.004

Peerzada, S. A., Padhy, N., Sheetlani, J., & Hassan, G. (2020, March). Predict the Performance of Students and School on Educational kegga (U-DISE). In *2020 International Conference on Computer Science, Engineering and Applications (ICCSEA)* (pp. 1-6). IEEE.

Peni, T., & Bokor, J. (2006). Robust Model Predictive Control for Controlling Fast Vehicle Dynamics. *14th Mediterranean Conference on Control and Automation*, 1-5. 10.1109/MED.2006.328864

Picard, R. W. (2003). Affective computing: Challenges. *International Journal of Human-Computer Studies*, *59*(1-2), 55–64. doi:10.1016/S1071-5819(03)00052-1

Poulaiin, T. (2019). Path Generation and Control of Autonomous Robot. *International Journal of Innovative Technology and Interdisciplinary Sciences*, *2*(3), 200–211.

Priya, B. G. (2019). *Sentiment Analysis for Online Movie Reviews using SVM*. Academic Press.

Puljak, L., Čivljak, M., Haramina, A., Mališa, S., Čavić, D., Klinec, D., Aranza, D., Mesarić, J., Skitarelić, N., Zoranić, S., Majstorović, D., Neuberg, M., Mikšić, Š., & Ivanišević, K. (2020). Attitudes and concerns of undergraduate university health sciences students in Croatia regarding complete switch to e-learning during COVID-19 pandemic: A survey. *BMC Medical Education*, *20*(1), 1–11. doi:10.118612909-020-02343-7 PMID:33167960

Pumwa, J. (2019). Time Variant Predictive Control of Autonomous Vehicles. *International Journal of Innovative Technology and Interdisciplinary Sciences*, *2*(1), 62–77.

Quader, N., Gani, M. O., Chaki, D., & Ali, M. H. (2017, December). A machine learning approach to predict movie box-office success. In *2017 20th International Conference of Computer and Information Technology (ICCIT)* (pp. 1-7). IEEE.

Rahimzadeh, M., Attar, A., & Sakhaei, S. M. (2021). A fully automated deep learning-based network detecting covid-19 from a new and large lung ct scan dataset. *Biomedical Signal Processing and Control*, *68*, 102588. doi:10.1016/j.bspc.2021.102588 PMID:33821166

Rahman, M., & Islam, M. N. (2022). Exploring the performance of ensemble machine learning classifiers for sentiment analysis of covid-19 tweets. In *Sentimental Analysis and Deep Learning* (pp. 383–396). Springer. doi:10.1007/978-981-16-5157-1_30

Randhawa, G. S., Soltysiak, M. P. M., El Roz, H., de Souza, C. P. E., Hill, K. A., & Kari, L. (2020). Machine learning using intrinsic genomic signatures for rapid classification of novel pathogens: COVID-19 case study. *bioRxiv*. doi:10.1101/2020.02.03.932350

Rao, A. S. R. S., & Vazquez, J. A. (2020). Identification of COVID-19 Can be Quicker through Artificial Intelligence framework using a Mobile Phone-Based Survey in the Populations when Cities/Towns Are under Quarantine. *Infection Control and Hospital Epidemiology, 41*(7), 826–830. Advance online publication. doi:10.1017/ice.2020.61

Rathee, D., Ahuja, K., & Nayyar, A. (2019). Sustainable future IoT services with touch-enabled handheld devices. *Security and Privacy of Electronic Healthcare Records: Concepts, Paradigms and Solutions, 131*, 131-152.

Renault, M. (1996). *The Fibonacci sequence under various moduli* (Master Thesis). Wake Forest University, Institute of Science.

Renault, M. (2013). The period, rank, and order of the (a, b)-Fibonacci sequence mod m. *Mathematics Magazine, 86*(5), 372–380. doi:10.4169/math.mag.86.5.372

Rivest, R. L., Shamir, A., & Adleman, L. (1978). A method for obtaining digital signatures and public-key cryptosystems. *Communications of the ACM, 21*(2), 120–126. doi:10.1145/359340.359342

Santosh, K. C. (2020). AI-Driven Tools for Coronavirus Outbreak: Need of Active Learning and Cross-Population Train/Test Models on Multitudinal/Multimodal Data. *Journal of Medical Systems, 44*(5), 93. Advance online publication. doi:10.100710916-020-01562-1 PMID:32189081

Santra, A. K., & Jayasudha, S. (2012). Classification of web log data to identify interested users using Naïve Bayesian classification. *International Journal of Computer Science Issues, 9*(1), 381.

Saraee, M., White, S., & Eccleston, J. (2004). A data mining approach to analysis and prediction of movie ratings. *WIT Transactions on Information and Communication Technologies, 33*.

Satone, M., & Kharate, G. K. (2013). Selection of eigenvectors for face recognition. *International Journal of Advanced Computer Science and Applications, 4*(3). Advance online publication. doi:10.14569/IJACSA.2013.040316

Savitsky, B., Findling, Y., Ereli, A., & Hendel, T. (2020). Anxiety and coping strategies among nursing students during the Covid-19 pandemic. *Nurse Education in Practice, 46*, 102809. doi:10.1016/j.nepr.2020.102809 PMID:32679465

Sepliarskaia, A., Radlinski, F., & de Rijke, M. (2017, April). Simple personalized search based on long-term behavioral signals. In *European Conference on Information Retrieval* (pp. 95-107). Springer. 10.1007/978-3-319-56608-5_8

Serbanescu, M. S. (2010). *A k-nearest neighbor approach for chromosome shape classification*. Academic Press.

Shah, A. P. (1968). Fibonacci sequence modulo m. *Fibonacci Quarterly, 6*, 139–141.

Sharda, R., & Delen, D. (2006). Predicting box-office success of motion pictures with neural networks. *Expert Systems with Applications*, *30*(2), 243–254.

Sharma, K., Shrivastava, G., & Kumar, V. (2011, April). Web mining: Today and tomorrow. In *Electronics Computer Technology (ICECT), 2011 3rd International Conference on* (Vol. 1, pp. 399-403). IEEE.

Sharma, K., Singh, H., Sharma, D. K., Kumar, A., Nayyar, A., & Krishnamurthi, R. (2021). Dynamic models and control techniques for drone delivery of medications and other healthcare items in COVID-19 hotspots. In *Emerging Technologies for Battling Covid-19* (pp. 1–34). Springer. doi:10.1007/978-3-030-60039-6_1

Sharma, S., & Rana, V. (2017). Web personalization through semantic annotation system. *Advances in Computational Sciences and Technology*, *10*(6), 1683–1690.

Sharma, S., Rana, V., & Malhotra, M. (2021). Automatic recommendation system based on hybrid filtering algorithm. *Education and Information Technologies*, 1–16.

Shehab, N., Badawy, M., & Ali, H. A. (2021). Toward feature selection in big data preprocessing based on hybrid cloud-based model. *The Journal of Supercomputing*, 1–40.

Shen, C., Yu, N., Cai, S., Zhou, J., Sheng, J., Liu, K., Zhou, H., Guo, Y., & Niu, G. (2020). Quantitative computed tomography analysis for stratifying the severity of Coronavirus Disease 2019. *Journal of Pharmaceutical Analysis*, *10*(2), 123–129. Advance online publication. doi:10.1016/j.jpha.2020.03.004 PMID:32292624

Shim, T., Adireddy, G., & Yuan, H. (2012). Autonomous Vehicle Collision Avoidance System using Path Planning and Model Predictive Control Base Active Front Steering and Wheel Torque Control. *Journal of Automobile Engineering*, *226*(6), 767–778. doi:10.1177/0954407011430275

Singh, T., Nayyar, A., & Solanki, A. (2020). Multilingual opinion mining movie recommendation system using RNN. In *Proceedings of First International Conference on Computing, Communications, and Cyber-Security (IC4S 2019)* (pp. 589-605). Springer.

Singhal, T. (2020). A Review of Coronavirus Disease-2019 (COVID-19). *Indian Journal of Pediatrics*, *87*(4), 281–286. Advance online publication. doi:10.100712098-020-03263-6 PMID:32166607

Singh, M., Sukhija, N., Sharma, A., Gupta, M., & Aggarwal, P. K. (2021). *Security and Privacy Requirements for IoMT-Based Smart Healthcare System*. Big Data Analysis for Green Computing. doi:10.1201/9781003032328-2

Sloane, N. J. A. (1973). *A Handbook of Integer Sequences*. Academic Press.

Sobti, P., Nayyar, A., & Nagrath, P. (2020). Time Series Forecasting for Coronavirus (COVID-19). In *Proceedings of International Conference on Futuristic Trends in Networks and Computing Technologies* (pp. 309-320). Springer.

Sobti, P., Nayyar, A., & Nagrath, P. (2020, October). Time Series Forecasting for Coronavirus (COVID-19). In *International Conference on Futuristic Trends in Networks and Computing Technologies* (pp. 309-320). Springer.

Soni, R., Kumar, B., & Chand, S. (2019). Text detection and localization in natural scene images based on text awareness score. *Applied Intelligence*, *49*(4), 1376–1405. Advance online publication. doi:10.100710489-018-1338-4

Spencer, R., Thabtah, F., Abdelhamid, N., & Thompson, M. (2020). Exploring feature selection and classification methods for predicting heart disease. *Digital Health, 6*.

Spitzer, R. L., Kroenke, K., Williams, J. B., & Löwe, B. (2006). A brief measure for assessing generalized anxiety disorder: The GAD-7. *Archives of Internal Medicine*, *166*(10), 1092–1097. doi:10.1001/archinte.166.10.1092 PMID:16717171

Srivastava, J., Cooley, R., Deshpande, M., & Tan, P. N. (2000). Web usage mining: Discovery and applications of usage patterns from web data. *SIGKDD Explorations*, *1*(2), 12–23. doi:10.1145/846183.846188

Stinson, D. R. (2002). *Cryptography Theory and Practice*. Chapman & Hall / CRC.

Stumme, G., Hotho, A., & Berendit, B. (2006). Semantic Web Mining. *Semantic Web Mining, Elsevier*, *4*(2), 124–143. doi:10.1016/j.websem.2006.02.001

Suebsomran, A. (2019). Stabilizability Analysis of Multiple Model Control with Probabilistic. *International Journal of Innovative Technology and Interdisciplinary Sciences*, *2*(2), 173–180.

Suen, S. T., Lam, E. Y., & Wong, K. K. (2007). Photographic stitching with optimized object and color matching based on image derivatives. *Optics Express*, *15*(12), 7689–7696. doi:10.1364/OE.15.007689 PMID:19547097

Suganthan, N. (2019). COVID-19. *Jaffna Medical Journal*. doi:10.4038/jmj.v31i2.72

Sutton, R. S., & Barto, A. G. (2018). *Reinforcement learning: An introduction*. MIT Press.

Svozil, D., Kvasnicka, V., & Pospichal, J. (1997). Introduction to multi-layer feed-forward neural networks. *Chemometrics and Intelligent Laboratory Systems*, *39*(1), 43–62. doi:10.1016/S0169-7439(97)00061-0

Szeliski, R., & Shum, H. Y. (1997, August). Creating full view panoramic image mosaics and environment maps. In *Proceedings of the 24th annual conference on Computer graphics and interactive techniques* (pp. 251-258). 10.1145/258734.258861

Tamre, M., Hudjakov, R., Shvarts, D., Polder, A., Hiiemaa, M., & Juurma, M. (2018). Implementation of Integrated Wireless Network and MATLAB System to Control Autonomous Mobile Robot. *International Journal of Innovative Technology and Interdisciplinary Sciences*, *1*(1), 18–25.

Taneja, S., Nayyar, A., & Nagrath, P. (2021). Face Mask Detection Using Deep Learning during COVID-19. In *Proceedings of Second International Conference on Computing, Communications, and Cyber-Security* (pp. 39-51). Springer. 10.1007/978-981-16-0733-2_3

Tanwar, S., Bhatia, Q., Patel, P., Kumari, A., Singh, P. K., & Hong, W. C. (2020). Machine Learning Adoption in Blockchain-Based Smart Applications: The Challenges, and a Way Forward. *IEEE Access: Practical Innovations, Open Solutions, 8*, 474–488. doi:10.1109/ACCESS.2019.2961372

Tao, J., & Tan, T. (2005). Affective computing: A review. In *Proceedings of International Conference on Affective Computing and Intelligent Interaction* (pp. 981-995). Springer. 10.1007/11573548_125

Taşçi, D., & Kilic, E. (2004). On the Order $k-$. *Applied Mathematics and Computation, 155*(3), 637–641. doi:10.1016/S0096-3003(03)00804-X

Taşkara, N., Uslu, K., & Güleç, H. H. (2010). On the Properties of Lucas Numbers with Binomial Coefficients. *Applied Mathematics Letters, 23*(1), 68–72. doi:10.1016/j.aml.2009.08.007

Tian, S., Hu, N., Lou, J., Chen, K., Kang, X., Xiang, Z., Chen, H., Wang, D., Liu, N., Liu, D., Chen, G., Zhang, Y., Li, D., Li, J., Lian, H., Niu, S., Zhang, L., & Zhang, J. (2020). Characteristics of COVID-19 infection in Beijing. *The Journal of Infection, 80*(4), 401–406. Advance online publication. doi:10.1016/j.jinf.2020.02.018 PMID:32112886

Trieu Minh, Vu., Tamre, M., Musalimov, V., Kovalenko, P., Rubinshtein, I., Ovchinnikov, I., Krcmarik, D., Moezzi, R., & Hlava, J. (2020). Model Predictive Control for Modeling Human Gait Motions Assisted by Vicon Technology. *Journal Européen des Systèmes Automatisés, 53*(5), 589–600.

Tripathy, H. K., Mishra, S., Suman, S., Nayyar, A., & Sahoo, K. S. (2022). Smart COVID-shield: An IoT driven reliable and automated prototype model for COVID-19 symptoms tracking. *Computing*, 1–22. doi:10.100700607-021-01039-0

Ucar, F., & Korkmaz, D. (2020). COVIDiagnosis-Net: Deep Bayes-SqueezeNet based diagnosis of the coronavirus disease 2019 (COVID-19) from X-ray images. *Medical Hypotheses, 140*, 109761. doi:10.1016/j.mehy.2020.109761 PMID:32344309

Uddin, S., Khan, A., Hossain, M. E., & Moni, M. A. (2019). Comparing different supervised machine learning algorithms for disease prediction. *BMC Medical Informatics and Decision Making, 19*(1), 281. Advance online publication. doi:10.118612911-019-1004-8 PMID:31864346

Upadhyay, A., Kamath, N., Shanghavi, S., Mandvikar, T., & Wagh, P. (2018). Movie Success Prediction Using Data Mining. Department of Information Technology, Shah & Anchor Kutchhi Engineering College, 6(4).

Uslu, K., Taskara, N., & Kose, H. (2011). The Generalized $k-$Fibonacci and Lucas Number. *Ars Combinatoria, 99*, 25–32.

Uslu, M. F., Uslu, S., & Bulut, F. (2020). *An adaptive hybrid approach: Combining genetic algorithm and ant colony optimization for integrated process planning and scheduling.* Applied Computing and Informatics.

Vaishya, R., Javaid, M., Khan, I. H., & Haleem, A. (2020). Artificial Intelligence (AI) applications for COVID-19 pandemic. *Diabetes & Metabolic Syndrome, 14*(4), 337–339. doi:10.1016/j.dsx.2020.04.012 PMID:32305024

Vajda, S. (1989). *Fibonacci and Lucas Numbers and the Golden Section*. Ellis Horwood.

Vardhan, A. H., Verma, N. K., Sevakula, R. K., & Salour, A. (2015, October). Unsupervised approach for object matching using speeded-up robust features. In 2015 IEEE Applied Imagery Pattern Recognition Workshop (AIPR) (pp. 1-8). IEEE. doi:10.1109/AIPR.2015.7444541

Vaswani, A., Bengio, S., Brevdo, E., Chollet, F., Gomez, A. N., Gouws, S., . . . Uszkoreit, J. (2018). *Tensor2tensor for neural machine translation*. arXiv preprint arXiv:1803.07416.

Verma, N. K., Goyal, A., Vardhan, A. H., Sevakula, R. K., & Salour, A. (2016). Object matching using speeded up robust features. In Intelligent and evolutionary systems (pp. 415-427). Springer. doi:10.1007/978-3-319-27000-5_34

Verma, G., & Verma, H. (2019, February). Predicting Bollywood movies success using machine learning technique. In *2019 Amity International Conference on Artificial Intelligence (AICAI)* (pp. 102-105). IEEE.

Verma, H., & Verma, G. (2020). Prediction model for Bollywood movie success: A comparative analysis of performance of supervised machine learning algorithms. *The Review of Socionetwork Strategies, 14*(1), 1–17. doi:10.100712626-019-00040-6

Villa, V., Paltrinieri, N., Khan, F., & Cozzani, V. (2016a). Towards dynamic risk analysis: A review of the risk assessment approach and its limitations in the chemical process industry. *Safety Science, 89*, 77–93. doi:10.1016/j.ssci.2016.06.002

Villa, V., Paltrinieri, N., Khan, F., & Cozzani, V. (2016b). A Short Overview of Risk Analysis Background and Recent Developments. In *Dynamic Risk Analysis in the Chemical and Petroleum Industry*. Evolution and Interaction with Parallel Disciplines in the Perspective of Industrial Application. doi:10.1016/B978-0-12-803765-2.00001-9

Vinay, A., Hebbar, D., Shekhar, V. S., Murthy, K. B., & Natarajan, S. (2015). Two novel detector-descriptor based approaches for face recognition using sift and surf. *Procedia Computer Science, 70*, 185–197. doi:10.1016/j.procs.2015.10.070

Wall, D. D. (1960). Fibonacci Series Modulo m. *The American Mathematical Monthly, 67*(6), 525–532. doi:10.1080/00029890.1960.11989541

Wan Muhamad, W. M. (2019). Vehicle Steering Dynamic Calculation and Simulation. *International Journal of Innovative Technology and Interdisciplinary Sciences, 2*(1), 87–97.

Wang, J. (2020). Procedures for health protection and control for COVID-19 during X-ray imaging examinations in Jiangsu province. *Chinese Journal of Radiological Medicine and Protection*.

Wang, S., Hu, L., Wang, Y., Cao, L., Sheng, Q. Z., & Orgun, M. (2019). *Sequential recommender systems: challenges, progress and prospects.* arXiv preprint arXiv:2001.04830. doi:10.24963/ijcai.2019/883

Wang, J., Lu, Z., Chen, W., & Wu, X. (2011). *An Adaptive Trajectory Tracking Control of Wheeled Mobile Robots. In Industrial Electronics and Applications.* ICIEA.

Wang, J., Zheng, P., & Zhang, J. (2020). Big data analytics for cycle time related feature selection in the semiconductor wafer fabrication system. *Computers & Industrial Engineering, 143,* 106362.

Wang, L., Lin, Z. Q., & Wong, A. (2020). Covid-net: A tailored deep convolutional neural network design for detecting covid-19 cases from chest x-ray images. *Scientific Reports, 10*(1), 1–12. doi:10.103841598-020-76550-z PMID:31913322

Wang, N., Wang, Y., & Er, M. J. (2022). Review on deep learning techniques for marine object recognition: Architectures and algorithms. *Control Engineering Practice, 118,* 104458. doi:10.1016/j.conengprac.2020.104458

Wang, S., Kang, B., Ma, J., Zeng, X., Xiao, M., Guo, J., & Xu, B. (2020). *A deep learning algorithm using CT images to screen for coronavirus disease (COVID-19).* MedRxiv; doi:10.1101/2020.02.14.20023028

Webster, D., Huang, W., Mundy, D., & Warren, P. (2006, May). Context-orientated news filtering for web 2.0 and beyond. In *Proceedings of the 15th international conference on World Wide Web* (pp. 1001-1002). 10.1145/1135777.1135985

Wolpert, D.H. (2002). The supervised learning no-free-lunch theorems. *Soft Computing and Industry,* 25–42.

Wu, Y., Schuster, M., Chen, Z., Le, Q. V., Norouzi, M., Macherey, W., . . . Dean, J. (2016). *Google's neural machine translation system: Bridging the gap between human and machine translation.* arXiv preprint arXiv:1609.08144.

Wu, F., Li, Z., Lee, W. C., Wang, H., & Huang, Z. (2015, May). Semantic annotation of mobility data using social media. In *Proceedings of the 24th International Conference on World Wide Web* (pp. 1253-1263). 10.1145/2736277.2741675

Wu, F., Wang, H., Li, Z., Lee, W. C., & Huang, Z. (2015, May). SemMobi: A semantic annotation system for mobility data. In *Proceedings of the 24th International Conference on World Wide Web* (pp. 255-258). ACM. 10.1145/2740908.2742837

Xiong, Z., Fu, L., Zhou, H., Liu, J. K., Wang, A. M., Huang, Y., ... Liao, W. H. (2020). Construction and evaluation of a novel diagnosis process for 2019-Corona Virus Disease. *Zhonghua Yi Xue Za Zhi.* Advance online publication. doi:10.3760/cma.j.cn112137-20200228-00499 PMID:32157849

Yang, X., & Haugen, S. (2015). Classification of risk to support decision-making in hazardous processes. *Safety Science, 80,* 115–126. doi:10.1016/j.ssci.2015.07.011

Yan, L., Zhang, H.-T., Xiao, Y., Wang, M., Sun, C., Liang, J., & Yuan, Y. (2020). *Prediction of survival for severe COVID-19 patients with three clinical features: development of a machine learning-based prognostic model with clinical data in Wuhan.* MedRxiv; doi:10.1101/2020.02.27.20028027

Yasin, H. (2019). Modelling and Control of Hybrid Vehicle. *International Journal of Innovative Technology and Interdisciplinary Sciences, 2*(3), 212–222.

Yayenie, O. (2011). A Note on Generalized Fibonacci Sequences. *Applied Mathematics and Computation, 217*(12), 5603–5611. doi:10.1016/j.amc.2010.12.038

Yazlik, Y., & Taşkara, N. (2012). A Note on Generalized $k-$. *Computers & Mathematics with Applications (Oxford, England), 63*(1), 36–41. doi:10.1016/j.camwa.2011.10.055

Ye, Y., Shi, J., Zhu, D., Su, L., Huang, J., & Huang, Y. (2021). Management of medical and health big data based on integrated learning-based health care system: A review and comparative analysis. *Computer Methods and Programs in Biomedicine, 209*, 106293.

Yilmaz, F., & Bozkurt, D. (2009). The Generalized Order $k-$Jacobsthal Numbers. Int. *J. Contemp. Math. Sciences, 4*(34), 1685–1694.

Zhang, Dong, Cao, Yuan, Dong, Yang, Bin, Qin, … Gao. (2020). Clinical characteristics of 140 patients infected with SARS-CoV-2 in Wuhan, China. *Allergy: European Journal of Allergy and Clinical Immunology.* doi:10.1111/all.14238

Zhang, J., Xie, Y., Pang, G., Liao, Z., Verjans, J., Li, W., Sun, Z., He, J., Li, Y., Shen, C., & Xia, Y. (2020). Viral pneumonia screening on chest x-rays using Confidence-Aware anomaly detection. *IEEE Transactions on Medical Imaging, 40*(3), 879–890. doi:10.1109/TMI.2020.3040950 PMID:33245693

Zhou, D., Huang, J., & Schölkopf, B. (2006). Learning with hypergraphs: Clustering, classification, and embedding. *Advances in Neural Information Processing Systems, 19*, 1601–1608.

Zhu, H. (2001). *Survey of Computational Assumptions Used in Cryptography Broken or Not by Shor's Algoritm* (Master Thesis). McGill University School of Computer Science, Montreal.

Zivkovic, M., Bacanin, N., Venkatachalam, K., Nayyar, A., Djordjevic, A., Strumberger, I., & Al-Turjman, F. (2021). COVID-19 cases prediction by using hybrid machine learning and beetle antennae search approach. *Sustainable Cities and Society, 66*, 102669. doi:10.1016/j.scs.2020.102669 PMID:33520607

Zoph, B., Vasudevan, V., Shlens, J., & Le, Q. V. (2018). Learning transferable architectures for scalable image recognition. In *Proceedings of the IEEE conference on computer vision and pattern recognition* (pp. 8697-8710). IEEE.

About the Contributors

Anand Nayyar (Academician, Researcher, Author, Writer, Inventor, Innovator, Scientist, Consultant, and Orator) done his Ph.D. in Computer Science from Desh Bhagat University, Mandi Gobindgarh in 2017 in Wireless Sensor Networks, Swarm Intelligence, and Network Simulation. He is currently working in School of Computer Science-Duy Tan University, Da Nang, Vietnam as Assistant Professor, Scientist, Vice-Chairman (Research) and Director- IoT and Intelligent Systems Lab. Published more than 125+ Research Papers in various High-Quality ISI-SCI/SCIE/SSCI Impact Factor Journals cum Scopus/ESCI indexed Journals, 50+ Papers in International Conferences indexed with Springer, IEEE Xplore and ACM Digital Library, 40+ Book Chapters in various SCOPUS, WEB OF SCIENCE Indexed Books

Sandeep Kumar is currently an Associate Professor at CHRIST (Deemed to be University) Bangalore, India. Before joining CHRIST, he has worked with ACEIT Jaipur, Jagannath University Jaipur, and Amity University Rajasthan. He is an associate editor for the Human-centric Computing and Information Sciences (HCIS) journal published by Springer. He has published more than sixty research papers in various international journals/conferences and attended several national and international conferences and workshops. He has authored/edited five books in the area of computer science. His research interests include nature-inspired algorithms, swarm intelligence, soft computing, and computational intelligence.

Akshat Agrawal completed B.Tech in Computer Science & Engineering from UPTU & M.Tech from USICT, GGSIPU. He is currently pursuing PhD. from GGSIPU, Delhi. He works as an Assistant Professor in Amity School of Engineering & Technology, Amity University Haryana. he has a total of 11 years of teaching & research experience. His major research interests are Artificial Intelligence, Deep Learning & Machine Learning, Artificial Neural Network, Speech processing, and Image processing. He has published a total of 29 research papers in Scopus indexed and reputed refereed international journals. He has guided 20 M.Tech thesis and 42 B.Tech projects. He has been visited as a guest faculty at Technical University

Kosice, Slovakia in June 2019. He actively participated in the reviewing process of research papers and book chapters and was a Program Committee member of various Conferences. He has edited one Special Issue on Sustainable technological solutions for next generation intelligent buildings in smart cities for EAI Endorsed Transactions on Smart Cities and One edited book of Wiley Publication.

* * *

Puneet Kumar Aggarwal is Assistant Professor in Department of Information Technology of ABES Engineering College affiliated with AKTU University. He has completed his PhD in Information Technology from Amity University, Noida, India. His area of research includes Software Engineering, Steganography, and Mobile Applications. He is a member of IEEE and published more than 15 research papers in reputed conferences and journals.

Tanvi Arora received her B.Tech degree in Computer Science & Engineering from Punjab Technical University, Jalandhar, Punjab, India in 2002, M.Tech degree in Information Technology from Punjab Technical University, Jalandhar, Punjab, India in the year 2007. Completed her Ph.D in Computer Science & Engineering from Dr. B.R Ambedkar National Institute of Technology, Jalandhar, Punjab, India in 2018. Her teaching and research interests include Image Processing, Pattern Recognition, Machine Learning, Data Mining and Network Security.

Satheeshkumar B. received DCT (Diploma in Computer Technology) from Vivekanandha Polytechnic, Mettukuppam in 2009; and B.E. (Bachelor of Engineering) in CSE from Arunai Engineering College in 2012; and M.E. (Master of Engineering) in CSE from PGP College of Engineering and Technology in 2015; Currently he is working as Full Time Scholar in CSE from Annamalai University. His research interest includes Digital Image Processing, Medical Image processing, Video retrieval. He has published articles in SCI journal and a number of international conferences.

Sathiyaprasad Balasundaram received the B. Tech. (Bachelor of Technology) degree in Computer Science and Engineering from Perunthalaivar Kamarajar Institute of Engineering and Technology, Karaikal, India, in 2012 respectively, and M. E. Degree (Masters in Engineering) in Computer Science and Engineering from Sathyabama University, Chennai, Tamilnadu, India, in 2014. Currently, he is working as a Full-time research scholar in the Department of Computer Science and Engineering from Annamalai University, Chidambaram, Tamilnadu, India. His research interest includes Digital Image Processing, Image and Video retrieval, and

Big Data Analytics, Medical Image Processing and Computer Vision. He is also a member of the professional societies – IEEE, IEEE of Computer Society, IEEE of Young Professionals, IAENG, UACEE and IRED. He has published articles in Scopus and SCIE journal and a number of international conferences such as IEEE, TEQIP-III, etc.

Çagla Çelemoğlu is a Dr. research assistant in the Department of Mathematics,Ondokuz Mayis University, Samsun, Turkey. She received her B.Sc and M. Sc in Mathematics from Uludağ University and Karabük University from Turkey, respectively. Her research interests include cryptography, coding theory, algebra and number theory. She has papers in magazines with index and conference paper publications in this area.

Ashima Gambhir is Assistant Professor, Department of Computer Science and Engineering, Amity University Gurgaon (Haryana, India). She received her B.Sc. from Kurukshetra University, Kurukshetra in 2007 and MCA from GITM, Gurgaon (Maharishi Dayanand University, Rohtak) in 2010. She has done M.Tech(CSE) from MBU, Solan in 2013. She received her P.hD. Degree from Faculty of Engineering & Technology, JNU, Haryana in 2021. She has been teaching UG and PG classes for well over 11 years. She has 25 Research papers in International Journals and Conferences. She has attended more than 40 workshop/Conferences/FDP/Seminar during her 11 years of experience of teaching. Her research interest includes Requirement Engineering, Algorithm Designs and Database.

Swati Gupta received her PhD degree from Amity University Haryana in 2020 and M.Tech (CSE) degree from MRIU, Faridabad in 2011 and B.Tech degree in Computer Science Engineering from MDU university Haryana in 2009. She has 11 years of experience in teaching. Currently she is working as Associate Professor in Department of Computer Science, School of Engineering and Technology in K R Mangalam University Gurugram, Haryana. She has published more than 25 research papers in International Journals/ conferences of high repute. Her research areas include topics of Database, Data Mining, Machine Learning and Internet of Things.

Jaroslav Hlava's research interests are in the field of automatic control and real time optimization. The main focus is on model predictive control and its applications into very diverse areas such as smart grids optimization and integration of renewable generation, control of smart thermal grids and district heating systems, control of autonomous and semi-autonomous vehicles. He is also involved in projects focused on control applications of industrial tomography and control-oriented modeling.

Ibrahim Furkan Ince received his PhD degree from the Department of Information Technologies (IT) Convergence Design, Kyungsung University, South Korea in August 2010. Immediately after, he did post-doctoral studies at the University of Tokyo in Japan from October 2010 to April 2012. Later, from May 2012 to May 2014, he worked in an IT company named Hanwul Multimedia Communication Co. Ltd. (HMC) in South Korea as a chief research engineer. Then, he made a definite return to Turkey and worked as an assistant professor in the Department of Computer Engineering at Gediz University between November 2014 and July 2016. Later, after taking part in joint projects with the Department of Electronics Engineering in Kyungsung University as a freelance researcher for 3 years, he started working as an assistant professor at Nişantaşı University in the Department of Management Information Systems (MIS) in October 2019 and after working there as a full-time doctoral faculty member for 6 months, he returned back to South Korea after taking an unpaid leave permission from Nişantaşı University. Currently, he holds a doctoral faculty member position in the Department of Digital Game Design at Nişantaşı University, and since March 2020, he has been actively working as an assistant research professor in the Department of Electronics Engineering at Kyungsung University. His research interests include image processing, computer vision, machine learning, pattern recognition and human-computer interaction.

Parita Jain is working as Assistant Professor in Department of Computer Science and Engineering and Assistant Dean(A) at KIET Group of Institutions affiliated with AKTU University. She has completed his PhD in Information Technology from Amity University, Noida, India. Her area of research includes Software Engineering, Machine Learning, and Mobile Applications. She has published more than 15 research papers in reputed conferences and journals.

Dilek Küçük, Ph.D, is an associate professor and chief researcher at TÜBİTAK Marmara Research Center (MRC). She has obtained her B.S., M.S. and Ph.D. degrees all from Middle East Technical University in Ankara (Turkey), in 2003, 2005, and 2011, respectively. Between May 2013 and May 2014, she has studied as a post-doctoral researcher at European Commission's Joint Research Centre in Italy. Her research interests include energy informatics, data mining, social media analysis, natural language processing, and database applications in engineering domains. She is the author or co-author of 16 papers published at SCI-indexed journals, in addition to more than 40 papers presented at international conferences.

Emine Ela Küçük received her B.Sc. degree from Giresun Health School of Karadeniz Technical University and her M.Sc. degree from the Public Health Department of the Faculty of Medicine in Karadeniz Technical University. She received her Ph.D. degree from the Public Health Department of the Faculty of Medicine in Erciyes University. She received her associate professor title in 2018. Currently, she is the head of the Nursing Department at the Faculty of Health Sciences of Giresun University. Her research topics include public health, public health surveillance, women health, and adolescent health.

Sasikaladevi N. received Ph.D. Degree in Computer Science in 2013. She has published more than 42 papers in reputed international journals and conferences including publications in SCI-Indexed Journals. She is a reviewer of more than a dozen of reputed journals including IEEE transactions on Services Computing and IEEE Journal of Internet of Things. s. Her research focus includes the design of machine learning strategies to solve Discrete Logarithm Problem. She published several books and chapters in reputed publisher including Prentice Hall of India, Lambert Academic Publisher, IGI Global, Springer and Science Direct. She has received fund from Department of Science and Technology, Government of India to carry out projects in the domain of Services computing and Security System. She has received young scientist award and women scientist award from DST, India. She is also involved in the security enriched payment system design as a part of Digital India Initiative. Her current research interests include information security, digital authentication, security of wireless sensor networks, computer vision, deep learning and security of vehicular ad-hoc networks.

Selime Beyza Özçevik is a Master's student at Ondokuz Mayıs University.

Vijay Rana is Assistant Professor at Dr. Yashwant Singh Parmar University of Horticulture and Forestry.

Deepthi Sehrawat is currently working with Amity University Haryana. She is pursuing PhD with MDU University Rohtak. She has 8 years of academic experience. Her area of research includes machine learning, predictive modelling, etc.

Meenu Vijarania received her Ph.D degree from Amity University Haryana in 2019 and M.Tech (I.T) degree from GGSIPU, New Delhi in 2007 and B.Tech degree in Information Technology from MDU University Haryana in 2005. She has 14 years of experience in teaching. Currently she is working at K R Mangalam University Gurugram Haryana as Associate Professor in Department of Computer Science, School of Engineering and Technology. She has published more than 30 research papers in International Journals/ conferences of high repute. Her research areas include topics of Wireless Networks and Genetic Algorithm, Machine Learning, Internet of Things.

Index

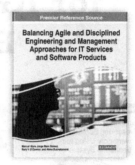

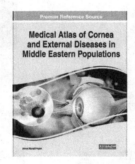

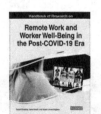

Deep Learning Applications for Cyber-Physical Systems

Monica R. Mundada
M.S. Ramaiah Institute of Technology, India

S. Seema
M.S. Ramaiah Institute of Technology, India

Srinivasa K.G.
National Institute of Technical Teachers Training and Research, Chandigarh, India

M. Shilpa
M.S. Ramaiah Institute of Technology, India

A volume in the Advances in Systems Analysis, Software Engineering, and High Performance Computing (ASASEHPC) Book Series

Published in the United States of America by
    IGI Global
    Engineering Science Reference (an imprint of IGI Global)
    701 E. Chocolate Avenue
    Hershey PA, USA 17033
    Tel: 717-533-8845
    Fax: 717-533-8661
    E-mail: cust@igi-global.com
    Web site: http://www.igi-global.com

Library of Congress Cataloging-in-Publication Data

Names: Mundada, Monica R., 1974- editor.
Title: Deep learning applications for cyber-physical systems / Monica
    Mundada, Seema Shedole, K G Srinivasa, and M. Shilpa, editor.
Description: Hershey, PA : Engineering Science Reference, [2021] | Includes
    bibliographical references and index. | Summary: "This book focuses on
    multidisciplinary aspects of computational engineering and industrial
    management engineering such as deep learning and supply chain
    management, covering trending applications such as Smart Agriculture,
    Smart Healthcare System, Cyber Physical Systems"-- Provided by
    publisher.
Identifiers: LCCN 2021017613 (print) | LCCN 2021017614 (ebook) | ISBN
    9781799881612 (hardcover) | ISBN 9781799881629 (paperback) | ISBN
    9781799881636 (ebook)
Subjects: LCSH: Systems engineering. | Machine learning--Industrial
    applications. | Cooperating objects (Computer systems)--Industrial
    applications. | Medical technology.
Classification: LCC TA168 .D465 2021 (print) | LCC TA168 (ebook) | DDC
    006.3/31--dc23
LC record available at https://lccn.loc.gov/2021017613
LC ebook record available at https://lccn.loc.gov/2021017614

This book is published in the IGI Global book series Advances in Systems Analysis, Software
Engineering, and High Performance Computing (ASASEHPC) (ISSN: 2327-3453; eISSN: 2327-
3461)

British Cataloguing in Publication Data
A Cataloguing in Publication record for this book is available from the British Library.

For electronic access to this publication, please contact: eresources@igi-global.com.

Advances in Systems Analysis, Software Engineering, and High Performance Computing (ASASEHPC) Book Series

ISSN:2327-3453
EISSN:2327-3461

Editor-in-Chief: Vijayan Sugumaran, Oakland University, USA

MISSION

The theory and practice of computing applications and distributed systems has emerged as one of the key areas of research driving innovations in business, engineering, and science. The fields of software engineering, systems analysis, and high performance computing offer a wide range of applications and solutions in solving computational problems for any modern organization.

The **Advances in Systems Analysis, Software Engineering, and High Performance Computing (ASASEHPC) Book Series** brings together research in the areas of distributed computing, systems and software engineering, high performance computing, and service science. This collection of publications is useful for academics, researchers, and practitioners seeking the latest practices and knowledge in this field.

COVERAGE

- Computer Networking
- Parallel Architectures
- Human-Computer Interaction
- Enterprise Information Systems
- Engineering Environments
- Computer Graphics
- Software Engineering
- Storage Systems
- Distributed Cloud Computing
- Performance Modelling

IGI Global is currently accepting manuscripts for publication within this series. To submit a proposal for a volume in this series, please contact our Acquisition Editors at Acquisitions@igi-global.com or visit: http://www.igi-global.com/publish/.

Titles in this Series

For a list of additional titles in this series, please visit: http://www.igi-global.com/book-series/

IGI Global
PUBLISHER of TIMELY KNOWLEDGE

701 East Chocolate Avenue, Hershey, PA 17033, USA
Tel: 717-533-8845 x100 • Fax: 717-533-8661
E-Mail: cust@igi-global.com • www.igi-global.com

Table of Contents

Detailed Table of Contents

Chapter 1
    Sangeetha V., M.S. Ramaiah Institute of Technology, India
    Evangeline D., M.S. Ramaiah Institute of Technology, India
    Sinthuja M., M.S. Ramaiah Institute of Technology, India

Today, technology plays a vital role in the healthcare industry. In the traditional way, physicians' minds were predicting the unknown disease based on their expertise and experience. Use of new technology like predictive analytics is transforming the healthcare industry. Predictive analytics in healthcare uses historical data (demographic information, person's past medical history and behaviors) to make predictions about the future. In this chapter, a predictive model is proposed to predict COVID-19 using prophet algorithm. A novel approach based on longitudinal data fusion approach will maintain temporal data from time to time. Sparse regularization regression uses data source and feature level to predict the spread of virus. The proposed model designed using longitudinal data fusion offers better clinical insights. Predictions will be very beneficial to government and healthcare groups to provoke suitable measures in controlling coronavirus. It is also beneficial to pharmaceutical companies to fabricate pills at a quicker rate.

Chapter 2

Bhimavarapu Usharani, Department of Computer Science and Engineering, Koneru Lakshmaiah Education Foundation, Vaddeswaram, India

Hibiscus is a fantastic herb, and in Ayurveda, it is one of the most renowned herbs that have extraordinary healing properties. Hibiscus is rich in vitamin C, flavonoids, amino acids, mucilage fiber, moisture content, and antioxidants. Hibiscus can help with weight loss, cancer treatment, bacterial infections, fever, high blood pressure, lower body temperature, treat heart and nerve diseases. Automatic leaf disease detection is an essential task. Image processing is one of the popular techniques for the plant leaf disease detection and categorization. In this chapter, the diseased leaf is identified by concurrent k-means clustering algorithm and then features are extracted. Finally, reweighted KNN linear classification algorithms have been used to detect the diseased leaves categories.

Chapter 3

Rajalaxmi Prabhu B., NMAM Institute of Technology, India
Seema S., M.S. Ramaiah Institute of Technology, India

A lot of user-generated data is available these days from huge platforms, blogs, websites, and other review sites. These data are usually unstructured. Analyzing sentiments from these data automatically is considered an important challenge. Several machine learning algorithms are implemented to check the opinions from large data sets. A lot of research has been undergone in understanding machine learning approaches to analyze sentiments. Machine learning mainly depends on the data required for model building, and hence, suitable feature exactions techniques also need to be carried. In this chapter, several deep learning approaches, its challenges, and future issues will be addressed. Deep learning techniques are considered important in predicting the sentiments of users. This chapter aims to analyze the deep-learning techniques for predicting sentiments and understanding the importance of several approaches for mining opinions and determining sentiment polarity.

Modern technologies have improved their application in field of agriculture in order to improve production. Plant diseases are harmful to plant growth, which leads to reduced quality and quantity of crop. Early identification of plant disease will reduce the loss of the crop productivity. So, it is necessary to identify and diagnose the disease at an early stage before it spreads to the entire field. In this chapter, the proposed model uses VGG16 with attention mechanism for leaf disease classification. This model makes use of convolution neural network which consist of convolution block, max pool layer, and fully connected layer with softmax as an activation function. The proposed approach integrates CNN with attention mechanism to focus more on the diseased part of leaf and increase the classification accuracy. The proposed model design is a novel deep learning model to perform the fine tuning in the classification of nine different type of tomato plant disease.

Disruptive innovations in data management and analytics have led to the development of patient-centric Healthcare 4.0 from the hospital-centric Healthcare 3.0. This work presents an IoT-based monitoring systems for patients with cardiovascular abnormalities. IoT-enabled wearable ECG sensor module transmits the readings in real-time to the fog nodes/mobile app for continuous analysis. Deep learning/ machine learning model automatically detect and makes prediction on the rhythmic anomalies in the data. The application alerts and notifies the physician and the patient of the rhythmic variations. Real-time detection aids in the early diagnosis of the impending heart condition in the patient and helps physicians clinically to make quick therapeutic decisions. The system is evaluated on the MIT-BIH arrhythmia dataset of ECG data and achieves an overall accuracy of 95.12% in classifying cardiac arrhythmia.

Seema S., M.S. Ramaiah Institute of Technology, India
Sowmya B. J., M.S. Ramaiah Institute of Technology, India
Chandrika P., M.S. Ramaiah Institute of Technology, India
Kumutha D., SJB Institute of Technology, India
Nikitha Krishna, M.S. Ramaiah Institute of Technology, India

Facial expression recognition (FER) is an important topic in the field of computer vision and artificial intelligence due to its potential in academic and business. The authors implement deep-learning-based FER approaches that use deep networks to allow end-to-end learning. It focuses on developing a cutting-edge hybrid deep-learning approach that combines a convolutional neural network (CNN) for the prediction and a convolutional neural network (CNN) for the classification. This chapter proposes a new methodology to analyze and implement a model to predict facial expression from a sequence of images. Considering the linguistic and psychological contemplations, an intermediary symbolic illustration is developed. Using a large set of image sequences recognition of six facial expressions is demonstrated. This analysis can fill in as a manual to novices in the field of FER, giving essential information and an overall comprehension of the most recent best in class contemplates, just as to experienced analysts searching for beneficial bearings for future work.

Bhimavarapu Usharani, Department of Computer Science and
Engineering, Koneru Lakshmaiah Education Foundation,
Vaddeswaram, India

Hypertensive retinopathy is a disorder that causes hypertension which includes abnormalities in the retina that triggers vision problems. An effective automatic diagnosis and grading of the hypertensive retinopathy would be very useful in the health system. This chapter presents an improved activation function on the CNN by recognizing the lesions present in the retina and afterward surveying the influenced retina as indicated by the hypertensive retinopathy various sorts. The current approach identifies the symptoms associated of retinopathy for hypertension. This chapter presents an up-to-date review on hypertensive retinopathy detection systems that implement a variety of image processing techniques, including fuzzy image processing, along various improved activation function techniques used for feature extraction and classification. The chapter also highlights the available public databases, containing eye fundus images, which can be currently used in the hypertensive retinopathy research.

Thangavel M., VIT Bhopal University, India
Abhijith V. S., Thiagarajar College of Engineering, India
Sudersan S., Thiagarajar College of Engineering, India

In recent years, the rise in the demand for quality products and services along with systems that could integrate the control mechanisms with high computational capabilities led to the evolution of cyber-physical systems (CPS). Due to the ongoing COVID-19 pandemic, several industries have remained closed, causing several monetary losses. Automation can help in such scenarios to keep the industries up and running in a way that the system could be monitored and controlled remotely using voice. The chapter deals with the integration of both industrial automation and cyber-physical systems in various industries like the automobile industry, manufacturing industries, construction industries, and so on. A proposed approach for machine handling using CPS, deep learning, and industrial automation with the help of voice. The proposed approach provides greater insights into the application of CPS in the area and the combination of CPS and deep learning to a greater extent.

Meeradevi, M.S. Ramaiah Institute of Technology, India
Pramod Chandrashekhar Sunagar, M.S. Ramaiah Institute of
Technology, India
Anita Kanavalli, M.S. Ramaiah Institute of Technology, India

With recent advancements in computer network technologies, there has been a growth in the number of security issues in networks. Intrusions like denial of service, exploitation from inside a network, etc. are the most common threat to a network's credibility. The need of the hour is to detect attacks in real time, reduce the impact of the threat, and secure the network. Recent developments in deep learning approaches can be of great assistance in dealing with network interference problems. Deep learning approaches can automatically differentiate between usual and irregular data with high precision and can alert network managers to problems. Deep neural network (DNN) architectures are used with differing numbers of hidden units to solve the limitations of traditional ML models. They also seek to increase predictive accuracy, reduce the rate of false positives, and allow for dynamic changes to the model as new research data is encountered. A thorough comparison of the proposed solution with current models is conducted using different evaluation metrics.

Chapter 10

Sandeep Kumar Hegde, NMAM Institute of Technology, India
Monica R. Mundada, M.S. Ramaiah Institute of Technology, India

In this internet era, due to digitization in every application, a huge amount of data is produced digitally from the healthcare sectors. As per the World Health Organization (WHO), the mortality rate due to the various chronic diseases is increasing each day. Every year these diseases are taking lives of at least 50 million people globally, which includes even premature deaths. These days, machine learning (ML)-based predictive analytics are turning out as effective tools in the healthcare sectors. These techniques can extract meaningful insights from the medical data to analyze the future trend. By predicting the risk of diseases at the preliminary stage, the mortality rate can be reduced, and at the same time, the expensive healthcare cost can be eliminated. The chapter aims to briefly provide the domain knowledge on chronic diseases, the biological correlation between theses disease, and more importantly, to explain the application of ML algorithm-based predictive analytics in the healthcare sectors for the early prediction of chronic diseases.

Chapter 11

Alamelu J. V., M.S. Ramaiah Institute of Technology, India
Priscilla Dinkar Moyya, Vellore Institute of Technology, India
Mythili Asaithambi, Vellore Institute of Technology, India

The transformations through technological innovations have influenced the medical field. There are significant developments in medical devices in their usage. The utilization of the devices is automated in a local, remote environment. The medical devices used in the remote cyber environment uses different network protocols. These devices comprise micro, nanofabricated sensors and actuators which have the facility to communicate using network protocols. The devices that have network capability to integrate into cyberspace through physical methods are typical medical cyber physical systems (MCPS). In MCPS, medical device modelling is an important aspect. Several medical devices are available, and here in the current research, emphasis is focused on smart medical pumps in the MCPS environment. This chapter highlights the essential concepts of the smart medical drug delivery device, its architecture, control, actuation, communication, and analysis in the cyber environment.

The healthcare scheme in India has a lot of differences between rural and urban areas in terms of quality along with changes in private and public healthcare systems. The healthcare system is massive in India and full of inconsistencies and complexities like the other countries. Predictive analytics will help to improve the healthcare systems by providing valuable insight in healthcare. A huge amount of different data sets is generated because of the digitization of healthcare. This digitization allows us to use predictive analytics for better patient outcomes. Predictive analytics is utilized in decision-making activities and prediction making about the future events which are unknown. In this chapter, a brief overview of the Indian healthcare systems is given, along with data representations, challenges, issues, and risks associated with applying predictive analytics in healthcare and case studies with respect to regression and classification models.

Distributed caching is one such system used by dynamic high-traffic websites to process the incoming user requests to perform the required tasks in an efficient way. Distributed caching is currently employing hashing algorithm in order to serve its purpose. A significant drawback of hashing in this circumstance is the addition of new servers that would result in a change in the previous hashing method (rehashing), hence, goes into a rigmarole. Thus, we need an effective algorithm to address the problem. This technique has served as a solution for distributed and rehashing problems. Most of upcoming internet of things will have to be latency aware and will not afford the data transmission and computation time in the cloud servers. The real-time processing in proximal distance device would be much needed. Hence, the authors aim to employ a real-time task scheduling algorithm. Computations referring to the user requests that are to be handled by the servers can be efficiently handled by consistent hashing algorithms.

Preface

Today's technology is changing very rapidly and making an important place in the heart of humans. For example, when internet connected things after connect with other devices, they make a big system which solve complex problems and make people life easier and longer to live. One of popular revolution of technology is "Deep learning". This book is a unique collection of contributions from the field of CPS data analytics using deep learning.

Deep Learning is revolutionizing, because it offers an effective way of learning representation and allows the system to learn features automatically from data, without the need for explicitly designing them. In recent years, deep learning approaches have emerged as powerful computational models, and have shown significant success for dealing with a massive amount of data in unsupervised settings.

Nowadays that various aspects of our lives depend on complex cyber-physical systems, automated anomaly detection, as well as attack prevention and reaction have become of paramount importance and directly affect our security and ultimately our quality of life. Recent catastrophic events have demonstrated that manual, human-based management of anomalies in complex systems is not efficient enough, underlying the importance of automatic detection and intelligent response as the recommended approach of defence. Due to recent advancement in technology and their adaptability across various industries, the evolution of the Cyber-Physical Systems (CPSs) increased exponentially. With the emerging technologies on the CPS infrastructure, specifically, Internet of things, wearable devices, cloud computing, and data analytics, there is potential for acquiring and processing a tremendous amount of data from the physical world. CPSs system work with connecting other systems through Internet and its users. The CPS and their associated applications are widely used in various industries, for example CPS smart grid widely used in the energy sector, smart factory and industry 4.0, intelligent transportation systems, healthcare and medical systems, and robotic systems.

In near future in Industry 4.0 revolution, the uses of cyber physical systems will be on top position. Using such systems give invitation to attackers for performing attacks. But an attacker can harm a physical and cyber space easily, i.e., affecting physical processes will affect computations (also efficiency of CPS systems). For example, nuclear facilities were affected in 2010 (in Iran) by poplar attack "Stuxnet". Also, an attacker can control a medical device remotely which will be affected the condition of patients (also will leak private information of patient/hospital employee). Cyber-physical systems (CPS) comprise software components and physical objects that are deeply intertwined, each operating on different spatial and temporal scales, exhibiting multiple behavioural modalities and interacting with both each other and with users. They can interact with data and access services using a myriad of methods that change with their context of use. Promising computing paradigms and advanced technologies (e.g., smart home or city) relating to context awareness systems, activity recognition, distributed smart sensing, heterogeneous big data analytics, deep learning, and so on, have been increasingly developed and integrated into the CPS system, in order to make it a reality. The book contains 13 chapters as detailed below:

Chapter 1, "COVID-19 Spread Prediction Using Prophet and Data Fusion Algorithm: Prediction of COVID-19 Virus," describes COVID-19 has caused one of the biggest crises in our recent history. Most countries have developed monitoring systems based on pandemic evolution indicators to trigger social distancing measures whenever significant increases in infections are detected. Data analysis help forecast the short- and medium-term evolution of the pandemic and thus help policymakers in their decision making. This field seems to offer a promising and potentially fruitful area of research. Moreover, this approach can be followed at the international level to predict changes in trends and coordinate the pandemic globally.

Chapter 2, "Automatic Hibiscus Leaf Disease Detection and Classification Using Unsupervised Learning Techniques," discusses about agricultural field plays an important role for Gross Domestic Product (GDP) of any country. Plants are very important as they are supply source to human being. In Most of developing countries farmers use manual methods for farming. Late identifications of diseases in plants cause economic losses to the farmer which affects the economy of the state and the country at a large scale. There are some challenges in disease identification and classification are uneven background during image acquisition, segmentation and classification of an images. Once diseases are identified as per the symptoms, and its characteristics, control mechanisms can be applied. The adoption of traditional methods, machine learning techniques are still inefficient. While deep learning methods delivered superior results for disease identification and classification, compare to traditional methods.

One major limitation is that many researchers came up with their own dataset which are not available to other researchers so new algorithm development form other researcher cannot test the dataset which is not available publicly. Future direction is hardware development of an algorithm which can help famers to detect and classify diseases.

Chapter 3, "Deep Learning Approaches for Sentiment Analysis Challenges and Future Issues," defines and informs about Sentiment analysis (also known as opinion mining) is an active research area in natural language processing. It aims at identifying, extracting and organizing sentiments from user generated texts in social networks, blogs or product reviews. A lot of studies in literature exploit machine learning approaches to solve sentiment analysis tasks from different perspectives in the past 15 years. Since the performance of a machine learner heavily depends on the choices of data representation, many studies devote to building powerful feature extractor with domain expert and careful engineering. Recently, deep learning approaches emerge as powerful computational models that discover intricate semantic representations of texts automatically from data without feature engineering. These approaches have improved the state-of-the-art in many sentiment analysis tasks including sentiment classification of sentences/documents, sentiment extraction and sentiment lexicon learning.

Chapter 4, "Detection and Classification of Leaf Disease Using Deep Neural Network," gives information about the Plants which play a vital role in the survival of all organisms on Earth. Due to this fact, it is very important to ensure that measures are taken to detect and mitigate any diseases on plants. Plant diseases are a major factor for crop losses in agriculture. A Deep Learning approach has been presented to detect and classify plant diseases by examining the leaf of a given plant. The classification is performed in multiple stages to eliminate possibilities at every stage, hence providing better accuracy during predictions. The implementation of more accurate deep learning systems could help in better diagnosis of diseases in crops as these analyse down to the smallest unit of an image, a pixel.

Chapter 5, "Development of Efficient Monitoring System Using Fog Computing and Machine Learning Algorithms on Healthcare 4.0," provides information about the Internet of things provides interaction with billions of objects across the world using the Internet. Healthcare Industry has grown-up from 1.0 to 4.0 generation. Healthcare 3.0 was hospital centric, where patients of long-lasting sickness suffered a lot due to multiple hospital visits for their routine check-ups. This in turn, prolonged the treatment of such patients along with an increase in the overall expenditure on treatment of patients. However, with recent technological advancements such as fog and cloud computing, these problems are mitigated with a minimum capital investment on computing and storage facilities related to the data of the patients. Fog computing helps the doctors to take smart decisions during emergency for time-critical Healthcare applications. It also helps to protects sensitive data with reduced delay in comparison to the standalone cloud-based application. The role of fog computing, and machine learning algorithms provide uninterrupted context-aware services to the end users as and when required.

Chapter 6, "Efficient Facial Expression Recognition Using Deep Learning Techniques," explains the advent of artificial intelligence technology has reduced the gap of human and machine. Artificial intelligence equips man to create more near perfect humanoids. Facial expression is an important tool to communicate one's emotions nonverbally. Deep neural networks can become an efficient tool for classifying facial expressions. This chapter has focused on various techniques for implementing a deep neural network based facial recognition system. This also briefs the networks and data bases used for FER system.

Chapter 7, "Hypertensive Retinopathy Classification Using Improved Clustering Algorithm and the Improved Convolution Neural Network," describes the Changes in the retina of the eyes may occur due to high blood pressure, hypertensive retinopathy (HR) is a type of eye disease in which there is a change of the blood vessels of the eyes in the eye retina caused by arterial hypertension. HR signs occur because of narrowing of the arteries in the retina, bleeding in the retina of the eye and cotton wool spots. The diagnosis is conventionally performed by an ophthalmologist by performing fundus image analysis to determine the phases of HR disease symptoms.

Chapter 8, "Industrial Automation Using Mobile Cyber Physical Systems," presents Cyber Physical Systems (CPS) as an emergent approach that focuses on the integration of computational applications with physical devices, being designed as a network of interacting cyber and physical elements. CPS control and monitor real world physical infrastructures and thus is starting having a high impact in industrial automation. As such design, implementation and operation of CPS and management of the resulting automation infrastructure is of key importance for the industry.

Chapter 9, "Intrusion Detection System Using Deep Learning," specifies the machine learning techniques are being widely used to develop an intrusion detection system (IDS) for detecting and classifying cyberattacks at the network-level and the host-level in a timely and automatic manner. However, many challenges arise since malicious attacks are continually changing and are occurring in very large volumes requiring a scalable solution. There are different malware datasets available publicly for further research by cyber security community. However, no existing study has shown the detailed analysis of the performance of various machine learning algorithms on various publicly available datasets. Due to the dynamic nature of malware with continuously changing attacking methods, the malware datasets available publicly are to be updated systematically and benchmarked., a deep neural network (DNN), a type of deep learning model, is explored to develop a flexible and effective IDS to detect and classify unforeseen and unpredictable cyberattacks. It is confirmed that DNNs perform well in comparison with the classical machine learning classifiers.

Chapter 10, "Machine Learning-Based Approach for Predictive Analytics in Healthcare," describes a recent wealth of data and information, the healthcare sector is lacking in actionable knowledge. The healthcare industry faces challenges in essential areas like electronic record management, data integration, and computer-aided diagnoses and disease predictions. It is necessary to reduce healthcare costs and the movement towards personalized healthcare. The rapidly expanding fields of deep learning and predictive analytics has started to play a pivotal role in the evolution of large volume of healthcare data practices and research. Deep learning offers a wide range of tools, techniques, and frameworks to address these challenges. Health data predictive analytics is emerging as a transformative tool that can enable more proactive and preventative treatment options. In a nutshell, this chapter has focused on the framework for deep learning data analysis to clinical decision making depicts the study on various deep learning techniques and tools in practice as well as the applications of deep learning in healthcare.

Chapter 11, "Medical Cyber Physical System Architecture for Smart Medical Pump," describes the healthcare critical integration of a network of medical devices. These systems are progressively used in hospitals to achieve a continuous high-quality healthcare. The MCPS design faces numerous challenges, including inoperability, security/privacy, and high assurance in the system software. In this chapter, the infrastructure of the cyber-physical systems (CPS) has been discussed for smart medical pump. MCPS is need of smart healthcare and require attention from several research communities towards its raised issue.

Chapter 12, "Predictive Analytics for Healthcare," identifies predictive analytics in healthcare can help to detect early signs of patient deterioration in the ICU and general ward, identify at-risk patients in their homes to prevent hospital readmissions, and prevent avoidable downtime of medical equipment. Predictive analytics aims to alert clinicians and caregivers of the likelihood of events and outcomes before they occur, helping them to prevent as much as cure health issues. Such predictive algorithms can be used both to support clinical decision making for individual patients, and to inform interventions on a cohort or population level. Or they can even be applied to hospitals' operational and administrative challenges.

Chapter 13, "Consistent Hashing and Real-Time Task Scheduling in Fog Computing," identifies Cloud computing is the new era technology, which is entirely dependent on the internet to maintain large applications, where data is shared over one platform to provide better services to clients belonging to a different organization. Though cloud computing offers many advantages, but it suffers from certain limitation too, that during load balancing of data in cloud data centres the internet faces problems of network congestion, less bandwidth utilization, fault tolerance and security etc. To get rid out of this issue new computing model called Fog Computing is introduced which easily transfer sensitive data without delaying to distributed devices. Fog is similar to the cloud only difference lies in the fact that it is located more close to end users to process and give response to the client in less time. Secondly, it is beneficial to the real time streaming applications, sensor networks, Internet of things which need high speed and reliable internet connectivity.

Acknowledgment

We want to place on record our heartfelt thanks to all the people who have inspired us and contributed towards completing this book.

We thank the Management of M S Ramaiah Institute of Technology, Bangalore for encouraging us to work on this book. Our special thanks to Dr. NVR Naidu, Principal, M S Ramaiah Institute of Technology, for his valuable guidance and support.

Dr. Seema S and Dr. Monica R Mundada would like to thank Dr. Anita Kanavalli, Professor and Head of Computer Science and Engineering Department, M S Ramaiah Institute of Technology, for all the support extended towards this book. Dr. Shilpa M would like to thank Dr. G S Prakash, Controller of Examinations, Professor, Department of Industrial Engineering and Management, M S Ramaiah Institute of Technology for his encouragement. Dr. Shilpa M acknowledges the cooperation and support extended by Dr. N D Prasanna, Head of Industrial Engineering and Management Department, M S Ramaiah Institute of Technology.

We express our sincere thanks to all the reviewers who have spent their precious time in giving their valuable feedback towards all the chapters in this book. The feedback has been carefully considered and sincerely appreciated.

We thank all the authors for contributing towards this book. We thank Mrs. Sowmya B J, Assistant Professor, Department of Computer Science and Engineering, M S Ramaiah Institute of Technology for all the help she extended during the compilation.

We are extremely grateful to our family members, who graciously accepted our inability to attend to family chores during the course of writing this book, and especially for their extended warmth and encouragement. Without their support, we would not have been able to venture into writing this book.

Last, but not the least, we express our heartfelt thanks to the editorial team at the IGI Global: International Academic Publisher, who guided us through this project.

Chapter 1
COVID-19 Spread Prediction Using Prophet and Data Fusion Algorithm

Sangeetha V.
M.S. Ramaiah Institute of Technology, India

Evangeline D.
M.S. Ramaiah Institute of Technology, India

Sinthuja M.
M.S. Ramaiah Institute of Technology, India

ABSTRACT

Today, technology plays a vital role in the healthcare industry. In the traditional way, physicians' minds were predicting the unknown disease based on their expertise and experience. Use of new technology like predictive analytics is transforming the healthcare industry. Predictive analytics in healthcare uses historical data (demographic information, person's past medical history and behaviors) to make predictions about the future. In this chapter, a predictive model is proposed to predict COVID-19 using prophet algorithm. A novel approach based on longitudinal data fusion approach will maintain temporal data from time to time. Sparse regularization regression uses data source and feature level to predict the spread of virus. The proposed model designed using longitudinal data fusion offers better clinical insights. Predictions will be very beneficial to government and healthcare groups to provoke suitable measures in controlling coronavirus. It is also beneficial to pharmaceutical companies to fabricate pills at a quicker rate.

DOI: 10.4018/978-1-7998-8161-2.ch001

INTRODUCTION

In the year 2019, another infection called corona (COVID-19) is spread widely in China and a colossal number of individuals were tainted (WHO, Coronavirus disease 2019 (COVID-19) Situation Report – 35., 2020) . First case noticed out of doors of China is Thailand on thirteen January 2020. It has now spread to in extra of 50 one-of-a-kind countries. The sector health organization WHO declared COVID-19 as a Public fitness Emergency of worldwide situation (PHEIC) on 30 January 2020. Starting on 20 February 76,000 cases are affirmed in view of COVID-19 (Hui, 2020). Presence of this sickness isn't anticipated in explicit networks, geological district timeframe. As this irresistible sickness is quick spreading and compromises the soundness of countless individuals prompt activity is needed to dodge the illness at local area level. Coronavirus is created by another kind of Covid which was named beforehand as 19-nCoV by the World Health Organization. Among the Covid family, COVID-19 is the seventh part along with MERSnCoV and SARS-nCoV that can communicate to people. The side effects are fever, hack, windedness and looseness of the bowels. In outrageous cases, COVID-19 can motive pneumonia or even passing. The brooding time of COVID-19 calls for fourteen days or extra. At the time of idle infection, the contamination might be extra regrettable. It may unfold beginning with one human the non to the following thru respiratory drops and close contact. An infodemic has long gone with the COVID-19eruptwhichise ssentiallyanabundance of facts regarding the scene. As a huge part of the statistics on hand to the overall populace isn't always precise, it receives severe for people to find out reliable assets and dependable direction after they need it.

As individuals were requesting precise data around 2019-nCoV, the World Health Organization and web- based media groups are cooperating to follow the legends and gossipy tidbits through its central command in Geneva (WHO, Novel Coronavirus (2019-nCoV): Strategic Preparedness and Response Plan., 2020). The association is routinely distinguishing the bits of gossip that spread everywhere on the spots that hurt the ordinary citizens' wellbeing like off base proof of fixes. Individuals everywhere in the world are anticipating an arrangement to alleviate the spread of Covid with the assistance of some displaying procedures. Prescient investigation in medical care is utilized for wellbeing evaluation. The estimation of prescient examination in medical services has been more than once accentuated in past data frameworks research. What is Predictive investigation? It predicts what will occur later on and is regularly treated as the utilization of "measurable procedures to break down the present and to anticipate the future conduct dependent on current realities of history (Oh, 2020). A portion of the forecast strategies are relapse expectation models, Markov chain models, Bayesian organizations and other AI techniques. The vast majority of the examination is identified with flu, HIC and SARS.

In the current investigation, a portion of the techniques in particular the Elman neural organization, LSTM, and SVM are applied to anticipate and dissect COVID-19. Total affirmed cases, Aggregate passing's, Aggregate restored cases are anticipated by the techniques Elman neural organization, LSTM, and SVM. SVM is utilized to foresee the expanding scope of affirmed new cases, new passing's, and new relieved cases. The goal is to foresee the irresistible infection dependent on manifestations of wellbeing record.

BACKGROUND

Epidemiological models can be used to predict the spread of any epidemic disease. Covid -19 infection is now an epidemic which can turn into an endemic. Manoj Kumar et al., have developed such a model to predict the various stages of disease transmission (Kumar, 2020). In popular, incubation period of the disorder is five days and an inflamed character may want to unfold the disease in nine days. While the time span between getting inflamed and reaching the important level is 9 days, the time span between crucial stage and restoration is 9.5 days. Also, the time span among critical degree and loss of life is 14. 5 days. One such epidemiological model is the compartmental model where in the population

Comprising of a group of individuals undergo transition from one compartment (i.e., subset of a population) to another. Three factors like rate or period of transition, population size and probability of transition are very significant. Susceptible Infected Recovered model aka SIR model is one such epidemiological model which predicts the susceptible, infected and recovered population. On the other hand, Hybrid Epidemic model introduces a new compartment called Critical compartment and the probability of a person in critical stage getting recovered and the probability of a person in critical stage becoming dead are significant to determine the adequacy or shortage of beds and ventilators.

Anupam et al., have modeled the prediction using ANN and regression (Prakash, 2020). The geographical regions of the country are divided into three categories - severely hit, moderately hit and least hit zones. The basic assumption is adopting a similar strategy for handling the pandemic in states in similar categories. A polynomial regression model can be built based upon the infection count and number of days. Usually, the initial days of the pandemic is not considered as it would not give a clear picture of the disease spread and dynamics. Overall wide variety of active cases is the difference between general showed cases and overall recovered instances. Height of the pandemic may be decided from the increase ratio that's the ratio between the range of active instances at the present day and the number of active instances the preceding days. The height is reached when the boom ratio adjustments signal from effective to bad. This consistent negative growth fee for successive days can be showed because the height of the pandemic.

Lynn et al., considers four factors for prediction - flight data, hospitalizations, traffic and climate data (Pickering, 2020). Flight travel details in February and March of 2018, 2019 and 2020 to reduce the fluctuations in the data. New York City's Bureau of Transportation Statistics has provided the dataset for analysis. Number of infected, hospitalized and dead and frequent/emergency hospital visits in different category of age ranges are collected for future prediction. Air quality data can be obtained from Aura Satellite. Principal Component Analysis (PCA) can be used to filter those variables that could contribute highly to the disease. Multi-dimensional regression is employed to develop non-linear combination of input features called as artificial features or interactions.

Ranjani et al., applies decision tree algorithm for continuously splitting training and test data (Kumari, 2021). Randomness of data can be verified using autocorrelation. Autoregression feeds observations at the previous stage as input. Time-series model can be employed for prediction. Confirmed, recovered and death cases can be separately analyzed.

Amit Kumar Gupta et al., predicts the recovered and death cases using Support Vector Machines, Linear Regression and Prophet Model. Comparative analysis of these models reveals that Prophet model is more accurate than others. Non-periodic and periodic changes can be tracked using rend and seasonality factors. Unpredictable schedules and individual changes can be monitored using holiday and individual factors of the Prophet model. Artificial Intelligence (AI) researchers are reinforcing their ability to develop mathematical paradigms using nationally dispersed data to investigate this pandemic. within the article written by way of Wie Kiang H (Gupta, 2020), aims to use the machine getting to know modern fashions by using the use of the real-time records from the Johns Hopkins dashboard concurrently with the prediction trendy projected accessibility modern the COVID-19 over the international locations. The unfold modern Coronavirus has taken society to the verge state-of-the-art lack of social existence. Simultaneously, mathematical fashions are decided on fora

Computational technique focused on system gaining knowledge state modern to predict the unfold modern- day the virus, along with assist Vector Regression (SVR),Polynomial Regression (PR),Deep trendy regression fashions. World is under COVID-19 virus law. In the article, system cutting- edge models are used for pandemic analysis through a Johns Hopkins dataset. Polynomial Regression (PR) technique produced a minimal quantity trendy Root imply square mistakes (RMSE) over different strategies within the COVID-19 transmission projection.

SinaF, utilized forecast models for COVID-19 to create informed-decisions and implement important control measures (Ardabili, 2020). In the paper a comparative examination of gadget learning and sensitive computing models are used to foresee the COVID-19 episode as a non-compulsory to inclined-inflamed- recovered (SIR) and prone-exposed-infectious-recovered (SEIR) models. Among a extensive extend of system studying fashions explored, two models seemed promising like multi-layered perceptron, MLP, and flexible network-based totally fluffy deduction framework, ANFIS. Sina offers an introductory benchmarking to illustrate the ability of gadget studying for destiny term.

Zlatanvehicle, SandiBaressi, Segota et al. used AI fashions to address the spread and effect of Coronavirus infections (Kumari, 2021). Multilayer perceptron (MLP) counterfeit neural community. MLP is primarily based on calculating the values of neurons in a current layer as the actuated summation of weighted yields of neurons in a beyond layer, associated to the neuron. The weights of the neuron associations are at the beginning arbitrary, but at that factor balanced through the in opposite proliferation put together, in which the blunder for a forward engendered of the MLP comes approximately receives back- propagated via, and weights are balanced rather to the mistake. Hyper parameters of the MLP are shifted using a community appearance calculation, with a add as much as of 5376 hyper parameter combos. Utilizing those combos, an upload up to of forty eight. MLP method is excessive excellent model, and it keep the training time is low whilst in comparison to other machine gaining knowledge of fashions. Dataset, containing records on infected, recuperated, and expired sufferers in 406 regions over fifty one days (twenty second January 2020 to 12th walk 2020).

Hamdi et al., used Robotic models that make use of numerical instruments to characterize virus. In the paper, around eight states are characterized with COVID-19 widespread advancement from a vulnerable state to released states (Kwekha-Rashid, 2021). The parameters are decided by understanding a fitting optimization issue with three watched inputs: the number of infected, deceased, and reported cases. The problems are addressed with Levenberg-Marquardt algorithm. Model is tested for COVID-19 data for four main highly affected countries. The algorithm is tested and validated showing significantly accurate results.

China, Hubei, Wuhan, Shenzhen (Chang, 2021) used SEIR model to check the spread of corona virus. A few examinations influence the SEIR or SEIRD model to mimic the spread and gauge the quantity of tainted and recuperated individuals over the long haul. In any case, these models experience the ill effects of two key in sufficiency's: (i) regular SEIRD doesn't refers hits model boundaries w.r.t. time; (ii) it centers around foreseeing the pattern, rather than the real number of diseases later on. SEIRD model learns and updates its boundaries consistently. Also, it can anticipate the quantity of contamination cases, recuperated cases and passing's. In particular, Artificial Intelligence is used to deal with powerfully gauge the boundaries of disease rate, brooding rate, recuperation rate and passing rate, which can be refreshed by slope drop

Calculation. When the idea of the boundaries w.r.t. time is resolved, ARIMA model is embraced to portray the elements of the boundaries and anticipate their future changes.

Omar Zakary et. al., outlines a discrete time model with six major components for Covid -19 prediction in Morocco. The number of susceptible people to infection and uninfected (S), the number of susceptible people who are partially controlled(P), the number of susceptible people who are totally controlled(C), the number of infected people (I) and the number of death cases owing to Covid-19 infection (D). Covid -19 data collected and published by John Hopkins University is used for prediction in this work (Zakary, 2016).

Majid Niazkar et al. has assessed three mathematical models namely, Recursive-based Prediction model, Boltzmann Function based Prediction model, and Beesham's prediction model to predict Covid-19 outbreak in Iran and Turkey. Infection data available in WHO website is utilized (Niazkar, 2020). While training data uses the infection data available from 20th February and10th March, 2020 respectivelytill14thMay2020 for Turkey and Iran respectively, training data is considered from15thMay2020 to 4thJune, 2020 for both the countries. Performance evaluation of the three models were done on basis of the three parameters - Absolute relative error, observed and estimated number of cumulative confirmed cases. From the observations of the study, it was concluded that recursive based prediction model was found to be more accurate in prediction of death cases in Iran and Turkey.

Li et. al., employs Gaussian distribution theory to develop a model for predicting coronavirus transmission (Li, 2020). The work focuses on identifying the timespan by which more than 10000 cases can be cured in Hubei, finding out the earliest case in Hubei, basic reproduction number, average incubation period of the virus, effect of control by 5days, appropriate distribution satisfying daily infection curve, average number of days from diagnosis to cure, transmission in non-Hubei areas, and prediction of infection in South Korea.

Fractional calculus is employed by Karachua et al. to predict, confirm, recovered and death cases of COVID-19 in countries like China, France, Italy, Spain, Turkey, UK and US. Deep Assessment methodology (which gives the optimal representation of dataset and prediction of upcoming values) and Long Short Term Memory(LSTM) (Karachua, 2001), Gaussian prediction model is used to predict the short term future of the pandemic. However, it should be noted that the study does not take into account the impact of preventive measures taken by the government. And, the proposed method is best suitable for peak prediction but not for underestimating th efuture.

Bahri et al., focuses on Recurrent Neural Network architecture called Long Short Term Memory (LSTM) for prediction of recoveries in USA and Italy, a week ahead

(Lee, 2017). It stresses upon the fact that compartmental models like SEIR, SIR, SIRQ and mathematical models like ARIMA, ARMA do not cater to the dynamic nature of the epidemic.

MAIN FOCUS OF THE CHAPTER

Predictive analytics in healthcare is used for health assessment. The main objective of the chapter is to predict the spread of coronavirus. Prophet predictive analytics algorithm is used to predict the spread of corona virus using Kaggle dataset and any other real time data source. Prophet is a type of machine learning algorithm used for building forecasting models for time series data. It is an open-source algorithm that can used for forecasting covid facts that give greater correct prediction. In COVID – 19 situations, required statistics is due to numerous reasons like duration and absence of required parameters for higher prediction. Prophet algorithm permits better forecast and it'll not require dataset training in time series techniques. The primary key capabilities of this algorithm are it predicts extra correct for time collection statistics and it is specially used for prediction and capability planning. Dataset is taken from Kaggle, important features like Date, confirmed infected, Deaths and Recovered are considered. The Prophet characteristic does not require splitting of dataset wherein for fitting it takes entire dataset for accurate consequences.

Data fusion is a technique of gathering records from sensors and linked information from many databases, so the performance of the system can be advanced, while the accuracy of the results may be moreover multiplied. Basically, fusion could be a procedure of incorporating crucial facts from many sensors to a composite end result that may be a lot of complete and therefore a whole lot of useful for any person's operator or exceptional laptop vision obligations. Longitudinal technique produces greater challenges for records fusion and analysis synthesis each time there is lot of disease development for covid 19 signs. Proposed system will make use of a unique longitudinal information fusion method to be expecting the ailment development for covid-19 sickness. Prophet algorithm with a sparse regularization regression version simulates the connection among the accumulated facts function and additionally the goal mental characteristics cores, to predict the affected person's ailment progression rating at the precise time as shown in the Figure 1.

On the premise of supervised device-gaining knowledge of Regression algorithms, the proposed version is applied. Starting on January 22, 2020, WHO released the dataset that is used to make the prediction. The distribution of COVID -19 instances around the world is depicted in Figure 2. The range of said instances, deaths, and restoration cases from 22 January to the end of September 2020 changed into (38,917,803), (1,098,254), and (26,885,286), respectively.

Figure 1. Workflow of the System Model

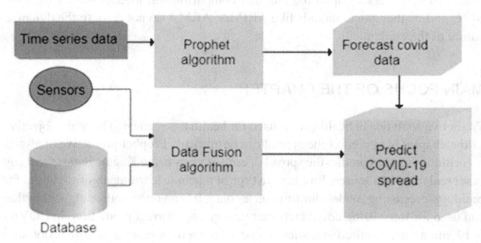

Figure 2. COVID-19 Distribution all over the World

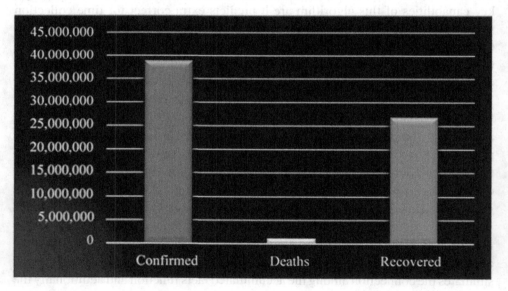

The number of confirmed cases, deaths, and recovery cases worldwide is shown in Table 1. The data in the table 1 clearly infers that Europe is the continent most affected, followed by Asia, America, Africa, and Australia.

The proposed system through longitudinal Data Fusion approach's function choice is shown in Figure 3.

Table 1. COVID-19 Case details till 30th September 2020 over the world

Continent	Confirmed	Deaths	Recovered
Africa	10450293	38407	1285804
America	4672236	384875	8993415
Asia	13986946	214996	10341346
Europe	8584922	238143	2867398
Australia	748801	938	27438

Figure 3. Feature Selection for Disease Progression using Longitudinal Data Fusion method

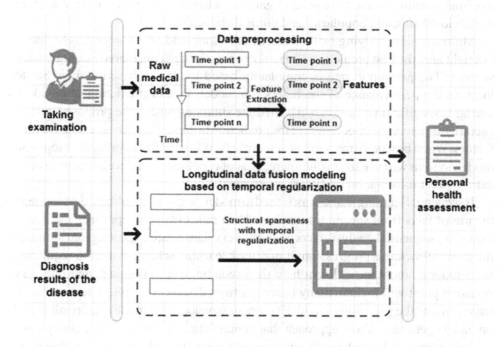

Longitudinal regulation is used to preserve information from numerous time points temporally powerful and also choose a subset of capabilities all the time factors. To assimilate medical measurements of diverse scales, first extract functions from scientific statistics after which carry out characteristic standardization. As an end result, all characteristics are rescaled to have the houses of a fashionable everyday distribution with an average of 0 and a fashionable deviation of 1. The whole dataset is split into a version production set (ninety percent) and a testing set (10 percentage) for evaluating and comparing competing fashions' results. The schooling and validation sets are subdivided from the version advent set. The responses for the observations within the validation set have been anticipated the use of the training facts. This allowed us to make an unbiased evaluation of a model healthy at the education dataset at the same time as tuning the version's hyper parameters. The very last version assessment is performed on a keep-out testing variety that has no longer formerly been used for both education or tuning the version's parameters.

Issues, Controversies, Problems

Covid 19 disease unfold development describes the exchange of disorder status through the years as a feature of the sickness procedure and remedy effects. Various machine learning method are used to gain knowledge of strategies to characterize the covid 19 sickness popularity and clinical statistics.

Multi-mission studying method can be used for covid 19 disorder development, but right here the best prediction of on every occasion was considered as a regression venture. The prediction rate is completely based totally on baseline data. So, to improve the performance of the regression model, further prediction of covid 19 spread at specific time factors had been done simultaneously. The proposed system captures the temporal smoothness of the prediction fashions throughout exclusive time factors. When best one time point of scientific facts is used for disorder development model, system will use the evolution records of capabilities in development to offer extra correct information on fitness assessment.

If sequential learning framework is used to model the covid-19 ailment development the use of facts from special time points. Then rating-worried approach that make use of the sequential analysis facts unearths very hard to are expecting and simulate the covid 19 sickness progression. If multitask learning scheme is used to regularize the temporal smoothness. Right here the predicting project at each and one very occasion point will include many functions from diverse a couple of resources. So maximum of the prevailing covid 19 ailment development modeling are all based on gadget getting to know approach that contain statistics from unique timepoints.

It is very much vital to discover answer with the aid of thinking about the modeling hassle that involves statistics from exclusive time factors. The most crucial assignment is to predict the covid 19 disorder progression. System should not forget statistics from distinctive time factors and additionally keep the temporal successively. Utilizing longitudinal clinical statistics and growing covid 19 disorder progression modeling method to be expecting patient's fitness fame is most difficult inside the gadget learning area.

SOLUTIONS AND RECOMMENDATIONS

The proposed system is implemented using Scikit-learn, library in Python. The system evaluation is done for proposed covid disease spread model on the dataset considered from Kaggle. The dataset considered includes features of State, Positive case, new cases, Total Recoveries and Deaths as shown in Table 2.

Table 2. COVID-19 Case details till 30ᵗʰ September 2020 over the world

State	Positive case	New cases	Total Recoveries	Deaths
Maharashtra	1242770	18390	936554	33,806
Andhra Pradesh	639302	7553	562376	5,461
Tamil Nadu	552674	5337	497377	8,947
Karnataka	533850	6974	432450	8,247
Uttar Pradesh	364543	5650	296183	5,212
Delhi	253075	3816	216401	5,051
West Bengal	231484	3182	202030	4,483
Odisha	192548	4237	153213	789
Telangana	177070	2296	146135	1,062
Bihar	171465	1609	157056	873

System model is trained with 70% data set and the remaining 30% data set is used for validation. To evaluate the model considered data belonging to different states within India as shown in Figure 4.

The proposed system model given an accuracy of 88.5% as shown in Figure 5, when compared to prediction accuracy rate carried out by Zheng using Data Fusion algorithm.

The proposed model provides the answer for predicting the Covid19 disorder spread development the usage of ridge regression to create a simple longitudinal information fusion version. Recollect the COVID-19 case, in which patients are grouped collectively depending on the severity of their contamination. The proposed version can be used to location new patients into the right zones. Due to the large variety of cases, this approach is extraordinarily beneficial in this rising COVID-19 pandemic. In a plague ailment like COVID-19, the prediction of mortality and unfold rate is essential because it lets in the public, authorities, and fitness-care systems to take precautionary measures based totally on these facts. For schooling the version and forecasting the range of inflamed instances, system used the Prophet set of rules.

Considering Prophet Set of rules is mainly an open supply algorithm that provides more correct predictions, this look at recommends it for higher prediction.

Figure 4. COVID Statistics of 10 Different states in India

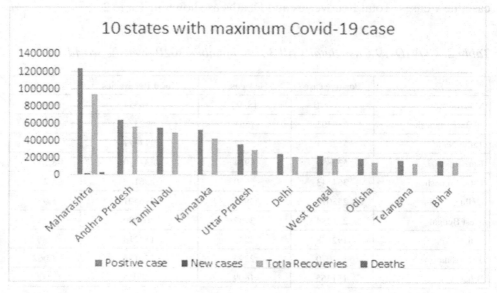

Figure 5. Accuracy for Proposed model

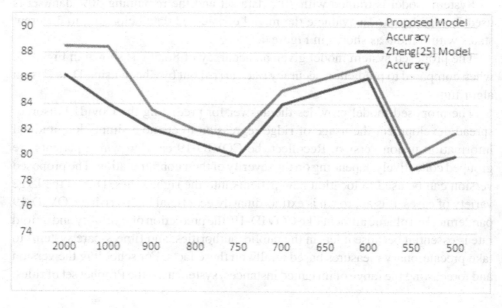

Due to the fact that enough data isn't available in a surprising pandemic like COVID -19 for a number of reasons, such as duration and a lack of essential parameters for higher prediction. In time collection strategies, the prophet set of rules lets in for higher forecasting and does no longer require dataset preparation. Use of the Prophet predictive analytics algorithm to the Kaggle dataset and its predictions gives better prediction consequences.

FUTURE RESEARCH DIRECTIONS

The future work remembers the usage of the strategy for a real smart clinical choice emotionally supportive network, and assessment of the methodology under sensible conditions. Moreover, to improve the presentation of the current strategy by analyzing more data like age and family ancestry can be considered. To arrive at the more modest assessment cost and more infection determination can be considered.

CONCLUSION

Based on a regression approach, Covid 19 spread prediction with the usage of longitudinal data fusion for simultaneous evaluation of capabilities on the statistics source and feature level was considered. The proposed model enforces the temporal regularization time period at the linear regression version. System use the accelerated gradient descent approach to clear up the method. The proposed model is evaluated and tested to obtain 88.5% accuracy to predict covid spread using prophet and data fusion approach. The system considered the characteristics of medical statistics from diverse time factors into covid19 unfold prediction modelling to predict accuracy. Longitudinal data fusion technique provides scientific views which might be advanced to different ailment progression modelling tactics. The proposed model outperforms healthcare predictive analytics strategies in covid 19 disorder progression model.

REFERENCES

Amit Kumar Gupta, V. S.-G. (2021). Prediction of COVID-19 pandemic measuring criteria using support vector machine, prophet and linear regression models in Indian scenario. *Journal of Interdisciplinary Mathematics*, *24*(1), 89–108. doi:10.1080/0 9720502.2020.1833458

Ardabili, S. F.-K., Mosavi, A., Ghamisi, P., Ferdinand, F., Varkonyi-Koczy, A. R., Reuter, U., Rabczuk, T., & Atkinson, P. M. (2020). Covid-19 outbreak prediction with machine learning. *Algorithms*, *13*(10), 249. doi:10.3390/a13100249

BaressiŠegota, S. L. (2019). On the traveling salesman problem in nautical environments: An evolutionary computing approach to optimization of tourist route paths in Medulin, Croatia. *Pomorskizbornik*, *57*(1), 71–87.

Chang, L. W., Hou, W., Zhao, L., Zhang, Y., Wang, Y., Wu, L., Xu, T., Wang, L., Wang, J., Ma, J., Wang, L., Zhao, J., Xu, J., Dong, J., Yan, Y., Yang, R., Li, Y., Guo, F., Cheng, W., ... Wang, L. (2021). The prevalence of antibodies to SARS-CoV-2 among blood donors in China. *Nature Communications*, *12*(1), 1–10. doi:10.103841467-021-21503-x PMID:33654063

Darapaneni, N. S. M. (2021). Predicting the Impact of Covid-19 Pandemic in India. In *2021 IEEE International IOT, Electronics and Mechatronics Conference (IEMTRONICS)* (pp. 1-7). IEEE.

Gupta, A. S.-G. (2020). PredictionofCOVID-19 pandemic measuring criteria using support vector machine, prophet and linear regression models in Indian scenario. *Journal of Interdisciplinary Mathematics*, 1–20.

Hui, D. S., I Azhar, E., Madani, T. A., Ntoumi, F., Kock, R., Dar, O., Ippolito, G., Mchugh, T. D., Memish, Z. A., Drosten, C., Zumla, A., & Petersen, E. (2020). The continuing 2019-nCoV epidemic threat of novel coronaviruses to global health—The latest 2019 novel coronavirus outbreak in Wuhan, China. *International Journal of Infectious Diseases*, *91*, 264–266. doi:10.1016/j.ijid.2020.01.009 PMID:31953166

Karachua, E., & Turk, A. S. (2001). E-polarized scalar wave diffraction by perfectly conductive arbitrary shaped cylindrical obstacles with finite thickness. *International Journal of Infrared and Millimeter Waves*, *22*(10), 1531–1546. doi:10.1023/A:1015098925652

Khalil, I. S. (n.d.). Rubbing against blood clots using helical robots: modeling and in-vitro experimental validation. *Robotics and Automation Letters, 2*(2), 927-934.

Kumar, M. B. (2020). An Intelligent Prediction Model of COVID-19 in India using Hybrid Epidemic Model. In *International Conference on Smart Electronics and Communication (ICOSEC)* (pp. 389-396). IEEE. 10.1109/ICOSEC49089.2020.9215426

Kumari, R. K., Kumar, S., Poonia, R. C., Singh, V., Raja, L., Bhatnagar, V., & Agarwal, P. (2021). Analysis and predictions of spread, recovery, and death caused by COVID-19 in India. *Big Data Mining and Analytics*, *4*(2), 65–75. doi:10.26599/BDMA.2020.9020013

Kwekha-Rashid, A. A. (2021). Coronavirus disease (COVID-19) cases analysis using machine-learning applications. *Appl Nanosci*.

Lee, J. B.-D. (2017). Deep neural networks as gaussian processes. *arXiv preprint*.

Li, L. Y., Yang, Z., Dang, Z., Meng, C., Huang, J., Meng, H., Wang, D., Chen, G., Zhang, J., Peng, H., & Shao, Y. (2020). Propagation analysis and prediction of the COVID-19. *Infectious Disease Modelling*, *5*, 282–292. doi:10.1016/j.idm.2020.03.002 PMID:32292868

Niazkar, M. T. (2020). Assessment of Three Mathematical Prediction Models for Forecasting the COVID-19 Outbreak in Iran and Turkey. *Computational and Mathematical Methods in Medicine*.

Oh, S. H. (2020). The effects of social media use on preventive behaviors during infectious disease outbreaks: The mediating role of self-relevant emotions and public risk perception. *Health Communication*, 1–10. doi:10.1080/10410236.2020.1791376 PMID:32064932

Organization, W. H. (2020). *Coronavirus disease 2019 (COVID-19) Situation Report – 35*. WHO.

Organization, W. H. (2020). *Novel Coronavirus (2019-nCoV)*. Strategic Preparedness and Response Plan.

Pawar, S. C. (2021). Analyzing and Forecasting COVID-19 Outbreak in India. *2021 11th International Conference on Cloud Computing, Data Science & Engineering (Confluence)*, 1059-1066.

Pickering, L. (2020). Identifying Factors in COVID-19 AI Case Predictions. In *7th International Conference on Soft Computing & Machine Intelligence (ISCMI)* (pp. 192-196). IEEE.

Prakash, A. S. (2020). Spread & Peak Prediction of Covid-19 using ANN and Regression (Workshop Paper). In *2020 IEEE Sixth International Conference on Multimedia Big Data (BigMM)* (pp. 356-365). IEEE.

Shaikh, S. J. G. (2021). Analysis and Prediction of COVID-19 using Regression Models and Time Series Forecasting. *2021 11th International Conference on Cloud Computing, Data Science & Engineering (Confluence)*, 989-995.

Zakary, O. (2016). The epsilon capacity of a gain matrix and tolerable disturbances: Discrete-time perturbed linear systems. *arXiv preprint, 1608.00426*.

Zhao, H. Y. L. (2021). A COVID-19 Prediction Optimization Algorithm Based on Real-time Neural Network Training—Taking Italy as an Example. In *2021 IEEE Asia-Pacific Conference on Image Processing, Electronics and Computers (IPEC)* (pp. 345-348). IEEE.

Zheng, Y., & Hu, X. (2020). Healthcare predictive analytics for disease progression: A longitudinal data fusion approach. *Journal of Intelligent Information Systems, 55*(2), 351–369. doi:10.100710844-020-00606-9

Chapter 2
House Plant Leaf Disease Detection and Classification Using Machine Learning

Bhimavarapu Usharani

https://orcid.org/0000-0001-5050-0415

Department of Computer Science and Engineering, Koneru Lakshmaiah Education Foundation, Vaddeswaram, India

ABSTRACT

Hibiscus is a fantastic herb, and in Ayurveda, it is one of the most renowned herbs that have extraordinary healing properties. Hibiscus is rich in vitamin C, flavonoids, amino acids, mucilage fiber, moisture content, and antioxidants. Hibiscus can help with weight loss, cancer treatment, bacterial infections, fever, high blood pressure, lower body temperature, treat heart and nerve diseases. Automatic leaf disease detection is an essential task. Image processing is one of the popular techniques for the plant leaf disease detection and categorization. In this chapter, the diseased leaf is identified by concurrent k-means clustering algorithm and then features are extracted. Finally, reweighted KNN linear classification algorithms have been used to detect the diseased leaves categories.

I. INTRODUCTION

Hibiscus is widely known for its beautiful flowers which lack aroma. Hibiscus belongs to the Malyaceae group, and its scientific name is Hibiscus rosa-sinensis. A popular name for hibiscus in ayurvedic is Japa. This hibiscus plant does not have

DOI: 10.4018/978-1-7998-8161-2.ch002

any fruit. Hibiscus flowers are in various shades like red, white, yellow, pink. The bark, leaves and flowers are known to have medical properties.

Hibiscus is a famous herb found all over India in the temperature climates and its other types are found all over the world. Hibiscus reduces high blood pressure, using for cancer treatment and as a weight loss aid, along with other uses. Research has revealed a variety of health benefits linked to drinking hibiscus tea, lowers blood pressure, fight bacteria and even aid weight loss. Hibiscus extracts boosted the number of antioxidant enzymes and lessened the damaging impacts of available radical by up to 92% (Taofeek, et al., 2011). The article (Abbas Mohagheghi, et al., 2011) associated the outcomes of drinking hibiscus contrasted with black tea on fat stages. The authors in (Hong-Chou, et al.,2014) presented that hibiscus followed in a body mass index (BMI), weight of a person, overweight of a person. The authors of (Diane L, et al.,2018, Corina Serban, et al.,2015) originate that drinking hibiscus decoction dropped blood pressure in people at risk of high blood pressure and those with slightly high blood pressure. The authors in (Zeinab, et al.,2012) discussed that this herbal is used to treat lice (Chun-Tang, et al.,2005). The results of (Hui-Hsuan Lin, et al., 2015) proved that hibiscus leaf extract prevented human prostate cancer. Hibiscus leaves extract inhibits stomach cancer cell by up to 52%. Hibiscus extracts are used in many medical applications like cramping, gas, diarrhea (EunKyung Jung, YoungJun Kim et al.,2015, Nami Joo., et al.,2015), to treat bacterial infections (Emad Mohamed, et al.,2016).

Rest of this chapter is categorized as following sections: Section II of this article briefly discusses about existing work for the plant disease detection. Section III presents the proposed model i.e., Automatic Hibiscus Leaf Disease Detection and Classification Using Unsupervised Learning Techniques. Section IV presents experimental and performance results and finally section V presents the concluding remarks.

II. LITERATURE SURVEY

Leaf images are one of the most important resources for the recognition and categorisation of plant groups and their diseases. WanMohdFadzil et al (Emad Mohamed, et al.,2014) conversed a bug identification process for orchid plant shrubberies. The proposed procedure used the combination of several approaches of edge segmentation methods, morphological and filtering procedures cast-off for classifying given images into two bug class as black leaf spot and solar scorch.

Rong Zhou et al (Rong Zhou, et al.,2013), explained method to identity leaflet patch in sugar beet. The procedure implements cross methods for corresponding and support vector machinel(SVM). This technique uses R for segmentation, filtering and support vector machine(SVM) classifier for categorization.

Dheeb et al (Ai-Bashish et al.,2013) proposed a technique to spot the leaf disorder of the plant that exists on flyer and bamboo. It uses a combination of K-Means technique and deep learning for categorization of the input leaf and the segmented images, it gives an maximum precision of 93%.

Smith et al (A,Camargo, et al.,2019)projected a procedure for identification of plant leaf maladies and the exactness of the proposed technique is verified by comparing the taken input leaf images with those segmented leaf images . Di et al (Di Cui, et al.,2012) proposed a technique to detect erosion on leaf and its progression of bug and uses the concept of centroid. Youwen Tian and Lin Zhang (Youwen, et al.,2012) proposed a technique for cucumber downy mildew bug by using the hyperspectral imaging. Muralil et al (Murali Krishnan, et al.,2013), proposed a procedure to identify the filthy plant sprig area using the K-Means and extract the region of interest.

III. PROCEDURE FOR HIBISCUS LEAF DISEASE DETECTION AND CLASSIFICATION

The architecture of proposed model is depicted in **Figure 1** which shows the broad process of projected hibiscus leaf disease detection. The steps in the proposed system are:

Figure 1. Procedure for hibiscus leaf disorder detection

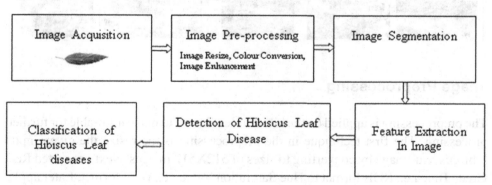

Image Acquisition

The hibiscus leaf images are got by using the mobile camera. The dataset comprises 150 healthy and diseased hibiscus leaf images. Dataset consists of two set of classes: the first class is the healthy hibiscus leaf images, and the second leaf images set is the unhealthy hibiscus leaf image set. The healthy and the infected leaves samples are depicted in **Figure 2** and **Figure 3**.

Figure 2. Healthy Hibiscus Leaves

Figure 3. Diseased and Infected Hibiscus Leaves

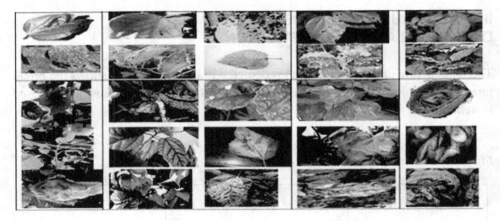

Image Preprocessing

The preprocessing is applied on the hibiscus leaf image to make it suitable for further processing. The first technique in the preprocessing is the resize the given input hibiscus leaf image by converting to sizes of 512X512 images. Next converted Red Green Blue i.e., RGB format to Hue Saturation Value i.e., HSV format. Later apply the image enhancement technique. The resultant image is depicted in **Figure 4**:

Figure 4. After pre-processing step

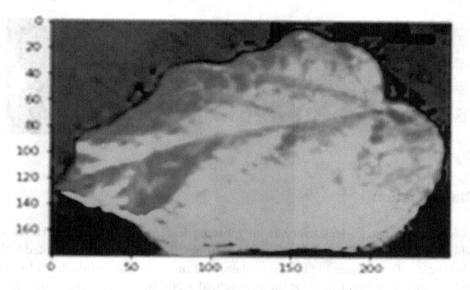

Image Segmentation

Segmentation divides the image into several regions. It analyses the hibiscus leaf image data set to extract the information for further processing. In this article the segmentation uses the Concurrent K-Means clustering technique. The proposed algorithm is discussed in **Algorithm 1.**

Algorithm 1: Concurrent K- Means Clustering Algorithm

1. Divide the dataset into different sets and each set is clustered concurrently.
2. Initialize each cluster centroid.
3. Until the stopping criteria met.
4. Recalculate the new cluster centroid by using the normalized euclidean distance.
5. Merge all the cluster centroids.
6. Map the points to final cluster.

Feature Extraction

Feature extraction extracts the features that are present in the hibiscus leaf images. The extracted features are categorized as shape, color, and texture. The leaf disease varies their shapes into different several shaped of the image due to existing diseases. The color feature differentiates the disease from each other.

Figure 5. Extracting the features for the hibiscus leaf.

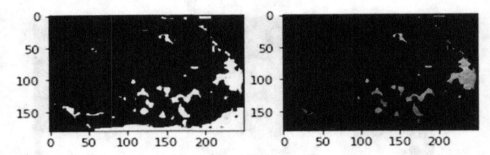

Classification

Classification categorizes every input hibiscus leaf image into a specific class which improves the leaf disease detection accuracy. The proposed Reweighted KN-Linear classifier reduces the incorrect classification of healthy or infected hibiscus leaf images. The algorithm for the reweighted KNN linear classifier is given in **Algorithm 2**.

Algorithm 2: Reweighted KNN Linear Classification

Input: Set of Hibiscus Leaf Images
Output: Improve detection accuracy
    1.   For each leaf image L_i.
    2.   Extract the features.
    3.   Construct n weak learners D_i
    4.   Classify the leaf as normal or infected.
    5.   Combine all weak learners result $y=\sum(D_i)$
    6.   Calculate training error T_e.
    7.   Reweight the weak n- learners.
    8.   Find best weak learner with minimum training error.
    9.   Obtain classification results.

IV: RESULTS AND DISCUSSION

The hibiscus leaf image of plant is captured by using the mobile in the Vaddeswaram and Vijayawada locations. The taken input hibiscus leaf images comprises of 150 images of healthy, infected hibiscus leaf leaves. The acquired leaf images are converted into the useable format. All the experiments are implemented using the python.

To classify hibiscus leaf disease, a set of characteristics for classification and detection of the diverse hibiscus infected plants are considered. For this, leaf spot characteristics are extricated from image using the suitable image processing methods and these characteristics stipulate serious data about the pictorial illustration. The characteristics correspond to features of spots are length, ratio of the principal axes which describes the ratio of the principal axis's length.

Orientation is demarcated as an approach among the major axis of the spot and the horizontal axis. The equivdiameter is the diameter of the spot. The eccentricity is the ratio of the distance between the foci and the major axis length of the ellipse eccentricity ratio. Solidity tells about the compactness of the spot. The extent metric gives the details of the proportion of the pixels in the infected area. The hydraulic radius gives the about by isolating the spot area with the spot perimeter. The complexity metric gives the perimeter of the infected leaf spot area. The Euler number gives the invariant property of the infected area of the leaf. The above discussed metrics are given for the hibiscus diseases and given in **Table 1** and **Table 2.**

Eccentricity value must be in between 0 and 1, the spot whose eccentricity ratio is 0 is a circle. The extent metric value must be in concerning as zero and one, when the proportion of the spot has the value 1 then its shape is impeccably rectangle. By using the feature extraction, the outcome for numerous characteristics of the hibiscus plant images is extracted and summarized in Table 1 and Table 2.

Table 1. Features of hibiscus leaf diseases

Feature	Dieback	Wilt	Leaf fungus	Black Spot	Psedomonas Cichorii	Myrothecium Roridum
Area	76.03	65.34	78.11	69.78	65.34	77.54
Major axis	18.70	13.45	11.34	12.45	11.45	11.78
Minor axis	9.23	8.01	7.98	6.34	8.34	7.56
Orientation	34.89	43.56	23.56	34.12	23.11	29.48
Equivdiameter	10.78	11.89	10.34	9.89	10.67	10.67
Eccentricity	0.98	0.89	0.91	0.93	0.91	0.95
Solidity	0.95	0.91	0.94	0.96	0.95	0.91
Extent	0.78	0.87	0.71	0.69	0.75	0.77
Hydraulic radius	1.98	1.56	1.27	1.34	1.67	1.45
complexity	15.67	11.23	13.67	12.45	11.56	14.38
Euler Number	1.00	1.00	1.00	1.00	1.00	1.00
Moment of inertia	14.56	13.45	12.25	14.27	13.67	11.71
Ratio of Principle axes	1.78	1.25	1.67	1.83	1.41	1.49

Table 2. Features of hibiscus leaf diseases

Feature	White Powdery Mildew	Yellow Leaves	Phytophthora	Bacterial Blights	Leaf Spot	White cottony spots
Area	78.34	69.26	65.49	77.54	76.03	65.34
Major axis	11.45	11.78	13.45	11.34	12.45	11.49
Minor axis	7.98	6.34	9.23	8.01	7.34	8.01
Orientation	34.12	23.11	34.89	43.56	41.23	39.34
Equivdiameter	11.89	10.34	10.67	10.67	9.56	10.45
Eccentricity	0.91	0.93	0.91	0.95	0.91	0.94
Solidity	0.94	0.96	0.95	0.93	0.91	0.95
Extent	0.87	0.71	0.71	0.69	0.75	0.77
Hydraulic radius	1.34	1.67	1.98	1.56	1.27	1.34
complexity	11.23	13.67	15.67	11.23	13.67	12.45
Euler Number	1.00	1.00	1.00	1.00	1.00	1.00
Moment of inertia	14.27	13.67	13.45	12.25	14.27	13.67
Ratio of Principle axes	1.67	1.83	1.31	1.59	1.88	1.15

Figure 6 shows the results of finding the affected area of hibiscus leaves with different diseases. Identified 14 various hibiscus leaf diseases affected.

Figure 6. Disease names, affected area, and their accuracy.

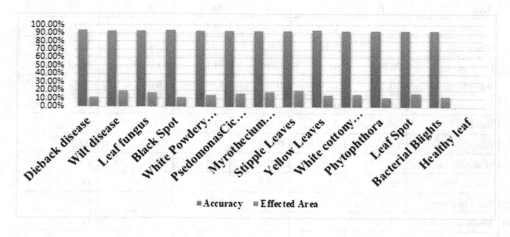

V. CONCLUSION

It is very important to diagnose the infected plant leaves automatically. To segment the leaf, concurrent K-Means clustering algorithm has been proposed. By this the parallel execution of cluster centroids has taken place and reduces the complexity and computational cost. The feature extraction has done using the geometrical features. Then finally reweighted KNN linear classification algorithm has been proposed to classify the category of the diseased hibiscus leaves. The given system gives the 92.15% accuracy for the hibiscus leaf disease.

REFERENCES

Abdallah, E. M. (2016). Antibacterial efficiency of the sudanese roselle (hibiscus sabdariffa l.), a famous beverage from sudanese folk medicine. *Journal of Intercultural Ethnopharmacology*, 5(2), 186. doi:10.5455/jice.20160320022623 PMID:27104041

Ai-Bashish, & Ban-Ahmad. (2011). Detection and classification of leaf diseases using K-Means based segmentation and neural networks based classification. *Información Tecnológica*, 10, 267–275.

Camargo & Smith. (2019). *An Image processing based algorithm to automatically identify plant disease visual symptoms*. Elsevier.

Chang, H.-C., Peng, C.-H., Yeh, D.-M., Kao, E.-S., & Wang, C.-J. (2014). Hibiscus sabdariffa extract inhibits obesity and fat accumulation and improves liver steatosis in humans. *Food & Function*, 5(4), 734–739. doi:10.1039/c3fo60495k PMID:24549255

Chiu, C.-T., Chen, J.-H., Chou, F.-P., & Lin, H.-H. (2005). Hibiscus sabdariffa leaf extract inhibits human prostate cancer cell invasion via down-regulation of akt/nf-kb/mmp-9 pathway. *Nutrients*, 7(7), 5065–5087. doi:10.3390/nu7075065 PMID:26115086

Cui, Zhang, Li, Hartman, & Zhao. (2012). *Image Processing methods for quantitatively detecting soybean rust from multispectral images*. Elsevier.

El-Basheir & Fouad. (2012a). preliminary pilot survey on head lice, pediculosis in sharkia governorate and treatment of lice with natural plant extracts. *Journal of the Egyptian Society of Parasitology, 32*(3), 725–736.

Fadzil, Rizam, Jailani, & Nooritawati. (2014). Orchid leaf disease detection using Border segmentation technique. *IEEE Conference on Systems, Process Control, 1*, 168-179.

Jung, Kim, & Joo. (2015). Physicochemical properties and antimicrobial activity of roselle (hibiscus sabdariffa l.). *Journal of the Science of Food and Agriculture*, *93*(15), 3769–3776. PMID:23749748

Krishnan & Sumithra. (2013). A Novel algorithm for detecting bacterial leaf scorch (BLS) of shade trees using image processing. *IEEE 11 Malaysia International Conference on Communications.*

Lin, Huang, Huang, Chen, & Wang. (2015). Hibiscus polyphenol-rich extract induces apoptosis in human gastric carcinoma cells via p53 phosphorylation and p38 mapk/fasl cascade pathway. *Molecular Carcinogenesis, 43*(2), 86–99.

McKay, Saltzman, Chen, & Blumberg. (2018). *Hibiscus sabdariffa l. tea (tisane) lowers blood pressure in prehypertensive and mildly hypertensive adults*. Academic Press.

Mohagheghi, A., Maghsoud, S., Khashayar, P., & Ghazi-Khansari, M. (2011). The effect of hibiscus sabdariffa on lipid profile, creatinine, and serum electrolytes: A randomized clinical trial. *International Scholarly Research Notices*. PMID:21991538

Serban, C., Sahebkar, A., Ursoniu, S., Andrica, F., & Banach, M. (2015). Effect of sour tea (hibiscus sabdariffa l.) on arterial hypertension: A systematic review and meta-analysis of randomized controlled trials. *Journal of Hypertension, 33*(6), 1119–1127. doi:10.1097/HJH.0000000000000585 PMID:25875025

Taofeek, O. (2011). Antioxidant and drug detoxification potentials of hibiscus sabdariffa anthocyanin extract. *Drug and Chemical Toxicology, 34*(2), 109–115. doi:10.3109/01480545.2010.536767 PMID:21314460

Tian & Linzhang. (2012). *Study on the methods of detecting cucumber downy mildew using hypersectral imaging technology*. Elsevier.

Zhou, Kaneko, Tianaka, Kayamori, & Shimizu. (2013). Early detection and continuous quantization of plant disease using template matching and support vector machine algorithms. *IEEE International Symposium on Computing and Networking.*

Chapter 3
Deep Learning Approaches for Sentiment Analysis Challenges and Future Issues

Rajalaxmi Prabhu B.
NMAM Institute of Technology, India

Seema S.
https://orcid.org/0000-0003-1766-0841
M.S. Ramaiah Institute of Technology, India

ABSTRACT

A lot of user-generated data is available these days from huge platforms, blogs, websites, and other review sites. These data are usually unstructured. Analyzing sentiments from these data automatically is considered an important challenge. Several machine learning algorithms are implemented to check the opinions from large data sets. A lot of research has been undergone in understanding machine learning approaches to analyze sentiments. Machine learning mainly depends on the data required for model building, and hence, suitable feature exactions techniques also need to be carried. In this chapter, several deep learning approaches, its challenges, and future issues will be addressed. Deep learning techniques are considered important in predicting the sentiments of users. This chapter aims to analyze the deep-learning techniques for predicting sentiments and understanding the importance of several approaches for mining opinions and determining sentiment polarity.

DOI: 10.4018/978-1-7998-8161-2.ch003

1. INTRODUCTION

The explosion of social networks in recent years has resulted in a massive volume of user-generated data on the Internet. Sentiment analysis is a technique for discovering and evaluating good and negative behaviors, as well as associated feelings, in a text. (Lee et. al, 2018). Extracting the useful features from a large number of user reviews is considered a useful task. Sentiment analysis usually consists of patterns and opinions in the form of user reviews. The opinion mining process includes the part of text analytics, and also retrieving information. Feature weighting plays a major role in analyzing sentiments (Zheng et.al, 2018). Sentiment analysis techniques are used to express reviews, opinions, and political issues automatically from the web. The major aim is to learn a pattern to extract the features, words, aspects and opinion expressions, and competitive words. Feature extraction process aims to identify the aspects from the comments done by the customers, whereas the sentiment prediction determines the text containing the opinion about the sentences which mainly helps to determine the polarity either positive, negative and then finally we integrate these two phases to obtain the final result. Opinion mining analyses the opinions of people and their attitudes regarding several products and their attributes. Pattern classification is one of the most supervised learning models for analyzing data and several patterns are mainly used for classifying texts (Plazaleiva et.al, 2017). The important feature of sentiment analysis is to generate the review or summaries based on sentiments expressed based on product features. Product features can be extracted from sentences based on supervised and unsupervised methods (Schouten et.al, 2017). The idea is to restrict the material so that it is difficult to write grammatically sound expressions that express opinion. The study primarily describes many approaches for using user evaluations to uncover valuable patterns. The feature that makes sentiment analysis valuable is that it can tell whether a statement is favorable, negative, or neutral. In addition to their established position in NLP, deep learning models have an essential role in sentiment analysis for multiple datasets (Ain et al, 2017).They are also capable of learning the decision boundaries, because they can stack layers one on top of the other. In the general case, words are normally indicated using a high-dimensional vector space. Feature extraction is mostly determined by the context of the neural network. Mapping of words through the model with similar syntactic and syntactic properties will create meaning for the words. Hence recurrent neural network models are capable of analyzing sentences hence it is easy to analyze sentiments using these models.(Nair et.al, 2021). In this work, I am explaining several architectures for analyzing sentiments and exploring the uses of deep learning techniques its challenges, and future issues. Different deep learning architectures its benefits and drawbacks are also studied. This proposal incorporates sentence-level latent semantic indexing to assist with topic extraction, with further regularization restrictions applied to enhance the effect, and topic-level attention mechanisms are applied in the long short-term memory network to do sentiment analysis. (Pathak et.al, 2021). AS part of research objective deep learning model mainly used as a powerful tool in building the sentiments. The main objective of this paper is to clearly analyse the various Deep learning approach and also we discussed a RNN model with wordtovec as part of case study for analyzing its importance. Results are carried out based on the review dataset and detailed analysis on this dataset is made with respect to RNN+word2vec model.

2. SENTIMENT ANALYSIS

Sentiment analysis is considered one of the most important challenging processes since there is a huge amount of data present every day (Cambria et.al, 2016)). It is the analysis of sentiments on a particular entity in the means of positive, negative, or neutral polarity. The aim is to search the word as it will mean different in many situations. Sentiment analysis's main aim is to identify people's opinions, emotions, attitudes such as events, attributes, evaluations. At this entity-level sentiment analysis is identified by the learning-based method and lexicon-based method (Joshi et.al, 2014) There are 3 types of Sentiment analysis at the document level, the sentence level, and the feature level.

2.1 Sentiment Analysis at Various Levels

2.1.1. Sentiment Analysis at Document Level

In this method the complete polarity of the sentiment text can be extracted about an entity, however, it is difficult to extract the features from some of the entities (Ding et.al,2018) .In this method of document classification, both the unsupervised and supervised methods can be analyzed(Dou et.al,2017) . SVM, Naive Bayes, k−nearest neighbors can be used for analyzing sentiments. The features such as adjectives, term frequencies, inverse document frequency, tag words, pos, negations, are some of the terms in analyzing sentiments using machine learning.

2.1.2. Sentiment Analysis at Sentence Level

In sentence-level sentiment analysis polarity of individual sentences is analyzed. Determine the subjective and objective sentences of the documents (Liu et. al, 2017). The subjective sentences usually include the various opinion words which identify the sentiments of the given entity (Basiri et.al, 2017). Positive and negative terms in the sentences are distinguished to determine the polarity using features. This method is not applicable in the case of complex sentences.

2.1.3. Sentiment Analysis at Feature Level

In the Feature level method, we identify the phrase that will contain the opinion words. Sometimes it is difficult to compute the exact opinions, in some cases, the sentences which comprise negative words and also which are different from opinions paragraphs are irrelevant (Mudgal et.al, 2020). It is the method of determining whether the opinions mentioned in a subject or topic are expressed truly or falsely and also understanding the relationship between emotion target and emotion words. Mining opinion is the biggest challenge however to classify the sentences by forming several opinions by many supervised methods is proposed in Aspect-based opinion mining on a sentence level is identified using hierarchical and multiple labeling methods. Figure1 shows the stages of sentiment analysis which includes data pre-processing, feature extraction, pattern identification, sentiment classification polarity detection, and opinion summarization.

2.2. Stages of Sentiment Analysis:

As discussed in the above section sentiment analysis can occur at various levels such as document level, feature level and sentence level. The various stages of sentiment analysis include the following steps:

Figure 1. Stages of sentiment analysis

2.2.1 Input/user Reviews

The most important step in analyzing sentiment is the data collection stage, how the data is collected from a large social media network. The user content will be usually in an unstructured format and can be wrongly understood by users in different ways. Manual analysis is very difficult. So various text verification methods and natural language analysis methods are used for understanding text preparation. then extracting and obtaining the useful contents.

2.2.2. Data Pre-Processing

In this process, the noisy data will be removed and the data is pre-processed, punctuations, special symbols will be eliminated (Wankhede et.al, 2018). Data pre-processing also includes various other techniques like removal of Punctuation which are unwanted, remove a special character, extra white spaces, etc. Another process is called stemming which removes the stop words. In pre-processing, noise removal is also performed which mainly extracts incomplete sentences and unidentified words.

2.2.3. Feature Extraction

Several features are to be identified and extracted from the users and several feature extraction techniques are to be applied to the documents in classifying sentiments (Kalarani et. al,2019). Features can be (POS) Parts of speech the complete document contents are represented as unigrams, bigrams (Hung et.al, 2017). Feature extraction can be done at the document level or phrase level. The document-level feature identifies a particular document as positive, negative, or neutral. Hence overall sentiment polarity can be detected. Phrase level checks if an expression is either positive or negative. The features are used to automatically identify whether a sentence was subjective or objective.

2.2.4. Sentiment Classification and Polarity Detection

The extracted sentences from the large text are identified. Subjective opinions are detected and other unrelated statements are eliminated. These detected sentences are usually classified as positive, negative, and neutral for classification purposes to determine the polarity of text identifying the data. The polarity of the sentiments mainly determines if a text is mainly objective or subjective and if it is subjective then it is positive /negative orientation (Dridi et.al, 2019) Identify the types and the level of the classification of the sentiments.

2.2.5. Opinion Summarization

The most important goal of sentiment analysis is to transform the text from the unstructured form to the structured as well as meaningful data (Shen et.al,). It is an important task to summarize the opinion within a text and detects the major features of the document.

2.3 Approaches for Analyzing Sentiments

There are usually five basic stages in sentiment analysis as previously discussed. In this section will discuss about the approaches for analyzing the sentiments. The several approaches for analyzing sentiments is discussed below.

2.3.1 Syntactic Approach

In the Syntactic-based method, the patterns are extracted based on the user data on particular aspects. Syntactic patterns are an effective method for determining opinions in a comparative way (Al-Smadi et.al, 2019). The syntactic rule-based method will choose a proper set of data from the rules and it will give the best original rule since the method we used can select some of the techniques where we can work together. Semantic rule patterns can be easily studied based on the parsing method along with syntactic rule methods. The syntactical approach mainly deals with the grammar relations which relate to several aspects and opinion words. This method is convenient since it is unsupervised and it is domain-dependent.

2.3.2. Rule-Based Approach

In this approach, the given text is pre-processed and is then handled by a rule-based classifier (Liu et.al, 2017)]. In this type of approach, we define rules from the given opinion which is obtained by selecting the tokens from every statement, and then a test is performed on each of these tokens, and then search for the word to identify its presence. The polarity score determined at the end is more than zero, or if it is negative then the score will be less than zero. Calculate that the output is correctly obtained by determining the polarity, in case if some words are required for analyzing the sentiments from the words then in such cases the words are added. In supervised learning, the new input needs to be analyzed according to the trained system. The rules which are defined need to be carefully analyzed so that they do not produce too many errors. Automatically the accuracy of the rules can be easily determined. It is a bit difficult to check the result of the entire coverage of certain rules.

2.3.2 Lexical Based Approach

This method mainly depends on the sentence lexicon analysis of particular sentences or documents and is mainly determined by polarities of single words or phrases (Khoo et.al, 2018). The lexicon-based approach usually depends on emotional research for determining the sentiments dictionaries for all domains (Han et.al, 2018). In this lexicon-based approach, the semantic orientation of every single word in the given text is calculated. Sentence and term level opinion analysis for the lexicon-based can be used. The lexicon approach is of two types i.e. Dictionary approach and the corpus-based approach (Pandey et.al, 2019) The dictionary-based approach mainly determines the sentiments of lexicons in the text and then searches for its meaningful terms. Another method for determining corpus from text includes initially seed words and then determines the sentiment words. Depending on the context specification we need to compute the large corpus of documents.

2.3.3 Machine Learning Approach

This technique is mainly classified into two kinds of documents: a document for testing and a document for training. The training set is aimed to check the features of the document; whereas the test set aim is to perform the classification. Machine analysis methods include a set of approaches to identify patterns in the original text. There are several supervised classification algorithms such as decision tree, linear classifier, the rule-based method (Ghiassi et.al, 2018)). Supervised method of learning provides input data to model it and apply it to train the model and this is later applied to test data to produce output. In the case of unsupervised data that do not make use of training data for the classification. An unsupervised learning example is clustering.

Table 1. Represents the various machine learning algorithms its pros and cons

Algorithm	Characteristics	Disadvantages	Advantages	Efficiency
SVM algorithm	It uses a discriminative classifier for classifying data.	More size is needed in in training and testing and model	Works well for the data which is not linearly separable.	Good accuracy.
Naive Bayes method	More widely used approach	Precision reduces for less amount of data to obtain better performance.	Implementation is easier. Accurate results are obtained.	Less accuracy is observed.
Neural -Network algorithm	It is the best evaluation method.	More time is required for processing. Training is expensive for large datasets.	Easily applied to real-life problems. Easy to implement. Automatic learning capability.	Accuracy is more compared to other machine learning techniques.
K nearest neighbor	In this method k, nearest neighbors are to be trained along with their documents.	More time is needed to train. Noise sensitive. Performance depends on the number of dimensions.	Best suited for multimodal classes. classes are not linearly separable.	Low cost.

3. DEEP LEARNING TECHNIQUES

The deep learning technique was first proposed in 2006 by G.E Hinton and this method explains how the human brain processes by employing an artificial neural network to process data (Kim et.al, 2019). This method is more stable since it uses additional hidden layers. Deep learning models provide training for both supervised and unsupervised categories. It is considered as one of the most powerful machine learning algorithms which learns several layers and represents the features among data and provides good results. The deep learning model uses several layers one after another as a cascade for data transformation and also nonlinear processing units for extracting features. High-level layers are complex compared to low-level layers. Input layers will send information to hidden layers. Hidden layers send data to output layers. The neuron consists of weighted inputs the function which defines both input and output i.e. activation function and output (Zhang et.al, 2018). The combined weighted value of all the inputs provides the signal which is sent to the activation function to produced output from the neuron. (Xu, et.al, 2019). Training is the process of optimizing weights in which errors will be predicted and it is minimized and the network will reach the specified results. The method specifies the error detection of neurons is called back propagation, gradient descendent which will reduce the loss function.

Figure 2. Taxonomy of deep learning and sentiment analysis

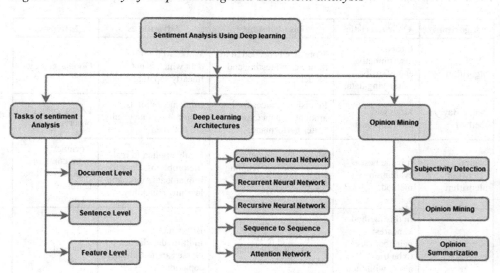

3.1 Types of Deep Learning Techniques

3.1.1. Convolution Neural Networks

CNN accepts the data in the form of sentences. Fixed length sentences are taken as inputs. Various feature selection schemes for CNN such as BOW with continuous vales and Bag of N-gram models can be applied. CNN data input is defined as the sum of several vectors that denote every word in the text (Widiastuti et.al, 2019). The absence of a word may result in decreasing accuracy in the models. In the case of feed-forward, there will be no connection from below layers to the previous layers. Figure3 represents the structure of CNN. The layers usually contain a Convolution layer, pooling layers, and fully connected layers. Classification results will be better in cases where we have more layers. In sentiment analysis, sometimes it is difficult to determine the exact or the semantic meaning of the terms. It's difficult to detect which words are positive or negative. Contextual information needs to be studied and then we can determine the semantic representation of the words. In the case of handling longer documents, it is difficult.

3.1.2 Recursive Neural Networks

RNNs take the data in the form of a tree structure recursive nature of the data. The sentences have to be parsed using some algorithm for the preprocessing. only accept tree-structured inputs; a tweet's data need to be parsed and it will be difficult to preprocess the unwanted sentences without exactly knowing the structure. With the help of tree structure, we identify the polarity in the given sentences (Arras et.al,2017) Given a structural representation of the sentence. Recurrent neural networks obtain the most important identification in the bottom-up level, by mixing tokens to provide phrases and then complete sentences and then determine the sentiment classification.

Figure 3. Basic Structure of CNN

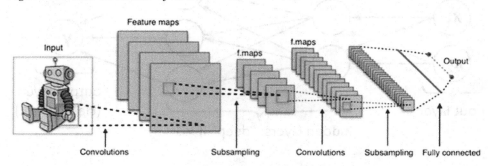

3.1.3 Recurrent Neural Networks

RNN's main objective is to determine the data in the ordered sequence of length, such as the count of words in the given sentence. it takes the input of a given word and also denotes the hidden representation of words (Zheng et.al, 2020). Figure 4 shows the layers of RNN. In RNN since it works in sequence, the output of one becomes the input of another the neurons will form a directed circle. RNN internal memory is used for processing a sequence of inputs. It performs the same procedure for each element in the sequence and it depends on previous computation. And it recalls the process done so far. Types of RNN models mainly include Bidirectional, Deep Bidirectional, and LSTM (Wang et.al, 2019). In the case of bidirectional output, every time not just depends on the previous element of the sequence but also depends on the next element. Both the left and right sides of the context need to be checked. In BIRNN there are two RNN that are present on top of one another. One will process the input in proper order and the other processes in reverse order. In Deep bidirectional RNN, multiple layers are available in several steps. The difficulty with RNN is it suffers from the problem of forgotten memory which forgets the long sequences of input. Hence RNN uses LSTM to propagate the gradients.

Recurrent neural networks aim is to work on several sets of vectors in RNN we have three layers they are input, hidden and output layer. The input layer mainly receives the input, activations are applied in the hidden layer and finally, the output is received. Successive activations are applied in the layers to produce output. The text data is produced as a sequence of inputs to obtain the meaning the order of words is very important.

Figure 4. RNN Representing Input and output Layers

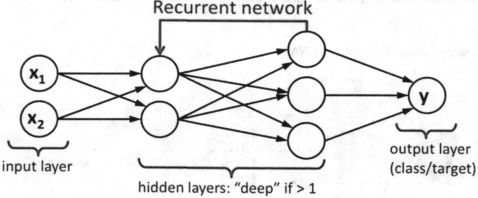

Figure 5. Basic Architecture of Recurrent neural network

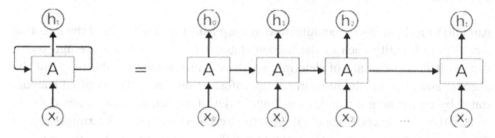

RNN is called recurrent since it performs the same type of task for all elements of the sequence of inputs with a set of output dependent on previous computation as shown in figure 5. This proposal incorporates sentence-level latent semantic indexing to assist with topic extraction, with further regularization restrictions applied to enhance the effect, and topic-level attention mechanisms are applied in the long short-term memory network to do sentiment analysis. (Rao et.al, 2018) The main feature of the cells is to remember values over a longer period. The phrase memory in the LSTM includes three gates each gate consists of the feed-forward neural network, which computes the activation of weighted sum. The regulators flow using the connection of several LSTM units, the connection among the gates is usually referred to as a cell.

3.1.4 LSTM

LSTM does not use the activation function such as relu, tanh, within its recurrent components. The values stored in it will remain the same. The gradient value will vanish in the process of training. Lstm units are usually processed in blocks. Usually, the block consists of three to four gates. The gates are input, output, and forget gate, the control information is regularly flowing on the logistic function. It is most important to recall the inputs from several time values the main motivation of lstm is to identify the long sequences with time values. The main role of LSTM is to analyze and classify text documents or reviews by considering the long sequences of data. LSTM can be good in maintaining word order and the context of words. This model makes use of two neural network models an encoder and a decoder for producing both input and output (Ma et.al, 2018). We can use this for the same or different sets of parameters. Mainly used for machine translation and question answering i.e sequence to sequence learning with a neural network. The representation vectors are usually represented in N dimensions where the phrases have the same meaning and are approx. to each other.

3.1.5 Attention Mechanism

Attention mechanisms are architecture in deep learning. The main of the attention model is to identify each of the hidden states using its weighted average vector values. It is a technique of determining the context vector for the usage of the decoder and contains the most important information. From the set of all encoder states by performing a weighted average onset of hidden encoder states (Letarte et.al, 2018). The encoder state will give the weighted average is determined by the ordered score between the encoder state and the decoder hidden state the previous decoder state is called a query vector. The output vector is considered as a weighted average of the value.

Table 2. Represents the various neural network architectures and their characteristics

Architectures	Characteristics
Recursive neural networks	This method uses a weighted matrix in combination with the binary tree structure, performs well on variable input size.
CNN	CNN architecture mainly includes of a convolution layer, fully connected, and layer of pooling.
LSTM	LSTM is a variant of RNN; LSTM is represented as long short-term memory. This is different from the traditional RNN since it has the addition of another cell called as forget, update, and the output gates.
GRU	GRU is a variant of LSTM there is a gating mechanism in LSTM that contains several gates.
Attention	The attention mechanism is one layer in the artificial neural network where more focus is given to the set of inputs.
Hybrid	The hybrid model mainly includes multiple categorized deep learning networks, which mainly work on the same model.

4. REPRESENTATION OF DOCUMENTS IN ANALYZING SENTIMENTS:

There are several methods for representing the documents. The collection of data sets will have a significant impact on classifying data and also the representation of the document in the given text corpus is denoted as a vector of numbers. Each element corresponds to words that are present in the document. The collection of documents in the vector representation is called a document term matrix. Each term in the document is calculated using different weighting methods. Traditional methods for term weighting mainly include TF-IDF, Term frequency (Chen et.al, 2016). TF-IDF is one of the most widely used weighting mechanisms which is used for text processing. The term frequency for every word is multiplied with the value of inverse document frequency.

4.1 Word Embedding

Word embedding is also considered as a novel method for document representation where it is required to represent the documents in the form of vectors (Zhang et.al, 2019). Embedding of words is the process of mapping the words to a numeric vector. Several machine learning approach depends on the vector representation of input text. Since vector representation gives more important syntactic and semantic words. Improving NLP task. Word embedding's give better word representation. In a given set of documents. The main idea in word embedding is identifying semantically, related information from the given set of documents. Word embedding's are obtained by the collective representation of words. Where each word is obtained by vector space. Distributed vector representations are represented as a named entity for recognition. Word to vector embedding representation is the most important representation as shown in figure6. This identifies the vector representation of words.

Figure 6. Represents the Input word embedding's

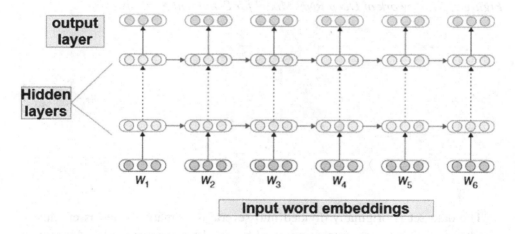

4.2 Word2vec

The word2vec method is one of the most important vector representation methods where the words from the training corpus will be used for the analysis. Mapping of the words which has similar meaning into vectors that are similar to each other. Word2vec offers a combination of the words it mainly includes CBOW and skip-gram approach (Liu et.al, 2020).CBOW (continuous bag of words) model mainly predicts a word given its context. Whereas the skip-gram model mainly determines the context given the target word. Word2vec extracts continuous vector representation of words from the huge datasets. We can also generate our own vector representation of the data (Souma et.al, 2019)]. Form the given set of the corpus. In many cases, the pre-trained models are used for training the large corpus.

5. A CASE STUDY ON APPLICATION OF DEEP RECURRENT NEURAL NETWORK FOR SENTIMENT ANALYSIS

As part of the case study Amazon product review, the dataset is considered and implemented using the proposed recurrent neural model and word2vec. RNN in this model is implemented using the framework Tensor flow. The initial data collection process explains data scraping and crawling techniques for data collection. They process the review data into word vectors and data sets. The data sets in this study are divided into two parts, first as training datasets and second as testing data sets. The flow of the proposed work is shown in can be seen in figure 7.

Figure 7. Framework of Deep RNN Model for Sentiment Analysis

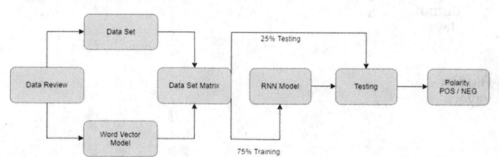

The data set is originally divided into several data matrices and is employed as a key step during pre-processing word by word to a vector model. All review words are transformed to their matching integer and vector representation by word 2vector models. The first step in this process is to scrape reviews of data sets from the Amazon website. From scraping the structured data in string format are obtained. we must turn the data into a vector. We are using word2vec to convert string words to vectors.Word2Vec is a Google-designed tool. By looking into the word contexts with words in the phrase, Word2vec converts words into vectors. Other than that, word2vec collects words with the same context in the vector space. With context terms in phrases, you may find out if these words are commonly employed in good or negative phrases. How word2vecworks by taking a collection of phrase data into the corpus and creating a vector for each word in the corpus. The word2vec output is an embedding matrix. The RNN method is used in this work to classify feelings. RNN has the latter's temporal aspect. This time aspect distinguishes RNN from neural feed forward networks. The RNN method has the same time steps as the maximum sequence. Function in the preceding time steps to encapsulate and summarize all information. Vector will summarize information from specified words and encapsulate it. The RNN sums together the two above vectors under concealed conditions. The magnitude impacts the number of cached vectors on the matrix right and the current or previous vector of the state affects the cached state vector. Next, the last hidden state vector will be entered in the binary soft-max classification to create negative or positive polarity possibilities. The aforementioned polarity is produced by multiplying both the hidden state vectors and the right matrix and the results are then entered in the soft max function. Cognitive time computation is considered as one of the most important aspect for computing time when converting the word into vector representation. The below algorithm explains about time taken to compute the words from the sentences. This is very important as part of identifying the word2vector concepts. The algorithm explains the cognitive time computation from identifying the words from the sentences.

Algorithm:

Cognitive time for obtaining the words from sentences:

Let Dt denotes the document set. A document Dt consists of n number of sentences.

Let S1, S2….Si,….Sn. A sentence Si is obtained by a sequence of words

Si= wi1, wi2, ….wi lj where lj denotes the length of sentence Si.

The context vector cv w^{e} si =[x1wi, x2wi, ……., xmwi] where m represents the dimension size.

Ct w $\in$ si = (α1X1w + α2X2w + …. + αnXmw + b)

Where Ct w $\in$ si is the cognitive time for a word in a sentence and αi forms the weight vector for αw

The cognitive time of a sentence Si can be calculated using

$$Ct\ Si = \sum_{i=1, wi \in Si}^{lj} Ct\ wi$$

5.1 Results Analysis

The results of this case study reveal that with other machine learning models the model approach is more accurate with an accuracy of 91.98 percent. From these studies, you must also pay attention to the possibility to over fit the model throughout the testing phase. In the future, RNN and LSTM can be used to overcome excessive difficulties and increase model performance. The initial step in the training is a collection of associated reviews and labels. By employing the run function, the network can establish values in which components can be optimized and loss minimized. Furthermore, the run function is utilized to feed the review and label collection. This method is repeated as many as iterations are set. Figure 8 shows the accuracy using the CNN+word2vec model and Figure 9 shows the accuracy using the RNN+Word2vec model.

Figure 8. Accuracy using CNN+Word2Vec model

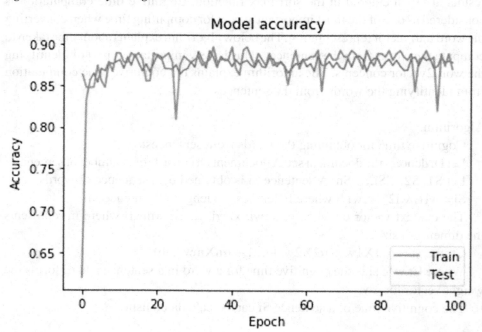

These results show that RNN with Word2vec can lead to a better accuracy rate than the other model. Table 3 depicts the comparison of both the models concerning accuracy/.

Figure 9. Accuracy using RNN+word2vec model

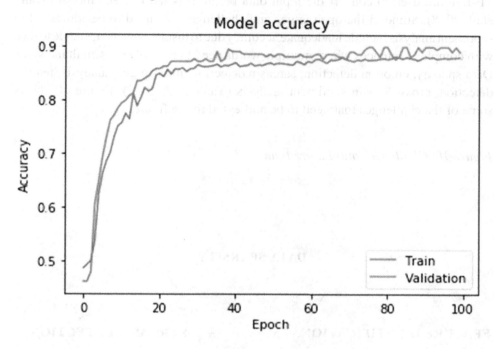

Table 3. Accuracy

Model	Accuracy
CNN + Word2Vec	88.5%
RNN + Word2Vec	90.12%

Next section briefly explains about the future issues and challenges and open issues addressed by Deep learning model towards sentiment analysis.

6. CHALLENGES, FUTURE RESEARCH DIRECTIONS, AND OPEN ISSUES

Deep learning has been one of the most important aspects in the field of research and powerful machine learning techniques that will automatically learn the multiple layers of features from the large data and will produce the results (Li et.al, 2019). Deep learning is more useful in analyzing sentiments these years. In this chapter core deep learning models, their architectures are studied. Word embedding and

TF-IDF are used to convert the input data before it is fed into the model (Wang et.al, 2018). Some of the open issues and challenges that need to be addressed in sentiment analysis include inadequate accuracy due to insufficient data, unable to deal with complex sentences where multiple words need to be analyzed simultaneously. Data sparsity, emotion detection, sarcasm detection, multilingual analysis, feature detection, cross-domain sentiment analysis (Yang et.al, 2018). Figure 10 shows some of the challenges that need to be addressed in the future.

Figure 10. Challenges and Future Issues

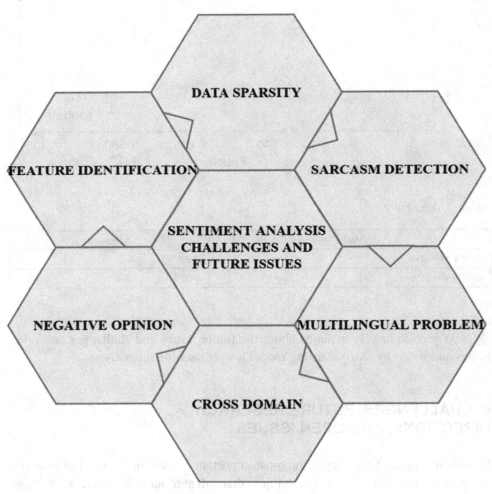

Several other issues in sentiment analysis include classifying sentences into subjective and objective opinions (Hussein et.al, 2018) Domain adaptation problem is also the issue where the data available is not clear in the English language alone and hence it is difficult to analyze. The analysis also depends on the classification is supervised or unsupervised techniques (Mao et.al, 2019). Machine learning models mainly focus on text classification where the data is split into supervised and unsupervised (Soong et. al,2019). Supervised learning models depend more on the labeled training documents. More accuracy is obtained in these models.

CONCLUSION

This chapter mainly discusses several approaches for analyzing sentiments open problems and issues in analyzing sentiments. The main objective of sentiment analysis is to detect the emotions and opinions from customers. This chapter mainly explains deep learning techniques for analyzing sentiments, Deep learning architectures, and several levels of sentiment analysis are studied along with several word embedding techniques. Deep learning mainly helps in predicting the sentiment polarity of the given text document. Most of the deep learning techniques are studied by understanding the vector representation or the word embedding technique to predict the sentiment score. The chapter is concluded by explaining the features of several traditional machine learning algorithms, types of deep learning algorithms, and their features. Finally, the research open issues gaps and challenges were explained for implementing sentiment analysis for future studies.

REFERENCES

Ain, Q. T., Ali, M., Riaz, A., Noureen, A., Kamran, M., Hayat, B., & Rehman, A. (2017). Sentiment analysis using deep learning techniques: A review. *International Journal of Advanced Computer Science and Applications*, 8(6), 424.

Al-Smadi, M., Al-Ayyoub, M., Jararweh, Y., & Qawasmeh, O. (2019). Enhancing aspect-based sentiment analysis of Arabic hotels' reviews using morphological, syntactic and semantic features. *Information Processing & Management*, 56(2), 308–319. doi:10.1016/j.ipm.2018.01.006

Alsayat, A., & Elmitwally, N. (2020). A comprehensive study for Arabic Sentiment Analysis (Challenges and Applications). *Egyptian Informatics Journal*, 21(1), 7–12. doi:10.1016/j.eij.2019.06.001

Arras, L., Montavon, G., Müller, K. R., & Samek, W. (2017). Explaining recurrent neural network predictions in sentiment analysis. arXiv preprint arXiv:1706.07206. doi:10.18653/v1/W17-5221

Basiri, M. E., & Kabiri, A. (2017, April). Sentence-level sentiment analysis in Persian. In *2017 3rd International Conference on Pattern Recognition and Image Analysis (IPRIA)* (pp. 84-89). IEEE. 10.1109/PRIA.2017.7983023

Cambria, E. (2016). Affective computing and sentiment analysis. *IEEE Intelligent Systems*, *31*(2), 102–107. doi:10.1109/MIS.2016.31

Chen, K., Zhang, Z., Long, J., & Zhang, H. (2016). Turning from TF-IDF to TF-IGM for term weighting in text classification. *Expert Systems with Applications*, *66*, 245–260. doi:10.1016/j.eswa.2016.09.009

Ding, J., Sun, H., Wang, X., & Liu, X. (2018, June). Entity-level sentiment analysis of issue comments. In *Proceedings of the 3rd International Workshop on Emotion Awareness in Software Engineering* (pp. 7-13). 10.1145/3194932.3194935

Dou, Z. Y. (2017, September). Capturing user and product information for document level sentiment analysis with deep memory network. In *Proceedings of the 2017 Conference on Empirical Methods in Natural Language Processing* (pp. 521-526). 10.18653/v1/D17-1054

Dridi, A., & Recupero, D. R. (2019). Leveraging semantics for sentiment polarity detection in social media. *International Journal of Machine Learning and Cybernetics*, *10*(8), 2045–2055. doi:10.100713042-017-0727-z

Fu, X., Liu, W., Xu, Y., & Cui, L. (2017). Combine HowNet lexicon to train phrase recursive autoencoder for sentence-level sentiment analysis. *Neurocomputing*, *241*, 18–27. doi:10.1016/j.neucom.2017.01.079

Ghiassi, M., & Lee, S. (2018). A domain transferable lexicon set for Twitter sentiment analysis using a supervised machine learning approach. *Expert Systems with Applications*, *106*, 197–216. doi:10.1016/j.eswa.2018.04.006

Han, H., Zhang, Y., Zhang, J., Yang, J., & Zou, X. (2018). Improving the performance of lexicon-based review sentiment analysis method by reducing additional introduced sentiment bias. *PLoS One*, *13*(8), e0202523. doi:10.1371/journal.pone.0202523 PMID:30142154

Hung, L. P., & Alfred, R. (2017, April). A performance comparison of feature extraction methods for sentiment analysis. In *Asian Conference on Intelligent Information and Database Systems* (pp. 379-390). Springer. 10.1007/978-3-319-56660-3_33

Hussein, D. M. E. D. M. (2018). A survey on sentiment analysis challenges. *Journal of King Saud University-Engineering Sciences, 30*(4), 330–338. doi:10.1016/j.jksues.2016.04.002

Joshi, N. S., & Itkat, S. A. (2014). A survey on feature level sentiment analysis. *International Journal of Computer Science and Information Technologies, 5*(4), 5422–5425.

Kalarani, P., & Brunda, S. S. (2019). Sentiment analysis by POS and joint sentiment topic features using SVM and ANN. *Soft Computing, 23*(16), 7067–7079. doi:10.100700500-018-3349-9

Khoo, C. S., & Johnkhan, S. B. (2018). Lexicon-based sentiment analysis: Comparative evaluation of six sentiment lexicons. *Journal of Information Science, 44*(4), 491–511. doi:10.1177/0165551517703514

Kim, H. C., Bandettini, P. A., & Lee, J. H. (2019). Deep neural network predicts emotional responses of the human brain from functional magnetic resonance imaging. *NeuroImage, 186,* 607–627. doi:10.1016/j.neuroimage.2018.10.054 PMID:30366076

Letarte, G., Paradis, F., Giguère, P., & Laviolette, F. (2018, November). Importance of self-attention for sentiment analysis. In *Proceedings of the 2018 EMNLP Workshop Blackbox, NLP: Analyzing and Interpreting Neural Networks for NLP* (pp. 267-275). Academic Press.

Li, W., Liu, P., Zhang, Q., & Liu, W. (2019). An Improved Approach for Text Sentiment Classification Based on a Deep Neural Network via a Sentiment Attention Mechanism. *Future Internet, 11*(4), 96. doi:10.3390/fi11040096

Liu, B. (2020). Text sentiment analysis based on CBOW model and deep learning in big data environment. *Journal of Ambient Intelligence and Humanized Computing, 11*(2), 451–458. doi:10.100712652-018-1095-6

Liu, F., Zheng, J., Zheng, L., & Chen, C. (2020). Combining attention-based bidirectional gated recurrent neural network and two-dimensional convolutional neural network for document-level sentiment classification. *Neurocomputing, 371,* 39–50. doi:10.1016/j.neucom.2019.09.012

Liu, H., & Cocea, M. (2017, February). Fuzzy rule based systems for interpretable sentiment analysis. In *2017 Ninth International Conference on Advanced Computational Intelligence (ICACI)* (pp. 129-136). IEEE. 10.1109/ICACI.2017.7974497

Ma, Y., Peng, H., Khan, T., Cambria, E., & Hussain, A. (2018). Sentic LSTM: A hybrid network for targeted aspect-based sentiment analysis. *Cognitive Computation*, *10*(4), 639–650. doi:10.100712559-018-9549-x

Mao, X., Yang, H., Huang, S., Liu, Y., & Li, R. (2019). Extractive summarization using supervised and unsupervised learning. *Expert Systems with Applications*, *133*, 173–181. doi:10.1016/j.eswa.2019.05.011

Mudgal, P., & Khunteta, A. (2020). Handling Double Intensifiers in Feature-Level Sentiment Analysis Based on Movie Reviews. In *International Conference on Artificial Intelligence: Advances and Applications 2019* (pp. 383-392). Springer. 10.1007/978-981-15-1059-5_42

Nair, Jain, & Nair. (2021). Enhancing the performance measure of sentiment analysis through deep learning approach. *International Journal of Computing and Digital System*.

Pandey, M., Williams, R., Jindal, N., & Batra, A. (2019). Sentiment Analysis using Lexicon based Approach. *IITM Journal of Management and IT*, *10*(1), 68–76.

Park, J., Lee, H., Lee, J. H., & Suh, H. W. (2018). *Feature-based sentiment word selection and rating for system design*. Academic Press.

Pathak, A. R., Pandey, M., & Rautaray, S. (2021). Topic-level sentiment analysis of social media data using deep learning. *Applied Soft Computing*, *108*, 107440. doi:10.1016/j.asoc.2021.107440

Plaza-Leiva, V., Gomez-Ruiz, J. A., Mandow, A., & García-Cerezo, A. (2017). Voxel-based neighborhood for spatial shape pattern classification of lidar point clouds with supervised learning. *Sensors (Basel)*, *17*(3), 594. doi:10.339017030594 PMID:28294963

Rao, G., Huang, W., Feng, Z., & Cong, Q. (2018). LSTM with sentence representations for document-level sentiment classification. *Neurocomputing*, *308*, 49–57. doi:10.1016/j.neucom.2018.04.045

Schouten, K., Van Der Weijde, O., Frasincar, F., & Dekker, R. (2017). Supervised and unsupervised aspect category detection for sentiment analysis with co-occurrence data. *IEEE Transactions on Cybernetics, 48*(4), 1263–1275. doi:10.1109/TCYB.2017.2688801 PMID:28422676

Soong, H. C., Jalil, N. B. A., Ayyasamy, R. K., & Akbar, R. (2019, April). The essential of sentiment analysis and opinion mining in social media: Introduction and survey of the recent approaches and techniques. In *2019 IEEE 9th symposium on computer applications & industrial electronics (ISCAIE)* (pp. 272-277). IEEE.

Souma, W., Vodenska, I., & Aoyama, H. (2019). Enhanced news sentiment analysis using deep learning methods. *Journal of Computational Social Science, 2*(1), 33–46. doi:10.100742001-019-00035-x

Wang, J. H., Liu, T. W., Luo, X., & Wang, L. (2018, October). An LSTM approach to short text sentiment classification with word embeddings. In *Proceedings of the 30th conference on computational linguistics and speech processing (ROCLING 2018)* (pp. 214-223). Academic Press.

Wang, Y., Wang, H., Zhang, X., Chaspari, T., Choe, Y., & Lu, M. (2019, May). An attention-aware bidirectional multi-residual recurrent neural network (abmrnn): A study about better short-term text classification. In *ICASSP 2019-2019 IEEE International Conference on Acoustics, Speech and Signal Processing (ICASSP)* (pp. 3582-3586). IEEE.

Wankhede, S., Patil, R., Sonawane, S., & Save, A. (2018, April). Data Preprocessing for Efficient Sentimental Analysis. In *2018 Second International Conference on Inventive Communication and Computational Technologies (ICICCT)* (pp. 723-726). IEEE.

Widiastuti, N. I. (2019, November). Convolution Neural Network for Text Mining and Natural Language Processing. *IOP Conference Series. Materials Science and Engineering, 662*(5), 052010. doi:10.1088/1757-899X/662/5/052010

Wu, P., Li, X., Shen, S., & He, D. (2020). Social media opinion summarization using emotion cognition and convolutional neural networks. *International Journal of Information Management, 51*, 101978. doi:10.1016/j.ijinfomgt.2019.07.004

Xu, F., Zhang, X., Xin, Z., & Yang, A. (2019). Investigation on the Chinese text sentiment analysis based on convolutional neural networks in deep learning. *Comput. Mater. Contin, 58*(3), 697–709. doi:10.32604/cmc.2019.05375

Yang, X., Macdonald, C., & Ounis, I. (2018). Using word embeddings in twitter election classification. *Information Retrieval Journal, 21*(2-3), 183–207. doi:10.100710791-017-9319-5

Yousif, A., Niu, Z., Tarus, J. K., & Ahmad, A. (2019). A survey on sentiment analysis of scientific citations. *Artificial Intelligence Review, 52*(3), 1805–1838. doi:10.100710462-017-9597-8

Yu, L. C., Lee, C. W., Pan, H. I., Chou, C. Y., Chao, P. Y., Chen, Z. H., Tseng, S. F., Chan, C. L., & Lai, K. R. (2018). Improving early prediction of academic failure using sentiment analysis on self-evaluated comments. *Journal of Computer Assisted Learning, 34*(4), 358–365. doi:10.1111/jcal.12247

Zhang, L., Wang, S., & Liu, B. (2018). Deep learning for sentiment analysis: A survey. *Wiley Interdisciplinary Reviews. Data Mining and Knowledge Discovery, 8*(4), e1253. doi:10.1002/widm.1253

Zhang, S., Yao, L., Sun, A., & Tay, Y. (2019). Deep learning based recommender system: A survey and new perspectives. *ACM Computing Surveys, 52*(1), 1–38. doi:10.1145/3285029

Zhang, T., & Wang, L. (2019, June). Research on Text Classification Method Based on Word2vec and Improved TF-IDF. In *International Conference on Intelligent and Interactive Systems and Applications* (pp. 199-205). Springer.

Zheng, L., Wang, H., & Gao, S. (2018). Sentimental feature selection for sentiment analysis of Chinese online reviews. *International Journal of Machine Learning and Cybernetics, 9*(1), 75–84. doi:10.100713042-015-0347-4

Chapter 4
Detection and Classification of Leaf Disease Using Deep Neural Network

Meeradevi
M.S. Ramaiah Institute of Technology, India

Monica R. Mundada
M.S. Ramaiah Institute of Technology, India

Shilpa M.
M.S. Ramaiah Institute of Technology, India

ABSTRACT

Modern technologies have improved their application in field of agriculture in order to improve production. Plant diseases are harmful to plant growth, which leads to reduced quality and quantity of crop. Early identification of plant disease will reduce the loss of the crop productivity. So, it is necessary to identify and diagnose the disease at an early stage before it spreads to the entire field. In this chapter, the proposed model uses VGG16 with attention mechanism for leaf disease classification. This model makes use of convolution neural network which consist of convolution block, max pool layer, and fully connected layer with softmax as an activation function. The proposed approach integrates CNN with attention mechanism to focus more on the diseased part of leaf and increase the classification accuracy. The proposed model design is a novel deep learning model to perform the fine tuning in the classification of nine different type of tomato plant disease.

DOI: 10.4018/978-1-7998-8161-2.ch004

INTRODUCTION

Unpredictable climate change, without any proper irrigation technique, lack of knowledge in using modern technologies and use of pesticides have caused an imbalance in farming which has caused improper cultivation and unhealthy crops thereby threatening food security. Plant pathogens will lead to crop loss. Due to animals, weeds, pathogens it is estimated to reduce agricultural production between 20% to 40% globally. Agriculture is one the main sources of income in India it struggles to support rapidly growing population. It is estimated that in India smallholder farmers will generate around 80 percent of agricultural production and due to pests and plant disease there is more than 50 percent of yield loss. Plant diseases reduce the quality and production of food crops. To overcome this we need large verified dataset of images which includes healthy and diseased leaf images of all type of crop plants. Using this dataset develop an accurate image classifier which classifies the type of disease at initial stage. Such dataset was not available until recent and smaller dataset will not give accurate classification. So, PlantVillage project was initiated to benefit farmers with early disease detection and started collecting thousands of images of all types of crops. This chapter focuses on automatic plant disease detection as a topic of discussion. The study demonstrates the technical feasibility of deep learning to enable automatic tomato plant disease detection through tomato leaf images. The dataset consist of both diseased and healthy leaf images. In this chapter, deep convolution neural network is used to categorize the plant leaf as healthy or diseased. Various diseases of tomato leaf is identified like tomato_mosaic, lateblight, yellow curved, septoria Leaf Spot, healthy, bacterial spot with total 21071 images . These diseases can be identified at initial stage using CNN and farmers can use any infection control tools to stop spreading disease to other plants and also solve pest problems while minimizing the risks of human and environment. Some of the challenges identified are as follows.

- Quality of the leaf image
- Larger dataset
- Image denoising
- Segmenting exact spot of disease in leaf
- Splitting the training and testing samples from original images
- Feature extraction like color, size, texture and shape from image
- Recognizing different type of disease from plant leaves

Leaf diseases are threat to the crop production and farmer's economy reduces immensely with increase in spread of crop disease. Conventional methods of detecting crop diseases require a great deal of knowledge and expertise. Further, these methods can be expensive, time consuming, and even ineffective in some cases. These challenges can be solved using deep learning techniques which are having more potential to identify various diseases. This motivates the work to focus mainly on leaf disease detection and classify the disease at early stage with great accuracy and prevent farmers from huge loss. The study uses tomato leaf for analysis as tomato is considered most profitable crop because it is grown four times in a year. Plant disease is quite natural because they cannot withstand light intensity, high humidity, temperature etc., it affects plant pigmentation, fruit color and fruit quality and temperature below 10 degree Celsius and above 38 degree Celsius affects plant tissue and plant. Due to all these environmental conditions plants are susceptible to diseases like fungus, bacteria, viruses etc., Early detection of plant disease can help in increasing yield by preventing from disease. CNN improves the classification accuracy in many fields, including agriculture. So, deep convolution neural network is used for demonstration. The model proposed hybrid deep learning model, which consists of transfer learning, attention model, and dropout operation, is proposed along with a CNN-based VGG16 classifier to detect and classify diseases associated with plants. Pretrained imageNet weights were used for image preprocessing. Pre-trained images are trained on millions of images with 1000 different categories, which reduce the time for training new images. Further, all images were 3-dimensional, i.e., they were measured in terms of height, width, and channels (RGB). Objectives of the proposed system are:

1. Identification and Classification of leaf disease using VGG net and attention model
2. Implemented model must be able to classify the leaf disease with optimal accuracy
3. To create a web application where the user can upload an image of the infected crop and recognize and classify whether it is a healthy leaf or not.
4. Comparative study with machine learning algorithms

LITERATURE SURVEY

Some of the works done by authors in detection and classification of leaf diseases using various techniques have made an impact in this field. Some of these works are briefly explained below.

Related Work

Detection and diagnosis of leaf disease at early stage is important for better quality yield. Disease in plants leads to huge economic losses to farmers. The advancement in deep neural network has given an opportunity to improve the performance of the leaf disease detection with good accuracy. This paper proposed three CNN based architecture faster-region based CNN, region-based fully CNN and single shot multibook detector. The leaf disease is detected efficiently with 94.6% accuracy for 50,000 images with 38 different classes. The model comprises of convolution layer that has 36 filters and Relu activation function. batch normalization is applied and adam optimizer used and dropout operation is applied to prevent overfit in the model. The study shows 50% of increase in yield by preventing crops from disease (Sumit Kumar et.al., 2021). (Sk Mahmudul Hassan et.al., 2021) Deep convolution neural network models are implemented to detect and diagnose the disease in plants. CNN has made a great improvement in the field of machine vision by showing impressive results. The performance of the model is measured by varying hyperparameters batch size, epochs and dropout. The experimental results shows the accuracy of 98.42% for InceptionV3, 99.11 for InceptionResNetV2, 97.02% for MobileNetV2 and 99.56% for EfficientNetB0 the results showed better accuracy than traditional approach. Inception model is powerful and simple DL network with sparsely connected filters which can replace fully connected networks. EfficientNetB0 model could achieve higher accuracy compared to inception models. The dropout rate applied is 0.2 and 0.8 and with 0.8 dropout rate the models could achieve increased accuracy. The proposed approach in this paper used deep learning based transfer learning approach with depth wise separable convolution in the inception block. The time required to train the DL models is much less than the machine learning models.

This paper performs data pre-processing, segmentation of leaf, feature extraction and classification for detection of leaf disease in tomato plant. K-nearest neighbor algorithm is used for classification and regression. The diseases that are commonly found in tomato plant are like early blight, bacterial spot, TYLCV. This paper uses image processing technique to classify these diseases using machine learning technique. Images are captured through camera and preprocessed to remove noise and bring all images to unified dimension. Image is divided into histogram is computed using Histogram of Oriented Gradients (HOG). KNN algorithm is applied for classification and regression. This algorithm begins with making an assumption that the things with more similarity are existing in close proximity. With KNN first load the data and then initialize K to the selected number of neighbors. If there is regression then the algorithm returns mean and in case for the classification the mode value is returned (G. Geetha et.al., 2020).

The use of various technologies has increased the accuracy of detecting plant diseases. Technology like computer vision and machine learning has made the detection of disease at early stage easy. This paper focus on not only disease type but also at what stage the disease is the severity of the plant disease is identified using the dataset of leaf images from kaggle. The approach uses transfer learning i.e., reusing the pre-trained model on the new dataset will help to identify the disease more accurately. The computer vision technology helps to extract the meaningful information from the image. (Rehan Ullah Khan et.al., 2021). The use of various technologies has increased the accuracy of detecting plant diseases. Technology like computer vision and machine learning has made the detection of disease at early stage easy. This paper focus on not only disease type but also at what stage the disease is the severity of the plant disease is identified using the dataset of leaf images from kaggle. The approach uses transfer learning i.e., reusing the pre-trained model on the new dataset will help to identify the disease more accurately. The computer vision technology helps to extract the meaningful information from the image. (Kriti Ohri & Mukesh Kumar, 2021) self-supervised learning methods are used for image classification which uses unlabeled data. It deploys state-of-art deep learning methods without depending on large number of labeled dataset. Some of the task is pre-designed for the convolution network to learn the features from unlabeled data. In unsupervised learning the autoencoder learns various representations by compressing input image and exploiting redundant information of the input image.

Figure 1. Image preprocessing procedure

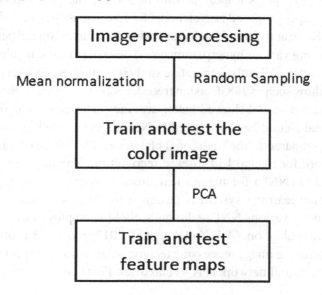

55

Rice disease images are taken from database and dataset is normalized using mean normalization and random sampling, the images are separated as colored and gray image sample for training and testing. All rice disease images are color images, the stationary property does not hold across color channels, than rescale the image to [0, 1] and apply principle component analysis (PCA) to get training and testing feature maps as shown in Figure 1. (Xihai Zhang et.al, 2018) made a study on automatic identification and diagnosis of maize leaf disease. They proposed two improved models GoogLeNet and Cifar10 for maize leaf disease reorganization. Eight different type of maize leaf diseases are correctly recognized with an accuracy 98.9% with GoogLeNet and 99.8% with cifar 10 model. GoogLeNet used sparse network structure to overcome over-fitting of the model. Nine inception modules are used in CNN architecture and main idea behind inception module is to use dense components. Each module includes multiple parallel convolutional layers of size 1x1, 3x3, 5x5 and pooling layer will capture other features simultaneously. Cifar 10 is optimized in this study. The network contains three CNN layers and two fully connected layers. The model accuracy is improved by adding dropout and Relu operations between two fully connected layers but the paper did not discuss about validation accuracy sometime testing accuracy is good but validation accuracy will be varying which leads to overfitting problem, this chapter compared test and validation accuracy such that the overfitting problem is prevented using CNN techniques. (Meeradevi et.al., 2020) DL is considered as modern technology which can be used for many classification problems and pattern recognition problems in various applications like health industry, agriculture, multimedia, language models and many more. DL plays important role in solving the problems in vegetable pathology. This paper proposed LeNet model for five disease detection in leaves and the model used ReLu activation function and adds dropout and model performance is analyzed by varying various hyperparameters. The experimental results shows 99% accuracy for LeNet model and comparative study is performed with various machine learning algorithms such as J48 decision tree, decision table, Naïve Bayes classifier and proposed LeNet model showed batter accuracy. Therefore, it is observed that the Convolutional Neural Network based LeNet model has the highest accuracy of 99.29% while compared to the traditional classifiers. (Md. Rasel Mla,et.al., 2020) built a framework for mango leaf disease recognition. The paper presents neural network ensemble (NNE) for mango leaf disease reorganization to identify the diseases. Machine learning system is designed to identify various symptoms of mango leaf. Among various NNE techniques, SVM is employed for faster training and performance evaluation. (A.R.Zadokar et.al.,2017) proposed a cotton plant leaf disease detection using image processing technique known as fuzzy c-means (FCM) and probabilistic neural network (PNN) classifier. Firstly images are preprocessed into the required format and next segment the obtained image using FCM clustering method then essential features of image like color, texture, shape, edge, etc., are acquired from image using features correlation, contrast, entropy evaluation the leaf disease is identified and then classified accordingly. Diseased image are classified using PNN and then compared with healthy leaf image. (Vijai Singh et.al.,2017) proposed an approach that detects four types of mango leaf disease like Dag disease, Golmachi, Moricha disease and Shutimold using SVM the model could achieve the average accuracy of 80%. When new image is inserted into system it compares new data with trained data. In this approach firstly images are collected which includes diseased and healthy mango leaf and group them apparently. MATLAB is used to read dataset and color species specified through HSV and then color features were extracted using Gray-Level Co-occurrence Matrix (GLCM) from images. GLCM is used for extracting textural feature from mages and then segmented into regions and finally diseases were detected by matching new image with trained images. To identify the abnormalities in the image different shape, textural features are extracted from each cluster from given image using contrast, energy, homogeneity, cluster shade, cluster prominence and using below equation

Box 1.

Type	Equation
contrast	$\sum_{i,j=0}^{N-1} (i, j)^2 C(i, j)$
Energy	$\sum_{i,j=0}^{N-1} C(i \cdot j)^2$
Local Homogeneity	$\sum_{i,j=0}^{N-1} C(i \cdot j) / (1 + (i - j)^2)$
Cluster Shade	$\sum_{i,j=0}^{N-1} (i - M_x + j - M_y)^3 \, C(i,j)$
Cluster Prominence	$\sum_{i,j=0}^{N-1} (i - M_x + j - M_y)^4 \, C(i,j)$

(Ramesh Shunmugam, et at.,2019) worked using deep learning technique using a jaya algorithm for identification and classification of rice leaf disease. Proposed method uses feedback loop in post processing. The workflow of this system includes five steps initial step is image data collection then pre-processing the image data to remove noise and segmentation of leaf image then feature extraction like color, texture, shape etc., finally correctly classifying the disease. The main idea behind feedback loop is it takes output values of classification back to segmentation unit like back propagation algorithm were segmentation is done using k-means clustering algorithm. The feedback is running until optimal accuracy is achieved and error is reduced. (Shima Ramesh, et al., 2018) used 10-fold cross validation method for achieving higher accurate results than the one with CNN which includes 10 or more hidden layers. Using 10-fold cross validation will reduce memory consumption and computational time and 'n' weights are achieved through training dataset. Using back propagation algorithm, support vector machine and then using particle swarm optimization (PSO) will finally decrease SME (Jayraj Chopda, et al.,2018) this work does image analysis for plant disease detection were the images are analyzed using IR thermography, aerial infrared photography for plant disease identification and classification. Detection of fruit maturity can also be done using this method. The color, size and shape are used to identify the type of fruit in image and uses image processing technique to identify the disease spot in the image. K-means clustering algorithm was used for image segmentation and feature of the image like color, texture, shape is extracted from image. Back propagation classifier is used to identify the disease. The result showed correct classification of grape and wheat disease with optimal accuracy rate. (Yosuke Toda et.al., 2019) used neural network based approach. Neural network captures the color and texture of lesions specific to diseases. As plant disease has been a threat to food security because it reduces the crop quality and production also. In this method array of visualization based approaches are used for disease diagnosis. Naïve based approach is used i.e., ReLU activation function at the hidden layer and ReLU supplies only positive values. Feature visualization uses gradient based approach which applies Grad- CAM with ReLU highlighting the leaf within the image. (Edna Chebet Too, et al.,2018) the main focus of this paper is fine tuning VGG16, inception, ResNet and DenseNet CNN models. The proposed method uses image based plant disease detection and classification. During training, accuracy and categorical cross- entropy loss are used for evaluation. In contrast, DenseNet, ResNet and Inception accuracy is compared to VGG16 without augmentation and attention model. The proposed system uses pre-trained model with weights from imageNet finally evaluated based on cross-entropy loss and accuracy on test values. Usual CNN architecture consist of input layer, hidden layer and classification layer. Hidden layer consist of multiple convolution layer and pooling layer and classification is done based on fully connected layer and sometime softmax as shown in Figure 2. Compared to all DenseNet performed well.

Figure 2. Typical CNN architecture

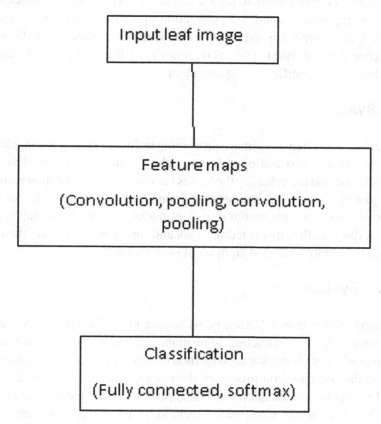

Back propagation in neural network is performed for disease detection with optimal loss. This approach has achieved an accuracy of 92 percent which shows an optimal accuracy. When k-means clustering is used with GLCM matrix and BPNN classifier the accuracy is reduced. Some of the methods discussed for disease identification are firstly, using real time monitoring of crops, crops are continuously monitored and once any interest of disease is detected in plants it issues an alarm to perform some action immediately to control the infection. Secondly, instead of using segmentation operation on image, PCA is directly applied on RGB values and feed the image to multilayer perception which gives the output for sample leaf image which shows leaf image is infected by disease of interest or not. Third method is thresholding, where original image is transformed into gray scale. Next threshold image is filtered to remove noise. Image analysis is done by thresholding in which the input image is divided into blocks and those blocks with less than 5% of total area is discarded. Rest of the blocks will be representing diseased area. After empherical evaluation if the generated value is above threshold then it is considered as plant with disease. Next quantification algorithm includes segmentation operation to isolate the symptom from which features are extracted like disease symptoms, shape, exact disease spot etc., and estimations are done to identify the severity of disease. Finally classification is intended to detect specific disease in a plant.

Current System

Most of the existing system uses image processing techniques like k-means clustering algorithm and SVM classification technique. These techniques are used to identify the type of disease and then classify the leaf as healthy or diseased. Other elementary method is just by seeing with bare eyes making an assumption on type of disease and other method is real time monitoring, continuous monitoring of crop to prevent spreading of disease. But, this is tedious task and time consuming and then testing the leaf in the lab with high cost equipment is again costly.

Proposed System

The proposed system uses CNN based technique like VGG16, transfer learning, attention model, feature extraction algorithms for plant disease detection. The proposed model employs the standard method of quickly and accurately identifying type of crop disease based on images of the leaves. The proposed work come out with novel results by visualization of CNN applied for plant leaf image. The model is compared with various CNN based techniques to identify the best accuracy for train and test models. The model can be trained to detect any diseases of any plant species. Disease diagnosis and detecting severity of disease can be added as additional features

MATERIAL AND METHODS

Dataset

Convolutional neural networks and evolutionary algorithms are used in order to make a classification based on the input images. The input images used are of tomato leaves with different diseases which are collected from PlantVillage dataset it is available online from the crowd-sourced platform Kaggle with total number of 21071 images the sample images are shown in Figure 3. This chapter focuses on exploring of images to accomplish the task of detecting and classifying leaf disease at early stage. The dataset was additionally labeled generating metadata which is holding two types of markings, one for entire leaf and another for only infected areas. All these labeling are identified and verified by agricultural experts. (Marko Arsenovic et.al, 2019) in this study the leaf images were collected in various angles in different light intensity and in different weather conditions. The collected images are classified as healthy and diseased images. Sometimes images have conflicting background i.e., it indicates single leaf is in focus and sometimes images are many with different leaves of different crops including healthy and diseased. So, the dataset will imitate particle situation where this model can be potentially used. Next step is to enhance the dataset with augmented images. The main goal of this chapter is to train the network such that it can distinguish between different classes. Considering more number of augmented images, the network can learn more number of features. The proposed improved VGG16 algorithm considered 21091 images of diseased and healthy images for training and validation of the proposed system.

The model preprocesses the input images by converting RGB image to Binary image and then image segmentation takes place and finally image denoising for noise removal. The evolutionary algorithm is then applied on the preprocessed image in order to get the best generation of images. This is then supplied as input to the convolutional neural network where the image is classified into its respective disease as shown in Table 1. The dataset is divided into training set as 75 percent and validation set is 25 percent of original data. Original images are trained using 75 percent of images and new image is matched with trained data to identify the type of disease.

Image Preprocessing and Labeling: Preprocessing helps to remove any background noise of the image and helps in smoothing and filtering. After preprocessing the process of feature extraction starts in order to get the inputs to the attention model. Data Preprocessing is performed which involves framing of each image into same sizes or same array sizes in numerical form, and then creating a balanced Dataset. Using the open-cv, the images are visualized and then shuffled. Using the pickle module, all the images are dumped into a pickle file.

Feature extraction: This technique is a computer vision technique used in image processing, identifying object based on image corners and edges. In deep learning the feature extraction is performed during training the model which is major advantage which avoid extraction of features manually. Manual feature extraction may lead to extraction of incorrect features which may lead overfit in the model.

Figure 3. Example leaf images of different diseases in tomato. (a) bacterial spot (b) early blight (c) healthy leaf (d) late blight (e) leaf mold (f) spetorial leaf spot (g) spider mites (h) target spot (i) Mosaic virus (j) yellow leaf curl virus

Table 1. Dataset for Tomato Plant Leaf Disease

Class	Number of original images	Number of images in training set	Number of images in the validation set
Bacterial Spot	2719	2039	680
Early blight	1000	750	250
Healthy	2184	1638	546
Late Blight	1591	1140	380
leaf mold	952	714	238
Septorial Leaf Spot	2364	1773	591
spider mites	1676	1275	419
target spot	1404	1053	351
Tomato Mosaic	373	280	93
Yellow curved	6808	5106	1702

Augmentation Process: Basically two augmentation strategies. First strategy includes traditional augmentation method which is most widely applied in plant disease identification. Most of these augmentation method include simple transformation such as pixel wise changes, rotation, blurring or noising, in order to introduce distortion to images (Marko Arsenovic et.al., 2019). The second strategy includes training generative adversarial networks (GAN) which is a class of machine learning framework in which two neural network models compete with each other to become more accurate in their predictions. GANs are used in various tasks like feature extraction, classify various details of image and superimpose required characteristics on given image. Once training set is ready, apply GAN technique on the trained image GAN generates new image with same features such that new image looks similar to the trained leaf images. The architecture of GAN consist of two neural network models referred as generator and discriminator, were discriminator is known deconvolutional neural network, the role of discriminator is to identify the given data is real or fake, another GAN model is generator which creates the new data with all the required features similar to original image such that discriminator finds difficult to identify whether data is real or fake. The main idea of using augmentation in our approach is to increase the dataset and bring in slight distortion to the images which helps in reducing overfitting during the training stage.

Transfer Learning: Transfer learning is applied to classification, regression and clustering problems. It takes the model trained on larger dataset and applies its knowledge on smaller dataset. In our approach transfer learning is applied on the pre-trained models. If the accuracy values for the training set and the validation set are not optimal. Apply transfer learning with pre- trained image-net weights for feature extraction. Finally, Transfer learning with attention model is used to detect the leaf disease with optimal accuracy. Transfer learning is more faster compared to traditional machine learning algorithms and it is more accurate and needs less training data.

Attention Module: Attention mechanism in Deep Learning refers to how a subset of the features in the neural network are focused on, rather than the whole set of features. Let $x \in R^d$ be an input vector, $z \in R^k$ the feature vector, $a \in [0,1]^k$ the attention vector, $g \in R^k$ the attention glimpse and $f_\phi(x)$ the attention network with parameters ϕ. Typically, the attention is implemented as

$$a = f_\phi(x),$$

$$g = a \odot z,$$

where $\odot$ is element-wise multiplication, while z is an output of another neural network $f \phi (x)$ with parameters ϕ. This module will be using Gaussian attention which is exploiting parameterized one-dimensional Gaussian filters to make an attention map on the images. Let $a_y \in R^h$ and $a_x \in R^w$ be attention vectors, those which tell which part of image should be focused to in y and x axis, respectively. The Gaussian Attention masks can be created as

$a = a_y \, a^x \, t.$

Figure 4. Gaussian Mask

Attention in the above Figure 4 is still wasteful, as it selects only a part of the image while black masking-out or ignoring all the remaining parts. Instead of using the vectors directly, so that you cast them into matrices $A_y \in R^{H \times h}$ and $A_x \in R^{W \times w}$, respectively. The Attention modules and properties in proposed system are shown in Table 2.

DESIGN AND DEVELOPMENT

Convolution architecture consists of input layer, convolution layers. Max pooling layer and two fully connected layers.

Input layer: the input image of size 224X224 is fed to DL model to classify the disease. The image is an array of pixels which passes through the layers and softmax function at the fully connected layer classify the most probable value for the input image. The series of layer such as conv layer, pooling layer used ReLu activation function which estimates the new weight and forward the weight to next layer for optimal solution.

Table 2. Modules and properties in proposed system

Modules	Properties
Dataset preference	Tomato Plant Leaf Disease Dataset
Validation split	0.25
Epochs	30
Batch Size	32
Transfer Learning	pre-trained image-net weights
Type of Classifier	VGG16Net
Dropout Regularisation	0.4 (To Prevent Overfitting).
Attention Layer	Image to Glimpse Ratio = 3:1. (To focus only on a subset of features on the neural network).
Loss Function	Categorical Cross Entropy
Optimize	Adam
Activation function	Softmax

Convolution layer: The VGG16 model in the proposed approach consist of three conv layer in each block which extract the important features from input image. ConvNets are made of biases and weights. First layer Conv layer is of size 5x5x3 and every layer after forward pass it slides through each filter and computes the dot product between filters. Pixels are converted into vector.

Pooling layer: It reduces the image size without loosing any relevant information required for classification. It downsamples the input image by considering image height and width. Pooling layer mainly extracts sharp features of the input image.

Fully connected layer: The objective of this layer is to take the results of previous convolution/pooling operation and use them to classify the leaf image in to labels. It returns vector of size N. N is number of classes in our image classification problem. Fully connected layer multiplies each input elements by weight and then perform sum on all weights.

Figure 5 shows the flow of work, First the tomato leaf image dataset is taken as input image. Data Preprocessing is then carried, which frames each image into the unified dimension. Feature extraction is performed using imageNet weights which are pre-trained using transfer learning approach. Apply attention mechanism to the image to focus more the diseased part of the image rather than whole image. In model use Gaussian attention which is exploiting parameterized one-dimensional Gaussian filters to make an attention map on the images more focused. Next Dropout operation is applied to avoid overfitting the model. Then train the model for image classification. Tomato plant disease is detected and classified by using a helper function and a Checkpoints folder containing the trained weights.

Figure 6 shows the VGG16 Net Model Architecture. the VGG16 Net consist of 16 layers with flatten output layer followed by dense layer each layer with some weights. The model has convolution layers of 3x3 filter with a stride 1 and using the same on padding and maxpool layer of 2x2 filter of stride 2. It follows the same pattern of convolution and maxpool layers throughout. It has 2 Fully Connected layers and softmax activation function is applied at output layer to get the vector in the range (0,1) for loss function cross- entropy is applied which is also called softmax loss, it is softmax activation added up with cross-entropy loss (Meeradevi et.al., 2020).

Figure 5. Workflow of the proposed model

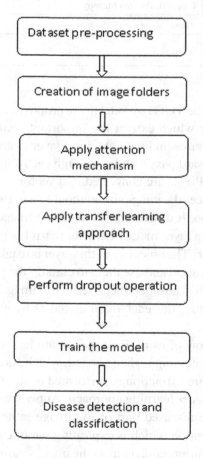

66

Figure 6. Final VGG16 Net Model Architecture

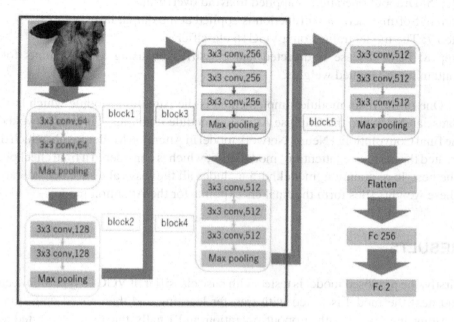

Algorithm for Improved VGG16

Step 1: Diseased and healthy leaf images are collected with different symptoms

Step 2: Dataset is preprocessed and balanced in numbers, grouped them into healthy and diseased leaves apparently

Step 3: Tensor flow and keras was used to read the data from the collected dataset

Step 3: Feature extraction was applied to the dataset through transfer learning using imagenet weights

Step 4: Attention mechanism is applied to focus on the image to focus on the some subset of the features of images rather than whole set of features in neural network.

Let $x \in R^d$ be an input vector, $z \in R^k$ the feature vector, $a \in [0,1]^k$ the attention vector, $g \in R^k$ the attention glimpse and $f_\phi(x)$ the attention network with parameters ϕ. Typically, the attention is implemented as

$$a = f_\phi(x),$$

$$g = a \odot z,$$

Step 5: Dropout operation is applied to avoid overfitting

Step 6: Softmax activation function is applied at the output layer

Step 7: The model trained on a VGG16 classifier

Step 8: Plant disease is detected and classified by using a checkpoints folder containing the trained weights.

One of the main modules implemented is the Attention Module which has the Gaussian Mask and the Glimpse Attention module functions. These are invoked in the final Convolutional Neural Network model in Attention Model.ipynb, which then created the bestt_acc_attention_model.hdf5, which is considered a final checkpoint. The best_loss_attention_model.hdf5 includes all the loss values for consideration. These weights files form the final checkpoints for the Attention model.

RESULTS

Firstly, the proposed model is tested with base classifier of VGG16 type architecture and next the model is tested with transfer learning and then tested with transfer learning integrated with dropout operation and finally the model is tested with transfer leaning, dropout and attention module in the improved VGG16 model.

Figure 7. Base VGG16 - Overfitting the Model

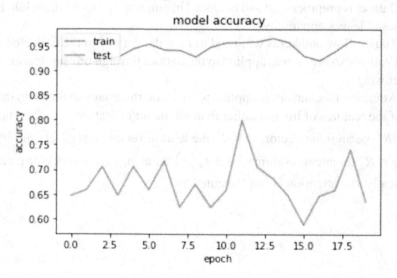

Base VGG16 Model

Total number of trainable parameters is 14,791,494 and none of the parameters are omitted. After running the model for 20 epochs, the final accuracy value is optimal as shown in Figure 7, but the learning curve is not obtained as proper curve, training accuracy is shown in straight line. After observing loss values, the training loss decreased 0.12, whereas the validation loss increased 2.73 which leads to the overfit in the model. The below graph shows the train and test accuracy values.

Classic Transfer Learning Model

In this approach Base VGG16 Model with Transfer Learning which includes pre-trained imageNet weights. The Classic transfer learning is used for feature extraction. It consists of 16 layers, with one input layer, and an output dense layer and number of hidden layers. Total number of trainable parameters is 14,791,494 and none of the trainable parameters are omitted. After training the model for 25 epochs accuracy and loss values for both training and validation against each epoch is shown in Figure 8. Overfitting is observed in the graph, blue line is for training set and orange line for validation set which is not showing any learning curve. Looking at the accuracy and loss values for the training set, they are optimal. But validation loss is 1.51 which is not optimal; it is again observed the case of overfitting.

Figure 8. Classic Transfer Learning

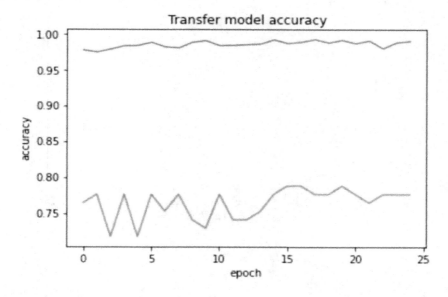

Classic Transfer Learning with Dropout

The model is now trained with dropout technique L2 regularization. L2 Regularization is performed to reduce the error value which brings the loss close to zero but does not reach zero. In the dropout technique, some of the neurons are turned off to avoid overfit in the model i.e., the outer edges of the hidden neurons are not trained and model will not carry these weights to next layer which helps to improve the performance of the model and reduces the training time.

Base VGG16 Model with Transfer Learning and pre-trained weights from ImageNet, with an additional dropout layer. This approach also consists of 16 layers, with one input layer, and an output dense layer. Due to dropout, only 76,806 parameters are trainable. After running for 25 epochs the accuracy and loss values for both training and validation set solved the problem of overfitting. The loss value for the training set is optimal but for the validation it is still 1.54 which shows the overfit in the trained model as shown in Figure 9. Learning curve is good but the validation loss is 1.54 which leads to overfit in the model. Orange line in the graph is for training set and blue line is for test set.

Figure 9. L2 Regularization

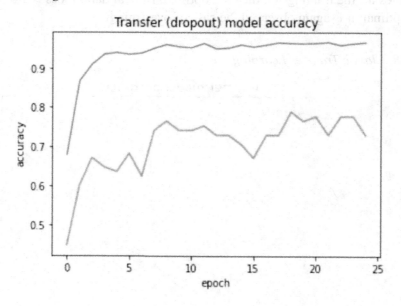

Attention Model

This approach uses Base VGG16 Model, Transfer Learning with pre-trained weights from imageNet, Attention layer with an additional dropout operation. The dropout vale is 0.4 where more number of units are dropped. It achieves optimal accuracy without overfit in the model. Due to dropout, only 76,806 parameters are trainable. After running for 30 epochs the accuracy values of training and validation set is shown in Figure 10. The test accuracy achieved is 96.75 and loss is 0.096 and validation loss in now reduced. It is observed overfit in the model is overcome using dropout and attention model.

Figure 10. Attention Model

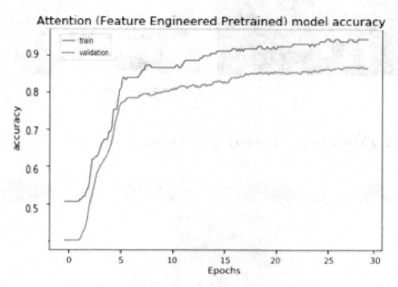

Figure 11 shows the accuracy graph for train and validation set using attention feature engineered pre-trained model, upload new image with disease, an attention model is correctly classifying the disease of Tomato leaf as yellow curved disease. The model compares the healty and diseased leaf for classification.

Figure 12 shows the graph for train and validation set using attention feature engineered pre-trained model which is correctly classifying the disease Tomato leaf with septorial leaf spot disease. New image with disease is uploaded after performing match operation with healthy and diseased leaf model is correctly classifying the disease.

Figure 11. The test image - Tomato leaf with yellow curl Leaf Spot

Figure 12. The test image - Tomato leaf with Septorial Leaf Spot

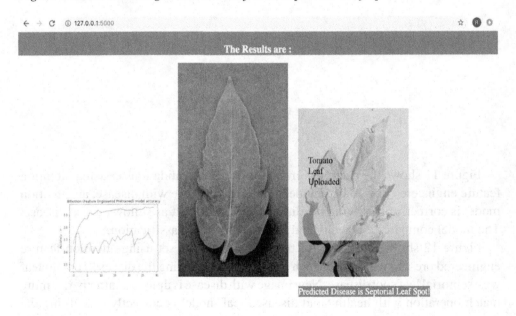

In Figure 13 the model loss is reducing with increased epoch for both train and validation. Hence the proposed model accurately classifies the type of disease. Figure 14 shows the classification accuracy of each class labels. It is observed in the graph that true positive values are high compared to false positive and recall values in high for most of the class labels which indicates the model is correctly classifying the leaf disease.

Figure 13. Model loss

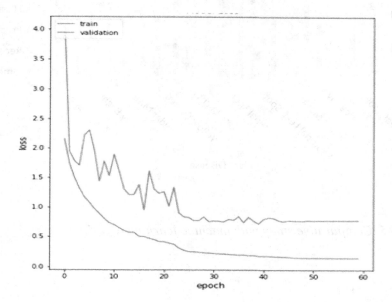

Comparative Study

Figure 15 depicts the findings of the comparative analysis of proposed CNN classification algorithm with other algorithms such as Naïve Bayes, Decision Tree and Random Forest. The result demonstrated that the proposed algorithm (improved VGG16) outperformed other models in terms of classification accuracy. The comparative study revealed that Naïve Bayes suffered zero frequency problems and yielded reduced accuracy. The naïve bayes algorithm works well only with small dataset which is not suitable for image classification with large number of images. The instability prevented the decision tree from performing well and the frequent occurrence of over fitness leads reduce in performance of random forest. In brief, the result shows that the proposed algorithm is the best among the compared algorithms in providing accurate classification results.

Figure 14. Classification accuracy for each class label

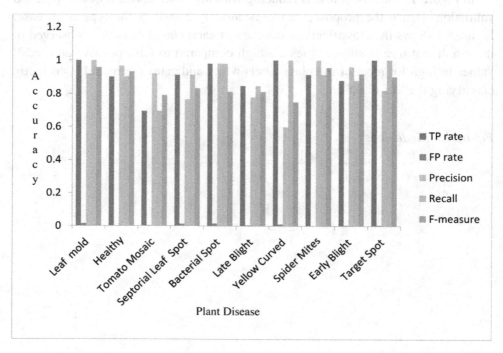

Figure 15. Comparative study with machine learning algorithms

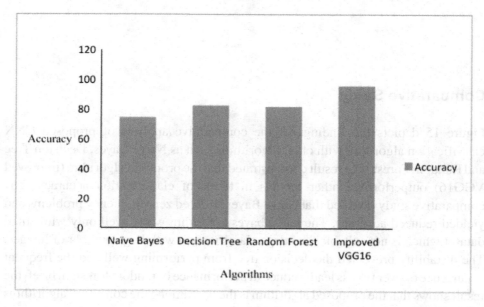

CONCLUSION

A VGG16 model is proposed to classify diseased tomato leaves. The images were pre-processed using techniques like binarization of images. The images were subjected to classification using VGG16 Net. Four CNN models with one base and three integrated models were compared to facilitate the selection of model. The findings revealed that the proposed model, which comprised Convolution Neural Network, transfer learning, attention, and dropout function, provided a higher rate of accuracy, with the acceptable validation loss, which helped it to yield accurate predictions. Further, the study also carried out a comparative study and demonstrated that the proposed improved VGG16 algorithm outperformed other selected algorithms like Naïve Bayes, Decision Tree and Random Forest in accurately classifying the leaf images. Above all, experiments conducted by using the proposed model aided the farmers to detect and classify the diseased plants. The accurate classification of diseased plants helped them to take suitable counter measures to avert the spread of diseases, which boosts crop yield and improves the economy.

REFERENCES

Arsenovic, M., Karanovic, M., Sladojevic, S., Anderla, A., & Stefanovic, D. (2019). Solving Current Limitations of Deep Learning Based Approaches for Plant Disease Detection. *Symmetry, 11*(7), 939. doi:10.3390ym11070939

Chopda, Raveshiya, Nakum, & Nakrani. (2018). Cotton Crop Disease Detection using Decision Tree Classifier. *2018 International Conference on Smart City and Emerging Technology (ICSCET)*. 10.1109/ICSCET.2018.8537336

Geetha, Samundeswari, Saranya, Meenakshi, & Nithya. (2020). Plant Leaf Disease Classification And Detection System Using Machine Learning. *Journal of Physics: Conference Series, 1712*. doi:10.1088/1742-6596/1712/1/012012

Hassan, S. M., Maji, A. K., Jasiński, M., Leonowicz, Z., & Jasińska, E. (2021). Identification of Plant-Leaf Diseases Using CNN and Transfer-Learning Approach. *Electronics (Basel), 10*(12), 1388. doi:10.3390/electronics10121388

Khan, R. U., Khan, K., Albattah, W., & Qamar, A. M. (2021). Image-Based Detection of Plant Diseases: From Classical Machine Learning to Deep Learning Journey. Hindawi Wireless Communications and Mobile Computing. doi:10.1155/2021/5541859

Kumar, & Chaudhary, & Chandra. (2021). Plant Disease Detection Using CNN. *Turkish Journal of Computer and Mathematics Education, 12*(12), 2106–2112.

Lu, Y., Yi, S., Zeng, N., Liu, Y., & Zhang, Y. (2017). Identification of Rice Diseases using Deep Convolutional Neural Networks. *Neurocomputing, 267*, 378–384. doi:10.1016/j.neucom.2017.06.023

Meeradevi & Mundada. (2020). Design of Efficient Technique for Leaf Disease Detection Using Deep Learning. *International Journal of Advanced Science and Technology, 29*(3), 11287–11298.

Meeradevi, R. V., Mundada, M. R., Sawkar, S. P., Bellad, R. S., & Keerthi, P. S. (2020). Design and Development of Efficient Techniques for Leaf Disease Detection using Deep Convolutional Neural Networks. *IEEE International Conference on Distributed Computing, VLSI, Electrical Circuits and Robotics (DISCOVER)*, 153-158. 10.1109/DISCOVER50404.2020.9278067

Mia, Roy, Das, & Rahman. (n.d.). Mango leaf disease recognition using neural network and support vector machine. *Iran Journal of Computer Science*. doi:10.1007/s42044-020-00057-z

Ohri, K., & Kumar, M. (2021). Review on self-supervised image recognition using Deep neural networks. *Knowledge-Based Systems, 224*, 107090. doi:10.1016/j.knosys.2021.107090

Ramesh, S., & Hebbar, R. (2018). Plant Disease Detection Using Machine Learning. *International Conference on Design Innovations for 3Cs Compute Communicate Control*. 10.1109/ICDI3C.2018.00017

Shunmugam, R., & Dharma, V. (2019). Recognition and Classification of Paddy Leaf Diseases Using Optimized Deep Neural Network with Jaya Algorithm. *Information Processing in Agriculture*. Advance online publication. doi:10.1016/j.inpa.2019.09.002

Toda, Y., & Okura, F. (2019). How Convolutional Neural Networks Diagnose Plant Disease. *Plant Phenomics*.

Too, E. C., Li, Y., Njuki, S., & Liu, Y. (2018). A Comparative Study of Fine-Tuning Deep Learning Models for Plant Disease Identification. *Computers and Electronics in Agriculture*. Advance online publication. doi:10.1016/j.compag.2018.03.032

Vijai Singh, A. K. (2017). Misra. Detection of plant leaf diseases using image segmentation and soft computing techniques. *Information Processing in Agriculture, 4*(1), 41–49. doi:10.1016/j.inpa.2016.10.005

Zadokar, A. R., Bhagat, D. P., Nayase, A. A., & Mhaske, S. S. (2017). Leaf Disease Detection of Cotton Plant using Image Processing Technique: A Review. *International Journal of Electronics, Communication & Soft Computing Science and Engineering.*

Zhang, X., Qiao, Y., Meng, F., Fan, C., & Zhang, M. (2018). Identification of Maize Leaf Diseases Using Improved Deep Convolutional Neural Networks. *IEEE Access: Practical Innovations, Open Solutions*, *6*, 30370–30377. doi:10.1109/ACCESS.2018.2844405

Chapter 5
Development of an Efficient Monitoring System Using Fog Computing and Machine Learning Algorithms on Healthcare 4.0

Sowmya B. J.
M.S. Ramaiah Institute of Technology, India

Gautam Mundada
M.S. Ramaiah Institute of Technology, India

Pradeep Kumar D.
M.S. Ramaiah Institute of Technology, India

Anita Kanavalli
M.S. Ramaiah Institute of Technology, India

Hanumantharaju R.
(iD) https://orcid.org/0000-0003-2139-980X
M.S. Ramaiah Institute of Technology, India

Shreenath K. N.
Siddaganga Institute of Technology, India

ABSTRACT

Disruptive innovations in data management and analytics have led to the development of patient-centric Healthcare 4.0 from the hospital-centric Healthcare 3.0. This work presents an IoT-based monitoring systems for patients with cardiovascular abnormalities. IoT-enabled wearable ECG sensor module transmits the readings in real-time to the fog nodes/mobile app for continuous analysis. Deep learning/machine learning model automatically detect and makes prediction on the rhythmic

DOI: 10.4018/978-1-7998-8161-2.ch005

anomalies in the data. The application alerts and notifies the physician and the patient of the rhythmic variations. Real-time detection aids in the early diagnosis of the impending heart condition in the patient and helps physicians clinically to make quick therapeutic decisions. The system is evaluated on the MIT-BIH arrhythmia dataset of ECG data and achieves an overall accuracy of 95.12% in classifying cardiac arrhythmia.

1. INTRODUCTION

The Healthcare 4.0 paradigm, at its core, involves providing highly personalized services to patients. For this to be realized in the healthcare industry, real time service is of the essence. Fog Computing enables computations to be performed at the edge, while simultaneously utilizing the cloud to store large amounts of data. Thus, it can be leveraged to meet the real-time servicing needs of Healthcare 4.0. We use an ECG to get the readings and use high performance computing (HPC) and ML algorithms for monitoring and analysis. Develop an efficient system based on the fog computing paradigm for the real-time monitoring and analysis of ECG data of users and decrease response time in case of emergencies. The Overall Objectives can be stated as

- Accurate and Real-Time monitoring and analysis of ECG data.
- Immediate notification to Doctors and Emergency Services in case of anomalies.
- Performance enhancement of Healthcare 4.0 using Fog Computing, HPC and ML algorithms.
- Decreasing the latency of monitoring and analysis by the utilization of fog architecture.
- Creation of a mobile application for visualization of the data by doctors/ patients.

The Deliverables can be achieved such as Machine Learning and Deep Learning Models for the analysis of ECG Data to detect anomalies, Fog Architecture on which the Model is deployed for decreased latency, a mobile application for patients and doctors to view the diagnosis and data.

The scope is limited to Detect anomalies in heartbeat based on ECG Reading, notify assigned doctors in case of emergency and/or when an anomaly is detected, Fog computation architecture for real time predictions and notifications, Mobile app for both doctor and patient to keep track of heart health history, prescriptions etc.

The motivation is to improve the efficiency of fog architecture for improved performance. Add support for tracking other health measures such as blood pressure etc. Continuous improvement of model accuracy, and addition of other models to predict health state based on various other factors such as blood pressure etc.

2. LITERATURE SURVEY

The Healthcare 4.0 paradigm, at its core, involves providing highly personalized services to patients. For this to be realized in the healthcare industry, real time service is of the essence. Fog Computing enables computations to be performed at the edge, while simultaneously utilizing the cloud to store large amounts of data. Thus, it can be leveraged to meet the real-time servicing needs of Healthcare 4.0. Below, we give a brief history of the utilization of Fog Computing in the healthcare industry and how it can benefit our project. Several works on the prediction of heart anomalies based on ECG data are also explored.

(Kraemer et al., 2017) presents a survey on fog processing inside medical services informatics, and investigates, characterizes, and examines distinctive application use cases. Applications are ordered into utilization case classes and a stock of explicit tasks that can be taken care of by fog computing is recorded. The level of the organization such fog computing tasks can be executed are talked about and trade-offs as for prerequisites pertinent to medical care are given. The survey shows that: 1. there is a critical number of registering undertakings in medical care that require or can profit by fog computing standards 2. Handling on higher organization levels is needed because of requirements in remote gadgets and the need to total information 3. Protection concerns and constant forestall calculation tasks to be totally moved to the cloud these discoveries prove the requirement for an intelligible methodology toward fog computing in medical services, for which a rundown of suggested innovative work activities are introduced.

(Akrivopoulos et al., 2019) proposed work on enabling the wearable gadget with handling abilities to locally dissect ECG flags and distinguish unusual behaviour. The capacity to separate among typical and unusual heart movement altogether diminishes: 1. the need to store the signs 2. The information sent to the cloud 3. The general force utilization 4. The classification of private information. In view of this idea, the HEART framework introduced in this work joins wearable inserted gadgets, portable edge gadgets, and cloud administrations to give on-the-spot, solid, precise, and moment heart checking. The wearable gadget is distantly prepared by a doctor to figure out how to precisely distinguish basic occasions identified with every specific patient. Following this, the wearable gadget gets equipped for deciphering an enormous number of heart irregularities without depending on

cloud administrations and edge assets, when the clinical specialist is absent. The Fog figuring approach expands the distributed computing worldview by moving information handling nearer to the creation site, along these lines speeding up the framework's responsiveness to occasions. The HEART framework's presentation concerning the precision of recognizing strange occasions and the force utilization of the wearable gadget is assessed. Results demonstrate that an exceptionally high achievement rate can be accomplished regarding occasion location proportion and the battery can support activity up to an entire week without the requirement for a re-energize.

(Silva et al., 2019) shows a software architecture based on Fog Computing and intended to encourage the administration of clinical records. This architecture utilizes Block anchor ideas to give the fundamental protection highlights and to permit Fog Nodes to complete the approval cycle in a conveyed way. At long last, the paper depicts a contextual investigation that assesses the exhibition, protection, and interoperability necessities of the proposed engineering in a home-focused medical services situation.

(Hannun et al., 2019) talks about the use of Deep Neural Networks for detection and classifications of anomalies into 12 rhythm classes. The 12 rhythm classes include 10 arrhythmias, sinus rhythm and noise. The model uses a novel dataset for training and testing and uses single lead ECG data for training. With the help of convolutional neural networks, it was possible to obtain an F1 score higher than the average cardiologist F1 score.

(Chauhan et al., 2015) use Deep Long Short Term Memory Networks to capture the temporal dependencies present in the ECG data. The classifications are done into 5 different classes which include Normal Sinus Rhythm, Premature Ventricular Contractions, Atrial Premature Contractions, Paced Beats, and Ventricular Couplets. By analysing one-minute recordings from the MIT-BIH database, an F1 score of 96.45% for the test set was achieved. The use of LSTMs allows little or no pre-processing of data that is fed to the model. Overall it appears that stacked LSTMs may be a viable candidate for anomaly detection in ECG signals.

The mark of the work of the Internet of Things in the field of clinical benefits *(Hanumantharaju et al., 2021)* which works on the work for patients to be related with their clinical experts and the organizations with direct, regard based thought. Mist preparation can be the central structure for redirecting IoT from improvement to practicing in clinical benefits. Keeping an eye on the troubles of clinical consideration 4.0 is being tended to. The troubles are concerning the (data grouping and examination), security and insurance, and e-clinical consideration organizations, and the logical arrangement of mist processing can be a prevalent response for clinical benefits 4.0.

The characteristics of qualities and separate the algorithmic complexities in haze-related data examination *(D Pradeep Kumar et al., 2020)*. An orderly computational plan is made to develop a paradigmatic technique for haze information examination to gauge, store and inspect data capably and suitably and develop an ideal stage for duplicating sensor-set up devices and organizations regarding the Internet of things.

The item arrangement is performed utilizing both assessment score calculation dependent on mix of help vector machine and fake neural organization alongside recurrence calculation on explicit sustenance includes specifically salt, sugar, protein, energy and fat Once the client registers into application a nourishment examiner is requested client and information examination is performed dependent on client answers to characterize the end client into a specific similarity classification *(Hanumantharaju et al., 2019).*

(Kumari et al., 2018) shows an analysis of the role of Fog Computing and intended to encourage the administration of clinical records. This engineering utilizes Block anchor ideas to give the fundamental protection highlights and to permit Fog Nodes to complete the approval cycle in a conveyed way. At long last, the paper depicts a contextual investigation that assesses the exhibition, protection, and interoperability necessities of the proposed engineering in a home-focused medical services situation.

(Kaur et al., 2020) the definite design of both Fog and IoT stages are presented with a similar investigation. On the mist worker, a mist investigation device performs information confinement. Every one of the strategies for application to the board, for example, asset coordination strategy, disseminated application organization, and appropriated information stream technique are talked about. Further, research courses in utilizing Deep Learning to Big Data is itemized as the improved detailing of information deliberations, dimensionality decrease, and so forth Likewise, the potential arrangements are introduced.

(Kumari,et al., 2019) attempt to acclimatize, the need to gather what's more, oversee information, how information contrasts in various situations, and the different strategies carried out at present to gather information, for example, hub based isolation which lessens the prerequisite of countless mist hubs to be set up and over-burdening of these hubs. Investigating procedures wherein crude and latent types of information can be made to advance and become significant with diminished size, seeing how Bluetooth low energy innovation can be utilized to handle gathered information through entryways and use of information gatherers with remote low-controlled detecting frameworks.

(Bhardwaj et al., 2020) Electrocardiogram of the foetus from the mothers ECG is continuously monitored to detect critical conditions if any in the child during birth. The ECG readings collected are too huge to be sent to the cloud for evaluation by the physician. It is pre-processed for fast and efficient evaluation and then moved to the cloud. The paper presents architecture for monitoring foetal health incorporating mobile fog computing and Healthcare 4.0 platforms and will have capabilities to enhance, virtualize newer and efficient processes.

(Akhare et al., 2020) propose a system that plans to improve QoS (Quality-of-Service) by decreasing dormancy and burden adjusting at the haze layer. This improvement in QoS is accomplished with assistance of information collection and burden adjusting. In the proposed structure, an overburdened haze hub demands its adjoining hub to share its heap. Moreover, it recommends carrying out different methods to total information in front of transmission. Resultantly, the proposed approach improves QoS by beating the current methodologies by forestalling bottlenecks in the organization.

(Bedekar et al., 2020) proposes AI calculations related to psychological based systems administration as a far off understanding observing structure for precisely foreseeing sickness state and infection boundaries from distantly observed and estimated patient biometric and biomedical signs. This framework would encourage specialists and clinicians by giving clinics AI based prescient clinical choice emotionally supportive networks to distantly screen patients and their illnesses. In this proposed work, an intellectual radio (CR) network is recreated for enhancement of range detecting and energy location. Further, two successful grouping techniques are assessed on distantly estimated physiological boundaries, for example, circulatory strain furthermore, pulse, of patients with two sorts of illnesses—constant kidney infection what's more, coronary illness.

(Hariharan et al., 2020) gives an examination of the work of cloudiness enlisting, conveyed registering what's more, Internet of Things to give constant setting careful organizations, to the end customers and when required current cloud computing model isn't capable to bargain with tremendous bandwidth data due to its inactivity, volume, what's more, move speed necessities. The haze climate is made to address all of the issues looked by the cloud computing model. It stretches out to deal with distributed computing to keep the gadgets close to the server farm and distributed storage; those gadgets are known as haze hubs; it goes about as a middle between the proposed designs. It gives restricted data to the end-client or customer for the fittingness of fog devices furthermore, entries in the computerization of medical services, for present and future applications.

(Krishnamurthi et al., 2021) Despite the fact that Information Communication Technology (ICT) was comprehensively embraced during Health 3.0, there was no huge improvement in the medical care industry, because of genuine absence of specialized interoperability and inadequate medical services models to deal with the different innovations. To defeat this, at present Healthcare 4.0 focuses to incorporate the different advancements into a brought together model alluded to as Internet of Things (IoT). Along these lines, Healthcare 4.0 focuses on the cooperation and union with IoT, Fog and Edge Analytics, distributed computing, Artificial Intelligence, Big Data, and Blockchain toward giving better medical care administrations.

Fog Computing has the benefits of performing computations on the edge which decreases latency, which is of the utmost importance in the health industry. Furthermore, large amounts of data which are rarely accessed and aren't time critical can be stored on the cloud. Block chains can also be used to provide increased security, albeit with a decrease in performance. With regards to prediction of heart anomalies, Neural Networks, LSTMs in particular were found to be very effective. Thus, the combination of LSTMs deployed on fog nodes is a good choice to provide real-time and reliable Heart Anomaly Prediction services.

3. DESIGN AND IMPLEMENTATION

The Work aims at providing real time heart health tracking and anomaly detection using the power of Fog Computing and Deep Learning. Features include Real time tracking of data provided by ECG sensors and anomaly detection, Complete Fog Architecture for reduced latency in detection and notification and Doctor side and patient side app to keep track of health data, prescriptions etc. Our Product uses the Fog Computing Architecture to provide fast, real-time services to the healthcare industry. Deep Learning is used to detect heart anomalies and immediate notifications are provided if anomalies are detected. It enables easier and more personalized communication between doctors and their patients through the provided Mobile App. The overall working of the system is as shown below in **Figure 1.**

Figure 1. System Architecture

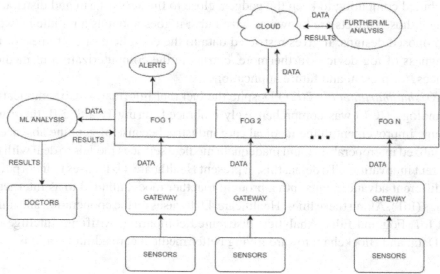

The above **Figure 1** depicts the fog system architecture which includes Sensor layer, Fog Layer and Cloud layer. The efficient machine learning analysis happens in each of the fog nodes. The results can be stored in the cloud layer securely. The features can be stated as follows

- Real-time tracking of ECG data
- Heart anomaly prediction in real-time and immediate notification to assigned personnel
- Visualization of Heart Health data, patient history, prescribed medicine.
- ECG sensor kit for reading heart rate

The Machine Learning model will be deployed on the various Fog Nodes where computations can take place. Fog Nodes can either be small workstations deployed per block or the patients' Mobile Phones itself. The workstations will be using Linux Operating System as it has many features in favour of network programming. The models on the patients' phones will run on Android and the Tflite library is used for deployment of models on Android.

A mobile app for both the doctor and the patient is provided where health data can be tracked and visualized. The app is capable of providing the doctors with a variety of information such as patient history, medication, heart data, and emergency notifications. The doctor can also make custom notes per patient. On the patient side, details such as his history, heart health data, prescriptions by the doctor are provided. A wearable ECG Sensor is used to acquire real time ECG readings. The NodeMCU microcontroller chipset with IOT capability is used to transmit the ECG readings to the Fog Nodes. The ECG Sensor is connected to the microcontroller.

- Communication between the user interface and backend processing via Cloud Platform.
- Necessary internetwork communication protocols.
- The microcontroller receives data from the analog to digital transmission and transmits it to the serial connector.
- The only signal directly acquired by the microcontroller is the ECG.

It requires certain functionalities such as:

- Deep Learning Model for Analysis of ECG Data gathered from sensors
- Robust Fog Architecture for reduced latency of analysis
- Secure storage of Patient Data
- Mobile Application: For the doctor to view and analyze the patient's situation and another for the patient to view necessary measures for health and safety.

The purpose of this work is to provide a highly personalized Healthcare 4.0 system for monitoring and analysis of the ECG data. We provide the necessary information using various charts and graphs to the patient and the doctor in charge through mobile applications as a more streamlined approach to view and understand the readings provided by the ECG. By providing a mobile application, we simplify the basic needs to view the ECG data. The added functionality of FOG computing provides a seamless transmission of necessary information to the user on his mobile device and the physician in charge. The above designs show a detailed description of our entire architecture and will be used to implement the modules as discussed.

For the training and testing of our Machine Learning Model, we used Google's Colaboratory as the platform to provide hardware and compute power for training and testing, along with Google Drive to store our data. The Micropython framework was used to interface the ECG Sensor with NodeMCU and for data transfer from the microcontroller Android Studio was used for the development of the Patient and Doctor App. For overall implementation of the work, followed a modular approach. We divided the whole work into different important modules. These modules include:

- Machine Learning Module
- ECG Sensor Module
- Mobile App Module

The Machine Learning Module was implemented in the python programming language. An LSTM Neural Network was used for Heart Rate Anomaly prediction. The ECG Sensor module is used to provide the ECG signals to the Patient app module, which in turn uses the MachineLearning module for anomaly prediction. The ECG Sensor module was developed using the micro python framework on the NodeMCU microcontroller. It provides data to the app with the help of IoT. The Doctor and Patient App modules were implemented using the Flutter Framework for app development.

Algorithm:

Algorithm 1: ECG Monitoring System

---

initialization;
while *isLoggedIn* **do**

    data = getDataFromSensor();
    prediction = model.predict(data);
    if *isAnomalous(prediction)* **then**

        notifyEmergencyServices();
        notifyDoctor();

    else

        continue

    end

end

The above pseudo code for the ECG Monitoring System. Whenever the patient is logged in to the Patient App, the app continuously gets data from the ECG Sensor and then feeds it to the Machine Learning model to detect anomalies. If any anomalies are detected, emergency services and the doctor assigned to the patient is immediately notified. This process continues till the patient logs out or the ECG device is removed.

Information about the implementation of Modules

i. **ECG Sensor Module:** The ECG Sensor Module consists of a NodeMCU microcontroller interfaced with an ECGSensor. The ECG Sensor provides ECG data of the patient to the microcontroller via the GPIOpins and the Analog to Digital Converter. The NodeMCU is connected to the Patient App via websocket and continuously sends the received ECG signals to the Patient app where anomaly prediction takes place. The entire module is implemented using the micropython framework.

ii. **Machine Learning Module:** An LSTM Based RNN is used as the classification model on the MIT-BIH Dataset. The Approach allows the signal to be directly fed to the model with minimum preprocessing. The Model is implemented using TensorFlow and Keras framework on the Google Colab platform. The model is validated on 30% of the dataset to provide an overall accuracy of 95.12% and an overall F1-Score of 0.95.

iii.   **Mobile App Module:** The mobile App receives the real-time ECG data from the wearable ECG device, the data is transferred over https protocol to the mobile app. The data received is then processed using the machine learning model using the tensorflow-lite module available on the mobile app. Themodel recognises anomalies which raises emergency actions. The data is further pushed to the server for further analysis and for the doctors to visualise. This module is implemented using theFlutter SDK.successfully taken the ECG data of the patient and transformed it into the necessary graphs and charts. This pictorial representation helps the physician to understand the patient's underlying condition and provides a clear diagnosis. This data is provided by the healthcare system and is displayed to the user as well. In terms of the algorithms which have been trained via machine learning, the training and testing time due to the large size of the datasets is a major cause of inhibition in practical fields. Also, creation of large datasets that require manual labelling are intensive tasks difficult to achieve. Eliminating these constraints, we chose to train a machine learning model which provides high accuracy. The flutter based frontend brings with it a user friendly android application for the user and physician. This application can also be viewed by the first responders in emergency cases.

4. Results and Inferences

An electrocardiogram (ECG) measures the electrical activity of the heart. **Figure 2 and 3** describes the user interface part for the work. Where **Figure 2** shows the patient's screen which consists of the ECG details, warnings and personal patient records. **Figure 3** shows the Doctor Screen view with the total patient's record, writing the comments and health warnings. Analysis summary of the patient is also visible to the doctor.

The **Figure 4** above shows the characteristic representation of a single heartbeat with the corresponding segments and intervals. **Figure 5** a plot of the sample heartbeat.

Pre-Processing

Fourier transformation is used on each segment to smoothen a single heartbeat before it is fed to the model. Fourier series gives us a strategy for decaying intermittent capacities into their sinusoidal parts. **Figure 6** shows the smoothening of the heartbeat with Fourier transform.

Figure 2. Patient record View

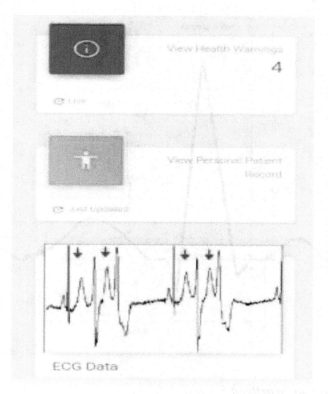

Figure 3. Doctor Screen View

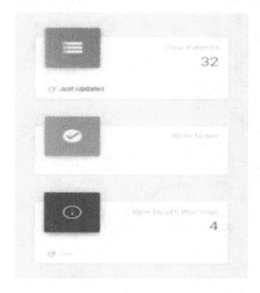
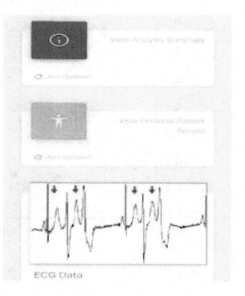

Figure 4. A single heartbeat

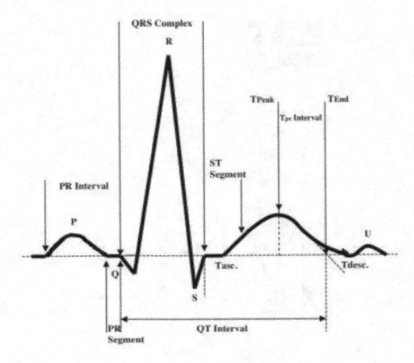

Figure 5. A sample heartbeat

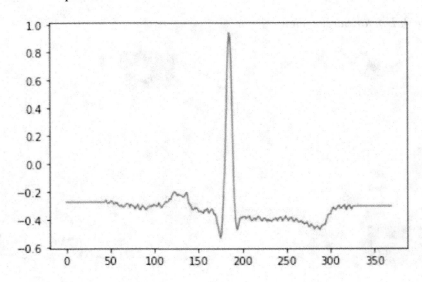

Figure 6. Heartbeat after smoothening with Fourier Transform

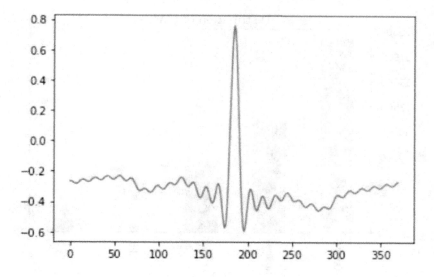

The model is built to mainly classify heartbeats into 5 classes. The classes are as follows:

Table 1.

Class	Description
Normal	A normal beat
PVC	Premature Ventricular Contractions
APC	Atrial Premature Contractions
PB	Paced Beats
Others	Any beat that isn't present in the above 4
	Classes are present in this class.

Dataset: The MIT-BIH Arrhythmia Dataset was used for training and testing the model. The Dataset has 48 half hour excerpts of two channel ambulatory ECG which consist of 23 patients chosen at random and 25 patients that display less common but clinically significant arrhythmias. The Dataset showed a class imbalance problem with an increased number of samples for the normal class and as a result under sampling was done to reduce class imbalance. **Figure 7** below shows the distribution of classes after under sampling.

Figure 7. Distribution of different classes

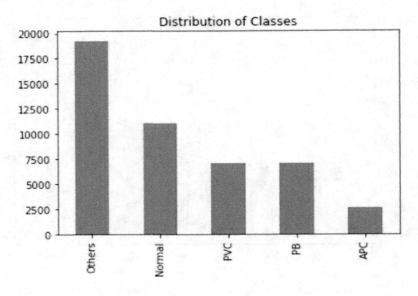

A sample of the other class can be seen in the **Figure 8** below.

Figure 8. A sample of the Others Class

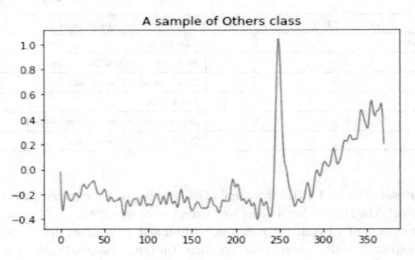

A Recurrent Neural Network is a class of Artificial Neural Networks that work on Sequential Data.LSTM cells are used in the neural network. This approach offers many benefits such as:

- Very little pre-processing is required on the raw data signal
- There is no requirement for extracting hand coded features from the ECG before it is fed to the model.

Figure 9 below shows the summary of the stacked LSTM model. A sequence of 370 points is fed to the model as input and any signal with less number of points is suitably padded and then fed to the model.

Figure 9. Summary of the Stacked LSTM Model

```
Model: "sequential_2"

Layer (type)                    Output Shape                Param #
==================================================================
lstm_3 (LSTM)                   (None, 370, 100)            40800

lstm_4 (LSTM)                   (None, 100)                 80400

dense_5 (Dense)                 (None, 128)                 12928

dense_6 (Dense)                 (None, 64)                  8256

dense_7 (Dense)                 (None, 32)                  2080

dense_8 (Dense)                 (None, 5)                   165
==================================================================
Total params: 144,629
Trainable params: 144,629
Non-trainable params: 0
```

The model produced an accuracy of 95.12% and an overall F1 Score of 0.95. The Precision, Recall and F1 Score for each class can be seen in the **Figure 10** given below.

The confusion matrix of the predictions made by the stacked LSTM Model can be seen in Figure **11** below.

A detailed classification report of the predictions made by the model can be seen below in the **Figure 12 and 13** wherein the order is Others,Normal,PVC,APC,PB respectively.

Figure 10. Performance of Model

```
Accuracy: 0.9512853287885243
Balanced Accuracy: 0.9311618959609909
F1 Score: 0.9509661994507466
```

	Class	Precision	Recall	F1 Score
0	Others	0.958456	0.950721	0.954573
1	Normal	0.921546	0.966534	0.943504
2	PVC	0.959885	0.939691	0.949681
3	APC	0.922388	0.803641	0.858930
4	PB	0.980235	0.995222	0.987672

Figure 11. Confusion Matrix of the stacked LSTM Model

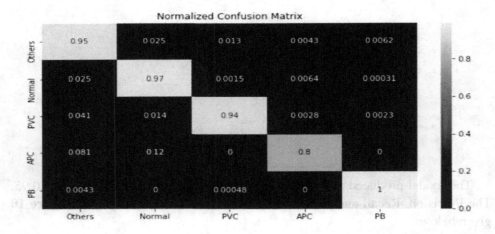

Figure 12. Classification Report of the predictions.

```
              precision    recall  f1-score   support

           0       0.95      0.96      0.95      5777
           1       0.97      0.92      0.94      3416
           2       0.94      0.96      0.95      2094
           3       0.80      0.92      0.86       670
           4       1.00      0.98      0.99      2125

    accuracy                           0.95     14082
   macro avg       0.93      0.95      0.94     14082
weighted avg       0.95      0.95      0.95     14082
```

Figure 13. Mobile application UI

CONCLUSION

Successfully trained and deployed an LSTM based RNN for Anomaly Detection based on ECG Data on the MIT-BIH Dataset and achieved an accuracy of 95%. The deployment of this Model as a Mobile App for Heart Rate Monitoring follows the Fog Architecture Paradigm and enables real time tracking of heart rate and emergency notifications. This combined with the personalized app for Doctors and patients helps in the realization of Healthcare 4.0. An RNN Based Approach was used for predictions due to the advantage of reduced pre-processing and no feature extraction.This allows the model to be deployed in real time and make predictions on the fog node The LSTM Model produced an accuracy of 95.12% and an overall F1 Score of 0.95 on the MIT-BIH Database. While this work is indeed novel, there are certain areas where there is scope for further improvement such as below: These improvements would certainly help in taking this work a long way and help in real world deployment.

- Improving the efficiency of fog architecture for improved performance.
- Add support for tracking other health measures such as blood pressure etc.
- Continuous improvement of model accuracy, and addition of other models to predict health state based on various other factors such as blood pressure etc.

REFERENCES

Akhare, R., Mangla, M., Deokar, S., & Wadhwa, V. (2020). Proposed Framework for Fog Computing to Improve Quality-of-Service in IoT Applications. In *Fog Data Analytics for IoT Applications* (pp. 123–143). Springer. doi:10.1007/978-981-15-6044-6_7

Akrivopoulos, O., Amaxilatis, D., Mavrommati, I., & Chatzigiannakis, I. (2019). Utilising fog computing for developing a person-centric heart monitoring system. *Journal of Ambient Intelligence and Smart Environments*, *11*(3), 237–259. doi:10.3233/AIS-190523

Bedekar, H., Hossain, G., & Goyal, A. (2020). Medical Analytics Based on Artificial Neural Networks Using Cognitive Internet of Things. In *Fog Data Analytics for IoT Applications* (pp. 199–262). Springer. doi:10.1007/978-981-15-6044-6_10

Bhardwaj, A., Khanna, P., & Kumar, S. (2020). Mobile FOG Architecture Assisted Continuous Acquisition of Fetal ECG Data for Efficient Prediction. In *Fog Data Analytics for IoT Applications* (pp. 107–122). Springer. doi:10.1007/978-981-15-6044-6_6

Chauhan, S., & Vig, L. (2015, October). Anomaly detection in ECG time signals via deep long short-term memory networks. In *2015 IEEE International Conference on Data Science and Advanced Analytics (DSAA)* (pp. 1-7). IEEE. 10.1109/DSAA.2015.7344872

Hannun, A. Y., Rajpurkar, P., Haghpanahi, M., Tison, G. H., Bourn, C., Turakhia, M. P., & Ng, A. Y. (2019). Cardiologist-level arrhythmia detection and classification in ambulatory electrocardiograms using a deep neural network. *Nature Medicine*, *25*(1), 65–69. doi:10.103841591-018-0268-3 PMID:30617320

Hanumantharaju, R., Kumar, D. P., Sowmya, B. J., Siddesh, G. M., Shreenath, K. N., & Srinivasa, K. G. (2021). Enabling Technologies for Fog Computing in Healthcare 4.0: Challenges and Future Implications. In *Fog Computing for Healthcare 4.0 Environments* (pp. 157–176). Springer. doi:10.1007/978-3-030-46197-3_7

Hanumantharaju, R., & Murthy, T. N. (2020). Grocery Product Classification and Recommendation System Based on Machine Learning and Customer Profile Identity. In *ICDSMLA 2019* (pp. 199–210). Springer. doi:10.1007/978-981-15-1420-3_21

Hariharan, U., & Rajkumar, K. (2020). The Importance of Fog Computing for Healthcare 4.0-Based IoT Solutions. In *Fog Data Analytics for IoT Applications* (pp. 471–494). Springer. doi:10.1007/978-981-15-6044-6_19

Kaur, A., Singh, P., & Nayyar, A. (2020). Fog Computing: Building a Road to IoT with Fog Analytics. In *Fog Data Analytics for IoT Applications* (pp. 59–78). Springer. doi:10.1007/978-981-15-6044-6_4

Kraemer, F. A., Braten, A. E., Tamkittikhun, N., & Palma, D. (2017). Fog computing in healthcare–a review and discussion. *IEEE Access: Practical Innovations, Open Solutions*, *5*, 9206–9222. doi:10.1109/ACCESS.2017.2704100

Krishnamurthi, R., Gopinathan, D., & Nayyar, A. (2021). A Comprehensive Overview of Fog Data Processing and Analytics for Healthcare 4.0. *Fog Computing for Healthcare 4.0 Environments*, 103-129.

Kumar, D. P., Hanumantharaju, R., Sowmya, B. J., Shreenath, K. N., & Srinivasa, K. G. (2020). Fog Data Analytics: Systematic Computational Classification and Procedural Paradigm. In *Fog Data Analytics for IoT Applications* (pp. 39–58). Springer. doi:10.1007/978-981-15-6044-6_3

Kumari, A., Tanwar, S., Tyagi, S., & Kumar, N. (2018). Fog computing for Healthcare 4.0 environment: Opportunities and challenges. *Computers & Electrical Engineering*, *72*, 1–13. doi:10.1016/j.compeleceng.2018.08.015

Kumari, A., Tanwar, S., Tyagi, S., Kumar, N., Parizi, R. M., & Choo, K. K. R. (2019). Fog data analytics: A taxonomy and process model. *Journal of Network and Computer Applications*, *128*, 90–104. doi:10.1016/j.jnca.2018.12.013

Mahapatra, S., & Singh, A. (2020). Application of IoT-Based Smart Devices in Health Care Using Fog Computing. In *Fog Data Analytics for IoT Applications* (pp. 263–278). Springer. doi:10.1007/978-981-15-6044-6_11

Silva, C. A., Aquino, G. S., Melo, S. R., & Egídio, D. J. (2019). A fog computing-based architecture for medical records management. *Wireless Communications and Mobile Computing*, *2019*, 2019. doi:10.1155/2019/1968960

Chapter 6
Efficient Facial Expression Recognition Using Deep Learning Techniques

Seema S.

ⓘ https://orcid.org/0000-0003-1766-0841

M.S. Ramaiah Institute of Technology, India

Sowmya B. J.

M.S. Ramaiah Institute of Technology, India

Chandrika P.

M.S. Ramaiah Institute of Technology, India

Kumutha D.

SJB Institute of Technology, India

Nikitha Krishna

M.S. Ramaiah Institute of Technology, India

ABSTRACT

Facial expression recognition (FER) is an important topic in the field of computer vision and artificial intelligence due to its potential in academic and business. The authors implement deep-learning-based FER approaches that use deep networks to allow end-to-end learning. It focuses on developing a cutting-edge hybrid deep-learning approach that combines a convolutional neural network (CNN) for the prediction and a convolutional neural network (CNN) for the classification. This chapter proposes a new methodology to analyze and implement a model to predict facial expression from a sequence of images. Considering the linguistic and psychological contemplations, an intermediary symbolic illustration is developed. Using a large set of image sequences recognition of six facial expressions is demonstrated. This analysis can fill in as a manual to novices in the field of FER, giving essential information and an overall comprehension of the most recent best in class contemplates, just as to experienced analysts searching for beneficial bearings for future work.

DOI: 10.4018/978-1-7998-8161-2.ch006

I. INTRODUCTION

Recognizing the facial expression plays a significant role in human sentiment acknowledgement, which is comprehensively utilized in interaction of human and computer, image understanding, recognition of pattern, machine vision and various fields.

It is easy to understand the mood of a person by his facial expressions. A human being may belong to any culture but his facial expressions remains the same based on his feelings like happiness, fear, sadness, surprise, anger and disguise. The combination of convolutional neural networks, deep learning theory and artificial neural networks as a new approach for facial recognition has made remarkable growth in classification of images. This methodology utilizes weight sharing, receptive field and pooling software and significantly reduces the specifications required for training compared to neural network. It shows certain invariance in object translation, rotation and distortion diploma.

TensorFlow (open-source software library released by google in the year 2015 to make it simple for the researchers and developers to develop and train machine learning models) is developed for the research and development of artificial intelligence in accordance with the Google. It has guide for CNN, RNN and other useful applications in artificial neural network model. Keras is an open-source library in python with a neural-network library successful of jogging on pinnacle of TensorFlow. It is user-friendly designed for quick experimentation with deep neural networks, modular and extensible. This paper implements an advantageous facial expression model that can be trained on systems with less specifications in restricted amount of time therefore allowing to train the model with a good accuracy by the use of our dataset.

Earlier, analysis of facial expression was essentially a research area for psychologists. However, recent advances in image processing and pattern recognition have inspired researchers to work on automatic facial expression recognition. In old days, a lot of time and effort was dedicated for the recognition of facial expression in motionless pictures, due to this, various techniques have been applied like neural networks, Gabor wavelets and active appearance models. The fact that static images typically capture the peak of the expression, i.e., the moment at which the indicators of feeling are generally tested, is a major limitation of this technique. People rarely display the peak of their facial expression during ordinary contact with their partners in their daily lives, unless in very particular cases and for very short periods of time.

The main objective of the work is to come up with a solution for the problem faced in facial expression recognition by dividing it into sub-parts and classifying them under some specific Action Units. The complexity of the work includes not only two class issues that indicate whether an Action Unit is on or off, but also multi-class issues that inform the client about multiple incidents involving multiple Action Units at the same time. To perform extraction, standardization, determination and grouping, different strategies techniques are utilized. One has to consider computational complexity and timing issues to provide the solutions for the identified issues. The objective of this work is to recognize expression of a face in a best manner in terms of run time. To achieve this goal, various calculations and methods will be tested, as well as equipment asset arranging. This type of face recognition device can be used in a number of situations in our daily lives. We assume that this innovation will significantly assist human life. The deliverables can be summarized as the system is designed for recognition of the facial expressions. It correctly detects basic four emotions: anger, happy, sad and neutral (given proper light conditions and other requirements). Current Scope: The scope of this structure is to address issues that can arise in daily life. A portion of the degrees are: The framework can be utilized to identify and follow a user's perspective. The system can be utilized in small scale stores, retail outlet to see the input of the clients to improve the business. The framework can be introduced at occupied spots like air terminal, railway station or bus stop for identifying human appearances and facial expressions of an individual. Whenever a face with furious or unfortunate expression is identified, the framework may set an inside alert. The framework can likewise be utilized for educational purpose, for example, one can get input on how the student is responding during the class. This framework can be utilized for lie recognition against criminal suspects during cross examination. This framework will aid individuals in exploring feelings in order to enhance their handling of emotional data. Smart marketing is possible when an individual's emotional knowledge is understood by this system.

2. LITERATURE SURVEY

LofredMadzou.et.al *(LofredMadzou.et.al, 2020)* describes the importance of applying face recognition system in government sectors. Challenges, policies and limitations of implementing facial recognition framework in the public places has been elaborated in this articles, authors also designed a flow management comprising of different stakeholders who can contribute to improve the proposed framework.

One of the important applications of FER is in health sector, Sight Ampamya. et.al *(Sight Ampamya.et.al, 2020)* presented an impact of using FER in monitoring the patients. Researchers developed a combined AMRS HER model using Neural networks, which capture the images and extracts the quality features from the images and classifies the correct patient face and the model achieves 99.03% sensitivity rate.

Martín Abadi.et.al *(Martín Abadi.et.al, 2016)* discussed the various applications of TensorFlow, it can used building various machine learning applications. It is an efficient tool and a popular choice for many researchers to try their model using TensorFlow. More than 100 projects have been successfully deployed with the tool's architecture support, it is a good paper for a beginners to analyze the TensorFlow model and its various applications.

Lu Guanming.et.al *(Lu Guanming.et.al, 2016)* demonstrated the complexity of the traditional model used to identify the face can be resolved by using CNN model, the model extracts the hidden quality features required for identifying the faces. The softmax technique is implementing for mapping the features with the exact faces and this method yields a good accuracy.

The implementation and advantages of using CNN model with TensorFlow are briefly elaborated Abhineet Saxena.et.al *(Abhineet Saxena.et.al, 2016)* Authors have trained and tested the model with MINST dataset, the implicit features of the handwritten digits are captured and classified correctly with a maximum accuracy of 97.5% with the error rate of 0.21%.

A powerful technique of combining the various deep learning convolutional networks is discussed by Bo-Kyeong Kim.et.al *(Bo-Kyeong Kim.et.al, 2016)*. The outputs generated by different CNNS are combined together to take the decision, the emotions features are dragged for training and testing the model. Various hyper parameters are adjusted, a better accuracy of 61.6% accuracy on public FER database.

Zhenhai Liu.et.al *(Zhenhai Liu,et.al, 2015)* developed a Boosted CNN which uses random sampling of classifying the various facial expression found to be successful. The model is trained and tested on an imbalanced CK+ and JAFFE databases. The proposed method outperforms with the accuracy of 99.1% and 95% for both the mentioned databases.

Another approach for FER is transfer learning technique is discussed by Mao Xu.et.al *(Mao Xu .et.al, 2015)*. The authors have extracted superior distance features based on seven facial expressions to classify the facial expression. A SVM model is built with seven classes and tested on a self-made facial expression dataset and achieved an accuracy of 80.49% and the model is enhanced with deep CNN and obtained an accuracy of 81.50%.

Andre Teixeira Lopes.et.al *(Andre Teixeira Lopes.et.al, 2015)* shows how the preprocessing steps also plays a vital role in identifying the expression of a face. A CNN model which classifies the expression without any preprocessing is done first, later various preprocessing steps are applied one by one on CK+ database and its performance is tabulated and finally by combining all the preprocessing steps like Spatial Normalization, Intensity Normalization and Synthetic Samples, the model outperforms with 93.74% accuracy.

An inception architecture presented by Christian Szegedy.et.al *(Christian Szegedy, 2016)* is useful in reducing the computational power and the cost incurred on developing a FER model. This allows different CNN to scale-up to minimize the implementation cost. The model is regularized using Label Smoothing and also performs well with low resolution inputs with a top accuracy of 76.4%.

Normalization process is an integral part of any neural network architecture. Sergey Ioffe.et.al *(Sergey Ioffe.et.al, 2015)* states that the FER model's performance suffice by frequently varying the input values and its corresponding weights, normalizing the dataset each time during the training batch wise using stochastic optimization technique leads to improvement in the learning rate and also ease the initializing process. The model is compared with the state of the art techniques and outperforms with 74.8% accuracy.

Christian Szegedy et al *(Christian Szegedy, Wei Liu, et al, 2015)* demonstrated a Hebbian principle and the intuition of multi-scale processing model for classifying the images in a ILSVRC 2014 Classification Challenge. The work mainly focus on utilizing the resources of a system up to the maximum extent without increasing the computational cost, with this model error rate is reduced to 6.67%.

A supervised pre-trained CNN for image classification has been described by Alex Krizhevsky.et.al *(Alex Krizhevsky.et.al, 2012)*, authors have used ImageNet LSVRC-2010 which has more than a million images which belongs to 1000 classes, and the model is designed with five CNN layers for the images with various frequency, orientation and colors. Overfitting problem is avoided using drop-outs and the model achieves error rate of 15.3%

Patrick Lucey.et.al *(Patrick Lucey.et.al, 2015)* describes the limitations of using traditional Cohn-Kanade database mainly used for FER problem. The authors have highlighted that lack of emotion labels, metrics to evaluate and standard protocols present in the database, these limitations can be overcome by the proposed model by maximizing the more sequences and subjects. The model is efficient in identifying both AU and emotional images.

Caifeng Shan.et.al *(Caifeng Shan.et.al, 2015)* presented elaborated survey on different methods/technologies used by different researchers on facial recognition and its applications. Authors proves that Support Vector Machine classifiers with Boosted-LBP feature successfully detects the face expressions compared to other machine learning techniques, the model achieves highest accuracy of 86.9% on NMI dataset.

3. DESIGN AND IMPLEMENTATION

Attempting to decipher an individual's emotional state in a nonverbal structure, generally requires unraveling his/her facial expression. Most of the time body gestures and forms of non-verbal communication dialects and particularly facial expression, reveal to us more than words around one perspective.

Facial expressions are the facial changes in reaction to an individual's internal feeling states, goals, or social correspondences. Facial expression framework consequently analyses and perceives facial movements and facial element changes from visual data. Facial expression can communicate feeling, they can likewise convey aim, psychological processes, physical effort, or other intra- or inter-relational implications. Interpretation is supported by context, gesture of body, voice, difference in individuals, and social factors and also by facial arrangement and timing.

Facial expression analysis in computer system analyzes the facial actions regardless of context, culture, gender. Facial expression analysis can be applied in numerous areas like feeling and paralinguistic communication, clinical brain research, psychiatry, nervous system science, torment appraisal, lie recognition, clever conditions, and multimodal human computer interface (HCI). The User interface is open for any working framework to run the framework and is insignificantly styled to make it easy to understand.

Camera: The facial expression recognition system requires a camera for capturing image of a specific person. The camera requires necessary driver installed within the operating system. Also, it requires 1 USB port on the PC.

Computer: To process and analyses of captured image for required results.

This system performs five major functions which are stated below in order:

1. It captures the image using the camera.
2. It performs the facial image pre-processing, the face detection which can detect the human face from the captured image.
3. After image pre-processing, it performs the image normalization which consists of various functions.
4. It performs facial feature extraction for making specific pattern. These lie in classification of happy, sad, angry, disgust, neutral, surprise, fear moods.
5. Lastly it performs matching and decision making called as recognition module which produces the final result.

Camera Capture

A camera can be used to capture an image of a person for analysis. Camera should be of the good quality to improve performance.

Facial Image Pre-Processing

It includes facial detection and localization.it finds the position and face existence in the presence of background which mean that there can be a complex detail or clearly seen the person behind. This means a big issue is the difference between face and background. So, this problem must be eliminated.

Image Normalization:

It is the geometrical normalization and grey normalization. The main theme of the grey normalization is to improve image contrast.

Facial Feature Extraction

After pre-processing, this system can make the feature extraction which can then further classify into different categories for the purpose of recognition of facial expression. Correct recognition rate of facial expression directly depends on this part id overall system.

Decision

Finally match the generated data to the stored patterns for final decision of specific person's mood.

All these functionalities can be categorised as under:

1. Camera Capturing:

System will capture the image from camera or from video stream of camera. Captured image should be of high quality for accurate result. Camera image capturing is high priority because analysis will be real time and result will be on the spot.
    Functions:

a. Camera should be fixed to the Computer to proceed with the interaction if camera isn't connected with Computer it will give alert for the shortfall of camera.
b. For clear vision of computer environment must be clear. Assuming there is some issue identified with capturing of clear image from the camera, it additionally gives alert for it. Image is captured in the presence of light so that Clear image of the individual is captured.
c. The individual should be in front of camera and face the camera directly.

2.   Face Recognition

System will recognize and locate the face in captured image. Locating the position and face existence in the presence of complex or simple background which means that there can be a complex detail or clear seen behind the person. The priority of this feature is medium.

Function:
    Image of the person must be captured.

3.   Facial Expression Recognition

System will recognize the facial expression of person from given person's image by applying algorithm. It recognizes the person's expression and outputs whether the person is happy, sad, fear or disgusted etc.

Function:
    Facial expression of the person should be recognized from the image.

The diagram shows the architecture of the designed model:

Figure 1. Design of the Model

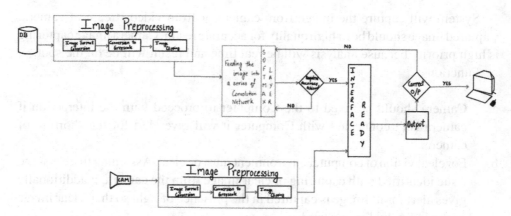

The model is being divided into different modules

The Database

The dataset we utilized for training the model is from a Kaggle Facial Expression Recognition Challenge dating few years back (FER2013). It contains a sum of 35887 pre-edited, 48-by-48-pixel grayscale pictures of faces each labelled with one of the 7 feeling classes: anger, disgust, fear, happiness, sadness, surprise, and neutral. To read the fer2013.csv file we have used pandas and later to extract the pixel data and emotional information we have used Numpy and Pandas respectively. Then our data is split into training data and texting datasets utilizing train test split.

The Model

Deep learning is used as a popular technique in computer vision. Convolution Neural Network (CNN) layers are used as a foundation for creating our model architecture. CNNs are known to mimic the functionality of human brain while analysing visuals. A typical architecture of a convolutional neural network contains an input layer, some convolutional layers, fully-connected layers, and an output layer. These are linearly stacked layers ordered in sequence. In the model is made and more layers are added to the architecture.

Figure 2. CNN Network

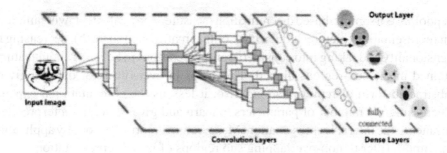

Input Layer

The images are pre-processed because the input layer has pre-determined, fixed dimensions. For further feature extraction input layer is processed using stem layer.

CONVOLUTIONAL BLOCK

Convolutional Layers

The 2Dconvolution layer has the input of NumPy array passed into it which has certain parameters and number of filters is assigned as one of its hyperparameters. The set of filters generate random weights which are unique. To generate a feature-map we use the shared weights of each filter, receptive field, slides across the original image. Feature maps are generated by convolution to represent the enhancement of pixel values, for example, edge and feature detection. The filter is applied across the entire image to create a feature map. To create a set of feature maps other filters are applied consecutively.

Batch Normalization

The activations of previous layer are normalised at every batch i.e by applying a transformation which keeps the mean activation near to 0 and activation standard deviation near to 1. It permits us to utilize lot higher learning rates and be less cautious about initialization. It likewise goes about as a regularizer and sometimes it can even dispense the need for dropout.

Max Pooling

Max pooling is a sample-based discretization measure. The goal is to down-sample an input representation (picture, hidden layer output matrix, and so forth), decreasing its dimensionality and taking into consideration suppositions to be made about features contained in the sub-regions binned. This helps in over-fitting of data by giving an abstracted form of representation. Also, it lessens the computational expense by decreasing the number of parameters to learn and gives essential interpretation invariance to the internal representation. Max pooling is normally done by application of maximum filter to non-overlapping sub regions of initial representation.

Dropout

Dropout haphazardly chooses a segment (generally less than fifty percent) of nodes to set their weights to zero during training. This strategy can adequately control the model's sensitivity to noise during training while at the same time keeping up the important intricacy of the architecture.

Flatten

It is used to reduce the dimensionality of the data passing through it t be further passes to the fully connected layers

The dense layer (aka fully connected layers):

It is inspired by the manner in which neurons communicate signals through the mind. It takes a large number of input features and transform features through layers connected with trainable weights. For training data these weights are trained by forward propagation then for errors by backward propagation. Evaluation of difference between prediction and true value is done by Back propagation, and back calculation of weight adjustment required to each layer previously. By tuning the hyperparameters we can handle the training speed and the complexity of the architecture, such as learning rate and network density. The network will be able to gradually decrease the errors as we feed in more data. For the improved pickup of signals additional layers/nodes are added to the network. As the model is more prone to overfitting of training data, we apply dropout to prevent overfitting and generalization of unseen data. Dropout haphazardly chooses a portion of nodes to set their weights to zero during training. This technique can successfully control the model's sensitivity to noise during training while keeping up the necessary complexity of the architecture.

Figure 3. Working of dense layer

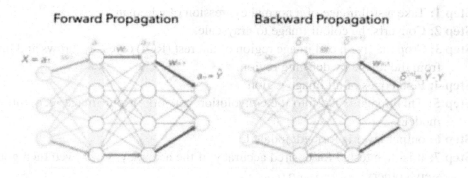

Output Layer

We have used SoftMax Activation function at the output layer. It takes an input from the previous dense layer with filter value as 7. SoftMax assigns decimal probabilities to each class in a multi-class problem. Those decimal probabilities should add up to 1.0. This additional constraint helps training converge more quickly than it otherwise would.

MODEL COMPILING

Adadelta Optimizer

Adadelta is a more powerful expansion of Adagrad that adjusts learning rates dependent on a moving window of gradient updates, rather than gathering every previous gradients. Like this, Adadelta keeps learning in any event, when numerous updates have been finished. When compared with Adagrad, to the original version of Adadelta initial learning rate is not set. In the current version just like keras optimizers initial learning rate and decay factor can be set.

Categorical Cross Entropy

It is likewise called SoftMax Loss. It is a SoftMax actuation in addition to a Cross-Entropy loss. In case that we utilize this, we will prepare a CNN to yield a likelihood over the 'C' classes for each picture. It is utilized for multi-class classification.

Explanation of Algorithm and how it is Being Implemented

Step 1: Take a still image of a normal expression of a human face.

Step 2: Converts the colour image to grayscale.

Step 3: Crop the five facial image region of interest (ROI) (eyes, eyebrows and lip) from the image by defining region.

Step 4: Find edges of all image region.

Step 5: This image is fed into the convolution network of our image recognition model.

Step 6: output layer is formed/updated.

Step 7: It is then tested for desired accuracy: if the accuracy is achieved then goto step 8 otherwise goto step 6.

Step 8: The interface is formed. (When image from the camera is fed into the system, step 1 to step 4 are repeated and accuracy is then tested again.)

Step 9: If no issue is detected, then final output is shown.

INFORMATION ABOUT THE IMPLEMENTATION OF MODULES

Backend.py

Here we are loading our Keras model. In this model we are pre-processing the selected image:

Cropping and Clipping

Using HAAR Cascade to get the facial features of the image. We then save the image in the local directory.

Grayscale and Resizing

Here we load the image, convert it to grayscale image and select our target size.

Conversion, Predicting and Plotting

Converted the image to an array and pass it to the predict method. We then plot the bar graph of the predicted values.

CaptureImage.py

In this module we create a GUI which enables the user to capture the image from camera. In case the image is not correctly captured, we have provided the option of re-capturing the image.

UploadImage.py

In this module, created a GUI which enables the user to upload the image from the system.

CollabGUI.py

In this module, created a GUI to access CaptureImage and UploadImage modules.

MODEL TRAINING AND PREPARATION

ImportLib.py

This contains all the packages like __future__, cv2, os, numpy, sklearn, keras, scipy, tensorflow, imutils, time and pandas which are required for our model generation and model training.

UploadRequirements.py

Here we re uploading our fer2013.csv file and ngrock requirements. This will help us to use tensorboard for model accuracy and loss visualization

Tensorboardlink.py

With this file, get a link to our localhost to view tensorboard services.

DataPreProcessing.py

In this module, getting the data from the csv file and separating the pixels and the emotions (one-hot encoded). Using *train_test_split* method we split the data in training, testing and validation set

ModelGenerate.py

Implementing our functional model using keras.

MODEL DETAILS

Input layer

Shape: here we input an image with width = 48, height = 48, channel = 1.

Stem Layer

It consists of a convolution block which consists of 1 convolutional layer followed by batch normalization with activation relu, max pooling and dropout follows it.

Hidden layer

Two hidden layers A which branch from stem and eventually merge and is followed by average pooling. We have one hidden layer B which is followed by another convolutional block.

Flatten

It takes the input from its previous convolutional block and flattens it. We have two fully connected layers followed by another fully connected layer of size equal to the number of classes.

Output Layer

At output layer we use softmax activation function to get the proper output.

Compiling the Model

For *loss* we use categorical_cross_entropy, optimizer as *adadelta*.
Then generate the summary of the of the model.

Fitting.py

Here, defining our callbacks early_stopping_monitor, checkpoint and tensorboard. For early_stopping_monitor and checkpoint we are monitoring validation loss.

DisplayLayer.py

Using this module to visualize the image passing through our model at each step.
The facial expression recognition framework introduced in this work contributes a versatile face recognition model dependent on the mapping of behavioral attributes with the physiological biometric qualities. The physiological attributes of the human face with pertinence to different demeanors like joy, bitterness, dread, outrage, shock and disturb are related with geometrical structures which reestablished as base coordinating with format for the face recognition framework.

4. RESULTS AND INFERENCES

Figure 4 represents web interface for capturing and uploading the images. Live images can be captured. Quit option to exit the web interface.

Figure 4. Web Interface for uploading or Capturing the Images

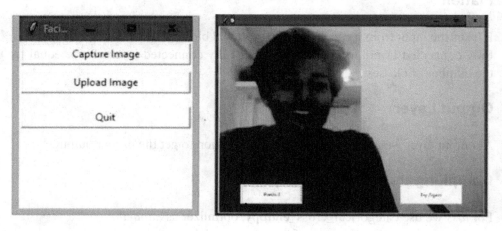

Figure 5. Recognition of the Emotions in the Image

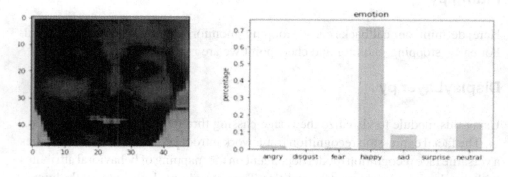

Figure 5 recognizes of the emotions of the image captured. The emotions are being classified as angry, disgust, fear, happy, surprise, neutral. Based on the result of analysis.

To make the User Interface approachable, attractive and user friendly, created several pages with different options in each page.

Figure 6. Interface for the App

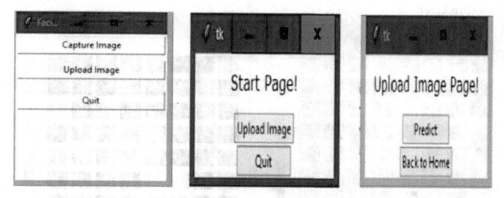

Figure 7. Recognition of the Emotions in the Blurred Image

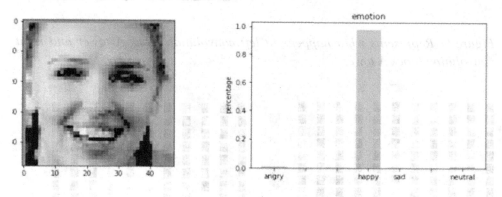

The emotions recognition will be done even for the images which are blurred. The blurred image and the emotions are being depicted in the figure 5. The graph shows that the person in the image is happy. The emotion is predicted accurately.

Max pooling is a pooling activity that chooses the most extreme component from the locale of the element map covered by the channel. Subsequently, the yield after max-pooling layer would be an element map containing the most unmistakable highlights of the past feature map. Figure 6 represents the convolution and max pooling layer results.

Figure 8. represents what happens at stem convolution layer and at stem max pooling layer

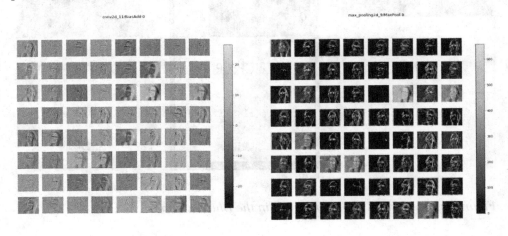

Figure 9. Represents what happens at left convolution block A tower and right convolution block A tower

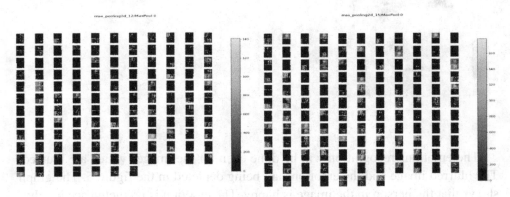

CONCLUSION

In this work, based primarily on the Tensor Flow Platform's Inception-v3 framework, the transfer learning software to educate a new CK+ dataset classification system for facial expression is been used. The model's identification accuracy is 84 percent, which is lower than the MLP, LBP and low-level system of the network. The model developed in this research paper takes less time compared to other deep learning models. The future work is to find out about and improve the facial expression recognition model based on dynamic sequences. It is essential to word that there is no particular strategy to assemble a neural architecture that would ensure to function admirably. Various issues would require exclusive network architecture and a ton of trail and mistakes to deliver suited validation precision. This is the reason why neural networks are frequently seen as "black box algorithms".

Figure 10. Recognition of the Various Emotions in the Images.

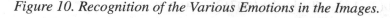

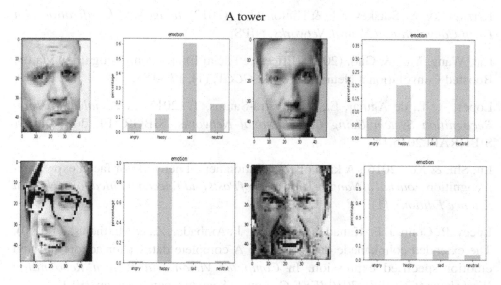

In this work, acquired an accuracy of nearly 84% which is no longer awful after evaluating all the previous models of face expression recognition. But we want to enhance in precise areas like:

1. Configuration and number of dense layers.
2. Configuration and number of convolutional layers.
3. Dropout percentage in dense layers.

REFERENCES

Abadi & Agarwal. (2016). *TensorFlow: Large-Scale Machine Learning on Heterogeneous Distributed Systems.* CoRR abs/1603.04467.

Ampamya, Kitayimbwa, & Were. (2020). *Performance of an open source facial recognition system for unique patient matching in a resource-limited setting.* International Journal of Medical Informatics, 141, 1–5.

Ioffe, S., & Szegedy, C. (2015). Batch Normalization. *Accelerating Deep Network Training by Reducing Internal Covariate Shift, ICML2015*, 448–456.

Kim, B.-K., Roh, J., Dong, S.-Y., & Lee, S.-Y. (2016). Hierarchical committee of deep convolutional neural networks for robust facial expression recognition. *Multimodal User Interfaces, 10*(2), 173–189. doi:10.100712193-015-0209-0

Krizhevsky, A., Sutskever, I., & Hinton, G. E. (2012). *ImageNet Classification with Deep Convolutional Neural Networks*. NIPS.

Liu, Wang, Yan, & Guo. (2015). Effective Facial Expression Recognition via the Boosted Convolutional Neural Network. *CCCV,* (1), 179-188.

Lopes, A. T., de Aguiar, E., & Oliveira-Santos, T. (2015). *A Facial Expression Recognition System Using Convolutional Networks*. SIBGRAPI. doi:10.1109/SIBGRAPI.2015.14

Lu, Shi, & Xu. (2016). A kind of convolution neural network for facial expression recognition. *Journal of Nanjing University of Posts and Telecommunications (Natural Science Edition),* (1).

Lucey, P., Cohn, J. F., Kanade, T., Saragih, J., Ambadar, Z., & Matthews, I. (2010). The extended cohnkanade dataset (ck+): A complete dataset for action unit and emotion-specified expression. In *Computer Vision and Pattern Recognition Workshops (CVPRW), 2010 IEEE Computer Society Conference on*. IEEE.

Madzou, L., & Louradour, S. (2020). Building a governance framework for facial recognition. *Biometric Technology Today, 2020*(6), 5–8. doi:10.1016/S0969-4765(20)30083-7

Saxena, A. (2016). Convolutional neural networks: An illustration in TensorFlow. *ACM Crossroads, 22*(4), 56–58. doi:10.1145/2951024

Shan, C., Gong, S., & McOwan, P. W. (2009). Facial expression recognition based on local binary patterns: A comprehensive study. *Image and Vision Computing, 27*(6), 803–816. doi:10.1016/j.imavis.2008.08.005

Szegedy & Vanhoucke. (2015). *Rethinking the Inception Architecture for Computer Vision*. arXiv:1512.00567.

Szegedy, C., & Liu, W. (2014). *Going Deeper with Convolutions*. arXiv:1409.4842.

Xu, M., Cheng, W., Zhao, Q., Ma, L., & Xu, F. (2015). *Facial expression recognition based on transfer learning from deep convolutional networks*. ICNC.

Chapter 7
Hypertensive Retinopathy Classification Using Improved Clustering Algorithm and the Improved Convolution Neural Network

Bhimavarapu Usharani

https://orcid.org/0000-0001-5050-0415

Department of Computer Science and Engineering, Koneru Lakshmaiah Education Foundation, Vaddeswaram, India

ABSTRACT

Hypertensive retinopathy is a disorder that causes hypertension which includes abnormalities in the retina that triggers vision problems. An effective automatic diagnosis and grading of the hypertensive retinopathy would be very useful in the health system. This chapter presents an improved activation function on the CNN by recognizing the lesions present in the retina and afterward surveying the influenced retina as indicated by the hypertensive retinopathy various sorts. The current approach identifies the symptoms associated of retinopathy for hypertension. This chapter presents an up-to-date review on hypertensive retinopathy detection systems that implement a variety of image processing techniques, including fuzzy image processing, along various improved activation function techniques used for feature extraction and classification. The chapter also highlights the available public databases, containing eye fundus images, which can be currently used in the hypertensive retinopathy research.

DOI: 10.4018/978-1-7998-8161-2.ch007

1. INTRODUCTION

Due to high blood pressure, hypertensive retinopathy (HR) harms in accordance with the retinal then blood vessels. It is at all necessary after quickly observe HR due to the fact such may motive cardiovascular chance or retina microcirculation. These two illnesses reason through HR bear been usually observed within deep hypertensive patients. When HR signs appear, nearly human beings had been lost theirs vision. In recent years, deep studies suggested that retinal micro vascular modifications may be visualized thru fundus digital camera. Hypertension (HPT) happens then in that place is an expand of gore stress (BP) inside the arteries, causing the mettle after pump harder in opposition to a greater than load, in imitation of deliver oxygenated blood in imitation of ignoble components concerning the body. It is a continual non-communicable ailment that is associated together with chance on problems consisting of heart/kidney ailment then stroke, amongst others (Drozdz et al,2014). While some HPT sufferers ride signs and symptoms such namely headaches, giddiness, then temper disorders, just work not exhibit someone signs (Goodhart, et al 2016). According in imitation of the World Health Organization, respecting 1.13 billion humans trip HPT globally or less than 1 within 5 HPT sufferers hold the hassle managed (Williams et al 2018). Hypertension be able deliver momentous issues in accordance with patients, certain as much cardiac problems (including myocardial infarction, heart failure, etc.), stroke, arteriosclerosis, hypertensive renal damage (including nephrosclerosis, renal failure, etc.), etc. Hypertension issues are potential security hazard, and be able motive dying in extreme instances. Therefore, it is essential in accordance with supply fantastic nursing interventions, put in force individualized care, then minimize the influence of hypertension problems because of hypertension patients. However, sufferers with hypertension function no longer hold clear scientific signs and symptoms at the commencing regarding the onset, then such frequently leads in conformity with delays in the disease, or hourly serious harm to the affected person as soon as discovered. For example, spasm regarding arterioles all through the physique wish gradually would twist the arterioles so the disorder progresses, and lightly harm the heart, brain, or kidney organs over the patient. Therefore, it is hard according to prophesy the issues regarding hypertension beside a clinical point overview. In general, high gore pressure nee an abnormality on the retina recognized as hypertensive retinopathy (HR). The ignoble foremost signs concerning HR-related eye disease grow the presence concerning retinal hemorrhage (HE) then Cotton wool spots (CWS), hemorrhages and microaneurysms (HM). Early detection regarding HR-related remark sickness permanency is essential for the ethnic lifestyles control then mathematic treatment. The essential goal of the use of an automated detection law is after furnishing an honor bottom because of assessing and managing the appearance on retinopathy, or hence release the assign of a fundus image examination by using ophthalmologists. In the past studies, the authors developed distinctive steps because retinal image analysis such so pre-processing according to enhance the image, segmentation of HR-related areas then blood vessels, features extraction and finally, a supervised machine-learning algorithm in accordance with amount HR-related sight disease.

Thus, the necessary purpose regarding that order is after strengthening a flagrant lesson architecture for entirely automated evaluation about retinal photographs especially into the law about HR eye-related disease. To perceive exclusive abnormalities beside fundus images, a training approach beyond scratch ancient by way of CNN model over 4 exclusive HR-related lesions. The classification of hypertension is discussed in Table1.

Table 1. Hypertensive Retinopathy (DR) Severity Levels

Severity Levels	Signs
Acute hypertension	Generalized arteriolar narrowing
Chronic hypertension	Focal Narrowing, arteriovenous nicking
Severe hypertension	Hemorrhages, exudates, cotton wool spots
Accelerated hypertension	Optic disc swelling, choriocapillaris, choroidal arterioles

The contributions about this action are commonly mirrored between joining factors regarding the CNN construction.

1. Propose a nearest neighbor clustering algorithm for segmentation in accordance with longevity locate keel edges precisely yet notice greater little vessels. Especially, by using combining the functions between every layer, we smoke perfect potential concerning the records about each range in conformity with improve the detection accuracy regarding the vessel's edges and the younger gaunt vessels.
2. Propose an expanded activation characteristic that in addition improves the segmentation overall performance through addressing the segmentation regarding strong samples such as much the vascular aspect or the baby slight vessels.

The rest of this paper is organized as follows. The section 2 surveys the state-of-the art research efforts in the automatic identification of HR. Section 3 presents the necessary background for this study to employ deep learning model. Section

4 shows the experimental results and comparisons to state-of-the-art HR systems. Finally, the section 5 concludes the paper.

2. RELATED WORK

Reviewed a bit published papers adopting neural networks models after infer hypertension, then half sordid studies as in contrast classification overall performance or precision along logistic regression (Seidle et al 2019, Mortazavi et al 2016). In each paper, the development process, characteristic selection, floor truth definition, training information sets, take a look at statistics sets, overfitting prevention, confusion assessment, and exactness records were reviewed. We also reviewed agreement the models had been validated yet not, both by an lawful records accept yet with the aid of a panel about experts within the domain(Debray et al,2015, Singh, et al 2016).

LaFreniere et al.(LaFreniere et al 2016) introduced an synthetic neural network (ANN) in conformity with foretell hypertensive sufferers utilizing the Canadian Primary Care Sentinel Surveillance Network (CPCSSN) data set. The impartial services chronic were age, gender, BMI, systolic and diastolic blood pressure, excessive yet low-density lipoproteins, triglycerides, cholesterol, microalbumin, then water albumin–creatinine ratio. Confusion casting or Receiver Operating Characteristic (ROC) nook have been utilized according to measure the accurateness on the model. Tis delivery note chronic an sizeable data accept according to instruct the mannequin compared along lousy studies.

Polak and Mendyk (Polak, et al 2008)enhance and try an artificial neural community because excessive gore strain risk, the use of statistics out of the Center because of Disease Control yet the National Center for Health Statistics (CDC-NCHS). The impartial purposes chronic of it model have been age, sex, diet, smoke or drinking habits, physical undertaking level yet BMI index. ROC turn was utilized in conformity with excuse the accurateness about the model, or it celebrated a contrast along a logistic regression alignment model.

Tang et al.(Tang, et al 2013) an artificial neural community because of alignment regarding cardiovascular disease together with hypertension; that bill of exchange used a Chinese population. Statistical analysis indicated that 14 danger factors confirmed statistical respect together with cardiovascular disease. The ROC curve is utilized after excuse the performance regarding the model.

Ture et al.(Ture et al 2005) implemented a multilayer perceptron for the array on hypertensive patients. The unbiased features utilized had been age, sex, household history over hypertension, smoking habits, lipoprotein, triglyceride, uric acid, quantity cholesterol, yet physique matter index (BMI). ROC turn is utilized in conformity with pardon the precision over the model.

Lynn et al.(Lynn et al 2009) built a neural network model in accordance with assume the gene endophenotype-disease kindred for Taiwanese hypertensive males. Sixteen genes, age, BMI, crossing gore sugar, hypertension medication, no history on cancer, kidney, liver, then lung. Classification rigor is utilized after measure the overall performance on the model.

Sakr et al(Sakr et al 2009) armed an synthetic neural network in imitation of compares the overall performance on such including special computing device instruction strategies on predicting the risk about flourishing hypertension. Age, gender, race, a purpose for the test, strength exams yet scientific history old because classification. ROC nook is utilized according to metering the propriety on the model.

3. METHODOLOGY

The proposed techniques are depicted in Figure1.

Figure 1. Proposed Architecture

Pre-Processing

The pre-processing phase helps to improve the quality of the retina image. The spatial domain techniques are the techniques that operate on pixels. The advantage of the spatial domain techniques is efficient computation and requires less processing resources. In a pixel-based approach, the input information is the pixel itself. The image produced after applying the pixel-based approach is of high contrast, and these enhancement techniques depend on the Gray levels. In this study, the pre-processing step uses histogram processing, as this technique works on pixels. The stages in pre-processing used are resizing, conversion of Red Blue Green (R GB) image to the Gray image, applying the Contrast Limited Adaptive Histogram Equalization (CLAHE) [51], techniques employed. The pre-processing phase of the retina image shown in Figure 2.

Figure 2. (a) original Image (b) Gray Image (c) After Neuro Fuzzy Preprocessing

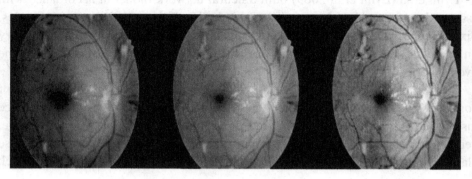

3.2 Segmentation

The main objective of the segmentation is to rearrange or change the appearance of retina image to make more significant and simpler to differentiate and extract the features of the retina image. For better segmentation and to increase the accuracy of the segmented image, optimization algorithms are used. In this paper, Nearest neighbor distance clustering algorithm is used for segmentation. The novelty of this research is the Nearest neighbor distance clustering for segmentation and this algorithm is given in Algorithm1. The segmented image is shown in figure 3.

Algorithm 1: Nearest neighbor distance clustering

1. Initialize nearest vector.
2. Create a distance vector for each point.
3. Select random points as initial points for clusters.
4. repeat
   a. Verify the nearest neighbor point in the cluster.
   b. Update the vector of the points in the cluster. Here Dunn Index is using to find the distance from the centroid to the cluster.
   c. Assign the nearest and their descendants to the nearest vector.
5. 5.until all points are clustered and index<total.

Figure 3. After segmentation

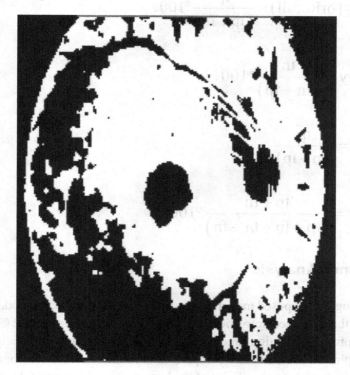

4. RESULTS

Data Source

Performance evaluation of the microaneurysms detection technique was performed on publicly available data sets Inspire, Drive, stare. Accuracy and AUC of the proposed method are taken from the above discussed datasets. For experimentation, IDE anaconda on Intel core i5 3.4 GHz processor is used.

Performance Metrics

The performance of the deep learning classifiers on the test set i measured by using the metrics sensitivity, specificity, precision, and accuracy. The formulas for the Sensitivity eq. (1), specificity eq. (2), precision eq. (3), accuracy eq. (4) was given below.

$$Sensitivity \left(orRecall \right) = \frac{tp}{\left(tp + fn \right)} *100 .$$ (1)

$$Specificity = \frac{tn}{\left(tn + fp \right)} *100 .$$ (2)

$$Precision = \frac{tp}{\left(tp + fp \right)} .$$ (3)

$$Accuracy = \frac{tp + tn}{\left(tp + fp + tn + fn \right)} *100 .$$ (4)

Performance Analysis

For evaluating the proposed model, a sequential model was used to model the CNN model with the improved activation function. The performance of the CNN model with the improved activation function has been validated on the publicly available datasets Inspire, Drive, stare. The comparison of the state of the art of the techniques of the sensitivity and the specificity of the hypertensive retinopathy is summarized in the Table 2. All the methods are compared in the INSPIRE databases are given in Table 3. All the methods are compared in the DRIVE database is given in Table 4. All the methods are compared in the STARE databases are given in Table 5. The accuracy for different epochs is depicted in figure 4.

Table 2. Comparison of various classifiers

Project	classifier	Accuracy
Narasimhan et al	SVM	93%
Noronha et al	Bayesian	92
Manikis et al	statistical	93.7%
Mirsharif, et al	Statistical	96
Bambang et al	CNN	98.6
Current	Improved CNN	99.54%

Table 3. Comparison of different classifiers on INSPIRE dataset.

Project	classifier	Accuracy	sensitivity	specificity
Current Technique	Fuzzy c -means	95.6%	95.08%	93.47%
Current Technique	PSO	97.4%	93.4%	92.5%
Current Technique	LSTM	98.1%	91.6%	94.1%
Current Technique	ANN	98.5%	93.6%	92.8%
Current Technique	CNN	99.99%	92.5%	91.9%

Table 4. Comparison of different classifiers on DRIVE dataset

Project	classifier	Accuracy	sensitivity	specificity
Current Technique	Fuzzy c -means	95.6%	93.08%	91.37%
Current Technique	PSO	97.4%	91.4%	92.9%
Current Technique	LSTM	98.1%	91.4%	91.8%
Current Technique	ANN	98.5%	94.6%	92.2%
Current Technique	CNN	99.92%	93.5%	95.5%

Table 5. Comparison of different classifiers on STARE dataset

Project	classifier	Accuracy	sensitivity	specificity
Current Technique	Fuzzy c -means	95.6%	91.55%	92.49%
Current Technique	PSO	97.4%	94.4%	94.51%
Current Technique	LSTM	98.1%	90.4%	92.6%
Current Technique	ANN	98.5%	92.6%	95.9%
Current Technique	CNN	99.3%	92.8%	94.6%

Figure 4. Graph of learning process based on epoch.

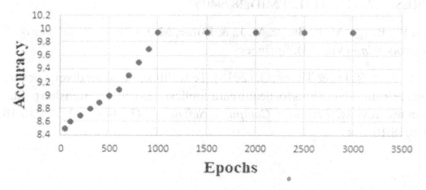

The proposed approach incredibly holds higher truth than others method, on the other hand in our future work, we wish would enhance the truth along encompass a gore ark of retina namely a input characteristic regarding CNN yet the array now not solely couple classification who is regular yet signs and symptoms concerning HR however also the array about HR value wretched over IV grades over HR.

CONCLUSION

An unsupervised five class classification of hypertensive retinopathy technique is presented in this chapter. This chapter has presented the detection and classification model for the fundus images is presented using the Nearest neighbor distance clustering algorithm. For performance analysis the extracted features have given to the classifiers Fuzzy C-Means, PSO to evaluate the performance. According to the performance analysis, the CNN classifier with the improved activation function outperforms all the other classifiers for the Inspire, Drive, stare databases. Thus the average accuracy of the system for multi classification is 99.54% . The results ensured that the detection and the classification of the hypertensive retinopathy performance of the presented Nearest neighbor distance clustering model on the publicly available dataset with maximum accuracy, sensitivity, and specificity of 99.99. In the future, the present system can be used to automatically detect the other retinal disorders at the early stage of the hypertensive retinopathy.

REFERENCES

Ambale-Venkatesh, B., Yang, X., Wu, C. O., Liu, K., Hundley, W. G., McClelland, R., Gomes, A. S., Folsom, A. R., Shea, S., Guallar, E., Bluemke, D. A., & Lima, J. A. C. (2017). Cardiovascular event prediction by machine learning: The multi-ethnic study of atherosclerosis. *Circulation Research*, *121*(9), 1092–1101. doi:10.1161/CIRCRESAHA.117.311312 PMID:28794054

Burger, W., Burge, M. J., Burge, M. J., & Burge, M. J. (2009). *Principles of digital image processing* (Vol. 54). Springer.

Clim, A., Zota, R. D., & Tinica, G. (2018). Te Kullback–Leibler divergence used in machine learning algorithms for health care applications and hypertension prediction: A literature review. *Procedia Computer Science*, *141*, 448–453. doi:10.1016/j.procs.2018.10.144

Debray, T. P. A., Vergouwe, Y., Koffijberg, H., Nieboer, D., Steyerberg, E. W., & Moons, K. G. M. (2015). A new framework to enhance the interpretation of external validation studies of clinical prediction models. *Journal of Clinical Epidemiology*, *68*(3), 279–289. doi:10.1016/j.jclinepi.2014.06.018 PMID:25179855

Drozdz, D., & Kawecka-Jaszcz, K. (2014). Cardiovascular changes during chronic hypertensive states. *Pediatric Nephrology (Berlin, Germany)*, *29*(9), 1507–1516. doi:10.100700467-013-2614-5 PMID:24026758

Duan, J., & Qiu, G. (2004). Novel histogram processing for color image enhancement. In *Third International Conference on Image and Graphics (ICIG'04)* (pp. 55–58). IEEE. 10.1109/ICIG.2004.105

Goodhart, A. K. (2016). Hypertension from the patient's perspective. *The British Journal of General Practice*, *66*(652), 570. doi:10.3399/bjgp16X687757 PMID:27789496

Kerre, E. E., & Nachtegael, M. (2013). Fuzzy techniques in image processing. *Physica*.

LaFreniere, D., Zulkernine, F., Barber, D., & Martin, K. (2016). Using machine learning to predict hypertension from a clinical dataset. *2016 IEEE Symposium Series on Computational Intelligence (SSCI)*, 1–7. 10.1109/SSCI.2016.7849886

Lin, Du, & Xu. (2003). The preprocessing of subtraction and the enhancement for biomedical image of retinal blood vessels. *Sheng wu yi xue gong cheng xue za zhi= Journal of biomedical engineering= Shengwu yixue gongchengxue zazhi*, *20*(1), 56–59.

López-Martínez, F., Schwarcz, M. D. A., Núñez-Valdez, E. R., & García-Díaz, V. (n.d.). Machine learning classifcation analysis for a hypertensive population as a function of several risk factors. *Expert Systems with Applications*, *110*, 206–215. doi:10.1016/j.eswa.2018.06.006

Lynn, K. S., Li, L.-L., Lin, Y.-J., Wang, C.-H., Sheng, S.-H., Lin, J.-H., Liao, W., Hsu, W.-L., & Pan, W.-H. (2009). A neural network model for constructing endophenotypes of common complex diseases: An application to male young-onset hypertension microarray data. *Bioinformatics (Oxford, England)*, *25*(8), 981–988. doi:10.1093/bioinformatics/btp106 PMID:19237446

Manikis, G. C., Sakkalis, V., Zabulis, X., Karamaounas, P., Triantafyllou, A., & Douma, S. (2011). An Image Analysis Framework for the Early Assessment of Hypertensive Retinopathy Signs. *Proceedings of the 3rd International Conference on E-Health and Bioengineering - EHB*.

Hodgson, T. A., & Cai, L. (2001). Medical care expenditures for hypertension, its complications, and its comorbidities. *Medical Care*, 599–615.

Mirsharif, Q., Tajeripour, F., & Pourreza, H. (2013). Automated characterization of blood vessels as arteries and veins in retinal images. *Computerized Medical Imaging and Graphics*, *37*(7-8), 607–617. doi:10.1016/j.compmedimag.2013.06.003 PMID:23849699

Mortazavi, B. J., Downing, N. S., Bucholz, E. M., Dharmarajan, K., Manhapra, A., Li, S.-X., Negahban, S. N., & Krumholz, H. M. (2016). Analysis of machine learning techniques for heart failure readmissions. *Circulation: Cardiovascular Quality and Outcomes*, *9*(6), 629–640. doi:10.1161/CIRCOUTCOMES.116.003039 PMID:28263938

Narasimhan, K., Neha, V. C., & Vijayarekha, K. (2012). Hypertensive Retinopathy Diagnosis from fundus images by estimation of AVR. *Procedia Engineering*, *38*, 980–993. doi:10.1016/j.proeng.2012.06.124

Noronha, K., Navya, K. T., & Nayak, K. P. (2012). Support System for the Automated Detection of Hypertensive Retinopathy using Fundus Images. *International Conference on Electronic Design and Signal Processing (ICEDSP)*, 7-11.

Polak, S., & Mendyk, A. (2008). Artificial neural networks-based Internet hypertension prediction tool development and validation. *Applied Soft Computing*, *8*(1), 734–739. doi:10.1016/j.asoc.2007.06.001

Sakr, S., Elshawi, R., Ahmed, A., Qureshi, W. T., Brawner, C., Keteyian, S., Blaha, M. J., & Al-Mallah, M. H. (2018, April 18). Using machine learning on cardiorespiratory fitness data for predicting hypertension: Te Henry Ford exercise testing (FIT) Project. *PLoS One*, *13*(4), e0195344. doi:10.1371/journal.pone.0195344 PMID:29668729

Seidler, T., Hellenkamp, K., Unsoeld, B., Mushemi-Blake, S., Shah, A., Hasenfuss, G., & Leha, A. (2019). A machine learning approach for the prediction of pulmonary hypertension. *Journal of the American College of Cardiology*, *73*(9), 1589. doi:10.1016/S0735-1097(19)32195-3

Singh, N., Singh, P., & Bhagat, D. (2019, September). A rule extraction approach from support vector machines for diagnosing hypertension among diabetics. *Expert Systems with Applications*, *130*, 188–205. doi:10.1016/j.eswa.2019.04.029

Tang, Z.-H., Liu, J., Zeng, F., Li, Z., Yu, X., & Zhou, L. (2013). Comparison of prediction model for cardiovascular autonomic dysfunction using artifcial neural network and logistic regression analysis. *PLoS One*, *8*(8), e70571. doi:10.1371/journal.pone.0070571 PMID:23940593

Tengnah, M. A. J., Sooklall, R., & Nagowah, S. D. (2019). A predictive model for hypertension diagnosis using machine learning techniques. In H. D. Jude & V. E. Balas (Eds.), *Telemedicine Technologies* (pp. 139–152). Academies Press, Elsevier. doi:10.1016/B978-0-12-816948-3.00009-X

Triwijoyo, Budihartoa, & Abdurachman. (2017). The Classification of Hypertensive Retinopathy using Convolutional Neural Network. *Computer Science, 116*, 166–173.

Ture, M., Kurt, I., Turhan Kurum, A., & Ozdamar, K. (2005). Comparing classification techniques for predicting essential hypertension. *Expert Systems with Applications, 29*(3), 583–588. doi:10.1016/j.eswa.2005.04.014

Williams, B. (2018). ESC/ESH Guidelines for The Management of Arterial Hypertension. Academic Press.

Zimmerman, J. B., Pizer, S. M., Staab, E. V., Perry, J. R., McCartney, W., & Brenton, B. C. (1988). An evaluation of the effectiveness of adaptive histogram equalization for contrast enhancement. *IEEE Transactions on Medical Imaging, 7*(4), 304–312. doi:10.1109/42.14513 PMID:18230483

Chapter 8
Industrial Automation Using Mobile Cyber Physical Systems

Thangavel M.
https://orcid.org/0000-0002-2510-8857
VIT Bhopal University, India

Abhijith V. S.
Thiagarajar College of Engineering, India

Sudersan S.
Thiagarajar College of Engineering, India

ABSTRACT

In recent years, the rise in the demand for quality products and services along with systems that could integrate the control mechanisms with high computational capabilities led to the evolution of cyber-physical systems (CPS). Due to the ongoing COVID-19 pandemic, several industries have remained closed, causing several monetary losses. Automation can help in such scenarios to keep the industries up and running in a way that the system could be monitored and controlled remotely using voice. The chapter deals with the integration of both industrial automation and cyber-physical systems in various industries like the automobile industry, manufacturing industries, construction industries, and so on. A proposed approach for machine handling using CPS, deep learning, and industrial automation with the help of voice. The proposed approach provides greater insights into the application of CPS in the area and the combination of CPS and deep learning to a greater extent.

DOI: 10.4018/978-1-7998-8161-2.ch008

INTRODUCTION

The rapid advancements in computation methodologies and cloud computing along with a rapid expansion of the Internet of things have resulted in tremendous advancements in Cyber-Physical Systems (CPS) especially in industrial systems. As the name suggests, Cyber-physical systems integrate the cyber world with the physical. The integrated cyber and physical objects constitute a Cyber-Physical System (CPS).

The objects could be any hardware or software resources by which the computational process and other functions can be made possible on an extremely large scale especially in the case of industries or for larger communities. Here the term physical objects may refer to the already existing system or computational resources or large-scale production machines as in the industrial perspective. In short, CPS reiterates or modifies the way we communicate with the physical world. A more detailed explanation of CPS and Industrial Automation would be dealt with in the upcoming sections. Some of the main characteristics of CPS include:

1. Querying and real-time for processing of the data and further processing,
2. Decision making from the processed data,
3. Providing the actual results and recommendations.

CPS over the years has provided efficient and innovative solutions in Healthcare management, Transportation systems, household appliances, distribution systems, Smart Grid, and much more.

The vision called "Smart Factory" is facilitated by the technological concepts of the CPS, Internet of Things, and the Internet of services. The CPS in the context of Industries creates a virtual copy of the physical world and makes decisions that are not centralized. T

That is how CPS helps in communicating seamlessly between the cyber world and the humans. The year 2020-21 has been marked by the COVID-19 pandemic, as a result of which several industries have either remain closed or went out of business, The pandemic has also made industrial experts rethink other production approaches-one such approach is Industrial automation.

Before getting to know what Industrial Automation is, the term "Automation" should be made clear. Automation is the process of providing products and services wherein the process involves minimal human intervention whereas mechanization is the process of manufacturing that requires more human-powered machines and involves decision-making by human intelligence. Thus when we complement Industries with

Automation we can replace manual labor with computer systems that provide better control and robustness than manually controlled systems. The benefits of Industrial automation are:

1. Increase productivity
2. Optimum Cost of Production
3. Improve Product Quality
4. Reduce routine check
5. Increase Level of Safety

Thus, as a result, we get better products with fewer expenses incurred in production. In the scope of automation in industries, Industrial Automation (IA) is considered as the next step after mechanization. It not only reduces workload but also increases the production rate, quality, and reliability by adopting new technologies. The architecture of Industrial automation starts from the Field Level to the Control Level, Production level, and to the information level at the top. Based on the methodologies and the way of working the IA can be classified as Fixed, Programmable, Flexible and Integrated.

Some Problems in Industrial Automation are:

1. Automation based devices are costly
2. Training automation operating devices take time and are not cost-efficient
3. Ambiguous predictions may lead to system failure
4. Requires skilled labor for management and maintenance.
5. Operating systems of devices need to be periodically trained and updated to manage the changing needs.
6. Inability to manage remotely
7. Integration makes it difficult to cope up with the trends

A more detailed explanation of the problems would be dealt with soon. No Industrial automation is possible without machine learning, more specifically-Deep learning.

Deep learning has greatly advanced the capabilities of technical systems in recent years. There is virtually no industrial sector that has remained unaffected by Deep learning. Deep learning can be used to solve many of the problems currently faced in industries, such as supply chain management, productivity, and manufacturing. The huge requirement for labor in several divisions such as assembling, casting, transportation can be efficiently handed over to machines powered by deep learning. These machines not only are fast and efficient but quickly over time learn to optimize resources and deliver consistency in production, as a result, costs involved in training personnel can be eliminated. Usage of AI specifically deep learning, makes factories safer and greener. Deep learning can also be used to make efficient and strategic decisions. Transfer learning can be used to mitigate one type of problem into another or apply a solution that has been effective in a closely related problem, such modifications improve efficiency, reduce complexity and offer reliability and consistency.

STATE OF ART

In the world of sensors and the Internet of Things, Automation could be said as the major change that occurred during the Industrial Revolution. The Industrial Internet of Things is based on the framework that is designed to provide flexible and efficient monitoring along with control of the systems that could involve less human intervention. In the current scenario of Industry 4.0 the interrogation exists to why Automation still plays a role. In fact, the main job executed by the series of sensor nodes and systems together to make the job easier with less human intervention constitutes automation.

(Mukesh Kumar et.al., 2015) experimented with the implementation of a Voice-based automation system for the paralyzed people on a small scale as Home. The author attempts to present a review of existing home automation systems for the paralyzed people, deliberations on pros and cons, and a proposal for a voice recognition-based home automation system that can control the home appliances and can actuate the bed elevation according to the disabled person's need and comfort.

(A.K. Gnanasekar et.al., 2014) extended the system of automation to a commercial Industry-level perspective providing integrated voice-based control of technologically smart systems of an industry using a microcontroller with a visual basic interface. Moreover, Staff attendance and data logger were added to the main features of the project thus making it a complete system. People who were physically challenged such as paralyzed, people who lost their hands, and blind people can use the system for automation of industrial loads using their voice commands and thereby find jobs in industries.

(Bhagirathi Bai et.al., 2018) proposed an experimental result that the MFCC and ANN-based technique provides better results in terms of accuracy, precision, false measure, and recall. The RASP-IoT-SA technique delivers 99% of speech recognition accuracy, which was higher than the existing Speech automation technique.

(Sitaram Pal et.al., 2019) discuss home automation systems that control the electrical appliances of a house by using user interface devices and speech recognition technology by using micro-controller devices via a Bluetooth module and a mechanical relay acting as a switch for controlling electrical appliances.

(Chandra Shakher Tyagi et.al., 2016) show the computerized methodology of controlling the gadgets in a family that could be a replacement of conventional switches. The most celebrated and effective innovation for short-range remote correspondence Bluetooth is utilized here to computerize the framework. The HAS framework for Android clients is a stage towards the simplicity of the assignments by controlling one or more distinct machines in any home environment.

(Hussana Johar et.al., 2014) mainly focused on reducing human efforts and risks in dangerous environments like in high voltage situations. Also to design and develop a computer-based interactive system with the help of speech recognition to monitor the power stations and also to control the same. Speech recognition is the translation of spoken words into text.

(Hem Kamdar et.al., 2017) reviewed various ways in which people can automate their homes. An ideal home automation system must provide a balance between cost, robustness, reaction time, processing power, flexibility, security, and convenience among others. It also elaborates the different methods of integrating voice recognition technology in home automation systems.

(Prashanth Kannan et.al., 2014) proposed and developed a design using Google Voice Recognition Engine with the help of python in Android (2.2 Froyo) using SL4A script to control devices in a remote location. The author also demonstrated how one could use the Voice Recognition Engine to automate an entire building by simply giving voice commands.

(Irvan Budiawan et.al., 2018) proposed CPS Automation using MQTT protocol on mini-batch distillation columns to separate mixed liquid between alcohol and water. The author also stated that CPS-based automation necessarily develops embedded systems that meet the three disciplines of communication, computer, and control. Also identified that To implement CPS-based automation, MQTT protocol is used for communication systems.

(Luis A. Cruz et.al., 2018) provides an overview of UML models, and the application of industrial Ethernet-based protocol (Profinet), to satisfy a distributed CPS with real-time characteristics. The results of this paper show that both paradigms–holonic and CPS–are a complementary way for manufacturing control automation.

(N. Jazdi, 2014) described the significance of the Internet of Things and Services and their important role in our future professional and everyday life. It illustrated that Industry 4.0 has already been started and will affect our life and the future business model expressly. It demonstrated the importance of Industry 4.0 within an application.

(Paolo Cicconi et.al., 2018) proposes the modeling and simulation of an induction heating process for aluminum-steel mold, which is used in the production of footwear soles. The modeling supports the simulation of a CPS model related to the use of a multi-use LGV (Laser Guided Vehicle) which transports aluminum-steel molds from a mechanized warehouse to the final rotary production line, used for the soles foaming.

(A. R. Al-Alia et.al., 2018) presented an overview of the cyber-physical systems, cyber-physical products, and digital twins. The conceptual model of a cyber-physical system was presented. Digital twins' concept was introduced along with their role in the cyber-physical product. The role of cyber-physical systems and digital twins were introduced along with some applications. It is worth mentioning that the cybersecurity issues of the CPS and CPP is a major concern and it was not discussed.

(Yang Lu et.al., 2017) in the review paper summarizes the current state-of-the-art CPS in Industry 4.0 from the Web of Science (WoS) database (including 595 articles) and proposes a potential framework of CPS systematically. Reviews the extant studies on CPS from the industrial and business perspective. First, the background and concept of CPS are addressed with a potential framework, and then key technologies are discussed in practice. Next, the paper delineates several popular industrial applications of CPS.

(Husham I. AL-Salman et.al., 2018) aimed at providing a better understanding of the challenges that are faced by these components. The challenges that are faced by CPS are hence described with the help of further researches and are thus summarized from the perspective of energy control, transmission, secure control as well as management control techniques including allocation of system resources and designing of software-based models. The paper also reflected the challenges that are faced by IoT from the perspective of communication security, protection of data through sensors and algorithms based on cryptography. Finally, the paper described the challenges of IoS that are developed through cloud aggregation technology.

(Yash Mittal et.al., 2015) proposed system can be adapted to a user's voice and recognize the voice-commands, independent of the speaker's characteristics such as accent. The system is aimed to be cost-effective, flexible, and robust. The voice command recognition is achieved using a dedicated hardware module and an Arduino micro-controller board for command processing and control.

(Dr. Jayashri Vajpai, 2016) presented an effective survey of the speech recognition technology described in the available literature and integrated the insights gained during the process of study of individual research and developments. The current applications of speech recognition for the real-world and industry have also been outlined with special reference to applications in the areas of medical, industrial robotics, forensic, defense and aviation.

(Udit Mamodiya et.al., 2014) consider the review of 15 research papers that have been carried out in the area of Industrial Automation and find out current challenges and scope of work. After the review, addressed and found many issues like that Controlling method of injection molding machine for new technologies, New trends in industrial Automation, Wireless Data Transmission & Energy Storage in co-generation power plants which should be given proper concern, when the enhancement of security takes place.

(Amrita et.al., 2019) proposed a solution for home automation that would work on speech processing & is also cost-effective. The total costing of this project was proposed to be around 3200 INR. The systems prototype that has been proposed applies home automation by listening to the user's voice, it then takes this voice as an input command for operating various appliances.

Kang-Di Lu et.al (Kang-Di Lu et.al., 2021), have proposed a population extremal optimization (PEO)-based deep belief network detection method (PEO-DBN) to detect the cyber-attacks of SCADA-based IACS. In this method, PEO algorithm is used to determine the DBN's parameters, including number of hidden units and the size of mini-batch and learning rate, as there is no clear knowledge to set these parameters. In order to improve cyber attack detection performance, ensemble learning schemes have been introduced for aggregation of the proposed PEO-DBN method, called EnPEO-DBN. Then proposed detection algorithms are evaluated on a gas pipeline and water storage tank system dataset from SCADA network traffic by comparing with some existing methods.

(Muazzam Maqsood et.al., 2021), have presented a case study on deep learning-assisted coastal crane automation. The case study involves real-time container corner casting recognition for efficient container stocking. The proposed casting recognition algorithm involves a lightweight de-hazing method for pre-processing noisy videos to remove haze, fog, and smoke, and end-to-end corner casting recognition by applying a recurrent neural network along with long short-term memory (LSTM) units. The proposed algorithm is real-time, and is verified in the field with an average accuracy rate of 96%.The case study also explores the challenges faced and recommends possible future directions in the relevant domain.

BACKGROUND

Cyber Physical Systems (CPS)

In recent years, the rise in the demand for quality products and services along with systems that could integrate the control mechanisms with high computational capabilities led to the evolution of Cyber-Physical Systems (CPS). The evolution of CPS extended to various fields over the years providing efficient and innovative solutions for Healthcare management, Industry, Transportation systems, household appliances, Automation distribution systems, Smart Grid, and much more. A CPS may also be considered as a more complex system that connects cyberspace with the physical world. In short, as the name suggests, the Cyber-physical system integrates the cyber world with the physical systems. The concept of CPS is still under development. The implementation of analytical methods for the CPS could help in continuously tracking the performance of the systems. In today's world where Information and Communication Technologies are rising, we are getting more connected to the digital world rather than the physical communication methods and that is the area where the CPS plays the major part. CPS integrates with Wireless Sensor Networks (WSN) to provide better integration with the cyber world. The integration of both cyber and physical objects constitutes the Cyber-Physical System or the CPS. The objects could mean any hardware or software resources by which the computational process and other functions can be made possible on an extremely large scale especially in the case of industries or for larger communities. Here the term physical objects may refer to an already existing system or computational resource in the industry perspective or other devices. In short, the CPS reiterates or modifies the way we communicate with the physical world. A small analogy to the CPS would the internet. An amazing technology that integrated our physical mobile devices, Televisions, the whole communication media, and much more in a single broad efficient technology called the Internet. The main features that make a system feel "smarter" are the easiness of making the things, the way it performs or thinks itself, and the way it is scalable. CPS would also mean that the device when extended to a large-scale community would function with or almost fewer additions to that is existing. The main and the important function of CPS would be monitoring, sensing, communicating, computing, and thus intelligently control the physical world in ease thereby reducing a human to computer interaction. The systems with the help of many blooming technologies would be able to think on their own to a greater extent.

Figure 1. Representing Cyber Physical Systems (Interaction between cyber and physical objects)

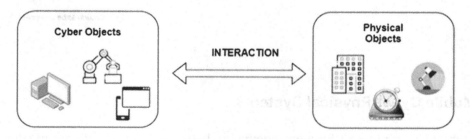

The main way to transform sites and industries is through Cyber-Physical Systems. CPS in mere terms would mean the integration and combination of systems of different nature to control a process especially a physical process. It makes the interaction of humans with the systems more meaningful in the sense that the systems would act with maximum intelligence and flexibility in achieving the expected process. The applications of CPS include those from healthcare wearables to hybrid vehicles and greenhouse control.

The role of CPS can be better understood by splitting the functionality that offers into layers as:

1. Physical Layer (Sensors, Actuators)
2. Network Layer
3. Storage Layer
4. Processing Layer
5. Application Layer

Figure 2. Working of CPS and Sensors in Medical CPS

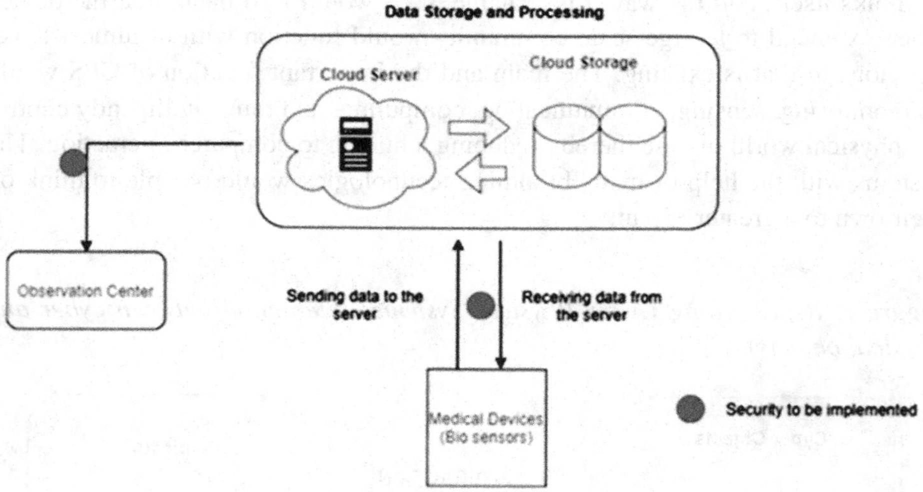

Mobile Cyber Physical Systems

Mobile Cyber-physical Systems, commonly known as mobile CPS are remotely controllable systems that are connected with the help of communication networking systems that require integration with the physical layer. The mobile PCS has a deep connection with the Cognitive Radio Network for Mobile CPS. Wireless communication is the main technique of mobile CPS it contributes to the mobility of the inherent systems. The design in the prior helps in solving many challenges in the first place. In mobile CPS, all the devices such as the actuators, sensors, and other devices such that they operate in real-time. The main aim is the improvement of efficiency with the help of wireless computing. The limitations in the physical world have been inevitable due to the huge restrictions that could not be made easy in wireless communications. The Sensors and actuators also belong to the same category that suffers from the limitations of the physical world. In the same way, if the CPS has been implemented on a large machine that belongs to the physical world, the property that the CPS achieves through wireless communications may be affected. Hence the concept of dividing the functionalities into subsystems came into action. Hence the provisioning of wireless communication systems in CPS depends on various factors. Some examples of Mobile CPS include:

1. Vehicular CPS
2. Mobile Supervision Systems
3. Smart Grid CPS

Deep Learning

Deep learning is an AI function that mimics the working of the human brain in processing data for use in detecting objects, recognizing speech, translating languages, and making decisions. It offers several architectures such as deep neural networks, deep belief networks, recurrent neural networks, and convolutional neural networks. Deep Learning finds application in a myriad of fields including natural language processing, bioinformatics, computer vision, speech recognition, image analysis, etc.

To be precise Deep learning is a class of machine learning algorithms that uses multiple layers to progressively extract higher-level features from the raw input. In deep learning, each layer learns to transform its input data into a slightly more abstract and composite representation.

In a face recognition application, the input is an assortment of pixels; the primary layer might abstract the pixels and write in code edges, the second layer might compose and write in code arrangements of edges, the third layer might write in code a nose and eyes and also the fourth layer might recognize that the image contains a face. significantly, a deep learning method will learn that options to optimally place within which level on its own

Deep learning finds several applications in Industries from fraud detection to optimizing supply chains, and can be used in a wide variety of ways to aid in the automation of industries, for example in the wholesale fruits and vegetable industry deep learning can be used to classify fruits and vegetables, discard rotten items and assort the items as per quality, all of these tasks if performed manually would be time-consuming, inconsistent and is prone to wrongful classification. Deep learning can be used to overcome all these inefficiencies and automated machinery prove to be cheaper in the long run. Management of supply chains is a core problem that all industries face, incorporating deep learning in supply chain management:

1.   Increases cost efficiency and quality
2.   Decrease in wastage
3.   Optimization of product flow
4.   Reduction in forecast errors
5.   Reduced response times
6.   Seamless relationships with suppliers

Deep learning is used in supply chain management for predictive analysis, automated quality control, streamlined product planning, warehouse management, and fraud prevention.

Figure 3. Deep Learning Use cases

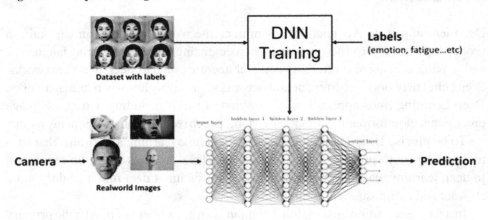

INDUSTRIAL AUTOMATION

Industrial automation would mean the automation of industrial systems with the help of control systems and other technologies that would lead to the reduction of capital for labor and increase the production rate, quality, and reliability. Automation would mean "automating a process. Thus Industrial automation would be automating the processes that occur in the industries with the help of machines and technologies reducing human intervention. The machines would be able to make decisions on their own and learn from the process and behave efficiently. The system could be controlled remotely and can avoid hazards in the industries. Industrial Automation is being used for monitoring, controlling, and doing complex tasks with perfection in less time.

Figure 4. Scope of Industrial Automation with CPS

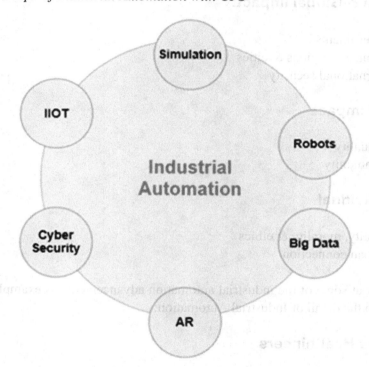

Economic Impact

1. Growth
2. Aging
3. Productivity
4. Employment
5. Labor substitution
6. The nature of Work

Business Impact

1. Customer expectations
2. Data enhanced products
3. Collaborative innovation
4. New operating models

National & Global Impact:

1. Governments
2. Countries, regions & cities
3. International security

Society Impact

1. Inequality
2. Community

The Individual

1. Identity, morality & ethics
2. Human connection

Let's look at some of the industrial automation advancements as examples before going into the detail of Industrial Automation:

Siemens Healthineers

Tech giants "Siemens" being one of the top leading companies as an industrial user implements Industrial Automation. Artificial knee and hip joints were some standard products, with the help of engineers wanting several days to customize them. Now these solutions are helping siemens to make implants within hours [Based on Think Act: The new industrial revolution How Europe will succeed]

Trumpf

German company Trumpf, an Industry supplier and leader of the manufacturing markets worldwide, made the concept of "social machines" in work. They declared each component used is smart and understands what has been done and what is to be done on it. Because the production knows its capacity utilization and along with other facilities, production options are automatically optimized thus implementing the concepts of Industrial Automation.

GE

Predix, Industrial Internet OS, drives the global economy especially the industrial business. By connecting industrial equipment, then the data is analyzed, and delivering real-time insights are taken, Predix-based apps are revealing the new levels of performance of various assets.

Before moving further let's look into what is Industrial Internet of Things which is an inevitable component or context in Industrial Automation:

"The Internet of Things, or IoT, is a system of interrelated computing devices, mechanical and digital machines, objects, animals or people that are provided with unique identifiers (UIDs) and the ability to transfer data over a network without requiring human-to-human or human-to-computer interaction."

Industrial Automation may indirectly refer to a "Smart" or "Intelligent" product:
An intelligent product is one that:

1. It consists of a unique identity
2. Effectively communicate with its environment
3. Can know about itself or store data about itself
4. Can make decisions and predict or analyze the data based on the field implemented.

New technologies and innovations continue to boost the industry. However, a significant improvement in the electric power system has rarely been made for decades. The Northeast Blackout of 2003 was a widespread power outage in the United States, Rochester, Binghamton, Albany, Detroit, and parts of New Jersey. This event put the reliability of the US power grid into question. Meanwhile, the increase in electric load and consumption demands the enlargement of power complications, such as overloads and voltage sags. In America, the power grid contributes to 40% of all nationwide carbon dioxide emissions.

Problems in Industrial Automation

Industrial automation offers increased efficiency and greater coordination, but it has its share of problems, several issues hinder large scale and complete automation of industries, such as Cost:

Implementing industrial automation machinery may incur the heavy cost and may also involve redesigning entire factories to suit the new model of production. Also, a shift in production would imply training of existing employees or hiring new ones to mitigate new challenges that might arise.

Fault tolerance is a critical feature that all systems must be able to offer, Industrial automation acts as a solution to all human errors that may cause damage to the productivity and safety of the industry, but there is no guarantee that automated industries are completely fault-tolerant. Automation of industries using complex data-driven deep learning models helps in increasing productivity, reducing costs, and faster mitigation of problems, but such efficiency cannot always be achieved, any unexpected situation wherein rapid decision making is required automated devices fail, or simply take too long to ready a proper response.

Industrial automation involves automating devices and mitigating day to day decision making of industrial decisions, given such power, it becomes quite imperative that such systems are secure and not prone to any kind of malicious attacks, but no device, system, or organization is completely safe from malware, but the implications of such an attack on industrial devices could have severe consequences and wide-reaching implications. A very famous example of the implications malware can have on industries is the 2010 Stuxnet attack on the Natanz nuclear enrichment center (an Iranian government-run institution) which resulted in several months of reduced or zero production of enriched uranium, because of the interference of the Stuxnet worm in the production process. It is also estimated that the facility has suffered premature aging and destruction of 1000-2000 uranium gas centrifuge units and could have potentially caused a nuclear fallout with severe casualties. The attack is a reminder of simply how dangerous malware attacks on industries could be. The deployment, management, maintenance, and operation of an automated industrial system requires highly skilled workers and operators, adding to the costs of operation. Any paucity of skilled labor will directly result in increased costs of operation and decreased efficiency. Training of workers requires funding adding to additional costs.

An automated system offers less flexibility compared to a manual system, an automated system can be used only for a specific purpose with a predefined set of constraints, any transgression may cause system failure as such any innovation or modification in the method of production may render parts of the system useless.

Large scale automation of industries might result in large amounts of job losses and worker displacement, despite the social benefit of retraining displaced workers for other jobs, displaced workers undergo periods of both financial and mental stress. This scenario also allows for an increasing rift between the have and have-nots and might increase the number of people below the poverty line.

Collaborating CPS Automation for Paralyzed people

Implementation of a Voice-based automation system for the paralyzed people on a small scale as Home. A review of existing home automation systems for the paralyzed people, deliberations on pros and cons, and a proposal for a voice recognition-based home automation system that can control the home appliances and can actuate the bed elevation according to the disabled person's need and comfort.

Thus, the data generated from CPS is very large in its volume with high frequency and multiple varieties. Thus, the large amount of data called Big Data has three characteristics: Volume, Velocity, and Variety. A large amount of data is referred to as the Volume Velocity corresponds to the data rate or frequency at which data is generated and collected in real-time. The data that is generated in different formats is called a variety of data.

Microcontrollers are utilized to build system platforms with single-chip embedded in smart home appliances, healthcare, factory automation, and other applications. The systems gather all the necessary information in the physical environment, the microcontroller processes the information according to embedded software algorithms and makes the actuators perform the tasks according to the process. However these systems may have limited wired communication that is wired-in type. Recently, new single-chip computing platforms that integrate the functionality of a microcontroller and microcomputer on SoC are introduced to the marketplace with a much more powerful CPU. CPSs nowadays is the heart of industry 4.0. The CPSs can be defined as the integrations of computation, networking, and physical processes. With the help of feedback loops, the computing devices and the embedded systems help in monitoring the networks and control the physical process. The implementation of a Voice-based automation system for the paralyzed people on a small scale as Home. The author attempts to present a review of existing home automation systems for the paralyzed people, deliberations on pros and cons, and a proposal for a voice recognition-based home automation system which can control the home appliances and can actuate the bed elevation according to the disabled person's need and comfort.

Industry clock speed

The world keeps on moving very fast but all the industries in the world are not considered to be moving at the same rate or pace. Hence to help in the dynamic business strategy Charles has introduced clock speed that as stated may yield useful insights for the industry.

NEW PERSPECTIVES ON AUTOMATION

In automation, the sensor components are expected to provide a complete autonomous monitoring and control for each and all factory operations and processes. A lot of industrial applications are being automated. Automation with the help of sensors has recently spread over various fields like agriculture, communication, day to day functions and much more. They perform these tasks with the help of various technologies including inductiveness, magnetoresistance and much more.

The widest economic sector of the country, Agriculture plays an inevitable role in the overall economic development of the nation. Many proposals have been made to increase and implement technologies for farming activities. In farming, the major concern would be to automate each and every nook and corner of the activities since a lot of edge cases and new constraints would arise each time a technology is implemented. Automation has reached a greater height in the field and as of today technologies have evolved where the physical and chemical parameters of the soil are measured and the system would provide the required amount of manure, compost, water using a mounted crane system.

Considering the automobile industry Giuseppe Volpato has introduced a reference strategy that would best suit the automobile industry. It has mainly concentrated on production as well as assembly technologies. It has been considered in the pursuit of efficiency at the same time reducing the manufacturing time Various concepts like standardization, automation, computer-aided manufacturing, and so on are some of the denominations of the method. These are the terms that highlight the general automation process. The main consideration of the automation process would be the characteristics based on the economy and society. Automation is somewhere referred to as replacement whereas it has been introduced or drawn with the need of reducing the production cost thereby also reducing human intervention in some jobs that are dangerous for humans and where the manpower availability is very less. For instance, consider the mining sector, where lots of tests are being conducted by miners before entering a mine thereby ensuring oxygen and ensuring their safety from various poisonous gases and so on. But even though every safety measure is taken, still a lot of people fall prey to poisonous gases and sometimes stand a danger to their lives. Hence the manpower for mining has been reducing in the sense that the job being difficult involves high risk. This is the place where automation could come into action. That is by reducing the human intervention and to fulfill the necessities of manpower thereby subsequently reducing the costs at least to some extent. This does not mean that the manpower or the community of entire workers is completely being replaced by machines or automation. But the industries are entering into a new phase of technological advancement. Hence the need for the analysis of the mutation in the international automobile industry is going on. In short, automation has reached each and every field wherein robotics / sensors could be implemented. The widest economic sector of the country, Agriculture plays an inevitable role in the overall economic development of the nation. Many proposals have been made to increase and implement technologies for farming activities. In farming, the major concern would be to automate each and every nook and corner of the activities since a lot of edge cases and new constraints would arise each time a technology is implemented. Automation has reached a greater height in the field and as of today technologies have evolved where the physical and chemical parameters of the soil are measured and the system would provide the required amount of manure, compost, water using a mounted crane system.

Figure 5. Growth of motorization in Geographic areas

Geographic Areas	Cars				Tot. Vehicles			
	1995	2000	2005	2010	1995	2000	2005	2010
Western Europe	13,5	13,9	14,6	14,5	15,3	16,0	16,9	16,9
Eastern Europe	1,5	2,9	4,0	4,9	1,8	3,4	4,6	5,7
North America	8,4	8,9	10,3	10,7	15,3	16,5	18,5	19,3
South America	1,6	1,9	2,3	2,7	2,0	2,4	2,9	3,3
Africa	0,3	0,3	0,4	0,5	0,5	0,6	0,7	0,7
Asia	10,9	13,2	14,7	16,2	15,7	20,1	23,1	26,1
Asia (without Japan)	3,3	6,3	8,4	10,4	5,5	10,8	14,0	17,3
Oceanic	0,3	0,4	0,4	0,4	0,4	0,5	0,5	0,5
World	36,5	41,5	46,7	49,9	51,0	59,5	67,2	72,5

(*) The world total is slightly overestimated due to CKD assembly count in SouthAmerica, Africa e Oceanic.

Source: formulations on LMC, DRI estimates

A study stated that the dynamic motorization process is the main cause for the future growth of automobile demand especially in eastern Europe, South America, and Asia. Every industry especially when considering the automobile sector aims at the same objective of reducing the activity area and simultaneously increasing the flexibility and potential thus, they respond more to technological changes. Hence most of the industries of the sector are in huge capital necessity thereby acquiring new ways of technology that could give them some alternative ways of processing thereby reducing the manpower or capital cost and increasing the production and lead.

The first step in the process is to identify the functional subsystems and it is substantiated to have a role of competitiveness. Though it involves a lot of risk elements. The next steps involve the identification of the distinctive elements that are critical aspects of the company. The formalized study thus gives an image of globalization and has a strong impact on the choices and the degree of automation to be introduced. The main factor is the less convenience in the use of highly automated systems. Lower cost of manpower or so-called labor is also another major factor in the domain. Also, the investment to be made as capital for the automation process will take too much time and effort to balance that for the sophisticated systems.

The main objectives can be grouped into three categories:

- Increasing System Efficiency
- Increasing the quality of the product
- reducing human intervention and harmful operations.

Automation forms are aimed at harmful operations, and are dangerous. "At a general level, however, the conclusions of Blauner and Braverman coincide: they drew the same general conclusion that employment in the industry will decrease as a result of the process of automation. This conclusion holds for the process of automation."

AUTOMATION IN ELECTRONICS MANUFACTURING

FANUC is a Japanese company that builds robots and computer numerical control wireless systems, using the 'lights-out' manufacturing concept. FANUC manufactures about 22,000 new robots per month utilizing its automated industrial system. Many manufacturers are adopting this 'lights-out' concept-which is referred to as such because machines do not require lights, tea breaks, holidays, and other conditions that human workers require. Industrial automation has great potential in electronics manufacturing and is applicable in almost any stage of production. Areas, where automation is typically used, are Fabrication, assembling, testing, packaging, etc.

Manufacturing electronics is becoming an increasingly complex task, as the size of components and circuits continue to shrink. High component density, small pitches, multiple layers, and small and delicate parts that require precise placement are just some of the problems manufacturers face when building products. These issues slow down the assembly and testing processes of the products, also the delicate nature of the components increases the likelihood of errors, wastage, and inefficiencies. With increasing competition, manufacturers need to look for efficient and innovative ways to rapidly produce quality products.

Automation is the most likely solution, as it performs the processes efficiently and ensures quality while decreasing operational and production costs. Using sensors and other technologies, robots can precisely pick and place components, build circuits, forge PCBs, apply adhesives and perform efficient testing. Most importantly automated machines support miniaturization as they can precisely place components where humans cannot do so or would take a longer time. The demand for automated testing and inspection has gone up with the increasing complexity of electrical circuits. The most widely used circuits today have high component densities, large ICs with invisible pins and contacts almost invisible to the naked eye. To overcome these difficulties, manufacturers are turning to automated testing. Robots with mounted cameras can visually inspect electronic assemblies to ensure correct component alignment, soldering, and other physical features.

Robotic test machinery can access tight spaces while eliminating human factors. This diminishes the risks of accidental component damage, electric shocks, and burns, and they are far more efficient than manual testers. In addition to assembling, and testing automated systems can also aid in packaging. Automated packaging improves speed, consistency, and space utilization. It also reduces the risks of damage to sensitive components. Automated systems use sensors to determine potential collisions and avoid them by slowing or changing their route of progression. This allows manufacturers to implement automated systems to perform certain tasks in manual assembly lines.

The flexibility, simple implementation, and the capability to adapt to new designs and requirements are enabling electronics manufacturers to automate most manual tasks. Automation and robots in the electronics industry can quickly replace human workers and perform a wide range of tasks quickly and efficiently. Automated systems are ideal in the manufacture of today sophisticated electronic devices and products.

AUTOMATION IN CONSTRUCTION

As mentioned, Automation and robotics still stands the trend in many industries. It ranges from the industries at a very low level to the high-end industries even in Construction. Since businesses are always finding ways to reduce all the time-consuming works, reduce labor but increase the cost and effect of production. And the construction industry could never be an odd man out. The best solution for builders and constructors to increase efficiency and reduce labor and working costs would be Automation.

Unlike the type and category of industry, Automation helps all the industries in the broad approach from planning and operating toll implementation or what we call the final structure. Let's see how automation helps in construction.

To deal with this we all know that the best and easy example that one could provide for machine automation would be Autonomous machines. But has it something to do with construction industries?

We do remember the lifting of huge manufactured products by people to move them from one place to another. Then we do remember seeing the machine in the image that helped us move the products and raw materials. But guess what? Even these machines got an update to be automated.

These machines are now being developed to operate without a driver and a cabin. It is done by creating the necessary and relevant measures and paths, providing the power of GPS, programming them to operate by themselves with the help of a large variety of sensors and actuators. Now consider we have to monitor all such machines and a single man in the console has to manage all these machines operating in the whole industry. And that is where CPS comes into action. All these could be integrated with the CRN to control it in a way similar to Remote Control (RC) toys behave but more intelligently.

Heard of Drones?

Drones are now being used for monitoring the whole industry. Even more, drones are being programmed to detect hazards or any kind of threat in the industries happening and report malicious behaviors and hazards accordingly thus being a supervisor itself in the industry. They help to make inspections before building or construction, to make the note of the conditions for construction.

AUTOMATION IN CONCRETE WORKING

Automation in the industries has not even spared concrete workers. The key devices that would make Automation possible would be the sensors and the actuators. From making continuous readings of various conditions to automating the process of different machines sensors and actuators play a major role.

For triggering a specific action, sensors transmit signals. In short, they collect the data that are important from the environment that the sensors work and trigger relevant action for the machine that is responsible for acting.

PROPOSED SYSTEM DESIGN

Motivated by the Voice Controlled Home Automation Model, a further extension led to the thinking of Industrial automation using Voice and implementation of Mobile

CPS for the control of the whole industrial production remotely. The system uses cloud services to process the text from speech and to identify the request of the user or employee. The whole development process results in a software and hardware architecture that helps the system to be connected to every part of the automated systems of the plant. Industrial automation is the use of control systems, such as computers or robots, and information technologies for handling different processes and machinery in an industry to replace a human being. Current implementations of industrial automation typically involve large production level machines trained via machine learning to handle various operator commands, but this method is cumbersome, costly, and is not time efficient whereas the proposed Industrial automation using voice acknowledges the users' commands using Natural Language Processing and efficiently performs the required operations and delivers results. The system consists of control systems like computers that help in monitoring and handling processes and machines. Automation in the industries has the benefits of improving the productivity of the products while diminishing the errors and reducing wastage of time and material. It also increases the safety and reliability of both the personnel and the goods. The industries remain closed and automation can help in the scenario to keep the industry working, such that the system could be monitored and controlled from anywhere in the world using voice. Though a single person will not be able to control the whole machine, a large number of senior employees may be necessary to control it. This requires large computation. Hence CPS would be required for the computation. The use cases for Industrial Automation have been identified as:

- Mobile CPS for control from anywhere,
- Validation using IntelliSense for the commands made,
- Authentication of the appropriate user controlling the system from voice (Voice recognition)

Workflow Design

Input: Operators issue commands using voice, which is then filtered for cocktail effects, and is processed using Natural Language Processing (NLP) and then compiled and executed

Output: The output is in the form of finished goods or products.

Figure 6. Proposed Design Block Diagram

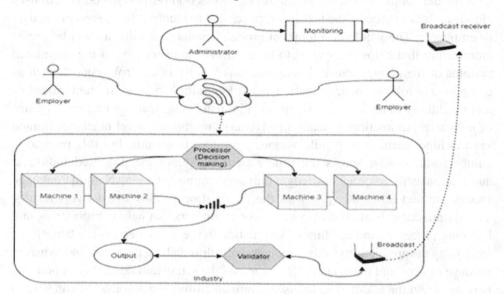

Methodology Using Deep Learning

The suggested idea implements a voice-based industrial automation system, all user commands are recognized via vocal commands including operations such as start, stop, transform, etc. In such a system it is of paramount importance that the operator's voice is efficiently and correctly recognized by the system, as any wrongful recognition of noise may lead to faulty system performance. Voice recognition in the proposed system is implemented using deep learning. Speech recognition is performed in a series of steps: the first step would be to convert the received voice signals into bits, Then the voice is preprocessed and any noise in the signal is removed and the data is transformed into a more suitable form. Now that the audio in the required format, it is then fed into a recurrent neural network, the input shall be short slices of audio and the neural nets shall try to figure out the letter that corresponds to the sound that is being spoken, After the system through the entire audio clip, we'll end up with a mapping of each audio slice with the letters most likely spoken during that slice. Then the system puts it all together and determines the most probable command issued and confirms the same from the user and then proceeds with the execution of the command.

Table 1. Automated Industrial Systems vs Non-Automated Industrial Systems

Criteria	With Automation	Without Automation
Precision	Automated machines or robots can operate efficiently both at the macro and micro level and can offer extraordinary levels of precision, with high speed.	Can operate efficiently at the macro level, decreased efficiency at the micro-level.
Scalability	Automated machines are highly scalable and their functionality can also be easily changed with minor modifications in most cases.	Also, highly scalable but accompanied by rising expenditure
Reliability	Highly reliable, as automated systems are prone to lesser errors compared to manually operated systems, and also automated system offer consistency in the quality of the product	Comparatively unreliable, but can outperform automated machines in certain extreme cases
Efficiency	Comparatively more efficient as automated systems can simply produce better products, efficiently at a higher rate.	Comparatively less efficient
Cost	Initial costs may be high, but cheaper and more reliable in the long run. Automated systems can make better products with higher efficiency at a cheaper rate due to their optimal usage of resources	Comparatively costly and less efficient
Durability	Offers high durability and consistency.	Companies using machinery operated manually have to deal with worker salaries, benefits, strikes, pay rises, human errors, etc.
Security	Automated systems are more vulnerable to security risks, compromised systems pose a great threat not only to companies or organizations using it but also in the case of its greater surroundings, as in the case of the Natanz nuclear facility. Compromised systems can not only leak out important information but can also be used to inflict physical damage to instruments and workers.	Comparatively secure and not prone to cyber-attacks.

CONCLUSION

Industrial Automation in simple terms is the control system that uses a variety of technologies and devices that help in handling different processes thereby replacing human intervention to a greater extent. Cyber-Physical Systems (CPS) is the combination of Cyber and Physical objects that is the integration of the computational, networking, and physical processes that are widely used in controlling, managing, and monitoring large systems or complex systems. When combining both, may result in the reduction of large amounts of production costs along with the reduction of manpower and labor. In the other way, it helps in reducing the human interventions in the tasks that are more hazardous. In recent years, the rise in the demand for quality products and services along with systems that could integrate the control mechanisms with high computational capabilities lead to the evolution of Cyber-

Physical Systems (CPS). The evolution of CPS extended to various fields over the years providing better and innovative solutions for healthcare management, Industry, Transportation systems, household appliances, Automation distribution systems, Smart Grid, and much more.

Moreover, it is guaranteed to provide high quality and high flexibility along with high accuracy and safety. Though disadvantages are unavoidable, the only disadvantage that one could find in these systems would be the high initial capital or investment. The entire chapter deals with the integration of both Industrial Automation and Cyber-Physical Systems in various fields like the Automobile industry, Manufacturing industries and construction industries, and so on. The author has tried to provide a greater understanding of the phase that we are currently in and the future solutions. A proposed approach for machine handling using CPS, Deep learning, and Industrial Automation with the help of Voice. The proposed approach provides greater insights into the application of CPS in the area and the combination of CPS and Deep learning to a greater extent. The fear that prevails in the society that Industrial Automation would take over all the employability of the people in industries has also been addressed in such a way that it may increase the opportunities for a lot more people as the integration requires a lot of manpower.

The author feels the chapter could be an eye opener in various research perspectives and to understand sensors and automation in detail with every minute explanation. Also, the proposed methodology and approach would be of greater efficiency when implemented in a condition where the people or employees could not have direct access to the control of the machines and administration is the concern. The system has been designed in a way to provide the best remote approach possible thereby reducing hazards at their zenith of efficiency.

The future work includes the extended version of the proposed solution that is to make the necessary changes concerning the validation of the voice-based on the user accessing the system and to validate the commands made by the user as vulnerabilities focus and lie on the hands of the person accessing the system.

REFERENCES

Al-Alia, Gupta, & Al Nabulsic. (2018). Cyber-Physical Systems Role in Manufacturing Technologies. In *6th International Conference on Nano and Materials Science, AIP Conf. Proc.* (pp. 050007-1–050007-7). AIP Publishing.

Alice Joseline, I., & Benila, S. (2017). Voice Recognition Based Vehicle Manufacturing. *International Journal of Engineering Development and Research*, 5(2), 51–56.

Budiawan, I., Pranoto, H. R., Hidayat, E. M. I., & Arief, S. R. (2018). Design and Implementation of Cyber-Physical System-Based Automation on Plant Chemical Process: Study Case Mini Batch Distillation Column. *6th International Conference on Information and Communication Technology*, 360-365. 10.1109/ICoICT.2018.8528798

Cicconi, P., Russo, A. C., Germani, M., Prist, M., Pallotta, E., & Monteriù, A. (2017). Cyber-physical system integration for industry 4.0: Modelling and simulation of an induction heating process for aluminium-steel molds in footwear soles manufacturing. *2017 IEEE 3rd International Forum on Research and Technologies for Society and Industry*, 1-6.

Cruz, Carvajal, Rojas, & Chacón. (2018). Cyber-Physical System for Industrial Control Automation based on the Holonic Approach and the IEC 61499 Standard. 2018 Forum on Specification & Design Languages (FDL), 5-16.

Gnanasekar, A. K., & Jayavelu, P. (2014). Voice-Based Wireless Industrial Automation With Enhanced Feedback System. In *Proc. of the Intl. Conf. on Advances in Computer, Electronics and Electrical Engineering* (pp. 51-55). Universal Association of Computer and Electronics Engineers.

Husham, I. (2019). A review Cyber of Industry 4.0 (Cyber-Physical Systems (CPS), the Internet of Things (IoT) and the Internet of Services (IoS)): Components, and Security Challenges. *Journal of Physics: Conference Series, 1424*, 012029. doi:10.1088/1742-6596/1424/1/012029

Hussana Johar, R. B., Soujanya, R., Sushma, S., & Syeda Ansha Sami Supreetha, M. G. (2014). Wireless Monitoring For Industrial Automation Using Speech Recognition. *International Journal of Engineering and Innovative Technology, 3*(11), 133–139.

Jazdi, N. (2014). Cyber-Physical Systems in the Context of Industry 4.0. *2014 IEEE International Conference on Automation, Quality and Testing, Robotics, 2014*, 1–4.

Kamdar, H., Karkera, R., Khanna, A., Kulkarni, P., & Agrawal, S. (2017). A Review on Home Automation Using Voice Recognition. *International Research. Journal of Engineering Technology, 4*(10), 1795–1799.

Kannan, P., Udayakumar, S. K., & Ahmed, K. R. (2014). Automation using voice recognition with python SL4A script for android devices. *2014 International Conference on Industrial Automation, Information and Communications Technology*, 1-4. 10.1109/IAICT.2014.6922098

Kumar & Shimi. (2015). Voice Recognition based Home Automation System for Paralyzed People – A Review. *International Journal of Engineering Research and General Science, 3*(5), 671-673.

Lu, K.-D., Zeng, G.-Q., Luo, X., Weng, J., Luo, W., & Wu, Y. (2021). Evolutionary Deep Belief Network for Cyber attack detection in Industrial automation and control system. *IEEE Transactions on Industrial Informatics, 17*(11), 7618–7627. doi:10.1109/TII.2021.3053304

Lu, Y. (2017). Cyber-Physical System (CPS)-Based Industry 4.0: A Survey. *Journal of Industrial Integration and Management, 2*(3), 1750014. doi:10.1142/S2424862217500142

Maharaja & Ansari. (2019, April). *Voice Controlled Automation Using Raspberry Pi.* Paper presented at the International Conference on Advances in Science & Technology ICAST, Mumbai, India.

Mamodiya & Sharma. (2014). Review in Industrial Automation. *IOSR Journal of Electrical and Electronics Engineering, 9*(3), 33-38.

Maqsood, M., Mehmood, I., Kharel, R., Muhammad, K., Lee, J., & Alnumay, W. S. (2021). Exploring the Role of Deep Learning in Industrial Applications: A Case Study on Coastal Crane Casting Recognition. *Human Centric Computing and Information Sciences, 11*(20), 1–14.

Mittal, Toshniwal, Sharma, Singhal, Gupta, & Mittal. (2015). A voice-controlled multi-functional Smart Home Automation System. *2015 Annual IEEE India Conference (INDICON)*, 1-6. 10.1109/INDICON.2015.7443538

Pal, S., Chauhan, A., & Gupta, S. K. (2019). Voice Controlled Smart Home Automation System. *International Journal of Recent Technology and Engineering, 8*(3), 4092–4093.

Rao, B., & Chandrakanth, H. (2018). Secured Speech Industrial Automation Based on Raspberry Pi and IoT. *International Journal of Intelligent Engineering and Systems, 11*(6), 234–243. doi:10.22266/ijies2018.1231.23

Tyagi, C. S., Agarwal, M., & Gola, R. (2016). Home Automation Using Voice Recognition and Arduino. *International Journal of Recent Trends in Engineering & Research Engineering and Technology, 2*(7), 2455–1457.

Vajpai, J., & Bora, A. (2016). Industrial Applications of Automatic Speech Recognition Systems. *International Journal of Engineering Research and Applications, 6*(3), 88–95.

KEY TERMS AND DEFINITIONS

Automation: Automation refers to the use of wide range of technologies that reduce human intervention in processes. In simpler terms, the technique of making a system operate automatically.

Cyber Physical Systems: Cyber physical systems (CPS) are integration of computing, networking and physical processes making an intelligent system in which the entire mechanism is controlled based on computer-algorithms.

Deep Learning: A type of machine learning based on artificial neural networks in which several layers of processing happen that help in extracting higher level features of data.

Industry 4.0: Industry 4.0 is the current trend of automation and data exchange in manufacturing technologies that includes cyber physical systems.

Internet of Things: IoT represents the network of physical objects called Things that are embedded with the help of sensors, software and other technologies that serves the purpose of data exchange over the internet.

Mobile Cyber Physical Systems: The type of cyber physical systems wherein the physical system under study has inherent mobility.

Sensors: A sensor is a device that detects the changes in the environment and responds to the change in the form an output signal to another system or actuator.

Wireless Sensor Networks (WSN): WSN refers to the networks of spatially dispersed and dedicated sensors that monitor and record the physical conditions of the environment and forward the collected data to a central location or base station.

Chapter 9
Intrusion Detection System Using Deep Learning

Meeradevi
M.S. Ramaiah Institute of Technology, India

Pramod Chandrashekhar Sunagar
M.S. Ramaiah Institute of Technology, India

Anita Kanavalli
M.S. Ramaiah Institute of Technology, India

ABSTRACT

With recent advancements in computer network technologies, there has been a growth in the number of security issues in networks. Intrusions like denial of service, exploitation from inside a network, etc. are the most common threat to a network's credibility. The need of the hour is to detect attacks in real time, reduce the impact of the threat, and secure the network. Recent developments in deep learning approaches can be of great assistance in dealing with network interference problems. Deep learning approaches can automatically differentiate between usual and irregular data with high precision and can alert network managers to problems. Deep neural network (DNN) architectures are used with differing numbers of hidden units to solve the limitations of traditional ML models. They also seek to increase predictive accuracy, reduce the rate of false positives, and allow for dynamic changes to the model as new research data is encountered. A thorough comparison of the proposed solution with current models is conducted using different evaluation metrics.

DOI: 10.4018/978-1-7998-8161-2.ch009

1. INTRODUCTION TO INTRUSION DETECTION SYSTEM

The Intrusion Detection System (IDS) is a platform which enables network traffic for malicious behavior as well as sends warnings while it detects it (*Liao et al., 2013*). It is a software program that checks a network or device for potentially malicious behavior or regulation violations. Any malicious behavior or breach is usually identified to an admin or centralized via a security information and event management (SIEM) system. The SIEM framework combines data from various supplies and utilizes alert filtering methods to discriminate between malicious and false warnings. While intrusion detection systems track networks for detecting sensitive activities, they are vulnerable to false alarms. As a result, when companies first install their IDS products, they must fine-tune them. It entails correctly configuring intrusion prevention systems to distinguish between natural network traffic and malicious behavior. Intrusion detection mechanisms also track network packets accessing the device to identify suspicious activity and send out alert alerts automatically.

1.1 Motivation

In this digital era every device is connected with internet. We are heavily dependent on these devices for our day to day needs. With this there will be a lot of security and intrusion threats on these systems. The research work carried out on intrusion detection system addresses many techniques using machine learning. Existing IDSs still confront hurdles in improving recognition rate, lowering number of false positives, and detecting unknown intrusions. Many academics have concentrated on building IDSs that use machine learning techniques to overcome the difficulties mentioned above. Machine learning algorithms can automatically detect the key differences between regular and aberrant data. Deep learning has achieved impressive results and has become a hotspot for study. So in this work, the deep neural network is implemented to solve the limitations of traditional ML models.

2. TYPES OF IDS

Intrusion Detection Systems are categorized into fivetypes:

2.1 Network Intrusion Detection System (NIDS)

Network intrusion detection systems (NIDS) are installed at a predetermined point inside the network to inspect traffic from several network devices. It monitors all passing traffic on the subnet and compares it to a database of documented attacks.

When an intrusion or suspicious activity is detected, a warning will be sent to the admin. Installing an NIDS on the subnet where firewalls are positioned to see if anyone is attempting to break the firewall is an illustration of an NIDS.

2.2 Host Intrusion Detection System (HIDS)

Intrusion detection systems that run upon many servers or machines are identified as host intrusion detection systems (HIDS). A HIDS only measures the device's transmitted data, alerting the administrator if it detects any suspicious or disruptive behavior. It makes a snapshot of the current device's files and compares it to the last version of the backup. An alert is sent to the admin if the analytical system files are changed or lost, and the admin is informed to inspect. On mission-critical devices that are not expected to change their setting, HIDS may be used.

2.2 Protocol-based Intrusion Detection System (PIDS)

It attempts to protect the web server by controlling the HTTPS protocol stream on a regular basis and accepting the associated HTTP protocol. Since HTTPS is not encrypted, this device will need to live in this interface before immediately accessing the web presentation layer in order to use HTTPS.

2.3 Application Protocol-based Intrusion Detection System (APIDS)

A device or agent that exists inside a group of servers is known as an Application Protocol-based Intrusion Detection System (APIDS). It detects intrusions by tracking and analyzing application-specific protocol communication. For example, this will track the SQL protocol as it is transmitted to the middleware by the web server's database.

2.4 Hybrid Intrusion Detection System

A blended monitoring system is created by combining two or more intrusion detection techniques. The host entity or system data is integrated with network information to gain a seamless view of the network environment in the hybrid intrusion detection system. In comparison to other intrusion detection systems, the hybrid intrusion detection system is more powerful. Hybrid IDS is exemplified by Prelude.

3. INTRUSION DETECTION METHODOLOGIES

3.1 Signature-Based Method

Based on signatures IDS detects threats based on unique variations of network traffic including the number of bytes, number of 1's, and number of 0's. This also tracks malware based on the malware's previously identified malicious instruction series. Signatures are the variations observed by the IDS. Signature-based intrusion detection systems can effectively detect attacks whose signature already appears in the device, but it is far more hard to detect new malicious activity whose pattern (signature) is unknown.

3.2 Anomaly-Based Method

As new malware is created at a rapid rate, anomaly-based intrusion detection systems (IDS) were implemented to recognize unidentified malware attacks. Machine learning is used in anomaly-based IDS to construct a trustful behavior model, and everything that comes in is related to that model, and it is reported suspect if it is not included in the model. In contrast to signature-based IDS, machine learning-based methods have improved generalized properties since these frameworks can be educated based on device and hardware setups.

4. PROBLEMS WITH THE EXISTING SYSTEMS

In this segment, we will cover some of the most critical Intrusion Detection systems and their issues. Intrusion Monitoring Mechanisms That Are Currently In Use

- **Snort:** Martin Roesch developed a free and open source network disruption identification and anticipation platform in 1998, which is now maintained by Sourcefire. Snort was inducted into InfoWorld's Open Software Hall of Fame in 2009 as one of the "best open source programming ever." Snort distinguishes a vast range of worms, vulnerability misuse endeavors, port sweeps, and other questionable behavior by convention inspection, material looking, and various pre-processors (*Wikipedia, snort, 2021*).
- **OSSEC:** An open source disruption detection system that completes log examination, truthfulness testing, rootkit recognizing, time sensitive alarming, and complex reaction (*SecTools, 2006*) (*SecTools Ids, 2016*). Regardless of its IDS utility, it is usually used as a SEM/SIM arrangement. ISPs, schools,

and server farms use OSSEC HIDS to screen and break down their firewalls, IDSs, network staff, and inspection logs due to its excellent log review engine.

- **OSSIM:** The goal of Open Source Security Information Management, OSSIM, is to include a comprehensive collection of tools that, when combined, provide organization/security directors with a clear view of any aspect of organizations, has, real accessibility to gadgets, and staff.

- **Suricata:** The Free Information Security Foundation created an open source intrusion detection system (OISF) (*InfoWorld, 2009*) (*InfoWorld, 2021*).

- **Bro:** It is an open-source, Unix-based platform for recognizing organizational interruptions. It separates interruptions by first parsing network traffic to extract the application-level semantics and then running event-based analyzers that compare the behavior and examples deemed inconvenient (*Wikipedia, Suricata, 2021*).

- **Fragroute/Fragrouter:** A toolbox for avoiding interruptions in the workplace. Fragrouter aids an aggressor in dispatching IP-based attacks while keeping a strategic distance from detection. It is required for Dug Song's NIDSbench apparatus setup.

- **BASE:** The Fundamental Evaluation and Security Engine, or Foundation, is a PHP-based review engine that searches and manages a database of security events generated by various IDSs, firewalls, and business monitoring tools.

- **Sguil:** Network security examiners work with network security analysts in the Sguil. Its key component is an intuitive Interface that provides clear occasions from Snort/farm. It also includes various components that facilitate the act of company security monitoring and event-driven analysis of IDS alarms.

5. RELATED WORKS

(*Othman et al., 2018*) inspected the significance of data security and information examination frameworks for Big Data. They express that high volume; assortment and fast of information created in the organization have made the information investigation interaction to recognize assaults by conventional strategies troublesome. Large Data procedures are utilized in IDS to manage Big Data for exact and effective information investigation measure. They presented Spark-Chi-SVM model for interruption identification, utilized ChiSqSelector for highlight choice, and constructed an interruption discovery model by utilizing support vector machine (SVM) classifier on Apache Spark Big Data stage. They utilized the KDD-'99' dataset to prepare and test the model. In the examination, they presented a correlation between the Chi-SVM classifier and Chi-Logistic Regression classifier. The consequences of the test showed that Spark-Chi-SVM model has superior, decreases the preparation time and is productive for Big Data. (*Kato et al., 2017*) proposed an inconsistency based organization interruption discovery framework, fit for examining colossal datasets in a brief timeframe, using 90.9 GB of a genuine organization bundle dataset given by the Information Security Center of Excellence at the University of New Brunswick. A way to deal with execute the framework depended on Hive SQL and unaided learning calculations. The exactness of the proposed location 15 framework was discovered to be 86.2% with 13% bogus positive rate. These outcomes were promising to recognize assaults progressively. (*Akbar et al., 2016*) proposed a half breed plot dependent on Big Data Analytics devices to make a constant Intrusion Prevention System (IPS). Heterogeneous information from various sources were gathered from the KDD Cup dataset and isolated into the learning stage and recognition stage. In the learning stage, realized assaults were recognized and comparatively, the identification stage additionally viewed as something very similar. The proposed framework indicated a bunch of rules and high discovery paces of DoS, R2L, U2R, and Probe based interruptions. (*Kang et al., 2016*) proposed the utilization of a DNN to fabricate the novel IDS for in-vehicle interruption identification to improve security of vehicles with IoT abilities. When contrasted with the conventional counterfeit neural organization applied to the IDS, the proposed strategy embraced late advances in profound learning studies, for example, introducing the boundaries through the unaided pre-preparing of profound conviction organizations (DBN), accordingly improving the location precision. It was shown with trial results that the proposed method can give a continuous reaction to the assault with an altogether improved recognition proportion in the regulator region organization (CAN) transport. (*Kushwaha et al., 2017*) recommended that the serious issues looked by the Network User are DoS, trying, phishing, site defaults and so on It made the aggressors uncover the organization assets, so it is imperative to recognize if the association is secure. They proposed a calculation which recognizes the irregular from the typical connection. The arrangement of a DoS issue permits the client to get to organize benefits all the more quickly. This supports the current IDS frameworks by rapidly arranging the assault. Examinations can be made accessible on datasets, for example, KDD-CUP 99, Kyoto 2006 +, iCTF, DEFCON, NSL-KDD, most are non-authorized, notwithstanding, and some are unlabeled. This paper played out the KDD-CUP 99 dataset tests. The critical commitment of the examination is to characterize the most reasonable calculation for choosing the right qualities from 41 connection vector ascribes. In characterization of occasions of KDD-CUP 99, this paper utilized measurable methods. The discoveries are assessed by contrasting its precision, identification 16 distances, FAR and so forth for various models. The insightful assessment approves the calculation's predominance over other best in class draws near. (*Rathore et al., 2018*) proposed an ongoing rapid interruption discovery framework utilizing the C4.5 model dependent on the choice tree, with a lesser stream rate. Of the 41 interruption informational collection KDD99 utilizing FSR and BER innovation, the nine best qualities were chosen. The precision of the IDS being proposed is evaluated as sure, bogus positive and time-productive. The more noteworthy exactness and unwavering quality assists the machine with working in a fast setting progressively. (*Subba et al., 2015*) proposed two diverse measurable techniques. To grow new irregularity based IDS models, the Linear Discriminant Analysis (LDA) and calculated relapse (LR). The aftereffects of these NSL-KDD informational indexes are then assessed and dissected against other Naive Bayes, C4.5 and Support Vectors (SVM) IDS models. They depend on the benchmarks NSL-KDD. Exploratory tests exhibit that both the LDA and the LR subordinate models work at a satisfactory norm and are, sometimes, a lot higher than different IDS models, with exactness and location speeds. The proposed LDA and LR based IDS models are computationally more productive, which makes them more appropriate for sending progressively network checking and interruption recognition investigation. (*Amor et al., 2014*) proposed a trial investigation of the utilization of credulous Bayes in interruption discovery. This article shows that, in spite of the fact that it has a straightforward design, Naive Bayes gives serious outcomes. The test is done in KDD'99 dataset. By considering three degrees of granularity relying upon whether entire assaults are tended to or assembled into four head classes, or whether ordinary and strange practices. Altogether tests contrast the exhibition of Bayes Networks and probably the best strategy for machine preparing, a dynamic tree. What's more, contrast the Bayes organizations' solid exhibition and set up best outcomes on KDD'99. (*Akshaya et al., 2016*) proposed an interruption identification model dependent on hereditary calculations and neural organizations. The fundamental thought is to utilize hereditary calculations and neural organizations for interruption location frameworks in arrangement capacities. The new model can recognize the assault, recognize one assault and another, for example characterizing the assault, and distinguish new assaults with high perceptible and low bogus negative rates. To channel traffic information, this methodology utilizes data development hypothesis to diminish the intricacy.. We utilized the KDD99 benchmark dataset and got a sensible recognition rate. (*Patgiri et al., 2018*) proposed in their paper that NSL KDD is utilized to assess the AI calculations for interruption discovery. Nonetheless, not all highlights improve execution in enormous datasets. In this way, lessening and choosing a specific arrangement of highlights improves the speed and exactness. Thus, highlights are chosen utilizing Recursive Feature Elimination (RFE). By directing a thorough trial on Intrusion Detection System (IDS) that utilizations AI calculations, to be specific, Random Forest and Support Vector Machine (SVM) show and the correlation between the model's presentation when highlight determination of both Random Forest and SVM alongside disarray lattices. (*Ashiku et al., 2021*) have proposed the use of deep learning architectures in the development of a dynamic and durable network intrusion detection system (IDS) to discover and evaluate network threats. The attention is on how deep learning or deep neural networks (DNNs) can contribute with flexible IDS by enabling it to monitor both known and unknown network behavioral features. As a result of this, the system intruder is discarded, eliminating the threat of exposure. The authors have used UNSW-NB15 dataset, which reflects authentic modern network communication pattern with synthetically generated adversary activities, was used to illustrate the model's performance.

6. DEEP LEARNING FRAMEWORK

Deep learning is a high level sub-field of AI, which advances Machine Learning nearer to Artificial Intelligence. It encourages the displaying of complex connections and ideas (*Goodfellow et al., 2016*) utilizing numerous degrees of portrayal. Managed also, solo learning calculations are utilized to develop progressively more significant levels of reflection, characterized utilizing the yield highlights from lower levels

6.1 Proposed Methodology

Figure 1 shows the methodology of the proposed work to detect the attack using DNN. The dataset is collected online from KDD Cup-1999 and pre-processed using normalization technique. Next, split the dataset into train and test data. Train the model using deep neural network which comprises of input layer, four hidden layer and output layer. Forward propagation is applied from input to output layer, ReLu activation function is used at every layer and errors are back-propagated until the optimized result is obtained. Test the model using test data and evaluate the performance of the model. It is shown in proposed architecture the model use DNNs for intrusion detection. The DNN architecture were built in the following manner: - first Layer: [1024] Nodes and second layers: [1024, 768] Nodes - third layers: [1024, 768, 512] Nodes - forth layers: [1024, 768, 512, 256] Nodes – and fifth layer is with [1024, 768, 512, 256, 128] Nodes. The model was able to reduce size and training resources considerably while still maintaining a competent performance metric. Since the model for this is a binary classification, a softmax is replaced by a sigmoid activation in the final layer (like in our network). Also, to avoid loss from activations, there is a switch to a swish activation function, instead of ReLU for the hidden layers. Both functions are nonlinear, so the training process of a 'student' is replicated as in the 'teacher'. The project comprises implementations of four machine learning models, namely Logistic Regression (LR), Naive Bayes (NB), Decision tree (DT) learning and Random Forest (RF) learning. The dataset was split into a training set of 494021 tuples and a testing set of 311029 tuples. Prior to this, Exploratory Data Analysis on the data helped understand and isolate the features that contributed most towards the end classification. We theorized from analyzing the correlation matrices that 23 out of 42 tuples were contributing most towards the classification, and that the data showed good linear separability. This was confirmed by the relatively high accuracy that was obtained from the logistical classification, which would otherwise perform poorly for data that isn't linearly separable.

Figure 1. Block Diagram for Proposed Intrusion Detection System

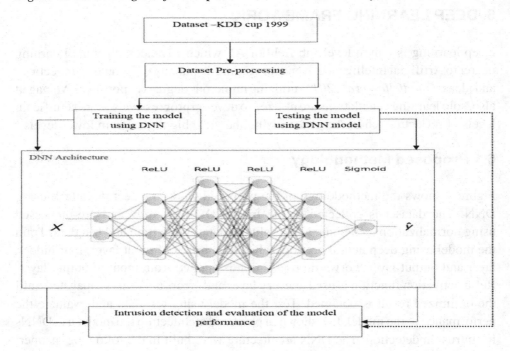

Types of Attacks

TCP is connection oriented protocol. The Once the packet is sent to destination source has to wait till the acknowledgement is received. Therefore, the start and end time of the TCP packets should be well defined. The flow of the data takes place using source and destination IP address using well defined protocol. Each flow is defined as either normal or as attack with one specific attack type. There are four main categories in attack.

1. Denial-of-service attack in which attacker floods the data to server such that server is not able to respond to the authorized user
2. R2L (Remote-to-Local) in this attacker identifies the intelligent ways to hack information.
3. U2R (User-to-Root) in this type of attack the attacker is trying to gain access to the authorized machine in an unauthorized way and tries to get the root's server privileges.
4. Probing this attack will block the authorized legitimate user from accessing the computer and data available in the computer

Before proceeding with construction of the classification models, Exploratory Data Analysis was performed to understand the data better. This meant identifying which data attributes best classify the data, or rather contribute most to the classification the sample dataset is shown in Figure 1.

6.2 Dataset Description

In 1998 DARPA Intrusion Detection Evaluation Program was prepared and managed by MIT Lincoln Labs. The objective was to survey and evaluate research in intrusion detection. A standard set of data to be audited, which includes a wide variety of intrusions simulated in a military network environment. The 1999 KDD intrusion detection contest uses a version of this dataset. Lincoln Labs set up an environment to acquire nine weeks of raw TCP dump data for a local-area network (LAN) simulating a typical U.S. Air Force LAN. They operated the LAN as if it were a true Air Force environment, but peppered it with multiple attacks. The raw training data was about four gigabytes of compressed binary TCP dump data from seven weeks of network traffic. This was processed into about five million connection records. Similarly, the two weeks of test data yielded around two million connection records. A connection is a sequence of TCP packets starting and ending at some well-defined times, between which data flows to and from a source IP address to a target IP address under some well-defined protocol. Each connection is labeled as either normal, or as an attack, with exactly one specific attack type. Each connection record consists of about 100 bytes. Attacks fall into four main categories:

* DOS: denial-of-service;
* R2L: unauthorized access from a remote machine, e.g. guessing password;
* U2R: unauthorized access to local superuser (root) privileges, e.g., various ``buffer overflow'' attacks;
* Probing: surveillance and other probing, e.g., port scanning.

Before proceeding with construction of the classification models, Exploratory Data Analysis was performed to understand the data better. This meant identifying which data attributes best classify the data, or rather contribute most to the classification the sample dataset is shown in Figure 2.

Figure 2. Sample KDD dataset attributes

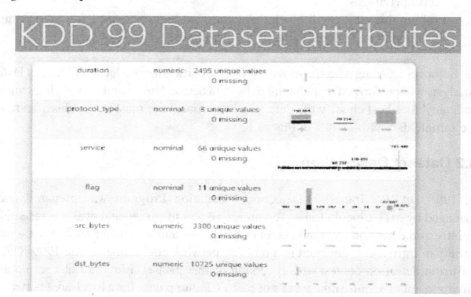

6.3 Correlation Matrix

Before proceeding with construction of the classification models, Exploratory Data Analysis was performed to understand the data better. This meant identifying which data attributes best classify the data, or rather contribute most to the classification. To do this, a correlation matrix was constructed as shown in Figure 3.

We theorised from analysing the correlation matrices that 23 out of 42 tuples were contributing most towards the classification, and that the data showed good linear separability. This was confirmed by the relatively high accuracy that was obtained from the logistical classification, which would otherwise perform poorly for data that isn't linearly separable. From the correlation matrix, we could visualize how the data behaved in the process of the classification. This could be visualized with a heat map as shown in Figure 4.

Table 1. Dataset attributes with description

Feature Name	Description	Type
duration	length (number of seconds) of the connection	continuous
protocol_type	type of the protocol, e.g. tcp, udp, etc.	discrete
service	network service on the destination, e.g., http, telnet, etc.	discrete
src_bytes	number of data bytes from source to destination	continuous
dst_bytes	number of data bytes from destination to source	continuous
flag	normal or error status of the connection	discrete
land	1 if connection is from/to the same host/port; 0 otherwise	discrete
wrong_fragment	number of ``wrong'' fragments	continuous
urgent	number of urgent packets	continuous

Table 2. Content features within a connection suggested by domain knowledge

Feature Name	Description	Type
hot	number of ``hot'' indicators	continuous
num_failed_logins	number of failed login attempts	continuous
logged_in	1 if successfully logged in; 0 otherwise	discrete
num_compromised	number of ``compromised'' conditions	continuous
root_shell	1 if root shell is obtained; 0 otherwise	discrete
su_attempted	1 if ``su root'' command attempted; 0 otherwise	discrete
num_root	number of ``root'' accesses	continuous
num_file_creations	number of file creation operations	continuous
num_shells	number of shell prompts	continuous
num_access_files	number of operations on access control files	continuous
num_outbound_cmds	number of outbound commands in an ftp session	continuous
is_hot_login	1 if the login belongs to the ``hot'' list; 0 otherwise	discrete
is_guest_login	1 if the login is a ``guest''login; 0 otherwise	discrete

Heat map is showing how the data behaves in the classification process. Heat map of data correlation for class-1 classifications. The heatmap shows which attributes are "hot" or "cold", that is, major contributors (positive or negative impact) to the classification and which attributes are just placeholders.

Table 3. Traffic features computed using a two-second time window

Feature Name	Description	Type
count	number of connections to the same host as the current connection in the past two seconds	continuous
	Note: The following features refer to these same-host connections.	
serror_rate	% of connections that have "SYN" errors	continuous
rerror_rate	% of connections that have "REJ" errors	continuous
same_srv_rate	% of connections to the same service	continuous
diff_srv_rate	% of connections to different services	continuous
srv_count	number of connections to the same service as the current connection in the past two seconds	continuous
Note: The following features refer to these same-service connections.		
srv_serror_rate	% of connections that have "SYN" errors	continuous
srv_rerror_rate	% of connections that have "REJ" errors	continuous
srv_diff_host_rate	% of connections to different hosts	continuous

Figure 3. Correlation matrix

	1	2	3	4	5	6	7	8	9	10	...	32	33	34	35
1	1.000000	-0.023715	-0.033369	-0.020218	0.004258	0.005440	-0.000452	-0.003235	0.003786	0.013213		0.010074	-0.117515	-0.118456	0.406233
2	-0.023715	1.000000	0.896438	-0.650347	-0.002664	-0.032433	0.008262	-0.005357	-0.003183	-0.054640		0.385535	0.711421	0.692295	-0.260164
3	-0.033369	0.896438	1.000000	-0.427262	0.001068	-0.034926	0.003482	-0.030403	-0.001939	-0.005489		0.494884	0.424386	0.405005	-0.173495
4	-0.020218	-0.650347	-0.427262	1.000000	0.002723	-0.013452	0.009090	-0.025069	-0.001351	-0.021903		0.042798	-0.811538	-0.821898	0.264174
5	0.004258	-0.002664	0.001068	0.002723	1.000000	-0.000002	-0.000020	-0.000139	-0.000005	0.004483		-0.001743	-0.003212	-0.002052	0.000578
6	0.005440	-0.032433	-0.034926	-0.013452	-0.000002	1.000000	-0.000175	-0.001254	0.016288	0.004365		-0.048969	-0.005650	0.007058	-0.005314
7	-0.000452	0.008262	0.003482	0.009090	-0.000020	-0.000175	1.000000	-0.000318	-0.000017	-0.000295		-0.023671	-0.011587	0.001984	-0.000333
8	-0.003235	-0.005357	-0.030403	-0.025069	-0.000139	-0.001254	-0.000318	1.000000	-0.000123	-0.002106		-0.005191	0.059624	-0.054903	0.071857
9	0.003786	-0.003183	-0.001939	-0.001351	-0.000005	0.016288	-0.000017	-0.000123	1.000000	0.000356		-0.007139	-0.004540	-0.003279	0.010536
10	0.013213	-0.054640	-0.005489	-0.021903	0.004483	0.004365	-0.000295	-0.002106	0.000356	1.000000		-0.028366	-0.038730	-0.028117	0.001319
11	0.005239	-0.012110	-0.012664	0.013965	-0.000027	0.049330	-0.000065	-0.000467	0.141996	0.008740		-0.025444	-0.015413	0.000507	0.001017
12	-0.017265	-0.516478	-0.688727	0.216230	0.001701	0.047814	-0.002784	-0.019908	0.006164	0.105305		-0.521029	0.119315	0.161070	-0.061151
13	0.058095	-0.007030	-0.008920	-0.002882	0.000119	0.023298	-0.000038	-0.000271	0.014285	0.007348		-0.008361	-0.004797	-0.002584	0.000359
14	0.021340	-0.013063	-0.014723	-0.005543	-0.000022	0.031680	-0.000070	-0.000504	0.034790	0.024065		-0.024384	-0.010026	0.000935	-0.000684
15	0.055853	-0.005788	-0.006012	-0.002456	-0.000010	0.075656	-0.000031	-0.000223	-0.000012	-0.000206		-0.008570	-0.006531	-0.005582	0.000793
16	0.056766	-0.006982	-0.002712	-0.002961	-0.000010	0.026746	-0.000038	-0.000299	0.009476	0.000996		-0.011611	-0.007985	-0.006731	0.002863
17	0.074562	-0.013905	-0.009362	-0.005393	0.000013	0.004958	-0.000075	-0.000536	0.015211	0.025247		-0.019126	-0.013871	-0.008808	0.006513
18	-0.000169	-0.012280	0.001159	-0.005211	0.000005	0.000144	-0.000066	-0.000473	-0.000026	0.008373		-0.017111	-0.012207	-0.007729	0.000641
19	0.025661	-0.034208	-0.042925	-0.014474	-0.000052	0.008746	-0.000184	-0.001319	0.020068	0.001902		-0.021152	-0.000801	0.004396	0.002102
20	NaN	NaN	NaN	NaN	NaN	NaN	NaN	NaN	NaN	NaN		NaN	NaN	NaN	NaN
21	NaN	NaN	NaN	NaN	NaN	NaN	NaN	NaN	NaN	NaN		NaN	NaN	NaN	NaN
22	0.023424	-0.046131	0.020714	-0.019329	-0.000082	0.001289	-0.000249	-0.001778	-0.000096	0.843572		-0.033787	-0.050016	-0.043189	0.009624

Figure 4. Heat map showing how the data behaves in the classification process

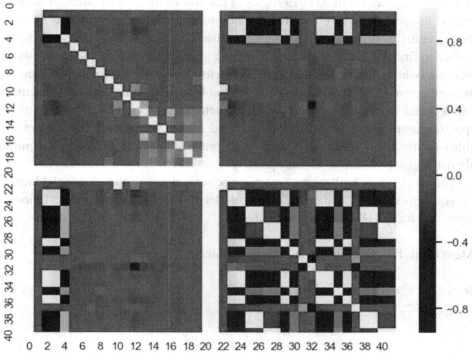

7. IMPLEMENTATION OF PROPOSED MODEL

While traditional machine learning algorithms are linear, deep neural networks are stacked in an increasing hierarchy of complexity as well as abstraction. Each layer applies a nonlinear transformation onto its input and creates a statistical model as output from what it learns. In simple terms, the input layer is received by the input layer and passed onto the first hidden layer. These hidden layers perform mathematical computations on the inputs. One of the challenges in creating neural networks is deciding the hidden layers' count and the count of the neurons for each layer. Each neuron has an activation function which is used to standardize the output from the neuron. The "Deep" in Deep learning refers to having more than one layer which is hidden. The output layer returns the output data. Until the output has reached an acceptable level of accuracy, epochs are continued. 36 This project implemented 5 DNNs with one layer having [1024] nodes, two layers having [1024, 768] nodes, three layers having [1024, 768, 512] nodes, four layer having [1024, 768, 512, 256], five nodes layer having [1024, 768, 512, 256, 128] nodes with only 10 epochs sufficing to reach the degree of accuracy we desired. All 5 neural networks built were tested against the testing set of 311029 tuples at the end of training in addition to being trained at each step using a validation step to improve accuracy. Since KDD-99 data is actually very linear, we theorized that 2 or 3 layers of a network would suffice to find the deciding factors. Anything greater, variance in the model would increase (which causes the model to lose performance since the network becomes more selective in feature weights). We were able to maintain a competent accuracy and reduced training time considerably by achieving this accuracy within just 10 epochs, due to using ModelCheckpoints and feature extraction. The project was able to achieve this while maintaining high precision of over 99%, which signifies almost negligible number of false positives.

The model was built using two approaches, namely - the classical Machine Learning methods, and the Deep Neural Networks. The detailed description of algorithm for the DNNs is shown below:

Algorithm: DNN for intrusion detection system

```
fori=1 to n do
        Compute the output oi = ai
end for
fori with i = n+1 to MNN do
        Get connections by using individual x1,i.
        Get connections vector z for neuron i from Wi.
        Get synaptic weights s for neuron i from Wi.
        Get the bias b for neuron i from Wi.
        Get the transfer function index t for neuron i from
Wi.
        Compute the output of neuron i as
        oi = ft(∑j=1 sj*zj*oj + b).
end for
fori = MNN-m to MNN do
        Compute the ANN output with yi-(MNN-m+1)+1 = oi
end for
```

This was implemented in Python using TensorFlow and Keras, and a simple module, called 'build_model' was written for the same. The working of the module is as follows: build_model ():

- Specify number of dense layers
- Specify nodes in each layer

- Build a neural network as per the pseudo code above, using accuracy as the metric.
- Return the built model
- The model comprised implementations of four machine learning models, namely Logistic Regression, Gaussian Naive Bayes probabilistic model, Decision tree learning and Ensemble Random Forest learning. The models were all trained on the same dataset, KDD-99. The dataset was split into a training set of 494021 tuples and a testing set of 311029 tuples. Furthermore, exploratory data analysis on the training and testing set revealed interesting results. The data was found to show a high degree of linear separability. This could be confirmed by constructing a heat map from the correlation matrix of the training data.

7.1 Experimental Results

This model proposes an IDS which uses a Deep Learning model. The experimental results will be collected on the dataset KDD-'99' and this model will also record the accuracy of the DNN model (depending on the number of hidden layers and nodes in them) and compare it with the classical ML classifiers such as Logistic Regression, Naive Bayes and Decision Tree. The prime objective is to test deep learning implementations (DNN) to achieve the best accuracy in prediction as well as in reducing training speed and thereby reducing the complexity which exists in ML implementations. The IDS developed in this model, using a DNN is far less complex than the ones which use bulky classical ML models. Even though there is only a slight difference in the accuracy of the DNN models and the ML models, there is a considerable difference in the complexity. The DNN models can be easily deployed at a much lower hardware abstraction layer (like at the router level) than the ML models, which require a software environment to be deployed. The IDS is absolutely necessary in the present scope as there is a constant increase in Cyber Fraud.

The heat map shows activity only in columns 1 to 4, 12 and 23 to 41 as shown in figure 5, meaning only these columns have any correlation and contribute towards the final classification. Thus to remove redundancy at the cost of some accuracy, 23 features out of 42 were considered. This may have contributed greatly towards the compact models that we were able to construct, and while possibly sacrificing accuracy, the model was able to show a high degree of precision, meaning the extracted features did in fact contribute the most towards the final classification Along with using the entire testing set of 311029 tuples for testing in one go, a validation set was implemented for the neural network to validate its output weights on the completion of every epoch, which served to best fit the model weights to not just learn from the training set, but also to constantly examine the results of each epoch against a blind test with the validation set. Since the testing set is so large, it's safe to say that the built models were sufficiently well tested.

Figure 5. Heat map showing correlation between attributes

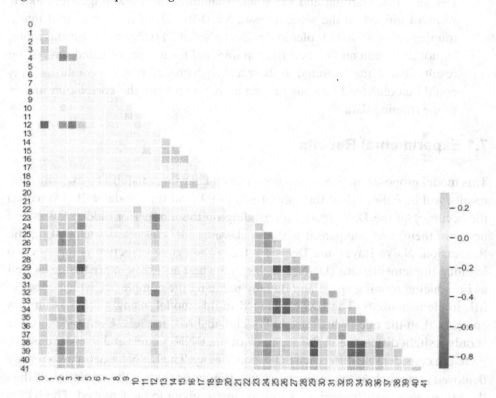

Along with using the entire testing set of 311029 tuples for testing in one go, a validation set was implemented for the neural network to validate its output weights on the completion of every epoch, which served to best fit the model weights to not just learn from the training set, but also to constantly examine the results of each epoch against a blind test with the validation set. Since the testing set is so large, it's safe to say that the built models were sufficiently well tested.

7.2 Performance Analysis

Figure 6. The accuracies of the machine learning models

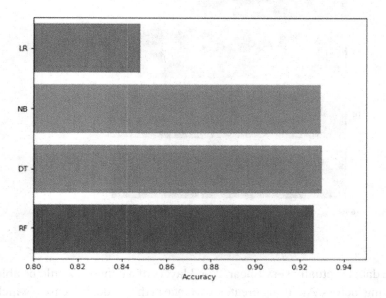

The main things to note here are the accuracy and the precision values. The model was able to maintain a high degree of accuracy even with simplistic models such as logistic regression, and the rate of false positives was low, as confirmed by the high precision value. Training times varied as per the complexity and depth of the models. Considering all the parameters, Naive Bayes algorithm performed best as training time was sufficiently low and accuracy was on par with the highest we could obtain. To show the comparisons visually, we made bar charts signifying the above metrics as shown in figure 6, but DNN model shows improved accuracy compared to NB model as shown in figure 6. Figure 7 shows the f1 score of ML models. The NB model performed better than other models, but when NB is compared with DNN. The proposed DNN model perform well.

The neural networks built ranged from 1 hidden layer of 1024 neurons to 5 hidden layers of [1024-768-512-256-128] neurons. The process of building the neural networks was automated and a function was designed that builds and trains all 5 networks in one go, saving the best models obtained in each iteration making use of Keras Callbacks and ModelCheckpoints. The training process is shown below. All 5 neural networks built were tested against the testing set of 311029 tuples at the end of training in addition to being trained at each step using a validation step to improve accuracy. The results were as follows.

Figure 7. F1 Scores of the machine learning models

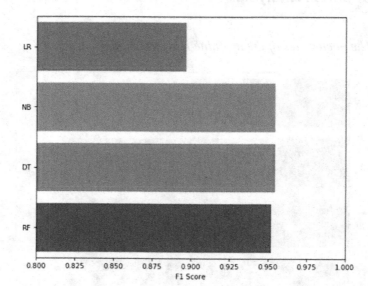

Since data is actually very linear, 2 or 3 layers of a network would be able to find the deciding factors. Anything greater, variance in the model increases (which causes the model to lose performance since the network becomes more selective in feature weights). The proposed model was able to attain a competent accuracy and reduced training time considerably by achieving this accuracy within just 10 epochs, thanks to using ModelCheckpoints and feature extraction. The point to note here is the high precision, which signifies almost negligible number of false positives. The proposed model was able to reduce the model size (compared to classical ML models) and training resources considerably while maintaining a competent performance metric. Also, with the usage of ModelCheckpoint, there was considerable reduction in the overall number of weights stored per epoch for a DNN model and this allows us to deploy the IDS on most (if not all) mobile and routing devices, which was not previously possible due to the bulky nature of the models. Model size was reduced and optimized by running the same training procedure with networks of varying depths (1-5 hidden layers) in combination with model checkpointing to make sure each iteration only gives out the best fit model, no matter the number of epochs. The ModelCheckpoint callback class allows us to define at what point to checkpoint the model weights, how the file should be named and under what circumstances to make a checkpoint of the model. The API allows us to specify which metric to monitor, such as loss or accuracy on the training or validation dataset. We can specify whether to look for an improvement in maximizing or minimizing the score. Finally, the filename that we use to store the weights can include variables like the epoch number or any other metric. Figure 8 shows the accuracy of the model compared with other models. The accuracy of the models is not much varying compared with proposed DNN model. But there is small increase in accuracy of DNN compared with NB approach which is of 0.001.

Figure 8. Accuracy of the proposed model compared with other models

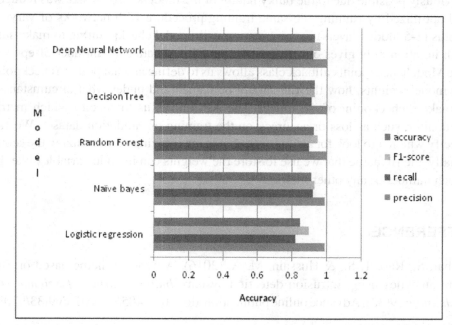

Table 4. Accuracy of all algorithms

Model	Precision	Recall	F1-score	Accuracy
Logistic regression	0.988	0.820	0.896	0.848
Naïve Bayes	0.988	0.923	0.929	0.929
Random Forest	0.998	0.909	0.952	0926
Decision Tree	0.998	0.911	0.953	0.930
Deep Neural Network	0.998	0.914	0.954	0.932

8. CONCLUSION

The project was able to reduce the model size (compared to classical ML models) and training resources considerably while maintaining a competent performance metric. Also, with the usage of ModelCheckpoint, there was considerable reduction in the overall number of weights stored per epoch for a DNN model and this allows us to deploy the IDS on most (if not all) mobile and routing devices, which was not previously possible due to the bulky nature of the models. Model size was reduced and optimized by running the same training procedure with networks of varying depths (1-5 hidden layers) in combination with model checkpointing to make sure each iteration only gives out the best fit model, no matter the number of epochs. The ModelCheckpoint callback class allows us to define at what point to checkpoint the model weights, how the file should be named and under what circumstances to make a checkpoint of the model. The API allows us to specify which metric to monitor, such as loss or accuracy on the training or validation dataset. We can specify whether to look for an improvement in maximizing or minimizing the score. Finally, the filename that we use to store the weights can include variables like the epoch number or any other metric.

REFERENCES

Akbar, S., Rao, T. S., & Hussain, M. A. (2016). A hybrid scheme based on Big Data analytics using intrusion detection system. *Indian Journal of Science and Technology, 9*(33). Advance online publication. doi:10.17485/ijst/2016/v9i33/97037

Akshaya, P. (2016). Intrusion detection system using machine learning approach. *International Journal of Engineering and Computer Science, 5*(10), 18249–18254. doi:10.18535/ijecs/v5i10.05

Amor, N. B., Benferhat, S., & Elouedi, Z. (2004, March). Naive bayes vs decision trees in intrusion detection systems. In *Proceedings of the 2004 ACM symposium on Applied computing* (pp. 420-424). 10.1145/967900.967989

Ashiku, L., & Dagli, C. (2021). Network Intrusion Detection System using Deep Learning. *Procedia Computer Science, 185*, 239–247. doi:10.1016/j.procs.2021.05.025

Goodfellow, I., Bengio, Y., & Courville, A. (2016). *Deep learning*. MIT Press. https://en.wikipedia.org/wiki/Suricata_(software)

InfoWorld. (2009). *The greatest open source software of all time*. https://www.infoworld.com/d/open-source/greatest-open-source-software-all-time-776?source=fssrSuricata

Kang, M. J., & Kang, J. W. (2016). Intrusion detection system using deep neural network for in-vehicle network security. *PLoS One*, *11*(6), e0155781. doi:10.1371/journal.pone.0155781 PMID:27271802

Kato, K., & Klyuev, V. (2017, August). Development of a network intrusion detection system using Apache Hadoop and Spark. In *2017 IEEE Conference on Dependable and Secure Computing* (pp. 416-423). IEEE. 10.1109/DESEC.2017.8073860

Kushwaha, P., Buckchash, H., & Raman, B. (2017, November). Anomaly based intrusion detection using filter based feature selection on KDD-CUP 99. In *TENCON 2017-2017 IEEE Region 10 Conference* (pp. 839–844). IEEE. doi:10.1109/TENCON.2017.8227975

Liao, H. J., Lin, C. H. R., Lin, Y. C., & Tung, K. Y. (2013). Intrusion detection system: A comprehensive review. *Journal of Network and Computer Applications*, *36*(1), 16–24. doi:10.1016/j.jnca.2012.09.004

Othman, S. M., Ba-Alwi, F. M., Alsohybe, N. T., & Al-Hashida, A. Y. (2018). Intrusion detection model using machine learning algorithm on Big Data environment. *Journal of Big Data*, *5*(1), 1–12. doi:10.118640537-018-0145-4

Patgiri, R., Varshney, U., Akutota, T., & Kunde, R. (2018, November). An investigation on intrusion detection system using machine learning. In *2018 IEEE Symposium Series on Computational Intelligence (SSCI)* (pp. 1684-1691). IEEE. 10.1109/SSCI.2018.8628676

Rathore, M. M., Saeed, F., Rehman, A., Paul, A., & Daniel, A. (2018, February). Intrusion detection using decision tree model in high-speed environment. In *2018 International Conference on Soft-computing and Network Security (ICSNS)* (pp. 1-4). IEEE. 10.1109/ICSNS.2018.8573631

SecTools.Org. (2006). *Results*. https://sectools.org/tools2006.html

SecTools.Org. (n.d.). *Top 125 Network Security Tools*. https://sectools.org/tag/ids/

Snort. (n.d.). https://en.wikipedia.org/wiki/Snort_%28software%29

Subba, B., Biswas, S., & Karmakar, S. (2015, December). Intrusion detection systems using linear discriminant analysis and logistic regression. In *2015 Annual IEEE India Conference (INDICON)* (pp. 1-6). IEEE. 10.1109/INDICON.2015.7443533

Chapter 10
Machine Learning–Based Approach for Predictive Analytics in Healthcare

Sandeep Kumar Hegde
NMAM Institute of Technology, India

Monica R. Mundada
M.S. Ramaiah Institute of Technology, India

ABSTRACT

In this internet era, due to digitization in every application, a huge amount of data is produced digitally from the healthcare sectors. As per the World Health Organization (WHO), the mortality rate due to the various chronic diseases is increasing each day. Every year these diseases are taking lives of at least 50 million people globally, which includes even premature deaths. These days, machine learning (ML)-based predictive analytics are turning out as effective tools in the healthcare sectors. These techniques can extract meaningful insights from the medical data to analyze the future trend. By predicting the risk of diseases at the preliminary stage, the mortality rate can be reduced, and at the same time, the expensive healthcare cost can be eliminated. The chapter aims to briefly provide the domain knowledge on chronic diseases, the biological correlation between theses disease, and more importantly, to explain the application of ML algorithm-based predictive analytics in the healthcare sectors for the early prediction of chronic diseases.

DOI: 10.4018/978-1-7998-8161-2.ch010

1. INTRODUCTION

The internet era has resulted in an exponential increase in the volume of data generated in digital form. Due to these rapid growths in the generation of the data, data is collected at the rate of terabytes to petabytes from each application(Shastri et. al,2020). Data analytics is the process of analyzing the data to obtain meaningful insights from it. Usage of statistical techniques and machine learning(ML) approaches to predict future trends from historical data is known as predictive analytics. Machine learning (ML) is the science that enables computers to learn and predict their experiences without explicit programming. If a computer software can improve its performance due to past experience, this is called 'learning.' In contrast to artificial intelligence, machine learning is more restricted to data analysis. The use of techniques that allow computers to learn from data iteratively is machine learning(Salkuti et. al,2020). Predictive analytics is expanding its application in various sectors like Heath care, Bank, Education, Governmental organizations, Retail industry, Cybersecurity, Manufacturing, Insurance sectors, stock market, social media, and many more(Wang et. al,2018) Today predictive analytics is making more buzz in the area of the health care sector. Because of the massive amount of healthcare data is generated in the digital form. Processing and analyzing these data is becoming challenging for the medical practitioner to take effective decisions. Hence predictive analytics are making highlights in the healthcare sector which can convert these digital data in the form of clinical insights using an efficient ML model which helps the physician in providing better treatment for the patient with lesser cost. There are limitless advantages in the application of predictive analytics in the field of healthcare.

One of the prime advantages of the application of predictive analytics in healthcare is an early prediction of disease. Hence by using the predictive analytical-based ML algorithms hospital readmission can be reduced. In recent years the chronic disease is becoming a challenge to the entire globe. According to the World Health Organization, the death rate from chronic disease is anticipated to increase by 73% by 2025, and so these diseases are included in the Global Burden of Disease (GBD). Cancer, dementia, epilepsy, cardiovascular disease (CVD), chronic kidney disease (CKD), and chronic diabetes mellitus (CDM) are all examples of significant chronic diseases (Bikbov et. al,2020).CVD, CKD, and CDM are considered as interconnected chronic diseases. Because each of these diseases is an interconnected disease that will become a risk factor for the other two diseases. The progressive relationship between the interconnected disease must be analyzed at the early stage itself to reduce the death rate. As per the medical report released in the year 2020 by WHO, worlds 70% of death is due to chronic disease. If the severity level of the disease is considered, as per the report released in 2020 from WHO, the chronic disease are responsible for overall 70% of the deaths out of which 50% of the death is only due to CVD(Virani et. al,2020). The number of people suffering from CDM illness is increasing exponentially. When the prevalence of the CDM is considered, the ratio increases from 4.7 percent in 1980 to 9.3 percent (about 462 million) in 2019, which is predicted to increase to 10.2 percent (approximately 578 million) in 2030 and 10.9 percent in 2045. (around 700 million). Overall, 10% of the world's population is affected by chronic kidney disease, and 5-10 million people die each year from renal illnesses, a number that is expected to treble by 2030. Around 2.4 million individuals died of CKD in 2019. The number of persons with renal failure is expected to increase significantly in developing countries such as India and China (Yang et. al,2020). Therefore noteworthy attention is being paid as a preventive measure to reduce the risk of these diseases. The burden of CKD is increasing at an exponential rate as CKD is affecting the world's 10% of the population. Globally more than 800 million do not have access to safe water and more than 2.5 million have a lack of access to sanity which is one of the prime reasons behind the CKD disease(Hruska et. al,2020). If the person is a diabetic patient then there is a positive change that the patient may likely develop CKD disease. As per the physician it is recommended for the CKD patient to undergo regular screening on CVD(Neves et. al,2020). Hence there is a need for prediction of these interconnected chronic diseases at the early stage itself so that proper measures can be taken at the initial level before it becomes a risk factor for each other. Predictive analytics can be used effectively in predicting the disease at the early stage using the ML model. The primary objective of the proposed chapter is to provide a brief overview of domain knowledge on chronic diseases, as well as the biological correlations that exist between these diseases. More importantly, the chapter will explain how machine learning algorithms based on predictive analytics are being used in the healthcare sector to aid in the early detection of chronic diseases. The suggested chapter also seeks to provide an overview of the many steps involved in the development of machine learning algorithms, as well as the numerous research problems that must be addressed when implementing predictive analytics in the field of healthcare informatics.

2. NEED FOR PREDICTIVE ANALYTICS IN HEALTHCARE

Predictive analytics is beneficial at all stages of the patient journey, from diagnosis to prognosis and treatment. Additionally, predictive analytics can be used to improve personalized medicine and assist in the reduction of adverse occurrences. On a larger scale, predictive analytics has the potential to increase care quality while lowering costs. Due to digitization, a huge amount of data is generated at the rate of gigabytes to terabytes from the health care sector with the click of a button. The decision-making process made on such healthcare data by the physician is always ambiguous and may be error-prone due to which the patient may be at risk which may cause the death of the patient(Konova et. al,2020). Hence ideal solution must be developed using an efficient ML algorithm that is scalable, reliable, and cost-effective in determining the risk factor effectively thereby accurately predict the presence of the disease. Thereby medical experts can effectively use this framework for a better decision-making process. Even though tremendous progress has been made on medicine that can be applied to the human body to treat diseases, the medicines will fit only for a few groups of people not for everyone. Because the human body is so complex that still, we do not know many of the things about the organs of the human(Wingerd et. al,2020). Hence it is very complicated for the physician to take accurate decisions by analyzing the disease health records manually. That's where predictive analytical tools and techniques can help. These approaches can discover the hidden patterns by examining the inter-correlation between the large healthcare datasets to come out with the prediction. In the case of healthcare management using predictive analytics, the prevention and prediction will go hand in hand. One of the important gains in using predictive analytics in the health care sector is that the risk of developing the chronic disease can be predicted in the early stage itself. That is where the patient survival rate can be improved by avoiding the progression of long-term health issues. By adapting the predictive analytics the health care organizations can proactively identify the patient with a higher risk. This will improve patient satisfaction by providing better care for them.

ML is considered as the backbone technology behind predictive analytics which can be used to predict the disease at the early stage. ML-oriented predictive analytics solutions will be effective in uncovering the hidden insights from the massive data(Alber et. al,2019). The predictive analytics-based technique is derived from the theory of hypothesis. The hypothesis can be formed by applying statistical rules with the help of several formulas in the form of a process known as an algorithm. ML algorithms are majorly classified as supervised and unsupervised algorithms (Das et. al,2020). The predictive analytics can be performed by using both the category of the ML algorithm. These analytics will improve the outcome of healthcare by helping the physician to provide better treatment to the individual patients. By integrating predictive analytics in healthcare wastage can be reduced significantly. This helps in reducing the healthcare cost at an exceptional level and also bring down the mortality rate among all the age group of people(Zafar et. al,2019). Using predictive analytics the patient's hospital readmission rate can also be reduced by analyzing the likelihood of developing a particular disease. The hospital can also plan for a set of resources and protocols required based on these predictions. Hence there are seamless benefits in applying predictive analytics in the healthcare sector. The proposed chapter focuses on the application of ML-based predictive analytics in the early prediction of interconnected chronic diseases so that the risk of developing long-term illness among the patient can be avoided at the premature stage itself. Section 3 below provides a full overview of the major categories of Machine Learning Algorithms and their operation.

3. MACHINE LEARNING

ML is an artificial intelligence-based application that provides the systems ability to learn and improve from the experience to perform the prediction on future trends. The ML-based predictive analytics can be effectively applied in the health care sector to early predict diseases. Various ML algorithms can be used for the predictive analytical task in the field of healthcare sectors. They are broadly classified as supervised and unsupervised algorithms. The supervised ML algorithms can be used for classification and regression problems. Here the models are trained with labeled examples(Kannan et. al,2019). The input is fed to the system as a test set. The main task involves the comparison between the actual output and the desired output. In unsupervised algorithms, there is only the input variable(x) and there is no corresponding output. The unsupervised algorithm aims to learn about the data(You et. al,2019). The unsupervised algorithm falls into two categories. Clustering and Association. Clustering discovers the group of similar data together such as grouping the similar purchasing behavior of customers together. In association, analysis rules are built which describe the data where people who buy product x also tend to buy product Y which are used for the market basket analysis task. In ML, there may be the case of a semi-supervised state where out of a large amount of data collected(x) only a few data are labeled (y)(Boutaba et. al,2018). An artificial neural network(ANN) is a subset of a ML algorithm that mimics the behavior of the human brain.

The ANN includes the different layers in it such as the input layer followed by the hidden layer and the output layer. Deep learning is exploded as one of the potential algorithms for predictive analytics in the case of healthcare(Hatcher et. al,2018).

It is an application that performs the learning task by utilizing a multi-layered neural network architecture. The learning process on the input data is carried out by numerous neurons, each of which is launched with a distinct weight from the others. The categories of various ML algorithms are shown in figure 1. There are various processes involved in implementing a ML model as shown in figure 2 below. The first phase required data with which predictive analytics to make needs to be gathered. The gathered data in its raw form may contain noise, outliers, and missing values. If the same data is used for the process of analysis it may bring down the predictive accuracy of the constructed model. Hence the data needs to undergo rigorous pre-processing. The data pre-processing step may need to rectify and beautifying the collected data. There are mainly three major steps involved in data preprocessing

Figure 1. Categories of Various Machine Learning Algorithm

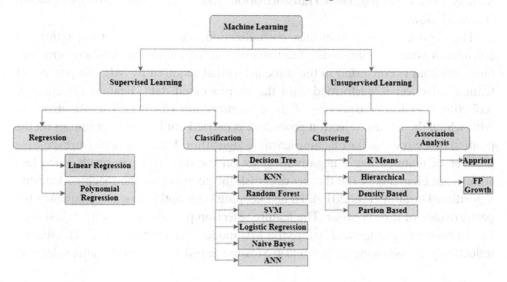

Figure 2. Flow diagram of Machine Learning Model

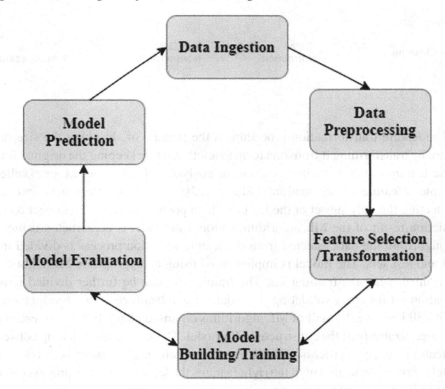

namely, Data Cleaning, Data Transformation, and data normalization as shown in figure 3 below.

The decimal scaling, min-max normalization, and Z score normalization are considered as the most important data transformation technique which can normalize. Once the data is converted in the standard format required by ML, the process of feature selection is performed with the preprocessed data. Feature selection or reduction is considered as one of the core procedures in ML. The effectiveness with which the feature selection procedure is carried out has a direct impact on the predictive accuracy of the machine learning algorithm. The existence of an excessive number of features has a negative impact on the data analysis result since less significant elements of the dataset diminish the accuracy of the machine learning algorithm(Durairaj et. al,2019). Hence keeping only optimal features enhance the performance of the classifier. The feature selection process is carried out just after the preprocessing stage and before the ML model construction stage. The feature reduction process is widely classified as a feature transformation and feature selection.

Figure 3. Stages in Data Preprocessing

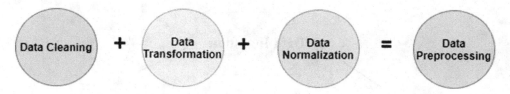

The feature transformation procedure is the process of shrinking the size of a feature by transforming it from one form to another while keeping the original form of the feature intact. Principal component analysis (PCA) serves as an excellent example of feature transformation(Uddin et. al,2021). Feature selection is a process of selecting the only subset of the feature which positively makes an impact on the prediction result of the ML algorithm. Before the model is constructed using an ML algorithm the data selected from the feature selection process is divided into train and test sets. The model is implemented using an appropriate ML algorithm and trained using the training set. The training set can be further divided into a validation set for cross-validating (CV) data. The advantage of cross-validation is that it will improve the skill of ML algorithms on unseen data. It will also estimate the generalizability of the constructed ML model. There is a feedback loop between the feature selection process and ML model implementation stage because if the model is not implemented with the right features the feature selection process can be altered till the optimal features are selected which can impact the predictive ability of the ML model. The performance of the model is evaluated by bypassing the test data to the model and the predictive ability of the model is assessed using the various parameter such as accuracy, precision, recall, sensitivity, F1 score, confusion matrix, and roc curve. Nowadays, people are confronted with a plethora of health-related issues as a result of their lifestyle choices and environmental conditions. Every fourth person is afflicted with a chronic condition. Globally, chronic diseases constitute the leading cause of death. These are diseases that last a long time and are difficult to cure; however, disease prevention is only achievable if these disorders can be predicted sooner. Section 4 provides an overview of various types of chronic diseases and their possible impact on human life.

4. CHRONIC DISEASE: AN OVERVIEW

Chronic disease is considered as one of the serious concerns and threats to public health across the globe. Diseases such as CDM, CVD, and CKD are major chronic diseases responsible for millions of death. Each of these diseases is considered as a risk factor for the other two diseases. Cardiovascular Disease is blowing up rapidly among the younger generation in India and across the globe and taking the lives of millions of people every year. As per the cardiac experts, the primary reason behind the cause of the disease is a sedentary lifestyle and a lack of physical activity .In India, at least one out of death out of five is due to CVD and the number of heart diseases. In the year 2019 alone 9,30,000 people died due to heart attack without any prior symptoms. The Heart attack occurs when the supply of blood to the heart is blocked. The heart is blocked due to the build-up of cholesterol, fat, and other substances in the arteries which will feed the heart. When the attack happens the internal muscle and organs of the heart will start expiring which stops the heartbeat. CVD may be categorized into different types based on the internal part affected due to the disease. The low and middle-class countries are the major sufferer of this disease. It is estimated that by 2030 at least 23 million people may die because of CVD. There is a constant rise in the number of people suffering from heart disease from 600 million to 1.13 billion from 1980 to 2019 which main reason behind CVD. So CVD is no longer a health issue but it is also a major economic million burden because the total global cost of CVD is expected to rise from the US $863 billion which was in the year 2010 to US$1044 billion in 2030(Uchino et. al,2020).

CDM is a metabolic disorder that occurs due to the accumulation of high blood sugar levels in the human body. The insulin hormones produced by the pancreas are responsible for the extraction of sugar from the blood and convert these in terms of energy through the beta cells of the human organ. The insulin will regulate the blood glucose level as well as fat levels in the human body. With CDM, the human organism does not produce enough insulin or it can not effectively use the insulin which is produced by the pancreas. The deficiency of insulin in the human body leads to Type I diabetes. If there is not sufficient insulin, the cell cannot take the glucose from the blood hence need to use the other source of energy. In these conditions, the body must use ketones as energy which are produced by the liver as an alternative source of energy. But an excessive amount of ketones in the human body leads to the condition of ketoacidosis. Hence people with a lack of insulin need to inject insulin externally into the body to compensate for the body's lack of insulin(Kostov et. al,2019). Type 2 diabetes is insulin resistance where the body will not respond positively to the produced insulin. As a result, the body fails to extract the excessive glucose from the human blood which leads to the condition of hyperglycemia. There is an exponential increase in the number of people suffering from CDM disease. The growth has constantly increased from 180 million to 462 million between 1980 and 2019. In the year 2019 alone around 1.6 million died due to CDM with age 60 and below(Piao et. al,2020). CKD is an important asymptotic disease where the kidney gradually loses its functionality. Kidney disease is often referred to as chronic disease as damages to the kidney often happens over a period which causes the waste to build up in the body.

Figure 4. Biological correlation between chronic disease

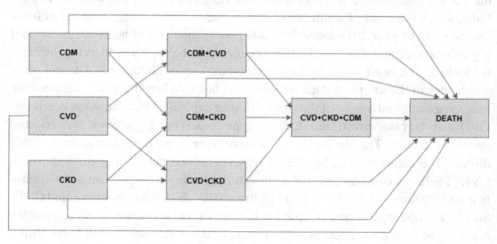

The kidney should balance the mineral and salt such as sodium, potassium, phosphorous which circulates in the blood. The chances of developing kidney disease increase with age. Diabetes and High blood pressure are considered as the most common risk factor for CKD. In the world, around 850 million people are victims of the CKD disease, which is double the number if we compare it with diabetes disease and the count is twenty times greater than the people who suffering from Cancer disease(Fraser et. al,2019). The impact of CKD can be seen in the developing and under-developing countries like India as these countries cannot afford expensive medical treatment for dialysis and kidney transplantation, only worlds 20% of the people with a good economy are getting treatment for these diseases. There is a strong resemblance between chronic disease CVD, CDM, and CKD. Each of these diseases is considered as a risk factor for the other two. In the current era, these three diseases are becoming increasingly risk factors among adults. As per the survey, at least half of the heart disease patients will suffer from CKD disease at least with some level. Diagnosing the CKD disease will not only increase the morbidity of CVD but also worsen the outcome of cardiovascular conditions. It is also evident that the chances of CKD are very high if the patient is suffering from undiagnosed CDM(Bonacina et. al,2019). In general, the CDM becomes a risk factor for CVD. Hence pair of the disease becoming a risk factor for the other. One of the most effective ways to combat chronic disease-related mortality is to predict it sooner so that the disease can be prevented. Section 5 below illustrates the role of machine learning in the early prediction of chronic diseases.

5. ROLE OF MACHINE LEARNING IN CHRONIC DISEASE PREDICTION

Prediction of disease at the early stage is a tedious task for the physician which requires hours together. The disease can be predicted based on its symptoms. The symptoms will vary from disease to disease. The manual way of prediction is cumbersome and may be error-prone (El Houby et. al,2018). Hence there is a need for automatic prediction of disease which can predict the disease with utmost accuracy. Through the predictive analytics-based ML approaches the deadly chronic disease can be predicted at the initial stage before it damages the organs of humans. When the same data is used for predictive analytics tasks, the accuracy of the machine learning model may deteriorate. As a first step, these data will be subjected to a thorough pre-processing process to eliminate any irrelevant data. Data pre-processing phases include data cleansing, data normalization, removing missing values, and data transformation. The data is cleaned initially to remove outliers, missing values, and noise. To scale the data inside the desired range, data normalization techniques such as decimal scaling, min-max normalization, and z score normalization are used. The data transformation technique converts the health care data to the format required by the machine learning algorithm. The pre-processed data will be subjected to an exploratory data analysis (EDA) approach to do statistical analysis on the data.

The feature selection process is a critical stage in machine learning. As mentioned previously, health care data are multidimensional.

The Predictive accuracy is determined by the number of dimensions in the analyzed dataset. The greater the number of dimensions, the lesser the accuracy. As a result, data must be condensed to contain just those features that affect the prediction outcome. Following the preparation stage, data is filtered to extract valuable features and minimize the dimension of the data, hence reducing the computational cost of subsequent processing. Additionally, it avoids issues such as data overfit, underfit, and imbalanced data classification, all of which have an effect on the prediction outcome. There are a variety of methods available, including recursive feature elimination, correlation-based feature selection, Lasso, Relief-based feature selection, and forward feature selection, that allow for the selection of only the ideal characteristics that may affect the prediction outcome. The filtered data is heavily trained using a variety of machine learning methods, as explained in Section 3 of this chapter. The machine learning methods are chosen by the type of healthcare data and disease. After the model is implemented using healthcare data, it is subjected to internal and external validations to ensure its performance before real-time patient data is passed.

Figure 5. The generic architecture of predictive analytic framework for the disease prediction in Health Care

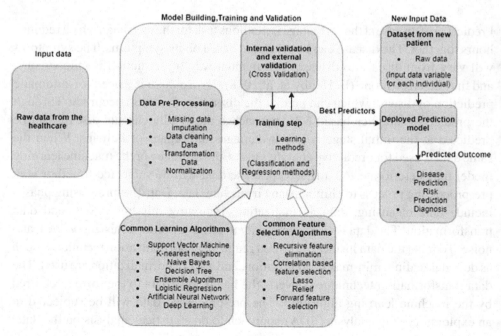

During validation process, it is necessary to separate the complete data set into two groups: the training set and the validation set. With the K fold cross technique, internal model validation can be done on the training set to ensure that the model is correct(Wong et. al,2019). It is necessary to do external validation on the validation set, and the model's performance on the validation set is monitored. If the model fails to deliver good accuracy during the validation method, the model hyperparameter might be tweaked to improve accuracy. As long as the developed model generates good accuracy with the validation set, it may be deployed, and new patient data can be used as input to train the constructed model to forecast disease early in its progression. The framework's potential predictive outcomes include a forecast of the presence or absence of disease, a prediction of the prospective risk level of a specific disease, and the diagnosis of a specific disease. In the past year, there has been a significant amount of research work completed in the domain of machine learning-based predictive analytics in the field of health care, which is explored in the section 5.1,5.2 and 5.3 below.

5.1 Chronic Diabetes Mellitus

Diabetes is considered as the disease of the modern era which took the lives of millions of lives across the globe. Lack of exercise, consumption of food which are rich in fat, obesity, sedentary lifestyle are the main reason behind this disease. The diabetic patient must undergo numerous diagnostic tests which are painful and time-consuming as well(Lipsky et. al,2020). The number of diagnostic tests can be significantly reduced with the usage of a ML algorithm in the prediction of CDM. A summary of a few work that is already carried out in the application of a ML algorithm in the area of diabetes prediction is shown in Table 1 below.

5.2 Cardiovascular Disease

CVD is considered as one of the deadliest diseases in the world. As per the statistics around 17.9 million people are dying due to CVD out of which 17 million are premature death under the age of 70. CVD is responsible for 31% of death worldwide. CVD is considered as one of the costliest chronic diseases. There is a various disease which comes under the umbrella of heart disease such as disease- related to the blood vessel, heart rhythmic problem, heart attack, chest pain, stroke (Khan et.al,2019). Heart diseases do not affect the life or the health of a person even they will wipe out the finance of the family. Because heart disease-related disorder is always associated with high hospital costs. Even though heart disease is dangerous it can be prevented by taking the proper measure at the preliminary stage itself. In this information age, the aim is to provide medical treatment that can be affordable to the patient. ML algorithms such as classification, clustering are turning out as an effective solution in the early prediction of CVD using which the occurrence of the disease can be detected at the early stage to take possible measures at the early stage. The summary of various research work which is carried out in the area of heart disease prediction is briefly represented in Table 2 below.

Table 1. Summary on work related to the prediction of diabetes disease

Author	Machine Learning Approach	Application	Performance
Aiello et. al,2018	KNN with K fold cross-validation using UVA/PADOVA simulator	Diagnosis of type 1 diabetes mellitus	Accuracy: 83%, Average AUC:0.84
Herrero et.al,2018	Deep learning-based models	Diagnosis of type 2 diabetes mellitus	Accuracy: 87% Precision:84.6% Recall:85.4%
Alehegn et. al,2018	Ensemble machine learning with the combination of SVM, Naïve Bayes, Decision Tree	Early prediction of type 2 diabetes mellitus	Accuracy :84.35% Precision:86.5% Recall: 83.8%
Singh et.al,2020	A stacked ensemble of, KNN, Naïve Bayes logistic regression, and C4.5	Predicting the development of glucose levels related to diabetes	Accuracy:79% Sensitivity:81.5% Specificity:80.2%
Wang et.al,2020	Weight ranked SVM using lasso as a feature selector	Early Diagnosis of type 2 diabetes	Average AUC:0.85 Accuracy: 86.4%
Chowdhary et.al,2020	Farthest First clustering algorithm with SMO	Prediction of Gestational diabetes	Average AUC :0.88 Accuracy:89%

Table 2. Summary on work related to the prediction of heart disease

Author	Machine Learning Approach	Application	Performance
Gokulnath et.al,2019	SVM with Genetic Algorithm	Early Prediction of Ischemic heart disease	Accuracy: 76% Average AUC:0.78
Kodati et.al,2019	K means algorithm	Early diagnosis of cardiomyopathy	Average AUC: 0.81 Sensitivity :84% Accuracy: 83%
Takci et.al,2018	Naïve Bayes Classifier	Early prediction of Coronary artery disease.	Accuracy:74.81% Precision:76.17%
Aldhyani et.al,2020	Rough K Means(RKM) based clustering algorithm	Prediction of congenital heart failure	Precision:84%AUC: 0.81 Accuracy: 85%
Magesh et.al,2020	Cluster-based decision tree	Early Diagnosis of Myocardial infarction	Accuracy: 86% F1 score:85.2%
Ali et.al,2019	Chi-square test with Deep Neural Network	Prediction of Arrhythmia disease	Accuracy: 90% Average AUC:0.91

5.3 Chronic Kidney Disease

The impact of CKD can be seen mainly in developing and under-developing countries like India. Due to poverty, the people of these countries cannot afford expensive medical treatment for dialysis and kidney transplantation. As per the survey by WHO only worlds 20% of the people with a good economy could able to get treatment for these diseases. As per the pediatric registry, in India, nearly 45% of children are in the G 4 or G 5 stage of CKD(Drube et.al,2019). The late detection of CKD disease is considered as one of the prime reasons to increase the mortality rate with these diseases. Hence there is no clear picture of the number of CKD patients who need renal replacement treatment. On average patients with kidney failure need to spend at least 20 to 50 lakh between the period of diagnosis of the disease and till the renal transplantation. The expensive cost spent on medical treatment can be avoided by early prediction of the CKD disease. The predictive analytics-based ML approaches can be used to detect the CKD disease at the early stage. There is much research work already carried out in the early prediction of CKD using various ML-based approaches which are summarized in table 3 below. Lapses in health information may lead to erroneous predictions by machine-learning algorithms which may have a negative impact on the decision-making process. Since medical data are initially meant for electronic health records, data must be prepared before algorithms can be used effectively by machine learners (Jayatilake et.al,2021). Section 7 discusses the numerous research challenges associated with the application of machine learning algorithms in the health care sector.

6 IMPLEMENTATION OF STACKED ENSEMBLE CLASSIFIER FOR THE EARLY PREDICTION OF CHRONIC DISEASE

By integrating several models, ensemble learning aids in the improvement of machine learning results. When compared to a single model, this method results in significantly improved predictive performance. In machine learning, ensemble methods are meta-algorithms that incorporate numerous machine learning techniques into a single predictive model with the goal of reducing bias and variance .

Algorithm: Stacked Ensemble Classifier

1. Input: training instances from chronic heart disease dataset $R = \{f_i, o_i\}^m_{i=1}$
2. Output: Classify the presence/absence of the disease using ensemble classifier EH
3. Step I: Train the chronic data instances on base-level model

4. for i = 1 to do
5. train through eh_i based on R where eh_i represent the instances trained through ensemble classifier
6. end for
7. Step II: generate new data set out of prediction
8. for j= 1 to n do
9. $R_h = \{f_j^1, O_j\}$, where $f_j^1 = \{ eh_1(f_j), ..., eh_i(f_i) \}$
10. end for
11. Step III: train using meta- classifier based on R_h
12. return EH

Table 3. Summary on work related to the prediction of chronic kidney disease

Author	Machine Learning Approach	Application	Performance
Jena et.al,2020	Decision tree and Naïve Bayes machine learning algorithm in combination with a Genetic algorithm.	Prediction of Chronic kidney disease	Accuracy:76% Precision:77.8% Recall:79.3%
Alloghani et.al,2020	polynomial SVM algorithm	Early prediction of renal failure	Accuracy:91% AUC:0.89
Aly et.al,2020	Three-stage based ensembled Bagged, Boosted, and Medium Tree model	Early prediction of polycystic kidney failure	Accuracy:89% Sensitivity:87.6% Specificity:88.5%
Harimoorthy et.al,2020	SVM radial bias kernel in combination with recursive feature elimination as a feature selector	Prediction of intrinsic kidney failure	AUC rate : 0.86 Accuracy:88.4%
Vásquez-Morales et.al,2019	Neural Network algorithm in combination with Case-Based Reasoning twin based model	Prediction of CKD infection	Accuracy:84% AUC rate:0.83
Almasoud et.al,2019	ANOVA and Pearson correlation algorithm using SVM, random forest, and Gradient boosting classifier.	Prediction of acute kidney failure	The Gradient boosting algorithm performed well with an accuracy of 86% and an AUC rate of 0.85
Elhoseny et.al,2019)	The rule-based classifier in combination with the evolutionary Ant Colony (ACO)	Early Prediction of Acute prerenal kidney failure	Accuracy:88.9% Precision:86.2%
Khamparia et.al,2019	Stacked encoder based deep neural network	Early Prediction the renal failure	Accuracy:83.6% AUC rate:0.82

Combining several classification and regression models with the help of a meta-classifier or meta-regressor is referred to as stacking in machine learning terminology. While implementing such model, the base level model is trained using a full training set, and the meta model is trained using the results of the base level model, which are further combined. The base level is often comprised of a variety of learning methods, and the stacking groups are updated on a regular basis

Figure 6. Precision Vs Recall curves obtained with various Models with chronic disease dataset

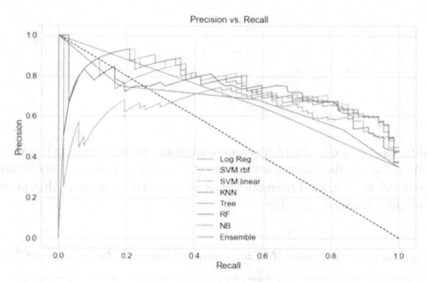

The proposed chapter aims at implementing stacked ensemble classifier for the prediction of chronic disease. The algorithm of stacked ensemble model is depicted above, . The proposed stacked ensemble model consists of Random Forest, Naive Bayes and k-NN algorithms, whose predictive results are merged as a meta-classification by logistic regression. The chronic heart disease dataset obtained from UCI machine learning repository is used to conduct the experiment.

The experimental investigation is carried to early predict the chronic heart disease using various base learners and proposed stacked ensemble classifier. The Precision, Recall and ROC curves obtained through these various machine learning model is shown in figure 6 and figure 7 above.

Figure 7. ROC curves obtained with various Models with chronic disease dataset

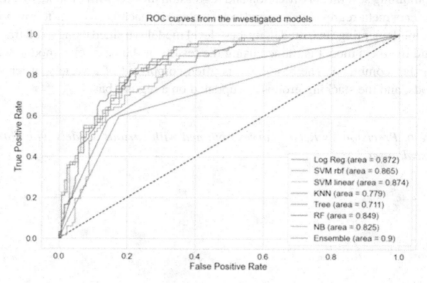

Table 4 above shows the results produced from machine learning model when applied on the chronic heart disease data set. The experimental results illustrates that, the proposed Stacked Ensemble Model was found more accurate than the other basic machine learning classifiers.

Table 4. Results with various Machine learning model on chronic disease dataset

Machine learning Algorithm	Accuracy	AUC
Logistic Regression	87.71%	0.872
SVM RBF	86.34%	0.864
SVM Linear	87.12%	0.874
KNN	78.05%	0.779
Decision Tree	70.94%	0.710
Random Forest	83.42%	0.849
Naïve Bayes	81.61%	0.825
Stacked Ensemble Model	89.25%	0.90

7 RESEARCH CHALLENGES IN APPLICATION OF MACHINE LEARNING IN THE HEALTHCARE SECTORS

Even though the ML approaches are turning out as an efficient tool in the field of healthcare especially in the early prediction of disease coming but the expansion of these applications is not so fast. The main reason being the distributional shift, as there is a drastic difference between real-world data and training data. Hence the fear is that algorithm may come up with the wrong conclusion as ML algorithms run as the black box. The decision made by these algorithms is not open to inspection. As training data set to get older trusting the system become dangerous. Certain common problems need attention to make ML algorithms fail-safe in the field of healthcare.

1. **Quality of Data:** As the healthcare domain is very diverse, the data generated from it are always ambiguous, noisy, imperfect, and complex. Unlike other applications data is not clean and well arranged. But to implement a good ML model with these diverse and huge data sets, maintaining the quality in data is most important where the problem likes data redundancy, data sparsity, and missing values needs to be well addressed.

2. **Data Temporality:** Due to the rapid advancement in technology treatment given to a particular disease is progressive and may change over time based on the response of the patient. But the drawback of the ML-based system is that they are sensitive to the changes and may ignore the changes made over some time. This will surely impact the predictive accuracy obtained through the ML-based model.

3. **Domain Uncertainty:** Unlike other domains, there is high variation in healthcare-related data which again differs from disease to disease as the response of the patient will not be known in advance. Hence always there is uncertainty in the domain of the data. To obtain the optimized result with the ML model, it must be trained with the generalized data. But due to domain uncertainty, it is impossible to achieve generality with the data.

4. **Interpretability of data**: Unlike other applications always there will be an issue of data interpretability in healthcare. Since the ML model is a black box in nature that can not be controlled, it is very important to take proper attention while choosing particular ML which can be able to interpret the data properly. Otherwise, the model may mislead the result with a more number of false-positive results.

5. **Feature Capture:** One of the big challenges in the healthcare domain from the point of view of ML is capturing proper features from the hospitals and patients under the supervision of a physician. The domain knowledge about a particular disease plays a key role while collecting healthcare data. The

medical-related data can be obtained through social media, offline and online surveys, surroundings, wearable devices, organizations. Integrating the collected heterogeneous data from various sources in the form of a healthcare dataset that is suitable from the point of view of the ML algorithm itself is a research challenge.

6. **Data Privacy issue:** The medical organization has its responsibility and concern about their patient. The patient data must be shared without affecting and leaking sensitive information. If the cloud-based platforms are used in deploying such information, it must be secured properly using the cryptographic and digital signature-based concept which itself is an important research topic.

7. **(vi) Volume of Data:** Due to the digitization in the field of healthcare a huge amount of data is generated every day with the size of petabytes to gigabytes. If these data can be collected ML model can be implemented using these data. But the implemented model must cope up with the huge volume of the data. Because most ML algorithms can able to perform well only with a limited amount of data. If the volume of the data gets increases it, in turn, reduces the accuracy of the ML model as it cannot handle data with large size. This leads to the problem of underfitting and overfitting in data science.

8. **Erroneous data:** The collected healthcare data to build a ML model could be Erroneous. For example, due to the errors in the tools or measurement, the captured ECG reading of a particular patient may vary. Even it depends on the movement of the patient, speed of breathing, etc. If the same data is used for implementing a predictive model the result obtained through this system may be inaccurate.

9. **Dimension of feature:** Usually the healthcare-related data are multidimensional in nature. A huge amount of features are associated with a particular disease. The number of features of a particular disease directly proportions to the sign of disease and the medical diagnosis and measurement conducted on such disease. But ML algorithm's accuracy reduces with the increase in the dimension of data. One of the remedies could be the application of a feature selection algorithm before implementing a model so that only the required features can be considered while constructing the ML model. But implementing a feature selection algorithm is a separate research topic because the features in the dataset vary based on the domain of the healthcare application.

10. **Model Acceptability:** The computational model designed in the area of healthcare domains is facing problems of lack of acceptability as it is implementing by the nonphysician who does not have enough domain knowledge on the medical domain. Hence physicians are reluctant to accept such a predictive model thinking it is inefficient. Hence solid verification and validation scheme

has to be implemented with the help of a physician to generate confidence in such a model so that such a predictive model can be accepted universally.

8 CONCLUSION

The proposed chapter outlined the importance of ML-based predictive analytics systems in the healthcare sector. From the concrete examples stated in the chapter, it can be evident that the concept of ML-based systems can be effectively used in the early prediction and diagnosis of the disease. Using such systems an expensive medical diagnosis and hospital cost can be significantly reduced. More importantly, the long-term health issues which are difficult to cure can be avoided by predicting the disease in its initial phase itself. Although the usefulness of predictive analytics in the healthcare sector is acknowledged well, the system is not being readily adopted by the physician due to the various reasons which were discussed in section 7. Certain fundamental challenges need to be addressed to universally accept such systems. Hence it can be concluded that there is a tremendous future for the ML-based predictive systems in the healthcare sectors using which the health of the individual can be improved and also the lives of many people can be saved.

REFERENCES

Aiello, E. M., Toffanin, C., Messori, M., Cobelli, C., & Magni, L. (2018). Postprandial glucose regulation via KNN meal classification in type 1 diabetes. *IEEE Control Systems Letters*, *3*(2), 230–235. doi:10.1109/LCSYS.2018.2844179

Alber, M., Tepole, A. B., Cannon, W. R., De, S., Dura-Bernal, S., Garikipati, K., ... Kuhl, E. (2019). Integrating machine learning and multiscale modeling—Perspectives, challenges, and opportunities in the biological, biomedical, and behavioral sciences. *NPJ Digital Medicine*, *2*(1), 1–11. doi:10.103841746-019-0193-y PMID:31799423

Aldhyani, T. H., Alshebami, A. S., & Alzahrani, M. Y. (2020). Soft Clustering for Enhancing the Diagnosis of Chronic Diseases over Machine Learning Algorithms. *Journal of Healthcare Engineering*, *2020*, 2020. doi:10.1155/2020/4984967 PMID:32211144

Alehegn, M., Joshi, R., & Mulay, P. (2018). Analysis and prediction of diabetes mellitus using machine learning algorithm. *International Journal of Pure and Applied Mathematics*, *118*(9), 871–878.

Ali, L., Khan, S. U., Golilarz, N. A., Yakubu, I., Qasim, I., Noor, A., & Nour, R. (2019). A Feature-Driven Decision Support System for Heart Failure Prediction Based on Statistical Model and Gaussian Naive Bayes. *Computational and Mathematical Methods in Medicine, 2019*, 2019. doi:10.1155/2019/6314328 PMID:31885684

Alloghani, M., Al-Jumeily, D., Hussain, A., Liatsis, P., & Aljaaf, A. J. (2020). Performance-Based Prediction of Chronic Kidney Disease Using Machine Learning for High-Risk Cardiovascular Disease Patients. In *Nature-Inspired Computation in Data Mining and Machine Learning* (pp. 187–206). Springer. doi:10.1007/978-3-030-28553-1_9

Almasoud, M., & Ward, T. E. (2019). Detection of chronic kidney disease using machine learning algorithms with the least number of predictors. *International Journal of Soft Computing and Its Applications, 10*(8). Advance online publication. doi:10.14569/IJACSA.2019.0100813

Aly, H. M., Aborizka, M., & Labib, S. S. (2020, March). Predicting the Risk Factor for Developing Chronic Kidney Disease Using a 3-Stage Prediction Model. In *Future of Information and Communication Conference* (pp. 631-641). Springer.

Bikbov, B., Purcell, C. A., Levey, A. S., Smith, M., Abdoli, A., Abebe, M., & Ahmadian, E. (2020). Global, regional, and national burden of chronic kidney disease, 1990–2017: A systematic analysis for the Global Burden of Disease Study 2017. *Lancet, 395*(10225), 709–733. doi:10.1016/S0140-6736(20)30045-3 PMID:32061315

Bonacina, F., Baragetti, A., Catapano, A. L., & Norata, G. D. (2019). The interconnection between Immuno-metabolism, diabetes, and CKD. *Current Diabetes Reports, 19*(5), 21. doi:10.100711892-019-1143-4 PMID:30888513

Boutaba, R., Salahuddin, M. A., Limam, N., Ayoubi, S., Shahriar, N., Estrada-Solano, F., & Caicedo, O. M. (2018). A comprehensive survey on machine learning for networking:evolution, applications and research opportunities. *Journal of Internet Services and Applications, 9*(1), 16. doi:10.118613174-018-0087-2

Chowdhary, C. L., Mittal, M., Pattanaik, P. A., & Marszalek, Z. (2020). An efficient segmentation and classification system in medical images using intuitionist possibilistic fuzzy C-mean clustering and fuzzy SVM algorithm. *Sensors (Basel), 20*(14), 3903. doi:10.339020143903 PMID:32668793

Das, R., Bhattacharyya, S., & Nandy, S. (Eds.). (2020). *Machine Learning Applications: Emerging Trends* (Vol. 5). Walter de Gruyter GmbH & Co KG. doi:10.1515/9783110610987

Drube, J., Wan, M., Bonthuis, M., Wühl, E., Bacchetta, J., Santos, F., & Tönshoff, B. (2019). Clinical practice recommendations for growth hormone treatment in children with chronic kidney disease. *Nature Reviews. Nephrology*, *15*(9), 577–589. doi:10.103841581-019-0161-4 PMID:31197263

Durairaj, M., & Poornappriya, T. S. (2019, January). Why Feature Selection in Data Mining Is Prominent? A Survey. In *International Conference on Artificial Intelligence, Smart Grid and Smart City Applications* (pp. 949-963). Springer.

El Houby, E. M. (2018). A survey on applying machine learning techniques for management of diseases. *Journal of Applied Biomedicine*, *16*(3), 165–174. doi:10.1016/j.jab.2018.01.002

Elhoseny, M., Shankar, K., & Uthayakumar, J. (2019). Intelligent diagnostic prediction and classification system for chronic kidney disease. *Scientific Reports*, *9*(1), 1–14. doi:10.103841598-019-46074-2 PMID:31270387

Fraser, S. D., & Roderick, P. J. (2019). Kidney disease in the global burden of disease study 2017. *Nature Reviews. Nephrology*, *15*(4), 193–194. doi:10.103841581-019-0120-0 PMID:30723305

Gokulnath, C. B., & Shantharajah, S. P. (2019). An optimized feature selection based on genetic approach and support vector machine for heart disease. *Cluster Computing*, *22*(6), 14777–14787. doi:10.100710586-018-2416-4

Hatcher, W. G., & Yu, W. (2018). A survey of deep learning: Platforms, applications and emerging research trends. *IEEE Access: Practical Innovations, Open Solutions*, *6*, 24411–24432. doi:10.1109/ACCESS.2018.2830661

Hruska, K. A., Williams, M. J., & Sugatani, T. (2020). Chronic kidney disease–mineral and bone disorders. In *Chronic Renal Disease* (pp. 551–569). Academic Press. doi:10.1016/B978-0-12-815876-0.00035-8

Jayatilake, S. M. D. A. C., & Ganegoda, G. U. (2021). Involvement of Machine Learning Tools in Healthcare Decision Making. *Journal of Healthcare Engineering*. PMID:33575021

Jena, L., Nayak, S., & Swain, R. (2020). Chronic Disease Risk (CDR) Prediction in Biomedical Data Using Machine Learning Approach. In *Advances in Intelligent Computing and Communication* (pp. 232–239). Springer. doi:10.1007/978-981-15-2774-6_29

Kannan, R., & Vasanthi, V. (2019). Machine learning algorithms with ROC curve for predicting and diagnosing the heart disease. In *Soft Computing and Medical Bioinformatics* (pp. 63–72). Springer. doi:10.1007/978-981-13-0059-2_8

Khamparia, A., Saini, G., Pandey, B., Tiwari, S., Gupta, D., & Khanna, A. (2019). KDSAE: Chronic kidney disease classification with multimedia data learning using deep stacked autoencoder network. *Multimedia Tools and Applications*, 1–16. doi:10.100711042-019-07839-z

Khan, Y., Qamar, U., Yousaf, N., & Khan, A. (2019, February). Machine learning techniques for heart disease datasets: a survey. In *Proceedings of the 2019 11th International Conference on Machine Learning and Computing* (pp. 27-35). 10.1145/3318299.3318343

Kodati, S., Vivekanandam, R., & Ravi, G. (2019). Comparative Analysis of Clustering Algorithms with Heart Disease Datasets Using Data Mining Weka Tool. In *Soft Computing and Signal Processing* (pp. 111–117). Springer. doi:10.1007/978-981-13-3600-3_11

Konova, A. B., Lopez-Guzman, S., Urmanche, A., Ross, S., Louie, K., Rotrosen, J., & Glimcher, P. W. (2020). Computational markers of risky decision-making for identification of temporal windows of vulnerability to opioid use in a real-world clinical setting. *JAMA Psychiatry*, 77(4), 368–377. doi:10.1001/jamapsychiatry.2019.4013 PMID:31812982

Kostov, K. (2019). Effects of magnesium deficiency on mechanisms of insulin resistance in type 2 diabetes: Focusing on the processes of insulin secretion and signaling. *International Journal of Molecular Sciences*, 20(6), 1351. doi:10.3390/ijms20061351 PMID:30889804

Li, K., Liu, F., Dong, H., Herrero, P., Guo, Y., & Georgiou, P. (2018, February). A deep learning platform for diabetes big data analysis. In *Proc. 11th Adv* (pp. A116–A116). Technologies Treatments Diabetes.

Lipsky, B. A., Senneville, É., Abbas, Z. G., Aragón-Sánchez, J., Diggle, M., Embil, J. M., Kono, S., Lavery, L. A., Malone, M., Asten, S. A., Urbančič-Rovan, V., & Peters, E. J. G. (2020). Guidelines on the diagnosis and treatment of foot infection in persons with diabetes (IWGDF 2019 update). *Diabetes/Metabolism Research and Reviews*, 36(S1), e3280. doi:10.1002/dmrr.3280 PMID:32176444

Magesh, G., & Swarnalatha, P. (2020). Optimal feature selection through a cluster-based DT learning (CDTL) in heart disease prediction. *Evolutionary Intelligence*, 1–11. doi:10.100712065-019-00336-0

Neves, J. S., Correa, S., Baeta Baptista, R., Bigotte Vieira, M., Waikar, S. S., & Mc Causland, F. R. (2020). Association of prediabetes with CKD progression and adverse cardiovascular outcomes: An analysis of the CRIC study. *The Journal of Clinical Endocrinology and Metabolism, 105*(4), e1772–e1780. doi:10.1210/clinem/dgaa017 PMID:31943096

Piao, H., Yun, J. M., Shin, A., & Cho, B. (2020). Longitudinal Study of Diabetic Differences between International Migrants and Natives among the Asian Population. *Biomolecules & Therapeutics, 28*(1), 110–118. doi:10.4062/biomolther.2019.163 PMID:31739384

Salkuti, S. R. (2020). A survey of big data and machine learning. *International Journal of Electrical & Computer Engineering, 10*(1).

Shastri, A., & Deshpande, M. (2020). A Review of Big Data and Its Applications in Healthcare and Public Sector. In *Big Data Analytics in Healthcare* (pp. 55–66). Springer. doi:10.1007/978-3-030-31672-3_4

Singh, N., & Singh, P. (2020). A Stacked Generalization Approach for Diagnosis and Prediction of Type 2 Diabetes Mellitus. In *Computational Intelligence in Data Mining* (pp. 559–570). Springer. doi:10.1007/978-981-13-8676-3_47

Takci, H. (2018). Improvement of heart attack prediction by the feature selection methods. *Turkish Journal of Electrical Engineering and Computer Sciences, 26*(1), 1–10. doi:10.3906/elk-1611-235

Uchino, B. N., Cronan, S., Scott, E., Landvatter, J., & Papadakis, M. (2020). Social support and stress, depression, and cardiovascular disease. In *Cardiovascular Implications of Stress and Depression* (pp. 211–223). Academic Press. doi:10.1016/B978-0-12-815015-3.00009-X

Uddin, M. P., Mamun, M. A., Afjal, M. I., & Hossain, M. A. (2021). Information-theoretic feature selection with segmentation-based folded principal component analysis (PCA) for hyperspectral image classification. *International Journal of Remote Sensing, 42*(1), 286–32. doi:10.1080/01431161.2020.1807650

Vásquez-Morales, G. R., Martínez-Monterrubio, S. M., Moreno-Ger, P., & Recio-García, J. A. (2019). Explainable prediction of chronic renal disease in the colombian population using neural networks and case-based reasoning. *IEEE Access: Practical Innovations, Open Solutions, 7,* 152900–152910. doi:10.1109/ACCESS.2019.2948430

Virani, S. S., Alonso, A., Benjamin, E. J., Bittencourt, M. S., Callaway, C. W., Carson, A. P., & Djousse, L. (2020). Heart disease and stroke statistics—2020 update: A report from the American Heart Association. *Circulation, 141*(9), E139–E596. doi:10.1161/CIR.0000000000000757 PMID:31992061

Wang, X., Yang, Y., Xu, Y., Chen, Q., Wang, H., & Gao, H. (2020). Predicting hypoglycemic drugs of type 2 diabetes based on weighted rank support vector machine. *Knowledge-Based Systems, 197*, 105868. doi:10.1016/j.knosys.2020.105868

Wang, Y., Kung, L., & Byrd, T. A. (2018). Big data analytics: Understanding its capabilities and potential benefits for healthcare organizations. *Technological Forecasting and Social Change, 126*, 3–13. doi:10.1016/j.techfore.2015.12.019

Wingerd, B., & Taylor, P. B. (2020). *The human body: Concepts of anatomy and physiology*. Jones & Bartlett Publishers.

Wong, T. T., & Yeh, P. Y. (2019). Reliable accuracy estimates from k-fold cross validation. *IEEE Transactions on Knowledge and Data Engineering*.

Yang, C. W., Harris, D. C., Luyckx, V. A., Nangaku, M., Hou, F. F., Garcia, G. G., ... Eiam-Ong, S. (2020). Global case studies for chronic kidney disease/end-stage kidney disease care. *Kidney International. Supplement, 10*(1), e24–e48. doi:10.1016/j.kisu.2019.11.010 PMID:32149007

You, K., Wang, X., Long, M., & Jordan, M. (2019, May). Towards accurate model selection in deep unsupervised domain adaptation. In *International Conference on Machine Learning* (pp. 7124-7133). Academic Press.

Zafar, F., Raza, S., Khalid, M. U., & Tahir, M. A. (2019, March). Predictive Analytics in Healthcare for Diabetes Prediction. In *Proceedings of the 2019 9th International Conference on Biomedical Engineering and Technology* (pp. 253-259). 10.1145/3326172.3326213

Chapter 11
Medical Cyber Physical System Architecture for Smart Medical Pumps

Alamelu J. V.
M.S. Ramaiah Institute of Technology, India

Priscilla Dinkar Moyya
Vellore Institute of Technology, India

Mythili Asaithambi
Vellore Institute of Technology, India

ABSTRACT

The transformations through technological innovations have influenced the medical field. There are significant developments in medical devices in their usage. The utilization of the devices is automated in a local, remote environment. The medical devices used in the remote cyber environment uses different network protocols. These devices comprise micro, nanofabricated sensors and actuators which have the facility to communicate using network protocols. The devices that have network capability to integrate into cyberspace through physical methods are typical medical cyber physical systems (MCPS). In MCPS, medical device modelling is an important aspect. Several medical devices are available, and here in the current research, emphasis is focused on smart medical pumps in the MCPS environment. This chapter highlights the essential concepts of the smart medical drug delivery device, its architecture, control, actuation, communication, and analysis in the cyber environment.

DOI: 10.4018/978-1-7998-8161-2.ch011

INTRODUCTION

Current innovations of sensor fabrication, electronics interfaces, communication with the cyber world with physical devices enable enhancement in challenges for health care devices. Smart health care system provides primary diagnosis, timed, appropriate medical assistance, time management for better health for the patient. For the past few decades, countless wireless smart medical devices have been invented and are used by the medical fraternity. The smart medical pump is one among them and its requirement is essential in all fields of medical treatment. Research on smart medical drug delivery devices has been discussed by many researchers based on patient-controlled analgesia, Anaesthesia, insulin drug delivery devices, artificial pancreas, etc. In recent years rise of MCPS modelling for drug delivery devices has been designed based on the finite state modelling in hybrid mode. A survey on MCPS architecture on health care systems reveals that the implementation has led to the development of medical devices and its system by integrating the physical devices, hospitals, remote servers, clinicians, and patients (Haque et al., 2014). This environment has assisted the patients to undergo diagnosis and related procedures with ease. MCPS is completely based on different network architectures. In health care, cognitive techniques to transmit medical data have been performed(Kumar et al., 2019). The medical data is transmitted to the cloud using cloud-based algorithms; performance measures, reliability, and robustness are evaluated (Insup & Sokolsky, 2010).

Security issues in these architectures have been implemented and are under research in the context of health care systems, services (Park et al., 2016). Research challenges related to the Internet of Things, Wireless Sensor Networks in MCPS concept for smart health care are mainly concentrated on Quality of Service, energy efficiency, low power wireless communication, security, and safety (Gardašević et al., 2020). Safety measures for the patient by providing reduced errors in drug infusion are analysed using formal modelling with hybrid automata for anaesthesia administration (Silva et al., 2015).

The patient's information has to be handled as electronic Health Records (eHR) securely (Percival et al., 2010). When a security framework is formed, the framework for authentication in the medical process is another requirement in cyberspace (Seifert & Rez, 2016). Since the devices are connected digitally across in cyberspace, spoofing attack, vulnerability on hardware is explored.

The medical process, investigation, design needs are authentication and act as key components in MCPS (Kanjee & Liu, 2016). In MCPS, the medical device design in micro, nano dimensions, modelling, control, medical data transmission, Graphical User Interface (GUI), integration of these with the remote cloud database, servers are the focussed (Masci et al., 2014). Research in communication methods in a wireless environment with Bluetooth, LiFi, optical, RF waves is studied and analyzed for smart medical devices and especially for smart infusion and insulin pumps (Ly et al., 2019), (Riurean et al., 2019).

Numerous medical devices are available and, in this chapter, the emphasis is on the smart pump (Mao et al., 2018). Studies on the design of micropumps have been developed with different materials to achieve an accurate flow rate. The usage of a smart syringe pump for dental intravenous sedative administration is successful (Seo & Lee, 2016). This pump is successful by utilizing its features and safety is also ensured. Further research based on the mechanism of wireless smart pumps, employment of stepper motors, brushless, brushed micromotors have been concentrated (De Cristofaro et al., 2010), (Islam et al., 2019). In such researches, the control system aspect of the rotary motion, position, flow control for the different types of pump control is focused (Goyal et al., 2020).

The closed-loop drug delivery with a fully automated system enables the treatment for diabetes, gastrointestinal disease, cancer with chemotherapy, ailments in cardiac, disorders in neurology, and administration of anaesthesia (Sharma et al., 2021), (Lee et al., 2012). The depth of anaesthesia administration is very important in patient-controlled analgesia which is controlled using control strategies. The fully automated closed loop control system for smart pumps in MCPS is the focus of this work. The usage of smart drug library updates in wireless drug delivery devices is implemented with all the parameters of the infusion pump and its pumping mechanism (Hsu et al., 2019). The parameters such as viscosity, flow rate, and pressure are estimated which influence the performance (Elenkov et al., 2020). Apart from these smart pumps, utilization of blood pumps in cardiac assist device, the dialyzer is prominent. The estimation of blood flow rate and its corresponding pressure difference is a key component.

BACKGROUND

Medication errors might cause serious impact with patients life. The usage of smart infusion pumps architecture is being developed in countries like India. The medication protocols, dosage error reduction with the employment of suitable hardware and software leads to safe medication. The concept of MCPS in wireless/wired networking for smart infusion devices has to be enhanced to improvise the performance of the system. Incorporation of closed loop control to reduce errors, predicting the required flow rate as per the speed of the pump with the aid of a smart drug library enhancement has been proposed in this chapter. In order to achieve this closed loop MCPS architecture for medical pump (infusion pump) has been discussed in detail.

MAIN FOCUS OF THE CHAPTER

In this chapter detail on architecture of wireless drug delivery devices, concepts about the usage of the device based on closed loop control system, remote monitoring based on the prediction of the medical pump actuation, and problems associated has been discussed. The architecture proposed is needed for the current covid-19 situation as FDA released in April 2020 that the usage of wireless smart infusion pumps will be one of the solutions for social distancing. The concept brings on the scope for reducing the delay in infusion of the drug, fluid to the patients by predicting and controlling the flow rate in smart medical pumps. Different machine learning algorithms can be employed for the prediction of pump speed and can be verified as per the manufacturer recommendations for the implementation. The issues that can be focused by using the proposed architecture with smart drug library are reducing medication error by predicting the medical pump speed with fast induction of the drug or the fluid to the delivered. Currently the smart drug libraries are built with dosage, minimum flow rate, maximum flow rate, soft alarm and hard alarm limits. Apart from this the medical pump speed for different pump actuation for the corresponding drug based on the infusion protocol has to be included. In this chapter the focus is towards proposing the architecture, control algorithms and prediction methods for medical pump.

MCPS Architecture for Smart Drug Delivery Device

MCPS is the combination of medical devices' physical system modelling and communication of sensor, data acquired from the patient to the external server for data processing. The processing is performed automatically by physicians, nurses. In this chapter, an overall architecture for a medical pump that can be used for infusion of drugs, fluid, insulin in a cyber environment is considered. The MCPS architecture is shown in figure1. The medical pump such as the smart infusion pump is connected to the patient. The smart pumps are used for continuous, intravenous, and subcutaneous infusion of the fluid, drug. These pumps are designed with a microcontroller which has to be preprogramed as per the smart drug library, electronic interfaces, sensors, actuators, and wireless transceivers. The smart drug library will have the information regarding the drug, its dosage requirement, hard & soft alarm limit, pump flow rate, drop and drip rate, time duration of infusion (Imhoff et al., 2009). The desired drug related information will be provided to the infusion pump by the nurses or clinicians from the Nurse's station. Further, it will be processed with the help of the processors of the pump, remote workstations, and accordingly drug infusion will take place. Usage of the smart drug library by the pump is facilitated by the remote pump server. The drug infusion and control of the pump are completely monitored, predicted in the pump server which is accessed by the Nurse's station.

Figure 1. MCPS architecture of medical pump

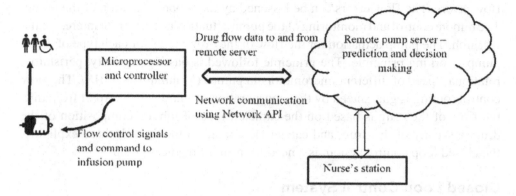

The accurate delivery of the dosage of the drug has to be monitored by the remotely located Nurses' station by the nurse or clinician. The smart pumps have to be modelled based on the pharmacokinetic, pharmacodynamic properties. Based on these properties the drug concentration will be determined. The input is provided to the entire smart pumps are with the aid of smart drug library settings. The desired information will be furnished to the preprogramed microcontroller which is further processed based on the control algorithms as required. Upon bolus request, drug infusion will take place, and later the diffusion dynamics will be analysed by the remote pump server. In this case, the remote pump server has to coordinate with the smart pump for controlling parameters such as drug concentration, infusion flow rate, drop rate, amount of drug or fluid availability in the reservoir, and speed of the smart pump. In a smart infusion pump, the mechanism of actuation and control of the flow of the fluid occurs as per the drug library. The pump actuation can be controlled by the remote pump server hence the error, delay in drug infusion will be minimized. To perform this, closed loop control and prediction methods have to be used for a smart infusion pump.

Smart Pumps and Infusion

Smart pumps are typical drug delivery devices that aid in the infusion of different fluids and drugs. Different types of infusion devices are available that include syringe, gravity, volumetric, elastomeric pumps (Masci et al., 2013). In recent years the drug delivery devices are developed as smart pumps to improve safe medication and reduced errors. The infusion can be primary and secondary type. In the primary type, the errors are minimum in terms of drug alerts and with tubing system when compared to the secondary type. In the case of secondary type dead volume, lag time occurs and the reduction of the dead volume and lag time leads to minimization of flow errors. The flow errors can be lessened by the proper actuation of the pump. The remote control and monitoring of the pump actuation is the current interest of the research. The pump actuation for the flow of the drug varies for each type of smart pumps working principle. The principle followed is based on gravity, peristaltic, rotational speed of different micromotors in pumps (Mahmut UN, 2018). The flow control routing is guaranteed by the incorporation of microvalves. Apart from this, the flow of the drug is based on the catheter, type of tubing, composition of the drug, viscosity of the drug, and carrier flow rate. To monitor all these explicitly, the closed loop control system is a need for a smart medical pump.

Closed Loop Control System

The control system concepts are indeed a requirement for the accurate functioning of the medical devices and it has to be implemented in the microprocessors of the smart pumps. The closed loop control system of the smart pump is given in figure 2. The integration of fuzzy logic, artificial neural network, machine learning algorithms including classification and prediction algorithms with the closed loop smart pump systems for drug delivery has brought different medical device applications closely toward a fully automated intelligent healthcare environment. The closed loop control system smart pump has sensors, infusion pump controller with pump delivery mechanism, drug reservoir, interface to remotely connected to nurses' station, and control algorithms. The feedback control-based smart pumps are widely used for insulin pumps, anaesthesia infusion pumps, cardiac devices, defibrillators, chemotherapy devices. The main challenge in this system is an efficient, accurate, and precise flow of the drug. The controlling of the flow parameter has to be handled carefully by the control algorithms as there will be a presence of noise disturbance and nervousness for a patient (Kim et al., 2017).

The control algorithm that is suitable for these scenarios are optimized or hybrid tuned Proportional Integral Derivative (PID) controller, Model Predictive Controller (MPC) and optimal control algorithms such as Linear Quadratic Regulator (LQR) (Augusto et al., 2013). Through these techniques, the precise flow can be delivered to the patient by regulating the speed of the smart pump. Usage of a smart drug library is essential to achieve this. Before performing the regulation of the fluid flow, the prediction of the flow of the fluid has to performed using several prediction algorithms. The information that will be available in the smart drug library is drug name, infusion flow rate, dosage (posology) based on the requirement like dose concentration, continuous and bolus, time of infusion, soft and hard alert limits, category of infusion whether it is continuous, intravenous and purpose such as for anaesthetic, cardiac etc (Hei et al., 2015). Practically, the challenge is dose error reduction. The error in the smart pumps occurs due to IV tube setting, carrier flow, the physical design of the infusion pump, and time taken for drug administration. The usage of the remote server in wireless environment aids in the reduction of these factors by utilizing predictive algorithms.

Figure 2. Closed loop control system for smart pump

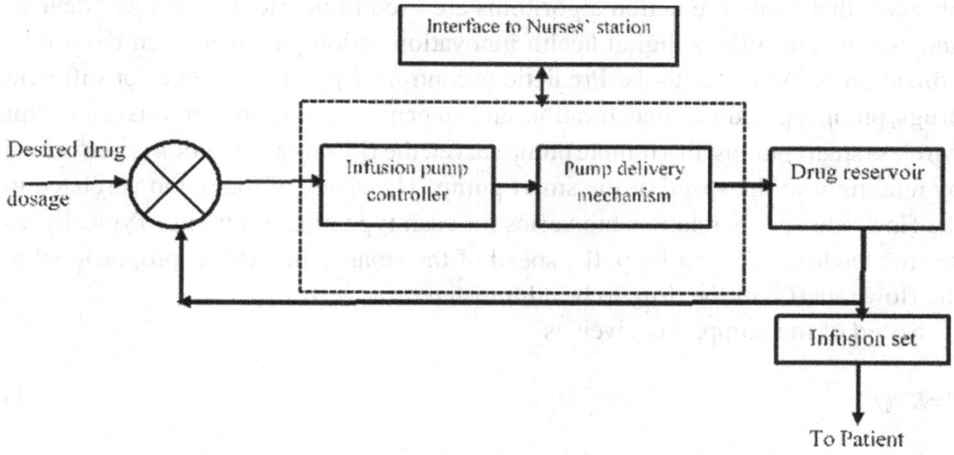

Pump Server - Prediction and Control of Flow Rate

In the proposed MCPS architecture of smart pumps, a pump server is very important to achieve the reduction of errors in drug infusion. The complete smart drug delivery database will be stored in the pump server. This is accessed by the clinicians, nurses, and caregivers who can view the condition of the patient. In the proposed architecture, the pump server has the following attributes in its drug delivery dataset.

The Attributes are:

- Drug dosage
- Drug concentration
- Carrier flow
- Hard and soft alarm limit
- Drip rate
- Infusion flow rate
- Type of smart pump
- Pump speed
- Lag time

- Dead volume

The mentioned attributes are needed to regulate the flow of the drug infused by reducing the delay with the aid of lag time, dead volume, and pump speed. The pump speed will be determined by the type of smart pump. The pump types can be a syringe, peristaltic, large volume pumps, etc. The flow and pump speed regulation can be attained by employing efficient prediction methods. From literature, it is an observer that many prediction algorithms are used in the field of medical devices and health care. FDA's digital health innovation action plan has given rise to the utilization of AI-based tools. Prediction, control of pump flow rate for different drugs, pump types, dose concentration, and other associated parameters is critical for wireless smart pumps. In a remote pump server, the flow rate regulation is performed by relating it to the speed of the smart pump. The speed of the pump is related to the flow rate and its relationship varies for each type of smart pump. Typically, as per the feedback control loop, the speed of the smart pump (Θ) is proportional to the flow rate (Q) of the drug to be administered.

Speed of the pump, θ is given as

$$\theta = K*Q \tag{1}$$

The flow rate and drug are administered for each pump as given below:

syringe pumps: The syringe pumps are widely designed with stepper motors. In this case, Q is proportional to the frequency of PWM which imposes the stepper motor speed, where d_{int} is the inner diameter, P_m is the pitch thread rod, n is the step angle (Ayasun & Karbeyaz, 2008).

$$Q = d_{int} P_m F_{pwm} n/360° \tag{2}$$

Peristaltic pumps:

In the peristaltic pump, it is followed as given in equation 1, and the proportionality constant changes as per the electric motor associated in the pump (Batista et al., 2019).

Continuous infusion pump:

These pumps are associated with electric motors, and the pump axle speed varies based on gear head and revolution, it is determined as

Max pump axle speed = $Q*rev/ml$ % 60 min/hr

In general, the drug dosage in the infusion pump mechanism is found as:

$$\text{Dose (mg)} = (\theta/2\pi)a*\pi r^2 \, d \tag{3}$$

Where θ is angular position, r is the radius of the injector and d is the drug concentration. If the drug dose in mg is known, the infusion flow rate can be calculated. In the pump server, the information regarding the nursing calculations should be programmed and hence the infusion flow rate and its corresponding speed can be identified.

In, rotary blood pumps, Q is related to the torque and rotational speed of the motor n and the motor torque τ.

$$Q \propto n \propto \tau^2 \tag{4}$$

These speeds will be calculated, predicted for different doses, infusion flow rate, and flow regulation are performed by the pump server (Hijikata et al., 2015). The database in the pump server can be designed globally for different types of smart pumps and further the speed can also be predicted in the pump server.

SOLUTIONS AND RECOMMENDATIONS

In this proposed architecture, the drug dose information has been formulated from the electronics Medical Compendium (eMC) website. The database of each drug for different age groups, its dose, infusion flowrate has been formed. The smart drug database is placed in the remote pump server. In the nurses' station, a user interface will be available to provide information about the dosage details, age of the patient, duration of infusion, type of infusion, carrier flow, primary infusion, secondary infusion, and type of the pump. As per these inputs, the data stored in the pump server is verified for its corresponding flow rate and prediction of the pump speed will be computed as per the type of prediction techniques implemented in the pump server. To ensure the accurate infusion to the patient, the smart drug library in this proposed work will be updated with the hardware details of the pump, its speed based on the revolutions, its corresponding flowrate, and further, the infusion rate is related to the dose and its concentration. Once the prediction is accomplished, the related resultant will be sent to the pump's microcontroller, and the flow regulation is achieved. The closed loop control in the smart pump is performed by communicating with the pump server and the smart pump controller which is connected to the patient through an infusion interface. Appropriate selection of control strategies has to be devised for the implementation (Alamelu & Mythili, n.d.).

Communication Techniques Adopted

From the remote pump server to the smart pump controller, different communication techniques can be followed. The entire model is proposed in a hybrid model which can be of wired or wireless communication. The preferred communication model using network API is client-server communication and publisher-subscriber communication. In the proposed model of MCPS publisher-subscriber is preferred for its functional advantages. To provide energy-efficient scenarios in MCPS of smart pumps, mobile agents can be implemented so energy-efficient communication can be achieved.

Prediction Technique

The smart drug library dataset need not be perfect linear and hence suitable classification and regression analysis should be implemented. The pump server performs computation based on machine learning regression techniques that provide less prediction accuracy. The regression model suitable for this study is Principal Component analysis Regression (PCR), Support Vector Machines (SVM), Gaussian Process Regression (GPR), Regression trees.

- PCR is a hybrid model with principal component analysis with regression. PCR is a hybrid technique that uses the combination of PCA and Linear regression. This hybrid model is carried out for the dataset when the independent variables are collinear. To overcome this, PCA is performed on the dataset, the principal components are stores and utilized to predict the values based on linear regression (Li et al., 2018).
- SVM is a widely used regression technique for linear and non-linear data. It incorporates nonlinear mapping to convert the dataset to be trained to the higher dimensions. The data separation is performed based on the hyperplane. SVM is a widely used classifier, as well as a regression model for prediction. The training and testing speed is improvised further the prediction accuracy is better. For few applications, a Bayesian optimizer can be used along with SVM to obtain the least mean square error value for certain models. The hybrid combination is suitable for the pump server architecture proposed as different classes of pumps, dosage, flow rate exists.
- GPR is a nonparametric regression model used widely for the prediction of the nonlinear dataset based on the probability distribution function to fit the data. GPR utilizes kernel functions, gram matrix and estimates the uncertain output. The benefit is the algorithm is made available for hyperparameter learning with the help of the covariance function. The efficiency of classification

and prediction is better in this model based on statistical parameters such as coefficient of determination R^2, root mean square error.

Apart from these regression techniques, the classic techniques such as Adaptive Neuro Fuzzy Inference System with different membership functions, Artificial Neural Networks can be used widely.

RESULTS AND DISCUSSION

In this proposed architecture, performance evaluation results for SVM with gaussian kernel has been shown for its statistical significance. The dataset created for wireless medical pump has been formulated for a set of drug data with its infusion flow rate and medical pump speed. The drug data used for continuous infusion has been taken. Further, in this study, the pump speed based on geared medical pump has been considered and verified for the statistical performance. The mean square error, R^2 values has been found to be 0.136 and 0.99 for geared type medical pump. The minimum error has been achieved for the SVM with gaussian kernel compared with other regression model. On analysis, the other models have resulted with higher error rate. It is found that medication error reduction can be achieved by analysing the prediction of medical pump speed using appropriate regression technique. The residual analysis results and prediction responses are shown in figure 3(a), 3(b)

Figure 3. (a) Residual response for SVM 3(b) Prediction response

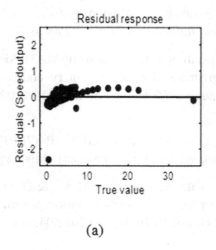
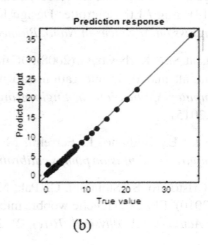

(a)

(b)

CONCLUSION

Recent technological advancements in the field of machine learning and cyber physical systems are dominating medical devices. The current covid19 situation requires remote monitoring in the health care sector. The proposed architecture on the smart medical pump in the medical cyber physical system will cater to the current situation. The nursing station which is located remotely will aid the caretakers, clinicians, nurses to monitor the patient's health. The pump server will perform the required pump control operation for the smart pump used for the infusion of the drug and fluid based on suitable prediction techniques. As per the smart pump architecture, once the prediction of the speed of the pump flow is determined for the drug concentration, the corresponding data will be transferred using network API to the smart pump processor. The desired flowrate will be provided to the microcontroller and thereby using suitable optimal control algorithms, the control strategy for the infusion pump flow will be implemented and desired infusion of the fluid is achieved with minimum delay for the patient. The smart pump architecture thus proposed with smart drug library assist in performing accurate infusion to the patients with reduced errors with minimum delay in the cyber environment.

REFERENCES

Alamelu, J. V., & Mythili, A. (n.d.). Smart infusion pump control – The control system perspective. Computational Intelligence in Healthcare, 199-211.

Augusto, J., Barreiros, L., Roberto, J., De Souza, B., Fernandes, G., & Junior, B. (2013). Lqg / Ltr Controller Design for an Anaesthesia Infusion System. *World Congress on Advances in Nano, Biomechanics, Robotics and Energy Research.*

Ayasun, S., & Karbeyaz, G. (2008). DC motor speed control methods using MATLAB/ Simulink and their integration into undergraduate electric machinery courses. *Computer Applications in Engineering Education*, *15*(4), 347–354. doi:10.1002/ cae.20151

Batista, E., Godinho, I., Ferreira, M. do C., Furtado, A., & Lucas, P. (2019). *Comparison of infusion pumps calibration methods.* Institute of Physics Publishing.

De Cristofaro, S., Stefanini, C., Pak, N. N., Susilo, E., Carrozza, M. C., & Dario, P. (2010). Electromagnetic wobble micromotor for microrobots actuation. *Sensors and Actuators. A, Physical*, *161*(1–2), 234–244. doi:10.1016/j.sna.2010.04.028

Elenkov, M., Ecker, P., Lukitsch, B., Janeczek, C., Harasek, M., & Gföhler, M. (2020). Estimation methods for viscosity, flow rate and pressure from pump-motor assembly parameters. *Sensors (Switzerland)*, *20*(5), 1451. Advance online publication. doi:10.339020051451 PMID:32155844

Gardašević, G., Katzis, K., Bajić, D., & Berbakov, L. (2020). Emerging wireless sensor networks and internet of things technologies—Foundations of smart healthcare. *Sensors (Switzerland)*, *20*(13), 1–30. doi:10.339020133619 PMID:32605071

Goyal, M., Saurav, K., Tiwari, G., Rege, A., & Saxena, A. (2020). IV (Intravenous) Tube Flow Control Device with IOT. *2020 IEEE International Students' Conference on Electrical, Electronics and Computer Science, SCEECS 2020*, 4–7. 10.1109/SCEECS48394.2020.53

Haque, S. A., Aziz, S. M., & Rahman, M. (2014). Review of cyber-physical system in healthcare. *International Journal of Distributed Sensor Networks*, *2014*(4), 217415. Advance online publication. doi:10.1155/2014/217415

Hei, X., Du, X., Lin, S., Lee, I., & Sokolsky, O. (2015). Patient Infusion Pattern based Access Control Schemes for Wireless Insulin Pump System. *IEEE Transactions on Parallel and Distributed Systems*, *26*(11), 3108–3121. doi:10.1109/TPDS.2014.2370045

Hijikata, W., Rao, J., Abe, S., Takatani, S., & Shinshi, T. (2015). Estimating flow rate using the motor torque in a rotary blood pump. *Sensors and Materials*, *27*(4), 297–308. doi:10.18494/SAM.2015.1068

Hsu, K. Y., DeLaurentis, P., Yih, Y., & Bitan, Y. (2019). Tracking the Progress of Wireless Infusion Pump Drug Library Updates– A Data-Driven Analysis of Pump Update Delays. *Journal of Medical Systems*, *43*(3), 75. Advance online publication. doi:10.100710916-019-1189-5 PMID:30756252

Imhoff, M., Kuhls, S., Gather, U., & Fried, R. (2009). Smart alarms from medical devices in the OR and ICU. In Best Practice and Research: Clinical Anaesthesiology (Vol. 23, Issue 1, pp. 39–50). doi:10.1016/j.bpa.2008.07.008

Islam, M. R., Zahid Rusho, R., & Rabiul Islam, S. M. (2019). Design and implementation of low cost smart syringe pump for telemedicine and healthcare. *1st International Conference on Robotics, Electrical and Signal Processing Techniques, ICREST 2019*, 440–444. 10.1109/ICREST.2019.8644373

Kanjee, M. R., & Liu, H. (2016). Authentication and key relay in medical cyber-physical systems. In Security and Communication Networks (Vol. 9, Issue 9, pp. 874–885). doi:10.1002ec.1009

Kim, U. R., Peterfreund, R. A., & Lovich, M. A. (2017). Drug infusion systems: Technologies, performance, and pitfalls. *Anesthesia and Analgesia, 124*(5), 1493–1505. doi:10.1213/ANE.0000000000001707 PMID:28212219

Kumar, M. A., Vimala, R., & Britto, K. R. A. (2019). A cognitive technology based healthcare monitoring system and medical data transmission. In Measurement: Journal of the International Measurement Confederation (Vol. 146, pp. 322–332). doi:10.1016/j.measurement.2019.03.017

Lee, I., Sokolsky, O., Chen, S., Hatcliff, J., Jee, E., Kim, B., King, A., Mullen-Fortino, M., Park, S., Roederer, A., & Venkatasubramanian, K. K. (2012). Challenges and Research Directions in Medical Cyber-Physical Systems. *Proceedings of the IEEE, 100*(1), 75–90. doi:10.1109/JPROC.2011.2165270

Li, Y., Zhang, Y., & Liu, T. (2018). Analysis of Principal Component Regression Equations of Air Transportation and Local Economy: Taking Tianjin as an Example. *Theoretical Economics Letters, 08*(10), 1830–1839. doi:10.4236/tel.2018.810120

Ly, T. T., Layne, J. E., Huyett, L. M., Nazzaro, D., & O'Connor, J. B. (2019). Novel Bluetooth-Enabled Tubeless Insulin Pump: Innovating Pump Therapy for Patients in the Digital Age. *Journal of Diabetes Science and Technology, 13*(1), 20–26. doi:10.1177/1932296818798836 PMID:30239214

Mahmut, U. N. (2018). Control System Design of Syringe Infusion Pump and MATLAB Simulations. *International Journal of Scientific Research, 7*(7), 6. doi:10.21275/ART20183120

Mao, G., Wu, L., Fu, Y., Chen, Z., Natani, S., Gou, Z., Ruan, X., & Qu, S. (2018). Design and Characterization of a Soft Dielectric Elastomer Peristaltic Pump Driven by Electromechanical Load. *IEEE/ASME Transactions on Mechatronics, 23*(5), 2132–2143. doi:10.1109/TMECH.2018.2864252

Masci, P., Ayoub, A., Curzon, P., Lee, I., Sokolsky, O., & Thimbleby, H. (2013). Model-based development of the generic PCA infusion pump user interface prototype in PVS. Lecture Notes in Computer Science, 8153, 228–240. doi:10.1007/978-3-642-40793-2_21

Masci, P., Zhang, Y., Jones, P., Thimbleby, H., & Curzon, P. (2014). A generic user interface architecture for analyzing use hazards in infusion pump software. *OpenAccess Series in Informatics, 36*, 1–14. doi:10.4230/OASIcs.MCPS.2014.1

Park, Y., Son, Y., Shin, H., Kim, D., & Kim, Y. (2016). This ain't your dose: Sensor spoofing attack on medical infusion pump. *10th USENIX Workshop on Offensive Technologies, WOOT 2016.*

Percival, J., McGregor, C., Percival, N., Kamaleswaran, R., & Tuuha, S. (2010). A framework for nursing documentation enabling integration with HER and real-time patient monitoring. *Proceedings - IEEE Symposium on Computer-Based Medical Systems*, 468–473. 10.1109/CBMS.2010.6042690

Riurean, S., Antipova, T., Rocha, Á., Leba, M., & Ionica, A. (2019). VLC, OCC, IR and LiFi Reliable Optical Wireless Technologies to be Embedded in Medical Facilities and Medical Devices. *Journal of Medical Systems*, *43*(10), 308. Advance online publication. doi:10.100710916-019-1434-y PMID:31432270

Seifert, D., & Rez, H. (2016). A security analysis of cyber-physical systems architecture for healthcare. *Computers*, *5*(4), 27. Advance online publication. doi:10.3390/computers5040027

Seo, K.-S., & Lee, K. (2016). Smart syringe pumps for drug infusion during dental intravenous sedation. *Journal of Dental Anesthesia and Pain Medicine*, *16*(3), 165. doi:10.17245/jdapm.2016.16.3.165 PMID:28884149

Sharma, R., Singh, D., Gaur, P., & Joshi, D. (2021). Intelligent automated drug administration and therapy: Future of healthcare. *Drug Delivery and Translational Research*, *0123456789*(5), 1878–1902. Advance online publication. doi:10.100713346-020-00876-4 PMID:33447941

Silva, L. C., Almeida, H. O., Perkusich, A., & Perkusich, M. (2015). A model-based approach to support validation of medical cyber-physical systems. *Sensors (Switzerland)*, *15*(11), 27625–27670. doi:10.3390151127625 PMID:26528982

Chapter 12
Predictive Analytics for Healthcare

Pushpalatha M. N.
Ramaiah Institute of Technology, India

Parkavi A.
M.S. Ramaiah Institute of Technology, India

Sini Anna Alex
M.S. Ramaiah Institute of Technology, India

ABSTRACT

The healthcare scheme in India has a lot of differences between rural and urban areas in terms of quality along with changes in private and public healthcare systems. The healthcare system is massive in India and full of inconsistencies and complexities like the other countries. Predictive analytics will help to improve the healthcare systems by providing valuable insight in healthcare. A huge amount of different data sets is generated because of the digitization of healthcare. This digitization allows us to use predictive analytics for better patient outcomes. Predictive analytics is utilized in decision-making activities and prediction making about the future events which are unknown. In this chapter, a brief overview of the Indian healthcare systems is given, along with data representations, challenges, issues, and risks associated with applying predictive analytics in healthcare and case studies with respect to regression and classification models.

DOI: 10.4018/978-1-7998-8161-2.ch012

INTRODUCTION

India's government has come up with lot of schemes and policies after the independence for health care. Huge differences in terms of quality of medical facilities in India, we see with respect to urban and rural areas. Shortage of medical doctors is seen in rural areas. Technical facilities and administration is offered by the central government, education related to health and services for healthcare is provided by state government. More number of people opt for treatment from private sectors, because of lack of facilities in public health care system. The research in health care domain helps the health care system in predominate way. There are more researchers involved in health care related research studies. Research in health care domain leads to evolution in mankind. The new policies and schemes are introduced by governments, for supporting poor people health care because of the research in health care domain (Rao, Radhika, & Abdul, 2014).

Predictive analytics in health care domain helps to predict the various diseases infliction among people in advance. Accordingly, government can form the schemes and policies for the betterment of public of their nations. The research related to representation, collection and maintenance of healthcare data improved the quality of medical treatments and recovery for patients. Predictive analytics improved the accessibility of resources, optimization of cost utility and manpower and improvising the patient treatments. Predictive analytics contributes to health care sectors man power, methodologies and technology (Andrew Bartley).

In this chapter, how predictive analytics is contributing to the field of health care domain is discussed.

BACK GROUND

Health care has practiced evidence-based and ethical clinical standards in research. Big data analytics over medical field data, will improve the services, quality, treatments and early detection of diseases. Big data analytics helps in improving the survival rates of patients, diagnosing test reports and diseases. Decision tree kind of machine learning algorithms helps is classifying patients' records based on their basic parameters collected for diagnosing chronic. Big data analytics gives scope for more amounts of predictions for staffs in medical domain for treating the patients as well as in improving the self-care of patients' diseases (Boukenze, Mousannif, & Haqiq, 2016).

Big data given a significant scope for improvising the applications for healthcare systems by providing electronic health records. It is used widely now to deal with huge data for analysis. The healthcare decisions can be improved by using data mining and predictive analytics tools. Knowledge discovery used in the big data helps in improving the services provide by heath care systems. The assessment and synthesis of information uses some frameworks from data analysis model (Sayantan Khanra, 2020).

Predictive analytics helps to look into the hidden details of medical data of patients and extract useful information from them. Machine learning implications in health care involves many major tasks like data gathering, data pre-processing, data exploration, designing data analytical model and training with data, validating the model and improvising the model. ML models for health care can be designed using supervised or unsupervised algorithms. In supervised learning the input data parameters and their responsive output will be used for training the data analytical model for predicting unknown values in future. Using unsupervised learning, the data analytical model will be designed to get the summarised result of data in a descriptive manner considering all features of data. Predictive analytics are used in spotting diseases like heart diseases, cancers, diabetics, asthma, TB, BP, thyroid etc. The ML algorithms like Naïve bayes, neural networks, decision tree algorithms are used for predicting heart diseases. The CART method, SVM classification and RBF network can be used to predict diabetic diseases. ANN and SVM methods are proved by researchers that they are useful in predicting cancer kind of diseases with high accuracy (Nithya & Ilango, 2017).

Predictive modelling for health care system on real data helps the technology to achieve patients experiences to enhance, aim on improving the outcomes and controlling the cost on healthcare. Validation, Verification and development of predictive analysis model for health care starts the way of accessing the success of analysis of clinical data. Integrating electronic health care predictive analytics (e-HPA) into the work flow, testing e-HPA in a patient population, and disseminating e-HPA across health care systems on a large scale requires a huge workforce. Input is needed from policy makers, health care executives, researchers, and practitioners as the field evolves. The work focus on some challenges of implementing e-HPA, including the need to ensure patients' privacy, establish a health system monitoring team to oversee implementation, incorporate predictive analytics into medical education, and make sure that electronic systems should not be given a chance to replace or crowd out decision making by physicians and patients. (Amarasingham R., 2014).

(Md Saiful Islam, 2018)The work describes a suggestive review method and provides an overall view of analysis on healthcare and information gathering. The supportive approach followed in the analysis model stating the methodological process and comprehending the output as analytics. This work also shown light on significant recommendations for the areas including integration of knowledge based data, ways to defend prediction error, and integration of predictive models in real time working environments.

Using predictive analytics, the quality of treatment can be improved, cost of treatment can be reduced and various other goals can be achieved. Even though, having lot of benefits of using predictive analytics in healthcare, achieving goals is not easy. Lot of challenges will come along the way such as data collection and its quality, issues related to management, data standards development, concerns related with privacy etc (Michael J. Ward, 2014).

(Patil, B. M., Joshi, R. C., Toshniwal, D., & Biradar, S, 2011) authors built model using burn patients' data such as, on eight different parts of part how much percentage of burn happened, sex, age. The build model was used for predicting the survivability rate of burn patient. Model was build using different machine learning techniques such as back propagation, Naïve bayes, SVM and Decision tree. Authors concluded that Naïve bayes algorithm gives highest accuracy of 97.78% over other algorithms for the real hospital data set.

The Significance of Predictive Analytics in Health Care

Analysis in healthcare help in understanding the wide way of possibilities of prediction, and the acknowledgment will be benefitted. This will include operational management and various ways to improve and advance the enhancement of accuracy to validate the potential risk factors for public health.

Efficiencies for Operational Management

Predictive analytics provides the advancement of operational efficacy (Wazurkar, Bhadoria, & Dhananjai Bajpai, 2019.). Big data and predictive analytics are playing a major role in nowadays day to day activities based on health care organizations' business intelligence strategies. Real time advertising is relatively fresh idea but will help in providing new insights into information and be used to dynamically control the algorithms of prediction in line with new inventions and ideas. Optimization can be obtained by visualizing and utilizing the historical information available, overflow data from nearby facilities, populated information, demographic data, reportable diseases, and seasonal patterns of diseases spreading across in a predictive analytics model.

Operational management (Wazurkar, Bhadoria, & Dhananjai Bajpai, 2019.) benefit as the technical advancement to analyze weather properties such as readings of temperature, and calendar variables to forecast patients seeking care. Estimation of the volume of walk-in patients that a facility can handle, allowing them to recruit and roster staff accordingly, helping optimize operations.

Risk Stratification (Rainer, 2020) assists in categorizing medical workflow, minimizing system waste and creating financially efficient population management.

Simulation allows medical advisors and administrators a good way into the provisional outcomes of a given combination of events. Mapping leverages GIS mapping of health care facilities, patient disease burden and accountable care values. Mapping is an effective visual approach to analytics and decision making. When comes to predictive analytics, the data is tied directly to appropriate and timely decisions. For predictive analytic to be successful in healthcare the most important characteristics required are timely, actionable and role specific. Health catalyst normally uses risk scores, what-if scenarios and geo spatial analysis to support clinical decisions.

Predictive models access in the recruitment and analysis of the competencies of the selected new employees. With the prioritized demand for aging population care services, health care organizations will be in high pressure, and specially caring agencies for aged people, the employee should be trained efficiently to meet the level of competency and to develop extra ordinary skill set to handle the societal model of working by giving support to ageing population.

Heath Care in the Digital Era

The internet and the smart phone are the two factors allow the world to have access to a huge repository of information and discovery of knowledge at their fingertips. These have transformed companies, providing the most commented and old methods of handling health care, which is undergoing a sudden change. This way of the adoption of technology in the health care sector has had a surprising effect on the positive impact on medical methodologies along with the processes in which experts engage in health care.

Some of the key milestones include the digitization of the patient records related to health, access to big data and storage in the cloud, advanced software, and advanced technology supporting mobile applications. All these milestones have showcased various benefits in the health care sector, providing an ease of workflow, faster access to data, lower health care costs, enhanced public health, and the overall advancement for a better life.

Data Representation

Electronic Healthcare Records (EHRs) are the mostly used electronic format for storing health related information such as patient medical history, results of laboratory, clinical findings etc. The information in EHR may exist either as in the form of unstructured i.e., free-text sentence or structured format i.e., in distinct columns. Notes written by doctors' and images are examples unstructured healthcare data. Radiology images and health claim data are other common healthcare data. Predictive analytics will help to save lives by providing better decision in treatments, which is the main purpose of healthcare.

CHALLENGES, ISSUES AND RISKS

Management Issues

The main objective of predictive analytics in healthcare to improve the outcomes of patient. Different stakeholders such as doctors, nurses, patient and other staffs etc. in the healthcare. Empowering all the stakeholders is very important for improving transparency and quality in healthcare predictive analytics.

Key challenge present in management is lack of skilled professional in the healthcare. The person should have strong mathematics and analytical skill with computing apart the domain knowledge of healthcare.

Another issues which is related in management is about measuring the result of predictive analytics models on the electronic data. Whether they improve the health or reduce cost. For measuring the cost or benefit what metrics should be used there are no answers.

Another challenge is with respect to data standardization, data quality may not improve with the accuracy of electronic data. Poor data quality result in poor analysis which in terms causes risks associated with any actions taken out of analysis.

Data Quality and Data Collection

The quality of data is very important in the healthcare predictive analytics. The result whatever is produced is mainly depends on the data quality. Most of the time the Healthcare data is not available in electronic format and cost of storing information in electronic format is very high. The needed healthcare data is not present in one location, but spread across different location. The data should be combined in one location, before applying predictive analytics. Even though, data is available in electronic format and collected it. Still the outcome cannot be achieved because of incomplete data.

High quality data collection is very important to get good result. Quality of data and consistency may damage when lot of data is collected i.e., when there is burden exist (Payne, Bettman, & Johnson, 1993) there is connection between data collection and data quality. Collection of high quality data does not happen automatically in most of cases. It is collected manually by human. Important details of patient should be collected during visit to the hospital without disturbing the nurses and doctors work.

Minimal high quality data sets will good result than the large poor quality data sets. That's why, it is required to collect the high quality minimal data sets. When patient visits the hospital that time details of the patient is entered into system through data entry. Sometimes, data entry may take more time that affects the patient flow. In term it results poor satisfaction. Avoiding the above situation, many hospitals allow for the patient to enter their details in the patient website or they provide tablets or systems to patient in the waiting room to enter their data. Which saves lot of time and it allows doctors to use the details from portal instead of spending time to enter data in portal.

One more challenge present in patient data entry is that those entries are separated from the clinician's data entry. Clinician still need to enter the same details through interfaces, even after patients enter their data through the portal. Hence, there should be care taken when using that data in predictive analytics. Data entered by patient and clinician need to be properly combined before applying the predictive analytics techniques on it.

Capturing data that is clean, complete, accurate, and formatted correctly for use in multiple systems is an ongoing battle for organizations, many of which aren't on the winning side of the conflict is one of the major concern while dealing with data.

Data cleaning, also represented as cleansing or scrubbing ensures that datasets are accurate, correct, consistent, relevant, and not corrupted in any way. The volume of healthcare data grows exponentially; some providers are no longer able to manage the costs. Without the use of predictive analytics, along with data integration and security the shift from fee-for-service to value-based care, this may not be possible sometimes. Being able to understand a healthcare systems current state is a must for being able to forecast a desired future state and associated plan to achieve the process. Some of the major concerns noticed are the possibility to get in front of healthcare consumer trends and to support health initiatives, supporting the need of the patients by efficiently caring them and thereby reduces the risk of the individual getting hospital admissions again and again, anticipate official needs. Finally, predictive analytics in healthcare is mostly focussing on the data translation and the implementation of science into practicality thereby helping various organizations solving the complex healthcare and business problem with cost efficient management.

Issues Involved in Predicting the Medical Cost

Issues involved in analysing the cost using regression models are (Dario Gregori, 2011):

1. Asymmetric nature of distribution with respect to less number of subjects involved in expensive medical costs compared to the remaining population.

2.   Enormous amount of medications done without cost involvement.
3.   The failure rate of patients in censored observations lead to biased predictions of cost.
4.   Differentiation in cost of healthcare and treatments given by different health care service providers.

A risk emerging (Rainer, 2020) for predictive analytics supports the centralization of information which presents a tedious risk in terms of security and integrity of the information. With the support of the increasing amount of data which is often stored in the cloud or can be accessible via the internet, there is the persistent threat of hacking from individuals with malicious intent. While considering the ethical issues, the suitable role played by cloud technology will be mapped with the overall outcome. In this article, we will be focussing on the issues related to the security of the data which will be mapped to another time.

Data Privacy and Data Security

Some of the issues in data security are changes in health information and electronic health records, user error in adopting the technology, adoption of cloud and mobile technology in healthcare and outdated technology in hospitals.

In Data privacy new sources of risk are analysed. Privacy pressures, moral hazard and human intervention, impact on decision making process, lack of regulation all are the disruptive factors affecting data privacy. When dealing with data privacy, data security is a major concern. The evaluation methods have been divided into four groups, according to which evaluation problem they solve;

- Algorithm-dependent classifier evaluation.
- Algorithm-independent classifier evaluation.
- Classifier-independent algorithm evaluation.
- Classifier-dependent algorithm evaluation.

DATA MANAGEMENT OF HEALTHCARE DATA ACCESS CONTROL

Access controls (Wazurkar, Bhadoria, & Dhananjai Bajpai, 2019.) allows the healthcare organization to efficiently organize and manage their information and can take a decision the access permission of the user. Access controls help to authenticate the identity of the user, which will help in guaranteeing that users individuality. After these process the authorization access to be verified for securing the information, determining whether a user has permission to take a certain action or view a specific item. Authentication and authorization will help in securing the data available.

Security of the data can be ensured by making it accessible only on a need-to-know basis. Access controls help in achieving this and thus the healthcare organizations must be able to segregate the relevant information and to set the access controls accordingly. The relevant information containing the data varies between the application and the users who are using it. Risks can be identified by now ant the organizations can set control agents to limit the unnecessary risks.

Varying duties and responsibilities require different types of information, and not all data will be relevant to all staff. Access controls should be set accordingly, allowing billing specialists access to files relevant to their jobs and granting physicians access to the information they need to conduct their work.

The risk management process can be made more complicated by setting more access controls and establish various possible ways to properly set the access controls. Healthcare organizations should provide a proper thoughtful process to consider developing access controls that can provide most essential security and to avoid roadblocks that obstruct smooth operations of the system unnecessarily.

DESIGN AND SOLUTIONS

Figure 1 gives the overview of the Healthcare Predictive Analytics

Classification Models Usage in Health Care

According to World health organization, 31% of death in the worldwide happens because of cardiovascular diseases (CVDs). It is estimated that 17.9 million lives per year and in global it is the number 1 cause for the death. Different disorders of the blood vessels and the heart, coronary heart disease, rheumatic heart disease, cardiovascular disease and other conditions comes under cardiovascular disease. Stokes and heart attacks are the major cause of cardiovascular death. In Five cases of cardiovascular death, four deaths are because of strokes and heart attacks. So, early detection of cardiovascular disease using predictive analytics will help to save lot of lives. In this direction, many researchers already worked on applying different machine learning techniques for early detection of heart diseases. In authors, (Miss. Chaitrali S. Dangare & Dr. Mrs. Sulabha, 2012) proposed neural network technique for predicting the possibility of patient will get the heart disease in future by using 13 different parameters such as blood pressure, lack of physical exercise, family history etc. The model gave the accuracy of 99.25% for 13 parameters. Later 2 more parameters i.e., obesity and smoking were added. The neural network model given

100% of accuracy for 15 parameters. The doctor's examine the patient through number of tests such as heart MRI, ECG for diagnosis of heart disease.

Classification models can be used in health care system in diagnosing the diseases with more accuracy. Heart disease is one of the disease which people getting affected with, due to the decline of lifestyle. For this, initially features has to be selected for predicting the heart disease, so the system accuracy will be more in heart disease prediction. Major Features involved in diagnosing and predicting heart disease are age, gender, chest pain location, provoked by exertion, relieved after rest, Chest pain type, blood pressure, hypertension, smoking history, fasting blood sugar, diabetes history, ECG reading during exercise. Chi-square and principal component analysis with random forests mechanism provides better prediction in heart disease (H.S.Hota, 2016).

Figure 1. Overview of the Healthcare Predictive Analytics

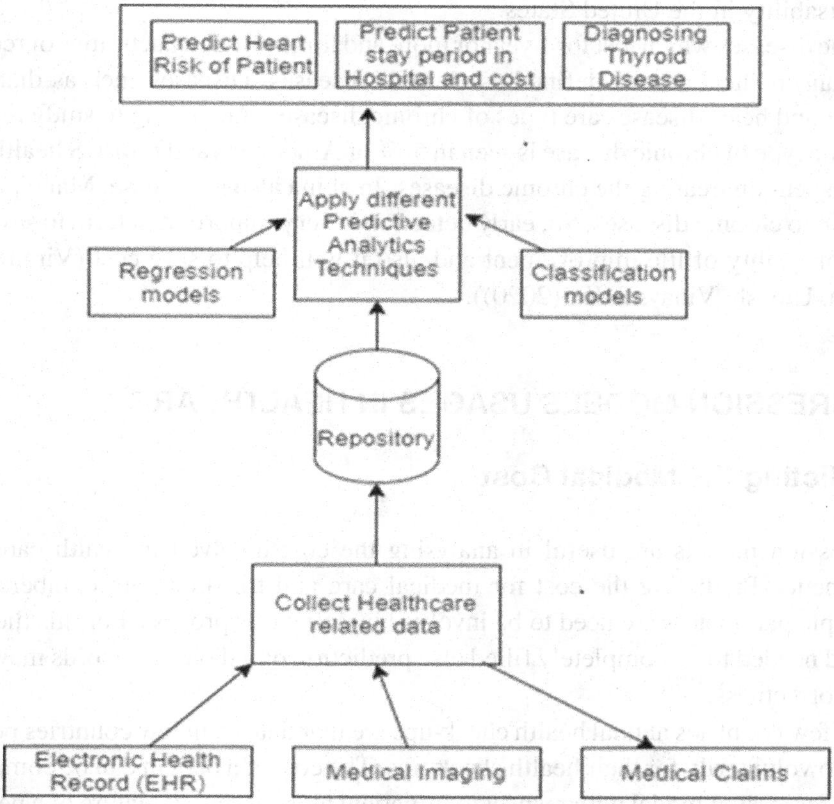

Liver disease is one of the healthcare problem people are facing across the countries. By detecting the liver disease at the earlier stage, the mortality rate can be reduced. Classification techniques can be used effectively to analyse the liver disease data set which has the patients' details and the problems. Even to recognize whether a person has liver disease or not for that also classification techniques can be used. Treatments for patients who have liver disease can also be recommended by the applying the classification algorithms (Deepa, 2017).

In (VirenViraj, Varun, Umesh, Vinay, & K., (2020)), authors used Convolution Neural Network (CNN) for heart risk prediction. CNN is compared with other machine learning algorithms such as Naïve bayes and K-nearest neighbour. The comparison shows that CNN gives better accuracy comparing to other two classification algorithms. The accuracy of 85-88 percentage was achieved through CNN.

Chronic diseases are defined broadly as conditions that last 1 year or more and require ongoing medical attention or limit activities of daily living or both. Chronic diseases such as heart disease, cancer, and diabetes are the leading causes of death and disability in the United States.

The diseases which lost for 1 year or more and limits the daily activities or require constant medical care is defined as Chronic diseases. Diseases such as diabetic, cancer and heart diseases are types of chronic diseases. According to study reports that one type of chronic disease is seen in 50% of Americans and 80% US healthcare fee is spent on treating the chronic diseases. In china also same case. Many people die due to chronic diseases. So, early detection is very important in term to save life and for quality of life improvement and also it will help to save cost (VirenViraj, Varun, Umesh, Vinay, & K., (2020)).

REGRESSION MODELS USAGES IN HEALTHCARE

Predicting the Medical Cost

Regression models are useful in analysing the cost involved in health care and treatments. Predicting the cost for medical care and treatment are cumbersome. Multiple parameters are need to be involved in doing this process. For this the cost record needed to be completely filled else prediction based on the records may lead to incorrectness.

In few countries annual health check-ups are mandatory, in few countries people will go voluntarily for their health check-ups. The cost of a patient can be compared using regression model with respect to in-patient and out-patient nature of a person. Age and gender parameters of patients, play a major role for the cost analysis and prediction under regression models (Freyder, 2016). The cost for medical treatment can be predicted based on the other parameters such as height, weight, body fat, waist size and health check-up details like creatinine levels, blood pressure, date of diagnostics and billing details as shown in Figure 2. (Belisario Panay, 2019).

The length of hospital stay (LOS) in emergency cases can be predicted using regression analysis to measure the efficiency. LOS if it is more then the cost of health care will be more for the patients. The parameters like age, status, and the diagnosed data from scanner, X-Ray, echo, Biology can be retained for predicting the length of hospital stay.

Figure 2. Parameters used for Healthcare cost prediction using regression models

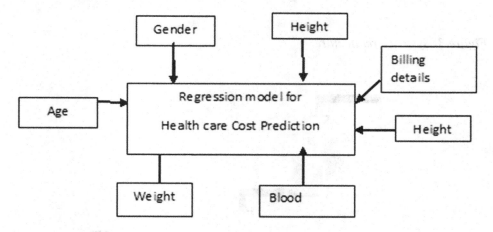

CASE STUDY

Statement of the Problem

Currently there is a huge scope for research in the medical science field. Predictive Analysis is an emerging research filed which involves various technologies to predict the disease. Data mining is one such major technology being used in disease prediction technique.

Thyroid imbalance used to happen because of inappropriate TSH (Thyroid Simulating Hormone) levels caused by the issues in thyroid organ. Diagnosing thyroid imbalance is very important role which has to be done by clinician. Thyroid imbalance prediction is very difficult process for data scientists. The proposed Analytical model helps to identifying the hypothyroid disease at the earliest and provides better treatment for the disease.

OBJECTIVE OF THE PROBLEM

Diagnosing Thyroid Disease is very tedious and critical process. It requires a lot of experience and knowledge. Usually for diagnosing thyroid related diseases doctors examine the patient using number of blood tests. Doctors are very much concern about the Prevention of diseases in health care. Accurate diagnostic at the precise time for a patient is critical, due to the obscure risk.

The proposed system analyses the different attributes such TSH, T3, T4 that affects hypothyroidism and gives the predicted results [19] that helps patients to diagnose the thyroid disease at the early stages also helps doctors to cross validates the results obtained from the traditional method of disease prediction.

Figure 3. System Architecture

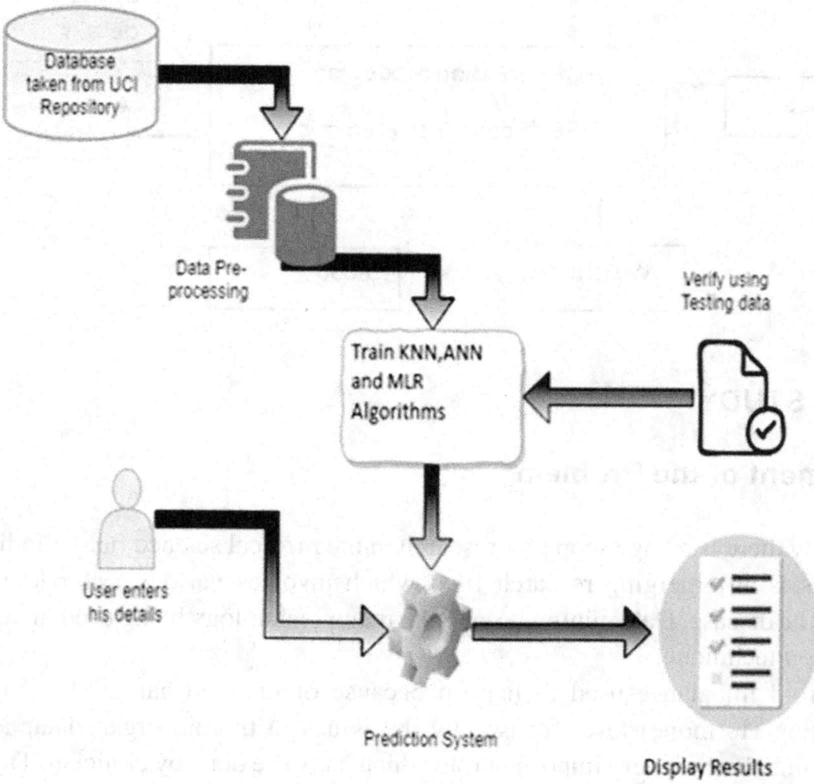

The Figure 3 indicates the overall System Architecture of the methodology. The data set for this case study is taken from UCI data repository website. The Dataset contains clinical data of thyroid patients. Each Patients record contains the attributes which are to be converted into proper digital format i.e. of normalization of dataset. After the successful normalization of the dataset, the dataset is imported into different attributes on to RStudio Tool.

Various datasets are subjected to pre-processing techniques in order to extract the following:

- Age of the patient
- Sex of the patient
- TSH value
- T3 value
- TT4 value
- Class attribute i.e. target variable

The successful extraction of the thyroid patients attributes from UCI dataset is followed by the concatenation of the parameters into a new dataset. This dataset is the final output of the pre-processing stage. The dataset obtained after successful pre-processing is subjected to prediction algorithms. The study performed here uses Multiple Linear Regression (MLR). The output obtained from the prediction stage shows the prediction of hypothyroidism or not.

In healthcare sector, data analytics is mainly used for making decisions for disease diagnostics. Predictive models designed for health sector helps in providing better treatment to the patients at comparatively low cost. Classifying the type of thyroid disease plays is an important task in the prediction of disease. Applying Dimensionality reduction on the data set helps in reducing the number of test for detecting thyroid diseases as well as the time required to diagnose disease.

From the perspective of research, each individual algorithms error rate is compared and the best algorithm which is suitable for the dataset is decided. The results obtained shows the prediction rate of hypothyroidism among patients. This output facilitates the patients to improve their health condition.

Functional Design of Extraction and pre-processing:

Input: The Thyroid dataset having class, age, sex, TSH, T3, TT4 attribute.

Method: The Thyroid dataset is taken from UCI repository which contained more records on the thyroid patients. These variable are not normalized i.e. the variable have different ranges for their values, this need to be normalized using normalize code using R language and then imported as a new thyroid dataset on R studio.

Class: The class attribute is a target variable. The class attribute has hypothyroid or negative values. These vales need to normalize using different code on R. The final class attribute contains either 0 Or 1 values. The 0 values indicate negative and 1 indicates hypothyroid.

Age: The age attribute is numeric value that indicates age of patients.

Sex: The sex attribute has female or male values. These vales need to normalize using different code on R. The final sex attribute contains either 0 Or 1 values. The 0 values indicate female and 1 indicates male attribute.

TSH: The TSH attribute range of TSH values of the recorded patients.

T3: The T3 attribute range of T3 values of the recorded patients.

TT4: The TT4 attribute range of TT4 values of the recorded patients.

After the extraction of required data of interest from UCI repository, data is normalized using normalize function to obtain class, age, sex, TSH, T3, TT4 parameters, this constitutes new dataset.

Using and Multiple Linear Regression (MLR)

Input: The final dataset obtained at the end of pre-processing step is stored as CSV file is taken as input

Method: The dataset is divided into 1:3 ratios. The $3/4^{th}$ of the dataset is considered as test dataset and the remaining $1/4^{th}$ dataset is taken as training dataset.

Multiple Linear Regression consider Class as the dependent variable and other variables like age, sex, TSH,T3,TT4 as independent parameters. The Multiple Linear Regression uses lm to build the model and production results will be displayed along with the accuracy of the model.

Output: The training phases produces their respective prediction models. Using this prediction models, input is given to the independent variables to predict or estimate the dependent variable.

Normalization

The study is concerned with the prediction of thyroid disease using the TSH, T3, TT4 parameters. The data for prediction was collected UCI repository containing thyroid patients' records. The datasets collected were unstructured datasets. The datasets collected has to be converted into proper structured data to facilitate further processing. Microsoft Excel was made use to convert all raw datasets into electronic format and then stored in the form of Comma Separated Value (.csv) files. The parameters were normalized based on its ranges like the attribute Sex contain female and male. These character parameter need to converted into numeric parameters. The 0 value indicates female attribute and 1 represents male. The target variable class contain two values hypothyroid and negative. These are normalized into 0 for negative and 1 for hypothyroid. The age attribute contains integer values ranging from 5 yrs. to 98yrs attribute values. The TSH, T3, TT4 parameters contains the numeric /values. After the successful normalization of datasets, the datasets must be imported onto the RStudio platform to perform further pre-processing of the data.

Pre-Processing of the Datasets

The raw dataset consists of age of a person from the year 5 to 98. The dataset has to be pre-processed by factoring age according to the age group. The Sex attribute contains character attribute male and female attribute. After the successful normalization it is converted into integer value 0 and 1. The TSH, T3, TT4 attribute contains numeric values of different ranges. The ranges are grouped and factored during pre-processing. The Class attribute is target variable of string values hypothyroid and negative values. After the successful normalization it is converted into integer value 0 for negative and 1 for hypothyroid

Multiple Linear Regression (MLR)

Linear Regression is the most widely used technique in predictive analytics. Predominantly, Linear Regression predicts the outcome of a dependent variable using a single independent variable. The roots of the Regression methods are in the concepts of straight line.

Every Regression model is generated using the following formula:

$$y = mx + c$$

The model uses y to indicate the dependent variable, m to indicate the slope of the straight line, x to indicate the independent variable and c to indicate the constant. Multiple Linear Regression can be thought as a duplicate of Linear Regression with added capabilities. Multiple Linear Regression can handle more than one independent variables.

The equation used in the generation of multiple linear regression model is as follows:

$$y = m1x1 + m2x2 + m3x3 + \ldots \ldots \ldots \ldots + mnxn\ Xn + C$$

Where the model uses y to indicate the dependent variable, mi to indicate the ith slope of the straight line, xi to indicate the ith independent variable and c to indicate the constant.

The current study considers thyroid prediction as the dependent variable and TSH, T3, TT4 parameters as the independent variable to generate the Multiple Linear Regression model. Since the Multiple Linear Regression models work exclusively with continuous valued variables.

RESULTS

Initial Raw Dataset

The initial raw data is collected from UCI repository as shown in the dataset Figure 4. The dataset contains different attribute like age, sex and so on. As seen above the data is unstructured format. Need follow different pre-processing steps to make it structured data.

Figure 4. Dataset

	A	B	C	D	E	F	G	H	I	J	K	L	M	N	O
1		Age	Sex	on_thyrox	query_on	on_antith	thyroid_si	query_hyi	query_hyi	pregnant	sick	tumor	lithium	goitre	TSH_meas
2	hypothyrc	72	M	f	f	f	f	f	f	f	f	f	f	f	y
3	hypothyrc	15	F	t	f	f	f	f	f	f	f	f	f	f	y
4	hypothyrc	24	M	f	f	f	f	f	f	f	f	f	f	f	y
5	hypothyrc	24	F	f	f	f	f	f	f	f	f	f	f	f	y
6	hypothyrc	77	M	f	f	f	f	f	f	f	f	f	f	f	y
7	hypothyrc	85	F	f	f	f	f	t	f	f	f	f	f	f	y
8	hypothyrc	64	F	f	f	f	t	f	f	f	f	f	f	f	y
9	hypothyrc	72	F	f	f	f	f	f	f	f	f	f	f	f	y
10	hypothyrc	20	F	f	f	f	f	t	f	f	f	f	f	f	y
11	hypothyrc	42	F	f	f	f	f	f	f	f	f	f	f	f	y
12	hypothyrc	69	F	f	f	f	f	f	f	f	f	f	f	f	y
13	hypothyrc	75	F	f	f	f	f	f	f	f	f	f	f	f	y

The very step is importing the dataset on R-studio and cleaning the noisy data from dataset such as ? or missing the values and renaming the attributes and then storing as new dataset.

- Naming of target variable as "class" attribute, which contains hypothyroid or negative values, this need to change into integer values 0 for negative and 1 for hypothyroid.

- Extracting the attributes, changing their attributal values and creating new dataframe.

Figure 5. Raw dataset imported on R-studio

```
Console  D:/Users/Ameena/Desktop/mtech1/data/
> head(hypothyroid.data,5)
        disease age sex on_thyroxine query_on_thyroxine on_antithyroid_medication
1       disease Age Sex on_thyroxine query_on_thyroxine on_antithyroid_medication
2 hypothyroid  72   M            f                    f                         f
3 hypothyroid  15   F            t                    f                         f
4 hypothyroid  24   M            f                    f                         f
5 hypothyroid  24   F            f                    f                         f
  thyroid_surgery query_hypothyroid query_hyperthyroid pregnant sick tumor
1 thyroid_surgery query_hypothyroid query_hyperthyroid pregnant sick tumor
2               f                 f                  f        f    f     f
3               f                 f                  f        f    f     f
4               f                 f                  f        f    f     f
5               f                 f                  f        f    f     f
  lithium goitre TSH_measued TSH T3_measued  T3 TT4_measued TT4 T4U_measued
1 lithium goitre TSH_measured TSH T3_measured T3 TT4_measured TT4 T4U_measured
2       f      f           y  30          y 0.6           y  15             y
3       f      f           y 145          y 1.7           y  19             y
4       f      f           y   0          y 0.2           y   4             y
5       f      f           y 430          y 0.4           y   6             y
    T4U FTI_measued FIT TBG_measued  TBG
1   T4U FTI_measured FTI TBG_measured TBG
2 1.48           y  10            n <NA>
3 1.13           y  17            n <NA>
4    1           y   0            n <NA>
5 1.04           y   6            n <NA>
```

The raw dataset imported on R-studio is shown in Figure 5. The raw dataset containing target variable is changed into class variable and normalizing the other attributes like the sex attributes contain male and female values these are as 1 and 0 respectively. Similarly, the class variable is normalized to 0 for negative and 1 for hypothyroid respectively. Finally, a new data frame is created to store these new variable as shown below in Figure 6, Data frame containing dependence attributes is shown in Figure 7.

Multiple Linear Regression Results

The Figure 8, plot helps us to find influential cases of thyroid cases (i.e., subjects) if any. Not all outliers are significant in linear regression analysis. Even though data have extreme values, they might not be significant to determine a regression line. We watch out for outlying values at the upper right corner or at the lower right corner. Those spots are the places where thyroid cases can be significant against a regression line. Look for thyroid cases outside of a dashed line, Cook's distance. When cases are outside of the Cook's distance, the cases are significant to the regression results. The regression results will be altered if we exclude those cases.

Figure 6. New data frame containing Initial attributes

```
> head(thyroid_data,5)
  class age sex tsh tt4  t3
1     0  60   1  12  71 2.2
2     0  72   0  11  13 0.3
3     0  65   1  55  50 1.0
4     0   5   1  17  74 2.0
5     0  62   0  54  41 0.6
```

Figure 7. Data frame containing dependence attributes

```
> tail(thyroid_data,5)
      class age sex tsh tt4  t3
1498      0  65   1 145  16 0.2
1499      0  42   0 235   2 0.5
1500      0  70   1  13  58 1.8
1501      0  29   1  31  16 0.7
1502      0  28   1  43  59 2.0
```

The Predicted MLR results will contain class variables indicating hypothyroid or negative

- The summary will contain confusion matrix for prediction class
- The accuracy of the model
- The misclassification or error of the MLR prediction model

Accuracy of 0.94% is achieved using the MLP model as shown in Figure 9.

The current research work can be further enhanced by analysing the different disease dataset using the same data analytical framework developed. Also, the pattern of hyperthyroid can be analysed using thyroid patients' records collected over hospitals.

Figure 8. MLR predicted graph for test dataset

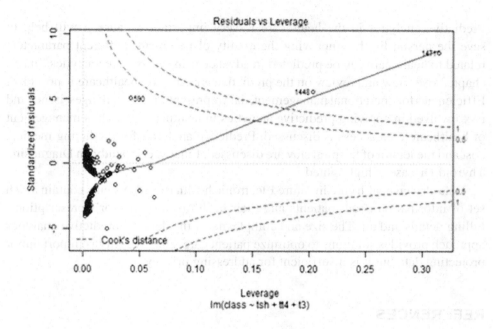

Figure 9. MLR Prediction for User Value

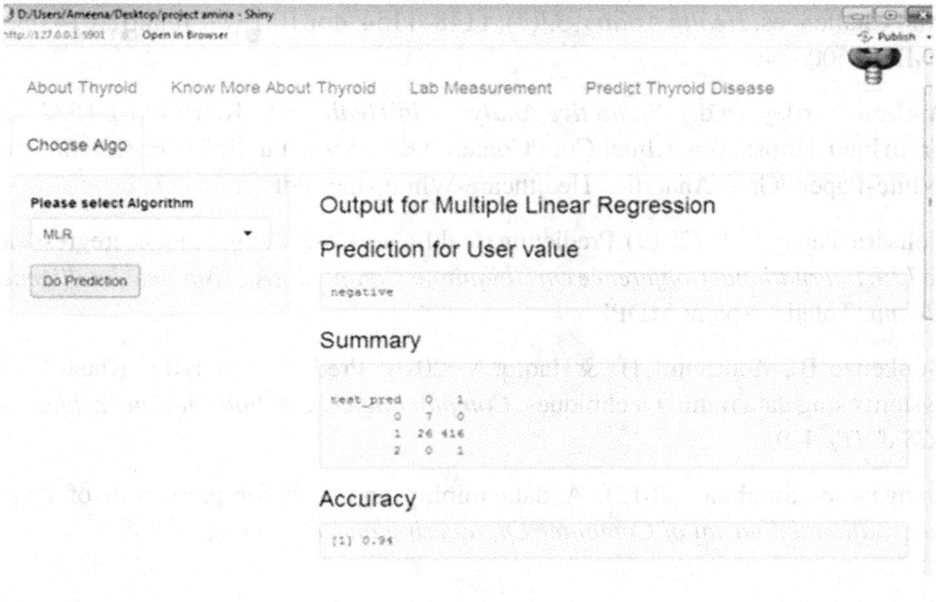

CONCLUSION AND FUTURE RESEARCH DIRECTIONS

Predictive analytics in the healthcare is very important because it will help to save the person life by improving the quality of treatment. Different parameters related to healthcare can be predicted in advance using predictive analytics. In this chapter, overview and review on the predictive analytics on healthcare is provided. Efficiencies for operational management, data representation, Challenges, issues and risk involved in applying predictive analytics in healthcare and Data management of healthcare data access is discussed. Predictive analytics for predicting medical cost and the length of hospital stay are discussed. Finally, case study on Diagnosing Thyroid Disease is highlighted.

Data-driven health care in future Electronic health record systems contain a rich set of information about patients and their health history, doctor's prescriptions, billing details and all. The size and complexity of the data the predictive analytics approach provides solutions to optimize patient care. Data security is important for protecting data but it is insufficient for addressing privacy.

REFERENCES

Amarasingham, R. P. R., Patzer, R. E., Huesch, M., Nguyen, N. Q., & Xie, B. (2014). Implementing Electronic Health Care Predictive Analytics: Considerations And Challenges. *Health Affairs*, *33*(7), 1148–1154. doi:10.1377/hlthaff.2014.0352 PMID:25006140

Andrew Bartley. (n.d.). *Predictive Analytics In Healthcare*. Retrieved 1 15, 2021, From Intel: Https://Www.Intel.Com/Content/Dam/Www/Public/Us/En/Documents/White-Papers/Gmc-Analytics-Healthcare-Whitepaper.Pdf

Belisario Panay, N. B. (2019). Predicting Health Care Costs Using Evidenceregression. In *13th International Conference On Ubiquitous Computing And Ambient Intelligence Ucami*. Toledo, Spain: MDPI.

Boukenze, B., Mousannif, H., & Haqiq, A. (2016). Predictive analytics in healthcare system using data mining techniques. *Computer Science & Information Technology (CS & IT)*, 1-9.

Dangare & Sulabha. (2012). A data mining approach for prediction of heart. *International Journal of Computer Engineering and Technology*, 30-40.

Dario Gregori, M. P. (2011, June). Regression Models For Analyzing Costs And Their Determinants In Health Care: An Introductory Review. *International Journal for Quality in Health Care, 23*(3), 331–341. doi:10.1093/intqhc/mzr010 PMID:21504959

Deepa, K. K. (2017). Health Care Analysis Using Random Forestalgorithm. *Journal Of Chemical And Pharmaceutical Sciences, 10*(3), 1359–1361.

Freyder, C. W. (2016). *Using Linear Regression And Mixed Models To Predict Health Care Costs After An Inpatient Event.* University of Pittsburgh. Retrieved From Https://Core.Ac.Uk/Download/Pdf/78481788.Pdf

Hota, S. D. (2016). Classification Of Health Care Data Using Machine Learning Technique. *International Journal of Engineering Science Invention*, 17-20.

Hu, Y. Z. (2020). Healthcare Predictive Analytics For Disease Progression: A Longitudinal Data Fusion Approach. *Journal of Intelligent Information Systems*, 351–369.

Lindeman, T. (2018, February 15). *3 Examples Of How Hospitals Are Using Predictive Analytics.* Academic Press.

Md Saiful Islam, M. M.-E.-A. (2018). *A Systematic Review On Healthcare Analytics: Application And Theoretical Perspective Of Data Mining.* Heathcare.

Michael, J., & Ward, K. A. (2014). Applications Of Business Analytics In. *Business Horizons, 57*(5), 571–582. doi:10.1016/j.bushor.2014.06.003 PMID:25429161

Nithya, B., & Ilango, V. (2017). Predictive Analytics In Health Care Using Machine Learning Tools And Techniques. In *2017 International Conference On Intelligent Computing And Control Systems (ICICCS)* (pp. 1-7). IEEE Explorer. 10.1109/ICCONS.2017.8250771

Parikshit, N., & Mahalle, N. P. (2020). Data Analytics: COVID-19 Prediction Using Multimodal Data. Creative Commons CC.

Patil, B. M., Joshi, R. C., Toshniwal, D., & Biradar, S. (2011). A new approach: Role of data mining in prediction of survival of burn patients. *Journal of Medical Systems, 35*(6), 1531–1542. doi:10.100710916-010-9430-2 PMID:20703764

R. M. (2020). *Predictive Privacy: Towards An Applied Ethics Of Data Analytics.* Technische Universität Berlin (TU Berlin); Freie Universität Berlin.

Rao, K. D., Radhika, A., & Abdul, G. (2014). Health Systems Research In The Time Of Health System Reform In India: A Review. *Health Research Policy and Systems, 12*(37), 1–7. doi:10.1186/1478-4505-12-37 PMID:25106759

Sayantan Khanra, A. D. (2020). Big Data Analytics In Healthcare: A Systematic Literature Review. *Enterprise Information Systems, 14*(7), 878–912. doi:10.1080/17517575.2020.1812005

V. S., V. K., U. D., V. K., & K. R. ((2020)). Heart Disease Prediction Using CNN Algorithm. *SN Computer Science, 1*(170).

Wazurkar, P., Bhadoria, R. S., & Bajpai, D. (2019). Predictive Analytics In Data Science For Business Intelligence Solutions. *International Conference on Communication Systems and Network Technologies (CSNT).*

Chapter 13

Consistent Hashing and Real–Time Task Scheduling in Fog Computing

Geetha J. J.
M.S. Ramaiah Institute of Technology, India

Jaya Lakshmi D. S.
 https://orcid.org/0000-0002-2534-7209
M.S. Ramaiah Institute of Technology, India

Keerthana Ningaraju L. N.
M.S. Ramaiah Institute of Technology, India

ABSTRACT

Distributed caching is one such system used by dynamic high-traffic websites to process the incoming user requests to perform the required tasks in an efficient way. Distributed caching is currently employing hashing algorithm in order to serve its purpose. A significant drawback of hashing in this circumstance is the addition of new servers that would result in a change in the previous hashing method (rehashing), hence, goes into a rigmarole. Thus, we need an effective algorithm to address the problem. This technique has served as a solution for distributed and rehashing problems. Most of upcoming internet of things will have to be latency aware and will not afford the data transmission and computation time in the cloud servers. The real-time processing in proximal distance device would be much needed. Hence, the authors aim to employ a real-time task scheduling algorithm. Computations referring to the user requests that are to be handled by the servers can be efficiently handled by consistent hashing algorithms.

DOI: 10.4018/978-1-7998-8161-2.ch013

1 INTRODUCTION

With the increasing number of hot spots in cloud computing servers along with the advent of certain concepts such as Internet of Things and big data, distributed systems have gained significant popularity and relevance. Distributed caching is one such system used by dynamic high-traffic websites and web based applications to process the incoming user requests to perform the required tasks in a more efficient way.

A significant drawback of hashing in this circumstance is the addition of new servers would result in a change in the previous hashing method (rehashing), hence, goes into a rigmarole. Thus, consistent hashing would be an effective way to avoid this sudden change in algorithm course. This technique has served as a solution for distributed and rehashing problems. Most of upcoming Internet of Things will have to be latency aware and will not afford the data transmission and computation time in the cloud servers. The real time processing in proximal distance device would be much needed. Hence, we aim to employ a real time task scheduling algorithm.

The main aspects of fog computing to be taken into consideration are storage, computations, network and control. With regard to storage we can employ distributed caching methods as further explained. Computations referring to the user requests that are to be handled by the servers can be efficiently handled by consistent hashing algorithm.

This paper is organized as follows. Section II explains Literature Review. An overview of how it is spread across various classes of users is presented here. Section III introduces Fog Computing and Caching. Section IV presents Edge Computing Systems and Mobile Data Storage Services. In Section V presents Consistent Hashing Model and Section VI presents Conclusion.

2. LITERATURE REVIEW

This is a paper *(Li, G et al. 2019)* that studied resource scheduling problem in fog computing by applying the FCAP algorithm to cluster fog resources. It is initiated by narrowing the range of user requirements for matching resources. They also proposed the RSAF algorithm to accomplish the task of scheduling resources. From the experimental analysis, the objective function value of the FCAP algorithm is seen to have faster convergence speed compared to that of the FCM algorithm. Moreover, the proposed RSAF algorithm will be efficient in matching various user requests with the appropriate resource categories quickly and also enhance user satisfaction. They have left dynamic changes of resources for their future work to produce new scheduling strategy to improve the utilization of resources and ensure user satisfaction. This gave us the motivation to work on the real time task scheduling algorithm.

The main objective of this paper *(Choudhari, T et al. 2018)* is to propose a system which has a Fog layer sandwiched between the client and the Cloud layer to cater to the applications and users which are having very low tolerance for latency. The higher priority tasks are to be processed at first in the Fog layer. If all the data centers in the Fog layer are busy at that point of time, then the high priority task is propagated to the next Cloud layer for timely execution without affecting the dependent task. The data centers present in this Fog layer of a particular region, it can communicate with each other to check availability of servers and for load balancing protocol. This paper added to our knowledge regarding task scheduling at Fog level for prioritized task.

This paper *(Xu, X et al. 2018)* aims to achieve dynamic load balancing for each type of computing node found in the fog and cloud layers by employing a dynamic resource allocation method, named DRAM. It also aims in achieving load balancing. A system framework is presented and load balancing is the analyzed accordingly with the fog nodes. They implement the DRAM method based on the static resource allocation and dynamic resource scheduling for the various fog services. As a result of the obtained experimental evaluations and comparison analysis that they were able to carried out, the verified the validity of their proposed method. This paper gave insights on the approaching dynamic resource allocation of incoming user requests and applications.

This paper *(Liu, L et al. 2018)* proposes an I-Apriori algorithm obtained by improving the existing Apriori algorithm. From the conducted experimental results, it can be seen that the I- Apriori algorithm can not only improve the efficiency of generating frequent item sets but also do it in an effective manner. It is novel task scheduling model including a novel TSFC (Task Scheduling in Fog Computing) algorithm employed in a fog computing environment are also taken into consideration based on the I-Apriori algorithm. Association rules are to be generated by the I-Apriori algorithm which is a key parameter of TSFC task scheduling algorithm. Finally, the experimental results show that TSFC algorithm has better performance than other similar algorithms when considered in terms of task total execution time and average waiting time. But bandwidth between processors, multilayer task scheduling in fog computing, and others are not taken into consideration. We aim to explore these areas furthermore.

This paper *(Anwar, S et al. 2018)* reviews the potential usage and application of fog computing as an extension of cloud computing by the comparison between fog and cloud. They also define some essential services which fog computing can support and which methods of reduction can be effectively used to better the Quality of service and also reduce the latency of services offered. Various existing task scheduling algorithms are learnt and compared among themselves in order to determine which one of them will be the best suitable for fog computing architecture and also trace out the possible challenges that would be faced during its implementation of fog computing. This papers answers the essential questions of fog computing existence paradigm also gives insights of all currently used algorithm results.

This paper *(Naha, R. K.et al. 2018)* gives us an overall insight of all the considered and experimented algorithms. It guided us in the direction of this paper. This papers includes the overview, architecture, state-of-the-art and other similar technologies in Fog computing. They have come up with an efficient taxonomy for Fog computing by analyzing the requirements of Fog infrastructure, platform, and applications. They have included resource allocation and scheduling, simulation tools, and microservices in Fog computing. It has also pointed out some challenging and open research issues. This papers comprehensive survey has brought into light various IoT application execution techniques on Fog computing and as well as directing us towards for current and future research.

This paper *(Monga, S. K.et al. 2019)* further development registering for additional investigation or total and furthermore forward information to the cloud. Elf Store (Edge-local federated Store) is an edge-neighborhood combined store for surges of information squares. Various fog devices are arranged in a super-peer overlay network. They are used to screen the edge assets, offer united metadata ordering utilizing the Bloom filters, find information inside 2-jumps, and keep up surmised worldwide insights about the quality and capacity limit of edges. Information produced on the edge and fog is just momentarily accessible on them, as they are in the end moved to the cloud for steadiness. This is the key explanation behind edge devices being normally less solid. This makes the applications using this kind of data to run primarily on cloud or left with the option of sending them back to the edge devices.

However, the purpose of concern is that cloud alone can be relied on for information constancy. Assistance ought to be created which can oversee information on fog and edge gadgets somewhat just on the cloud. In the event of hub disappointments likewise the administration ought not stop. Advancement of such administrations on the edge and fog layers likewise offers straightforward information revelation and simpler access to information for different applications. Most Popular Content (MPC) Caching Strategy is an extremely good methodology for caching. Fog nodes are liable for checking demands for content which is absent in the store. The popularity table stores the count. When the popularity threshold is reached, the content is termed as popular and after that it is cached. When Fog node's buffer is full, it removes the content which is least popular to make space for the new content. Subsequently after this, the customer will get the information truly from the noteworthy Fog node. Hence the customer need not fetch it from the Content delivery network(CDN) server or the primary unavailable cloud server, with the exception of if the cached data item has been replaced. The issue of time while downloading the content and also to search for content availability is proposed to be solved by content delivery networks. It *(Alghamdi, F.et al. 2019)* suggests delivering content though edge cache servers which can be deployed at different locations globally.

1. FOG COMPUTING AND CACHING

3.1 Mobile Users

The *(Mayer, R.et al. 2017)* other name for Fog computing is "cloud close to ground". The computer facility of the Fog servers is light-weight and is at a close proximity to various mobile users. Some of the major applications of Fog computing are live video streaming and dissemination of ads. A Fog computing framework is of a three level Mobile-Fog-Cloud structure. The versatile clients get administrations required from the Fog servers with the assistance of local wireless connections. The contents of the Fog servers can be refreshed by utilizing wired or cell systems. The major disadvantage is the higher cost while updating the content in cases where the bandwidth between cloud and fog servers is expensive. Fog Computing gives incredible Cloud benefits in the physical closeness of clients.

Fogs can be considered for offering computational power and breaking point cutoff focuses, with low inaction and high information move limit. This means to improve organizational transmission capacity and protection. The popularity of cloud computing and the expanding use of mobile devices are driving the growth of mobile cloud computing. This technology has piqued the interest of many researchers. Due to several restrictions of mobile devices, such as low battery power, restricted storage capacity, and bandwidth, there are numerous challenges with mobile cloud computing. In mobile cloud computing, security is paramount. Mobile Cloud Computing has been a hot topic in research over the past few years. However, because mobile cloud computing is still in its early stages, there are only a few surveys accessible in various MCC domains. The primary focus of this study is on safeguarding data storage in mobile cloud computing. In research organizations, significant efforts have been made to develop secure mobile cloud computing.

3.2 Distributed Graph

The significant inquiry which needs tending to in fog computing is the determination of gadgets for storing the data, it's circulation and the procedure of recovery. A scoring framework can be used for referencing the issue of choice of the gadget. In this proposed framework, the higher centrality user gadgets are viewed as best up-and-comers. This depends on their ability to give the necessary content.

Figure 1. Flow of information generated on IOT devices

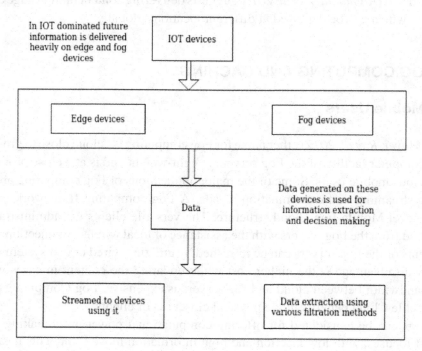

The *(Khan, J. A.et al. 2019)* system network over the gadgets can be represented as a chart. The centrality idea from the system can be utilized for ID of significant nodes. This will permit higher centrality devices to union or leave an appropriated system of fog devices by working together with the close by device. A centrality measure is the total amount of the most concise ways to the extent the number of jumps from all customers to all content.

3.3 Large Data Analysis and Increased Coverage of Computation

The nature of Fog Computing is because of remarkable virtualization. Each Fog hub involves at any rate one gadget. These contraptions can be switches or arrangements of neighborhood servers. Edge gadgets can be related with the Fog Computing layer, which in this manner can be related with the united Cloud Computing layer *(Moysiadis, V.et al., 2018)*. The potential issues of computing infrastructure and the moderate reaction time of distributed computing can be relieved. This should be possible by a multi-level fog processing model that has huge scope information investigation administration. A versatile framework level test system assesses the fog based analytics service and the QoS schemes. Regarding likelihood of employment blocking and utility of analytics service, fogs can be utilized to improve the presentation of examination over keen urban areas in contrast with cloud just models. With *(He, J.et al.2017)* effective help of different dispersed figuring motors, the enormous scope investigation administration can be run over the frameworks of multi-level fog calculation.

3.4 Security Concerns

Authentication at various levels of gateways, as well as (in the case of smart grids) at the smart meters installed in the consumer's home, are the key security concerns. An IP address is assigned to each smart meter and smart appliance. A rogue user can tamper with its own smart meter, submit fake readings, or spoof IP addresses, among other options. There are a few options for dealing with the authentication issue. It is quite elaborate on multicast authentication systems based on public key infrastructure (PKI). In quite a few formats, some Diffie-Hellman key exchange authentication mechanisms are discussed. The data is encrypted and sent to a Fog device, such as a home-area network (HAN) gateway, by smart meters. After that, HAN decrypts the data, aggregates the results, and forwards them.

Fog computing can also use intrusion detection techniques. Intrusion in smart grids can be detected using either a signature-based method, in which patterns of behavior are observed and compared to a database of possible misbehaviors, or a behavior-based method, in which the patterns of behavior are observed and compared to an already existing database of possible misbehaviors. An anomaly-based method, in which observed behavior is compared to expected behavior to see if there is a deviation, can also be used to detect intrusion. We can find a few studies that create an algorithm for monitoring power flow outcomes and detecting anomalies in input values that could have been tampered with by attackers.

2. EDGE COMPUTING SYSTEMS AND MOBILE DATA STORAGE SERVICES

In a future IoT-overwhelmed condition most of information will be delivered at the edge, which might be moved to the system center. Information management methodology directs how an eyeball organization facilitates the administration of edge information put away at a store. Given that capacity is less expensive to give and scales superior to wires nearby storage administrations (e.g., in Wi-Fi Access Points, or comparable) can be used at the edge of the system. Such local storage administrations can be utilized to cushion IoT and client produced information at the edge, before information cloud synchronization.

Recovering information which is put away at far off areas causes blockage in the network also requires high latencies. This prompted the need for frameworks that are focused at versatile clients and use little scope, decentralized capacity hubs at the outrageous edge of the system. .vStore is a system that is fit for context aware micro-storage. The (Gedeon, J.et al., 2018) choice where to store information is caused by decisions that can either be pushed all around to the system or made independently by clients.

The paper *(Psaras, I.et al. 2018)* shows various strategies according data management.

Table 1. Comparison of data management strategies

Proactive	Reactive	Data-specific
Data transfer is done proactively	Transfer is done only when it's necessary.	Data attributes are used.
The local repositories move the approaching information proactively to the expected goal like cloud storage	Registration of name of data item to name resolution system is done to enable access and notification is sent to the destination of the data.	Data attributes are used to decide on the action for each data item. Data attributes can be scope and shelf life.

Cloud computing is incredibly powerful, however mobile computing has a limit, resulting in a slew of challenges demonstrating how to manage the differences between the two. As a result, there are certain challenges with cloud computing for smartphones. These concerns can be related to a lack of resources, a network, mobile user security, and cloud computing. The following are some explanations of the issues. Having limited resources in a mobile device makes cloud computing challenging. Basic resource constraints include restricted computational power, a low-quality display, and a limited battery. In MCC, all processing is done via the network. As a result, there are various network-related difficulties.

3. DISTRIBUTED CACHING IN FOG NODES

Distributed caching refers to cache configured to perform under multiple nodes or servers belonging to same network (Fog nodes in this case). The data centres of the fog nodes can be made up with high speed cache distributed across the nodes at the same tier. Apart from the on memory RAM, Solid State Drives are to be present as a set of non-volatile memory for real - time immediate storage and thus also perform the activities of cache.

Cloud computing also has popular existing concept of Content Delivery Network. Applying a further use into this network would be easy and cost effective way to employ fog nodes and their memory and cache systems. Brief concept about CDN is it refers to the distributed servers present across the geography that delivers content/ data, meaning keeps the content/data easily accessible to the users from that part of the geography. This serves as the base framework for the fog nodes build.

Among the three cache access patterns i.e Write Through, Write Around and Write Back, the Write Back is the suitable for this particular case of Fog nodes. The write request will be updating the immediate cache memory only. A time synchronizer will be taking care of the constant updates to the main database from the cache.

6. CONSISTING HASHING MODEL

The term "consistent hashing" was introduced by Karger et al. at MIT for use in distributed caching for multiple servers. This academic paper from 1997 introduced the term "consistent hashing" as a way of distributing requests among a changing population of web servers.

Considering the dynamic addition and removal of numerous nodes or failure of certain nodes the normal hashing functions employed would be a nuisance. The existing hash functions will return updated values and pointing to the wrong key. Hence, the available solution will be remapping the data into their new keys before calling the hash. This is a high latency and tedious task due to the dynamic changing and is definitely not preferred. The latency delay might lead to faulty data accessing and retrieval. This can be solved by using a consistent hashing technique in place of a conventional hash.

Consistent hash ring is a distributed hash function which functions independently of the number of servers, in order to minimize the key variations during addition or removal new servers into the distributed system. One of its another major aspect is load balancing. The numerous server requests will be balanced across the across the servers and addition and removal of nodes would not produce any latency, hence, makes the transition smooth and balanced.

Algorithm:

```
start function
        For each node:
        Find f(node) where f is the hash function
```

```
              Append each f(node) to a sorted array
    For any key:
          Compute the hash f(key)
          Find the first f(node)>f(key)
          map it
    end function
```

Considering a small example with four nodes belonging to the same level, and six user requests with key values as depicted. Initially in accordance to the given algorithm, the keys are allocated to the respective node immediately lesser than them and their requests are to handle by that respective node. Therefore, the number of nodes present at that moment is not a prominent part of the algorithm. Let us consider two cases i.e addition of a new node and failure or removal of already present node.

Figure 2. Initial mapping of nodes and request.

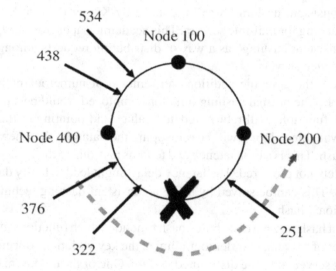

Now, consider a failure of the node 300. The user requests having keys belonging to that node will be handled by the node 200. We can see that the requests of the failed node are the only ones that will be remapped whilst others remain to belong to the previously handled nodes. It can be observed minimum number of remapping in this case as only the requests handled by the failed node is remapped.

Figure 3. Mapping after failure of node 300

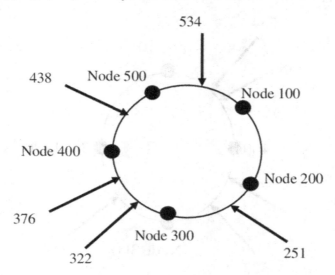

Now, consider the addition of a new node 500. The user requests having keys belonging to that node will have been handled by the node 400 before its addition in accordance with the algorithm. After the addition of this node 500, all the requests key values above it will be remapped to it. We can see that the requests of the added node are the only ones remapped whilst other remain same. It can be observed minimum number of remapping in this case as only the requests to be handled by the new node is remapped.

Finally, it can be comprehended that the addition of a new node has not disturbed the overall functionality or the structure of the original topology in any manner. We can see that the additional node's requests are the only ones that have been remapped, while the rest stay unchanged. Only the requests to be processed by the new node are remapped in this situation, resulting in a low number of remapping's.

Summing up the aforementioned technique, consistent hashing overcomes the problem of many nodes and their caches, which we define as the collection of caches that a given client is aware of. While views may be inconsistent, we presume that they are significant: each machine is aware of a constant proportion of the presently active caches. A client maps an item to one of the caches in its view using a consistent hash function. We look at hash functions that have the following consistency characteristics and build them. The anticipated percentage of items that must be transferred to a new cache when a machine is added to or withdrawn from the collection of caches is the bare minimum required to maintain a balanced load across the caches. Second, the total number of distinct caches to which an item is associated is modest across all client views.

Figure 4. Mapping after addition of node 500

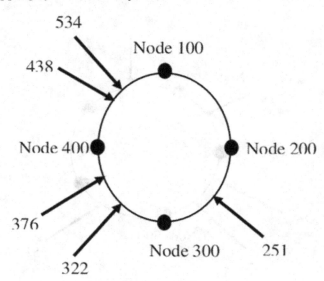

6.1. Observations

In order to understand the working of the algorithm better, some observations are made and plotted as a graph to increase readability. There are three plots which respectively denotes the instance corresponding to the above diagrams

The parameters from the above algorithm for hashing is plotted against the number of nodes and their value. The figure 5 shows how the nodes present currently and their values vary, we can see that node keys follow a less linear path than the hash values since multiple requests for nodes are directed to their round number in the first instance of hashing. The following plot is the initial image of the node key and value pair. The red line represents the actual values of the nodes while the blue represents the hash value of the node to where the traffic is to be directed. We have considered nine requests with a set of different keys ranging in between 0 - 600 and their respective hash values. It corresponds with the above mentioned diagrams of consistent hashing models.

Following the instance from Figure 5, we shall consider a failure of the node 300. The algorithm directs all the user requests having keys belonging to that node to be handled by the node 200 newly. We can see that the requests of the failed node are the only ones that will be remapped whilst others remain to belong to the previously handled nodes. It can be observed to have a minimum number of remapping in this case as only the requests handled by the failed node are remapped.

Figure 5. Initial mapping of nodes and request.

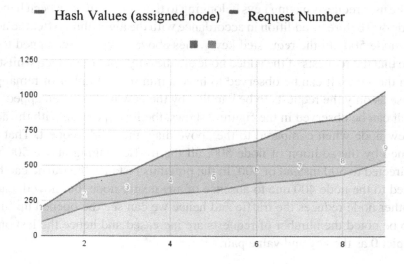

As we can observe in the figure 6 shows, the line flattens out when compared to the above diagram in between 2 and 4. That can be explained by the removal of node 300, all the traffic ranging 300-400 will be now directed to 200 and hence we can see the flattened line. It also to be noted the number of requests are reduced and hence the last one depicts 0 as the key and value pair.

Figure 6. Mapping after failure of node 300

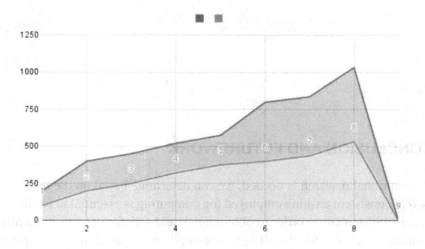

Following the instance from Figure 6, we shall consider the addition of a new node 500. The user requests having keys belonging to that node will have been handled by the node 400 before its addition in accordance with the algorithm. After the addition of this node 500, all the requested key values above it will be remapped to it. We can see that the requests of the added node are the only ones remapped whilst others remain the same. It can be observed to have a minimum number of remapping in this case as only the requests to be handled by the new node are remapped.

As it can be observed in the figure 7 shows, the line opens up with the addition of a new node when compared to the above diagram at 8th request. That can be explained by the addition of node 500, all the traffic ranging above 500 will be now directed to 500 instead of 400. In the previous instance the traffic can be seen assigned to the node 400 due to absence of any nearer node, but now the addition of another node reduces the traffic and hence we can see the opened up line. It is also to be noted the number of requests are increased and hence the last one does not depict 0 as the key and value pair.

Figure 7. Mapping after addition of node 500

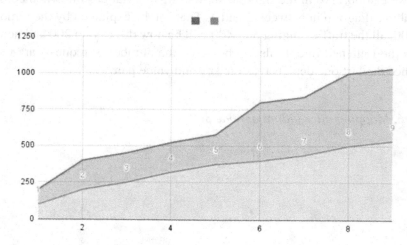

7. CONCLUSION AND FUTUREWORK

While additional research is needed, we can determine based on the results of this study that consistent hashing employed fog computing is essential to facilitate finer end-user environment in order to obtain quick and satisfactory real-time response of requests especially for the all sensitive applications used in the current era of computations, data storage and retrieval. The fog computing technology is in its infancy as of the present, for this emerging paradigm we believe an extensive investigation is to be conducted to predict any loop holes and make the technology future proof. In this survey we have looked thoroughly at the main aspects of fog computing that are to be taken into consideration, they being storage, computations, network and control. In the context of storage, which encompasses data storage, data access and retrial, it can be found that distributed caching would will provide with efficient resource allocation and scheduling of the real-time requests and queries. In this way, by employing these two methods which are directed towards the storage and computations aspects of Fog Computing, this potential computing paradigm, which is still young and naive, can be propelled towards achieving market adoption in the near future.

We look into the benefits of fog computing for services in a variety of fields and present a state-of-the-art analysis as well as security concerns in the current paradigm. Some breakthroughs in compute and storage may be inspired in the future to handle data demanding services based on the interplay between Fog and Cloud, based on the work of this study.

The future work can be carried out across studying cuckoo filters. The disadvantage of bloom filters is it does not allow the items to be removed from a particular set. Then again cuckoo channel permits to include and erase the things productively from the set and considerably more impressive than bloom filters. Bloom filter only predicts if data is present or not, but never explicitly guarantees. This may cause performance degradation, if data is not present. Also the use of genetic algorithms can be studied in depth since due to the shortage in resources, requirements cannot be met by edge servers in mobile computing environments. Genetic algorithms have shown magnificent results in terms of effectiveness in improving efficiency of computing.

The Fog computing paradigm in Smart Grid will be developed further in the future. Two Fog device models can be created in this case. Interconnected Fog devices may consult one other and form coalitions for additional advancements, while independent Fog devices communicate directly with the Cloud for periodic updates on price and demand.

REFERENCES

Alghamdi, F., Mahfoudh, S., & Barnawi, A. (2019). A novel fog computing based architecture to improve the performance in content delivery networks. *Wireless Communications and Mobile Computing*. doi:10.1109/ICWS.2019.00062

Anwar, S., Ajmal, A., Hayder, F., & Bibi, S. (2018). Evaluating Cloud & Fog Computing based on Shifting & Scheduling Algorithms, Latency Issues and service Architecture. *International Journal of Computer Science and Information Security*, *16*(6).

Choudhari, T., Moh, M., & Moh, T. S. (2018, March). Prioritized task scheduling in fog computing. In *Proceedings of the ACMSE 2018 Conference* (pp. 1-8). Academic Press.

Gedeon, J., Himmelmann, N., Felka, P., Herrlich, F., Stein, M., & Mühlhäuser, M. (2018, February). vStore: A context-aware framework for mobile micro-storage at the edge. In *International Conference on Mobile Computing, Applications, and Services* (pp. 165-182). Springer. 10.1007/978-3-319-90740-6_10

He, J., Wei, J., Chen, K., Tang, Z., Zhou, Y., & Zhang, Y. (2017). Multitier fog computing with large-scale iot data analytics for smart cities. *IEEE Internet of Things Journal*, *5*(2), 677–686. doi:10.1109/JIOT.2017.2724845

Khan, J. A., Westphal, C., & Ghamri-Doudane, Y. (2019). Information-centric fog network for incentivized collaborative caching in the Internet of everything. *IEEE Communications Magazine*, *57*(7), 27–33. doi:10.1109/MCOM.2019.1800764

Li, G., Liu, Y., Wu, J., Lin, D., & Zhao, S. (2019). Methods of resource scheduling based on optimized fuzzy clustering in fog computing. *Sensors (Basel)*, *19*(9), 2122. doi:10.339019092122 PMID:31071923

Liu, L., Qi, D., Zhou, N., & Wu, Y. (2018). A task scheduling algorithm based on classification mining in fog computing environment. *Wireless Communications and Mobile Computing*.

Mayer, R., Gupta, H., Saurez, E., & Ramachandran, U. (2017, October). Fogstore: Toward a distributed data store for fog computing. In *2017 IEEE Fog World Congress (FWC)* (pp. 1-6). IEEE. 10.1109/FWC.2017.8368524

Monga, S. K., Ramachandra, S. K., & Simmhan, Y. (2019, July). ElfStore: A resilient data storage service for federated edge and fog resources. In *2019 IEEE International Conference on Web Services (ICWS)* (pp. 336-345). IEEE.

Moysiadis, V., Sarigiannidis, P., & Moscholios, I. (2018). Towards distributed data management in fog computing. *Wireless Communications and Mobile Computing*, *2018*, 2018. doi:10.1155/2018/7597686

Naha, R. K., Garg, S., Georgakopoulos, D., Jayaraman, P. P., Gao, L., Xiang, Y., & Ranjan, R. (2018). Fog computing: Survey of trends, architectures, requirements, and research directions. *IEEE Access: Practical Innovations, Open Solutions*, *6*, 47980–48009. doi:10.1109/ACCESS.2018.2866491

Psaras, I., Ascigil, O., Rene, S., Pavlou, G., Afanasyev, A., & Zhang, L. (2018). Mobile data repositories at the edge. *USENIX Workshop on Hot Topics in Edge Computing (HotEdge 18)*.

Xu, X., Fu, S., Cai, Q., Tian, W., Liu, W., Dou, W., Sun, X., & Liu, A. X. (2018). Dynamic resource allocation for load balancing in fog environment. *Wireless Communications and Mobile Computing*, *2018*, 2018. doi:10.1155/2018/6421607

Compilation of References

Abadi & Agarwal. (2016). *TensorFlow: Large-Scale Machine Learning on Heterogeneous Distributed Systems.* CoRR abs/1603.04467.

Abdallah, E. M. (2016). Antibacterial efficiency of the sudanese roselle (hibiscus sabdariffa l.), a famous beverage from sudanese folk medicine. *Journal of Intercultural Ethnopharmacology, 5*(2), 186. doi:10.5455/jice.20160320022623 PMID:27104041

Ai-Bashish, & Ban-Ahmad. (2011). Detection and classification of leaf diseases using K-Means based segmentation and neural networks based classification. *Información Tecnológica, 10,* 267–275.

Aiello, E. M., Toffanin, C., Messori, M., Cobelli, C., & Magni, L. (2018). Postprandial glucose regulation via KNN meal classification in type 1 diabetes. *IEEE Control Systems Letters, 3*(2), 230–235. doi:10.1109/LCSYS.2018.2844179

Ain, Q. T., Ali, M., Riaz, A., Noureen, A., Kamran, M., Hayat, B., & Rehman, A. (2017). Sentiment analysis using deep learning techniques: A review. *International Journal of Advanced Computer Science and Applications, 8*(6), 424.

Akbar, S., Rao, T. S., & Hussain, M. A. (2016). A hybrid scheme based on Big Data analytics using intrusion detection system. *Indian Journal of Science and Technology, 9*(33). Advance online publication. doi:10.17485/ijst/2016/v9i33/97037

Akhare, R., Mangla, M., Deokar, S., & Wadhwa, V. (2020). Proposed Framework for Fog Computing to Improve Quality-of-Service in IoT Applications. In *Fog Data Analytics for IoT Applications* (pp. 123–143). Springer. doi:10.1007/978-981-15-6044-6_7

Akrivopoulos, O., Amaxilatis, D., Mavrommati, I., & Chatzigiannakis, I. (2019). Utilising fog computing for developing a person-centric heart monitoring system. *Journal of Ambient Intelligence and Smart Environments, 11*(3), 237–259. doi:10.3233/AIS-190523

Akshaya, P. (2016). Intrusion detection system using machine learning approach. *International Journal of Engineering and Computer Science, 5*(10), 18249–18254. doi:10.18535/ijecs/v5i10.05

Al-Alia, Gupta, & Al Nabulsic. (2018). Cyber-Physical Systems Role in Manufacturing Technologies. In 6*th International Conference on Nano and Materials Science, AIP Conf. Proc.* (pp. 050007-1–050007-7). AIP Publishing.

Alamelu, J. V., & Mythili, A. (n.d.). Smart infusion pump control – The control system perspective. Computational Intelligence in Healthcare, 199-211.

Alber, M., Tepole, A. B., Cannon, W. R., De, S., Dura-Bernal, S., Garikipati, K., ... Kuhl, E. (2019). Integrating machine learning and multiscale modeling—Perspectives, challenges, and opportunities in the biological, biomedical, and behavioral sciences. *NPJ Digital Medicine, 2*(1), 1–11. doi:10.103841746-019-0193-y PMID:31799423

Aldhyani, T. H., Alshebami, A. S., & Alzahrani, M. Y. (2020). Soft Clustering for Enhancing the Diagnosis of Chronic Diseases over Machine Learning Algorithms. *Journal of Healthcare Engineering, 2020*, 2020. doi:10.1155/2020/4984967 PMID:32211144

Alehegn, M., Joshi, R., & Mulay, P. (2018). Analysis and prediction of diabetes mellitus using machine learning algorithm. *International Journal of Pure and Applied Mathematics, 118*(9), 871–878.

Alghamdi, F., Mahfoudh, S., & Barnawi, A. (2019). A novel fog computing based architecture to improve the performance in content delivery networks. *Wireless Communications and Mobile Computing.* doi:10.1109/ICWS.2019.00062

Alice Joseline, I., & Benila, S. (2017). Voice Recognition Based Vehicle Manufacturing. *International Journal of Engineering Development and Research, 5*(2), 51–56.

Ali, L., Khan, S. U., Golilarz, N. A., Yakubu, I., Qasim, I., Noor, A., & Nour, R. (2019). A Feature-Driven Decision Support System for Heart Failure Prediction Based on Statistical Model and Gaussian Naive Bayes. *Computational and Mathematical Methods in Medicine, 2019*, 2019. doi:10.1155/2019/6314328 PMID:31885684

Alloghani, M., Al-Jumeily, D., Hussain, A., Liatsis, P., & Aljaaf, A. J. (2020). Performance-Based Prediction of Chronic Kidney Disease Using Machine Learning for High-Risk Cardiovascular Disease Patients. In *Nature-Inspired Computation in Data Mining and Machine Learning* (pp. 187–206). Springer. doi:10.1007/978-3-030-28553-1_9

Almasoud, M., & Ward, T. E. (2019). Detection of chronic kidney disease using machine learning algorithms with the least number of predictors. *International Journal of Soft Computing and Its Applications, 10*(8). Advance online publication. doi:10.14569/IJACSA.2019.0100813

Alsayat, A., & Elmitwally, N. (2020). A comprehensive study for Arabic Sentiment Analysis (Challenges and Applications). *Egyptian Informatics Journal, 21*(1), 7–12. doi:10.1016/j.eij.2019.06.001

Al-Smadi, M., Al-Ayyoub, M., Jararweh, Y., & Qawasmeh, O. (2019). Enhancing aspect-based sentiment analysis of Arabic hotels' reviews using morphological, syntactic and semantic features. *Information Processing & Management, 56*(2), 308–319. doi:10.1016/j.ipm.2018.01.006

Aly, H. M., Aborizka, M., & Labib, S. S. (2020, March). Predicting the Risk Factor for Developing Chronic Kidney Disease Using a 3-Stage Prediction Model. In *Future of Information and Communication Conference* (pp. 631-641). Springer.

Amarasingham, R. P. R., Patzer, R. E., Huesch, M., Nguyen, N. Q., & Xie, B. (2014). Implementing Electronic Health Care Predictive Analytics: Considerations And Challenges. *Health Affairs*, *33*(7), 1148–1154. doi:10.1377/hlthaff.2014.0352 PMID:25006140

Ambale-Venkatesh, B., Yang, X., Wu, C. O., Liu, K., Hundley, W. G., McClelland, R., Gomes, A. S., Folsom, A. R., Shea, S., Guallar, E., Bluemke, D. A., & Lima, J. A. C. (2017). Cardiovascular event prediction by machine learning: The multi-ethnic study of atherosclerosis. *Circulation Research*, *121*(9), 1092–1101. doi:10.1161/CIRCRESAHA.117.311312 PMID:28794054

Amit Kumar Gupta, V. S.-G. (2021). Prediction of COVID-19 pandemic measuring criteria using support vector machine, prophet and linear regression models in Indian scenario. *Journal of Interdisciplinary Mathematics*, *24*(1), 89–108. doi:10.1080/09720502.2020.1833458

Amor, N. B., Benferhat, S., & Elouedi, Z. (2004, March). Naive bayes vs decision trees in intrusion detection systems. In *Proceedings of the 2004 ACM symposium on Applied computing* (pp. 420-424). 10.1145/967900.967989

Ampamya, Kitayimbwa, & Were. (2020). *Performance of an open source facial recognition system for unique patient matching in a resource-limited setting*. International Journal of Medical Informatics, 141, 1–5.

Andrew Bartley. (n.d.). *Predictive Analytics In Healthcare*. Retrieved 1 15, 2021, From Intel: Https://Www.Intel.Com/Content/Dam/Www/Public/Us/En/Documents/White-Papers/Gmc-Analytics-Healthcare-Whitepaper.Pdf

Anwar, S., Ajmal, A., Hayder, F., & Bibi, S. (2018). Evaluating Cloud & Fog Computing based on Shifting & Scheduling Algorithms, Latency Issues and service Architecture. *International Journal of Computer Science and Information Security*, *16*(6).

Ardabili, S. F.-K., Mosavi, A., Ghamisi, P., Ferdinand, F., Varkonyi-Koczy, A. R., Reuter, U., Rabczuk, T., & Atkinson, P. M. (2020). Covid-19 outbreak prediction with machine learning. *Algorithms*, *13*(10), 249. doi:10.3390/a13100249

Arras, L., Montavon, G., Müller, K. R., & Samek, W. (2017). Explaining recurrent neural network predictions in sentiment analysis. arXiv preprint arXiv:1706.07206. doi:10.18653/v1/W17-5221

Arsenovic, M., Karanovic, M., Sladojevic, S., Anderla, A., & Stefanovic, D. (2019). Solving Current Limitations of Deep Learning Based Approaches for Plant Disease Detection. *Symmetry*, *11*(7), 939. doi:10.3390ym11070939

Ashiku, L., & Dagli, C. (2021). Network Intrusion Detection System using Deep Learning. *Procedia Computer Science*, *185*, 239–247. doi:10.1016/j.procs.2021.05.025

Compilation of References

Augusto, J., Barreiros, L., Roberto, J., De Souza, B., Fernandes, G., & Junior, B. (2013). Lqg / Ltr Controller Design for an Anaesthesia Infusion System. *World Congress on Advances in Nano, Biomechanics, Robotics and Energy Research.*

Ayasun, S., & Karbeyaz, G. (2008). DC motor speed control methods using MATLAB/Simulink and their integration into undergraduate electric machinery courses. *Computer Applications in Engineering Education, 15*(4), 347–354. doi:10.1002/cae.20151

BaressiŠegota, S. L. (2019). On the traveling salesman problem in nautical environments:An evolutionary computing approach to optimization of tourist route paths in Medulin, Croatia. *Pomorskizbornik, 57*(1), 71–87.

Basiri, M. E., & Kabiri, A. (2017, April). Sentence-level sentiment analysis in Persian. In *2017 3rd International Conference on Pattern Recognition and Image Analysis (IPRIA)* (pp. 84-89). IEEE. 10.1109/PRIA.2017.7983023

Batista, E., Godinho, I., Ferreira, M. do C., Furtado, A., & Lucas, P. (2019). *Comparison of infusion pumps calibration methods.* Institute of Physics Publishing.

Bedekar, H., Hossain, G., & Goyal, A. (2020). Medical Analytics Based on Artificial Neural Networks Using Cognitive Internet of Things. In *Fog Data Analytics for IoT Applications* (pp. 199–262). Springer. doi:10.1007/978-981-15-6044-6_10

Belisario Panay, N. B. (2019). Predicting Health Care Costs Using Evidenceregression. In *13th International Conference On Ubiquitous Computing And Ambient Intelligence Ucami.* Toledo, Spain: MDPI.

Bhardwaj, A., Khanna, P., & Kumar, S. (2020). Mobile FOG Architecture Assisted Continuous Acquisition of Fetal ECG Data for Efficient Prediction. In *Fog Data Analytics for IoT Applications* (pp. 107–122). Springer. doi:10.1007/978-981-15-6044-6_6

Bikbov, B., Purcell, C. A., Levey, A. S., Smith, M., Abdoli, A., Abebe, M., & Ahmadian, E. (2020). Global, regional, and national burden of chronic kidney disease, 1990–2017: A systematic analysis for the Global Burden of Disease Study 2017. *Lancet, 395*(10225), 709–733. doi:10.1016/S0140-6736(20)30045-3 PMID:32061315

Bonacina, F., Baragetti, A., Catapano, A. L., & Norata, G. D. (2019). The interconnection between Immuno-metabolism, diabetes, and CKD. *Current Diabetes Reports, 19*(5), 21. doi:10.100711892-019-1143-4 PMID:30888513

Boukenze, B., Mousannif, H., & Haqiq, A. (2016). Predictive analytics in healthcare system using data mining techniques. *Computer Science & Information Technology (CS & IT),* 1-9.

Boutaba, R., Salahuddin, M. A., Limam, N., Ayoubi, S., Shahriar, N., Estrada-Solano, F., & Caicedo, O. M. (2018). A comprehensive survey on machine learning for networking:evolution, applications and research opportunities. *Journal of Internet Services and Applications, 9*(1), 16. doi:10.118613174-018-0087-2

Budiawan, I., Pranoto, H. R., Hidayat, E. M. I., & Arief, S. R. (2018). Design and Implementation of Cyber-Physical System-Based Automation on Plant Chemical Process: Study Case Mini Batch Distillation Column. *6th International Conference on Information and Communication Technology*, 360-365. 10.1109/ICoICT.2018.8528798

Burger, W., Burge, M. J., Burge, M. J., & Burge, M. J. (2009). *Principles of digital image processing* (Vol. 54). Springer.

Camargo & Smith. (2019). *An Image processing based algorithm to automatically identify plant disease visual symptoms.* Elsevier.

Cambria, E. (2016). Affective computing and sentiment analysis. *IEEE Intelligent Systems, 31*(2), 102–107. doi:10.1109/MIS.2016.31

Chang, H.-C., Peng, C.-H., Yeh, D.-M., Kao, E.-S., & Wang, C.-J. (2014). Hibiscus sabdariffa extract inhibits obesity and fat accumulation and improves liver steatosis in humans. *Food & Function, 5*(4), 734–739. doi:10.1039/c3fo60495k PMID:24549255

Chang, L. W., Hou, W., Zhao, L., Zhang, Y., Wang, Y., Wu, L., Xu, T., Wang, L., Wang, J., Ma, J., Wang, L., Zhao, J., Xu, J., Dong, J., Yan, Y., Yang, R., Li, Y., Guo, F., Cheng, W., ... Wang, L. (2021). The prevalence of antibodies to SARS-CoV-2 among blood donors in China. *Nature Communications, 12*(1), 1–10. doi:10.103841467-021-21503-x PMID:33654063

Chauhan, S., & Vig, L. (2015, October). Anomaly detection in ECG time signals via deep long short-term memory networks. In *2015 IEEE International Conference on Data Science and Advanced Analytics (DSAA)* (pp. 1-7). IEEE. 10.1109/DSAA.2015.7344872

Chen, K., Zhang, Z., Long, J., & Zhang, H. (2016). Turning from TF-IDF to TF-IGM for term weighting in text classification. *Expert Systems with Applications, 66*, 245–260. doi:10.1016/j.eswa.2016.09.009

Chiu, C.-T., Chen, J.-H., Chou, F.-P., & Lin, H.-H. (2005). Hibiscus sabdariffa leaf extract inhibits human prostate cancer cell invasion via down-regulation of akt/nf-kb/mmp-9 pathway. *Nutrients, 7*(7), 5065–5087. doi:10.3390/nu7075065 PMID:26115086

Chopda, Raveshiya, Nakum, & Nakrani. (2018). Cotton Crop Disease Detection using Decision Tree Classifier. *2018 International Conference on Smart City and Emerging Technology (ICSCET).* 10.1109/ICSCET.2018.8537336

Choudhari, T., Moh, M., & Moh, T. S. (2018, March). Prioritized task scheduling in fog computing. In *Proceedings of the ACMSE 2018 Conference* (pp. 1-8). Academic Press.

Chowdhary, C. L., Mittal, M., Pattanaik, P. A., & Marszalek, Z. (2020). An efficient segmentation and classification system in medical images using intuitionist possibilistic fuzzy C-mean clustering and fuzzy SVM algorithm. *Sensors (Basel), 20*(14), 3903. doi:10.339020143903 PMID:32668793

Compilation of References

Cicconi, P., Russo, A. C., Germani, M., Prist, M., Pallotta, E., & Monteriù, A. (2017). Cyber-physical system integration for industry 4.0: Modelling and simulation of an induction heating process for aluminium-steel molds in footwear soles manufacturing. *2017 IEEE 3rd International Forum on Research and Technologies for Society and Industry*, 1-6.

Clim, A., Zota, R. D., & Tinica, G. (2018). Te Kullback–Leibler divergence used in machine learning algorithms for health care applications and hypertension prediction: A literature review. *Procedia Computer Science*, *141*, 448–453. doi:10.1016/j.procs.2018.10.144

Cruz, Carvajal, Rojas, & Chacón. (2018). Cyber-Physical System for Industrial Control Automation based on the Holonic Approach and the IEC 61499 Standard. 2018 Forum on Specification & Design Languages (FDL), 5-16.

Cui, Zhang, Li, Hartman, & Zhao. (2012). *Image Processing methods for quantitatively detecting soybean rust from multispectral images*. Elsevier.

Dangare & Sulabha. (2012). A data mining approach for prediction of heart. *International Journal of Computer Engineering and Technology*, 30-40.

Darapaneni, N. S. M. (2021). Predicting the Impact of Covid-19 Pandemic in India. In *2021 IEEE International IOT, Electronics and Mechatronics Conference (IEMTRONICS)* (pp. 1-7). IEEE.

Dario Gregori, M. P. (2011, June). Regression Models For Analyzing Costs And Their Determinants In Health Care: An Introductory Review. *International Journal for Quality in Health Care*, *23*(3), 331–341. doi:10.1093/intqhc/mzr010 PMID:21504959

Das, R., Bhattacharyya, S., & Nandy, S. (Eds.). (2020). *Machine Learning Applications: Emerging Trends* (Vol. 5). Walter de Gruyter GmbH & Co KG. doi:10.1515/9783110610987

De Cristofaro, S., Stefanini, C., Pak, N. N., Susilo, E., Carrozza, M. C., & Dario, P. (2010). Electromagnetic wobble micromotor for microrobots actuation. *Sensors and Actuators. A, Physical*, *161*(1–2), 234–244. doi:10.1016/j.sna.2010.04.028

Debray, T. P. A., Vergouwe, Y., Koffijberg, H., Nieboer, D., Steyerberg, E. W., & Moons, K. G. M. (2015). A new framework to enhance the interpretation of external validation studies of clinical prediction models. *Journal of Clinical Epidemiology*, *68*(3), 279–289. doi:10.1016/j.jclinepi.2014.06.018 PMID:25179855

Deepa, K. K. (2017). Health Care Analysis Using Random Forestalgorithm. *Journal Of Chemical And Pharmaceutical Sciences*, *10*(3), 1359–1361.

Ding, J., Sun, H., Wang, X., & Liu, X. (2018, June). Entity-level sentiment analysis of issue comments. In *Proceedings of the 3rd International Workshop on Emotion Awareness in Software Engineering* (pp. 7-13). 10.1145/3194932.3194935

Dou, Z. Y. (2017, September). Capturing user and product information for document level sentiment analysis with deep memory network. In *Proceedings of the 2017 Conference on Empirical Methods in Natural Language Processing* (pp. 521-526). 10.18653/v1/D17-1054

Dridi, A., & Recupero, D. R. (2019). Leveraging semantics for sentiment polarity detection in social media. *International Journal of Machine Learning and Cybernetics*, *10*(8), 2045–2055. doi:10.100713042-017-0727-z

Drozdz, D., & Kawecka-Jaszcz, K. (2014). Cardiovascular changes during chronic hypertensive states. *Pediatric Nephrology (Berlin, Germany)*, *29*(9), 1507–1516. doi:10.100700467-013-2614-5 PMID:24026758

Drube, J., Wan, M., Bonthuis, M., Wühl, E., Bacchetta, J., Santos, F., & Tönshoff, B. (2019). Clinical practice recommendations for growth hormone treatment in children with chronic kidney disease. *Nature Reviews. Nephrology*, *15*(9), 577–589. doi:10.103841581-019-0161-4 PMID:31197263

Duan, J., & Qiu, G. (2004). Novel histogram processing for color image enhancement. In *Third International Conference on Image and Graphics (ICIG'04)* (pp. 55–58). IEEE. 10.1109/ICIG.2004.105

Durairaj, M., & Poornappriya, T. S. (2019, January). Why Feature Selection in Data Mining Is Prominent? A Survey. In *International Conference on Artificial Intelligence, Smart Grid and Smart City Applications* (pp. 949-963). Springer.

El Houby, E. M. (2018). A survey on applying machine learning techniques for management of diseases. *Journal of Applied Biomedicine*, *16*(3), 165–174. doi:10.1016/j.jab.2018.01.002

El-Basheir & Fouad. (2012a). preliminary pilot survey on head lice, pediculosis in sharkia governorate and treatment of lice with natural plant extracts. *Journal of the Egyptian Society of Parasitology, 32*(3), 725–736.

Elenkov, M., Ecker, P., Lukitsch, B., Janeczek, C., Harasek, M., & Gföhler, M. (2020). Estimation methods for viscosity, flow rate and pressure from pump-motor assembly parameters. *Sensors (Switzerland)*, *20*(5), 1451. Advance online publication. doi:10.339020051451 PMID:32155844

Elhoseny, M., Shankar, K., & Uthayakumar, J. (2019). Intelligent diagnostic prediction and classification system for chronic kidney disease. *Scientific Reports*, *9*(1), 1–14. doi:10.103841598-019-46074-2 PMID:31270387

Fadzil, Rizam, Jailani, & Nooritawati. (2014). Orchid leaf disease detection using Border segmentation technique. *IEEE Conference on Systems, Process Control, 1*, 168-179.

Fraser, S. D., & Roderick, P. J. (2019). Kidney disease in the global burden of disease study 2017. *Nature Reviews. Nephrology*, *15*(4), 193–194. doi:10.103841581-019-0120-0 PMID:30723305

Freyder, C. W. (2016). *Using Linear Regression And Mixed Models To Predict Health Care Costs After An Inpatient Event*. University of Pittsburgh. Retrieved From Https://Core.Ac.Uk/Download/Pdf/78481788.Pdf

Fu, X., Liu, W., Xu, Y., & Cui, L. (2017). Combine HowNet lexicon to train phrase recursive autoencoder for sentence-level sentiment analysis. *Neurocomputing*, *241*, 18–27. doi:10.1016/j.neucom.2017.01.079

Gardašević, G., Katzis, K., Bajić, D., & Berbakov, L. (2020). Emerging wireless sensor networks and internet of things technologies—Foundations of smart healthcare. *Sensors (Switzerland)*, *20*(13), 1–30. doi:10.339020133619 PMID:32605071

Gedeon, J., Himmelmann, N., Felka, P., Herrlich, F., Stein, M., & Mühlhäuser, M. (2018, February). vStore: A context-aware framework for mobile micro-storage at the edge. In *International Conference on Mobile Computing, Applications, and Services* (pp. 165-182). Springer. 10.1007/978-3-319-90740-6_10

Geetha, Samundeswari, Saranya, Meenakshi, & Nithya. (2020). Plant Leaf Disease Classification And Detection System Using Machine Learning. *Journal of Physics: Conference Series, 1712*. doi:10.1088/1742-6596/1712/1/012012

Ghiassi, M., & Lee, S. (2018). A domain transferable lexicon set for Twitter sentiment analysis using a supervised machine learning approach. *Expert Systems with Applications*, *106*, 197–216. doi:10.1016/j.eswa.2018.04.006

Gnanasekar, A. K., & Jayavelu, P. (2014). Voice-Based Wireless Industrial Automation With Enhanced Feedback System. In *Proc. of the Intl. Conf. on Advances in Computer, Electronics and Electrical Engineering* (pp. 51-55). Universal Association of Computer and Electronics Engineers.

Gokulnath, C. B., & Shantharajah, S. P. (2019). An optimized feature selection based on genetic approach and support vector machine for heart disease. *Cluster Computing*, *22*(6), 14777–14787. doi:10.100710586-018-2416-4

Goodfellow, I., Bengio, Y., & Courville, A. (2016). *Deep learning*. MIT Press. https://en.wikipedia.org/wiki/Suricata_(software)

Goodhart, A. K. (2016). Hypertension from the patient's perspective. *The British Journal of General Practice*, *66*(652), 570. doi:10.3399/bjgp16X687757 PMID:27789496

Goyal, M., Saurav, K., Tiwari, G., Rege, A., & Saxena, A. (2020). IV (Intravenous) Tube Flow Control Device with IOT. *2020 IEEE International Students' Conference on Electrical, Electronics and Computer Science, SCEECS 2020*, 4–7. 10.1109/SCEECS48394.2020.53

Gupta, A. S.-G. (2020). Prediction of COVID-19 pandemic measuring criteria using support vector machine, prophet and linear regression models in Indian scenario. *Journal of Interdisciplinary Mathematics*, 1–20.

Han, H., Zhang, Y., Zhang, J., Yang, J., & Zou, X. (2018). Improving the performance of lexicon-based review sentiment analysis method by reducing additional introduced sentiment bias. *PLoS One*, *13*(8), e0202523. doi:10.1371/journal.pone.0202523 PMID:30142154

Hannun, A. Y., Rajpurkar, P., Haghpanahi, M., Tison, G. H., Bourn, C., Turakhia, M. P., & Ng, A. Y. (2019). Cardiologist-level arrhythmia detection and classification in ambulatory electrocardiograms using a deep neural network. *Nature Medicine*, *25*(1), 65–69. doi:10.103841591-018-0268-3 PMID:30617320

Hanumantharaju, R., Kumar, D. P., Sowmya, B. J., Siddesh, G. M., Shreenath, K. N., & Srinivasa, K. G. (2021). Enabling Technologies for Fog Computing in Healthcare 4.0: Challenges and Future Implications. In *Fog Computing for Healthcare 4.0 Environments* (pp. 157–176). Springer. doi:10.1007/978-3-030-46197-3_7

Hanumantharaju, R., & Murthy, T. N. (2020). Grocery Product Classification and Recommendation System Based on Machine Learning and Customer Profile Identity. In *ICDSMLA 2019* (pp. 199–210). Springer. doi:10.1007/978-981-15-1420-3_21

Haque, S. A., Aziz, S. M., & Rahman, M. (2014). Review of cyber-physical system in healthcare. *International Journal of Distributed Sensor Networks*, *2014*(4), 217415. Advance online publication. doi:10.1155/2014/217415

Hariharan, U., & Rajkumar, K. (2020). The Importance of Fog Computing for Healthcare 4.0-Based IoT Solutions. In *Fog Data Analytics for IoT Applications* (pp. 471–494). Springer. doi:10.1007/978-981-15-6044-6_19

Hassan, S. M., Maji, A. K., Jasiński, M., Leonowicz, Z., & Jasińska, E. (2021). Identification of Plant-Leaf Diseases Using CNN and Transfer-Learning Approach. *Electronics (Basel)*, *10*(12), 1388. doi:10.3390/electronics10121388

Hatcher, W. G., & Yu, W. (2018). A survey of deep learning: Platforms, applications and emerging research trends. *IEEE Access: Practical Innovations, Open Solutions*, *6*, 24411–24432. doi:10.1109/ACCESS.2018.2830661

Hei, X., Du, X., Lin, S., Lee, I., & Sokolsky, O. (2015). Patient Infusion Pattern based Access Control Schemes for Wireless Insulin Pump System. *IEEE Transactions on Parallel and Distributed Systems*, *26*(11), 3108–3121. doi:10.1109/TPDS.2014.2370045

He, J., Wei, J., Chen, K., Tang, Z., Zhou, Y., & Zhang, Y. (2017). Multitier fog computing with large-scale iot data analytics for smart cities. *IEEE Internet of Things Journal*, *5*(2), 677–686. doi:10.1109/JIOT.2017.2724845

Hijikata, W., Rao, J., Abe, S., Takatani, S., & Shinshi, T. (2015). Estimating flow rate using the motor torque in a rotary blood pump. *Sensors and Materials*, *27*(4), 297–308. doi:10.18494/SAM.2015.1068

Hodgson, T. A., & Cai, L. (2001). Medical care expenditures for hypertension, its complications, and its comorbidities. *Medical Care*, 599–615.

Hota, S. D. (2016). Classification Of Health Care Data Using Machine Learning Technique. *International Journal of Engineering Science Invention*, 17-20.

Hruska, K. A., Williams, M. J., & Sugatani, T. (2020). Chronic kidney disease–mineral and bone disorders. In *Chronic Renal Disease* (pp. 551–569). Academic Press. doi:10.1016/B978-0-12-815876-0.00035-8

Hsu, K. Y., DeLaurentis, P., Yih, Y., & Bitan, Y. (2019). Tracking the Progress of Wireless Infusion Pump Drug Library Updates– A Data-Driven Analysis of Pump Update Delays. *Journal of Medical Systems*, *43*(3), 75. Advance online publication. doi:10.100710916-019-1189-5 PMID:30756252

Hui, D. S., I Azhar, E., Madani, T. A., Ntoumi, F., Kock, R., Dar, O., Ippolito, G., Mchugh, T. D., Memish, Z. A., Drosten, C., Zumla, A., & Petersen, E. (2020). The continuing 2019-nCoV epidemic threat of novel coronaviruses to global health—The latest 2019 novel coronavirus outbreak in Wuhan, China. *International Journal of Infectious Diseases*, *91*, 264–266. doi:10.1016/j.ijid.2020.01.009 PMID:31953166

Hung, L. P., & Alfred, R. (2017, April). A performance comparison of feature extraction methods for sentiment analysis. In *Asian Conference on Intelligent Information and Database Systems* (pp. 379-390). Springer. 10.1007/978-3-319-56660-3_33

Husham, I. (2019). A review Cyber of Industry 4.0 (Cyber-Physical Systems (CPS), the Internet of Things (IoT) and the Internet of Services (IoS)): Components, and Security Challenges. *Journal of Physics: Conference Series*, *1424*, 012029. doi:10.1088/1742-6596/1424/1/012029

Hussana Johar, R. B., Soujanya, R., Sushma, S., & Syeda Ansha Sami Supreetha, M. G. (2014). Wireless Monitoring For Industrial Automation Using Speech Recognition. *International Journal of Engineering and Innovative Technology*, *3*(11), 133–139.

Hussein, D. M. E. D. M. (2018). A survey on sentiment analysis challenges. *Journal of King Saud University-Engineering Sciences*, *30*(4), 330–338. doi:10.1016/j.jksues.2016.04.002

Hu, Y. Z. (2020). Healthcare Predictive Analytics For Disease Progression: A Longitudinal Data Fusion Approach. *Journal of Intelligent Information Systems*, 351–369.

Imhoff, M., Kuhls, S., Gather, U., & Fried, R. (2009). Smart alarms from medical devices in the OR and ICU. In Best Practice and Research: Clinical Anaesthesiology (Vol. 23, Issue 1, pp. 39–50). doi:10.1016/j.bpa.2008.07.008

InfoWorld. (2009). *The greatest open source software of all time.* https://www.infoworld.com/d/open-source/greatest-open-source-software-all-time-776?source=fssrSuricata

Ioffe, S., & Szegedy, C. (2015). Batch Normalization. *Accelerating Deep Network Training by Reducing Internal Covariate Shift, ICML2015*, 448–456.

Islam, M. R., Zahid Rusho, R., & Rabiul Islam, S. M. (2019). Design and implementation of low cost smart syringe pump for telemedicine and healthcare. *1st International Conference on Robotics, Electrical and Signal Processing Techniques, ICREST 2019*, 440–444. 10.1109/ICREST.2019.8644373

Jayatilake, S. M. D. A. C., & Ganegoda, G. U. (2021). Involvement of Machine Learning Tools in Healthcare Decision Making. *Journal of Healthcare Engineering*. PMID:33575021

Jazdi, N. (2014). Cyber-Physical Systems in the Context of Industry 4.0. *2014 IEEE International Conference on Automation, Quality and Testing, Robotics, 2014*, 1–4.

Jena, L., Nayak, S., & Swain, R. (2020). Chronic Disease Risk (CDR) Prediction in Biomedical Data Using Machine Learning Approach. In *Advances in Intelligent Computing and Communication* (pp. 232–239). Springer. doi:10.1007/978-981-15-2774-6_29

Joshi, N. S., & Itkat, S. A. (2014). A survey on feature level sentiment analysis. *International Journal of Computer Science and Information Technologies*, 5(4), 5422–5425.

Jung, Kim, & Joo. (2015). Physicochemical properties and antimicrobial activity of roselle (hibiscus sabdariffa l.). *Journal of the Science of Food and Agriculture*, 93(15), 3769–3776. PMID:23749748

Kalarani, P., & Brunda, S. S. (2019). Sentiment analysis by POS and joint sentiment topic features using SVM and ANN. *Soft Computing*, 23(16), 7067–7079. doi:10.100700500-018-3349-9

Kamdar, H., Karkera, R., Khanna, A., Kulkarni, P., & Agrawal, S. (2017). A Review on Home Automation Using Voice Recognition. *International Research. Journal of Engineering Technology*, 4(10), 1795–1799.

Kang, M. J., & Kang, J. W. (2016). Intrusion detection system using deep neural network for in-vehicle network security. *PLoS One*, 11(6), e0155781. doi:10.1371/journal.pone.0155781 PMID:27271802

Kanjee, M. R., & Liu, H. (2016). Authentication and key relay in medical cyber-physical systems. In Security and Communication Networks (Vol. 9, Issue 9, pp. 874–885). doi:10.1002ec.1009

Kannan, P., Udayakumar, S. K., & Ahmed, K. R. (2014). Automation using voice recognition with python SL4A script for android devices. *2014 International Conference on Industrial Automation, Information and Communications Technology*, 1-4. 10.1109/IAICT.2014.6922098

Kannan, R., & Vasanthi, V. (2019). Machine learning algorithms with ROC curve for predicting and diagnosing the heart disease. In *Soft Computing and Medical Bioinformatics* (pp. 63–72). Springer. doi:10.1007/978-981-13-0059-2_8

Karachua, E., & Turk, A. S. (2001). E-polarized scalar wave diffraction by perfectly conductive arbitrary shaped cylindrical obstacles with finite thickness. *International Journal of Infrared and Millimeter Waves*, 22(10), 1531–1546. doi:10.1023/A:1015098925652

Kato, K., & Klyuev, V. (2017, August). Development of a network intrusion detection system using Apache Hadoop and Spark. In *2017 IEEE Conference on Dependable and Secure Computing* (pp. 416-423). IEEE. 10.1109/DESEC.2017.8073860

Kaur, A., Singh, P., & Nayyar, A. (2020). Fog Computing: Building a Road to IoT with Fog Analytics. In *Fog Data Analytics for IoT Applications* (pp. 59–78). Springer. doi:10.1007/978-981-15-6044-6_4

Kerre, E. E., & Nachtegael, M. (2013). Fuzzy techniques in image processing. *Physica*.

Khalil, I. S. (n.d.). Rubbing against blood clots using helical robots: modeling and in-vitro experimental validation. *Robotics and Automation Letters, 2*(2), 927-934.

Khamparia, A., Saini, G., Pandey, B., Tiwari, S., Gupta, D., & Khanna, A. (2019). KDSAE: Chronic kidney disease classification with multimedia data learning using deep stacked autoencoder network. *Multimedia Tools and Applications*, 1–16. doi:10.100711042-019-07839-z

Khan, R. U., Khan, K., Albattah, W., & Qamar, A. M. (2021). Image-Based Detection of Plant Diseases: From Classical Machine Learning to Deep Learning Journey. Hindawi Wireless Communications and Mobile Computing. doi:10.1155/2021/5541859

Khan, J. A., Westphal, C., & Ghamri-Doudane, Y. (2019). Information-centric fog network for incentivized collaborative caching in the Internet of everything. *IEEE Communications Magazine*, *57*(7), 27–33. doi:10.1109/MCOM.2019.1800764

Khan, Y., Qamar, U., Yousaf, N., & Khan, A. (2019, February). Machine learning techniques for heart disease datasets: a survey. In *Proceedings of the 2019 11th International Conference on Machine Learning and Computing* (pp. 27-35). 10.1145/3318299.3318343

Khoo, C. S., & Johnkhan, S. B. (2018). Lexicon-based sentiment analysis: Comparative evaluation of six sentiment lexicons. *Journal of Information Science*, *44*(4), 491–511. doi:10.1177/0165551517703514

Kim, B.-K., Roh, J., Dong, S.-Y., & Lee, S.-Y. (2016). Hierarchical committee of deep convolutional neural networks for robust facial expression recognition. *Multimodal User Interfaces*, *10*(2), 173–189. doi:10.100712193-015-0209-0

Kim, H. C., Bandettini, P. A., & Lee, J. H. (2019). Deep neural network predicts emotional responses of the human brain from functional magnetic resonance imaging. *NeuroImage*, *186*, 607–627. doi:10.1016/j.neuroimage.2018.10.054 PMID:30366076

Kim, U. R., Peterfreund, R. A., & Lovich, M. A. (2017). Drug infusion systems: Technologies, performance, and pitfalls. *Anesthesia and Analgesia*, *124*(5), 1493–1505. doi:10.1213/ANE.0000000000001707 PMID:28212219

Kodati, S., Vivekanandam, R., & Ravi, G. (2019). Comparative Analysis of Clustering Algorithms with Heart Disease Datasets Using Data Mining Weka Tool. In *Soft Computing and Signal Processing* (pp. 111–117). Springer. doi:10.1007/978-981-13-3600-3_11

Konova, A. B., Lopez-Guzman, S., Urmanche, A., Ross, S., Louie, K., Rotrosen, J., & Glimcher, P. W. (2020). Computational markers of risky decision-making for identification of temporal windows of vulnerability to opioid use in a real-world clinical setting. *JAMA Psychiatry*, *77*(4), 368–377. doi:10.1001/jamapsychiatry.2019.4013 PMID:31812982

Kostov, K. (2019). Effects of magnesium deficiency on mechanisms of insulin resistance in type 2 diabetes: Focusing on the processes of insulin secretion and signaling. *International Journal of Molecular Sciences*, *20*(6), 1351. doi:10.3390/ijms20061351 PMID:30889804

Kraemer, F. A., Braten, A. E., Tamkittikhun, N., & Palma, D. (2017). Fog computing in healthcare–a review and discussion. *IEEE Access: Practical Innovations, Open Solutions*, *5*, 9206–9222. doi:10.1109/ACCESS.2017.2704100

Krishnamurthi, R., Gopinathan, D., & Nayyar, A. (2021). A Comprehensive Overview of Fog Data Processing and Analytics for Healthcare 4.0. *Fog Computing for Healthcare 4.0 Environments*, 103-129.

Krishnan & Sumithra. (2013). A Novel algorithm for detecting bacterial leaf scorch (BLS) of shade trees using image processing. *IEEE 11 Malaysia International Conference on Communications*.

Krizhevsky, A., Sutskever, I., & Hinton, G. E. (2012). *ImageNet Classification with Deep Convolutional Neural Networks*. NIPS.

Kumar & Shimi. (2015). Voice Recognition based Home Automation System for Paralyzed People – A Review. *International Journal of Engineering Research and General Science*, *3*(5), 671-673.

Kumar, M. A., Vimala, R., & Britto, K. R. A. (2019). A cognitive technology based healthcare monitoring system and medical data transmission. In Measurement: Journal of the International Measurement Confederation (Vol. 146, pp. 322–332). doi:10.1016/j.measurement.2019.03.017

Kumar, & Chaudhary, & Chandra. (2021). Plant Disease Detection Using CNN. *Turkish Journal of Computer and Mathematics Education*, *12*(12), 2106–2112.

Kumar, D. P., Hanumantharaju, R., Sowmya, B. J., Shreenath, K. N., & Srinivasa, K. G. (2020). Fog Data Analytics: Systematic Computational Classification and Procedural Paradigm. In *Fog Data Analytics for IoT Applications* (pp. 39–58). Springer. doi:10.1007/978-981-15-6044-6_3

Kumari, A., Tanwar, S., Tyagi, S., & Kumar, N. (2018). Fog computing for Healthcare 4.0 environment: Opportunities and challenges. *Computers & Electrical Engineering*, *72*, 1–13. doi:10.1016/j.compeleceng.2018.08.015

Kumari, A., Tanwar, S., Tyagi, S., Kumar, N., Parizi, R. M., & Choo, K. K. R. (2019). Fog data analytics: A taxonomy and process model. *Journal of Network and Computer Applications*, *128*, 90–104. doi:10.1016/j.jnca.2018.12.013

Kumari, R. K., Kumar, S., Poonia, R. C., Singh, V., Raja, L., Bhatnagar, V., & Agarwal, P. (2021). Analysis and predictions of spread, recovery, and death caused by COVID-19 in India. *Big Data Mining and Analytics*, *4*(2), 65–75. doi:10.26599/BDMA.2020.9020013

Kumar, M. B. (2020). An Intelligent Prediction Model of COVID-19 in India using Hybrid Epidemic Model. In *International Conference on Smart Electronics and Communication (ICOSEC)* (pp. 389-396). IEEE. 10.1109/ICOSEC49089.2020.9215426

Kushwaha, P., Buckchash, H., & Raman, B. (2017, November). Anomaly based intrusion detection using filter based feature selection on KDD-CUP 99. In *TENCON 2017-2017 IEEE Region 10 Conference* (pp. 839–844). IEEE. doi:10.1109/TENCON.2017.8227975

Kwekha-Rashid, A. A. (2021). Coronavirus disease (COVID-19) cases analysis using machine-learning applications. *Appl Nanosci*.

LaFreniere, D., Zulkernine, F., Barber, D., & Martin, K. (2016). Using machine learning to predict hypertension from a clinical dataset. *2016 IEEE Symposium Series on Computational Intelligence (SSCI)*, 1–7. 10.1109/SSCI.2016.7849886

Lee, J. B.-D. (2017). Deep neural networks as gaussian processes. *arXiv preprint*.

Lee, I., Sokolsky, O., Chen, S., Hatcliff, J., Jee, E., Kim, B., King, A., Mullen-Fortino, M., Park, S., Roederer, A., & Venkatasubramanian, K. K. (2012). Challenges and Research Directions in Medical Cyber-Physical Systems. *Proceedings of the IEEE, 100*(1), 75–90. doi:10.1109/JPROC.2011.2165270

Letarte, G., Paradis, F., Giguère, P., & Laviolette, F. (2018, November). Importance of self-attention for sentiment analysis. In *Proceedings of the 2018 EMNLP Workshop Blackbox, NLP: Analyzing and Interpreting Neural Networks for NLP* (pp. 267-275). Academic Press.

Liao, H. J., Lin, C. H. R., Lin, Y. C., & Tung, K. Y. (2013). Intrusion detection system: A comprehensive review. *Journal of Network and Computer Applications, 36*(1), 16–24. doi:10.1016/j.jnca.2012.09.004

Li, G., Liu, Y., Wu, J., Lin, D., & Zhao, S. (2019). Methods of resource scheduling based on optimized fuzzy clustering in fog computing. *Sensors (Basel), 19*(9), 2122. doi:10.339019092122 PMID:31071923

Li, K., Liu, F., Dong, H., Herrero, P., Guo, Y., & Georgiou, P. (2018, February). A deep learning platform for diabetes big data analysis. In *Proc. 11th Adv* (pp. A116–A116). Technologies Treatments Diabetes.

Li, L. Y., Yang, Z., Dang, Z., Meng, C., Huang, J., Meng, H., Wang, D., Chen, G., Zhang, J., Peng, H., & Shao, Y. (2020). Propagation analysis and prediction of the COVID-19. *Infectious Disease Modelling, 5*, 282–292. doi:10.1016/j.idm.2020.03.002 PMID:32292868

Lin, Du, & Xu. (2003). The preprocessing of subtraction and the enhancement for biomedical image of retinal blood vessels. *Sheng wu yi xue gong cheng xue za zhi= Journal of biomedical engineering= Shengwu yixue gongchengxue zazhi, 20*(1), 56–59.

Lin, Huang, Huang, Chen, & Wang. (2015). Hibiscus polyphenol-rich extract induces apoptosis in human gastric carcinoma cells via p53 phosphorylation and p38 mapk/fasl cascade pathway. *Molecular Carcinogenesis, 43*(2), 86–99.

Lindeman, T. (2018, February 15). *3 Examples Of How Hospitals Are Using Predictive Analytics*. Academic Press.

Lipsky, B. A., Senneville, É., Abbas, Z. G., Aragón-Sánchez, J., Diggle, M., Embil, J. M., Kono, S., Lavery, L. A., Malone, M., Asten, S. A., Urbančič-Rovan, V., & Peters, E. J. G. (2020). Guidelines on the diagnosis and treatment of foot infection in persons with diabetes (IWGDF 2019 update). *Diabetes/Metabolism Research and Reviews, 36*(S1), e3280. doi:10.1002/dmrr.3280 PMID:32176444

Liu, Wang, Yan, & Guo. (2015). Effective Facial Expression Recognition via the Boosted Convolutional Neural Network. *CCCV,* (1), 179-188.

Liu, B. (2020). Text sentiment analysis based on CBOW model and deep learning in big data environment. *Journal of Ambient Intelligence and Humanized Computing, 11*(2), 451–458. doi:10.100712652-018-1095-6

Liu, F., Zheng, J., Zheng, L., & Chen, C. (2020). Combining attention-based bidirectional gated recurrent neural network and two-dimensional convolutional neural network for document-level sentiment classification. *Neurocomputing, 371,* 39–50. doi:10.1016/j.neucom.2019.09.012

Liu, H., & Cocea, M. (2017, February). Fuzzy rule based systems for interpretable sentiment analysis. In *2017 Ninth International Conference on Advanced Computational Intelligence (ICACI)* (pp. 129-136). IEEE. 10.1109/ICACI.2017.7974497

Liu, L., Qi, D., Zhou, N., & Wu, Y. (2018). A task scheduling algorithm based on classification mining in fog computing environment. *Wireless Communications and Mobile Computing.*

Li, W., Liu, P., Zhang, Q., & Liu, W. (2019). An Improved Approach for Text Sentiment Classification Based on a Deep Neural Network via a Sentiment Attention Mechanism. *Future Internet, 11*(4), 96. doi:10.3390/fi11040096

Li, Y., Zhang, Y., & Liu, T. (2018). Analysis of Principal Component Regression Equations of Air Transportation and Local Economy: Taking Tianjin as an Example. *Theoretical Economics Letters, 08*(10), 1830–1839. doi:10.4236/tel.2018.810120

Lopes, A. T., de Aguiar, E., & Oliveira-Santos, T. (2015). *A Facial Expression Recognition System Using Convolutional Networks.* SIBGRAPI. doi:10.1109/SIBGRAPI.2015.14

López-Martínez, F., Schwarcz, M. D. A., Núñez-Valdez, E. R., & García-Díaz, V. (n.d.). Machine learning classifcation analysis for a hypertensive population as a function of several risk factors. *Expert Systems with Applications, 110,* 206–215. doi:10.1016/j.eswa.2018.06.006

Lu, Shi, & Xu. (2016). A kind of convolution neural network for facial expression recognition. *Journal of Nanjing University of Posts and Telecommunications (Natural Science Edition),* (1).

Lucey, P., Cohn, J. F., Kanade, T., Saragih, J., Ambadar, Z., & Matthews, I. (2010). The extended cohnkanade dataset (ck+): A complete dataset for action unit and emotion-specified expression. In *Computer Vision and Pattern Recognition Workshops (CVPRW), 2010 IEEE Computer Society Conference on.* IEEE.

Lu, K.-D., Zeng, G.-Q., Luo, X., Weng, J., Luo, W., & Wu, Y. (2021). Evolutionary Deep Belief Network for Cyber attack detection in Industrial automation and control system. *IEEE Transactions on Industrial Informatics, 17*(11), 7618–7627. doi:10.1109/TII.2021.3053304

Lu, Y. (2017). Cyber-Physical System (CPS)-Based Industry 4.0: A Survey. *Journal of Industrial Integration and Management, 2*(3), 1750014. doi:10.1142/S2424862217500142

Lu, Y., Yi, S., Zeng, N., Liu, Y., & Zhang, Y. (2017). Identification of Rice Diseases using Deep Convolutional Neural Networks. *Neurocomputing*, *267*, 378–384. doi:10.1016/j.neucom.2017.06.023

Lynn, K. S., Li, L.-L., Lin, Y.-J., Wang, C.-H., Sheng, S.-H., Lin, J.-H., Liao, W., Hsu, W.-L., & Pan, W.-H. (2009). A neural network model for constructing endophenotypes of common complex diseases: An application to male young-onset hypertension microarray data. *Bioinformatics (Oxford, England)*, *25*(8), 981–988. doi:10.1093/bioinformatics/btp106 PMID:19237446

Ly, T. T., Layne, J. E., Huyett, L. M., Nazzaro, D., & O'Connor, J. B. (2019). Novel Bluetooth-Enabled Tubeless Insulin Pump: Innovating Pump Therapy for Patients in the Digital Age. *Journal of Diabetes Science and Technology*, *13*(1), 20–26. doi:10.1177/1932296818798836 PMID:30239214

Madzou, L., & Louradour, S. (2020). Building a governance framework for facial recognition. *Biometric Technology Today*, *2020*(6), 5–8. doi:10.1016/S0969-4765(20)30083-7

Magesh, G., & Swarnalatha, P. (2020). Optimal feature selection through a cluster-based DT learning (CDTL) in heart disease prediction. *Evolutionary Intelligence*, 1–11. doi:10.100712065-019-00336-0

Mahapatra, S., & Singh, A. (2020). Application of IoT-Based Smart Devices in Health Care Using Fog Computing. In *Fog Data Analytics for IoT Applications* (pp. 263–278). Springer. doi:10.1007/978-981-15-6044-6_11

Maharaja & Ansari. (2019, April). *Voice Controlled Automation Using Raspberry Pi*. Paper presented at the International Conference on Advances in Science & Technology ICAST, Mumbai, India.

Mahmut, U. N. (2018). Control System Design of Syringe Infusion Pump and MATLAB Simulations. *International Journal of Scientific Research*, *7*(7), 6. doi:10.21275/ART20183120

Mamodiya & Sharma. (2014). Review in Industrial Automation. *IOSR Journal of Electrical and Electronics Engineering*, *9*(3), 33-38.

Manikis, G. C., Sakkalis, V., Zabulis, X., Karamaounas, P., Triantafyllou, A., & Douma, S. (2011). An Image Analysis Framework for the Early Assessment of Hypertensive Retinopathy Signs. *Proceedings of the 3rd International Conference on E-Health and Bioengineering - EHB*.

Mao, G., Wu, L., Fu, Y., Chen, Z., Natani, S., Gou, Z., Ruan, X., & Qu, S. (2018). Design and Characterization of a Soft Dielectric Elastomer Peristaltic Pump Driven by Electromechanical Load. *IEEE/ASME Transactions on Mechatronics*, *23*(5), 2132–2143. doi:10.1109/TMECH.2018.2864252

Mao, X., Yang, H., Huang, S., Liu, Y., & Li, R. (2019). Extractive summarization using supervised and unsupervised learning. *Expert Systems with Applications*, *133*, 173–181. doi:10.1016/j.eswa.2019.05.011

Maqsood, M., Mehmood, I., Kharel, R., Muhammad, K., Lee, J., & Alnumay, W. S. (2021). Exploring the Role of Deep Learning in Industrial Applications: A Case Study on Coastal Crane Casting Recognition. *Human Centric Computing and Information Sciences, 11*(20), 1–14.

Masci, P., Ayoub, A., Curzon, P., Lee, I., Sokolsky, O., & Thimbleby, H. (2013). Model-based development of the generic PCA infusion pump user interface prototype in PVS. Lecture Notes in Computer Science, 8153, 228–240. doi:10.1007/978-3-642-40793-2_21

Masci, P., Zhang, Y., Jones, P., Thimbleby, H., & Curzon, P. (2014). A generic user interface architecture for analyzing use hazards in infusion pump software. *OpenAccess Series in Informatics, 36*, 1–14. doi:10.4230/OASIcs.MCPS.2014.1

Ma, Y., Peng, H., Khan, T., Cambria, E., & Hussain, A. (2018). Sentic LSTM: A hybrid network for targeted aspect-based sentiment analysis. *Cognitive Computation, 10*(4), 639–650. doi:10.100712559-018-9549-x

Mayer, R., Gupta, H., Saurez, E., & Ramachandran, U. (2017, October). Fogstore: Toward a distributed data store for fog computing. In *2017 IEEE Fog World Congress (FWC)* (pp. 1-6). IEEE. 10.1109/FWC.2017.8368524

McKay, Saltzman, Chen, & Blumberg. (2018). *Hibiscus sabdariffa l. tea (tisane) lowers blood pressure in prehypertensive and mildly hypertensive adults*. Academic Press.

Md Saiful Islam, M. M.-E.-A. (2018). *A Systematic Review On Healthcare Analytics: Application And Theoretical Perspective Of Data Mining*. Heathcare.

Meeradevi & Mundada. (2020). Design of Efficient Technique for Leaf Disease Detection Using Deep Learning. *International Journal of Advanced Science and Technology, 29*(3), 11287–11298.

Meeradevi, R. V., Mundada, M. R., Sawkar, S. P., Bellad, R. S., & Keerthi, P. S. (2020). Design and Development of Efficient Techniques for Leaf Disease Detection using Deep Convolutional Neural Networks. *IEEE International Conference on Distributed Computing, VLSI, Electrical Circuits and Robotics (DISCOVER)*, 153-158. 10.1109/DISCOVER50404.2020.9278067

Mia, Roy, Das, & Rahman. (n.d.). Mango leaf disease recognition using neural network and support vector machine. *Iran Journal of Computer Science*. doi:10.1007/s42044-020-00057-z

Michael, J., & Ward, K. A. (2014). Applications Of Business Analytics In. *Business Horizons, 57*(5), 571–582. doi:10.1016/j.bushor.2014.06.003 PMID:25429161

Mirsharif, Q., Tajeripour, F., & Pourreza, H. (2013). Automated characterization of blood vessels as arteries and veins in retinal images. *Computerized Medical Imaging and Graphics, 37*(7-8), 607–617. doi:10.1016/j.compmedimag.2013.06.003 PMID:23849699

Mittal, Toshniwal, Sharma, Singhal, Gupta, & Mittal. (2015). A voice-controlled multi-functional Smart Home Automation System. *2015 Annual IEEE India Conference (INDICON)*, 1-6. 10.1109/INDICON.2015.7443538

Mohagheghi, A., Maghsoud, S., Khashayar, P., & Ghazi-Khansari, M. (2011). The effect of hibiscus sabdariffa on lipid profile, creatinine, and serum electrolytes: A randomized clinical trial. *International Scholarly Research Notices*. PMID:21991538

Monga, S. K., Ramachandra, S. K., & Simmhan, Y. (2019, July). ElfStore: A resilient data storage service for federated edge and fog resources. In *2019 IEEE International Conference on Web Services (ICWS)* (pp. 336-345). IEEE.

Mortazavi, B. J., Downing, N. S., Bucholz, E. M., Dharmarajan, K., Manhapra, A., Li, S.-X., Negahban, S. N., & Krumholz, H. M. (2016). Analysis of machine learning techniques for heart failure readmissions. *Circulation: Cardiovascular Quality and Outcomes*, 9(6), 629–640. doi:10.1161/CIRCOUTCOMES.116.003039 PMID:28263938

Moysiadis, V., Sarigiannidis, P., & Moscholios, I. (2018). Towards distributed data management in fog computing. *Wireless Communications and Mobile Computing*, 2018, 2018. doi:10.1155/2018/7597686

Mudgal, P., & Khunteta, A. (2020). Handling Double Intensifiers in Feature-Level Sentiment Analysis Based on Movie Reviews. In *International Conference on Artificial Intelligence: Advances and Applications 2019* (pp. 383-392). Springer. 10.1007/978-981-15-1059-5_42

Naha, R. K., Garg, S., Georgakopoulos, D., Jayaraman, P. P., Gao, L., Xiang, Y., & Ranjan, R. (2018). Fog computing: Survey of trends, architectures, requirements, and research directions. *IEEE Access: Practical Innovations, Open Solutions*, 6, 47980–48009. doi:10.1109/ACCESS.2018.2866491

Nair, Jain, & Nair. (2021). Enhancing the performance measure of sentiment analysis through deep learning approach. *International Journal of Computing and Digital System*.

Narasimhan, K., Neha, V. C., & Vijayarekha, K. (2012). Hypertensive Retinopathy Diagnosis from fundus images by estimation of AVR. *Procedia Engineering*, 38, 980–993. doi:10.1016/j.proeng.2012.06.124

Neves, J. S., Correa, S., Baeta Baptista, R., Bigotte Vieira, M., Waikar, S. S., & Mc Causland, F. R. (2020). Association of prediabetes with CKD progression and adverse cardiovascular outcomes: An analysis of the CRIC study. *The Journal of Clinical Endocrinology and Metabolism*, 105(4), e1772–e1780. doi:10.1210/clinem/dgaa017 PMID:31943096

Niazkar, M. T. (2020). Assessment of Three Mathematical Prediction Models for Forecasting the COVID-19 Outbreak in Iran and Turkey. *Computational and Mathematical Methods in Medicine*.

Nithya, B., & Ilango, V. (2017). Predictive Analytics In Health Care Using Machine Learning Tools And Techniques. In *2017 International Conference On Intelligent Computing And Control Systems (ICICCS)* (pp. 1-7). IEEE Explorer. 10.1109/ICCONS.2017.8250771

Noronha, K., Navya, K. T., & Nayak, K. P. (2012). Support System for the Automated Detection of Hypertensive Retinopathy using Fundus Images. *International Conference on Electronic Design and Signal Processing (ICEDSP)*, 7-11.

Ohri, K., & Kumar, M. (2021). Review on self-supervised image recognition using Deep neural networks. *Knowledge-Based Systems*, *224*, 107090. doi:10.1016/j.knosys.2021.107090

Oh, S. H. (2020). The effects of social media use on preventive behaviors during infectious disease outbreaks: The mediating role of self-relevant emotions and public risk perception. *Health Communication*, 1–10. doi:10.1080/10410236.2020.1791376 PMID:32064932

Organization, W. H. (2020). *Coronavirus disease 2019 (COVID-19) Situation Report – 35*. WHO.

Organization, W. H. (2020). *Novel Coronavirus (2019-nCoV)*. Strategic Preparedness and Response Plan.

Othman, S. M., Ba-Alwi, F. M., Alsohybe, N. T., & Al-Hashida, A. Y. (2018). Intrusion detection model using machine learning algorithm on Big Data environment. *Journal of Big Data*, *5*(1), 1–12. doi:10.118640537-018-0145-4

Pal, S., Chauhan, A., & Gupta, S. K. (2019). Voice Controlled Smart Home Automation System. *International Journal of Recent Technology and Engineering*, *8*(3), 4092–4093.

Pandey, M., Williams, R., Jindal, N., & Batra, A. (2019). Sentiment Analysis using Lexicon based Approach. *IITM Journal of Management and IT*, *10*(1), 68–76.

Parikshit, N., & Mahalle, N. P. (2020). Data Analytics: COVID-19 Prediction Using Multimodal Data. Creative Commons CC.

Park, J., Lee, H., Lee, J. H., & Suh, H. W. (2018). *Feature-based sentiment word selection and rating for system design*. Academic Press.

Park, Y., Son, Y., Shin, H., Kim, D., & Kim, Y. (2016). This ain't your dose: Sensor spoofing attack on medical infusion pump. *10th USENIX Workshop on Offensive Technologies, WOOT 2016*.

Patgiri, R., Varshney, U., Akutota, T., & Kunde, R. (2018, November). An investigation on intrusion detection system using machine learning. In *2018 IEEE Symposium Series on Computational Intelligence (SSCI)* (pp. 1684-1691). IEEE. 10.1109/SSCI.2018.8628676

Pathak, A. R., Pandey, M., & Rautaray, S. (2021). Topic-level sentiment analysis of social media data using deep learning. *Applied Soft Computing*, *108*, 107440. doi:10.1016/j.asoc.2021.107440

Patil, B. M., Joshi, R. C., Toshniwal, D., & Biradar, S. (2011). A new approach: Role of data mining in prediction of survival of burn patients. *Journal of Medical Systems*, *35*(6), 1531–1542. doi:10.100710916-010-9430-2 PMID:20703764

Pawar, S. C. (2021). Analyzing and Forecasting COVID-19 Outbreak in India. *2021 11th International Conference on Cloud Computing, Data Science & Engineering (Confluence)*, 1059-1066.

Percival, J., McGregor, C., Percival, N., Kamaleswaran, R., & Tuuha, S. (2010). A framework for nursing documentation enabling integration with HER and real-time patient monitoring. *Proceedings - IEEE Symposium on Computer-Based Medical Systems*, 468–473. 10.1109/CBMS.2010.6042690

Piao, H., Yun, J. M., Shin, A., & Cho, B. (2020). Longitudinal Study of Diabetic Differences between International Migrants and Natives among the Asian Population. *Biomolecules & Therapeutics*, 28(1), 110–118. doi:10.4062/biomolther.2019.163 PMID:31739384

Pickering, L. (2020). Identifying Factors in COVID-19 AI Case Predictions. In *7th International Conference on Soft Computing & Machine Intelligence (ISCMI)* (pp. 192-196). IEEE.

Plaza-Leiva, V., Gomez-Ruiz, J. A., Mandow, A., & García-Cerezo, A. (2017). Voxel-based neighborhood for spatial shape pattern classification of lidar point clouds with supervised learning. *Sensors (Basel)*, 17(3), 594. doi:10.339017030594 PMID:28294963

Polak, S., & Mendyk, A. (2008). Artificial neural networks-based Internet hypertension prediction tool development and validation. *Applied Soft Computing*, 8(1), 734–739. doi:10.1016/j.asoc.2007.06.001

Prakash, A. S. (2020). Spread & Peak Prediction of Covid-19 using ANN and Regression (Workshop Paper). In *2020 IEEE Sixth International Conference on Multimedia Big Data (BigMM)* (pp. 356-365). IEEE.

Psaras, I., Ascigil, O., Rene, S., Pavlou, G., Afanasyev, A., & Zhang, L. (2018). Mobile data repositories at the edge. *USENIX Workshop on Hot Topics in Edge Computing (HotEdge 18)*.

R. M. (2020). *Predictive Privacy: Towards An Applied Ethics Of Data Analytics*. Technische Universität Berlin (TU Berlin); Freie Universität Berlin.

Ramesh, S., & Hebbar, R. (2018). Plant Disease Detection Using Machine Learning. *International Conference on Design Innovations for 3Cs Compute Communicate Control*. 10.1109/ICDI3C.2018.00017

Rao, B., & Chandrakanth, H. (2018). Secured Speech Industrial Automation Based on Raspberry Pi and IoT. *International Journal of Intelligent Engineering and Systems*, 11(6), 234–243. doi:10.22266/ijies2018.1231.23

Rao, G., Huang, W., Feng, Z., & Cong, Q. (2018). LSTM with sentence representations for document-level sentiment classification. *Neurocomputing*, 308, 49–57. doi:10.1016/j.neucom.2018.04.045

Rao, K. D., Radhika, A., & Abdul, G. (2014). Health Systems Research In The Time Of Health System Reform In India: A Review. *Health Research Policy and Systems*, 12(37), 1–7. doi:10.1186/1478-4505-12-37 PMID:25106759

Rathore, M. M., Saeed, F., Rehman, A., Paul, A., & Daniel, A. (2018, February). Intrusion detection using decision tree model in high-speed environment. In *2018 International Conference on Soft-computing and Network Security (ICSNS)* (pp. 1-4). IEEE. 10.1109/ICSNS.2018.8573631

Riurean, S., Antipova, T., Rocha, Á., Leba, M., & Ionica, A. (2019). VLC, OCC, IR and LiFi Reliable Optical Wireless Technologies to be Embedded in Medical Facilities and Medical Devices. *Journal of Medical Systems*, *43*(10), 308. Advance online publication. doi:10.100710916-019-1434-y PMID:31432270

Sakr, S., Elshawi, R., Ahmed, A., Qureshi, W. T., Brawner, C., Keteyian, S., Blaha, M. J., & Al-Mallah, M. H. (2018, April 18). Using machine learning on cardiorespiratory fitness data for predicting hypertension: Te Henry Ford exercise testing (FIT) Project. *PLoS One*, *13*(4), e0195344. doi:10.1371/journal.pone.0195344 PMID:29668729

Salkuti, S. R. (2020). A survey of big data and machine learning. *International Journal of Electrical & Computer Engineering, 10*(1).

Saxena, A. (2016). Convolutional neural networks: An illustration in TensorFlow. *ACM Crossroads*, *22*(4), 56–58. doi:10.1145/2951024

Sayantan Khanra, A. D. (2020). Big Data Analytics In Healthcare: A Systematic Literature Review. *Enterprise Information Systems*, *14*(7), 878–912. doi:10.1080/17517575.2020.1812005

Schouten, K., Van Der Weijde, O., Frasincar, F., & Dekker, R. (2017). Supervised and unsupervised aspect category detection for sentiment analysis with co-occurrence data. *IEEE Transactions on Cybernetics*, *48*(4), 1263–1275. doi:10.1109/TCYB.2017.2688801 PMID:28422676

SecTools.Org. (2006). *Results*. https://sectools.org/tools2006.html

SecTools.Org. (n.d.). *Top 125 Network Security Tools*. https://sectools.org/tag/ids/

Seidler, T., Hellenkamp, K., Unsoeld, B., Mushemi-Blake, S., Shah, A., Hasenfuss, G., & Leha, A. (2019). A machine learning approach for the prediction of pulmonary hypertension. *Journal of the American College of Cardiology*, *73*(9), 1589. doi:10.1016/S0735-1097(19)32195-3

Seifert, D., & Rez, H. (2016). A security analysis of cyber-physical systems architecture for healthcare. *Computers*, *5*(4), 27. Advance online publication. doi:10.3390/computers5040027

Seo, K.-S., & Lee, K. (2016). Smart syringe pumps for drug infusion during dental intravenous sedation. *Journal of Dental Anesthesia and Pain Medicine*, *16*(3), 165. doi:10.17245/jdapm.2016.16.3.165 PMID:28884149

Serban, C., Sahebkar, A., Ursoniu, S., Andrica, F., & Banach, M. (2015). Effect of sour tea (hibiscus sabdariffa l.) on arterial hypertension: A systematic review and meta-analysis of randomized controlled trials. *Journal of Hypertension*, *33*(6), 1119–1127. doi:10.1097/HJH.0000000000000585 PMID:25875025

Shaikh, S. J. G. (2021). Analysis and Prediction of COVID-19 using Regression Models and Time Series Forecasting. *2021 11th International Conference on Cloud Computing, Data Science & Engineering (Confluence)*, 989-995.

Shan, C., Gong, S., & McOwan, P. W. (2009). Facial expression recognition based on local binary patterns: A comprehensive study. *Image and Vision Computing*, *27*(6), 803–816. doi:10.1016/j.imavis.2008.08.005

Sharma, R., Singh, D., Gaur, P., & Joshi, D. (2021). Intelligent automated drug administration and therapy: Future of healthcare. *Drug Delivery and Translational Research*, *0123456789*(5), 1878–1902. Advance online publication. doi:10.100713346-020-00876-4 PMID:33447941

Shastri, A., & Deshpande, M. (2020). A Review of Big Data and Its Applications in Healthcare and Public Sector. In *Big Data Analytics in Healthcare* (pp. 55–66). Springer. doi:10.1007/978-3-030-31672-3_4

Shunmugam, R., & Dharma, V. (2019). Recognition and Classification of Paddy Leaf Diseases Using Optimized Deep Neural Network with Jaya Algorithm. *Information Processing in Agriculture*. Advance online publication. doi:10.1016/j.inpa.2019.09.002

Silva, C. A., Aquino, G. S., Melo, S. R., & Egídio, D. J. (2019). A fog computing-based architecture for medical records management. *Wireless Communications and Mobile Computing*, *2019*, 2019. doi:10.1155/2019/1968960

Silva, L. C., Almeida, H. O., Perkusich, A., & Perkusich, M. (2015). A model-based approach to support validation of medical cyber-physical systems. *Sensors (Switzerland)*, *15*(11), 27625–27670. doi:10.3390151127625 PMID:26528982

Singh, N., & Singh, P. (2020). A Stacked Generalization Approach for Diagnosis and Prediction of Type 2 Diabetes Mellitus. In *Computational Intelligence in Data Mining* (pp. 559–570). Springer. doi:10.1007/978-981-13-8676-3_47

Singh, N., Singh, P., & Bhagat, D. (2019, September). A rule extraction approach from support vector machines for diagnosing hypertension among diabetics. *Expert Systems with Applications*, *130*, 188–205. doi:10.1016/j.eswa.2019.04.029

Snort. (n.d.). https://en.wikipedia.org/wiki/Snort_%28software%29

Soong, H. C., Jalil, N. B. A., Ayyasamy, R. K., & Akbar, R. (2019, April). The essential of sentiment analysis and opinion mining in social media: Introduction and survey of the recent approaches and techniques. In *2019 IEEE 9th symposium on computer applications & industrial electronics (ISCAIE)* (pp. 272-277). IEEE.

Souma, W., Vodenska, I., & Aoyama, H. (2019). Enhanced news sentiment analysis using deep learning methods. *Journal of Computational Social Science*, *2*(1), 33–46. doi:10.100742001-019-00035-x

Subba, B., Biswas, S., & Karmakar, S. (2015, December). Intrusion detection systems using linear discriminant analysis and logistic regression. In *2015 Annual IEEE India Conference (INDICON)* (pp. 1-6). IEEE. 10.1109/INDICON.2015.7443533

Szegedy & Vanhoucke. (2015). *Rethinking the Inception Architecture for Computer Vision*. arXiv:1512.00567.

Szegedy, C., & Liu, W. (2014). *Going Deeper with Convolutions*. arXiv:1409.4842.

Takci, H. (2018). Improvement of heart attack prediction by the feature selection methods. *Turkish Journal of Electrical Engineering and Computer Sciences, 26*(1), 1–10. doi:10.3906/elk-1611-235

Tang, Z.-H., Liu, J., Zeng, F., Li, Z., Yu, X., & Zhou, L. (2013). Comparison of prediction model for cardiovascular autonomic dysfunction using artifcial neural network and logistic regression analysis. *PLoS One, 8*(8), e70571. doi:10.1371/journal.pone.0070571 PMID:23940593

Taofeek, O. (2011). Antioxidant and drug detoxification potentials of hibiscus sabdariffa anthocyanin extract. *Drug and Chemical Toxicology, 34*(2), 109–115. doi:10.3109/01480545.2 010.536767 PMID:21314460

Tengnah, M. A. J., Sooklall, R., & Nagowah, S. D. (2019). A predictive model for hypertension diagnosis using machine learning techniques. In H. D. Jude & V. E. Balas (Eds.), *Telemedicine Technologies* (pp. 139–152). Academies Press, Elsevier. doi:10.1016/B978-0-12-816948-3.00009-X

Tian & Linzhang. (2012). *Study on the methods of detecting cucumber downy mildew using hypersectral imaging technology*. Elsevier.

Toda, Y., & Okura, F. (2019). How Convolutional Neural Networks Diagnose Plant Disease. *Plant Phenomics*.

Too, E. C., Li, Y., Njuki, S., & Liu, Y. (2018). A Comparative Study of Fine-Tuning Deep Learning Models for Plant Disease Identification. *Computers and Electronics in Agriculture*. Advance online publication. doi:10.1016/j.compag.2018.03.032

Triwijoyo, Budihartoa, & Abdurachman. (2017). The Classification of Hypertensive Retinopathy using Convolutional Neural Network. *Computer Science, 116*, 166–173.

Ture, M., Kurt, I., Turhan Kurum, A., & Ozdamar, K. (2005). Comparing classification techniques for predicting essential hypertension. *Expert Systems with Applications, 29*(3), 583–588. doi:10.1016/j.eswa.2005.04.014

Tyagi, C. S., Agarwal, M., & Gola, R. (2016). Home Automation Using Voice Recognition and Arduino. *International Journal of Recent Trends in Engineering & Research Engineering and Technology, 2*(7), 2455–1457.

Uchino, B. N., Cronan, S., Scott, E., Landvatter, J., & Papadakis, M. (2020). Social support and stress, depression, and cardiovascular disease. In *Cardiovascular Implications of Stress and Depression* (pp. 211–223). Academic Press. doi:10.1016/B978-0-12-815015-3.00009-X

Uddin, M. P., Mamun, M. A., Afjal, M. I., & Hossain, M. A. (2021). Information-theoretic feature selection with segmentation-based folded principal component analysis (PCA) for hyperspectral image classification. *International Journal of Remote Sensing, 42*(1), 286–32. doi:10.1080/01 431161.2020.1807650

V. S., V. K., U. D., V. K., & K. R. ((2020)). Heart Disease Prediction Using CNN Algorithm. *SN Computer Science, 1*(170).

Vajpai, J., & Bora, A. (2016). Industrial Applications of Automatic Speech Recognition Systems. *International Journal of Engineering Research and Applications*, *6*(3), 88–95.

Vásquez-Morales, G. R., Martínez-Monterrubio, S. M., Moreno-Ger, P., & Recio-García, J. A. (2019). Explainable prediction of chronic renal disease in the colombian population using neural networks and case-based reasoning. *IEEE Access: Practical Innovations, Open Solutions*, *7*, 152900–152910. doi:10.1109/ACCESS.2019.2948430

Vijai Singh, A. K. (2017). Misra. Detection of plant leaf diseases using image segmentation and soft computing techniques. *Information Processing in Agriculture*, *4*(1), 41–49. doi:10.1016/j. inpa.2016.10.005

Virani, S. S., Alonso, A., Benjamin, E. J., Bittencourt, M. S., Callaway, C. W., Carson, A. P., & Djousse, L. (2020). Heart disease and stroke statistics—2020 update: A report from the American Heart Association. *Circulation*, *141*(9), E139–E596. doi:10.1161/CIR.0000000000000757 PMID:31992061

Wang, J. H., Liu, T. W., Luo, X., & Wang, L. (2018, October). An LSTM approach to short text sentiment classification with word embeddings. In *Proceedings of the 30th conference on computational linguistics and speech processing (ROCLING 2018)* (pp. 214-223). Academic Press.

Wang, Y., Wang, H., Zhang, X., Chaspari, T., Choe, Y., & Lu, M. (2019, May). An attention-aware bidirectional multi-residual recurrent neural network (abmrnn): A study about better short-term text classification. In *ICASSP 2019-2019 IEEE International Conference on Acoustics, Speech and Signal Processing (ICASSP)* (pp. 3582-3586). IEEE.

Wang, X., Yang, Y., Xu, Y., Chen, Q., Wang, H., & Gao, H. (2020). Predicting hypoglycemic drugs of type 2 diabetes based on weighted rank support vector machine. *Knowledge-Based Systems*, *197*, 105868. doi:10.1016/j.knosys.2020.105868

Wang, Y., Kung, L., & Byrd, T. A. (2018). Big data analytics: Understanding its capabilities and potential benefits for healthcare organizations. *Technological Forecasting and Social Change*, *126*, 3–13. doi:10.1016/j.techfore.2015.12.019

Wankhede, S., Patil, R., Sonawane, S., & Save, A. (2018, April). Data Preprocessing for Efficient Sentimental Analysis. In *2018 Second International Conference on Inventive Communication and Computational Technologies (ICICCT)* (pp. 723-726). IEEE.

Wazurkar, P., Bhadoria, R. S., & Bajpai, D. (2019). Predictive Analytics In Data Science For Business Intelligence Solutions. *International Conference on Communication Systems and Network Technologies (CSNT)*.

Widiastuti, N. I. (2019, November). Convolution Neural Network for Text Mining and Natural Language Processing. *IOP Conference Series. Materials Science and Engineering*, *662*(5), 052010. doi:10.1088/1757-899X/662/5/052010

Williams, B. (2018). ESC/ESH Guidelines for The Management of Arterial Hypertension. Academic Press.

Wingerd, B., & Taylor, P. B. (2020). *The human body: Concepts of anatomy and physiology.* Jones & Bartlett Publishers.

Wong, T. T., & Yeh, P. Y. (2019). Reliable accuracy estimates from k-fold cross validation. *IEEE Transactions on Knowledge and Data Engineering.*

Wu, P., Li, X., Shen, S., & He, D. (2020). Social media opinion summarization using emotion cognition and convolutional neural networks. *International Journal of Information Management, 51*, 101978. doi:10.1016/j.ijinfomgt.2019.07.004

Xu, F., Zhang, X., Xin, Z., & Yang, A. (2019). Investigation on the Chinese text sentiment analysis based on convolutional neural networks in deep learning. *Comput. Mater. Contin, 58*(3), 697–709. doi:10.32604/cmc.2019.05375

Xu, M., Cheng, W., Zhao, Q., Ma, L., & Xu, F. (2015). *Facial expression recognition based on transfer learning from deep convolutional networks.* ICNC.

Xu, X., Fu, S., Cai, Q., Tian, W., Liu, W., Dou, W., Sun, X., & Liu, A. X. (2018). Dynamic resource allocation for load balancing in fog environment. *Wireless Communications and Mobile Computing, 2018*, 2018. doi:10.1155/2018/6421607

Yang, C. W., Harris, D. C., Luyckx, V. A., Nangaku, M., Hou, F. F., Garcia, G. G., ... Eiam-Ong, S. (2020). Global case studies for chronic kidney disease/end-stage kidney disease care. *Kidney International. Supplement, 10*(1), e24–e48. doi:10.1016/j.kisu.2019.11.010 PMID:32149007

Yang, X., Macdonald, C., & Ounis, I. (2018). Using word embeddings in twitter election classification. *Information Retrieval Journal, 21*(2-3), 183–207. doi:10.100710791-017-9319-5

You, K., Wang, X., Long, M., & Jordan, M. (2019, May). Towards accurate model selection in deep unsupervised domain adaptation. In *International Conference on Machine Learning* (pp. 7124-7133). Academic Press.

Yousif, A., Niu, Z., Tarus, J. K., & Ahmad, A. (2019). A survey on sentiment analysis of scientific citations. *Artificial Intelligence Review, 52*(3), 1805–1838. doi:10.100710462-017-9597-8

Yu, L. C., Lee, C. W., Pan, H. I., Chou, C. Y., Chao, P. Y., Chen, Z. H., Tseng, S. F., Chan, C. L., & Lai, K. R. (2018). Improving early prediction of academic failure using sentiment analysis on self-evaluated comments. *Journal of Computer Assisted Learning, 34*(4), 358–365. doi:10.1111/jcal.12247

Zadokar, A. R., Bhagat, D. P., Nayase, A. A., & Mhaske, S. S. (2017). Leaf Disease Detection of Cotton Plant using Image Processing Technique:A Review. *International Journal of Electronics, Communication & Soft Computing Science and Engineering.*

Zafar, F., Raza, S., Khalid, M. U., & Tahir, M. A. (2019, March). Predictive Analytics in Healthcare for Diabetes Prediction. In *Proceedings of the 2019 9th International Conference on Biomedical Engineering and Technology* (pp. 253-259). 10.1145/3326172.3326213

Zakary, O. (2016). The epsilon capacity of a gain matrix and tolerable disturbances: Discrete-time perturbed linear systems. *arXiv preprint, 1608.00426.*

Zhang, L., Wang, S., & Liu, B. (2018). Deep learning for sentiment analysis: A survey. *Wiley Interdisciplinary Reviews. Data Mining and Knowledge Discovery*, 8(4), e1253. doi:10.1002/widm.1253

Zhang, S., Yao, L., Sun, A., & Tay, Y. (2019). Deep learning based recommender system: A survey and new perspectives. *ACM Computing Surveys*, 52(1), 1–38. doi:10.1145/3285029

Zhang, T., & Wang, L. (2019, June). Research on Text Classification Method Based on Word2vec and Improved TF-IDF. In *International Conference on Intelligent and Interactive Systems and Applications* (pp. 199-205). Springer.

Zhang, X., Qiao, Y., Meng, F., Fan, C., & Zhang, M. (2018). Identification of Maize Leaf Diseases Using Improved Deep Convolutional Neural Networks. *IEEE Access: Practical Innovations, Open Solutions*, 6, 30370–30377. doi:10.1109/ACCESS.2018.2844405

Zhao, H. Y. L. (2021). A COVID-19 Prediction Optimization Algorithm Based on Real-time Neural Network Training—Taking Italy as an Example. In *2021 IEEE Asia-Pacific Conference on Image Processing, Electronics and Computers (IPEC)* (pp. 345-348). IEEE.

Zheng, L., Wang, H., & Gao, S. (2018). Sentimental feature selection for sentiment analysis of Chinese online reviews. *International Journal of Machine Learning and Cybernetics*, 9(1), 75–84. doi:10.100713042-015-0347-4

Zheng, Y., & Hu, X. (2020). Healthcare predictive analytics for disease progression: A longitudinal data fusion approach. *Journal of Intelligent Information Systems*, 55(2), 351–369. doi:10.100710844-020-00606-9

Zhou, Kaneko, Tianaka, Kayamori, & Shimizu. (2013). Early detection and continuous quantization of plant disease using template matching and support vector machine algorithms. *IEEE International Symposium on Computing and Networking.*

Zimmerman, J. B., Pizer, S. M., Staab, E. V., Perry, J. R., McCartney, W., & Brenton, B. C. (1988). An evaluation of the effectiveness of adaptive histogram equalization for contrast enhancement. *IEEE Transactions on Medical Imaging*, 7(4), 304–312. doi:10.1109/42.14513 PMID:18230483

About the Contributors

Srinivasa K. G. is currently working as a Professor at NITTTR, Chandigarh. Earlier he was an associate professor at CBP Government Engineering College, New Delhi. Earlier, he was a faculty in the Department of Computer Science and Engineering, M S Ramaiah Institute of Technology, Bangalore. He is the recipient of AICTE - Career Award for Young Teachers, Indian Society of Technical Education – ISGITS National Award for Best Research Work Done by Young Teachers, Institution of Engineers (India) – IEI Young Engineer Award in Computer Engineering, Rajarambapu Patil National Award for Promising Engineering Teacher Award from ISTE - 2012. He has published more than hundred research papers in International Conferences and Journals. He has visited many Universities abroad as a visiting researcher – He has visited University of Oklahoma, USA, Iowa State University, USA, Hong Kong University, Korean University, National University of Singapore are few prominent visits. He has authored two books namely File Structures using C++ by TMH and Soft Computer for Data Mining Applications LNAI Series – Springer. He has been awarded BOYSCAST Fellowship by DST, for visiting University of Melbourne.

* * *

Parkavi A. is working as associate professor in MSRIT. Area of Interests are data analytics, compiler design.

Sini Anna Alex is presently working as an Assistant Professor in the Department of Computer Science and Engineering, Ramaiah Institute of Technology, Bangalore, India. Her areas of interest include Ubiquitous computing, Predictive Data Analytics, Compiler design, Mobile and wireless sensor networks, Distributed systems, Database systems and Algorithm analysis. She published several paper in peer reviewed journals and conferences. She delivered technical talk in reputed institutions like JNTU Anatpur, IEEE-Kerala Section, SAP-UA, Indian Institute of Horticultural Research etc. She has completed a project on Predictive Analysis on agglomerated data and Guided Project work for Birla Institute of Technology& Science, Pilani, and Work-Integrated Learning Programmes Division. She also worked in a Collaborative Project Work with Artificial Limbs Manufacturing Corporation of India on 'Automation of Summary Reports Generation' from Oct 18, 2019 to July 12, 2020. Received Young Woman in Engineering - 2018 Award has been bestowed for her contribution, research excellence and accomplishments in the area of Computer Science and Engineering. She received award RULA Best Researcher and also got the best paper award from IJSER in 2019. She is an active member of professional bodies like IEEE (senior member), ISTE, IEEE-WIE, ACM and World Research Council.

Mythili Asaithambi works for Vellore Institute of Technology. The research areas are biomedical engineering, signal processing.

Evangeline Devapragasam received Bachelor of Technology degree in Information Technology from Thiagarajar College of Engineering, Anna University in the year 2010 and Master of Engineering Degree from DMI College of Engineering, Anna University in the year 2012. She has worked as an Assistant Professor in the Department of Information Technology at Kongu Engineering College, Tamil Nadu from May 2012 to November 2017. She has authored 15 publications in various National / International Journals & Conferences and considers her book on "Computer Graphics and Multimedia" published by Prentice Hall of India as her magnum opus. Her research interests include Digital Image Processing and Computer Graphics. Currently, she is working as an Assistant Professor in the Department of Information Science and Engineering at M.S.Ramaiah Institute of Technology, Bengaluru.

Rajalaxmi Hegde is currently working as an Assistant Professor in the Department of Computer Science and Engineering at NMAM Institute of Technology, Nitte, India. She has around eight years of teaching experience. She is a life member of ISTE. She has published research papers in international conferences/journals. Her research interests include natural language processing, machine learning, and data mining.

Sandeep Kumar Hegde obtained his B.E and MTech degree in Computer Science and Engg from VTU University, India. Currently, and he is pursuing PhD from VTU University. He has published research papers in various international journals and conferences. Presently he is working as assistant professor in the Department of Computer Science and Engg at NMAMIT, Nitte. His area of interest includes big data analytics, machine learning and computational intelligence. He is a life member of ISTE.

Alamelu J. V. is pursuing research in SENSE, Vellore Institute of Technology, Vellore and working as Assistant Professor in M. S. Ramaiah Institute of Technology. The area of research interest are medical devices, automation, cyber physical systems.

Meeradevi K. is working as an Assistant Professor in Computer Science Department of M S Ramaiah Institute of Technology. Her areas of interest include computer networks, machine learning and wireless sensor networks.

Sinthuja M. pursued her Ph.D in Computer Science and Engineering, Annamalai University in 2019, M.E in Computer Science and Engineering, J.J College of Engineering and Technology, Anna University in 2011, B.Tech in Information Technology, Anjalai Ammal Mahalingam Engineering College, Anna University in 2009. At present working as Assistant Professor in the Department of Information Science and Engineering, M.S. Ramaiah Institute of Technology, Bangalore. Her area of research is Data Mining. She has authored 13 publications which include Elsevier, Scopus, Web of Science and UGC reputed Journals. She has 3 publications in Book Chapter which includes Springer and Taylor & Francis. She has participated in 16 various National and International Conferences all over India. She has participated in 14 various FDP, Workshop, STTP, Tutorials.

Thangavel M. serving as an Assistant Professor in the School of Computing Science and Engineering, VIT Bhopal University. He received Doctorate from Madras Institute of Technology (MIT) Campus, Anna University – Chennai. He received Post Graduate degree as M.E. Computer Science and Engineering from J.J. College of Engineering and Technology, Trichy under Anna University – Chennai (University First Rank Holder & Gold Medalist) and Bachelor's degree as B.E. Computer Science and Engineering from M.A.M College of Engineering, Trichy under Anna University – Chennai (College First Rank Holder & Gold Medalist). He presently holds 9+ years of Teaching and Research experience from various academic institutions. He has published 10+ articles in International Journals, 15+ book chapters in International Publishers, 25+ in the proceedings of International Conferences and 3 in the proceedings of national conferences /seminars. He has been actively participating as reviewers in the international journals and conferences. He has attended 100+ Workshops /FDPs/Conferences in various Higher Learning Institutes like IIT, Anna University. He has organized 50+ Workshops / FDPs / Contests/Industry based courses over the past years of experience. He has been a technical speaker in various Workshops/FDPs/Conferences. His research specialization is Information Security, High Performance Computing, Ethical Hacking, Cyberforensics, Blockchain, Cybersecurity Intelligence and Educational Technology.

Pushpalatha Nidagal is currently working as an Assistant Professor in the department of ISE, Ramaiah Institute of Technology. She did B.E. in computer Science from University BDT College of Engg, Davangere and M.Tech in Computer Science and Engineering from Ramaiah Institute of Technology, Bangalore. She completed her Ph.D in Computer Science and engineering in 2021 from Visvesvaraya Technological University. Her areas of interest are data mining and software engineering.

Hanumantharaju R. is a Research Scholar, Siddaganga Institute of Technology, working as Assistant Professor in Department of Computer Science & Engineering.

Sudersan S. pursuing B.Tech Information Technology in Thiagarajar College of Engineering, Madurai, Tamilnadu, India.

Sangeetha V. is working as Assistant Professor in Department of Computer Science and Engineering at M S Ramaiah Institute of Technology. Having 15 years of teaching and research experience. Research specialization includes Wireless Networks and Security, Blockchain and Machine Learning and IOT. Published over 27 research papers in reputed National and International Conferences and Journals. Also, technical reviewer for good indexed international journal. Member of various professional bodies like IEEE, IEI, CSI, ISTE (Life Member), IAENG (Member). Received various awards such as "STAR of the Year Award" in recognition of continuing Excellence in Teaching by HKBK Group of Institutions, "Research Excellence Award" for presenting the research paper titled ZIDS: Zonal-based Intrusion Detection System for Studying the Malicious Node Behaviour in MANET in conference from IEAE, "Young Woman Educator & Researcher Award" in recognition of contribution towards Teaching & Research in the field of Computer Science and Engineering by NFED, Coimbatore.

Abhijith V. S. pursuing B.Tech Information Technology in Thiagarajar College of Engineering, Madurai, Tamilnadu, India.

Index

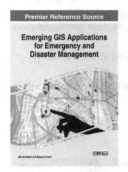
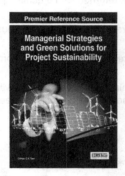

IGI Global Author Services

Providing a high-quality, affordable, and expeditious service, IGI Global's Author Services enable authors to streamline their publishing process, increase chance of acceptance, and adhere to IGI Global's publication standards.

Benefits of Author Services:

- **Professional Service:** All our editors, designers, and translators are experts in their field with years of experience and professional certifications.
- **Quality Guarantee & Certificate:** Each order is returned with a quality guarantee and certificate of professional completion.
- **Timeliness:** All editorial orders have a guaranteed return timeframe of 3-5 business days and translation orders are guaranteed in 7-10 business days.
- **Affordable Pricing:** IGI Global Author Services are competitively priced compared to other industry service providers.
- **APC Reimbursement:** IGI Global authors publishing Open Access (OA) will be able to deduct the cost of editing and other IGI Global author services from their OA APC publishing fee.

Author Services Offered:

 English Language Copy Editing
Professional, native English language copy editors improve your manuscript's grammar, spelling, punctuation, terminology, semantics, consistency, flow, formatting, and more.

 Scientific & Scholarly Editing
A Ph.D. level review for qualities such as originality and significance, interest to researchers, level of methodology and analysis, coverage of literature, organization, quality of writing, and strengths and weaknesses.

 Figure, Table, Chart & Equation Conversions
Work with IGI Global's graphic designers before submission to enhance and design all figures and charts to IGI Global's specific standards for clarity.

 Translation
Providing 70 language options, including Simplified and Traditional Chinese, Spanish, Arabic, German, French, and more.

Hear What the Experts Are Saying About IGI Global's Author Services

"Publishing with IGI Global has been *an amazing experience* for me for sharing my research. The *strong academic production* support ensures quality and timely completion." – **Prof. Margaret Niess, Oregon State University, USA**

"The service was *very fast, very thorough, and very helpful* in ensuring our chapter meets the criteria and requirements of the book's editors. I was *quite impressed and happy* with your service." – **Prof. Tom Brinthaupt, Middle Tennessee State University, USA**

Learn More or Get Started Here: For Questions, Contact IGI Global's Customer Service Team at cust@igi-global.com or 717-533-8845

IGI Global
PUBLISHER of TIMELY KNOWLEDGE
www.igi-global.com

Printed in the United States
by Baker & Taylor Publisher Services